ELLEN GOULD WHITE

THE GREAT CONTROVERSY

GIHON PUBLISHING

THE GREAT CONTROVERSY

ELLEN G. WHITE

1911 EDITION

PUBLISHER

DAIMLERSTR. 12
73635 RUDERSBERG

LITERATUR@GIHON.DE

PRINTED IN GERMANY

ISBN: 978-3-939979-38-8

Contents

Page numbers of the English edition (GC) of 1911
in parentheses next to the page numbers

INTRODUCTION

Before the entrance of sin, Adam enjoyed open communion with his Maker; but since man separated himself from God by transgression, the human race has been cut off from this high privilege. By the plan of redemption, however, a way has been opened whereby the inhabitants of the earth may still have connection with heaven. God has communicated with men by His Spirit, and divine light has been imparted to the world by revelations to His chosen servants. »Holy men of God spake as they were moved by the Holy Ghost.« 2 Peter 1:21

During the first twenty-five hundred years of human history, there was no written revelation. Those who had been taught of God, communicated their knowledge to others, and it was handed down from father to son, through successive generations. The preparation of the written word began in the time of Moses. Inspired revelations were then embodied in an inspired book. This work continued during the long period of sixteen hundred years-from Moses, the historian of creation and the law, to John, the recorder of the most sublime truths of the gospel.

The Bible points to God as its author; yet it was written by human hands; and in the varied style of its different books it presents the characteristics of the several writers. The truths revealed are all »given by inspiration of God« 2 Timothy 3:16 yet they are expressed in the words of men. The Infinite One by His Holy Spirit has shed light into the minds and hearts of His servants. He has given dreams and visions, symbols and figures; and those to whom the truth was thus revealed have themselves embodied the thought in human language.

The Ten Commandments were spoken by God Himself, and were written by His own hand. They are of divine, and not of human composition. But the Bible, with its God-given truths expressed in the language of men, presents a union of the divine and the human. Such a union existed in the nature of Christ, who was the Son of God and the Son of man. Thus it is true of the Bible, as it was of Christ, that »the Word was made flesh, and dwelt among us.« John 1:14

Written in different ages, by men who differed widely in rank and occupation, and in mental and spiritual endowments, the books of the Bible present a wide contrast in style, as well as a diversity in the nature of the subjects unfolded. Different forms of expression are employed by different writers; often the same truth is more strikingly presented by one than by another. And as several writers present a subject under varied aspects and relations, there may appear, to the superficial, careless, or prejudiced reader, to be discrepancy or contradiction, where the thoughtful, reverent student, with clearer insight, discerns the underlying harmony.

As presented through different individuals, the truth is brought out in its varied aspects. One writer is more strongly impressed with one phase of the subject; he grasps those points that harmonize with his experience or with his power of perception and appreciation; another seizes upon a different phase; and each, under the guidance of the Holy Spirit, presents what is most forcibly impressed upon his own mind-a different aspect of the truth in each, but a perfect harmony through all. And the truths thus revealed unite to form a perfect whole, adapted to meet the wants of men in all the circumstances and experiences of life.

God has been pleased to communicate His truth to the world by human agencies, and He Himself, by His Holy Spirit, qualified men and enabled them to do this work. He guided the mind in the selection of what to speak and what to write. The treasure was entrusted to earthen vessels, yet it is, nonetheless, from Heaven. The testimony is conveyed through the imperfect expression of human language, yet it is the testimony of God; and the obedient, believing child of God beholds in it the glory of a divine power, full of grace and truth.

In His word, God has committed to men the knowledge necessary for salvation. The Holy Scriptures are to be accepted as an authoritative, infallible revelation of His will. They are the standard of character, the revealer of doctrines, and the test of experience. »Every scripture inspired of God is also profitable for teaching, for reproof, for correction, for instruction which is in righteousness; that the man of God may be complete, furnished completely unto every good work.« 2 Timothy 3:16, 17, R.V.

Yet the fact that God has revealed His will to men through His word, has not rendered needless the continued presence and guiding of the Holy Spirit. On the contrary, the Spirit was promised by our Saviour, to open the word to His servants, to illuminate and apply its teachings. And since it was the Spirit of God that inspired the Bible, it is impossible that the teaching of the Spirit should ever be contrary to that of the word.

The Spirit was not given-nor can it ever be bestowedto supersede the Bible; for the Scriptures explicitly state that the word of God is the standard by which all teaching and experience must be tested. Says the apostle John, »Believe not every spirit, but try the spirits whether they are of God: because many false prophets are gone out into the world.« 1 John 4:1 And Isaiah declares, »To the law and to the testimony: if they speak not according to this word, it is because there is no light in them.« Isaiah 8:20

Great reproach has been cast upon the work of the Holy Spirit by the errors of a class that, claiming its enlightenment, profess to have no further need of guidance from the word of God. They are governed by impressions which they regard as the voice of God in the soul. But the spirit that controls them is not the Spirit of God. This following of impressions, to the neglect of the Scriptures, can lead only to confusion, to deception and ruin. It serves only to further the designs of the evil one. Since the ministry of the Holy Spirit is of vital importance to the church of Christ, it is one of the devices of Satan, through the errors of extremists and fanatics, to cast contempt upon the work of the Spirit and cause the people of God to neglect this source of strength which our Lord Himself has provided.

In harmony with the word of God, His Spirit was to continue its work throughout the period of the gospel dispensation. During the ages while the Scriptures of both the Old and the New Testament were being given, the Holy Spirit did not cease to communicate light to individual minds, apart from the revelations to be embodied in the Sacred Canon. The Bible itself relates how, through the Holy Spirit, men received warning, reproof, counsel, and instruction, in matters in no way relating to the giving of the Scriptures. And mention is made of prophets in different ages, of whose utterances nothing is recorded. In like manner, after the close of the canon of the Scripture, the Holy Spirit was still to continue its work, to enlighten, warn, and comfort the children of God.

Jesus promised His disciples, »The Comforter which is the Holy Ghost, whom the Father will send in My name, He shall teach you all things, and bring all things to your remembrance, whatsoever

I have said unto you.« »When He, the Spirit of truth, is come, He will guide you into all truth: ... and He will show you things to come.« John 14:26; 16:13 Scripture plainly teaches that these promises, so far from being limited to apostolic days, extend to the church of Christ in all ages. The Saviour assures His followers, »I am with you alway, even unto the end of the world.« Matthew 28:20 And Paul declares that the gifts and manifestations of the Spirit were set in the church »for the perfecting of the saints, for the work of the ministry, for the edifying of the body of Christ: till we all come in the unity of the faith, and of the knowledge of the Son of God, unto a perfect man, unto the measure of the stature of the fullness of Christ.« Ephesians 4:12,13

For the believers at Ephesus the apostle prayed, »That the God of our Lord Jesus Christ, the Father of glory, may give unto you the Spirit of wisdom and revelation in the knowledge of Him: the eyes of your understanding being enlightened; that ye may know what is the hope of His calling, and ... what is the exceeding greatness of His power to usward who believe.« Ephesians 1:17-19 The ministry of the divine Spirit in enlightening the understanding and opening to the mind the deep things of God's holy word, was the blessing which Paul thus besought for the Ephesian church.

After the wonderful manifestation of the Holy Spirit on the Day of Pentecost, Peter exhorted the people to repentance and baptism in the name of Christ, for the remission of their sins; and he said: »Ye shall receive the gift of the Holy Ghost. For the promise is unto you, and to your children, and to all that are afar off, even as many as the Lord our God shall call.« Acts 2:38,39

In immediate connection with the scenes of the great day of God, the Lord by the prophet Joel has promised a special manifestation of His Spirit. Joel 2:28 This prophecy received a partial fulfillment in the outpouring of the Spirit on the Day of Pentecost; but it will reach its full accomplishment in the manifestation of divine grace which will attend the closing work of the gospel.

The great controversy between good and evil will increase in intensity to the very close of time. In all ages the wrath of Satan has been manifested against the church of Christ; and God has bestowed His grace and Spirit upon His people to strengthen them to stand against the power of the evil one. When the apostles of Christ were to bear His gospel to the world and to record it for all future ages, they were especially endowed with the enlightenment of the Spirit. But as the church approaches her final deliverance, Satan is to work with greater power. He comes down »having great wrath, because he knoweth that he hath but a short time.« Revelation 12:12 He will work »with all power and signs and lying wonders.« 2.Thessalonians 2:9 For six thousand years that mastermind that once was highest among the angels of God has been wholly bent to the work of deception and ruin. And all the depths of satanic skill and subtlety acquired, all the cruelty developed, during these struggles of the ages, will be brought to bear against God's people in the final conflict. And in this time of peril the followers of Christ are to bear to the world the warning of the Lord's second advent; and a people are to be prepared to stand before Him at His coming, »without spot, and blameless.« 2 Peter 3:14 At this time the special endowment of divine grace and power is not less needful to the church than in apostolic days.

Through the illumination of the Holy Spirit, the scenes of the long-continued conflict between good and evil have been opened to the writer of these pages. From time to time I have been permitted to behold the working, in different ages, of the great controversy between Christ, the Prince of life, the Author of our salvation, and Satan, the prince of evil, the author of sin, the first transgressor of God's holy law. Satan's enmity against Christ has been manifested against His followers. The same hatred of the principles of God's law, the same policy of deception, by which error is made to appear as truth, by which human laws are substituted for the law of God, and men are led to worship the creature rather than the Creator, may be traced in all the history of the past. Satan's efforts to misrepresent the character of God, to cause men to cherish a false conception of the Creator, and thus to regard Him with fear and hate rather than with love; his endeavors to set aside the divine law, leading the people to think themselves free from its requirements; and his persecution of those who dare to resist his deceptions, have been steadfastly pursued in all ages. They may be traced in the history of patriarchs, prophets, and apostles, of martyrs and reformers.

In the great final conflict, Satan will employ the same policy, manifest the same spirit, and work for the same end as in all preceding ages. That which has been, will be, except that the coming struggle will be marked with a terrible intensity such as the world has never witnessed. Satan's deceptions will be more subtle, his assaults more determined. If it were possible, he would lead astray the elect. Mark 13:22, R.V.

As the Spirit of God has opened to my mind the great truths of His word, and the scenes of the past and the future, I have been bidden to make known to others that which has thus been revealed-to trace the history of the controversy in past ages, and especially so to present it as to shed a light on the fast-approaching struggle of the future. In pursuance of this purpose, I have endeavored to select and group together events in the history of the church in such a manner as to trace the unfolding of the great testing truths that at different periods have been given to the world, that have excited the wrath of Satan, and the enmity of a world-loving church, and that have been maintained by the witness of those who »loved not their lives unto the death.«

In these records we may see a foreshadowing of the conflict before us. Regarding them in the light of God‘s word, and by the illumination of His Spirit, we may see unveiled the devices of the wicked one, and the dangers which they must shun who would be found »without fault« before the Lord at His coming.

The great events which have marked the progress of reform in past ages are matters of history, well known and universally acknowledged by the Protestant world; they are facts which none can gainsay. This history I have presented briefly, in accordance with the scope of the book, and the brevity which must necessarily be observed, the facts having been condensed into as little space as seemed consistent with a proper understanding of their application. In some cases where a historian has so grouped together events as to afford, in brief, a comprehensive view of the subject, or has summarized details in a convenient manner, his words have been quoted; but in some instances no specific credit has been given, since the quotations are not given for the purpose of citing that writer as authority, but because his statement affords a ready and forcible presentation of the subject. In narrating the experience and views of those carrying forward the work of reform in our own time, similar use has been made of their published works.

It is not so much the object of this book to present new truths concerning the struggles of former times, as to bring out facts and principles which have a bearing on coming events. Yet viewed as a part of the controversy between the forces of light and darkness, all these records of the past are seen to have a new significance; and through them a light is cast upon the future, illumining the pathway of those who, like the reformers of past ages, will be called, even at the peril of all earthly good, to witness »for the word of God, and for the testimony of Jesus Christ.«

To unfold the scenes of the great controversy between truth and error; to reveal the wiles of Satan, and the means by which he may be successfully resisted; to present a satisfactory solution of the great problem of evil, shedding such a light upon the origin and the final disposition of sin as to make fully manifest the justice and benevolence of God in all His dealings with His creatures; and to show the holy, unchanging nature of His law, is the object of this book. That through its influence souls may be delivered from the power of darkness, and become »partakers of the inheritance of the saints in light,« to the praise of Him who loved us, and gave Himself for us, is the earnest prayer of the writer.

Ellen Gould White

Chapter 1

The Destruction of Jerusalem

»If thou hadst known, even thou, at least in this thy day, the things which belong unto thy peace! but now they are hid from thine eyes. For the days shall come upon thee, that thine enemies shall cast a trench about thee, and compass thee round, and keep thee in on every side, and shall lay thee even with the ground, and thy children within thee; and they shall not leave in thee one stone upon another; because thou knewest not the time of thy visitation.« Luke 19:42-44

From the crest of Olivet, Jesus looked upon Jerusalem. Fair and peaceful was the scene spread out before Him. It was the season of the Passover, and from all lands the children of Jacob had gathered there to celebrate the great national festival. In the midst of gardens and vineyards, and green slopes studded with pilgrims' tents, rose the terraced hills, the stately palaces, and massive bulwarks of Israel's capital. The daughter of Zion seemed in her pride to say, I sit a queen and shall see no sorrow; as lovely then, and deeming herself as secure in Heaven's favor, as when, ages before, the royal minstrel sang: »Beautiful for situation, the joy of the whole earth, is Mount Zion, ... the city of the great King.« Psalm 48:2 In full view were the magnificent buildings of the temple. The rays of the setting sun lighted up the snowy whiteness of its marble walls and gleamed from golden gate and tower and pinnacle. »The perfection of beauty« it stood, the pride of the Jewish nation. What child of Israel could gaze upon the scene without a thrill of joy and admiration! But far other thoughts occupied the mind of Jesus. »When He was come near, He beheld the city, and wept over it.« Luke 19:41

Amid the universal rejoicing of the triumphal entry, while palm branches waved, while glad hosannas awoke the echoes of the hills, and thousands of voices declared Him king, the world's Redeemer was overwhelmed with a sudden and mysterious sorrow. He, the Son of God, the Promised One of Israel, whose power had conquered death and called its captives from the grave, was in tears, not of ordinary grief, but of intense, irrepressible agony. His tears were not for Himself, though He well knew whither His feet were tending. Before Him lay Gethsemane, the scene of His approaching agony. The sheepgate also was in sight, through which for centuries the victims for sacrifice had been led, and which was to open for Him when He should be »brought as a lamb to the slaughter.« Isaiah 53:7 Not far distant was Calvary, the place of crucifixion. Upon the path which Christ was soon to tread must fall the horror of great darkness as He should make His soul an offering for sin. Yet it was not the contemplation of these scenes that cast the shadow upon Him in this hour of gladness. No foreboding of His own superhuman anguish clouded that unselfish spirit. He wept for the doomed thousands of Jerusalem because of the blindness and impenitence of those whom He came to bless and to save.

The history of more than a thousand years of God's special favor and guardian care, manifested to the chosen people, was open to the eye of Jesus. There was Mount Moriah, where the son of promise, an unresisting victim, had been bound to the altar emblem of the offering of the Son of God. There the covenant of blessing, the glorious Messianic promise, had been confirmed to the father of the faithful. Genesis 22:9,16-18 There the flames of the sacrifice ascending to heaven from the threshing floor of Ornan had turned aside the sword of the destroying angel 1 Chronicles 21 fitting symbol of the Saviour's sacrifice and mediation for guilty men. Jerusalem had been honored of God above all the earth. The Lord had »chosen Zion,« He had »desired it for His habitation.« Psalm 132:13 There, for ages, holy prophets had uttered their messages of warning. There priests had waved their censers, and the cloud of incense, with the prayers of the worshipers, had ascended before God. There daily the blood of slain lambs had been offered, pointing forward to the Lamb of God. There Jehovah had revealed His presence in the cloud of glory above the mercy seat. There rested the base of that mystic ladder connecting earth with heaven Genesis 28:12; John 1:51 that ladder upon which angels of God descended and ascended, and which opened to the world the way into the holiest of all. Had Israel as a nation preserved her allegiance to Heaven, Jerusalem would have stood forever, the elect of God. Jeremiah 17:21-25 But the history of that favored people was a record of backsliding and rebellion. They had resisted Heaven's grace, abused their privileges, and slighted their opportunities.

Although Israel had »mocked the messengers of God, and despised His words, and misused His prophets« 2 Chronicles 36:16 He had still manifested Himself to them, as »the Lord God, merciful and gracious, long-suffering, and abundant in goodness and truth« Exodus 34:6 notwithstanding repeated rejections, His mercy had continued its pleadings. With more than a father's pitying love for the son of his care, God had »sent to them by His messengers, rising up betimes, and sending; because He had compassion on His people, and on His dwelling place.« 2 Chronicles 36:15 When remonstrance, entreaty, and rebuke had failed, He sent to them the best gift of heaven; nay, He poured out all heaven in that one Gift.

The Son of God Himself was sent to plead with the impenitent city. It was Christ that had brought Israel as a goodly vine out of Egypt. Psalm 80:8 His own hand had cast out the heathen before it. He had planted it »in a very fruitful hill.« His guardian care had hedged it about. His servants had been sent to nurture it. »What could have been done more to My vineyard,« He exclaims, »that I have not done in it?« Isaiah 5:1-4 Though when He looked that it should bring forth grapes, it brought forth wild grapes, yet with a still yearning hope of fruitfulness He came in person to His vineyard, if haply it might be saved from destruction. He digged about His vine; He pruned and cherished it. He was unwearied in His efforts to save this vine of His own planting.

For three years the Lord of light and glory had gone in and out among His people. He »went about doing good, and healing all that were oppressed of the devil,« binding up the brokenhearted, setting at liberty them that were bound, restoring sight to the blind, causing the lame to walk and the deaf to hear, cleansing the lepers, raising the dead, and preaching the gospel to the poor. Acts 10:38; Luke 4:18; Matthew 11:5 To all classes alike was addressed the gracious call: »Come unto Me, all ye that labor and are heavy-laden, and I will give you rest.« Matthew 11:28

Though rewarded with evil for good, and hatred for His love, Psalm 109:5 He had steadfastly pursued His mission of mercy. Never were those repelled that sought His grace. A homeless wanderer, reproach and penury His daily lot, He lived to minister to the needs and lighten the woes of men, to plead with them to accept the gift of life. The waves of mercy, beaten back by those stubborn hearts, returned in a stronger tide of pitying, inexpressible [19/20] love. But Israel had turned from her best Friend and only Helper. The pleadings of His love had been despised, His counsels spurned, His warnings ridiculed.

The hour of hope and pardon was fast passing; the cup of God's long-deferred wrath was almost full. The cloud that had been gathering through ages of apostasy and rebellion, now black with woe, was about to burst upon a guilty people; and He who alone could save them from their impending fate had been slighted, abused, rejected, and was soon to be crucified. When Christ should hang upon the cross of Calvary, Israel's day as a nation favored and blessed of God would be ended. The loss of even one soul is a calamity infinitely outweighing the gains and treasures of a world; but as Christ looked upon Jerusalem, the doom of a whole city, a whole nation, was before Him that city, that nation, which had once been the chosen of God, His peculiar treasure.

Prophets had wept over the apostasy of Israel and the terrible desolations by which their sins were visited. Jeremiah wished that his eyes were a fountain of tears, that he might weep day and night for the slain of the daughter of his people, for the Lord's flock that was carried away captive. Jeremiah 9:1; 13:17 What, then, was the grief of Him whose prophetic glance took in, not years, but ages! He beheld the destroying angel with sword uplifted against the city which had so long been Jehovah's dwelling place. From the ridge of Olivet, the very spot afterward occupied by Titus and his army, He looked across the valley upon the sacred courts and porticoes, and with tear-dimmed eyes He saw, in awful perspective, the walls surrounded by alien hosts. He heard the tread of armies marshaling for war. He heard the voice of mothers and children crying for bread in the besieged city. He saw her holy and beautiful house, her palaces and towers, given to the flames, and where once they stood, only a heap of smoldering ruins.

Looking down the ages, He saw the covenant people scattered in every land, »like wrecks on a desert shore.« In the temporal retribution about to fall upon her children, He saw but the first draft from that cup of wrath which at the final judgment she must drain to its dregs. Divine pity, yearning love, found utterance in the mournful words: »O Jerusalem, Jerusalem, thou that killest the prophets, and stonest them which are sent unto thee, how often would I have

 gathered thy children together, even as a hen gathereth

her chickens under her wings, and ye would not!« O that thou, a nation favored above every other, hadst known the time of thy visitation, and the things that belong unto thy peace! I have stayed the angel of justice, I have called thee to repentance, but in vain. It is not merely servants, delegates, and prophets, whom thou hast refused and rejected, but the Holy One of Israel, thy Redeemer. If thou art destroyed, thou alone art responsible. »Ye will not come to Me, that ye might have life.« Matthew 23:37; John 5:40

Christ saw in Jerusalem a symbol of the world hardened in unbelief and rebellion, and hastening on to meet the retributive judgments of God. The woes of a fallen race, pressing upon His soul, forced from His lips that exceeding bitter cry. He saw the record of sin traced in human misery, tears, and blood; His heart was moved with infinite pity for the afflicted and suffering ones of earth; He yearned to relieve them all. But even His hand might not turn back the tide of human woe; few would seek their only Source of help. He was willing to pour out His soul unto death, to bring salvation within their reach; but few would come to Him that they might have life.

The Majesty of heaven in tears! the Son of the infinite God troubled in spirit, bowed down with anguish! The scene filled all heaven with wonder. That scene reveals to us the exceeding sinfulness of sin; it shows how hard a task it is, even for Infinite Power, to save the guilty from the consequences of transgressing the law of God. Jesus, looking down to the last generation, saw the world involved in a deception similar to that which caused the destruction of Jerusalem. The great sin of the Jews was their rejection of Christ; the great sin of the Christian world would be their rejection of the law of God, the foundation of His government in heaven and earth. The precepts of Jehovah would be despised and set at nought. Millions in bondage to sin, slaves of Satan, doomed to suffer the second death, would refuse to listen to the words of truth in their day of visitation. Terrible blindness! strange infatuation!

Two days before the Passover, when Christ had for the last time departed from the temple, after denouncing the hypocrisy of the Jewish rulers, He again went out with His disciples to the Mount of Olives and seated Himself with them upon the grassy slope overlooking the city. Once more He gazed upon its walls, its towers, and its palaces. Once more He beheld the temple in its dazzling splendor, a diadem of beauty crowning the sacred mount.

A thousand years before, the psalmist had magnified God's favor to Israel in making her holy house His dwelling place: »In Salem also is His tabernacle, and His dwelling place in Zion.« He »chose the tribe of Judah, the Mount Zion which He loved. And He built His sanctuary like high palaces.« Psalm 76:2; 78:68,69 The first temple had been erected during the most prosperous period of Israel's history. Vast stores of treasure for this purpose had been collected by King David, and the plans for its construction were made by divine inspiration. 1 Chronicles 28:12,19 Solomon, the wisest of Israel's monarchs, had completed the work. This temple was the most magnificent building which the world ever saw. Yet the Lord had declared by the prophet Haggai, concerning the second temple: »The glory of this latter house shall be greater than of the former.« »I will shake all nations, and the Desire of all nations shall come: and I will fill this house with glory, saith the Lord of hosts.« Haggai 2:9,7

After the destruction of the temple by Nebuchadnezzar it was rebuilt about five hundred years before the birth of Christ by a people who from a lifelong captivity had returned to a wasted and almost deserted country. There were then among them aged men who had seen the glory of Solomon's temple, and who wept at the foundation of the new building, that it must be so inferior to the former. The feeling that prevailed is forcibly described by the prophet: »Who is left among you that saw this house in her first glory? and how do ye see it now? is it not in your eyes in comparison of it as nothing?« Haggai 2:3; Ezra 3:12 Then was given the promise that the glory of this latter house should be greater than that of the former.

But the second temple had not equaled the first in magnificence; nor was it hallowed by those visible tokens of the divine presence which pertained to the first temple. There was no manifestation of supernatural power to mark its dedication. No cloud of glory was seen to fill the newly erected sanctuary. No fire from heaven descended to consume the sacrifice upon its altar. The Shekinah no longer abode between the cherubim in the most holy place; the ark, the mercy seat, and the tables of the testimony were not to be found therein. No voice sounded from heaven to make known to the inquiring priest the will of Jehovah.

For centuries the Jews had vainly endeavored to show wherein the promise of God given by Haggai had been fulfilled; yet pride and

unbelief blinded their minds to the true meaning of the

prophet's words. The second temple was not honored with the cloud of Jehovah's glory, but with the living presence of One in whom dwelt the fullness of the Godhead bodily who was God Himself manifest in the flesh. The »Desire of all nations« had indeed come to His temple when the Man of Nazareth taught and healed in the sacred courts. In the presence of Christ, and in this only, did the second temple exceed the first in glory. But Israel had put from her the proffered Gift of heaven. With the humble Teacher who had that day passed out from its golden gate, the glory had forever departed from the temple. Already were the Saviour's words fulfilled: »Your house is left unto you desolate.« Matthew 23:38

The disciples had been filled with awe and wonder at Christ's prediction of the overthrow of the temple, and they desired to understand more fully the meaning of His words. Wealth, labor, and architectural skill had for more than forty years been freely expended to enhance its splendors. Herod the Great had lavished upon it both Roman wealth and Jewish treasure, and even the emperor of the world had enriched it with his gifts. Massive blocks of white marble, of almost fabulous size, forwarded from Rome for this purpose, formed a part of its structure; and to these the disciples had called the attention of their Master, saying: »See what manner of stones and what buildings are here!« Mark 13:1

To these words, Jesus made the solemn and startling reply: »Verily I say unto you, There shall not be left here one stone upon another, that shall not be thrown down.« Matthew 24:2 With the overthrow of Jerusalem the disciples associated the events of Christ's personal coming in temporal glory to take the throne of universal empire, to punish the impenitent Jews, and to break from off the nation the Roman yoke. The Lord had told them that He would come the second time. Hence at the mention of judgments upon Jerusalem, their minds reverted to that coming; and as they were gathered about the Saviour upon the Mount of Olives, they asked: »When shall these things be? and what shall be the sign of Thy coming, and of the end of the world?« Verse 3

The future was mercifully veiled from the disciples. Had they at that time fully comprehended the two awful facts the Redeemer's sufferings and death, and the destruction of their city and temple they would have been overwhelmed with horror. Christ presented before them an outline of the prominent events to take place before the close of time. His words were not then fully understood; but their meaning was to be unfolded as His people should need the instruction therein given. The prophecy which He uttered was twofold in its meaning; while foreshadowing the destruction of Jerusalem, it prefigured also the terrors of the last great day.

Jesus declared to the listening disciples the judgments that were to fall upon apostate Israel, and especially the retributive vengeance that would come upon them for their rejection and crucifixion of the Messiah. Unmistakable signs would precede the awful climax. The dreaded hour would come suddenly and swiftly. And the Saviour warned His followers: »When ye therefore shall see the abomination of desolation, spoken of by Daniel the prophet, stand in the holy place, (whoso readeth, let him understand:) then let them which be in Judea flee into the mountains.« Matthew 24:15,16; Luke 21:20,21 When the idolatrous standards of the Romans should be set up in the holy ground, which extended some furlongs outside the city walls, then the followers of Christ were to find safety in flight. When the warning sign should be seen, those who would escape must make no delay. Throughout the land of Judea, as well as in Jerusalem itself, the signal for flight must be immediately obeyed. He who chanced to be upon the housetop must not go down into his house, even to save his most valued treasures. Those who were working in the fields or vineyards must not take time to return for the outer garment laid aside while they should be toiling in the heat of the day. They must not hesitate a moment, lest they be involved in the general destruction.

In the reign of Herod, Jerusalem had not only been greatly beautified, but by the erection of towers, walls, and fortresses, adding to the natural strength of its situation, it had been rendered apparently impregnable. He who would at this time have foretold publicly its destruction, would, like Noah in his day, have been called a crazed alarmist. But Christ had said: »Heaven and earth shall pass away, but My words shall not pass away.« Matthew 24:35 Because of her sins, wrath had been denounced against Jerusalem, and her stubborn unbelief rendered her doom certain.

The Lord had declared by the prophet Micah: »Hear this, I pray you, ye heads of the house of Jacob, and princes of the house of Israel, that abhor judgment, and pervert all equity. They build up Zion with blood, and Jerusalem with iniquity. The heads thereof judge

for reward, and the priests thereof teach for hire, and

the prophets thereof divine for money: yet will they lean upon the Lord, and say, Is not the Lord among us? none evil can come upon us.« Micah 3:9-11

These words faithfully described the corrupt and self-righteous inhabitants of Jerusalem. While claiming to observe rigidly the precepts of God's law, they were transgressing all its principles. They hated Christ because His purity and holiness revealed their iniquity; and they accused Him of being the cause of all the troubles which had come upon them in consequence of their sins. Though they knew Him to be sinless, they had declared that His death was necessary to their safety as a nation. »If we let Him thus alone,« said the Jewish leaders, »all men will believe on Him: and the Romans shall come and take away both our place and nation.« John 11:48 If Christ were sacrificed, they might once more become a strong, united people. Thus they reasoned, and they concurred in the decision of their high priest, that it would be better for one man to die than for the whole nation to perish.

Thus the Jewish leaders had built up »Zion with blood, and Jerusalem with iniquity.« Micah 3:10 And yet, while they slew their Saviour because He reproved their sins, such was their self-righteousness that they regarded themselves as God's favored people and expected the Lord to deliver them from their enemies. »Therefore,« continued the prophet, »shall Zion for your sake be plowed as a field, and Jerusalem shall become heaps, and the mountain of the house as the high places of the forest.« Verse 12

For nearly forty years after the doom of Jerusalem had been pronounced by Christ Himself, the Lord delayed His judgments upon the city and the nation. Wonderful was the long-suffering of God toward the rejectors of His gospel and the murderers of His Son. The parable of the unfruitful tree represented God's dealings with the Jewish nation. The command had gone forth, »Cut it down; why cumbereth it the ground?« Luke 13:7 but divine mercy had spared it yet a little longer. There were still many among the Jews who were ignorant of the character and the work of Christ. And the children had not enjoyed the opportunities or received the light which their parents had spurned. Through the preaching of the apostles and their associates, God would cause light to shine upon them; they would be permitted to see how prophecy had been fulfilled, not only in the birth and life of Christ, but in His death and resurrection. The children [27/28] were not condemned for the sins of the parents; but when, with a knowledge of all the light given to their parents, the children rejected the additional light granted to themselves, they became partakers of the parents' sins, and filled up the measure of their iniquity.

The long-suffering of God toward Jerusalem only confirmed the Jews in their stubborn impenitence. In their hatred and cruelty toward the disciples of Jesus they rejected the last offer of mercy. Then God withdrew His protection from them and removed His restraining power from Satan and his angels, and the nation was left to the control of the leader she had chosen. Her children had spurned the grace of Christ, which would have enabled them to subdue their evil impulses, and now these became the conquerors. Satan aroused the fiercest and most debased passions of the soul. Men did not reason; they were beyond reason controlled by impulse and blind rage. They became satanic in their cruelty. In the family and in the nation, among the highest and the lowest classes alike, there was suspicion, envy, hatred, strife, rebellion, murder. There was no safety anywhere. Friends and kindred betrayed one another. Parents slew their children, and children their parents. The rulers of the people had no power to rule themselves. Uncontrolled passions made them tyrants. The Jews had accepted false testimony to condemn the innocent Son of God. Now false accusations made their own lives uncertain. By their actions they had long been saying: »Cause the Holy One of Israel to cease from before us.« Isaiah 30:11 Now their desire was granted. The fear of God no longer disturbed them. Satan was at the head of the nation, and the highest civil and religious authorities were under his sway.

The leaders of the opposing factions at times united to plunder and torture their wretched victims, and again they fell upon each other's forces and slaughtered without mercy. Even the sanctity of the temple could not restrain their horrible ferocity. The worshipers were stricken down before the altar, and the sanctuary was polluted with the bodies of the slain. Yet in their blind and blasphemous presumption the instigators of this hellish work publicly declared that they had no fear that Jerusalem would be destroyed, for it was God's own city. To establish their power more firmly, they bribed false prophets to proclaim, even while Roman legions were besieging the temple, that the people were to wait for deliverance from God. To the

 last, multitudes held fast to the belief that the Most

High would interpose for the defeat of their adversaries. But Israel had spurned the divine protection, and now she had no defense. Unhappy Jerusalem! rent by internal dissensions, the blood of her children slain by one another's hands crimsoning her streets, while alien armies beat down her fortifications and slew her men of war!

All the predictions given by Christ concerning the destruction of Jerusalem were fulfilled to the letter. The Jews experienced the truth of His words of warning: »With what measure ye mete, it shall be measured to you again.« Matthew 7:2

Signs and wonders appeared, foreboding disaster and doom. In the midst of the night an unnatural light shone over the temple and the altar. Upon the clouds at sunset were pictured chariots and men of war gathering for battle. The priests ministering by night in the sanctuary were terrified by mysterious sounds; the earth trembled, and a multitude of voices were heard crying: »Let us depart hence.« The great eastern gate, which was so heavy that it could hardly be shut by a score of men, and which was secured by immense bars of iron fastened deep in the pavement of solid stone, opened at midnight, without visible agency. Milman, The History of the Jews, book 13

For seven years a man continued to go up and down the streets of Jerusalem, declaring the woes that were to come upon the city. By day and by night he chanted the wild dirge: »A voice from the east! a voice from the west! a voice from the four winds! a voice against Jerusalem and against the temple! a voice against the bridegrooms and the brides! a voice against the whole people!« Ibid. This strange being was imprisoned and scourged, but no complaint escaped his lips. To insult and abuse he answered only: »Woe, woe to Jerusalem!« »woe, woe to the inhabitants thereof!« His warning cry ceased not until he was slain in the siege he had foretold.

Not one Christian perished in the destruction of Jerusalem. Christ had given His disciples warning, and all who believed His words watched for the promised sign. »When ye shall see Jerusalem compassed with armies,« said Jesus, »then know that the desolation thereof is nigh. Then let them which are in Judea flee to the mountains; and let them which are in the midst of it depart out.« Luke 21:20, 21 After the Romans under Cestius had surrounded the city, they unexpectedly abandoned the siege when everything seemed favorable for an immediate attack. The besieged, despairing of successful resistance, were on the point of surrender, when the Roman general withdrew his forces without the least apparent reason. But God's merciful providence was directing events for the good of His own people. The promised sign had been given to the waiting Christians, and now an opportunity was offered for all who would, to obey the Saviour's warning. Events were so overruled that neither Jews nor Romans should hinder the flight of the Christians. Upon the retreat of Cestius, the Jews, sallying from Jerusalem, pursued after his retiring army; and while both forces were thus fully engaged, the Christians had an opportunity to leave the city. At this time the country also had been cleared of enemies who might have endeavored to intercept them. At the time of the siege, the Jews were assembled at Jerusalem to keep the Feast of Tabernacles, and thus the Christians throughout the land were able to make their escape unmolested. Without delay they fled to a place of safety the city of Pella, in the land of Perea, beyond Jordan.

The Jewish forces, pursuing after Cestius and his army, fell upon their rear with such fierceness as to threaten them with total destruction. It was with great difficulty that the Romans succeeded in making their retreat. The Jews escaped almost without loss, and with their spoils returned in triumph to Jerusalem. Yet this apparent success brought them only evil. It inspired them with that spirit of stubborn resistance to the Romans which speedily brought unutterable woe upon the doomed city.

Terrible were the calamities that fell upon Jerusalem when the siege was resumed by Titus. The city was invested at the time of the Passover, when millions of Jews were assembled within its walls. Their stores of provision, which if carefully preserved would have supplied the inhabitants for years, had previously been destroyed through the jealousy and revenge of the contending factions, and now all the horrors of starvation were experienced. A measure of wheat was sold for a talent. So fierce were the pangs of hunger that men would gnaw the leather of their belts and sandals and the covering of their shields. Great numbers of the people would steal out at night to gather wild plants growing outside the city walls, though many were seized and put to death with cruel torture, and often those who returned in safety were robbed of what they had gleaned at so great peril. The most inhuman tortures were inflicted by those in power, to force from the want-stricken people the last scanty supplies which they might have

concealed. And these cruelties were not infrequently

practiced by men who were themselves well fed, and who were merely desirous of laying up a store of provision for the future.

Thousands perished from famine and pestilence. Natural affection seemed to have been destroyed. Husbands robbed their wives, and wives their husbands. Children would be seen snatching the food from the mouths of their aged parents. The question of the prophet, »Can a woman forget her sucking child?« received the answer within the walls of that doomed city: »The hands of the pitiful women have sodden their own children: they were their meat in the destruction of the daughter of my people.« Isaiah 49:15; Lamentations 4:10 Again was fulfilled the warning prophecy given fourteen centuries before: »The tender and delicate woman among you, which would not adventure to set the sole of her foot upon the ground for delicateness and tenderness, her eye shall be evil toward the husband of her bosom, and toward her son, and toward her daughter, ... and toward her children which she shall bear: for she shall eat them for want of all things secretly in the siege and straitness, wherewith thine enemy shall distress thee in thy gates.« Deuteronomy 28:56,57

The Roman leaders endeavored to strike terror to the Jews and thus cause them to surrender. Those prisoners who resisted when taken, were scourged, tortured, and crucified before the wall of the city. Hundreds were daily put to death in this manner, and the dreadful work continued until, along the Valley of Jehoshaphat and at Calvary, crosses were erected in so great numbers that there was scarcely room to move among them. So terribly was visited that awful imprecation uttered before the judgment seat of Pilate: »His blood be on us, and on our children.« Matthew 27:25

Titus would willingly have put an end to the fearful scene, and thus have spared Jerusalem the full measure of her doom. He was filled with horror as he saw the bodies of the dead lying in heaps in the valleys. Like one entranced, he looked from the crest of Olivet upon the magnificent temple and gave command that not one stone of it be touched. Before attempting to gain possession of this stronghold, he made an earnest appeal to the Jewish leaders not to force him to defile the sacred place with blood. If they would come forth and fight in any other place, no Roman should violate the sanctity of the temple. Josephus himself, in a most eloquent appeal, entreated them to surrender, to save themselves, their city, and their place of worship. But his words were answered with bitter curs- [32/33] es. Darts were hurled at him, their last human mediator, as he stood pleading with them. The Jews had rejected the entreaties of the Son of God, and now expostulation and entreaty only made them more determined to resist to the last. In vain were the efforts of Titus to save the temple; One greater than he had declared that not one stone was to be left upon another.

The blind obstinacy of the Jewish leaders, and the detestable crimes perpetrated within the besieged city, excited the horror and indignation of the Romans, and Titus at last decided to take the temple by storm. He determined, however, that if possible it should be saved from destruction. But his commands were disregarded. After he had retired to his tent at night, the Jews, sallying from the temple, attacked the soldiers without. In the struggle, a firebrand was flung by a soldier through an opening in the porch, and immediately the cedar-lined chambers about the holy house were in a blaze. Titus rushed to the place, followed by his generals and legionaries, and commanded the soldiers to quench the flames. His words were unheeded. In their fury the soldiers hurled blazing brands into the chambers adjoining the temple, and then with their swords they slaughtered in great numbers those who had found shelter there. Blood flowed down the temple steps like water. Thousands upon thousands of Jews perished. Above the sound of battle, voices were heard shouting: »Ichabod!« the glory is departed.

»Titus found it impossible to check the rage of the soldiery; he entered with his officers, and surveyed the interior of the sacred edifice. The splendor filled them with wonder; and as the flames had not yet penetrated to the holy place, he made a last effort to save it, and springing forth, again exhorted the soldiers to stay the progress of the conflagration. The centurion Liberalis endeavored to force obedience with his staff of office; but even respect for the emperor gave way to the furious animosity against the Jews, to the fierce excitement of battle, and to the insatiable hope of plunder. The soldiers saw everything around them radiant with gold, which shone dazzlingly in the wild light of the flames; they supposed that incalculable treasures were laid up in the sanctuary. A soldier, unperceived, thrust a lighted torch between the hinges of the door: the whole building was in flames in an instant. The blinding smoke and fire forced the officers to retreat, and the noble edifice was left to its fate.

»It was an appalling spectacle to the Roman what was it to the Jew? The whole summit of the hill which commanded the city, blazed like a volcano. One after another the buildings fell in, with a tremendous crash, and were swallowed up in the fiery abyss. The roofs of cedar were like sheets of flame; the gilded pinnacles shone like spikes of red light; the gate towers sent up tall columns of flame and smoke. The neighboring hills were lighted up; and dark groups of people were seen watching in horrible anxiety the progress of the destruction: the walls and heights of the upper city were crowded with faces, some pale with the agony of despair, others scowling unavailing vengeance. The shouts of the Roman soldiery as they ran to and fro, and the howlings of the insurgents who were perishing in the flames, mingled with the roaring of the conflagration and the thundering sound of falling timbers. The echoes of the mountains replied or brought back the shrieks of the people on the heights; all along the walls resounded screams and wailings; men who were expiring with famine rallied their remaining strength to utter a cry of anguish and desolation. »The slaughter within was even more dreadful than the spectacle from without. Men and women, old and young, insurgents and priests, those who fought and those who entreated mercy, were hewn down in indiscriminate carnage. The number of the slain exceeded that of the slayers. The legionaries had to clamber over heaps of dead to carry on the work of extermination.« Milman, The History of the Jews, book 16

After the destruction of the temple, the whole city soon fell into the hands of the Romans. The leaders of the Jews forsook their impregnable towers, and Titus found them solitary. He gazed upon them with amazement, and declared that God had given them into his hands; for no engines, however powerful, could have prevailed against those stupendous battlements. Both the city and the temple were razed to their foundations, and the ground upon which the holy house had stood was »plowed like a field.« Jeremiah 26:18 In the siege and the slaughter that followed, more than a million of the people perished; the survivors were carried away as captives, sold as slaves, dragged to Rome to grace the conqueror's triumph, thrown to wild beasts in the amphitheaters, or scattered as homeless wanderers throughout the earth.

The Jews had forged their own fetters; they had filled for themselves the cup of vengeance. In the utter destruction that befell them as a nation, and in all the woes that followed them in their dispersion, they were but reaping the harvest which their own hands had sown. Says the prophet: »O Israel, thou hast destroyed thyself;« »for thou hast fallen by thine iniquity.« Hosea 13:9; 14:1 Their sufferings are often represented as a punishment visited upon them by the direct decree of God. It is thus that the great deceiver seeks to conceal his own work. By stubborn rejection of divine love and mercy, the Jews had caused the protection of God to be withdrawn from them, and Satan was permitted to rule them according to his will. The horrible cruelties enacted in the destruction of Jerusalem are a demonstration of Satan's vindictive power over those who yield to his control.

We cannot know how much we owe to Christ for the peace and protection which we enjoy. It is the restraining power of God that prevents mankind from passing fully under the control of Satan. The disobedient and unthankful have great reason for gratitude for God's mercy and long-suffering in holding in check the cruel, malignant power of the evil one. But when men pass the limits of divine forbearance, that restraint is removed. God does not stand toward the sinner as an executioner of the sentence against transgression; but He leaves the rejectors of His mercy to themselves, to reap that which they have sown. Every ray of light rejected, every warning despised or unheeded, every passion indulged, every transgression of the law of God, is a seed sown which yields its unfailing harvest. The Spirit of God, persistently resisted, is at last withdrawn from the sinner, and then there is left no power to control the evil passions of the soul, and no protection from the malice and enmity of Satan. The destruction of Jerusalem is a fearful and solemn warning to all who are trifling with the offers of divine grace and resisting the pleadings of divine mercy. Never was there given a more decisive testimony to God's hatred of sin and to the certain punishment that will fall upon the guilty.

The Saviour's prophecy concerning the visitation of judgments upon Jerusalem is to have another fulfillment, of which that terrible desolation was but a faint shadow. In the fate of the chosen city we may behold the doom of a world that has rejected God's mercy and trampled upon His law. Dark are the records of human misery that earth has witnessed during its long centuries of crime. The heart sickens, and the mind grows faint in contemplation. Terrible have been the results of rejecting the authority of Heaven.

But a scene yet darker is presented in the revelations of the future. The records of the past, the long procession of tumults, conflicts, and revolutions, the »battle of the warrior ... with confused noise, and garments rolled in blood« Isaiah 9:5 what are these, in contrast with the terrors of that day when the restraining Spirit of God shall be wholly withdrawn from the wicked, no longer to hold in check the outburst of human passion and satanic wrath! The world will then behold, as never before, the results of Satan's rule.

But in that day, as in the time of Jerusalem's destruction, God's people will be delivered, everyone that shall be found written among the living. Isaiah 4:3 Christ has declared that He will come the second time to gather His faithful ones to Himself: »Then shall all the tribes of the earth mourn, and they shall see the Son of man coming in the clouds of heaven with power and great glory. And He shall send His angels with a great sound of a trumpet, and they shall gather together His elect from the four winds, from one end of heaven to the other.« Matthew 24:30,31 Then shall they that obey not the gospel be consumed with the spirit of His mouth and be destroyed with the brightness of His coming. 2.Thessalonians 2:8 Like Israel of old the wicked destroy themselves; they fall by their iniquity. By a life of sin, they have placed themselves so out of harmony with God, their natures have become so debased with evil, that the manifestation of His glory is to them a consuming fire.

Let men beware lest they neglect the lesson conveyed to them in the words of Christ. As He warned His disciples of Jerusalem's destruction, giving them a sign of the approaching ruin, that they might make their escape; so He has warned the world of the day of final destruction and has given them tokens of its approach, that all who will may flee from the wrath to come. Jesus declares: »There shall be signs in the sun, and in the moon, and in the stars; and upon the earth distress of nations.« Luke 21:25; Matthew 24:29; Mark 13:24-26; Revelation 6:12-17 Those who behold these harbingers of His coming are to »know that it is near, even at the doors.« Matthew 24:33 »Watch ye therefore,« are His words of admonition. Mark 13:35 They that heed the warning shall not be left in darkness, that that day should overtake them unawares. But to them that will not watch, »the day of the Lord so cometh as a thief in the night.« 1 Thessalonians 5:2-5

The world is no more ready to credit the message for this time than were the Jews to receive the Saviour's warning [36/37] concerning Jerusalem. Come when it may, the day of God will come unawares to the ungodly. When life is going on in its unvarying round; when men are absorbed in pleasure, in business, in traffic, in money-making; when religious leaders are magnifying the world's progress and enlightenment, and the people are lulled in a false security then, as the midnight thief steals within the unguarded dwelling, so shall sudden destruction come upon the careless and ungodly, »and they shall not escape.« Verse 3

Destruction of Jerusalem and the Temple

Chapter 2

Persecution in the First Centuries

When Jesus revealed to His disciples the fate of Jerusalem and the scenes of the second advent, He foretold also the experience of His people from the time when He should be taken from them, to His return in power and glory for their deliverance. From Olivet the Saviour beheld the storms about to fall upon the apostolic church; and penetrating deeper into the future, His eye discerned the fierce, wasting tempests that were to beat upon His followers in the coming ages of darkness and persecution. In a few brief utterances of awful significance He foretold the portion which the rulers of this world would mete out to the church of God. Matthew 24:9, 21-22 The followers of Christ must tread the same path of humiliation, reproach, and suffering which their Master trod. The enmity that burst forth against the world's Redeemer would be manifested against all who should believe on His name.

The history of the early church testified to the fulfillment of the Saviour's words. The powers of earth and hell arrayed themselves against Christ in the person of His followers. Paganism foresaw that should the gospel triumph, her temples and altars would be swept away; therefore she summoned her forces to destroy Christianity. The fires of persecution were kindled. Christians were stripped of their possessions and driven from their homes. They »endured a great fight of afflictions.« Hebrews 10:32 They »had trial of cruel mockings and scourgings, yea, moreover of bonds and imprisonment.« Hebrews 11:36 Great numbers sealed their testimony with their blood. Noble and slave, rich and poor, learned and ignorant, were alike slain without mercy. These persecutions, beginning under Nero about the time of the martyrdom of Paul, continued with greater or less fury for centuries. Christians were falsely accused of the most dreadful crimes and declared to be the cause of great calamities – famine, pestilence, and earthquake. As they became the objects of popular hatred and suspicion, informers stood ready, for the sake of gain, to betray the innocent.

They were condemned as rebels against the empire, as foes of religion, and pests to society. Great numbers were thrown to wild beasts or burned alive in the amphitheaters. Some were crucified; others were covered with the skins of wild animals and thrust into the arena to be torn by dogs. Their punishment was often made the chief entertainment at public fetes. Vast multitudes assembled to enjoy the sight and greeted their dying agonies with laughter and applause.

Wherever they sought refuge, the followers of Christ were hunted like beasts of prey. They were forced to seek concealment in desolate and solitary places. »Destitute, afflicted, tormented; (of whom the world was not worthy:) they wandered in deserts, and in mountains, and in dens and caves of the earth.« Verses 37-38 The catacombs afforded shelter for thousands. Beneath the hills outside the city of Rome, long galleries had been tunneled through earth and rock; the dark and intricate network of passages extended for miles beyond the city walls. In these underground retreats the followers of Christ buried their dead; and here also, when suspected and proscribed, they found a home. When the Life-giver shall awaken those who have fought the good fight, many a martyr for Christ's sake will come forth from those gloomy caverns.

Under the fiercest persecution these witnesses for Jesus kept their faith unsullied. Though deprived of every comfort, shut away from the light of the sun, making their home in the dark but friendly bosom of the earth, they uttered no complaint. With words of faith, patience, and hope they encouraged one another to endure privation and distress. The loss of every earthly blessing could not force

Kolosseum in Rome

Nero Claudius Caesar (37-68)

them to renounce their belief in Christ. Trials and persecution were but steps bringing them nearer their rest and their reward.

Like God's servants of old, many were »tortured, not accepting deliverance; that they might obtain a better resurrection.« Verse 35 These called to mind the words of their Master, that when persecuted for Christ's sake, they were to be exceeding glad, for great would be their reward in heaven; for so the prophets had been persecuted before them. They rejoiced that they were accounted worthy to suffer for the truth, and songs of triumph ascended from the midst of crackling flames. Looking upward by faith, they saw Christ and angels leaning over the battlements of heaven, gazing upon them with the deepest interest and regarding their steadfastness with approval. A voice came down to them from the throne of God: »Be thou faithful unto death, and I will give thee a crown of life.« Revelation 2:10

In vain were Satan's efforts to destroy the church of Christ by violence. The great controversy in which the disciples of Jesus yielded up their lives did not cease when these faithful standard-bearers fell at their post. By defeat they conquered. God's workmen were slain, but His work went steadily forward. The gospel continued to spread and the number of its adherents to increase. It penetrated into regions that were inaccessible even to the eagles of Rome. Said a Christian, expostulating with the heathen rulers who were urging forward the persecution: You may »kill us, torture us, condemn us ... Your injustice is the proof that we are innocent. ... Nor does your cruelty ... avail you.« It was but a stronger invitation to bring others to their persuasion. »The oftener we are mown down by you, the more in number we grow; the blood of Christians is seed.« Tertullian, Apology, chapter 50

Thousands were imprisoned and slain, but others sprang up to fill their places. And those who were martyred for their faith were secured to Christ and accounted of Him as conquerors. They had fought the good fight, and they were to receive the crown of glory when Christ should come. The sufferings which they endured brought Christians nearer to one another and to their Redeemer. Their living example and dying testimony were a constant witness for the truth; and where least expected, the subjects of Satan were leaving his service and enlisting under the banner of Christ. Satan therefore laid his plans to war more successfully against the government of God by planting his banner in the Christian church. If the followers of Christ could be deceived and led to displease God, then their strength, fortitude, and firmness would fail, and they would fall an easy prey.

The great adversary now endeavored to gain by artifice what he had failed to secure by force. Persecution ceased, and in its stead were substituted the dangerous allurements of temporal prosperity and worldly honor. Idolaters were led to receive a part of the Christian faith, while they rejected other essential truths. They professed to accept Jesus as the Son of God and to believe in His death and resurrection, but they had no conviction of sin and felt no need of repentance or of a change of heart. With some concessions on their part they proposed that Christians should make concessions, that all might unite on the platform of belief in Christ.

Now the church was in fearful peril. Prison, torture, fire, and sword were blessings in comparison with this. Some of the Christians stood firm, declaring that they could make no compromise. Others were in favor of yielding or modifying some features of their faith and uniting with those who had accepted a part of Christianity, urging that this might be the means of their full conversion. That was a time of deep anguish to the faithful followers of Christ. Under a cloak of pretended Christianity, Satan was insinuating himself into the church, to corrupt their faith and turn their minds from the word of truth.

Most of the Christians at last consented to lower their standard, and a union was formed between Christianity and paganism. Although the worshipers of idols professed to be converted, and united with the church, they still clung to their idolatry, only changing the objects of their worship to images of Jesus, and even of Mary and the saints. The foul leaven of idolatry, thus brought into the church, continued its baleful work. Unsound doctrines, superstitious rites, and idolatrous ceremonies were incorporated into her faith and worship. As the followers of Christ united with idolaters, the Christian religion became corrupted, and the church lost her purity and power. There were some, however, who were not misled by these delusions. They still maintained their fidelity to the Author of truth and worshiped God alone.

There have ever been two classes among those who profess to be followers of Christ. While one class study the Saviour's life and earnestly seek to correct their defects and conform to the Pattern,
 the other class shun the plain, practical truths which

expose their errors. Even in her best estate the church was not composed wholly of the true, pure, and sincere. Our Saviour taught that those who willfully indulge in sin are not to be received into the church; yet He connected with Himself men who were faulty in character, and granted them the benefits of His teachings and example, that they might have an opportunity to see their errors and correct them. Among the twelve apostles was a traitor. Judas was accepted, not because of his defects of character, but notwithstanding them. He was connected with the disciples, that, through the instruction and example of Christ, he might learn what constitutes Christian character, and thus be led to see his errors, to repent, and, by the aid of divine grace, to purify his soul »in obeying the truth.« But Judas did not walk in the light so graciously permitted to shine upon him. By indulgence in sin he invited the temptations of Satan. His evil traits of character became predominant. He yielded his mind to the control of the powers of darkness, he became angry when his faults were reproved, and thus he was led to commit the fearful crime of betraying his Master. So do all who cherish evil under a profession of godliness hate those who disturb their peace by condemning their course of sin. When a favorable opportunity is presented, they will, like Judas, betray those who for their good have sought to reprove them.

The apostles encountered those in the church who professed godliness while they were secretly cherishing iniquity. Ananias and Sapphira acted the part of deceivers, pretending to make an entire sacrifice for God, when they were covetously withholding a portion for themselves. The Spirit of truth revealed to the apostles the real character of these pretenders, and the judgments of God rid the church of this foul blot upon its purity. This signal evidence of the discerning Spirit of Christ in the church was a terror to hypocrites and evildoers. They could not long remain in connection with those who were, in habit and disposition, constant representatives of Christ; and as trials and persecution came upon His followers, those only who were willing to forsake all for the truth's sake desired to become His disciples. Thus, as long as persecution continued, the church remained comparatively pure. But as it ceased, converts were added who were less sincere and devoted, and the way was open for Satan to obtain a foothold. But there is no union between the Prince of light and the prince of darkness, and there can be no union between their followers. When Christians consented to unite with those who were but half converted from paganism, they entered upon a path which led further and further from the truth. Satan exulted that he had succeeded in deceiving so large a number of the followers of Christ. He then brought his power to bear more fully upon these, and inspired them to persecute those who remained true to God. None understood so well how to oppose the true Christian faith as did those who had once been its defenders; and these apostate Christians, uniting with their half-pagan companions, directed their warfare against the most essential features of the doctrines of Christ.

It required a desperate struggle for those who would be faithful to stand firm against the deceptions and abominations which were disguised in sacerdotal garments and introduced into the church. The Bible was not accepted as the standard of faith. The doctrine of religious freedom was termed heresy, and its upholders were hated and proscribed.

After a long and severe conflict, the faithful few decided to dissolve all union with the apostate church if she still refused to free herself from falsehood and idolatry. They saw that separation was an absolute necessity if they would obey the word of God. They dared not tolerate errors fatal to their own souls, and set an example which would imperil the faith of their children and children's children. To secure peace and unity they were ready to make any concession consistent with fidelity to God; but they felt that even peace would be too dearly purchased at the sacrifice of principle. If unity could be secured only by the compromise of truth and righteousness, then let there be difference, and even war.

Well would it be for the church and the world if the principles that actuated those steadfast souls were revived in the hearts of God's professed people. There is an alarming indifference in regard to the doctrines which are the pillars of the Christian faith. The opinion is gaining ground, that, after all, these are not of vital importance. This degeneracy is strengthening the hands of the agents of Satan, so that false theories and fatal delusions which the faithful in ages past imperiled their lives to resist and expose, are now regarded with favor by thousands who claim to be followers of Christ.

The early Christians were indeed a peculiar people. Their blameless deportment and unswerving faith were a continual reproof that disturbed the sinner's peace. Though few in numbers, without wealth, position, or honorary titles, they were a terror to evildoers wherever their character and doctrines were known. Therefore they were hated by the wicked, even as Abel was hated by the ungodly Cain. For the same reason that Cain slew Abel, did those who sought to throw off the restraint of the Holy Spirit, put to death God's people. It was for the same reason that the Jews rejected and crucified the Saviour – because the purity and holiness of His character was a constant rebuke to their selfishness and corruption.

From the days of Christ until now His faithful disciples have excited the hatred and opposition of those who love and follow the ways of sin. How, then, can the gospel be called a message of peace? When Isaiah foretold the birth of the Messiah, he ascribed to Him the title, »Prince of Peace.« When angels announced to the shepherds that Christ was born, they sang above the plains of Bethlehem: »Glory to God in the highest, and on earth peace, good will toward men.« Luke 2:14 There is a seeming contradiction between these prophetic declarations and the words of Christ: »I came not to send peace, but a sword.« Matthew 10:34 But, rightly understood, the two are in perfect harmony. The gospel is a message of peace. Christianity is a system which, received and obeyed, would spread peace, harmony, and happiness throughout the earth. The religion of Christ will unite in close brotherhood all who accept its teachings. It was the mission of Jesus to reconcile men to God, and thus to one another. But the world at large are under the control of Satan, Christ's bitterest foe. The gospel presents to them principles of life which are wholly at variance with their habits and desires, and they rise in rebellion against it. They hate the purity which reveals and condemns their sins, and they persecute and destroy those who would urge upon them its just and holy claims. It is in this sense – because the exalted truths it brings occasion hatred and strife – that the gospel is called a sword.

The mysterious providence which permits the righteous to suffer persecution at the hand of the wicked has been a cause of great perplexity to many who are weak in faith. Some are even ready to cast away their confidence in God because He suffers the basest of men to prosper, while the best and purest are afflicted and tormented by their cruel power. How, it is asked, can One who is just and merciful, and who is also infinite in power, tolerate such injustice and oppression? This is a question with which we have nothing to do. God has given us sufficient evidence of His love, and we are not to doubt His goodness because we cannot understand the workings of His providence. Said the Saviour to His disciples, foreseeing the doubts that would press upon their souls in days of trial and darkness: »Remember the word that I said unto you, The servant is not greater than his lord. If they have persecuted Me, they will also persecute you.« John 15:20 Jesus suffered for us more than any of His followers can be made to suffer through the cruelty of wicked men. Those who are called to endure torture and martyrdom are but following in the steps of God's dear Son.

»The Lord is not slack concerning His promise.« 2 Peter 3:9 He does not forget or neglect His children; but He permits the wicked to reveal their true character, that none who desire to do His will may be deceived concerning them. Again, the righteous are placed in the furnace of affliction, that they themselves may be purified; that their example may convince others of the reality of faith and godliness; and also that their consistent course may condemn the ungodly and unbelieving.

God permits the wicked to prosper and to reveal their enmity against Him, that when they shall have filled up the measure of their iniquity all may see His justice and mercy in their utter destruction. The day of His vengeance hastens, when all who have transgressed His law and oppressed His people will meet the just recompense of their deeds; when every act of cruelty or injustice toward God's faithful ones will be punished as though done to Christ Himself.

There is another and more important question that should engage the attention of the churches of today. The apostle Paul declares that »all that will live godly in Christ Jesus shall suffer persecution.« 2 Timothy 3:12 Why is it, then, that persecution seems in a great degree to slumber? The only reason is that the church has conformed to the world's standard and therefore awakens no opposition. The religion which is current in our day is not of the pure and holy character that marked the Christian faith in the days of Christ and His apostles. It is only because of the spirit of compromise with sin, because the great truths of the word of God are so indifferently regarded, because there is so little vital godliness in the church, that Christianity is apparently so popular with the world. Let there be a revival of the faith and power of the early church, and the spirit of persecution will be revived, and the fires of persecution will be rekindled.

Chapter 3

An Era of Spiritual Darkness

The apostle Paul, in his second letter to the Thessalonians, foretold the great apostasy which would result in the establishment of the papal power. He declared that the day of Christ should not come, »except there come a falling away first, and that man of sin be revealed, the son of perdition; who opposeth and exalteth himself above all that is called God, or that is worshiped; so that he as God sitteth in the temple of God, showing himself that he is God.« And furthermore, the apostle warns his brethren that »the mystery of iniquity doth already work.« 2 Thessalonians 2:3,4,7 Even at that early date he saw, creeping into the church, errors that would prepare the way for the development of the papacy.

Little by little, at first in stealth and silence, and then more openly as it increased in strength and gained control of the minds of men, »the mystery of iniquity« carried forward its deceptive and blasphemous work. Almost imperceptibly the customs of heathenism found their way into the Christian church. The spirit of compromise and conformity was restrained for a time by the fierce persecutions which the church endured under paganism. But as persecution ceased, and Christianity entered the courts and palaces of kings, she laid aside the humble simplicity of Christ and His apostles for the pomp and pride of pagan priests and rulers; and in place of the requirements of God, she substituted human theories and traditions. The nominal conversion of Constantine, in the early part of the fourth century, caused great rejoicing; and the world, cloaked with a form of righteousness, walked into the church. Now the work of corruption rapidly progressed. Paganism, while appearing to be vanquished, became the conqueror. Her spirit controlled the church. Her doctrines, ceremonies, and superstitions were incorporated into the faith and worship of the professed followers of Christ.

This compromise between paganism and Christianity resulted in the development of »the man of sin« foretold in prophecy as opposing and exalting himself above God. That gigantic [49/50] system of false religionis a masterpiece of Satan's power – a monument of his efforts to seat himself upon the throne to rule the earth according to his will.

Satan once endeavored to form a compromise with Christ. He came to the Son of God in the wilderness of temptation, and showing Him all the kingdoms of the world and the glory of them, offered to give all into His hands if He would but acknowledge the supremacy of the prince of darkness. Christ rebuked the presumptuous tempter and forced him to depart. But Satan meets with greater success in presenting the same temptations to man. To secure worldly gains and honors, the church was led to seek the favor and support of the great men of earth; and having thus rejected Christ, she was induced to yield allegiance to the representative of Satan – the bishop of Rome.

It is one of the leading doctrines of Romanism that the pope is the visible head of the universal church of Christ, invested with supreme authority over bishops and pastors in all parts of the world. More than this, the pope has been given the very titles of Deity. He has been styled »Lord God the Pope«, see Appendix and has been declared infallible. He demands the homage of all men. The same claim urged by Satan in the wilderness of temptation is still urged by him through the Church of Rome, and vast numbers are ready to yield him homage. But those who fear and reverence God meet this heaven-daring assumption as Christ met the solicitations of the wily foe: »Thou shalt worship the Lord thy God, and Him only shalt thou serve.« Luke 4:8 God has never given a hint in His word that He has appointed any man to be the head of the church. The doctrine of papal supremacy is directly opposed to the teachings of the Scriptures. The pope can have no power over Christ's church except by usurpation. Romanists have persisted in bringing against Protestants the charge of heresy and willful separation from the true church. But these accusations apply rather to themselves. They are the ones who laid down the banner of Christ and departed from »the faith which was once delivered unto the saints.« Jude 3 Satan well knew that the Holy Scriptures would enable men to discern his deceptions and withstand his power. It was by the word that even the Saviour of the world had resisted his attacks. At every assault, Christ presented the shield of eternal truth, saying, »It is written.«

To every suggestion of the adversary, He opposed the wisdom

and power of the word. In order for Satan to maintain

his sway over men, and establish the authority of the papal usurper, he must keep them in ignorance of the Scriptures. The Bible would exalt God and place finite men in their true position; therefore its sacred truths must be concealed and suppressed. This logic was adopted by the Roman Church. For hundreds of years the circulation of the Bible was prohibited. The people were forbidden to read it or to have it in their houses, and unprincipled priests and prelates interpreted its teachings to sustain their pretensions. Thus the pope came to be almost universally acknowledged as the vicegerent of God on earth, endowed with authority over church and state.

The detector of error having been removed, Satan worked according to his will. Prophecy had declared that the papacy was to »think to change times and laws.« Daniel 7:25 This work it was not slow to attempt. To afford converts from heathenism a substitute for the worship of idols, and thus to promote their nominal acceptance of Christianity, the adoration of images and relics was gradually introduced into the Christian worship. The decree of a general council see Appendix finally established this system of idolatry. To complete the sacrilegious work, Rome presumed to expunge from the law of God the second commandment, forbidding image worship, and to divide the tenth commandment, in order to preserve the number.

The spirit of concession to paganism opened the way for a still further disregard of Heaven's authority. Satan, working through unconsecrated leaders of the church, tampered with the fourth commandment also, and essayed to set aside the ancient Sabbath, the day which God had blessed and sanctified, Genesis 2:2-3 and in its stead to exalt the festival observed by the heathen as »the venerable day of the sun.«

This change was not at first attempted openly. In the first centuries the true Sabbath had been kept by all Christians. They were jealous for the honor of God, and, believing that His law is immutable, they zealously guarded the sacredness of its precepts. But with great subtlety Satan worked through his agents to bring about his object. That the attention of the people might be called to the Sunday, it was made a festival in honor of the resurrection of Christ. Religious services were held upon it; yet it was regarded as a day of recreation, the Sabbath being still sacredly observed. To prepare the way for the work which he designed to accomplish, Satan had led the Jews, before the advent of Christ, to load down the Sabbath [51/52] with the most rigorous exactions, making its observance a burden. Now, taking advantage of the false light in which he had thus caused it to be regarded, he cast contempt upon it as a Jewish institution. While Christians generally continued to observe the Sunday as a joyous festival, he led them, in order to show their hatred of Judaism, to make the Sabbath a fast, a day of sadness and gloom.

In the early part of the fourth century the emperor Constantine issued a decree making Sunday a public festival throughout the Roman Empire. see Appendix The day of the sun was reverenced by his pagan subjects and was honored by Christians; it was the emperor's policy to unite the conflicting interests of heathenism and Christianity. He was urged to do this by the bishops of the church, who, inspired by ambition and thirst for power, perceived that if the same day was observed by both Christians and heathen, it would promote the nominal acceptance of Christianity by pagans and thus advance the power and glory of the church. But while many God-fearing Christians were gradually led to regard Sunday as possessing a degree of sacredness, they still held the true Sabbath as the holy of the Lord and observed it in obedience to the fourth commandment.

The archdeceiver had not completed his work. He was resolved to gather the Christian world under his banner and to exercise his power through his vicegerent, the proud pontiff who claimed to be the representative of Christ. Through half-converted pagans, ambitious prelates, and world-loving churchmen he accomplished his purpose. Vast councils were held from time to time, in which the dignitaries of the church were convened from all the world. In nearly every council the Sabbath which God had instituted was pressed down a little lower, while the Sunday was correspondingly exalted. Thus the pagan festival came finally to be honored as a divine institution, while the Bible Sabbath was pronounced a relic of Judaism, and its observers were declared to be accursed.

The great apostate had succeeded in exalting himself »above all that is called God, or that is worshiped.« 2 Thessalonians 2:4 He had dared to change the only precept of the divine law that unmistakably points all mankind to the true and living God. In the fourth commandment, God is revealed as the Creator of the heavens and the earth, and is thereby distinguished from all false gods. It was as a memorial of the work of creation that the seventh day was sanctified

 as a rest day for man. It was designed to keep the living God ever before the minds of men as the source of being and the object of reverence and worship. Satan strives to turn men from their allegiance to God, and from rendering obedience to His law; therefore he directs his efforts especially against that commandment which points to God as the Creator.

Protestants now urge that the resurrection of Christ on Sunday made it the Christian Sabbath. But Scripture evidence is lacking. No such honor was given to the day by Christ or His apostles. The observance of Sunday as a Christian institution had its origin in that »mystery of lawlessness« 2.Thessalonians 2:7, R.V. which, even in Paul's day, had begun its work. Where and when did the Lord adopt this child of the papacy? What valid reason can be given for a change which the Scriptures do not sanction?

In the sixth century the papacy had become firmly established. Its seat of power was fixed in the imperial city, and the bishop of Rome was declared to be the head over the entire church. Paganism had given place to the papacy. The dragon had given to the beast »his power, and his seat, and great authority.« Revelation 13:2 And now began the 1260 years of papal oppression foretold in the prophecies of Daniel and the Revelation. Daniel 7:25; Revelation 13:5-7; see Appendix Christians were forced to choose either to yield their integrity and accept the papal ceremonies and worship, or to wear away their lives in dungeons or suffer death by the rack, the fagot, or the headsman's ax. Now were fulfilled the words of Jesus: »Ye shall be betrayed both by parents, and brethren, and kinsfolks, and friends; and some of you shall they cause to be put to death. And ye shall be hated of all men for My name's sake.« Luke 21:16-17 Persecution opened upon the faithful with greater fury than ever before, and the world became a vast battlefield. For hundreds of years the church of Christ found refuge in seclusion and obscurity. Thus says the prophet: »The woman fled into the wilderness, where she hath a place prepared of God, that they should feed her there a thousand two hundred and three-score days.« Revelation 12:6

The accession of the Roman Church to power marked the beginning of the Dark Ages. As her power increased, the darkness deepened. Faith was transferred from Christ, the true foundation, to the pope of Rome. Instead of trusting in the Son of God for forgiveness of sins and for eternal salvation, the people looked to the pope, and to the priests and prelates to whom he delegated authority. They were taught that the pope was their earthly mediator and that none could approach God except through him; and, further, that he stood in the place of God to them and was therefore to be implicitly obeyed. A deviation from his requirements was sufficient cause for the severest punishment to be visited upon the bodies and souls of the offenders. Thus the minds of the people were turned away from God to fallible, erring, and cruel men, nay, more, to the prince of darkness himself, who exercised his power through them. Sin was disguised in a garb of sanctity. When the Scriptures are suppressed, and man comes to regard himself as supreme, we need look only for fraud, deception, and debasing iniquity. With the elevation of human laws and traditions was manifest the corruption that ever results from setting aside the law of God.

Those were days of peril for the church of Christ. The faithful standard-bearers were few indeed. Though the truth was not left without witnesses, yet at times it seemed that error and superstition would wholly prevail, and true religion would be banished from the earth. The gospel was lost sight of, but the forms of religion were multiplied, and the people were burdened with rigorous exactions. They were taught not only to look to the pope as their mediator, but to trust to works of their own to atone for sin. Long pilgrimages, acts of penance, the worship of relics, the erection of churches, shrines, and altars, the payment of large sums to the church – these and many similar acts were enjoined to appease the wrath of God or to secure His favor; as if God were like men, to be angered at trifles, or pacified by gifts or acts of penance!

Notwithstanding that vice prevailed, even among the leaders of the Roman Church, her influence seemed steadily to increase. About the close of the eighth century, papists put forth the claim that in the first ages of the church the bishops of Rome had possessed the same spiritual power which they now assumed. To establish this claim, some means must be employed to give it a show of authority; and this was readily suggested by the father of lies. Ancient writings were forged by monks. Decrees of councils before unheard of were discovered, establishing the universal supremacy of the pope from the earliest times. And a church that had rejected the truth greedily accepted these deceptions. see Appendix

The few faithful builders upon the true foundation 1 Corinthians 3:10-11 were perplexed and hindered as the rubbish of false doctrine obstructed the work. Like the builders upon the wall of Jerusalem in Nehemiah's day, some were ready to say: »The strength of the bearers of burdens is decayed, and there is much rubbish; so that we are not able to build.« Nehemiah 4:10 Wearied with the constant struggle against persecution, fraud, iniquity, and every other obstacle that Satan could devise to hinder their progress, some who had been faithful builders became disheartened; and for the sake of peace and security for their property and their lives, they turned away from the true foundation. Others, undaunted by the opposition of their enemies, fearlessly declared: »Be not ye afraid of them: remember the Lord, which is great and terrible«; verse 14 and they proceeded with the work, everyone with his sword girded by his side. Ephesians 6:17 The same spirit of hatred and opposition to the truth has inspired the enemies of God in every age, and the same vigilance and fidelity have been required in His servants. The words of Christ to the first disciples are applicable to His followers to the close of time: »What I say unto you I say unto all, Watch.« Mark 13:37 The darkness seemed to grow more dense. Image worship became more general. Candles were burned before images, and prayers were offered to them. The most absurd and superstitious customs prevailed. The minds of men were so completely controlled by superstition that reason itself seemed to have lost its sway. While priests and bishops were themselves pleasure-loving, sensual, and corrupt, it could only be expected that the people who looked to them for guidance would be sunken in ignorance and vice.

Another step in papal assumption was taken, when, in the eleventh century, Pope Gregory VII proclaimed the perfection of the Roman Church. Among the propositions which he put forth was one declaring that the church had never erred, nor would it ever err, according to the Scriptures. But the Scripture proofs did not accompany the assertion. The proud pontiff also claimed the power to depose emperors, and declared that no sentence which he pronounced could be reversed by anyone, but that it was his prerogative to reverse the decisions of all others. see Appendix

A striking illustration of the tyrannical character of this advocate of infallibility was given in his treatment of the German emperor, Henry IV. For presuming to disregard the pope's authority, this monarch was declared to be excommunicated and dethroned. Terrified by the desertion and threats of his own princes, who were encouraged in rebellion against him by the papal mandate, Henry felt the necessity of making his peace with Rome. In company with his wife and a faithful servant he crossed the Alps in midwinter, that he might humble himself before the pope. Upon reaching the castle whither Gregory had withdrawn, he was conducted, without his guards, into an outer court, and there, in the severe cold of winter, with uncovered head and naked feet, and in a miserable dress, he awaited the pope's permission to come into his presence. Not until he had continued three days fasting and making confession, did the pontiff condescend to grant him pardon. Even then it was only upon condition that the emperor should await the sanction of the pope before resuming the insignia or exercising the power of royalty. And Gregory, elated with his triumph, boasted that it was his duty to pull down the pride of kings.

How striking the contrast between the overbearing pride of this haughty pontiff and the meekness and gentleness of Christ, who represents Himself as pleading at the door of the heart for admittance, that He may come in to bring pardon and peace, and who taught His disciples: »Whosoever will be chief among you, let him be your servant.« Matthew 20:27

The advancing centuries witnessed a constant increase of error in the doctrines put forth from Rome. Even before the establishment of the papacy the teachings of heathen philosophers had received attention and exerted an influence in the church. Many who professed conversion still clung to the tenets of their pagan philosophy, and not only continued its study themselves, but urged it upon others as a means of extending their influence among the heathen. Serious errors were thus introduced into the Christian faith. Prominent among these was the belief in man's natural immortality and his consciousness in death. This doctrine laid the foundation upon which Rome established the invocation of saints and the adoration of the Virgin Mary. From this sprang also the heresy of eternal torment for the finally impenitent, which was early incorporated into the papal faith.

Then the way was prepared for the introduction of still another invention of paganism, which Rome named purgatory, and employed to terrify the credulous and superstitious multitudes. By this heresy is affirmed the existence of a place of torment, in which

the souls of such as have not merited eternal damnation are to suffer punishment for their sins, and from which, when freed from impurity, they are admitted to heaven. see Appendix

Still another fabrication was needed to enable Rome to profit by the fears and the vices of her adherents. This was supplied by the doctrine of indulgences. Full remission of sins, past, present, and future, and release from all the pains and penalties incurred, were promised to all who would enlist in the pontiff's wars to extend his temporal dominion, to punish his enemies, or to exterminate those who dared deny his spiritual supremacy. The people were also taught that by the payment of money to the church they might free themselves from sin, and also release the souls of their deceased friends who were confined in the tormenting flames. By such means did Rome fill her coffers and sustain the magnificence, luxury, and vice of the pretended representatives of Him who had not where to lay His head. see Appendix

The Scriptural ordinance of the Lord's Supper had been supplanted by the idolatrous sacrifice of the mass. Papal priests pretended, by their senseless mummery, to convert the simple bread and wine into the actual »body and blood of Christ.« Cardinal Wiseman, The Real Presence of the Body and Blood of Our Lord Jesus Christ in the Blessed Eucharist, Proved From Scripture, lecture 8, sec. 3, par. 26. With blasphemous presumption, they openly claimed the power of creating God, the Creator of all things. Christians were required, on pain of death, to avow their faith in this horrible, Heaven-insulting heresy. Multitudes who refused were given to the flames. see Appendix

In the thirteenth century was established that most terrible of all the engines of the papacy – the Inquisition. The prince of darkness wrought with the leaders of the papal hierarchy. In their secret councils Satan and his angels controlled the minds of evil men, while unseen in the midst stood an angel of God, taking the fearful record of their iniquitous decrees and writing the history of deeds too horrible to appear to human eyes. »Babylon the great« was »drunken with the blood of the saints.« The mangled forms of millions of martyrs cried to God for vengeance upon that apostate power.

Popery had become the world's despot. Kings and emperors bowed to the decrees of the Roman pontiff. The destinies of men, both for time and for eternity, seemed under his control. For hundreds of years the doctrines of Rome had been extensively and implicitly received, its rites reverently performed, its festivals generally observed. Its clergy were honored and liberally sustained. Never since has the Roman Church attained to greater dignity, magnificence, or power.

But »the noon of the papacy was the midnight of the world.« J. A. Wylie, The History of Protestantism, b. 1, ch. 4 The Holy Scriptures were almost unknown, not only to the people, but to the priests. Like the Pharisees of old, the papal leaders hated the light which would reveal their sins. God's law, the standard of righteousness, having been removed, they exercised power without limit, and practiced vice without restraint. Fraud, avarice, and profligacy prevailed. Men shrank from no crime by which they could gain wealth or position. The palaces of popes and prelates were scenes of the vilest debauchery. Some of the reigning pontiffs were guilty of crimes so revolting that secular rulers endeavored to depose these dignitaries of the church as monsters too vile to be tolerated. For centuries Europe had made no progress in learning, arts, or civilization. A moral and intellectual paralysis had fallen upon Christendom.

The condition of the world under the Romish power presented a fearful and striking fulfillment of the words of the prophet Hosea: »My people are destroyed for lack of knowledge: because thou hast rejected knowledge, I will also reject thee: ... seeing thou hast forgotten the law of thy God, I will also forget thy children.« »There is no truth, nor mercy, nor knowledge of God in the land. By swearing, and lying, and killing, and stealing, and committing adultery, they break out, and blood toucheth blood.« Hosea 4:6, 1, 2 Such were the results of banishing the word of God.

Chapter 4

The Waldenses

Amid the gloom that settled upon the earth during the long period of papal supremacy, the light of truth could not be wholly extinguished. In every age there were witnesses for God – men who cherished faith in Christ as the only mediator between God and man, who held the Bible as the only rule of life, and who hallowed the true Sabbath. How much the world owes to these men, posterity will never know. They were branded as heretics, their motives impugned, their characters maligned, their writings suppressed, misrepresented, or mutilated. Yet they stood firm, and from age to age maintained their faith in its purity, as a sacred heritage for the generations to come.

The history of God's people during the ages of darkness that followed upon Rome's supremacy is written in heaven, but they have little place in human records. Few traces of their existence can be found, except in the accusations of their persecutors. It was the policy of Rome to obliterate every trace of dissent from her doctrines or decrees. Everything heretical, whether persons or writings, she sought to destroy. Expressions of doubt, or questions as to the authority of papal dogmas, were enough to forfeit the life of rich or poor, high or low. Rome endeavored also to destroy every record of her cruelty toward dissenters. Papal councils decreed that books and writings containing such records should be committed to the flames. Before the invention of printing, books were few in number, and in a form not favorable for preservation; therefore there was little to prevent the Romanists from carrying out their purpose.

No church within the limits of Romish jurisdiction was long left undisturbed in the enjoyment of freedom of conscience. No sooner had the papacy obtained power than she stretched out her arms to crush all that refused to acknowledge her sway, and one after another the churches submitted to her dominion. In Great Britain primitive Christianity had very early taken root. The gospel received by the Britons in the first centuries was then uncorrupted by Romish apostasy. Persecution from pagan emperors, which extended even to these far-off shores, was the only gift that the first churches of Britain received from Rome. Many of the Christians, fleeing from persecution in England, found refuge in Scotland; thence the truth was carried to Ireland, and in all these countries it was received with gladness.

When the Saxons invaded Britain, heathenism gained control. The conquerors disdained to be instructed by their slaves, and the Christians were forced to retreat to the mountains and the wild moors. Yet the light, hidden for a time, continued to burn. In Scotland, a century later, it shone out with a brightness that extended to fardistant lands. From Ireland came the pious Columba and his colaborers, who, gathering about them the scattered believers on the lonely island of Iona, made this the center of their missionary labors. Among these evangelists was an observer of the Bible Sabbath, and thus this truth was introduced among the people. A school was established at Iona, from which missionaries went out, not only to Scotland and England, but to Germany, Switzerland, and even Italy.

But Rome had fixed her eyes on Britain, and resolved to bring it under her supremacy. In the sixth century her missionaries undertook the conversion of the heathen Saxons. They were received with favor by the proud barbarians, and they induced many thousands to profess the Romish faith. As the work progressed, the papal leaders and their converts encountered the primitive Christians. A striking contrast was presented. The latter were simple, humble, and Scriptural in character, doctrine, and manners, while the former manifested the superstition, pomp, and arrogance of popery. The emissary of Rome demanded that these Christian churches acknowledge the supremacy of the sovereign pontiff. The Britons meekly replied that they desired to love all men, but that the pope was not entitled to supremacy in the church, and they could render to him only that submission which was due to every follower of Christ. Repeated attempts were made to secure their allegiance to Rome; but these humble Christians, amazed at the pride displayed by her emissaries, steadfastly replied that they knew no other master than Christ. Now the true spirit of the papacy was revealed. Said the Romish leader: »If you will not receive brethren who bring you peace, you shall receive enemies who will bring you war. If you will not unite with us in showing the Saxons the way of life, you shall receive from them the stroke of death.« J. H. Merle D'Aubigne, History

 the Reformation of the Sixteenth Century, b. 17, ch. 2. These were no idle threats. War, intrigue, and deception were employed against these witnesses for a Bible faith, until the churches of Britain were destroyed, or forced to submit to the authority of the pope.

In lands beyond the jurisdiction of Rome there existed for many centuries bodies of Christians who remained almost wholly free from papal corruption. They were surrounded by heathenism and in the lapse of ages were affected by its errors; but they continued to regard the Bible as the only rule of faith and adhered to many of its truths. These Christians believed in the perpetuity of the law of God and observed the Sabbath of the fourth commandment. Churches that held to this faith and practice existed in Central Africa and among the Armenians of Asia.

But of those who resisted the encroachments of the papal power, the Waldenses stood foremost. In the very land where popery had fixed its seat, there its falsehood and corruption were most steadfastly resisted. For centuries the churches of Piedmont maintained their independence; but the time came at last when Rome insisted upon their submission. After ineffectual struggles against her tyranny, the leaders of these churches reluctantly acknowledged the supremacy of the power to which the whole world seemed to pay homage. There were some, however, who refused to yield to the authority of pope or prelate. They were determined to maintain their allegiance to God and to preserve the purity and simplicity of their faith. A separation took place. Those who adhered to the ancient faith now withdrew; some, forsaking their native Alps, raised the banner of truth in foreign lands; others retreated to the secluded glens and rocky fastnesses of the mountains, and there preserved their freedom to worship God.

The faith which for centuries was held and taught by the Waldensian Christians was in marked contrast to the false doctrines put forth from Rome. Their religious belief was founded upon the written word of God, the true system of Christianity. But those humble peasants, in their obscure retreats, shut away from the world, and bound to daily toil among their flocks and their vineyards, had not by themselves arrived at the truth in opposition to the dogmas and heresies of the apostate church. Theirs was not a faith newly received. Their religious belief was their inheritance from their fathers. They contended for the faith of the apostolic church, – »the faith which was once delivered unto the saints.« Jude 3 »The church in the wilderness,« and not the proud hierarchy enthroned in the world's great capital, was the true church of Christ, the guardian of the treasures of truth which God has committed to His people to be given to the world.

Among the leading causes that had led to the separation of the true church from Rome was the hatred of the latter toward the Bible Sabbath. As foretold by prophecy, the papal power cast down the truth to the ground. The law of God was trampled in the dust, while the traditions and customs of men were exalted. The churches that were under the rule of the papacy were early compelled to honor the Sunday as a holy day. Amid the prevailing error and superstition, many, even of the true people of God, became so bewildered that while they observed the Sabbath, they refrained from labor also on the Sunday. But this did not satisfy the papal leaders. They demanded not only that Sunday be hallowed, but that the Sabbath be profaned; and they denounced in the strongest language those who dared to show it honor. It was only by fleeing from the power of Rome that any could obey God's law in peace. see Appendix

The Waldenses were among the first of the peoples of Europe to obtain a translation of the Holy Scriptures. (See Appendix.) Hundreds of years before the Reformation they possessed the Bible in manuscript in their native tongue. They had the truth unadulterated, and this rendered them the special objects of hatred and persecution. They declared the Church of Rome to be the apostate Babylon of the Apocalypse, and at the peril of their lives they stood up to resist her corruptions. While, under the pressure of long-continued persecution, some compromised their faith, little by little yielding its distinctive principles, others held fast the truth. Through ages of darkness and apostasy there were Waldenses who denied the supremacy of Rome, who rejected image worship as idolatry, and who kept the true Sabbath. Under the fiercest tempests of opposition they maintained their faith. Though gashed by the Savoyard spear, and scorched by the Romish fagot, they stood unflinchingly for God's word and His honor.

Behind the lofty bulwarks of the mountains – in all ages the refuge of the persecuted and oppressed – the Waldenses found a hiding place. Here the light of truth was kept burning amid the darkness of the Middle Ages. Here, for a thousand years, witnesses for the truth maintained the ancient faith.

God had provided for His people a sanctuary of awful grandeur, befitting the mighty truths committed to their trust. To those faithful exiles the mountains were an emblem of the immutable righteousness of Jehovah. They pointed their children to the heights towering above them in unchanging majesty, and spoke to them of Him with whom there is no variableness nor shadow of turning, whose word is as enduring as the everlasting hills. God had set fast the mountains and girded them with strength; no arm but that of Infinite Power could move them out of their place. In like manner He had established His law, the foundation of His government in heaven and upon earth. The arm of man might reach his fellow men and destroy their lives; but that arm could as readily uproot the mountains from their foundations, and hurl them into the sea, as it could change one precept of the law of Jehovah, or blot out one of His promises to those who do His will. In their fidelity to His law, God's servants should be as firm as the unchanging hills.

The mountains that girded their lowly valleys were a constant witness to God's creative power, and a never-failing assurance of His protecting care. Those pilgrims learned to love the silent symbols of Jehovah's presence. They indulged no repining because of the hardships of their lot; they were never lonely amid the mountain solitudes. They thanked God that He had provided for them an asylum from the wrath and cruelty of men. They rejoiced in their freedom to worship before Him. Often when pursued by their enemies, the strength of the hills proved a sure defense. From many a lofty cliff they chanted the praise of God, and the armies of Rome could not silence their songs of thanksgiving. Pure, simple, and fervent was the piety of these followers of Christ. The principles of truth they valued above houses and lands, friends, kindred, even life itself. These principles they earnestly sought to impress upon the hearts of the young. From earliest childhood the youth were instructed in the Scriptures and taught to regard sacredly the claims of the law of God. Copies of the Bible were rare; therefore its precious words were committed to memory. Many were able to repeat large portions of both the Old and the New Testament. Thoughts of God were associated alike with the sublime scenery of nature and with the humble blessings of daily life. Little children learned to look with gratitude to God as the giver of every favor and every comfort.

Parents, tender and affectionate as they were, loved their children too wisely to accustom them to self-indulgence. Before them was a life of trial and hardship, perhaps a martyr's death. They were educated from childhood to endure hardness, to submit to control, and yet to think and act for themselves. Very early they were taught to bear responsibilities, to be guarded in speech, and to understand the wisdom of silence. One indiscreet word let fall in the hearing of their enemies might imperil not only the life of the speaker, but the lives of hundreds of his brethren; for as wolves hunting their prey did the enemies of truth pursue those who dared to claim freedom of religious faith.

The Waldenses had sacrificed their worldly prosperity for the truth's sake, and with persevering patience they toiled for their bread. Every spot of tillable land among the mountains was carefully improved; the valleys and the less fertile hillsides were made to yield their increase. Economy and severe self-denial formed a part of the education which the children received as their only legacy. They were taught that God designs life to be a discipline, and that their wants could be supplied only by personal labor, by forethought, care, and faith. The process was laborious and wearisome, but it was whole some, just what man needs in his fallen state, the school which God has provided for his training and development. While the youth were inured to toil and hardship, the culture of the intellect was not neglected. They were taught that all their powers belonged to God, and that all were to be improved and developed for His service.

The Vaudois churches, in their purity and simplicity, resembled the church of apostolic times. Rejecting the supremacy of the pope and prelate, they held the Bible as the only supreme, infallible authority. Their pastors, unlike the lordly priests of Rome, followed the example of their Master, who »came not to be ministered unto, but to minister.« They fed the flock of God, leading them to the green pastures and living fountains of His holy word. Far from the monuments of human pomp and pride the people assembled, not in magnificent churches or grand cathedrals, but beneath the shadow of the mountains, in the Alpine valleys, or, in time of danger, in some rocky stronghold, to listen to the words of truth from the servants of Christ. The pastors not only preached the gospel, but they visited the sick, catechized the children, admonished the erring, and labored to settle disputes and promote harmony and brotherly love. In times of peace they were sustained by the freewill offerings of the people; but, like Paul the tentmaker, each learned some trade or profession by which, if necessary, to provide for his own support. From their pastors the youth received instruction. While attention was given to
 branches of general learning, the Bible was made the

chief study. The Gospels of Matthew and John were committed to memory, with many of the Epistles. They were employed also in copying the Scriptures. Some manuscripts contained the whole Bible, others only brief selections, to which some simple explanations of the text were added by those who were able to expound the Scriptures. Thus were brought forth the treasures of truth so long concealed by those who sought to exalt themselves above God.

By patient, untiring labor, sometimes in the deep, dark caverns of the earth, by the light of torches, the Sacred Scriptures were written out, verse by verse, chapter by chapter. Thus the work went on, the revealed will of God shining out like pure gold; how much brighter, clearer, and more powerful because of the trials undergone for its sake only those could realize who were engaged in the work. Angels from heaven surrounded these faithful workers.

Satan had urged on the papal priests and prelates to bury the word of truth beneath the rubbish of error, heresy, and superstition; but in a most wonderful manner it was preserved uncorrupted through all the ages of darkness. It bore not the stamp of man, but the impress of God. Men have been unwearied in their efforts to obscure the plain, simple meaning of the Scriptures, and to make them contradict their own testimony; but like the ark upon the billowy deep, the word of God outrides the storms that threaten it with destruction. As the mine has rich veins of gold and silver hidden beneath the surface, so that all must dig who would discover its precious stores, so the Holy Scriptures have treasures of truth that are revealed only to the earnest, humble, prayerful seeker. God designed the Bible to be a lessonbook to all mankind, in childhood, youth, and manhood, and to be studied through all time. He gave His word to men as a revelation of Himself. Every new truth discerned is a fresh disclosure of the character of its Author. The study of the Scriptures is the means divinely ordained to bring men into closer connection with their Creator and to give them a clearer knowledge of His will. It is the medium of communication between God and man.

While the Waldenses regarded the fear of the Lord as the beginning of wisdom, they were not blind to the importance of a contact with the world, a knowledge of men and of active life, in expanding the mind and quickening the perceptions. From their schools in the mountains some of the youth were sent to institutions of learning in the cities of France or Italy, where was a more extended field for [69/70] study, thought, and observation than in their native Alps. The youth thus sent forth were exposed to temptation, they witnessed vice, they encountered Satan's wily agents, who urged upon them the most subtle heresies and the most dangerous deceptions. But their education from childhood had been of a character to prepare them for all this.

In the schools whither they went, they were not to make confidants of any. Their garments were so prepared as to conceal their greatest treasure – the precious manuscripts of the Scriptures. These, the fruit of months and years of toil, they carried with them, and whenever they could do so without exciting suspicion, they cautiously placed some portion in the way of those whose hearts seemed open to receive the truth. From their mother's knee the Waldensian youth had been trained with this purpose in view; they understood their work and faithfully performed it. Converts to the true faith were won in these institutions of learning, and frequently its principles were found to be permeating the entire school; yet the papal leaders could not, by the closest inquiry, trace the so-called corrupting heresy to its source.

The spirit of Christ is a missionary spirit. The very first impulse of the renewed heart is to bring others also to the Saviour. Such was the spirit of the Vaudois Christians. They felt that God required more of them than merely to preserve the truth in its purity in their own churches; that a solemn responsibility rested upon them to let their light shine forth to those who were in darkness; by the mighty power of God's word they sought to break the bondage which Rome had imposed. The Vaudois ministers were trained as missionaries, everyone who expected to enter the ministry being required first to gain an experience as an evangelist. Each was to serve three years in some mission field before taking charge of a church at home. This service, requiring at the outset self-denial and sacrifice, was a fitting introduction to the pastor's life in those times that tried men's souls. The youth who received ordination to the sacred office saw before them, not the prospect of earthly wealth and glory, but a life of toil and danger, and possibly a martyr's fate. The missionaries went out two and two, as Jesus sent forth His disciples. With each young man was usually associated a man of age and experience, the youth being under the guidance of his companion, who was held responsible for his training, and whose instruction he was required to heed. These colaborers were not always together, but often met for prayer and counsel, thus strengthening each other in the faith.

To have made known the object of their mission would have ensured its defeat; therefore they carefully concealed their real character. Every minister possessed a knowledge of some trade or profession, and the missionaries prosecuted their work under cover of a secular calling. Usually they chose that of merchant or peddler. »They carried silks, jewelry, and other articles, at that time not easily purchasable save at distant marts; and they were welcomed as merchants where they would have been spurned as missionaries.« Wylie, b. 1, ch. 7. All the while their hearts were uplifted to God for wisdom to present a treasure more precious than gold or gems. They secretly carried about with them copies of the Bible, in whole or in part; and whenever an opportunity was presented, they called the attention of their customers to these manuscripts. Often an interest to read God's word was thus awakened, and some portion was gladly left with those who desired to receive it. The work of these missionaries began in the plains and valleys at the foot of their own mountains, but it extended far beyond these limits. With naked feet and in garments coarse and travel-stained as were those of their Master, they passed through great cities and penetrated to distant lands. Everywhere they scattered the precious seed. Churches sprang up in their path, and the blood of martyrs witnessed for the truth. The day of God will reveal a rich harvest of souls garnered by the labors of these faithful men. Veiled and silent, the word of God was making its way through Christendom and meeting a glad reception in the homes and hearts of men.

To the Waldenses the Scriptures were not merely a record of God's dealings with men in the past, and a revelation of the responsibilities and duties of the present, but an unfolding of the perils and glories of the future. They believed that the end of all things was not far distant, and as they studied the Bible with prayer and tears they were the more deeply impressed with its precious utterances and with their duty to make known to others its saving truths. They saw the plan of salvation clearly revealed in the sacred pages, and they found comfort, hope, and peace in believing in Jesus. As the light illuminated their understanding and made glad their hearts, they longed to shed its beams upon those who were in the darkness of papal error.

They saw that under the guidance of pope and priest, multitudes were vainly endeavoring to obtain pardon by afflicting their bodies for the sin of their souls. Taught to trust to their good works to save them, they were ever looking to themselves, their minds [71/72] dwelling upon their sinful condition, seeing themselves exposed to the wrath of God, afflicting soul and body, yet finding no relief. Thus conscientious souls were bound by the doctrines of Rome. Thousands abandoned friends and kindred, and spent their lives in convent cells. By oft-repeated fasts and cruel scourgings, by midnight vigils, by prostration for weary hours upon the cold, damp stones of their dreary abode, by long pilgrimages, by humiliating penance and fearful torture, thousands vainly sought to obtain peace of conscience. Oppressed with a sense of sin, and haunted with the fear of God's avenging wrath, many suffered on, until exhausted nature gave way, and without one ray of light or hope they sank into the tomb. The Waldenses longed to break to these starving souls the bread of life, to open to them the messages of peace in the promises of God, and to point them to Christ as their only hope of salvation. The doctrine that good works can atone for the transgression of God's law they held to be based upon falsehood. Reliance upon human merit intercepts the view of Christ's infinite love. Jesus died as a sacrifice for man because the fallen race can do nothing to recommend themselves to God. The merits of a crucified and risen Saviour are the foundation of the Christian's faith. The dependence of the soul upon Christ is as real, and its connection with Him must be as close, as that of a limb to the body, or of a branch to the vine.

The teachings of popes and priests had led men to look upon the character of God, and even of Christ, as stern, gloomy, and forbidding. The Saviour was represented as so far devoid of sympathy with man in his fallen state that the mediation of priests and saints must be invoked. Those whose minds had been enlightened by the word of God longed to point these souls to Jesus as their compassionate, loving Saviour, standing with outstretched arms, inviting all to come to Him with their burden of sin, their care and weariness. They longed to clear away the obstructions which Satan had piled up that men might not see the promises, and come directly to God, confessing their sins, and obtaining pardon and peace.

Eagerly did the Vaudois missionary unfold to the inquiring mind the precious truths of the gospel. Cautiously he produced the carefully written portions of the Holy Scriptures. It was his greatest joy to give hope to the conscientious, sin-stricken soul, who could see only a God of vengeance, waiting to execute justice. With quivering lip and tearful eye did he, often on bended knees, open to his brethren the precious promises that reveal the sinner's only hope. Thus the light of truth penetrated many a darkened mind, rolling back the cloud of gloom, until the Sun of Righteousness shone into the heart with healing in His beams. It was often the case that some portion of Scripture was read again and again, the hearer desiring it to be repeated, as if he would assure himself that he had heard aright. Especially was the repetition of these words eagerly desired: »The blood of Jesus Christ His Son cleanseth us from all sin.« 1 John 1:7 »As Moses lifted up the serpent in the wilderness, even so must the Son of man be lifted up: that whosoever believeth in Him should not perish, but have eternal life.« John 3:14-15 Many were undeceived in regard to the claims of Rome. They saw how vain is the mediation of men or angels in behalf of the sinner. As the true light dawned upon their minds they exclaimed with rejoicing: »Christ is my priest; His blood is my sacrifice; His altar is my confessional.« They cast themselves wholly upon the merits of Jesus, repeating the words, »Without faith it is impossible to please Him.« Hebrews 11:6 »There is none other name under heaven given among men, whereby we must be saved.« Acts 4:12

The assurance of a Saviour's love seemed too much for some of these poor tempest-tossed souls to realize. So great was the relief which it brought, such a flood of light was shed upon them, that they seemed transported to heaven. Their hands were laid confidingly in the hand of Christ; their feet were planted upon the Rock of Ages. All fear of death was banished. They could now covet the prison and the fagot if they might thereby honor the name of their Redeemer.

In secret places the word of God was thus brought forth and read, sometimes to a single soul, sometimes to a little company who were longing for light and truth. Often the entire night was spent in this manner. So great would be the wonder and admiration of the listeners that the messenger of mercy was not infrequently compelled to cease his reading until the understanding could grasp the tidings of salvation. Often would words like these be uttered: »Will God indeed accept my offering? Will He smile upon me? Will He pardon me?« The answer was read: »Come unto Me, all ye that labor and are heavy-laden, and I will give you rest.« Matthew 11:28

Faith grasped the promise, and the glad response was heard: »No more long pilgrimages to make; no more painful journeys to holy shrines. I may come to Jesus just as I am, sinful and unholy, and He will not spurn the penitential prayer. 'Thy sins be forgiven thee.' Mine, even mine, may be forgiven!« A tide of sacred joy would fill the heart, and the name of Jesus would be magnified by praise and thanksgiving. Those happy souls returned to their homes to diffuse light, to repeat to others, as well as they could, their new experience; that they had found the true and living Way. There was a strange and solemn power in the words of Scripture that spoke directly to the hearts of those who were longing for the truth. It was the voice of God, and it carried conviction to those who heard.

The messenger of truth went on his way; but his appearance of humility, his sincerity, his earnestness and deep fervor, were subjects of frequent remark. In many instances his hearers had not asked him whence he came or whither he went. They had been so overwhelmed, at first with surprise, and afterward with gratitude and joy, that they had not thought to question him. When they had urged him to accompany them to their homes, he had replied that he must visit the lost sheep of the flock. Could he have been an angel from heaven? they queried. In many cases the messenger of truth was seen no more. He had made his way to other lands, or he was wearing out his life in some unknown dungeon, or perhaps his bones were whitening on the spot where he had witnessed for the truth. But the words he had left behindcould not be destroyed. They were doing their work in the hearts of men; the blessed results will be fully known only in the judgment.

The Waldensian missionaries were invading the kingdom of Satan, and the powers of darkness aroused to greater vigilance. Every effort to advance the truth was watched by the prince of evil, and he excited the fears of his agents. The papal leaders saw a portent of danger to their cause from the labors of these humble itinerants. If the light of truth were allowed to shine unobstructed, it would sweep away the heavy clouds of error that enveloped the people. It would direct the minds of men to God alone and would eventually destroy the supremacy of Rome. The very existence of this people, holding the faith of the ancient church, was a constant testimony to Rome's apostasy, and therefore excited the most bitter hatred and persecution. Their refusal to surrender the Scriptures was also an offense that Rome could not tolerate. She determined to blot them from the earth. Now began the most terrible crusades against God's people in their mountain homes. Inquisitors were put upon their track, and the scene of innocent Abel falling before the murderous Cain was often repeated.

Again and again were their fertile lands laid waste, their dwellings and chapels swept away, so that where once were flourishing fields and the homes of an innocent, industrious people, there remained only a desert. As the ravenous beast is rendered more furious by the taste of blood, so the rage of the papists was kindled to greater intensity by the sufferings of their victims. Many of these witnesses for a pure faith were pursued across the mountains and hunted down in the valleys where they were hidden, shut in by mighty forests and pinnacles of rock. No charge could be brought against the moral character of this proscribed class. Even their enemies declared them to be a peaceable, quiet, pious people. Their grand offense was that they would not worship God according to the will of the pope. For this crime every humiliation, insult, and torture that men or devils could invent was heaped upon them.

When Rome at one time determined to exterminate the hated sect, a bull was issued by the pope, condemning them as heretics, and delivering them to slaughter. see Appendix They were not accused as idlers, or dishonest, or disorderly; but it was declared that they had an appearance of piety and sanctity that seduced »the sheep of the true fold.« Therefore the pope ordered »that malicious and abominable sect of malignants,« if they »refuse to abjure, to be crushed like venomous snakes.« Wylie, b. 16, ch. 1 Did this haughty potentate expect to meet those words again? Did he know that they were registered in the books of heaven, to confront him at the judgment? »Inasmuch as ye have done it unto one of the least of these My brethren,« said Jesus, »ye have done it unto Me.« Matthew 25:40

This bull called upon all members of the church to join the crusade against the heretics. As an incentive to engage in this cruel work, it »absolved from all ecclesiastical pains and penalties, general and particular; it released all who joined the crusade from any oaths they might have taken; it legitimatized their title to any property they might have illegally acquired; and promised remission of all their sins to such as should kill any heretic. It annulled all contracts made in favor of Vaudois, ordered their domestics to abandon them, forbade all persons to give them any aid whatever, and empowered all persons to take possession of their property.« Wylie, b. 16, ch. 1 This document clearly reveals the master spirit behind the scenes. It is the roar of the dragon, and not the voice of Christ, that is heard therein. The papal leaders would not conform their characters to the great standard of God's law, but erected a standard to suit themselves, and determined to compel all to conform to this because Rome willed it. The most horrible tragedies were enacted. Corrupt and blasphemous priests and popes were doing the work which Satan appointed them. Mercy had no place in their natures. The same spirit that crucified Christ and slew the apostles, the same that moved the bloodthirsty Nero against the faithful in his day, was at work to rid the earth of those who were beloved of God. The persecutions visited for many centuries upon this God-fearing people were endured by them with a patience and constancy that honored their Redeemer. Notwithstanding the crusades against them, and the inhuman butchery to which they were subjected, they continued to send out their missionaries to scatter the precious truth. They were hunted to death; yet their blood watered the seed sown, and it failed not of yielding fruit. Thus the Waldenses witnessed for God centuries before the birth of Luther. Scattered over many lands, they planted the seeds of the Reformation that began in the time of Wycliffe, grew broad and deep in the days of Luther, and is to be carried forward to the close of time by those who also are willing to suffer all things for »the word of God, and for the testimony of Jesus Christ.« Revelation 1:9

Cruel massacre of Waldensians

Chapter 5

John Wycliffe

Before the Reformation there were at times but very few copies of the Bible in existence, but God had not suffered His word to be wholly destroyed. Its truths were not to be forever hidden. He could as easily unchain the words of life as He could open prison doors and unbolt iron gates to set His servants free. In the different countries of Europe men were moved by the Spirit of God to search for the truth as for hid treasures. Providentially guided to the Holy Scriptures, they studied the sacred pages with intense interest. They were willing to accept the light at any cost to themselves. Though they did not see all things clearly, they were enabled to perceive many long-buried truths. As Heaven-sent messengers they went forth, rending asunder the chains of error and superstition, and calling upon those who had been so long enslaved, to arise and assert their liberty.

Except among the Waldenses, the word of God had for ages been locked up in languages known only to the learned; but the time had come for the Scriptures to be translated and given to the people of different lands in their native tongue. The world had passed its midnight. The hours of darkness were wearing away, and in many lands appeared tokens of the coming dawn. In the fourteenth century arose in England the »morning star of the Reformation.« John Wycliffe was the herald of reform, not for England alone, but for all Christendom. The great protest against Rome which it was permitted him to utter was never to be silenced. That protest opened the struggle which was to result in the emancipation of individuals, of churches, and of nations.

Wycliffe received a liberal education, and with him the fear of the Lord was the beginning of wisdom. He was noted at college for his fervent piety as well as for his remarkable talents and sound scholarship. In his thirst for knowledge he sought to become acquainted with every branch of learning. He was educated in the scholastic philosophy, in the canons of the church, and in the civil law, especially that of his own country. In his after labors the value of this early training was apparent. A thorough acquaintance with the speculative philosophy of his time enabled him to expose its errors; and by his study of national and ecclesiastical law he was prepared to engage in the great struggle for civil and religious liberty. While he could wield the weapons drawn from the word of God, he had acquired the intellectual discipline of the schools, and he understood the tactics of the schoolmen. The power of his genius and the extent and thoroughness of his knowledge commanded the respect of both friends and foes. His adherents saw with satisfaction that their champion stood foremost among the leading minds of the nation; and his enemies were prevented from casting contempt upon the cause of reform by exposing the ignorance or weakness of its supporter.

While Wycliffe was still at college, he entered upon the study of the Scriptures. In those early times, when the Bible existed only in the ancient languages, scholars were enabled to find their way to the fountain of truth, which was closed to the uneducated classes. Thus already the way had been prepared for Wycliffe's future work as a Reformer. Men of learning had studied the word of God and had found the great truth of His free grace there revealed. In their teachings they had spread a knowledge of this truth, and had led others to turn to the living oracles.

When Wycliffe's attention was directed to the Scriptures, he entered upon their investigation with the same thoroughness which had enabled him to master the learning of the schools. Heretofore he had felt a great want, which neither his scholastic studies nor the teaching of the church could satisfy. In the word of God he found that which he had before sought in vain. Here he saw the plan of salvation revealed and Christ set forth as the only advocate for man. He gave himself to the service of Christ and determined to proclaim the truths he had discovered. Like after Reformers, Wycliffe did not, at the opening of his work, foresee whither it would lead him. He did not set himself deliberately in opposition to Rome. But devotion to truth could not but bring him in conflict with falsehood. The more clearly he discerned the errors of the papacy, the more earnestly he presented the teaching of the Bible. He saw that Rome had forsaken the word of God for human tradition; he fearlessly accused the priesthood of having banished the Scriptures, and demanded that the Bible be restored to the people and that its authority be again established in the church. He was an able and earnest teacher and an eloquent preacher, and his daily life was a demonstration of the truths he preached. His knowledge of the Scriptures, the force of his reasoning, the purity of his life, and his unbending courage and integrity won for him general esteem and confidence. Many of the people had become dissatisfied with their former faith as they saw the iniquity that prevailed in the Roman Church, and they hailed with unconcealed joy the truths brought to view by Wycliffe; but the papal leaders were filled with rage when they perceived that this Reformer was gaining an influence greater than their own.

Wycliffe was a keen detector of error, and he struck fearlessly against many of the abuses sanctioned by the authority of Rome. While acting as chaplain for the king, he took a bold stand against the payment of tribute claimed by the pope from the English monarch and showed that the papal assumption of authority over secular rulers was contrary to both reason and revelation. The demands of the pope had excited great indignation, and Wycliffe's teachings exerted an influence upon the leading minds of the nation. The king and the nobles united in denying the pontiff's claim to temporal authority and in refusing the payment of the tribute. Thus an effectual blow was struck against the papal supremacy in England.

Another evil against which the Reformer waged long and resolute battle was the institution of the orders of mendicant friars. These friars swarmed in England, casting a blight upon the greatness and prosperity of the nation. Industry, education, morals, all felt the withering influence. The monk's life of idleness and beggary was not only a heavy drain upon the resources of the people, but it brought useful labor into contempt. The youth were demoralized and corrupted. By the influence of the friars many were induced to enter a cloister and devote themselves to a monastic life, and this not only without the consent of their parents, but even without their knowledge and contrary to their commands. One of the early Fathers of the Roman Church, urging the claims of monasticism above the obligations of filial love and duty, had declared: »Though thy father should lie before thy door weeping and lamenting, and thy mother should show the body that bore thee and the breasts that nursed thee, see that thou trample them underfoot, and go onward straightway to Christ.« By this »monstrous inhumanity,« as Luther afterward styled it, »savoring more of the wolf and the tyrant than of the Christian and the man,« were the hearts of children steeled against their parents. Barnas Sears, The Life of Luther, pp. 70, 69 Thus did the papal leaders, like the Pharisees of old, make the commandment of God of none effect by their tradition. Thus homes were made desolate and parents were deprived of the society of their sons and daughters.

Even the students in the universities were deceived by the false representations of the monks and induced to join their orders. Many afterward repented this step, seeing that they had blighted their own lives and had brought sorrow upon their parents; but once fast in the snare it was impossible for them to obtain their freedom. Many parents, fearing the influence of the monks, refused to send their sons to the universities. There was a marked falling off in the number of students in attendance at the great centers of learning. The schools languished, and ignorance prevailed.

The pope had bestowed on these monks the power to hear confessions and to grant pardon. This became a source of great evil. Bent on enhancing their gains, the friars were so ready to grant absolution that criminals of all descriptions resorted to them, and, as a result, the worst vices rapidly increased. The sick and the poor were left to suffer, while the gifts that should have relieved their wants went to the monks, who with threats demanded the alms of the people, denouncing the impiety of those who should withhold gifts from their orders. Notwithstanding their profession of poverty, the wealth of the friars was constantly increasing, and their magnificent edifices and luxurious tables made more apparent the growing poverty of the nation. And while spending their time in luxury and pleasure, they sent out in their stead ignorant men, who could only recount marvelous tales, legends, and jests to amuse the people and make them still more completely the dupes of the monks. Yet the friars continued to maintain their hold on the superstitious multitudes and led them to believe that all religious duty was comprised in acknowledging the supremacy of the pope, adoring the saints, and making gifts to the monks, and that this was sufficient to secure them a place in heaven.

Men of learning and piety had labored in vain to bring about a reform in these monastic orders; but Wycliffe, with clearer insight, struck at the root of the evil, declaring that the system itself was false and that it should be abolished. Discussion and inquiry were awakening. As the monks traversed the country, vending the pope's pardons, many were led to doubt the possibility of purchasing for-

giveness with money, and they questioned whether

they should not seek pardon from God rather than from the pontiff of Rome. see Appendix note for p. 59 Not a few were alarmed at the rapacity of the friars, whose greed seemed never to be satisfied. »The monks and priests of Rome,« said they, »are eating us away like a cancer. God must deliver us, or the people will perish.« D'Aubigne, b. 17, ch. 7 To cover their avarice, these begging monks claimed that they were following the Saviour's example, declaring that Jesus and His disciples had been supported by the charities of the people. This claim resulted in injury to their cause, for it led many to the Bible to learn the truth for themselves – a result which of all others was least desired by Rome. The minds of men were directed to the Source of truth, which it was her object to conceal.

Wycliffe began to write and publish tracts against the friars, not, however, seeking so much to enter into dispute with them as to call the minds of the people to the teachings of the Bible and its Author. He declared that the power of pardon or of excommunication is possessed by the pope in no greater degree than by common priests, and that no man can be truly excommunicated unless he has first brought upon himself the condemnation of God. In no more effectual way could he have undertaken the overthrow of that mammoth fabric of spiritual and temporal dominion which the pope had erected and in which the souls and bodies of millions were held captive.

Again Wycliffe was called to defend the rights of the English crown against the encroachments of Rome; and being appointed a royal ambassador, he spent two years in the Netherlands, in conference with the commissioners of the pope. Here he was brought into communication with ecclesiastics from France, Italy, and Spain, and he had an opportunity to look behind the scenes and gain a knowledge of many things which would have remained hidden from him in England. He learned much that was to give point to his after labors. In these representatives from the papal court he read the true character and aims of the hierarchy. He returned to England to repeat his former teachings more openly and with greater zeal, declaring that covetousness, pride, and deception were the gods of Rome.

In one of his tracts he said, speaking of the pope and his collectors: »They draw out of our land poor men's livelihood, and many thousand marks, by the year, of the king's money, for sacraments and spiritual things, that is cursed heresy of simony, and maketh all Christendom assent and maintain this heresy. And certes though our realm had a huge hill of gold, and never other man took thereof but only this proud worldly priest's collector, by process of time this hill must be spended; for he taketh ever money out of our land, and sendeth nought again but God's curse for his simony.« John Lewis, History of the Life and Sufferings of J. Wiclif, p. 37.

Soon after his return to England, Wycliffe received from the king the appointment to the rectory of Lutterworth. This was an assurance that the monarch at least had not been displeased by his plain speaking. Wycliffe's influence was felt in shaping the action of the court, as well as in molding the belief of the nation.

The papal thunders were soon hurled against him. Three bulls were dispatched to England, – to the university, to the king, and to the prelates, – all commanding immediate and decisive measures to silence the teacher of heresy. Augustus Neander, General History of the Christian Religion and Church, period 6, sec. 2, pt. 1, par. 8; see also Appendix. Before the arrival of the bulls, however, the bishops, in their zeal, had summoned Wycliffe before them for trial. But two of the most powerful princes in the kingdom accompanied him to the tribunal; and the people, surrounding the building and rushing in, so intimidated the judges that the proceedings were for the time suspended, and he was allowed to go his way in peace. A little later, Edward III, whom in his old age the prelates were seeking to influence against the Reformer, died, and Wycliffe's former protector became regent of the kingdom.

But the arrival of the papal bulls laid upon all England a peremptory command for the arrest and imprisonment of the heretic. These measures pointed directly to the stake. It appeared certain that Wycliffe must soon fall a prey to the vengeance of Rome. But He who declared to one of old, »Fear not: ... I am thy shield«, Genesis 15:1 again stretched out His hand to protect His servant. Death came, not to the Reformer, but to the pontiff who had decreed his destruction. Gregory XI died, and the ecclesiastics who had assembled for Wycliffe's trial, dispersed.

God's providence still further overruled events to give opportunity for the growth of the Reformation. The death of Gregory was followed by the election of two rival popes. Two conflicting powers, each professedly infallible, now claimed obedience. see Appendix notes for p. 50 and 85 Each called upon the faithful to assist him in making war upon the other, enforcing his demands by terrible anathemas against his

 adversaries, and promises of rewards in heaven to his

supporters. This occurrence greatly weakened the power of the papacy. The rival factions had all they could do to attack each other, and Wycliffe for a time had rest. Anathemas and recriminations were flying from pope to pope, and torrents of blood were poured out to support their conflicting claims. Crimes and scandals flooded the church. Meanwhile the Reformer, in the quiet retirement of his parish of Lutterworth, was laboring diligently to point men from the contending popes to Jesus, the Prince of Peace.

The schism, with all the strife and corruption which it caused, prepared the way for the Reformation by enabling the people to see what the papacy really was. In a tract which he published, On the Schism of the Popes, Wycliffe called upon the people to consider whether these two priests were not speaking the truth in condemning each other as the anti-christ. »God,« said he, »would no longer suffer the fiend to reign in only one such priest, but ... made division among two, so that men, in Christ's name, may the more easily overcome them both.« R. Vaughan, Life and Opinions of John de Wycliffe, vol. 2, p. 6.

Wycliffe, like his Master, preached the gospel to the poor. Not content with spreading the light in their humble homes in his own parish of Lutterworth, he determined that it should be carried to every part of England. To accomplish this he organized a body of preachers, simple, devout men, who loved the truth and desired nothing so much as to extend it. These men went everywhere, teaching in the market places, in the streets of the great cities, and in the country lanes. They sought out the aged, the sick, and the poor, and opened to them the glad tidings of the grace of God.

As a professor of theology at Oxford, Wycliffe preached the word of God in the halls of the university. So faithfully did he present the truth to the students under his instruction, that he received the title of »the gospel doctor.« But the greatest work of his life was to be the translation of the Scriptures into the English language. In a work, On the Truth and Meaning of Scripture, he expressed his intention to translate the Bible, so that every man in England might read, in thc language in which he was born, the wonderful works of God. But suddenly his labors were stopped. Though not yet sixty years of age, unceasing toil, study, and the assaults of his enemies had told upon his strength and made him prematurely old. He was attacked by a dangerous illness. The tidings brought great joy to the friars. Now they thought he would bitterly repent the evil he had done the church, and they hurried to his chamber to listen to his confession. Representatives from the four religious orders, with four civil officers, gathered about the supposed dying man. »You have death on your lips,« they said; »be touched by your faults, and retract in our presence all that you have said to our injury.« The Reformer listened in silence; then he bade his attendant raise him in his bed, and, gazing steadily upon them as they stood waiting for his recantation, he said, in the firm, strong voice which had so often caused them to tremble: »I shall not die, but live; and again declare the evil deeds of the friars.« D'Aubigne, b. 17, ch. 7 Astonished and abashed, the monks hurried from the room.

Wycliffe's words were fulfilled. He lived to place in the hands of his countrymen the most powerful of all weapons against Rome - to give them the Bible, the Heaven-appointed agent to liberate, enlighten, and evangelize the people. There were many and great obstacles to surmount in the accomplishment of this work. Wycliffe was weighed down with infirmities; he knew that only a few years for labor remained for him; he saw the opposition which he must meet; but, encouraged by the promises of God's word, he went forward nothing daunted. In the full vigor of his intellectual powers, rich in experience, he had been preserved and prepared by God's special providence for this, the greatest of his labors. While all Christendom was filled with tumult, the Reformer in his rectory at Lutterworth, unheeding the storm that raged without, applied himself to his chosen task.

At last the work was completed – the first English translation of the Bible ever made. The word of God was opened to England. The Reformer feared not now the prison or the stake. He had placed in the hands of the English people a light which should never be extinguished. In giving the Bible to his countrymen, he had done more to break the fetters of ignorance and vice, more to liberate and elevate his country, than was ever achieved by the most brilliant victories on fields of battle.

The art of printing being still unknown, it was only by slow and wearisome labor that copies of the Bible could be multiplied. So great was the interest to obtain the book, that many willingly engaged in the work of transcribing it, but it was with difficulty that the copyists could supply the demand. Some of the more wealthy purchasers desired the whole Bible. Others bought only a portion. In many cases, several families united to purchase a copy. Thus Wycliffe's Bible soon found its way to the homes of the people.

The appeal to men's reason aroused them from their passive submission to papal dogmas. Wycliffe now taught the distinctive doctrines of Protestantism - salvation through faith in Christ, and the sole infallibility of the Scriptures. The preachers whom he had sent out circulated the Bible, together with the Reformer's writings, and with such success that the new faith was accepted by nearly one half of the people of England.

The appearance of the Scriptures brought dismay to the authorities of the church. They had now to meet an agency more powerful than Wycliffe – an agency against which their weapons would avail little. There was at this time no law in England prohibiting the Bible, for it had never before been published in the language of the people. Such laws were afterward enacted and rigorously enforced. Meanwhile, notwithstanding the efforts of the priests, there was for a season opportunity for the circulation of the word of God. Again the papal leaders plotted to silence the Reformer's voice. Before three tribunals he was successively summoned for trial, but without avail. First a synod of bishops declared his writings heretical, and, winning the young king, Richard II, to their side, they obtained a royal decree consigning to prison all who should hold the condemned doctrines.

Wycliffe appealed from the synod to Parliament; he fearlessly arraigned the hierarchy before the national council and demanded a reform of the enormous abuses sanctioned by the church. With convincing power he portrayed the usurpation and corruptions of the papal see. His enemies were brought to confusion. The friends and supporters of Wycliffe had been forced to yield, and it had been confidently expected that the Reformer himself, in his old age, alone and friendless, would bow to the combined authority of the crown and the miter. But instead of this the papists saw themselves defeated. Parliament, roused by the stirring appeals of Wycliffe, repealed the persecuting edict, and the Reformer was again at liberty.

A third time he was brought to trial, and now before the highest ecclesiastical tribunal in the kingdom. Here no favor would bc shown to heresy. Here at last Rome would triumph, and the Reformer's work would be stopped. So thought the papists. If they could but accomplish their purpose, Wycliffe would be forced to abjure his doctrines, or would leave the court only for the flames. But Wycliffe did not retract; he would not dissemble. He fearlessly maintained his teachings and repelled the accusations of his perse- [89/90] cutors. Losing sight of himself, of his position, of the occasion, he summoned his hearers before the divine tribunal, and weighed their sophistries and deceptions in the balances of eternal truth. The power of the Holy Spirit was felt in the council room. A spell from God was upon the hearers. They seemed to have no power to leave the place. As arrows from the Lord's quiver, the Reformer's words pierced their hearts. The charge of heresy, which they had brought against him, he with convincing power threw back upon themselves. Why, he demanded, did they dare to spread their errors? For the sake of gain, to make merchandise of the grace of God?

»With whom, think you,« he finally said, »are ye contending? with an old man on the brink of the grave? No! with Truth – Truth which is stronger than you, and will overcome you.« Wylie, b. 2, ch. 13 So saying, he withdrew from the assembly, and not one of his adversaries attempted to prevent him.

Wycliffe's work was almost done; the banner of truth which he had so long borne was soon to fall from his hand; but once more he was to bear witness for the gospel. The truth was to be proclaimed from the very stronghold of the kingdom of error. Wycliffe was summoned for trial before the papal tribunal at Rome, which had so often shed the blood of the saints. He was not blind to the danger that threatened him, yet he would have obeyed the summons had not a shock of palsy made it impossible for him to perform the journey. But though his voice was not to be heard at Rome, he could speak by letter, and this he determined to do. From his rectory the Reformer wrote to the pope a letter, which, while respectful in tone and Christian in spirit, was a keen rebuke to the pomp and pride of the papal see.

»Verily I do rejoice,« he said, »to open and declare unto every man the faith which I do hold, and especially unto the bishop of Rome: which, forasmuch as I do suppose to be sound and true, he will most willingly confirm my said faith, or if it be erroneous, amend the same.

»First, I suppose that the gospel of Christ is the whole body of God's law ... I do give and hold the bishop of Rome, forasmuch as he is the vicar of Christ here on earth, to be most bound, of all other men, unto that law of the gospel. For the greatness among Christ's disciples did not consist in worldly dignity or honors, but in the near and exact following of Christ in His life and manners ... Christ, for the time of His pilgrimage here, was a most poor man, abjecting and

 casting off all worldly rule and honor. ... »No faithful

man ought to follow either the pope himself or any of the holy men, but in such points as he hath followed the Lord Jesus Christ; for Peter and the sons of Zebedee, by desiring worldly honor, contrary to the following of Christ's steps, did offend, and therefore in those errors they are not to be followed. ... »The pope ought to leave unto the secular power all temporal dominion and rule, and thereunto effectually to move and exhort his whole clergy; for so did Christ, and especially by His apostles. Wherefore, if I have erred in any of these points, I will most humbly submit myself unto correction, even by death, if necessity so require; and if I could labor according to my will or desire in mine own person, I would surely present myself before the bishop of Rome; but the Lord hath otherwise visited me to the contrary, and hath taught me rather to obey God than men.« In closing he said: »Let us pray unto our God, that He will so stir up our Pope Urban VI, as he began, that he with his clergy may follow the Lord Jesus Christ in life and manners; and that they may teach the people effectually, and that they, likewise, may faithfully follow them in the same.« John Foxe, Acts and Monuments, vol. 3, pp. 49, 50

Thus Wycliffe presented to the pope and his cardinals the meekness and humility of Christ, exhibiting not only to themselves but to all Christendom the contrast between them and the Master whose representatives they professed to be. Wycliffe fully expected that his life would be the price of his fidelity. The king, the pope, and the bishops were united to accomplish his ruin, and it seemed certain that a few months at most would bring him to the stake. But his courage was unshaken. »Why do you talk of seeking the crown of martyrdom afar?« he said. »Preach the gospel of Christ to haughty prelates, and martyrdom will not fail you. What! I should live and be silent? ... Never! Let the blow fall, I await its coming.« D'Aubigne, b. 17, ch. 8

But God's providence still shielded His servant. The man who for a whole lifetime had stood boldly in defense of the truth, in daily peril of his life, was not to fall a victim of the hatred of its foes. Wycliffe had never sought to shield himself, but the Lord had been his protector; and now, when his enemies felt sure of their prey, God's hand removed him beyond their reach. In his church at Lutterworth, as he was about to dispense the communion, he fell, stricken with palsy, and in a short time yielded up his life. God had appointed to Wycliffe his work. He had put the word of truth in his mouth, and He set a guard about him that this word might come to the people. His life was protected, and his labors were prolonged, until a foundation was laid for the great work of the Reformation.

Wycliffe came from the obscurity of the Dark Ages. There were none who went before him from whose work he could shape his system of reform. Raised up like John the Baptist to accomplish a special mission, he was the herald of a new era. Yet in the system of truth which he presented there was a unity and completeness which Reformers who followed him did not exceed, and which some did not reach, even a hundred years later. So broad and deep was laid the foundation, so firm and true was the framework, that it needed not to be reconstructed by those who came after him.

The great movement that Wycliffe inaugurated, which was to liberate the conscience and the intellect, and set free the nations so long bound to the triumphal car of Rome, had its spring in the Bible. Here was the source of that stream of blessing, which, like the water of life, has flowed down the ages since the fourteenth century. Wycliffe accepted the Holy Scriptures with implicit faith as the inspired revelation of God's will, a sufficient rule of faith and practice. He had been educated to regard the Church of Rome as the divine, infallible authority, and to accept with unquestioning reverence the established teachings and customs of a thousand years; but he turned away from all these to listen to God's holy word. This was the authority which he urged the people to acknowledge. Instead of the church speaking through the pope, he declared the only true authority to be the voice of God speaking through His word. And he taught not only that the Bible is a perfect revelation of God's will, but that the Holy Spirit is its only interpreter, and that every man is, by the study of its teachings, to learn his duty for himself. Thus he turned the minds of men from the pope and the Church of Rome to the word of God.

Wycliffe was one of the greatest of the Reformers. In breadth of intellect, in clearness of thought, in firmness to maintain the truth, and in boldness to defend it, he was equaled by few who came after him. Purity of life, unwearying diligence in study and in labor, incorruptible integrity, and Christlike love and faithfulness in his ministry, characterized the first of the Reformers. And this notwithstanding the intellectual darkness and moral corruption of the age from which he emerged.

The character of Wycliffe is a testimony to the educating, transforming power of the Holy Scriptures. It was the Bible that made him

what he was. The effort to grasp the great truths of revelation imparts freshness and vigor to all the faculties. It expands the mind, sharpens the perceptions, and ripens the judgment. The study of the Bible will ennoble every thought, feeling, and aspiration as no other study can. It gives stability of purpose, patience, courage, and fortitude; it refines the character and sanctifies the soul. An earnest, reverent study of the Scriptures, bringing the mind of the student in direct contact with the infinite mind, would give to the world men of stronger and more active intellect, as well as of nobler principle, than has ever resulted from the ablest training that human philosophy affords. »The entrance of Thy words,« says the psalmist, »giveth light; it giveth understanding.« Psalm 119:130

The doctrines which had been taught by Wycliffe continued for a time to spread; his followers, known as Wycliffites and Lollards, not only traversed England, but scattered to other lands, carrying the knowledge of the gospel. Now that their leader was removed, the preachers labored with even greater zeal than before, and multitudes flocked to listen to their teachings. Some of the nobility, and even the wife of the king, were among the converts. In many places there was a marked reform in the manners of the people, and the idolatrous symbols of Romanism were removed from the churches. But soon the pitiless storm of persecution burst upon those who had dared to accept the Bible as their guide. The English monarchs, eager to strengthen their power by securing the support of Rome, did not hesitate to sacrifice the Reformers. For the first time in the history of England the stake was decreed against the disciples of the gospel. Martyrdom succeeded martyrdom. The advocates of truth, proscribed and tortured, could only pour their cries into the ear of the Lord of Sabaoth. Hunted as foes of the church and traitors to the realm, they continued to preach in secret places, finding shelter as best they could in the humble homes of the poor, and often hiding away even in dens and caves.

Notwithstanding the rage of persecution, a calm, devout, earnest, patient protest against the prevailing corruption of religious faith continued for centuries to be uttered. The Christians of that early time had only a partial knowledge of the truth, but they had learned to love and obey God's word, and they patiently suffered for its sake. Like the disciples in apostolic days, many sacrificed their worldly possessions for the cause of Christ. Those who were permitted to dwell in their homes gladly sheltered their banished brethren, and when they too were driven forth they cheerfully accepted the lot of the outcast. Thousands, it is true, terrified by the fury of their persecutors, purchased their freedom at the sacrifice of their faith, and went out of their prisons, clothed in penitents' robes, to publish their recantation. But the number was not small – and among them were men of noble birth as well as the humble and lowly – who bore fearless testimony to the truth in dungeon cells, in »Lollard towers,« and in the midst of torture and flame, rejoicing that they were counted worthy to know »the fellowship of His sufferings.«

The papists had failed to work their will with Wycliffe during his life, and their hatred could not be satisfied while his body rested quietly in the grave. By the decree of the Council of Constance, more than forty years after his death his bones were exhumed and publicly burned, and the ashes were thrown into a neighboring brook. »This brook,« says an old writer, »hath conveyed his ashes into Avon, Avon into Severn, Severn into the narrow seas, they into the main ocean. And thus the ashes of Wycliffe are the emblem of his doctrine, which now is dispersed all the world over.« T. Fuller, Church History of Britain, b. 4, sec. 2, par. 54. Little did his enemies realize the significance of their malicio us act.

It was through the writings of Wycliffe that John Huss, of Bohemia, was led to renounce many of the errors of Romanism and to enter upon the work of reform. Thus in these two countries, so widely separated, the seed of truth was sown. From Bohemia the work extended to other lands. The minds of men were directed to the long-forgotten word of God. A divine hand was preparing the way for the Great Reformation.

John Wycliffe (1321-1384)

Wycliffe and Lollards Preacher

Chapter 6

Huss and Jerome

The gospel had been planted in Bohemia as early as the ninth century. The Bible was translated, and public worship was conducted, in the language of the people. But as the power of the pope increased, so the word of God was obscured. Gregory VII, who had taken it upon himself to humble the pride of kings, was no less intent upon enslaving the people, and accordingly a bull was issued forbidding public worship to be conducted in the Bohemian tongue. The pope declared that »it was pleasing to the Omnipotent that His worship should be celebrated in an unknown language, and that many evils and heresies had arisen from not observing this rule.« Wylie, b. 3, ch. 1 Thus Rome decreed that the light of God's word should be extinguished and the people should be shut up in darkness. But Heaven had provided other agencies for the preservation of the church. Many of the Waldenses and Albigenses, driven by persecution from their homes in France and Italy, came to Bohemia. Though they dared not teach openly, they labored zealously in secret. Thus the true faith was preserved from century to century.

Before the days of Huss there were men in Bohemia who rose up to condemn openly the corruption in the church and the profligacy of the people. Their labors excited widespread interest. The fears of the hierarchy were roused, and persecution was opened against the disciples of the gospel. Driven to worship in the forests and the mountains, they were hunted by soldiers, and many were put to death. After a time it was decreed that all who departed from the Romish worship should be burned. But while the Christians yielded up their lives, they looked forward to the triumph of their cause. One of those who »taught that salvation was only to be found by faith in the crucified Saviour,« declared when dying: »The rage of the enemies of the truth now prevails against us, but it will not be forever; there shall arise one from among the common people, without sword or authority, and against him they shall not be able to prevail.« Ibid., b. 3, ch. 1 Luther's time was yet far distant; but already one was rising, whose testimony against Rome would stir the nations. John Huss was of humble birth, and was early left an orphan by the death of his father. His pious mother, regarding education and the fear of God as the most valuable of possessions, sought to secure this heritage for her son. Huss studied at the provincial school, and then repaired to the university at Prague, receiving admission as a charity scholar. He was accompanied on the journey to Prague by his mother; widowed and poor, she had no gifts of worldly wealth to bestow upon her son, but as they drew near to the great city, she kneeled down beside the fatherless youth and invoked for him the blessing of their Father in heaven. Little did that mother realize how her prayer was to be answered.

At the university, Huss soon distinguished himself by his untiring application and rapid progress, while his blameless life and gentle, winning deportment gained him universal esteem. He was a sincere adherent of the Roman Church and an earnest seeker for the spiritual blessings which it professes to bestow. On the occasion of a jubilee he went to confession, paid the last few coins in his scanty store, and joined in the processions, that he might share in the absolution promised. After completing his college course, he entered the priesthood, and rapidly attaining to eminence, he soon became attached to the court of the king. He was also made professor and afterward rector of the university where he had received his education. In a few years the humble charity scholar had become the pride of his country, and his name was renowned throughout Europe.

But it was in another field that Huss began the work of reform. Several years after taking priest's orders he was appointed preacher of the chapel of Bethlehem. The founder of this chapel had advocated, as a matter of great importance, the preaching of the Scriptures in the language of the people. Notwithstanding Rome's opposition to this practice, it had not been wholly discontinued in Bohemia. But there was great ignorance of the Bible, and the worst vices prevailed among the people of all ranks. These evils Huss unsparingly denounced, appealing to the word of God to enforce the principles of truth and purity which he inculcated. A citizen of Prague, Jerome, who afterward became so closely associated with Huss, had, on returning from England, brought with him the writings of Wycliffe. The queen of England, who had been a convert to Wycliffe's teachings, was a Bohemian princess, and through her influence also the Reformer's works were widely circulated in her native country.

Jan Hus (1370-1415)

Hieronymus (1365-1416)

These works Huss read with interest; he believed their author to be a sincere Christian and was inclined to regard with favor the reforms which he advocated. Already, though he knew it not, Huss had entered upon a path which was to lead him far away from Rome.

About this time there arrived in Prague two strangers from England, men of learning, who had received the light and had come to spread it in this distant land. Beginning with an open attack on the pope's supremacy, they were soon silenced by the authorities; but being unwilling to relinquish their purpose, they had recourse to other measures. Being artists as well as preachers, they proceeded to exercise their skill. In a place open to the public they drew two pictures. One represented the entrance of Christ into Jerusalem, »meek, and sitting upon an ass«, Matthew 21:5 and followed by His disciples in travel-worn garments and with naked feet. The other picture portrayed a pontifical procession – the pope arrayed in his rich robes and triple crown, mounted upon a horse magnificently adorned, preceded by trumpeters and followed by cardinals and prelates in dazzling array.

Here was a sermon which arrested the attention of all classes. Crowds came to gaze upon the drawings. None could fail to read the moral, and many were deeply impressed by the contrast between the meekness and humility of Christ the Master and the pride and arrogance of the pope, His professed servant. There was great commotion in Prague, and the strangers after a time found it necessary, for their own safety, to depart. But the lesson they had taught was not forgotten. The pictures made a deep impression on the mind of Huss and led him to a closer study of the Bible and of Wycliffe's writings. Though he was not prepared, even yet, to accept all the reforms advocated by Wycliffe, he saw more clearly the true character of the papacy, and with greater zeal denounced the pride, the ambition, and the corruption of the hierarchy. From Bohemia the light extended to Germany, for disturbances in the University of Prague caused the withdrawal of hundreds of German students. Many of them had received from Huss their first knowledge of the Bible, and on their return they spread the gospel in their fatherland.

Tidings of the work at Prague were carried to Rome, and Huss was soon summoned to appear before the pope. To obey would be to expose himself to certain death. The king and queen of Bohemia, the university, members of the nobility, and officers of the government united in an appeal to the pontiff that Huss be permitted to remain at Prague and to answer at Rome by deputy. Instead of granting this request, the pope proceeded to the trial and condemnation of Huss, and then declared the city of Prague to be under interdict.

In that age this sentence, whenever pronounced, created widespread alarm. The ceremonies by which it was accompanied were well adapted to strike terror to a people who looked upon the pope as the representative of God Himself, holding the keys of heaven and hell, and possessing power to invoke temporal as well as spiritual judgments. It was believed that the gates of heaven were closed against the region smitten with interdict; that until it should please the pope to remove the ban, the dead were shut out from the abodes of bliss. In token of this terrible calamity, all the services of religion were suspended. The churches were closed. Marriages were solemnized in the churchyard. The dead, denied burial in consecrated ground, were interred, without the rites of sepulture, in the ditches or the fields. Thus by measures which appealed to the imagination, Rome essayed to control the consciences of men.

The city of Prague was filled with tumult. A large class denounced Huss as the cause of all their calamities and demanded that he be given up to the vengeance of Rome. To quiet the storm, the Reformer withdrew for a time to his native village. Writing to the friends whom he had left at Prague, he said: »If I have withdrawn from the midst of you, it is to follow the precept and example of Jesus Christ, in order not to
 give room to the ill-minded to draw on themselves eter-

nal condemnation, and in order not to be to the pious a cause of affliction and persecution. I have retired also through an apprehension that impious priests might continue for a longer time to prohibit the preaching of the word of God amongst you; but I have not quitted you to deny the divine truth, for which, with God's assistance, I am willing to die.« Bonnechose, The Reformers Before the Reformation, vol. 1, p. 87

Huss did not cease his labors, but traveled through the surrounding country, preaching to eager crowds. Thus the measures to which the pope resorted to suppress the gospel were causing it to be the more widely extended. »We can do nothing against the truth, but for the truth.« 2.Corinthians 13:8

»The mind of Huss, at this stage of his career, would seem to have been the scene of a painful conflict. Although the church was seeking to overwhelm him by her thunderbolts, he had not renounced her authority. The Roman Church was still to him the spouse of Christ, and the pope was the representative and vicar of God. What Huss was warring against was the abuse of authority, not the principle itself. This brought on a terrible conflict between the convictions of his understanding and the claims of his conscience. If the authority was just and infallible, as he believed it to be, how came it that he felt compelled to disobey it? To obey, he saw, was to sin; but why should obedience to an infallible church lead to such an issue? This was the problem he could not solve; this was the doubt that tortured him hour by hour. The nearest approximation to a solution which he was able to make was that it had happened again, as once before in the days of the Saviour, that the priests of the church had become wicked persons and were using their lawful authority for unlawful ends. This led him to adopt for his own guidance, and to preach to others for theirs, the maxim that the precepts of Scripture, conveyed through the understanding, are to rule the conscience; in other words, that God speaking in the Bible, and not the church speaking through the priesthood, is the one infallible guide.« Wylie, b. 3, ch. 2

When after a time the excitement in Prague subsided, Huss returned to his chapel of Bethlehem, to continue with greater zeal and courage the preaching of the word of God. His enemies were active and powerful, but the queen and many of the nobles were his friends, and the people in great numbers sided with him. Comparing his pure and elevating teachings and holy life with the degrading dogmas which the Romanists preached, and the avarice and debauchery which they practiced, many regarded it an honor to be on his side.

Hitherto Huss had stood alone in his labors; but now Jerome, who while in England had accepted the teachings of Wycliffe, joined in the work of reform. The two were hereafter united in their lives, and in death they were not to be divided. Brilliancy of genius, eloquence and learning – gifts that win popular favor – were possessed in a pre-eminent degree by Jerome; but in those qualities which constitute real strength of character, Huss was the greater. His calm judgment served as a restraint upon the impulsive spirit of Jerome, who, with true humility, perceived his worth, and yielded to his counsels. Under their united labors the reform was more rapidly extended.

God permitted great light to shine upon the minds of these chosen men, revealing to them many of the errors of Rome; but they did not receive all the light that was to be given to the world. Through these, His servants, God was leading the people out of the darkness of Romanism; but there were many and great obstacles for them to meet, and He led them on, step by step, as they could bear it. They were not prepared to receive all the light at once. Like the full glory of the noontide sun to those who have long dwelt in darkness, it would, if presented, have caused them to turn away. Therefore He revealed it to the leaders little by little, as it could be received by the people. From century to century, other faithful workers were to follow, to lead the people on still further in the path of reform.

The schism in the church still continued. Three popes were now contending for the supremacy, and their strife filled Christendom with crime and tumult. Not content with hurling anathemas, they resorted to temporal weapons. Each cast about him to purchase arms and to obtain soldiers. Of course money must be had; and to procure this, the gifts, offices, and blessings of the church were offered for sale. see Appendix note for page 59 The priests also, imitating their superiors, resorted to simony and war to humble their rivals and strengthen their own power. With daily increasing boldness Huss thundered against the abominations which were tolerated in the name of religion; and the people openly accused the Romish leaders as the cause of the miseries that overwhelmed Christendom.

Again the city of Prague seemed on the verge of a bloody conflict. As in former ages, God's servant was accused as »he that troubleth Israel.« 1 Kings 18:17 The city was again placed under interdict, and Huss withdrew to his native village. The testimony so faithfully borne from his loved chapel of Bethlehem was ended. He was to speak from a wider stage, to all Christendom, before laying down his life as a witness for the truth.

To cure the evils that were distracting Europe, a general council was summoned to meet at Constance. The council was called at the desire of the emperor Sigismund, by one of the three rival popes, John XXIII. The demand for a council had been far from welcome to Pope John, whose character and policy could ill bear investigation, even by prelates as lax in morals as were the churchmen of those times. He dared not, however, oppose the will of Sigismund. see Appendix

The chief objects to be accomplished by the council were to heal the schism in the church and to root out heresy. Hence the two antipopes were summoned to appear before it, as well as the leading propagator of the new opinions, John Huss. The former, having regard to their own safety, did not attend in person, but were represented by their delegates. Pope John, while ostensibly the convoker of the council, came to it with many misgivings, suspecting the emperor's secret purpose to depose him, and fearing to be brought to account for the vices which had disgraced the tiara, as well as for the crimes which had secured it. Yet he made his entry into the city of Constance with great pomp, attended by ecclesiastics of the highest rank and followed by a train of courtiers. All the clergy and dignitaries of the city, with an immense crowd of citizens, went out to welcome him. Above his head was a golden canopy, borne by four of the chief magistrates. The host was carried before him, and the rich dresses of the cardinals and nobles made an imposing display.

Meanwhile another traveler was approaching Constance. Huss was conscious of the dangers which threatened him. He parted from his friends as if he were never to meet them again, and went on his journey feeling that it was leading him to the stake. Notwithstanding he had obtained a safe-conduct from the king of Bohemia, and received one also from the emperor Sigismund while on his journey, he made all his arrangements in view of the probability of his death.

In a letter addressed to his friends at Prague he said: »My brethren, ... I am departing with a safe-conduct from the king to meet my numerous and mortal enemies. ... I confide altogether in the all-powerful God, in my Saviour; I trust that He will listen to your ardent prayers, that He will infuse His prudence and His wisdom into my mouth, in order that I may resist them; and that He will accord me His Holy Spirit to fortify me in His truth, so that I may face with courage, temptations, prison, and, if necessary, a cruel death. Jesus Christ suffered for His well-beloved; and therefore ought we to be astonished that He has left us His example, in order that we may ourselves endure with patience all things for our own salvation? He is God, and we are His creatures; He is the Lord, and we are His servants; He is Master of the world, and we are contemptible mortals – yet He, suffered! Why, then, should we not suffer also, particularly when suffering is for us a purification? Therefore, beloved, if my death ought to contribute to His glory, pray that it may come quickly, and that He may enable me to support all my calamities with constancy. But if it be better that I return amongst you, let us pray to God that I may return without stain – that is, that I may not suppress one tittle of the truth of the gospel, in order to leave my brethren an excellent example to follow. Probably, therefore, you will nevermore behold my face at Prague; but should the will of the all-powerful God deign to restore me to you, let us then advance with a firmer heart in the knowledge and the love of His law.« Bonnechose, vol. 1, pp. 147, 148

In another letter, to a priest who had become a disciple of the gospel, Huss spoke with deep humility of his own errors, accusing himself »of having felt pleasure in wearing rich apparel and of having wasted hours in frivolous occupations.« He then added these touching admonitions: »May the glory of God and the salvation of souls occupy thy mind, and not the possession of benefices and estates. Beware of adorning thy house more than thy soul; and, above all, give thy care to the spiritual edifice. Be pious and humble with the poor, and consume not thy substance in feasting. Shouldst thou not amend thy life and refrain from superfluities, I fear that thou wilt be severely chastened, as I am myself. ... Thou knowest my doctrine, for thou hast received my instructions from thy childhood; it is therefore useless for me to write to thee any further. But I conjure thee, by the mercy of our Lord, not to imitate me in any of the vanities into which thou hast seen me fall.« On the cover of the letter he added: »I conjure thee, my friend, not to break this seal until thou shalt have acquired the certitude that I am dead.« Ibid., vol. 1, pp. 148, 149 On his journey, Huss everywhere beheld indications of the spread of his doctrines and the favor with which his cause was regarded. The people thronged to meet him, and in some towns the magistrates attended him through their streets. Upon arriving at Constance, Huss was granted full liberty. To the emperor's safe-conduct was added a personal assurance of protection by the pope. But, in violation of these solemn and repeated declarations, the Reformer was in a short time arrested, by order of the pope and cardinals, and thrust into a loathsome dungeon. Later he was transferred to a strong castle across the Rhine and there kept a prisoner. The pope, profiting little by his perfidy, was soon after committed to the same prison. Ibid., vol. 1, p. 247 He had been proved before the council to be guilty of the basest crimes, besides murder, simony, and adultery, »sins not fit to be named.« So the council itself declared, and he was finally deprived of the tiara and thrown into prison. The antipopes also were deposed, and a new pontiff was chosen.

Though the pope himself had been guilty of greater crimes than Huss had ever charged upon the priests, and for which he had demanded a reformation, yet the same council which degraded the pontiff proceeded to crush the Reformer. The imprisonment of Huss excited great indignation in Bohemia. Powerful noblemen addressed to the council earnest protests against this outrage. The emperor, who was loath to permit the violation of a safe-conduct, opposed the proceedings against him. But the enemies of the Reformer were malignant and determined. They appealed to the emperor's prejudices, to his fears, to his zeal for the church. They brought forward arguments of great length to prove that »faith ought not to be kept with heretics, nor persons suspected of heresy, though they are furnished with safeconducts from the emperor and kings.« Jacques Lenfant, History of the Council of Constance, vol. 1, p. 516 Thus they prevailed. Enfeebled by illness and imprisonment, – for the damp, foul air of his dungeon had brought on a fever which nearly ended his life, – Huss was at last brought before the council. Loaded with chains he stood in the presence of the emperor, whose honor and good faith had been pledged to protect him. During his long trial he firmly maintained the truth, and in the presence of the assembled dignitaries of church and state he uttered a solemn and faithful protest against the corruptions of the hierarchy. When required to choose whether he would recant his doctrines or suffer death, he accepted the martyr's fate.

The grace of God sustained him. During the weeks of suffering that passed before his final sentence, heaven's peace filled his soul. »I write this letter,« he said to a friend, »in my prison, and [106/107] with my fettered hand, expecting my sentence of death tomorrow. ... When, with the assistance of Jesus Christ, we shall again meet in the delicious peace of the future life, you will learn how merciful God has shown Himself toward me, how effectually He has supported me in the midst of my temptations and trials.« Bonnechose, vol. 2, p. 67

In the gloom of his dungeon he foresaw the triumph of the true faith. Returning in his dreams to the chapel at Prague where he had preached the gospel, he saw the pope and his bishops effacing the pictures of Christ which he had painted on its walls. »This vision distressed him: but on the next day he saw many painters occupied in restoring these figures in greater number and in brighter colors. As soon as their task was ended, the painters, who were surrounded by an immense crowd, exclaimed, 'Now let the popes and bishops come; they shall never efface them more!'« Said the Reformer, as he related his dream: »I maintain this for certain, that the image of Christ will never be effaced. They have wished to destroy it, but it shall be painted afresh in all hearts by much better preachers than myself.« D'Aubigne, b. 1, ch. 6 For the last time, Huss was brought before the council. It was a vast and brilliant assembly – the emperor, the princes of the empire, the royal deputies, the cardinals, bishops, and priests, and an immense crowd who had come as spectators of the events of the day. From all parts of Christendom had been gathered the witnesses of this first great sacrifice in the long struggle by which liberty of conscience was to be secured.

Being called upon for his final decision, Huss declared his refusal to abjure, and, fixing his penetrating glance upon the monarch whose plighted word had been so shamelessly violated, he declared: »I determined, of my own free will, to appear before this council, under the public protection and faith of the emperor here present.« Bonnechose, vol. 2, p. 84 A deep flush crimsoned the face of Sigismund as the eyes of all in the assembly turned upon him. Sentence having been pronounced, the ceremony of degradation began. The bishops clothed their prisoner in the sacerdotal habit, and as he took the priestly robe, he said: »Our Lord Jesus Christ was covered with a white robe, by way of insult, when Herod had Him conducted before Pilate.« Ibid., vol. 2, p. 86 Being again exhorted to retract, he replied, turning toward the people: »With what face, then, should I behold the heavens? How should I look on those multitudes of men to whom I have preached

 the pure gospel? No; I esteem their salvation more

than this poor body, now appointed unto death.« The vestments were removed one by one, each bishop pronouncing a curse as he performed his part of the ceremony. Finally »they put on his head a cap or pyramidal-shaped miter of paper, on which were painted frightful figures of demons, with the word 'Archheretic' conspicuous in front. 'Most joyfully,' said Huss, 'will I wear this crown of shame for Thy sake, O Jesus, who for me didst wear a crown of thorns.'«

When he was thus arrayed, »the prelates said, 'Now we devote thy soul to the devil.' 'And I,' said John Huss, lifting up his eyes toward heaven, 'do commit my spirit into Thy hands, O Lord Jesus, for Thou hast redeemed me.'« Wylie, b. 3, ch. 7 He was now delivered up to the secular authorities and led away to the place of execution. An immense procession followed, hundreds of men at arms, priests and bishops in their costly robes, and the inhabitants of Constance. When he had been fastened to the stake, and all was ready for the fire to be lighted, the martyr was once more exhorted to save himself by renouncing his errors. »What errors,« said Huss, »shall I renounce? I know myself guilty of none. I call God to witness that all that I have written and preached has been with the view of rescuing souls from sin and perdition; and, therefore, most joyfully will I confirm with my blood that truth which I have written and preached.« Ibid., b. 3, ch. 7 When the flames kindled about him, he began to sing, »Jesus, Thou Son of David, have mercy on me,« and so continued till his voice was silenced forever.

Even his enemies were struck with his heroic bearing. A zealous papist, describing the martyrdom of Huss, and of Jerome, who died soon after, said: »Both bore themselves with constant mind when their last hour approached. They prepared for the fire as if they were going to a marriage feast. They uttered no cry of pain. When the flames rose, they began to sing hymns; and scarce could the vehemency of the fire stop their singing.« Ibid., b. 3, ch. 7 When the body of Huss had been wholly consumed, his ashes, with the soil upon which they rested, were gathered up and cast into the Rhine, and thus borne onward to the ocean. His persecutors vainly imagined that they had rooted out the truths he preached. Little did they dream that the ashes that day borne away to the sea were to be as seed scattered in all the countries of the earth; that in lands yet unknown it would yield abundant fruit in witnesses for the truth. The voice which had spoken in the council hall of Constance had wakened echoes that would be heard through all coming ages. [109/110]

Huss was no more, but the truths for which he died could never perish. His example of faith and constancy would encourage multitudes to stand firm for the truth, in the face of torture and death. His execution had exhibited to the whole world the perfidious cruelty of Rome. The enemies of truth, though they knew it not, had been furthering the cause which they vainly sought to destroy.

Yet another stake was to be set up at Constance. The blood of another witness must testify for the truth. Jerome, upon bidding farewell to Huss on his departure for the council, had exhorted him to courage and firmness, declaring that if he should fall into any peril, he himself would fly to his assistance. Upon hearing of the Reformer's imprisonment, the faithful disciple immediately prepared to fulfill his promise. Without a safe-conduct he set out, with a single companion, for Constance. On arriving there he was convinced that he had only exposed himself to peril, without the possibility of doing anything for the deliverance of Huss. He fled from the city, but was arrested on the homeward journey and brought back loaded with fetters and under the custody of a band of soldiers. At his first appearance before the council his attempts to reply to the accusations brought against him were met with shouts, »To the flames with him! to the flames!« Bonnechose, vol. 1, p. 234 He was thrown into a dungeon, chained in a position which caused him great suffering, and fed on bread and water. After some months the cruelties of his imprisonment brought upon Jerome an illness that threatened his life, and his enemies, fearing that he might escape them, treated him with less severity, though he remained in prison for one year.

The death of Huss had not resulted as the papists had hoped. The violation of his safe-conduct had roused a storm of indignation, and as the safer course, the council determined, instead of burning Jerome, to force him, if possible, to retract. He was brought before the assembly, and offered the alternative to recant, or to die at the stake. Death at the beginning of his imprisonment would have been a mercy in comparison with the terrible sufferings which he had undergone; but now, weakened by illness, by the rigors of his prison house, and the torture of anxiety and suspense, separated from his friends, and disheartened by the death of Huss, Jerome's fortitude gave way, and he consented to submit to the council. He pledged himself to adhere to the Catholic faith, and accepted the action of the council in

 condemning the doctrines of Wycliffe and Huss, excepting, however, the »holy truths« which they had taught. Ibid, vol. 2, p. 141 By this expedient Jerome endeavored to silence the voice of conscience and escape his doom. But in the solitude of his dungeon he saw more clearly what he had done. He thought of the courage and fidelity of Huss, and in contrast pondered upon his own denial of the truth. He thought of the divine Master whom he had pledged himself to serve, and who for his sake endured the death of the cross. Before his retraction he had found comfort, amid all his sufferings, in the assurance of God's favor; but now remorse and doubts tortured his soul. He knew that still other retractions must be made before he could be at peace with Rome. The path upon which he was entering could end only in complete apostasy. His resolution was taken: To escape a brief period of suffering he would not deny his Lord. Soon he was again brought before the council. His submission had not satisfied his judges. Their thirst for blood, whetted by the death of Huss, clamored for fresh victims. Only by an unreserved surrender of the truth could Jerome preserve his life. But he had determined to avow his faith and follow his brother martyr to the flames.

He renounced his former recantation and, as a dying man, solemnly required an opportunity to make his defense. Fearing the effect of his words, the prelates insisted that he should merely affirm or deny the truth of the charges brought against him. Jerome protested against such cruelty and injustice. »You have held me shut up three hundred and forty days in a frightful prison,« he said, »in the midst of filth, noisomeness, stench, and the utmost want of everything; you then bring me out before you, and lending an ear to my mortal enemies, you refuse to hear me. ... If you be really wise men, and the lights of the world, take care not to sin against justice. As to me, I am only a feeble mortal; my life is but of little importance; and when I exhort you not to deliver an unjust sentence, I speak less for myself than for you.« Ibid., vol. 2, pp. 146, 147

His request was finally granted. In the presence of his judges, Jerome kneeled down and prayed that the divine Spirit might control his thoughts and words, that he might speak nothing contrary to the truth or unworthy of his Master. To him that day was fulfilled the promise of God to the first disciples: »Ye shall be brought before governors and kings for My sake. ... But when they deliver you up, take no thought how or what ye shall speak: for it shall be given you in that same hour what ye shall speak. For it is not ye that speak, but the Spirit of your Father which speaketh in you.« Matthew 10:18-20 The words of Jerome excited astonishment and admiration, even in his enemies. For a whole year he had been immured in a dungeon, unable to read or even to see, in great physical suffering and mental anxiety. Yet his arguments were presented with as much clearness and power as if he had had undisturbed opportunity for study. He pointed his hearers to the long line of holy men who had been condemned by unjust judges. In almost every generation have been those who, while seeking to elevate the people of their time, have been reproached and cast out, but who in later times have been shown to be deserving of honor. Christ Himself was condemned as a malefactor at an unrighteous tribunal.

At his retraction, Jerome had assented to the justice of the sentence condemning Huss; he now declared his repentance and bore witness to the innocence and holiness of the martyr. »I knew him from his childhood,« he said. »He was a most excellent man, just and holy; he was condemned, notwithstanding his innocence. ... I also – I am ready to die: I will not recoil before the torments that are prepared for me by my enemies and false witnesses, who will one day have to render an account of their impostures before the great God, whom nothing can deceive.« Bonnechose, vol. 2, p. 151

In self-reproach for his own denial of the truth, Jerome continued: »Of all the sins that I have committed since my youth, none weigh so heavily on my mind, and cause me such poignant remorse, as that which I committed in this fatal place, when I approved of the iniquitous sentence rendered against Wycliffe, and against the holy martyr, John Huss, my master and my friend. Yes! I confess it from my heart, and declare with horror that I disgracefully quailed when, through a dread of death, I condemned their doctrines. I therefore supplicate ... Almighty God to deign to pardon me my sins, and this one in particular, the most heinous of all.« Pointing to his judges, he said firmly: »You condemned Wycliffe and John Huss, not for having shaken the doctrine of the church, but simply because they branded with reprobation the scandals proceeding from the clergy – their pomp, their pride, and all the vices of the prelates and priests. The things which they have affirmed, and which are irrefutable, I also think and declare, like them.«

His words were interrupted. The prelates, trembling with rage, cried out: »What need is there of further proof? We behold with our own eyes the most obstinate of heretics!«

Unmoved by the tempest, Jerome exclaimed: »What! do you suppose that I fear to die? You have held me for a whole year in a frightful dungeon, more horrible than death itself. You have treated me more cruelly than a Turk, Jew, or pagan, and my flesh has literally rotted off my bones alive; and yet I make no complaint, for lamentation ill becomes a man of heart and spirit; but I cannot but express my astonishment at such great barbarity toward a Christian.« Ibid., vol. 2, pp. 151,153

Again the storm of rage burst out, and Jerome was hurried away to prison. Yet there were some in the assembly upon whom his words had made a deep impression and who desired to save his life. He was visited by dignitaries of the church and urged to submit himself to the council. The most brilliant prospects were presented before him as the reward of renouncing his opposition to Rome.

But like his Master when offered the glory of the world, Jerome remained steadfast. »Prove to me from the Holy Writings that I am in error,« he said, »and I will abjure it.« »The Holy Writings!« exclaimed one of his tempters, »is everything then to be judged by them? Who can understand them till the church has interpreted them?« »Are the traditions of men more worthy of faith than the gospel of our Saviour?« replied Jerome. »Paul did not exhort those to whom he wrote to listen to the traditions of men, but said, 'Search the Scriptures.'« »Heretic!« was the response, »I repent having pleaded so long with you. I see that you are urged on by the devil.« Wylie, b. 3, ch. 10

Erelong sentence of condemnation was passed upon him. He was led out to the same spot upon which Huss had yielded up his life. He went singing on his way, his countenance lighted up with joy and peace. His gaze was fixed upon Christ, and to him death had lost its terrors. When the executioner, about to kindle the pile, stepped behind him, the martyr exclaimed: »Come forward boldly; apply the fire before my face. Had I been afraid, I should not be here.«

His last words, uttered as the flames rose about him, were a prayer. »Lord, Almighty Father,« he cried, »have pity on me, and pardon me my sins; for Thou knowest that I have always loved Thy truth.« Bonnechose, vol. 2, p. 168 His voice ceased, but his lips continued to move in prayer. When the fire had done its work, the ashes of the martyr, with the earth upon which they rested, were gathered up, and like those of Huss, were thrown into the Rhine.

So perished God's faithful light bearers. But the light of the truths which they proclaimed – the light of their heroic example – could not be extinguished. As well might men attempt to turn back the sun in its course as to prevent the dawning of that day which was even then breaking upon the world.

The execution of Huss had kindled a flame of indignation and horror in Bohemia. It was felt by the whole nation that he had fallen a prey to the malice of the priests and the treachery of the emperor. He was declared to have been a faithful teacher of the truth, and the council that decreed his death was charged with the guilt of murder. His doctrines now attracted greater attention than ever before. By the papal edicts the writings of Wycliffe had been condemned to the flames. But those that had escaped destruction were now brought out from their hiding places and studied in connection with the Bible, or such parts of it as the people could obtain, and many were thus led to accept the reformed faith. The murderers of Huss did not stand quietly by and witness the triumph of his cause. The pope and the emperor united to crush out the movement, and the armies of Sigismund were hurled upon Bohemia. But a deliverer was raised up. Ziska, who soon after the opening of the war became totally blind, yet who was one of the ablest generals of his age, was the leader of the Bohemians. Trusting in the help of God and the righteousness of their cause, that people withstood the mightiest armies that could be brought against them. Again and again the emperor, raising fresh armies, invaded Bohemia, only to be ignominiously repulsed. The Hussites were raised above the fear of death, and nothing could stand against them. A few years after the opening of the war, the brave Ziska died; but his place was filled by Procopius, who was an equally brave and skillful general, and in some respects a more able leader.

The enemies of the Bohemians, knowing that the blind warrior was dead, deemed the opportunity favorable for recovering all that they had lost. The pope now proclaimed a crusade against the Hussites, and again an immense force was precipitated upon Bohemia, but only to suffer terrible defeat. Another crusade was proclaimed. In all the papal countries of Europe, men, money, and munitions of war were raised. Multitudes flocked to the papal standard, assured that at last an end would be made of the Hussite heretics. Confident of victory, the vast force entered Bohemia. The people rallied to repel them. The two armies approached each other until only a river lay between them. »The crusaders were in greatly superior force, but instead of

dashing across the stream, and closing in battle with

the Hussites whom they had come so far to meet, they stood gazing in silence at those warriors.« Wylie, b. 3, ch. 17 Then suddenly a mysterious terror fell upon the host. Without striking a blow, that mighty force broke and scattered as if dispelled by an unseen power. Great numbers were slaughtered by the Hussite army, which pursued the fugitives, and an immense booty fell into the hands of the victors, so that the war, instead of impoverishing, enriched the Bohemians.

A few years later, under a new pope, still another crusade was set on foot. As before, men and means were drawn from all the papal countries of Europe. Great were the inducements held out to those who should engage in this perilous enterprise. Full forgiveness of the most heinous crimes was ensured to every crusader. All who died in the war were promised a rich reward in heaven, and those who survived were to reap honor and riches on the field of battle. Again a vast army was collected, and, crossing the frontier they entered Bohemia. The Hussite forces fell back before them, thus drawing the invaders farther and farther into the country, and leading them to count the victory already won. At last the army of Procopius made a stand, and turning upon the foe, advanced to give them battle. The crusaders, now discovering their mistake, lay in their encampment awaiting the onset. As the sound of the approaching force was heard, even before the Hussites were in sight, a panic again fell upon the crusaders. Princes, generals, and common soldiers, casting away their armor, fled in all directions. In vain the papal legate, who was the leader of the invasion, endeavored to rally his terrified and disorganized forces. Despite his utmost endeavors, he himself was swept along in the tide of fugitives. The rout was complete, and again an immense booty fell into the hands of the victors. Thus the second time a vast army, sent forth by the most powerful nations of Europe, a host of brave, warlike men, trained and equipped for battle, fled without a blow before the defenders of a small and hitherto feeble nation. Here was a manifestation of divine power. The invaders were smitten with a supernatural terror. He who overthrew the hosts of Pharaoh in the Red Sea, who put to flight the armies of Midian before Gideon and his three hundred, who in one night laid low the forces of the proud Assyrian, had again stretched out His hand to wither the power of the oppressor. »There were they in great fear, where no fear was: for God hath scattered the bones of him that encampeth against thee: thou hast put them to shame, because God hath despised them.« Psalm 53:5

The papal leaders, despairing of conquering by force, at last resorted to diplomacy. A compromise was entered into, that while professing to grant to the Bohemians freedom of conscience, really betrayed them into the power of Rome. The Bohemians had specified four points as the condition of peace with Rome: the free preaching of the Bible; the right of the whole church to both the bread and the wine in the communion, and the use of the mother tongue in divine worship; the exclusion of the clergy from all secular offices and authority; and, in cases of crime, the jurisdiction of the civil courts over clergy and laity alike. The papal authorities at last »agreed that the four articles of the Hussites should be accepted, but that the right of explaining them, that is, of determining their precise import, should belong to the council - in other words, to the pope and the emperor.« Wylie, b. 3, ch. 18 On this basis a treaty was entered into, and Rome gained by dissimulation and fraud what she had failed to gain by conflict; for, placing her own interpretation upon the Hussite articles, as upon the Bible, she could pervert their meaning to suit her own purposes.

A large class in Bohemia, seeing that it betrayed their liberties, could not consent to the compact. Dissensions and divisions arose, leading to strife and bloodshed among themselves. In this strife the noble Procopius fell, and the liberties of Bohemia perished.

Sigismund, the betrayer of Huss and Jerome, now became king of Bohemia, and regardless of his oath to support the rights of the Bohemians, he proceeded to establish popery. But he had gained little by his subservience to Rome. For twenty years his life had been filled with labors and perils. His armies had been wasted and his treasuries drained by a long and fruitless struggle; and now, after reigning one year, he died, leaving his kingdom on the brink of civil war, and bequeathing to posterity a name branded with infamy. Tumults, strife, and bloodshed were protracted. Again foreign armies invaded Bohemia, and internal dissension continued to distract the nation. Those who remained faithful to the gospel were subjected to a bloody persecution. As their former brethren, entering into compact with Rome, imbibed her errors, those who adhered to the ancient faith had formed themselves into a distinct church, taking the name of »United Brethren.« This act drew upon them maledictions from all classes. Yet their firmness was unshaken. Forced to find refuge in the woods and caves, they still assembled to read God's word

 and unite in His worship.

Through messengers secretly sent out into different countries, they learned that here and there were »isolated confessors of the truth, a few in this city and a few in that, the object, like themselves, of persecution; and that amid the mountains of the Alps was an ancient church, resting on the foundations of Scripture, and protesting against the idolatrous corruptions of Rome.« Wylie, b. 3, ch. 19 This intelligence was received with great joy, and a correspondence was opened with the Waldensian Christians.

Steadfast to the gospel, the Bohemians waited through the night of their persecution, in the darkest hour still turning their eyes toward the horizon like men who watch for the morning. »Their lot was cast in evil days, but ... they remembered the words first uttered by Huss, and repeated by Jerome, that a century must revolve before the day should break. These were to the Taborites [Hussites] what the words of Joseph were to the tribes in the house of bondage: 'I die, and God will surely visit you, and bring you out.'« Ibid., b. 3, ch. 19

»The closing period of the fifteenth century witnessed the slow but sure increase of the churches of the Brethren. Although far from being unmolested, they yet enjoyed comparative rest. At the commencement of the sixteenth century their churches numbered two hundred in Bohemia and Moravia.« Ezra Hall Gillett, Life and Times of John Huss, vol. 2, p. 570 »So goodly was the remnant which, escaping the destructive fury of fire and sword, was permitted to see the dawning of that day which Huss had foretold.« Wylie, b. 3, ch. 19

John Hus at the Council of Constance (1415)

Preparation for burning of John Hus (1415)

Chapter 7

Luther's Separation From Rome

Foremost among those who were called to lead the church from the darkness of popery into the light of a purer faith, stood Martin Luther. Zealous, ardent, and devoted, knowing no fear but the fear of God, and acknowledging no foundation for religious faith but the Holy Scriptures, Luther was the man for his time; through him God accomplished a great work for the reformation of the church and the enlightenment of the world.

Like the first heralds of the gospel, Luther sprang from the ranks of poverty. His early years were spent in the humble home of a German peasant. By daily toil as a miner his father earned the means for his education. He intended him for a lawyer; but God purposed to make him a builder in the great temple that was rising so slowly through the centuries. Hardship, privation, and severe discipline were the school in which Infinite Wisdom prepared Luther for the important mission of his life.

Luther's father was a man of strong and active mind and great force of character, honest, resolute, and straightforward. He was true to his convictions of duty, let the consequences be what they might. His sterling good sense led him to regard the monastic system with distrust. He was highly displeased when Luther, without his consent, entered a monastery; and it was two years before the father was reconciled to his son, and even then his opinions remained the same.

Luther's parents bestowed great care upon the education and training of their children. They endeavored to instruct them in the knowledge of God and the practice of Christian virtues. The father's prayer often ascended in the hearing of his son that the child might remember the name of the Lord and one day aid in the advancement of His truth. Every advantage for moral or intellectual culture which their life of toil permitted them to enjoy was eagerly improved by these parents. Their efforts were earnest and persevering to prepare their children for a life of piety and usefulness. With their firmness and strength of character they sometimes exercised too great severity; but the Reformer himself, though conscious that in some respects they had erred, found in their discipline more to approve than to condemn.

At school, where he was sent at an early age, Luther was treated with harshness and even violence. So great was the poverty of his parents that upon going from home to school in another town he was for a time obliged to obtain his food by singing from door to door, and he often suffered from hunger. The gloomy, superstitious ideas of religion then prevailing filled him with fear. He would lie down at night with a sorrowful heart, looking forward with trembling to the dark future and in constant terror at the thought of God as a stern, unrelenting judge, a cruel tyrant, rather than a kind heavenly Father.

Yet under so many and so great discouragements Luther pressed resolutely forward toward the high standard of moral and intellectual excellence which attracted his soul. He thirsted for knowledge, and the earnest and practical character of his mind led him to desire the solid and useful rather than the showy and superficial.

When, at the age of eighteen, he entered the University of Erfurt, his situation was more favorable and his prospects were brighter than in his earlier years. His parents having by thrift and industry acquired a competence, they were able to render him all needed assistance. And the influence of judicious friends had somewhat lessened the gloomy effects of his former training. He applied himself to the study of the best authors, diligently treasuring their most weighty thoughts and making the wisdom of the wise his own. Even under the harsh discipline of his former instructors he had early given promise of distinction, and with favorable influences his mind rapidly developed. A retentive memory, a lively imagination, strong reasoning powers, and untiring application soon placed him in the foremost rank among his associates. Intellectual discipline ripened his understanding and aroused an activity of mind and a keenness of perception that were preparing him for the conflicts of his life.

The fear of the Lord dwelt in the heart of Luther, enabling him to maintain his steadfastness of purpose and leading him to deep humility before God. He had an abiding sense of his dependence upon divine aid, and he did not fail to begin each day with prayer, while his heart was continually breathing a petition for guidance and support. »To pray well,« he often said, »is the better half of study.« D'Aubigne, b. 2, ch. 2

While one day examining the books in the library of the university, Luther discovered a Latin Bible. Such a book he had never before seen. He was ignorant even of its existence. He had heard portions of the Gospels and Epistles, which were read to the people at public worship, and he supposed that these were the entire Bible. Now, for the first time, he looked upon the whole of God's word. With mingled awe and wonder he turned the sacred pages; with quickened pulse and throbbing heart he read for himself the words of life, pausing now and then to exclaim: »O that God would give me such a book for myself!« Ibid., b. 2, ch. 2 Angels of heaven were by his side, and rays of light from the throne of God revealed the treasures of truth to his understanding. He had ever feared to offend God, but now the deep conviction of his condition as a sinner took hold upon him as never before.

An earnest desire to be free from sin and to find peace with God led him at last to enter a cloister and devote himself to a monastic life. Here he was required to perform the lowest drudgery and to beg from house to house. He was at an age when respect and appreciation are most eagerly craved, and these menial offices were deeply mortifying to his natural feelings; but he patiently endured this humiliation, believing that it was necessary because of his sins.

Every moment that could be spared from his daily duties he employed in study, robbing himself of sleep and grudging even the time spent at his scanty meals. Above everything else he delighted in the study of God's word. He had found a Bible chained to the convent wall, and to this he often repaired. As his convictions of sin deepened, he sought by his own works to obtain pardon and peace. He led a most rigorous life, endeavoring by fasting, vigils, and scourgings to subdue the evils of his nature, from which the monastic life had brought no release. He shrank from no sacrifice by which he might attain to that purity of heart which would enable him to stand approved before God. »I was indeed a pious monk,« he afterward said, »and followed the rules of my order more strictly than I can express. If ever monk could obtain heaven by his monkish works, I should certainly have been entitled to it. ... If it had continued much longer, I should have carried my mortifications even to death.« Ibid., b. 2, ch. 3 As the result of this painful discipline he lost strength and suffered from fainting spasms, from the effects of which he never fully recovered. But with all his efforts his burdened soul found no relief. He was at last driven to the verge of despair.

When it appeared to Luther that all was lost, God raised up a friend and helper for him. The pious Staupitz opened the word of God to Luther's mind and bade him look away from himself, cease the contemplation of infinite punishment for the violation of God's law, and look to Jesus, his sin-pardoning Saviour. »Instead of torturing yourself on account of your sins, throw yourself into the Redeemer's arms. Trust in Him, in the righteousness of His life, in the atonement of His death. ... Listen to the Son of God. He became man to give you the assurance of divine favor.« »Love Him who first loved you.« Ibid., b. 2, ch. 4 Thus spoke this messenger of mercy. His words made a deep impression upon Luther's mind. After many a struggle with long-cherished errors, he was enabled to grasp the truth, and peace came to his troubled soul.

Luther was ordained a priest and was called from the cloister to a professorship in the University of Wittenberg. Here he applied himself to the study of the Scriptures in the original tongues. He began to lecture upon the Bible; and the book of Psalm, the Gospels, and the Epistles were opened to the understanding of crowds of delighted listeners. Staupitz, his friend and superior, urged him to ascend the pulpit and preach the word of God. Luther hesitated, feeling himself unworthy to speak to the people in Christ's stead. It was only after a long struggle that he yielded to the solicitations of his friends. Already he was mighty in the Scriptures, and the grace of God rested upon him. His eloquence captivated his hearers, the clearness and power with which he presented the truth convinced their understanding, and his fervor touched their hearts.

Luther was still a true son of the papal church and had no thought that he would ever be anything else. In the providence of God he was led to visit Rome. He pursued his journey on foot, lodging at the monasteries on the way. At a convent in Italy he was filled with wonder at the wealth, magnificence, and luxury that he witnessed. Endowed with a princely revenue, the monks dwelt in splendid apartments, attired themselves in the richest and most costly robes, and feasted at a sumptuous table. With painful misgivings Luther contrasted this scene with the self-denial and hardship of his own life. His mind was becoming perplexed.

At last he beheld in the distance the seven-hilled city. With deep emotion he prostrated himself upon the earth, exclaiming: »Holy Rome, I salute thee!« Ibid., b. 2, ch. 6

He entered the city, visited the churches, listened to the marvelous tales repeated by priests and monks, and performed all the ceremonies required. Everywhere he looked upon scenes that filled him with astonishment and horror. He saw that iniquity existed among all classes of the clergy. He heard indecent jokes from prelates, and was filled with horror at their awful profanity, even during mass. As he mingled with the monks and citizens he met dissipation, debauchery. Turn where he would, in the place of sanctity he found profanation. »No one can imagine,« he wrote, »what sins and infamous actions are committed in Rome; they must be seen and heard to be believed. Thus they are in the habit of saying, 'If there is a hell, Rome is built over it: it is an abyss whence issues every kind of sin.'« Ibid., b. 2, ch. 6

By a recent decretal an indulgence had been promised by the pope to all who should ascend upon their knees »Pilate's staircase,« said to have been descended by our Saviour on leaving the Roman judgment hall and to have been miraculously conveyed from Jerusalem to Rome. Luther was one day devoutly climbing these steps, when suddenly a voice like thunder seemed to say to him: »The just shall live by faith.« Romans 1:17 He sprang to his feet and hastened from the place in shame and horror. That text never lost its power upon his soul. From that time he saw more clearly than ever before the fallacy of trusting to human works for salvation, and the necessity of constant faith in the merits of Christ. His eyes had been opened, and were never again to be closed, to the delusions of the papacy. When he turned his face from Rome he had turned away also in heart, and from that time the separation grew wider, until he severed all connection with the papal church.

After his return from Rome, Luther received at the University of Wittenberg the degree of doctor of divinity. Now he was at liberty to devote himself, as never before, to the Scriptures that he loved. He had taken a solemn vow to study carefully and to preach with fidelity the word of God, not the sayings and doctrines of the popes, all the days of his life. He was no longer the mere monk or professor, but the authorized herald of the Bible. He had been called as a shepherd to feed the flock of God, that were hungering and thirsting for the truth. He firmly declared that Christians should receive no other doctrines than those which rest on the authority of the Sacred Scriptures. These words struck at the very foundation of papal supremacy. They contained the vital principle of the Reformation. Luther saw the danger of exalting human theories above the word of God. He fearlessly attacked the speculative infidelity of the schoolmen and opposed the philosophy and theology which had so long held a controlling influence upon the people. He denounced such studies as not only worthless but pernicious, and sought to turn the minds of his hearers from the sophistries of philosophers and theologians to the eternal truths set forth by prophets and apostles.

Precious was the message which he bore to the eager crowds that hung upon his words. Never before had such teachings fallen upon their ears. The glad tidings of a Saviour's love, the assurance of pardon and peace through His atoning blood, rejoiced their hearts and inspired within them an immortal hope. At Wittenberg a light was kindled whose rays should extend to the uttermost parts of the earth, and which was to increase in brightness to the close of time. But light and darkness cannot harmonize. Between truth and error there is an irrepressible conflict. To uphold and defend the one is to attack and overthrow the other. Our Saviour Himself declared: »I came not to send peace, but a sword.« Matthew 10:34 Said Luther, a few years after the opening of the Reformation: »God does not guide me, He pushes me forward. He carries me away. I am not master of myself. I desire to live in repose; but I am thrown into the midst of tumults and revolutions.« D'Aubigne, b. 5, ch. 2 He was now about to be urged into the contest.

The Roman Church had made merchandise of the grace of God. The tables of the money-changers Matthew 21:12 were set up beside her altars, and the air resounded with the shouts of buyers and sellers. Under the plea of raising funds for the erection of St. Peter's Church at Rome, indulgences for sin were publicly offered for sale by the authority of the pope. By the price of crime a temple was to be built up for God's worship – the cornerstone laid with the wages of iniquity! But the very means adopted for Rome's aggrandizement provoked the deadliest blow to her power and greatness. It was this that aroused the most determined and successful of the enemies of popery, and led to the battle which shook the papal throne and jostled the triple crown upon the pontiff's head. The official appointed to conduct the sale of indulgences in Germany – Tetzel by name – had been convicted of the basest offenses against society and against the law of God; but having escaped the punishment due for his crimes, he was employed to further the mercenary and unscrupulous projects of the pope.

With great effrontery he repeated the most glaring falsehoods and related marvelous tales to deceive an ignorant, credulous, and superstitious people. Had they possessed the word of God they would not have been thus deceived. It was to keep them under the control of the papacy, in order to swell the power and wealth of her ambitious leaders, that the Bible had been withheld from them. see John C. L. Gieseler, A Compendium of Ecclesiastical History, per. 4, sec. 1, par. 5

As Tetzel entered a town, a messenger went before him, announcing: »The grace of God and of the holy father is at your gates.« D'Aubigne, b. 3, ch. 1 And the people welcomed the blasphemous pretender as if he were God Himself come down from heaven to them.

The infamous traffic was set up in the church, and Tetzel, ascending the pulpit, extolled the indulgences as the most precious gift of God. He declared that by virtue of his certificates of pardon all the sins which the purchaser should afterward desire to commit would be forgiven him, and that »not even repentance is necessary.« Ibid., b. 3, ch. 1 More than this, he assured his hearers that the indulgences had power to save not only the living but the dead; that the very moment the money should clink against the bottom of his chest, the soul in whose behalf it had been paid would escape from purgatory and make its way to heaven. see K. R. Hagenbach, History of the Reformation, vol. 1, p. 96 When Simon Magus offered to purchase of the apostles the power to work miracles, Peter answered him: »Thy money perish with thee, because thou hast thought that the gift of God may be purchased with money.« Acts 8:20 But Tetzel's offer was grasped by eager thousands. Gold and silver flowed into his treasury. A salvation that could be bought with money was more easily obtained than that which requires repentance, faith, and diligent effort to resist and overcome sin. see Appendix note for p. 59

The doctrine of indulgences had been opposed by men of learning and piety in the Roman Church, and there were many who had no faith in pretensions so contrary to both reason and revelation. No prelate dared lift his voice against this iniquitous traffic; but the minds of men were becoming disturbed and uneasy, and many eagerly inquired if God would not work through some instrumentality for the purification of His church.

Luther, though still a papist of the straitest sort, was filled with horror at the blasphemous assumptions of the indulgence mongers.
 Many of his own congregation had purchased certifi-

cates of pardon, and they soon began to come to their pastor, confessing their various sins, and expecting absolution, not because they were penitent and wished to reform, but on the ground of the indulgence. Luther refused them absolution, and warned them that unless they should repent and reform their lives, they must perish in their sins. In great perplexity they repaired to Tetzel with the complaint that their confessor had refused his certificates; and some boldly demanded that their money be returned to them. The friar was filled with rage. He uttered the most terrible curses, caused fires to be lighted in the public squares, and declared that he »had received an order from the pope to burn all heretics who presumed to oppose his most holy indulgences.« D'Aubigne, b. 3, ch. 4

Luther now entered boldly upon his work as a champion of the truth. His voice was heard from the pulpit in earnest, solemn warning. He set before the people the offensive character of sin, and taught them that it is impossible for man, by his own works, to lessen its guilt or evade its punishment. Nothing but repentance toward God and faith in Christ can save the sinner. The grace of Christ cannot be purchased; it is a free gift. He counseled the people not to buy indulgences, but to look in faith to a crucified Redeemer. He related his own painful experience in vainly seeking by humiliation and penance to secure salvation, and assured his hearers that it was by looking away from himself and believing in Christ that he found peace and joy.

Martin Luther (1483-1546)

Johann von Staupitz (1465-1524)

As Tetzel continued his traffic and his impious pretensions, Luther determined upon a more effectual protest against these crying abuses. An occasion soon offered. The castle church of Wittenberg possessed many relics, which on certain holy days were exhibited to the people, and full remission of sins was granted to all who then visited the church and made confession.

Accordingly on these days the people in great numbers resorted thither. One of the most important of these occasions, the festival of All Saints, was approaching. On the preceding day, Luther, joining the crowds that were already making their way to the church, posted on its door a paper containing ninety-five propositions against the doctrine of indulgences. He declared his willingness to defend these theses next day at the university, against all who should see fit to attack them. His propositions attracted universal attention. They were read and reread, and repeated in every direction. Great excitement was created in the university and in the whole city. By these theses it was shown that the power to grant the pardon of sin, and to remit its penalty, had never been committed to the pope or to any other man. The whole scheme was a farce, – an artifice to extort money by playing upon the superstitions of the people, – a device of Satan to destroy the souls of all who should trust to its lying pretensions. It was also clearly shown that the gospel of Christ is the most valuable treasure of the church, and that the grace of God, therein revealed, is freely bestowed upon all who seek it by repentance and faith.

Luther's theses challenged discussion; but no one dared accept the challenge. The questions which he proposed had in a few days spread through all Germany, and in a few weeks they had sounded throughout Christendom. Many devoted Romanists, who had seen and lamented the terrible iniquity prevailing in the church, but had not known how to arrest its progress, read the propositions with great joy, recognizing in them the voice of God. They felt that the Lord had graciously set His hand to arrest the rapidly swelling tide of corruption that was issuing from the see of Rome. Princes and magistrates secretly rejoiced that a check was to be put upon the arrogant power which denied the right of appeal from its decisions. But the sin-loving and superstitious multitudes were terrified as the sophistries that had soothed their fears were swept away. Crafty ecclesiastics, interrupted in their work of sanctioning crime, and seeing their

 gains endangered, were enraged, and rallied to uphold

their pretensions. The Reformer had bitter accusers to meet. Some charged him with acting hastily and from impulse. Others accused him of presumption, declaring that he was not directed of God, but was acting from pride and forwardness. »Who does not know,« he responded, »that a man rarely puts forth any new idea without having some appearance of pride, and without being accused of exciting quarrels? ... Why were Christ and all the martyrs put to death? Because they seemed to be proud contemners of the wisdom of the time, and because they advanced novelties without having first humbly taken counsel of the oracles of the ancient opinions.« Again he declared: »Whatever I do will be done, not by the prudence of men, but by the counsel of God. If the work be of God, who shall stop it? if it be not, who can forward it? Not my will, nor theirs, nor ours; but Thy will, O holy Father, which art in heaven.« Ibid., b. 3, ch. 6

Though Luther had been moved by the Spirit of God to begin his work, he was not to carry it forward without severe conflicts. The reproaches of his enemies, their misrepresentation of his purposes, and their unjust and malicious reflections upon his character and motives, came in upon him like an overwhelming flood; and they were not without effect. He had felt confident that the leaders of the people, both in the church and in the schools, would gladly unite with him in efforts for reform. Words of encouragement from those in high position had inspired him with joy and hope. Already in anticipation he had seen a brighter day dawning for the church. But encouragement had changed to reproach and condemnation. Many dignitaries, of both church and state, were convicted of the truthfulness of his theses; but they soon saw that the acceptance of these truths would involve great changes. To enlighten and reform the people would be virtually to undermine the authority of Rome, to stop thousands of streams now flowing into her treasury, and thus greatly to curtail the extravagance and luxury of the papal leaders. Furthermore, to teach the people to think and act as responsible beings, looking to Christ alone for salvation, would overthrow the pontiff's throne and eventually destroy their own authority. For this reason they refused the knowledge tendered them of God and arrayed themselves against Christ and the truth by their opposition to the man whom He had sent to enlighten them. Luther trembled as he looked upon himself – one man opposed to the mightiest powers of earth. He sometimes doubted whether he had indeed been led of God to set himself against the authority of the church. »Who was I,« he writes, »to oppose the majesty of the pope, before whom ... the kings of the earth and the whole world trembled? ... No one can know what my heart suffered during these first two years, and into what despondency, I may say into what despair, I was sunk.« Ibid., b. 3, ch. 6 But he was not left to become utterly disheartened. When human support failed, he looked to God alone and learned that he could lean in perfect safety upon that all-powerful arm.

To a friend of the Reformation Luther wrote: »We cannot attain to the understanding of Scripture either by study or by the intellect. Your first duty is to begin by prayer. Entreat the Lord to grant you, of His great mercy, the true understanding of His word. There is no other interpreter of the word of God than the Author of this word, as He Himself has said, 'They shall be all taught of God.' Hope for nothing from your own labors, from your own understanding: trust solely in God, and in the influence of His Spirit. Believe this on the word of a man who has had experience.« Ibid., b. 3, ch. 7 Here is a lesson of vital importance to those who feel that God has called them to present to others the solemn truths for this time. These truths will stir the enmity of Satan and of men who love the fables that he has devised. In the conflict with the powers of evil there is need of something more than strength of intellect and human wisdom. When enemies appealed to custom and tradition, or to the assertions and authority of the pope, Luther met them with the Bible and the Bible only. Here were arguments which they could not answer; therefore the slaves of formalism and superstition clamored for his blood, as the Jews had clamored for the blood of Christ. »He is a heretic,« cried the Roman zealots. »It is high treason against the church to allow so horrible a heretic to live one hour longer. Let the scaffold be instantly erected for him!« Ibid., b. 3, ch. 9 But Luther did not fall a prey to their fury. God had a work for him to do, and angels of heaven were sent to protect him. Many, however, who had received from Luther the precious light were made the objects of Satan's wrath and for the truth's sake fearlessly suffered torture and death.

Luther's teachings attracted the attention of thoughtful minds throughout all Germany. From his sermons and writings issued beams of light which awakened and illuminated thousands. A living faith was taking the place of the dead formalism in which the church

 had so long been held. The people were daily losing

confidence in the superstitions of Romanism. The barriers of prejudice were giving way. The word of God, by which Luther tested every doctrine and every claim, was like a two-edged sword, cutting its way to the hearts of the people. Everywhere there was awakening a desire for spiritual progress. Everywhere was such a hungering and thirsting after righteousness as had not been known for ages. The eyes of the people, so long directed to human rites and earthly mediators, were now turning in penitence and faith to Christ and Him crucified.

This widespread interest aroused still further the fears of the papal authorities. Luther received a summons to appear at Rome to answer to the charge of heresy. The command filled his friends with terror. They knew full well the danger that threatened him in that corrupt city, already drunk with the blood of the martyrs of Jesus. They protested against his going to Rome and requested that he receive his examination in Germany.

This arrangement was finally effected, and the pope's legate was appointed to hear the case. In the instructions communicated by the pontiff to this official, it was stated that Luther had already been declared a heretic. The legate was therefore charged »to prosecute and constrain without any delay.« If he should remain steadfast, and the legate should fail to gain possession of his person, he was empowered »to proscribe him in every part of Germany; to banish, curse, and excommunicate all those who are attached to him.« Ibid., b. 4, ch. 2 And, further, the pope directed his legate, in order entirely to root out the pestilent heresy, to excommunicate all, of whatever dignity in church or state, except the emperor, who should neglect to seize Luther and his adherents, and deliver them up to the vengeance of Rome.

Here is displayed the true spirit of popery. Not a trace of Christian principle, or even of common justice, is to be seen in the whole document. Luther was at a great distance from Rome; he had had no opportunity to explain or defend his position; yet before his case had been investigated, he was summarily pronounced a heretic, and in the same day, exhorted, accused, judged, and condemned; and all this by the self-styled holy father, the only supreme, infallible authority in church or state! At this time, when Luther so much needed the sympathy and counsel of a true friend, God's providence sent Melanchthon to Wittenberg. Young in years, modest and diffident in his manners, Melanchthon's sound judgment, extensive knowledge, and winning eloquence, combined with the purity and uprightness of his character, won universal admiration and esteem. The brilliancy of his talents was not more marked than his gentleness of disposition. He soon became an earnest disciple of the gospel, and Luther's most trusted friend and valued supporter; his gentleness, caution, and exactness serving as a complement to Luther's courage and energy. Their union in the work added strength to the Reformation and was a source of great encouragement to Luther.

Augsburg had been fixed upon as the place of trial, and the Reformer set out on foot to perform the journey thither. Serious fears were entertained in his behalf. Threats had been made openly that he would be seized and murdered on the way, and his friends begged him not to venture. They even entreated him to leave Wittenberg for a time and find safety with those who would gladly protect him. But he would not leave the position where God had placed him. He must continue faithfully to maintain the truth, notwithstanding the storms that were beating upon him. His language was: »I am like Jeremiah, a man of strife and contention; but the more their threats increase, the more my joy is multiplied.c ... They have already destroyed my honor and my reputation. One single thing remains; it is my wretched body: let them take it; they will thus shorten my life by a few hours. But as for my soul, they cannot take that. He who desires to proclaim the word of Christ to the world, must expect death at every moment.« Ibid., b. 4, ch. 4 The tidings of Luther's arrival at Augsburg gave great satisfaction to the papal legate. The troublesome heretic who was exciting the attention of the whole world seemed now in the power of Rome, and the legate determined that he should not escape. The Reformer had failed to provide himself with a safe-conduct. His friends urged him not to appear before the legate without one, and they themselves undertook to procure it from the emperor. The legate intended to force Luther, if possible, to retract, or, failing in this, to cause him to be conveyed to Rome, to share the fate of Huss and Jerome. Therefore through his agents he endeavored to induce Luther to appear without a safe-conduct, trusting himself to his mercy. This the Reformer firmly declined to do. Not until he had received the document pledging him the emperor's protection, did he appear in the presence of the papal ambassador.

As a matter of policy, the Romanists had decided to attempt to win Luther by an appearance of gentleness. The legate, in his inter-

 views with him, professed great friendliness; but he demanded that Luther submit implicitly to the authority of the church, and yield every point without argument or question. He had not rightly estimated the character of the man with whom he had to deal. Luther, in reply, expressed his regard for the church, his desire for the truth, his readiness to answer all objections to what he had taught, and to submit his doctrines to the decision of certain leading universities. But at the same time he protested against the cardinal's course in requiring him to retract without having proved him in error.

The only response was: »Retract, retract!« The Reformer showed that his position was sustained by the Scriptures and firmly declared that he could not renounce the truth. The legate, unable to reply to Luther's arguments, overwhelmed him with a storm of reproaches, gibes, and flattery, interspersed with quotations from tradition and the sayings of the Fathers, granting the Reformer no opportunity to speak. Seeing that the conference, thus continued, would be utterly futile, Luther finally obtained a reluctant permission to present his answer in writing.

»In so doing,« said he, writing to a friend, »the oppressed find double gain; first, what is written may be submitted to the judgment of others; and second, one has a better chance of working on the fears, if not on the conscience, of an arrogant and babbling despot, who would otherwise overpower by his imperious language.« Martyn, The Life and Times of Luther, pp. 271, 272 At the next interview, Luther presented a clear, concise, and forcible exposition of his views, fully supported by many quotations from Scripture. This paper, after reading aloud, he handed to the cardinal, who, however, cast it contemptuously aside, declaring it to be a mass of idle words and irrelevant quotations. Luther, fully aroused, now met the haughty prelate on his own ground – the traditions and teachings of the church – and utterly overthrew his assumptions.

When the prelate saw that Luther's reasoning was unanswerable, he lost all self-control, and in a rage cried out: »Retract! or I will send you to Rome, there to appear before the judges commissioned to take cognizance of your cause. I will excommunicate you and all your partisans, and all who shall at any time countenance you, and will cast them out of the church.« And he finally declared, in a haughty and angry tone: »Retract, or return no more.« D'Aubigne, London ed., b. 4, ch. 8

The Reformer promptly withdrew with his friends, thus declaring plainly that no retraction was to be expected from him.

This was not what the cardinal had purposed. He had flattered himself that by violence he could awe Luther to submission. Now, left alone with his supporters, he looked from one to another in utter chagrin at the unexpected failure of his schemes.

Luther's efforts on this occasion were not without good results. The large assembly present had opportunity to compare the two men, and to judge for themselves of the spirit manifested by them, as well as of the strength and truthfulness of their positions. How marked the contrast! The Reformer, simple, humble, firm, stood up in the strength of God, having truth on his side; the pope's representative, self-important, overbearing, haughty, and unreasonable, was without a single argument from the Scriptures, yet vehemently crying: »Retract, or be sent to Rome for punishment.«

Notwithstanding Luther had secured a safe-conduct, the Romanists were plotting to seize and imprison him. His friends urged that as it was useless for him to prolong his stay, he should return to Wittenberg without delay, and that the utmost caution should be observed in order to conceal his intentions. He accordingly left Augsburg before daybreak, on horseback, accompanied only by a guide furnished him by the magistrate. With many forebodings he secretly made his way through the dark and silent streets of the city. Enemies, vigilant and cruel, were plotting his destruction. Would he escape the snares prepared for him? Those were moments of anxiety and earnest prayer. He reached a small gate in the wall of the city. It was opened for him, and with his guide he passed through without hindrance. Once safely outside, the fugitives hastened their flight, and before the legate learned of Luther's departure, he was beyond the reach of his persecutors. Satan and his emissaries were defeated. The man whom they had thought in their power was gone, escaped as a bird from the snare of the fowler.

At the news of Luther's escape the legate was overwhelmed with surprise and anger. He had expected to receive great honor for his wisdom and firmness in dealing with this disturber of the church; but his hope was disappointed. He gave expression to his wrath in a letter to Frederick, the elector of Saxony, bitterly denouncing Luther and demanding that Frederick send the Reformer to Rome or banish him from Saxony.

In defense, Luther urged that the legate or the pope show him his errors from the Scriptures, and pledged himself in the most solemn manner to renounce his doctrines if they could be shown to contradict the word of God. And he expressed his gratitude to God that he had been counted worthy to suffer in so holy a cause.

The elector had, as yet, little knowledge of the reformed doctrines, but he was deeply impressed by the candor, force, and clearness of Luther's words; and until the Reformer should be proved to be in error, Frederick resolved to stand as his protector. In reply to the legate's demand he wrote: »Since Dr. Martin has appeared before you at Augsburg, you should be satisfied. We did not expect that you would endeavor to make him retract without having convinced him of his errors. None of the learned men in our principality have informed me that Martin's doctrine is impious, anti-christian, or heretical.' The prince refused, moreover, to send Luther to Rome, or to expel him from his states.« D'Aubigne, b. 4, ch. 10

The elector saw that there was a general breaking down of the moral restraints of society. A great work of reform was needed. The complicated and expensive arrangements to restrain and punish crime would be unnecessary if men but acknowledged and obeyed the requirements of God and the dictates of an enlightened conscience. He saw that Luther was laboring to secure this object, and he secretly rejoiced that a better influence was making itself felt in the church.

He saw also that as a professor in the university Luther was eminently successful. Only a year had passed since the Reformer posted his theses on the castle church, yet there was already a great falling off in the number of pilgrims that visited the church at the festival of All Saints. Rome had been deprived of worshipers and offerings, but their place was filled by another class, who now came to Wittenberg, not pilgrims to adore her relics, but students to fill her halls of learning. The writings of Luther had kindled everywhere a new interest in the Holy Scriptures, and not only from all parts of Germany, but from other lands, students flocked to the university. Young men, coming in sight of Wittenberg for the first time, »raised their hands to heaven, and praised God for having caused the light of truth to shine forth from this city, as from Zion in times of old, and whence it spread even to the most distant countries.« Ibid., b. 4, ch. 10 Luther was as yet but partially converted from the errors of Romanism. But as he compared the Holy Oracles with the papal decrees and constitutions, he was filled with wonder. »I am reading,« he wrote, »the decrees of the pontiffs, and ... I do not know whether the pope is antichrist himself, or his apostle, so greatly is Christ misrepresented and crucified in them.« Ibid., b. 5, ch. 1 Yet at this time Luther was still a supporter of the Roman Church, and had no thought that he would ever separate from her communion.

The Reformer's writings and his doctrine were extending to every nation in Christendom. The work spread to Switzerland and Holland. Copies of his writings found their way to France and Spain. In England his teachings were received as the word of life. To Belgium and Italy also the truth had extended. Thousands were awakening from their deathlike stupor to the joy and hope of a life of faith.

Rome became more and more exasperated by the attacks of Luther, and it was declared by some of his fanatical opponents, even by doctors in Catholic universities, that he who should kill the rebellious monk would be without sin. One day a stranger, with a pistol hidden under his cloak, approached the Reformer and inquired why he went thus alone. »I am in God's hands,« answered Luther. »He is my strength and my shield. What can man do unto me?« Ibid., b. 6, ch.2 Upon hearing these words, the stranger turned pale and fled away as from the presence of the angels of heaven.

Rome was bent upon the destruction of Luther; but God was his defense. His doctrines were heard everywhere – »in cottages and convents, ... in the castles of the nobles, in the universities, and in the palaces of kings;« and noble men were rising on every hand to sustain his efforts. Ibid., b. 6, ch. 2

It was about this time that Luther, reading the works of Huss, found that the great truth of justification by faith, which he himself was seeking to uphold and teach, had been held by the Bohemian Reformer. »We have all,« said Luther, »Paul, Augustine, and myself, been Hussites without knowing it!« »God will surely visit it upon the world,« he continued, »that the truth was preached to it a century ago, and burned!« Wylie, b. 6, ch. 1

In an appeal to the emperor and nobility of Germany in behalf of the reformation of Christianity, Luther wrote concerning the pope: »It is a horrible thing to behold the man who styles himself Christ's vicegerent, displaying a magnificence that no emperor can equal. Is this being like the poor Jesus, or the humble Peter? He is, say they, the lord of the world! But Christ, whose vicar he boasts of being, has said, 'My kingdom is not of this world.' Can the dominions of a vicar extend beyond those of his superior?« D'Aubigne, b. 6, ch. 3

He wrote thus of the universities: »I am much afraid that the universities will prove to be the great gates of hell, unless they diligently labor in explaining the Holy Scriptures, and engraving them in the hearts of youth. I advise no one to place his child where the Scriptures do not reign paramount. Every institution in which men are not unceasingly occupied with the word of God must become corrupt.« Ibid., b. 6, ch. 3

This appeal was rapidly circulated throughout Germany and exerted a powerful influence upon the people. The whole nation was stirred, and multitudes were roused to rally around the standard of reform. Luther's opponents, burning with a desire for revenge, urged the pope to take decisive measures against him. It was decreed that his doctrines should be immediately condemned. Sixty days were granted the Reformer and his adherents, after which, if they did not recant, they were all to be excommunicated.

That was a terrible crisis for the Reformation. For centuries Rome's sentence of excommunication had struck terror to powerful monarchs; it had filled mighty empires with woe and desolation. Those upon whom its condemnation fell were universally regarded with dread and horror; they were cut off from intercourse with their fellows and treated as outlaws, to be hunted to extermination. Luther was not blind to the tempest about to burst upon him; but he stood firm, trusting in Christ to be his support and shield. With a martyr's faith and courage he wrote: »What is about to happen I know not, nor do I care to know. ... Let the blow light where it may, I am without fear. Not so much as a leaf falls, without the will of our Father. How much rather will He care for us! It is a light thing to die for the Word, since the Word which was made flesh hath Himself died. If we die with Him, we shall live with Him; and passing through that which He has passed through before us, we shall be where He is and dwell with Him forever.« Ibid., 3d London ed., Walther, 1840, b. 6, ch. 9

When the papal bull reached Luther, he said: »I despise and attack it, as impious, false. ... It is Christ Himself who is condemned therein. ... I rejoice in having to bear such ills for the best of causes. Already I feel greater liberty in my heart; for at last I know that the pope is antichrist, and that his throne is that of Satan himself.« D'Aubigne, b. 6, ch. 9

Yet the mandate of Rome was not without effect. Prison, torture, and sword were weapons potent to enforce obedience. The weak and superstitious trembled before the decree of the [141/142] pope; and while there was general sympathy for Luther, many felt that life was too dear to be risked in the cause of reform. Everything seemed to indicate that the Reformer's work was about to close.

But Luther was fearless still. Rome had hurled her anathemas against him, and the world looked on, nothing doubting that he would perish or be forced to yield. But with terrible power he flung back upon herself the sentence of condemnation and publicly declared his determination to abandon her forever. In the presence of a crowd of students, doctors, and citizens of all ranks Luther burned the pope's bull, with the canon laws, the decretals, and certain writings sustaining the papal power. »My enemies have been able, by burning my books,« he said, »to injure the cause of truth in the minds of the common people, and destroy their souls; for this reason I consumed their books in return. A serious struggle has just begun. Hitherto I have been only playing with the pope. I began this work in God's name; it will be ended without me, and by His might.« Ibid., b. 6, ch. 10

To the reproaches of his enemies who taunted him with the weakness of his cause, Luther answered: »Who knows if God has not chosen and called me, and if they ought not to fear that, by despising me, they despise God Himself? Moses was alone at the departure from Egypt; Elijah was alone in the reign of King Ahab; Isaiah alone in Jerusalem; Ezekiel alone in Babylon. ... God never selected as a prophet either the high priest or any other great personage; but ordinarily He chose low and despised men, once even the shepherd Amos. In every age, the saints have had to reprove the great, kings, princes, priests, and wise men, at the peril of their lives. ... I do not say that I am a prophet; but I say that they ought to fear precisely because I am alone and that they are many. I am sure of this, that the word of God is with me, and that it is not with them.« Ibid., b. 6, ch. 10

Yet it was not without a terrible struggle with himself that Luther decided upon a final separation from the church. It was about this time that he wrote: »I feel more and more every day how difficult it is to lay aside the scruples which one has imbibed in childhood. Oh, how much pain it has caused me, though I had the Scriptures on my side, to justify it to myself that I should dare to make a stand alone against the pope, and hold him forth as antichrist! What have the tribulations of my heart not been! How many times have I not asked myself with bitterness that question which was so frequent

 on the lips of the papists: 'Art thou alone wise? Can

everyone else be mistaken? How will it be, if, after all, it is thyself who art wrong, and who art involving in thy error so many souls, who will then be eternally damned?' 'Twas so I fought with myself and with Satan, till Christ, by His own infallible word, fortified my heart against these doubts.« Martyn, pp. 372, 373

The pope had threatened Luther with excommunication if he did not recant, and the threat was now fulfilled. A new bull appeared, declaring the Reformer's final separation from the Roman Church, denouncing him as accursed of Heaven, and including in the same condemnation all who should receive his doctrines. The great contest had been fully entered upon.

Opposition is the lot of all whom God employs to present truths specially applicable to their time. There was a present truth in the days of Luther, - a truth at that time of special importance; there is a present truth for the church today. He who does all things according to the counsel of His will has been pleased to place men under various circumstances and to enjoin upon them duties peculiar to the times in which they live and the conditions under which they are placed. If they would prize the light given them, broader views of truth would be opened before them. But truth is no more desired by the majority today than it was by the papists who opposed Luther. There is the same disposition to accept the theories and traditions of men instead of the word of God as in former ages. Those who present the truth for this time should not expect to be received with greater favor than were earlier reformers. The great controversy between truth and error, between Christ and Satan, is to increase in intensity to the close of this world's history.

Said Jesus to His disciples: »If ye were of the world, the world would love his own: but because ye are not of the world, but I have chosen you out of the world, therefore the world hateth you. Remember the word that I said unto you, The servant is not greater than his Lord. If they have persecuted Me, they will also persecute you; if they have kept My saying, they will keep yours also.« John 15:19-20 And on the other hand our Lord declared plainly: »Woe unto you, when all men shall speak well of you! for so did their fathers to the false prophets.« Luke 6:26 The spirit of the world is no more in harmony with the spirit of Christ today than in earlier times, and those who preach the word of God in its purity will be received with no greater favor now than then. The forms of oppo- [143/144] sition to the truth may change, the enmity may be less open because it is more subtle; but the same antagonism still exists and will be manifested to the end of time.

John Tetzel (1465-1519)

Bull against Luther

Drain Letter 1925

Chapter 8

Luther Before the Diet

A new emperor, Charles V, had ascended the throne of Germany, and the emissaries of Rome hastened to present their congratulations and induce the monarch to employ his power against the Reformation. On the other hand, the elector of Saxony, to whom Charles was in great degree indebted for his crown, entreated him to take no step against Luther until he should have granted him a hearing. The emperor was thus placed in a position of great perplexity and embarrassment. The papists would be satisfied with nothing short of an imperial edict sentencing Luther to death. The elector had declared firmly that »neither his imperial majesty nor any other person had shown that Luther's writings had been refuted;« therefore he requested »that Dr. Luther should be furnished with a safe-conduct, so that he might appear before a tribunal of learned, pious, and impartial judges.« D'Aubigne, b. 6, ch. 11

The attention of all parties was now directed to the assembly of the German states which convened at Worms soon after the accession of Charles to the empire. There were important political questions and interests to be considered by this national council; for the first time the princes of Germany were to meet their youthful monarch in deliberative assembly. From all parts of the fatherland had come the dignitaries of church and state. Secular lords, highborn, powerful, and jealous of their hereditary rights; princely ecclesiastics, flushed with their conscious superiority in rank and power; courtly knights and their armed retainers; and ambassadors from foreign and distant lands, – all gathered at Worms. Yet in that vast assembly the subject that excited the deepest interest was the cause of the Saxon Reformer.

Charles had previously directed the elector to bring Luther with him to the Diet, assuring him of protection, and promising a free discussion, with competent persons, of the questions in dispute. Luther was anxious to appear before the emperor. His health was at this time much impaired; yet he wrote to the elector: »If I cannot go to Worms in good health, I will be carried there, sick as I am. For if the emperor calls me, I cannot doubt that it is the call of God Himself. If they desire to use violence against me, and that is very probable (for it is not for their instruction that they order me to appear), I place the matter in the Lord's hands. He still lives and reigns who preserved the three young men in the burning fiery furnace. If He will not save me, my life is of little consequence. Let us only prevent the gospel from being exposed to the scorn of the wicked, and let us shed our blood for it, for fear they should triumph. It is not for me to decide whether my life or my death will contribute most to the salvation of all. ... You may expect everything from me ... except flight and recantation. Fly I cannot, and still less retract.« Ibid., b. 7, ch. 1

As the news was circulated at Worms that Luther was to appear before the Diet, a general excitement was created. Aleander, the papal legate to whom the case had been specially entrusted, was alarmed and enraged. He saw that the result would be disastrous to the papal cause. To institute inquiry into a case in which the pope had already pronounced sentence of condemnation would be to cast contempt upon the authority of the sovereign pontiff. Furthermore, he was apprehensive that the eloquent and powerful arguments of this man might turn away many of the princes from the cause of the pope. He therefore, in the most urgent manner, remonstrated with Charles against Luther's appearance at Worms. About this time the bull declaring Luther's excommunication was published; and this, coupled with the representations of the legate, induced the emperor to yield. He wrote to the elector that if Luther would not retract, he must remain at Wittenberg. Not content with this victory, Aleander labored with all the power and cunning at his command to secure Luther's condemnation. With a persistence worthy of a better cause, he urged the matter upon the attention of princes, prelates, and other members of the assembly, accusing the Reformer of »sedition, rebellion, impiety, and blasphemy.« But the vehemence and passion manifested by the legate revealed too plainly the spirit by which he was actuated. »He is moved by hatred and vengeance,« was the general remark, »much more than by zeal and piety.« Ibid., b. 7, ch.1 The majority of the Diet were more than ever inclined to regard Luther's cause with favor.

With redoubled zeal Aleander urged upon the emperor the duty of executing the papal edicts. But under the laws of Germany this could not be done without the concurrence of the princes;

and, overcome at last by the legate's importunity, Charles bade him present his case to the Diet. »It was a proud day for the nuncio. The assembly was a great one: the cause was even greater. Aleander was to plead for Rome, ... the mother and mistress of all churches.« He was to vindicate the princedom of Peter before the assembled principalities of Christendom. »He had the gift of eloquence, and he rose to the greatness of the occasion. Providence ordered it that Rome should appear and plead by the ablest of her orators in the presence of the most august of tribunals, before she was condemned.« Wylie, b. 6, ch. 4 With some misgivings those who favored the Reformer looked forward to the effect of Aleander's speech. The elector of Saxony was not present, but by his direction some of his councilors attended to take notes of the nuncio's address.

With all the power of learning and eloquence, Aleander set himself to overthrow the truth. Charge after charge he hurled against Luther as an enemy of the church and the state, the living and the dead, clergy and laity, councils and private Christians. »In Luther's errors there is enough,« he declared, to warrant the burning of »a hundred thousand heretics.«

In conclusion he endeavored to cast contempt upon the adherents of the reformed faith: »What are all these Lutherans? A crew of insolent pedagogues, corrupt priests, dissolute monks, ignorant lawyers, and degraded nobles, with the common people whom they have misled and perverted. How far superior to them is the Catholic party in number, ability, and power! A unanimous decree from this illustrious assembly will enlighten the simple, warn the imprudent, decide the waverers, and give strength to the weak.« D'Aubigne, b. 7, ch. 3

With such weapons the advocates of truth in every age have been attacked. The same arguments are still urged against all who dare to present, in opposition to established errors, the plain and direct teachings of God's word. »Who are these preachers of new doctrines?« exclaim those who desire a popular religion. »They are unlearned, few in numbers, and of the poorer class. Yet they claim to have the truth, and to be the chosen people of God. They are ignorant and deceived. How greatly superior in numbers and influence is our church! How many great and learned men are among us! How much more power is on our side!« These are the arguments that have a telling influence upon the world; but they are no more conclusive now than in the days of the Reformer. The Reformation did not, as many suppose, end with Luther. It is to be continued to the close of this world's history. Luther had a great work to do in reflecting to others the light which God had permitted to shine upon him; yet he did not receive all the light which was to be given to the world. From that time to this, new light has been continually shining upon the Scriptures, and new truths have been constantly unfolding.

The legate's address made a deep impression upon the Diet. There was no Luther present, with the clear and convincing truths of God's word, to vanquish the papal champion. No attempt was made to defend the Reformer. There was manifest a general disposition not only to condemn him and the doctrines which he taught, but if possible to uproot the heresy. Rome had enjoyed the most favorable opportunity to defend her cause. All that she could say in her own vindication had been said. But the apparent victory was the signal of defeat. Henceforth the contrast between truth and error would be more clearly seen, as they should take the field in open warfare. Never from that day would Rome stand as secure as she had stood.

While most of the members of the Diet would not have hesitated to yield up Luther to the vengeance of Rome, many of them saw and deplored the existing depravity in the church, and desired a suppression of the abuses suffered by the German people in consequence of the corruption and greed of the hierarchy. The legate had presented the papal rule in the most favorable light. Now the Lord moved upon a member of the Diet to give a true delineation of the effects of papal tyranny. With noble firmness, Duke George of Saxony stood up in that princely assembly and specified with terrible exactness the deceptions and abominations of popery, and their dire results. In closing he said: »These are some of the abuses that cry out against Rome. All shame has been put aside, and their only object is ... money, money, money, ... so that the preachers who should teach the truth, utter nothing but falsehoods, and are not only tolerated, but rewarded, because the greater their lies, the greater their gain. It is from this foul spring that such tainted waters flow. Debauchery stretches out the hand to avarice. ... Alas, it is the scandal caused by the clergy that hurls so many poor souls into eternal condemnation. A general reform must be effected.« Ibid., b. 7, ch. 4

A more able and forcible denunciation of the papal abuses could not have been presented by Luther himself; and the fact that the speaker was a determined enemy of the Reformer's gave greater influence to his words. Had the eyes of the assembly been opened, they would have beheld angels of God in the midst of them, shedding beams of light athwart the darkness of error and opening minds and hearts to the reception of truth. It was the power of the God of truth and wisdom that controlled even the adversaries of the reformation, and thus prepared the way for the great work about to be accomplished. Martin Luther was not present; but the voice of One greater than Luther had been heard in that assembly.

A committee was at once appointed by the Diet to prepare an enumeration of the papal oppressions that weighed so heavily on the German people. This list, containing a hundred and one specifications, was presented to the emperor, with a request that he would take immediate measures for the correction of these abuses. »What a loss of Christian souls,« said the petitioners, »what depredations, what extortions, on account of the scandals by which the spiritual head of Christendom is surrounded! It is our duty to prevent the ruin and dishonor of our people. For this reason we most humbly but most urgently entreat you to order a general reformation, and to undertake its accomplishment.« Ibid., b. 7, ch. 4

The council now demanded the Reformer's appearance before them. Notwithstanding the entreaties, protests, and threats of Aleander, the emperor at last consented, and Luther was summoned to appear before the Diet. With the summons was issued a safe-conduct, ensuring his return to a place of security. These were borne to Wittenberg by a herald, who was commissioned to conduct him to Worms. The friends of Luther were terrified and distressed. Knowing the prejudice and enmity against him, they feared that even his safeconduct would not be respected, and they entreated him not to imperil his life. He replied: »The papists do not desire my coming to Worms, but my condemnation and my death. It matters not. Pray not for me, but for the word of God. ... Christ will give me His Spirit to overcome these ministers of error. I despise them during my life; I shall triumph over them by my death. They are busy at Worms about compelling me to retract; and this shall be my retraction: I said formerly that the pope was Christ's vicar; now I assert that he is our Lord's adversary, and the devil's apostle.« Ibid., b. 7, ch. 6

Luther was not to make his perilous journey alone. Besides the imperial messenger, three of his firmest friends determined to accompany him. Melanchthon earnestly desired to join them. His heart was knit to Luther's, and he yearned to follow him, if need be, to prison or to death. But his entreaties were denied. Should Luther perish, the hopes of the Reformation must center upon his youthful colaborer. Said the Reformer as he parted from Melanchthon: »If I do not return, and my enemies put me to death, continue to teach, and stand fast in the truth. Labor in my stead. ... If you survive, my death will be of little consequence.« Ibid., b. 7, ch. 7 Students and citizens who had gathered to witness Luther's departure were deeply moved. A multitude whose hearts had been touched by the gospel, bade him farewell with weeping. Thus the Reformer and his companions set out from Wittenberg.

On the journey they saw that the minds of the people were oppressed by gloomy forebodings. At some towns no honors were proffered them. As they stopped for the night, a friendly priest expressed his fears by holding up before Luther the portrait of an Italian reformer who had suffered martyrdom. The next day they learned that Luther's writings had been condemned at Worms. Imperial messengers were proclaiming the emperor's decree and calling upon the people to bring the proscribed works to the magistrates. The herald, fearing for Luther's safety at the council, and thinking that already his resolution might be shaken, asked if he still wished to go forward. He answered: »Although interdicted in every city, I shall go on.« Ibid., b. 7, ch. 7

At Erfurt, Luther was received with honor. Surrounded by admiring crowds, he passed through the streets that he had often traversed with his beggar's wallet. He visited his convent cell, and thought upon the struggles through which the light now flooding Germany had been shed upon his soul. He was urged to preach. This he had been forbidden to do, but the herald granted him permission, and the friar who had once been made the drudge of the convent, now entered the pulpit. To a crowded assembly he spoke from the words of Christ, »Peace be unto you.« »Philosophers, doctors, and writers,« he said, »have endeavored to teach men the way to obtain everlasting life, and they have not succeeded. I will now tell it to you: ... God has raised one Man from the dead, the Lord Jesus Christ, that He might destroy death, extirpate sin, and shut the gates of hell. This is the work of salvation. ... Christ has vanquished! this is the joyful news; and we are saved by His work, and not by our own. ... Our Lord Jesus Christ said, 'Peace be unto you; behold My hands;' that is to say,

Behold, O man! it is I, I alone, who have taken away thy sin, and ransomed thee; and now thou hast peace, saith the Lord.«

He continued, showing that true faith will be manifested by a holy life. »Since God has saved us, let us so order our works that they may be acceptable to Him. Art thou rich? let thy goods administer to the necessities of the poor. Art thou poor? let thy services be acceptable to the rich. If thy labor is useful to thyself alone, the service that thou pretendest to render unto God is a lie.« Ibid., b. 7, ch. 7

The people listened as if spellbound. The bread of life was broken to those starving souls. Christ was lifted up before them as above popes, legates, emperors, and kings. Luther made no reference to his own perilous position. He did not seek to make himself the object of thought or sympathy. In the contemplation of Christ he had lost sight of self. He hid behind the Man of Calvary, seeking only to present Jesus as the sinner's Redeemer. As the Reformer proceeded on his journey, he was everywhere regarded with great interest. An eager multitude thronged about him, and friendly voices warned him of the purpose of the Romanists. »They will burn you,« said some, »and reduce your body to ashes, as they did with John Huss.« Luther answered, »Though they should kindle a fire all the way from Worms to Wittenberg, the flames of which reached to heaven, I would walk through it in the name of the Lord; I would appear before them; I would enter the jaws of this behemoth, and break his teeth, confessing the Lord Jesus Christ.« Ibid., b. 7, ch. 7

The news of his approach to Worms created great commotion. His friends trembled for his safety; his enemies feared for the success of their cause. Strenuous efforts were made to dissuade him from entering the city. At the instigation of the papists he was urged to repair to the castle of a friendly knight, where, it was declared, all difficulties could be amicably adjusted. Friends endeavored to excite his fears by describing the dangers that threatened him. All their efforts failed. Luther, still unshaken, declared: »Even should there be as many devils in Worms as tiles on the housetops, still I would enter it.« Ibid., b. 7, ch. 7

Upon his arrival at Worms, a vast crowd flocked to the gates to welcome him. So great a concourse had not assembled to greet the emperor himself. The excitement was intense, and from the midst of the throng a shrill and plaintive voice chanted a funeral dirge as a warning to Luther of the fate that awaited him. »God will be my defense,« said he, as he alighted from his carriage.

The papists had not believed that Luther would really venture to appear at Worms, and his arrival filled them with consternation. The emperor immediately summoned his councilors to consider what course should be pursued. One of the bishops, a rigid papist, declared: »We have long consulted on this matter. Let your imperial majesty get rid of this man at once. Did not Sigismund cause John Huss to be burnt? We are not bound either to give or to observe the safe-conduct of a heretic.« »No,« said the emperor, »we must keep our promise.« Ibid., b. 7, ch. 8 It was therefore decided that the Reformer should be heard.

All the city were eager to see this remarkable man, and a throng of visitors soon filled his lodgings. Luther had scarcely recovered from his recent illness; he was wearied from the journey, which had occupied two full weeks; he must prepare to meet the momentous events of the morrow, and he needed quiet and repose. But so great was the desire to see him that he had enjoyed only a few hours' rest when noblemen, knights, priests, and citizens gathered eagerly about him. Among these were many of the nobles who had so boldly demanded of the emperor a reform of ecclesiastical abuses and who, says Luther, »had all been freed by my gospel.« Martyn, p. 393 Enemies, as well as friends, came to look upon the dauntless monk; but he received them with unshaken calmness, replying to all with dignity and wisdom. His bearing was firm and courageous. His pale, thin face, marked with the traces of toil and illness, wore a kindly and even joyous expression. The solemnity and deep earnestness of his words gave him a power that even his enemies could not wholly withstand. Both friends and foes were filled with wonder. Some were convinced that a divine influence attended him; others declared, as had the Pharisees concerning Christ: »He hath a devil.«

On the following day Luther was summoned to attend the Diet. An imperial officer was appointed to conduct him to the hall of audience; yet it was with difficulty that he reached the place. Every avenue was crowded with spectators eager to look upon the monk who had dared resist the authority of the pope.

As he was about to enter the presence of his judges, an old general, the hero of many battles, said to him kindly: »Poor monk, poor monk, thou art now going to make a nobler stand than I or any other captains have ever made in the bloodiest of our battles. But if thy cause is just, and thou art sure of it, go forward in God's name, and fear nothing. God will not forsake thee.« D'Aubigne, b. 7, ch. 8

At length Luther stood before the council. The emperor occupied the throne. He was surrounded by the most illustrious personages in the empire. Never had any man appeared in the presence of a more imposing assembly than that before which Martin Luther was to answer for his faith. »This appearance was of itself a signal victory over the papacy. The pope had condemned the man, and he was now standing before a tribunal which, by this very act, set itself above the pope. The pope had laid him under an interdict, and cut him off from all human society; and yet he was summoned in respectful language, and received before the most august assembly in the world. The pope had condemned him to perpetual silence, and he was now about to speak before thousands of attentive hearers drawn together from the farthest parts of Christendom. An immense revolution had thus been effected by Luther's instrumentality. Rome was already descending from her throne, and it was the voice of a monk that caused this humiliation.« Ibid., b. 7, ch. 8

In the presence of that powerful and titled assembly the lowly born Reformer seemed awed and embarrassed. Several of the princes, observing his emotion, approached him, and one of them whispered: »Fear not them which kill the body, but are not able to kill the soul.« Another said: »When ye shall be brought before governors and kings for My sake, it shall be given you, by the Spirit of your Father, what ye shall say.« Thus the words of Christ were brought by the world's great men to strengthen His servant in the hour of trial.

Luther was conducted to a position directly in front of the emperor's throne. A deep silence fell upon the crowded assembly. Then an imperial officer arose and, pointing to a collection of Luther's writings, demanded that the Reformer answer two questions – whether he acknowledged them as his, and whether he proposed to retract the opinions which he had therein advanced. The titles of the books having been read, Luther replied that as to the first question, he acknowledged the books to be his. »As to the second,« he said, »seeing that it is a question which concerns faith and the salvation of souls, and in which the word of God, the greatest and most precious treasure either in heaven or earth, is involved, I should act imprudently were I to reply without reflection. I might affirm less than the circumstance demands, or more than truth requires, and so sin against this saying of Christ: 'Whosoever shall deny Me before men, him will I also deny before My Father which is in heaven.' Matthew 10:33 For this reason I entreat your imperial majesty, with all humility, to allow me time, that I may answer without offending against the word of God.« D'Aubigne, b. 7, ch. 8

In making this request, Luther moved wisely. His course convinced the assembly that he did not act from passion or impulse. Such calmness and self-command, unexpected in one who had shown himself bold and uncompromising, added to his power, and enabled him afterward to answer with a prudence, decision, wisdom, and dignity that surprised and disappointed his adversaries, and rebuked their insolence and pride.

The next day he was to appear to render his final answer. For a time his heart sank within him as he contemplated the forces that were combined against the truth. His faith faltered; fearfulness and trembling came upon him, and horror overwhelmed him. Dangers multiplied before him; his enemies seemed about to triumph, and the powers of darkness to prevail. Clouds gathered about him and seemed to separate him from God. He longed for the assurance that the Lord of hosts would be with him. In anguish of spirit he threw himself with his face upon the earth and poured out those broken, heart-rending cries, which none but God can fully understand. »O almighty and everlasting God,« he pleaded, »how terrible is this world! Behold, it openeth its mouth to swallow me up, and I have so little trust in Thee. ... If it is only in the strength of this world that I must put my trust, all is over. ... My last hour is come, my condemnation has been pronounced. ... O God, do Thou help me against all the wisdom of the world. Do this, ... Thou alone; ... for this is not my work, but Thine. I have nothing to do here, nothing to contend for with these great ones of the world. ... But the cause is Thine, ... and it is a righteous and eternal cause. O Lord, help me! Faithful and unchangeable God, in no man do I place my trust. ... All that is of man is uncertain; all that cometh of man fails. ... Thou hast chosen me for this work. ... Stand at my side, for the sake of Thy well-beloved Jesus Christ, who is my defense, my shield, and my strong tower.« Ibid., b. 7, ch. 8

An all-wise Providence had permitted Luther to realize his peril, that he might not trust to his own strength and rush presumptuously into danger. Yet it was not the fear of personal suffering, a dread of torture or death, which seemed immediately impending, that overwhelmed him with its terror. He had come to the crisis, and he felt his insufficiency to meet it. Through his weakness the cause of truth might suffer loss. Not for his own safety, but for the triumph of the gospel did he wrestle with God. Like Israel's, in that night struggle beside the lonely stream, was the anguish and conflict of his soul. Like Israel, he prevailed with God. In his utter helplessness his faith fastened upon Christ, the mighty Deliverer. He was strengthened with the assurance that he would not appear alone before the council. Peace returned to his soul, and he rejoiced that he was permitted to uplift the word of God before the rulers of the nations. With his mind stayed upon God, Luther prepared for the struggle before him. He thought upon the plan of his answer, examined passages in his own writings, and drew from the Holy Scriptures suitable proofs to sustain his positions. Then, laying his left hand on the Sacred Volume, which was open before him, he lifted his right hand to heaven and vowed »to remain faithful to the gospel, and freely to confess his faith, even should he seal his testimony with his blood.« Ibid., b. 7, ch. 8

When he was again ushered into the presence of the Diet, his countenance bore no trace of fear or embarrassment. Calm and peaceful, yet grandly brave and noble, he stood as God's witness among the great ones of the earth. The imperial officer now demanded his decision as to whether he desired to retract his doctrines. Luther made his answer in a subdued and humble tone, without violence or passion. His demeanor was diffident and respectful; yet he manifested a confidence and joy that surprised the assembly.

»Most serene emperor, illustrious princes, gracious lords,« said Luther, »I appear before you this day, in conformity with the order given me yesterday, and by God's mercies I conjure your majesty and your august highnesses to listen graciously to the defense of a cause which I am assured is just and true. If, through ignorance, I should transgress the usages and proprieties of courts, I entreat you to pardon me; for I was not brought up in the palaces of kings, but in the seclusion of a convent.« Ibid., b. 7, ch. 8

Then, proceeding to the question, he stated that his published works were not all of the same character. In some he had treated of faith and good works, and even his enemies declared them not only harmless but profitable. To retract these would be to condemn truths which all parties confessed. The second class consisted of writings exposing the corruptions and abuses of the papacy. To revoke these works would strengthen the tyranny of Rome and open a wider door to many and great impieties. In the third class of his books he had attacked individuals who had defended existing evils. Concerning these he freely confessed that he had been more violent than was becoming. He did not claim to be free from fault; but even these books he could not revoke, for such a course would embolden the enemies of truth, and they would then take occasion to crush God's people with still greater cruelty.

»Yet I am but a mere man, and not God,« he continued; »I shall therefore defend myself as Christ did: 'If I have spoken evil, bear witness of the evil.' ... By the mercy of God, I conjure you, most serene emperor, and you, most illustrious princes, and all men of every degree, to prove from the writings of the prophets and apostles that I have erred. As soon as I am convinced of this, I will retract every error, and be the first to lay hold of my books and throw them into the fire.« »What I have just said plainly shows, I hope, that I have carefully weighed and considered the dangers to which I expose myself; but far from being dismayed, I rejoice to see that the gospel is now, as in former times, a cause of trouble and dissension. This is the character, this is the destiny, of the word of God. 'I came not to send peace on earth, but a sword,' said Jesus Christ. God is wonderful and terrible in His counsels; beware lest, by presuming to quench dissensions, you should persecute the holy word of God, and draw down upon yourselves a frightful deluge of insurmountable dangers, of present disasters, and eternal desolation. ... I might quote many examples from the oracles of God. I might speak of the Pharaohs, the kings of Babylon, and those of Israel, whose labors never more effectually contributed to their own destruction than when they sought by counsels, to all appearance most wise, to strengthen their dominion. 'God removeth mountains, and they know it not.'« Ibid., b. 7, ch. 8

Luther had spoken in German; he was now requested to repeat the same words in Latin. Though exhausted by the previous effort, he complied, and again delivered his speech, with the same clearness and energy as at the first. God's providence directed in this matter. The minds of many of the princes were so blinded by error and superstition that at the first delivery they did not see the force of Luther's reasoning; but the repetition enabled them to perceive clearly the points presented. Those who stubbornly closed their eyes to the light, and determined not to be convinced of the truth, were enraged at the power of Luther's words. As he ceased speaking, the spokes-

man of the Diet said angrily: »You have not answered

the question put to you. ... You are required to give a clear and precise answer. ... Will you, or will you not, retract?«

The Reformer answered: »Since your most serene majesty and your high mightinesses require from me a clear, simple, and precise answer, I will give you one, and it is this: I cannot submit my faith either to the pope or to the councils, because it is clear as the day that they have frequently erred and contradicted each other. Unless therefore I am convinced by the testimony of Scripture or by the clearest reasoning, unless I am persuaded by means of the passages I have quoted, and unless they thus render my conscience bound by the word of God, I cannot and I will not retract, for it is unsafe for a Christian to speak against his conscience. Here I stand, I can do no other; may God help me. Amen.« Ibid., b. 7, ch. 8

Thus stood this righteous man upon the sure foundation of the word of God. The light of heaven illuminated his countenance. His greatness and purity of character, his peace and joy of heart, were manifest to all as he testified against the power of error and witnessed to the superiority of that faith that overcomes the world.

The whole assembly were for a time speechless with amazement. At his first answer Luther had spoken in a low tone, with a respectful, almost submissive bearing. The Romanists had interpreted this as evidence that his courage was beginning to fail. They regarded the request for delay as merely the prelude to his recantation. Charles himself, noting, half contemptuously, the monk's worn frame, his plain attire, and the simplicity of his address, had declared: »This monk will never make a heretic of me.« The courage and firmness which he now displayed, as well as the power and clearness of his reasoning, filled all parties with surprise. The emperor, moved to admiration, exclaimed: »This monk speaks with an intrepid heart and unshaken courage.« Many of the German princes looked with pride and joy upon this representative of their nation.

The partisans of Rome had been worsted; their cause appeared in a most unfavorable light. They sought to maintain their power, not by appealing to the Scriptures, but by a resort to threats, Rome's unfailing argument. Said the spokesman of the Diet: »If you do not retract, the emperor and the states of the empire will consult what course to adopt against an incorrigible heretic.« Luther's friend, who had with great joy listened to his noble defense, trembled at these words; but the doctor himself said calmly: »May God be my helper, for I can retract nothing.« Ibid., b. 7, ch. 8 He was directed to withdraw from the Diet while the princes consulted together. It was felt that a great crisis had come. Luther's persistent refusal to submit might affect the history of the church for ages. It was decided to give him one more opportunity to retract. For the last time he was brought into the assembly. Again the question was put, whether he would renounce his doctrines. »I have no other reply to make,« he said, »than that which I have already made.« It was evident that he could not be induced, either by promises or threats, to yield to the mandate of Rome.

The papal leaders were chagrined that their power, which had caused kings and nobles to tremble, should be thus despised by a humble monk; they longed to make him feel their wrath by torturing his life away. But Luther, understanding his danger, had spoken to all with Christian dignity and calmness. His words had been free from pride, passion, and misrepresentation. He had lost sight of himself, and the great men surrounding him, and felt only that he was in the presence of One infinitely superior to popes, prelates, kings, and emperors. Christ had spoken through Luther's testimony with a power and grandeur that for the time inspired both friends and foes with awe and wonder. The Spirit of God had been present in that council, im-

Luther before the Diet of Worms (17 April 1521)

pressing the hearts of the chiefs of the empire. Several of the princes boldly acknowledged the justice of Luther's cause. Many were convinced of the truth; but with some the impressions received were not lasting. There was another class who did not at the time express their convictions, but who, having searched the Scriptures for themselves, at a future time became fearless supporters of the Reformation.

The elector Frederick had looked forward anxiously to Luther's appearance before the Diet, and with deep emotion he listened to his speech. With joy and pride he witnessed the doctor's courage, firmness, and self-possession, and determined to stand more firmly in his defense. He contrasted the parties in contest, and saw that the wisdom of popes, kings, and prelates had been brought to nought by the power of truth. The papacy had sustained a defeat which would be felt among all nations and in all ages.

As the legate perceived the effect produced by Luther's speech, he feared, as never before, for the security of the Romish power, and resolved to employ every means at his command to effect the Reformer's overthrow. With all the eloquence and diplomatic skill for which he was so eminently distinguished, he represented to the youthful emperor the folly and danger of sacrificing, in the cause of an insignificant monk, the friendship and support of the powerful see of Rome.

His words were not without effect. On the day following Luther's answer, Charles caused a message to be presented to the Diet, announcing his determination to carry out the policy of his predecessors to maintain and protect the Catholic religion. Since Luther had refused to renounce his errors, the most vigorous measures should be employed against him and the heresies he taught. »A single monk, misled by his own folly, has risen against the faith of Christendom. To stay such impiety, I will sacrifice my kingdoms, my treasures, my friends, my body, my blood, my soul, and my life. I am about to dismiss the Augustine Luther, forbidding him to cause the least disorder among the people; I shall then proceed against him and his adherents as contumacious heretics, by excommunication, by interdict, and by every means calculated to destroy them. I call on the members of the states to behave like faithful Christians.« Ibid., b. 7, ch. 9 Nevertheless the emperor declared that Luther's safe-conduct must be respected, and that before proceedings against him could be instituted, he must be allowed to reach his home in safety.

Two conflicting opinions were now urged by the members of the Diet. The emissaries and representatives of the pope again demanded that the Reformer's safe-conduct should be disregarded. »The Rhine,« they said, »should receive his ashes, as it had received those of John Huss a century ago.« Ibid., b. 7, ch. 9

But princes of Germany, though themselves papists and avowed enemies to Luther, protested against such a breach of public faith, as a stain upon the honor of the nation. They pointed to the calamities which had followed the death of Huss, and declared that they dared not call down upon Germany, and upon the head of their youthful emperor, a repetition of those terrible evils.

Charles himself, in answer to the base proposal, said: »Though honor and faith should be banished from all the world, they ought to find a refuge in the hearts of princes.« Ibid., b. 7, ch. 9 He was still further urged by the most bitter of Luther's papal enemies to deal with the Reformer as Sigismund had dealt with Huss – abandon him to the mercies of the church; but recalling the scene when Huss in public assembly had pointed to his chains and reminded the monarch of his plighted faith, Charles V declared: »I should not like to blush like Sigismund.« Lenfant, vol. 1, p. 422

Yet Charles had deliberately rejected the truths presented by Luther. »I am firmly resolved to imitate the example of my ancestors,« wrote the monarch. D'Aubigne, b. 7, ch. 9 He had decided that he would not step out of the path of custom, even to walk in the ways of truth and righteousness. Because his fathers did, he would uphold the papacy, with all its cruelty and corruption. Thus he took his position, refusing to accept any light in advance of what his fathers had received, or to perform any duty that they had not performed.

There are many at the present day thus clinging to the customs and traditions of their fathers. When the Lord sends them additional light, they refuse to accept it, because, not having been granted to their fathers, it was not received by them. We are not placed where our fathers were; consequently our duties and responsibilities are not the same as theirs. We shall not be approved of God in looking to the example of our fathers to determine our duty instead of searching the word of truth for ourselves. Our responsibility is greater than was that of our ancestors. We are accountable for the light which they received, and which was handed down as an inheritance for us, and

 we are accountable also for the additional light which

is now shining upon us from the word of God. Said Christ of the unbelieving Jews: »If I had not come and spoken unto them, they had not had sin: but now they have no cloak for their sin.« John 15:22 The same divine power had spoken through Luther to the emperor and princes of Germany. And as the light shone forth from God's word, His Spirit pleaded for the last time with many in that assembly. As Pilate, centuries before, permitted pride and popularity to close his heart against the world's Redeemer; as the trembling Felix bade the messenger of truth, »Go thy way for this time; when I have a convenient season, I will call for thee;« as the proud Agrippa confessed, »Almost thou persuadest me to be a Christian« Acts 24:25; 26:28, yet turned away from the Heaven-sent message – so had Charles V, yielding to the dictates of worldly pride and policy, decided to reject the light of truth.

Rumors of the designs against Luther were widely circulated, causing great excitement throughout the city. The Reformer had made many friends, who, knowing the treacherous cruelty of Rome toward all who dared expose her corruptions, resolved that he should not be sacrificed. Hundreds of nobles pledged themselves to protect him. Not a few openly denounced the royal message of evincing a weak submission to the controlling power of Rome. On the gates of houses and in public places, placards were posted, some condemning and others sustaining Luther. On one of these were written merely the significant words of the wise man: »Woe to thee, O land, when thy king is a child.« Ecclesiastes 10:16 The popular enthusiasm in Luther's favor throughout all Germany convinced both the emperor and the Diet that any injustice shown him would endanger the peace of the empire and even the stability of the throne.

Frederick of Saxony maintained a studied reserve, carefully concealing his real feelings toward the Reformer, while at the same time he guarded him with tireless vigilance, watching all his movements and all those of his enemies. But there were many who made no attempt to conceal their sympathy with Luther. He was visited by princes, counts, barons, and other persons of distinction, both lay and ecclesiastical. »The doctor's little room,« wrote Spalatin, »could not contain all the visitors who presented themselves.« Martyn 1:404 The people gazed upon him as if he were more than human. Even those who had no faith in his doctrines could not but admire that lofty integrity which led him to brave death rather than violate his conscience.

Earnest efforts were made to obtain Luther's consent to a compromise with Rome. Nobles and princes represented to him that if he persisted in setting up his own judgment against that of the church and the councils he would soon be banished from the empire and would have no defense. To this appeal Luther answered: »The gospel of Christ cannot be preached without offense. ... Why then should the fear or apprehension of danger separate me from the Lord, and from that divine word which alone is truth? No; I would rather give up my body, my blood, and my life.« D'Aubigne, b. 7, ch. 10 Again he was urged to submit to the judgment of the emperor, and then he would have nothing to fear. »I consent,« said he in reply, »with all my heart, that the emperor, the princes, and even the meanest Christian, should examine and judge my works; but on one condition, that they take the word of God for their standard. Men have nothing to do but to obey it. Do not offer violence to my conscience, which is bound and chained up with the Holy Scriptures.« Ibid., b. 7, ch. 10

To another appeal he said: »I consent to renounce my safe-conduct. I place my person and my life in the emperor's hands, but the word of God – never!« Ibid., b. 7, ch. 10 He stated his willingness to submit to the decision of a general council, but only on condition that the council be required to decide according to the Scriptures. »In what concerns the word of God and the faith,« he added, »every Christian is as good a judge as the pope, though supported by a million councils, can be for him.« Martyn 1:410 Both friends and foes were at last convinced that further effort for reconciliation would be useless.

Had the Reformer yielded a single point, Satan and his hosts would have gained the victory. But his unwavering firmness was the means of emancipating the church, and beginning a new and better era. The influence of this one man, who dared to think and act for himself in religious matters, was to affect the church and the world, not only in his own time, but in all future generations. His firmness and fidelity would strengthen all, to the close of time, who should pass through a similar experience. The power and majesty of God stood forth above the counsel of men, above the mighty power of Satan.

Luther was soon commanded by the authority of the emperor to return home, and he knew that this notice would be speedily followed by his condemnation. Threatening clouds overhung his path; but as he departed from Worms, his heart was filled with joy and praise. »The devil himself,« said he, »guarded the pope's citadel; but

Christ has made a wide breach in it, and Satan was constrained to confess that the Lord is mightier than he.« D'Aubigne, b. 7, ch. 11

After his departure, still desirous that his firmness should not be mistaken for rebellion, Luther wrote to the emperor. »God, who is the searcher of hearts, is my witness,« he said, »that I am ready most earnestly to obey your majesty, in honor or in dishonor, in life or in death, and with no exception save the word of God, by which man lives. In all the affairs of this present life, my fidelity shall be unshaken, for here to lose or to gain is of no consequence to salvation. But when eternal interests are concerned, God wills not that man should submit unto man. For such submission in spiritual matters is a real worship, and ought to be rendered solely to the Creator.« Ibid., b. 7, ch. 11

On the journey from Worms, Luther's reception was even more flattering than during his progress thither. Princely ecclesiastics welcomed the excommunicated monk, and civil rulers honored the man whom the emperor had denounced. He was urged to preach, and, notwithstanding the imperial prohibition, he again entered the pulpit. »I never pledged myself to chain up the word of God,« he said, »nor will I.« Martyn 1:420

He had not been long absent from Worms, when the papists prevailed upon the emperor to issue an edict against him. In this decree Luther was denounced as »Satan himself under the form of a man and dressed in a monk's frock.« D'Aubigne, b. 7, ch. 11 It was commanded that as soon as his safe-conduct should expire, measures be taken to stop his work. All persons were forbidden to harbor him, to give him food or drink, or by word or act, in public or private, to aid or abet him. He was to be seized wherever he might be, and delivered to the authorities. His adherents also were to be imprisoned and their property confiscated. His writings were to be destroyed, and, finally, all who should dare to act contrary to this decree were included in its condemnation. The elector of Saxony and the princes most friendly to Luther had left Worms soon after his departure, and the emperor's decree received the sanction of the Diet. Now the Romanists were jubilant. They considered the fate of the Reformation sealed.

God had provided a way of escape for His servant in this hour of peril. A vigilant eye had followed Luther's movements, and a true and noble heart had resolved upon his rescue. It was plain that Rome would be satisfied with nothing short of his death; only by concealment could he be preserved from the jaws of the lion. God gave wisdom to Frederick of Saxony to devise a plan for the Reformer's preservation. With the co-operation of true friends the elector's purpose was carried out, and Luther was effectually hidden from friends and foes. Upon his homeward journey he was seized, separated from his attendants, and hurriedly conveyed through the forest to the castle of Wartburg, an isolated mountain fortress. Both his seizure and his concealment were so involved in mystery that even Frederick himself for a long time knew not whither he had been conducted. This ignorance was not without design; so long as the elector knew nothing of Luther's whereabouts, he could reveal nothing. He satisfied himself that the Reformer was safe, and with this knowledge he was content.

Spring, summer, and autumn passed, and winter came, and Luther still remained a prisoner. Aleander and his partisans exulted as the light of the gospel seemed about to be extinguished. But instead of this, the Reformer was filling his lamp from the storehouse of truth; and its light was to shine forth with brighter radiance. In the friendly security of the Wartburg, Luther for a time rejoiced in his release from the heat and turmoil of battle. But he could not long find satisfaction in quiet and repose. Accustomed to a life of activity and stern conflict, he could ill endure to remain inactive. In those solitary days the condition of the church rose up before him, and he cried in despair. »Alas! there is no one in this latter day of His anger, to stand like a wall before the Lord, and save Israel!« Ibid., b. 9, ch. 2

Again, his thoughts returned to himself, and he feared being charged with cowardice in withdrawing from the contest. Then he reproached himself for his indolence and self-indulgence. Yet at the same time he was daily accomplishing more than it seemed possible for one man to do. His pen was never idle. While his enemies flattered themselves that he was silenced, they were astonished and confused by tangible proof that he was still active. A host of tracts, issuing from his pen, circulated throughout Germany. He also performed a most important service for his countrymen by translating the New Testament into the German tongue. From his rocky Patmos he continued for nearly a whole year to proclaim the gospel and rebuke the sins and errors of the times.

But it was not merely to preserve Luther from the wrath of his enemies, nor even to afford him a season of quiet for these important labors, that God had withdrawn His servant from the stage of public life. There were results more precious than these to be secured. In the solitude and obscurity of his mountain retreat, Luther was removed from earthly supports and shut out from human praise. He was thus saved from the pride and self-confidence that are so often caused by success. By suffering and humiliation he was prepared again to walk safely upon the dizzy heights to which he had been so suddenly exalted. As men rejoice in the freedom which the truth brings them, they are inclined to extol those whom God has employed to break the chains of error and superstition. Satan seeks to divert men's thoughts and affections from God, and to fix them upon human agencies; he leads them to honor the mere instrument and to ignore the Hand that directs all the events of providence. Too often religious leaders who are thus praised and reverenced lose sight of their dependence upon God and are led to trust in themselves. As a result they seek to control the minds and consciences of the people, who are disposed to look to them for guidance instead of looking to the word of God. The work of reform is often retarded because of this spirit indulged by its supporters. From this danger, God would guard the cause of the Reformation. He desired that work to receive, not the impress of man, but that of God. The eyes of men had been turned to Luther as the expounder of the truth; he was removed that all eyes might be directed to the eternal Author of truth.

Kurfürst Friedrich I. from Saxony

Melanchton (1497-1560)

Chapter 9

The Swiss Reformer

In the choice of instrumentalities for the reforming of the church, the same divine plan is seen as in that for the planting of the church. The heavenly Teacher passed by the great men of the earth, the titled and wealthy, who were accustomed to receive praise and homage as leaders of the people. They were so proud and self-confident in their boasted superiority that they could not be molded to sympathize with their fellow men and to become colaborers with the humble Man of Nazareth. To the unlearned, toiling fishermen of Galilee was the call addressed: »Follow Me, and I will make you fishers of men.« Matthew 4:19 These disciples were humble and teachable. The less they had been influenced by the false teaching of their time, the more successfully could Christ instruct and train them for His service. So in the days of the Great Reformation. The leading Reformers were men from humble life – men who were most free of any of their time from pride of rank and from the influence of bigotry and priestcraft. It is God's plan to employ humble instruments to accomplish great results. Then the glory will not be given to men, but to Him who works through them to will and to do of His own good pleasure.

A few weeks after the birth of Luther in a miner's cabin in Saxony, Ulric Zwingli was born in a herdsman's cottage among the Alps. Zwingli's surroundings in childhood, and his early training, were such as to prepare him for his future mission. Reared amid scenes of natural grandeur, beauty, and awful sublimity, his mind was early impressed with a sense of the greatness, the power, and the majesty of God. The history of the brave deeds achieved upon his native mountains kindled his youthful aspirations. And at the side of his pious grandmother he listened to the few precious Bible stories which she had gleaned from amid the legends and traditions of the church. With eager interest he heard of the grand deeds of patriarchs and prophets, of the shepherds who watched their flocks on the hills of Palestine where angels talked with them, of the Babe of Bethlehem and the Man of Calvary.

Like John Luther, Zwingli's father desired an education for his son, and the boy was early sent from his native valley. His mind rapidly developed, and it soon became a question where to find teachers competent to instruct him. At the age of thirteen he went to Bern, which then possessed the most distinguished school in Switzerland. Here, however, a danger arose which threatened to blight the promise of his life. Determined efforts were put forth by the friars to allure him into a monastery. The Dominican and Franciscan monks were in rivalry for popular favor. This they endeavored to secure by the showy adornments of their churches, the pomp of their ceremonials, and the attractions of famous relics and miracle-working images.

The Dominicans of Bern saw that if they could win this talented young scholar, they would secure both gain and honor. His extreme youth, his natural ability as a speaker and writer, and his genius for music and poetry, would be more effective than all their pomp and display, in attracting the people to their services and increasing the revenues of their order. By deceit and flattery they endeavored to induce Zwingli to enter their convent. Luther, while a student at school, had buried himself in a convent cell, and he would have been lost to the world had not God's providence released him. Zwingli was not permitted to encounter the same peril. Providentially his father received information of the designs of the friars. He had no intention of allowing his son to follow the idle and worthless life of the monks. He saw that his future usefulness was at stake, and directed him to return home without delay. The command was obeyed; but the youth could not be long content in his native valley, and he soon resumed his studies, repairing, after a time, to Basel. It was here that Zwingli first heard the gospel of God's free grace. Wittembach, a teacher of the ancient languages, had, while studying Greek and Hebrew, been led to the Holy Scriptures, and thus rays of divine light were shed into the minds of the students under his instruction. He declared that there was a truth more ancient, and of infinitely greater worth, than the theories taught by schoolmen and philosophers. This ancient truth was that the death of Christ is the sinner's only ransom. To Zwingli these words were as the first ray of light that precedes the dawn.

Zwingli was soon called from Basel to enter upon his lifework. His first field of labor was in an Alpine parish, not far distant from his native valley. Having received ordination as a priest, he »devoted himself with his whole soul to the search after divine truth; [172/173] for he was well aware,« says a fellow Reformer, »how much he must know to whom the flock of Christ is entrusted.« Wylie, b. 8, ch. 5

The more he searched the Scriptures, the clearer appeared the contrast between their truths and the heresies of Rome. He submitted himself to the Bible as the word of God, the only sufficient, infallible rule. He saw that it must be its own interpreter. He dared not attempt to explain Scripture to sustain a preconceived theory or doctrine, but held it his duty to learn what is its direct and obvious teaching. He sought to avail himself of every help to obtain a full and correct understanding of its meaning, and he invoked the aid of the Holy Spirit, which would, he declared, reveal it to all who sought it in sincerity and with prayer. »The Scriptures,« said Zwingli, »come from God, not from man, and even that God who enlightens will give thee to understand that the speech comes from God. The word of God ... cannot fail; it is bright, it teaches itself, it discloses itself, it illumines the soul with all salvation and grace, comforts it in God, humbles it, so that it loses and even forfeits itself, and embraces God.« The truth of these words Zwingli himself had proved. Speaking of his experience at this time, he afterward wrote: »When ... I began to give myself wholly up to the Holy Scriptures, philosophy and theology (scholastic) would always keep suggesting quarrels to me. At last I came to this, that I thought, 'Thou must let all that lie, and learn the meaning of God purely out of His own simple word.' Then I began to ask God for His light, and the Scriptures began to be much easier to me.« Ibid., b. 8, ch. 6 The doctrine preached by Zwingli was not received from Luther. It was the doctrine of Christ. »If Luther preaches Christ,« said the Swiss Reformer, »he does what I am doing. Those whom he has brought to Christ are more numerous than those whom I have led. But this matters not. I will bear no other name than that of Christ, whose soldier I am, and who alone is my Chief. Never has one single word been written by me to Luther, nor by Luther to me. And why? ... That it might be shown how much the Spirit of God is in unison with itself, since both of us, without any collusion, teach the doctrine of Christ with such uniformity.« D'Aubigne, b. 8, ch. 9

In 1516 Zwingli was invited to become a preacher in the convent at Einsiedeln. Here he was to have a closer view of the corruptions of Rome and was to exert an influence as a Reformer that would be felt far beyond his native Alps. Among the chief attractions of Einsiedeln was an image of the Virgin which was said to have the power of working miracles. Above the gateway of the convent was the inscription, »Here a plenary remission of sins may be obtained.« Ibid., b. 8, ch. 5 Pilgrims at all seasons resorted to the shrine of the Virgin; but at the great yearly festival of its consecration multitudes came from all parts of Switzerland, and even from France and Germany. Zwingli, greatly afflicted at the sight, seized the opportunity to proclaim liberty through the gospel to these bondslaves of superstition.

»Do not imagine,« he said, »that God is in this temple more than in any other part of creation. Whatever be the country in which you dwell, God is around you, and hears you. ... Can unprofitable works, long pilgrimages, offerings, images, the invocation of the Virgin or of the saints, secure for you the grace of God? ... What avails the multitude of words with which we embody our prayers? What efficacy has a glossy cowl, a smooth-shorn head, a long and flowing robe, or gold-embroidered slippers? ... God looks at the heart, and our hearts are far from Him.« »Christ,« he said, »who was once offered upon the cross, is the sacrifice and victim, that had made satisfaction for the sins of believers to all eternity.« Ibid., b. 8, ch. 5 To many listeners these teachings were unwelcome. It was a bitter disappointment to them to be told that their toilsome journey had been made in vain. The pardon freely offered to them through Christ they could not comprehend. They were satisfied with the old way to heaven which Rome had marked out for them. They shrank from the perplexity of searching for anything better. It was easier to trust their salvation to the priests and the pope than to seek for purity of heart.

But another class received with gladness the tidings of redemption through Christ. The observances enjoined by Rome had failed to bring peace of soul, and in faith they accepted the Saviour's blood as their propitiation. These returned to their homes to reveal to others the precious light which they had received. The truth was thus carried from hamlet to hamlet, from town to town, and the number of pilgrims to the Virgin's shrine greatly lessened. There was a falling off in the offerings, and consequently in the salary of Zwingli, which was drawn from them. But this caused him only joy as he saw that the power of fanaticism and superstition was being broken.

The authorities of the church were not blind to the work which Zwingli was accomplishing; but for the present they forbore to interfere. Hoping yet to secure him to their cause, they endeavored to win him by flatteries; and meanwhile the truth was gaining a hold upon the hearts of the people. Zwingli's labors at Einsiedeln had prepared him for a wider field, and this he was soon to enter. After three years here he was called to the office of preacher in the cathedral at Zurich. This was then the most important town of the Swiss confederacy, and the influence exerted here would be widely felt. The ecclesiastics by whose invitation he came to Zurich were, however, desirous of preventing any innovations, and they accordingly proceeded to instruct him as to his duties. »You will make every exertion,« they said, »to collect the revenues of the chapter, without overlooking the least. You will exhort the faithful, both from the pulpit and in the confessional, to pay all tithes and dues, and to show by their offerings their affection to the church. You will be diligent in increasing the income arising from the sick, from masses, and in general from every ecclesiastical ordinance.« »As for the administration of the sacraments, the preaching, and the care of the flock,« added his instructors, »these are also the duties of the chaplain. But for these you may employ a substitute, and particularly in preaching. You should administer the sacraments to none but persons of note, and only when called upon; you are forbidden to do so without distinction of persons.« Ibid., b. 8, ch. 6

Zwingli listened in silence to this charge, and in reply, after expressing his gratitude for the honor of a call to this important station, he proceeded to explain the course which he proposed to adopt. »The life of Christ,« he said, »has been too long hidden from the people. I shall preach upon the whole of the Gospel of St. Matthew, ... drawing solely from the fountains of Scripture, sounding its depths, comparing one passage with another, and seeking for understanding by constant and earnest prayer. It is to God's glory, to the praise of His only Son, to the real salvation of souls, and to their edification in the true faith, that I shall consecrate my ministry.« Ibid., b. 8, ch. 6 Though some of the ecclesiastics disapproved his plan, and endeavored to dissuade him from it, Zwingli remained steadfast. He declared that he was about to introduce no new method, but the old method employed by the church in earlier and purer times.

Already an interest had been awakened in the truths he taught; and the people flocked in great numbers to listen to his preaching. Many who had long since ceased to attend service were among his hearers. He began his ministry by opening the Gospels and reading and explaining to his hearers the inspired narrative of the life, teachings, and death of Christ. Here, as at Einsiedeln, he presented the word of God as the only infallible authority and the death of Christ as the only complete sacrifice. »It is to Christ,« he said, »that I desire to lead you – to Christ, the true source of salvation.« Ibid., b. 8, ch. 6 Around the preacher crowded the people of all classes, from statesmen and scholars to the artisan and the peasant. With deep interest they listened to his words. He not only proclaimed the offer of a free salvation, but fearlessly rebuked the evils and corruptions of the times. Many returned from the cathedral praising God. »This man,« they said, »is a preacher of the truth. He will be our Moses, to lead us forth from this Egyptian darkness.« Ibid., b. 8, ch. 6

But though at first his labors were received with great enthusiasm, after a time opposition arose. The monks set themselves to hinder his work and condemn his teachings. Many assailed him with gibes and sneers; others resorted to insolence and threats. But Zwingli bore all with patience, saying: »If we desire to gain over the wicked to Jesus Christ, we must shut our eyes against many things.« Ibid., b. 8, ch. 6

About this time a new agency came in to advance the work of reform. One Lucian was sent to Zurich with some of Luther's writings, by a friend of the reformed faith at Basel, who suggested that the sale of these books might be a powerful means of scattering the light. »Ascertain,« he wrote to Zwingli, »whether this man possesses sufficient prudence and skill; if so, let him carry from city to city, from town to town, from village to village, and even from house to house, among the Swiss, the works of Luther, and especially his exposition of the Lord's

Ulrich Zwingli (1484-1531)

Zurich Bible 1531

Prayer written for the laity. The more they are known, the more purchasers they will find.« Ibid., b. 8, ch. 6 Thus the light found entrance.

At the time when God is preparing to break the shackles of ignorance and superstition, then it is that Satan works with greatest power to enshroud men in darkness and to bind their fetters still more firmly. As men were rising up in different lands to present to the people forgiveness and justification through the blood of Christ, Rome proceeded with renewed energy to open her market throughout Christendom, offering pardon for money. Every sin had its price, and men were granted free license for crime if the treasury of the church was kept well filled. Thus the two movements advanced, – one offering forgiveness of sin for money, the other forgiveness through Christ, – Rome licensing sin and making it her source of revenue; the Reformers condemning sin and pointing to Christ as the propitiation and deliverer.

In Germany the sale of indulgences had been committed to the Dominican friars and was conducted by the infamous Tetzel. In Switzerland the traffic was put into the hands of the Franciscans, under the control of Samson, an Italian monk. Samson had already done good service to the church, having secured immense sums from Germany and Switzerland to fill the papal treasury. Now he traversed Switzerland, attracting great crowds, despoiling the poor peasants of their scanty earnings, and exacting rich gifts from the wealthy classes. But the influence of the reform already made itself felt in curtailing, though it could not stop, the traffic. Zwingli was still at Einsiedeln when Samson, soon after entering Switzerland, arrived with his wares at a neighboring town. Being apprised of his mission, the Reformer immediately set out to oppose him. The two did not meet, but such was Zwingli's success in exposing the friar's pretensions that he was obliged to leave for other quarters.

At Zurich, Zwingli preached zealously against the pardonmongers; and when Samson approached the place, he was met by a messenger from the council with an intimation that he was expected to pass on. He finally secured an entrance by stratagem, but was sent away without the sale of a single pardon, and he soon after left Switzerland.

A strong impetus was given to the reform by the appearance of the plague, or Great Death, which swept over Switzerland in the year 1519. As men were thus brought face to face with the destroyer, many were led to feel how vain and worthless were the pardons which they had so

 lately purchased; and they longed for a surer foundation

for their faith. Zwingli at Zurich was smitten down; he was brought so low that all hope of his recovery was relinquished, and the report was widely circulated that he was dead. In that trying hour his hope and courage were unshaken. He looked in faith to the cross of Calvary, trusting in the all-sufficient propitiation for sin. When he came back from the gates of death, it was to preach the gospel with greater fervor than ever before; and his words exerted an unwonted power. The people welcomed with joy their beloved pastor, returned to them from the brink of the grave. They themselves had come from attending upon the sick and the dying, and they felt, as never before, the value of the gospel.

Zwingli had arrived at a clearer understanding of its truths, and had more fully experienced in himself its renewing power. The fall of man and the plan of redemption were the subjects upon which he dwelt. »In Adam,« he said, »we are all dead, sunk in corruption and condemnation.« Wylie, b. 8, ch. 9 »Christ ... has purchased for us a never-ending redemption. ... His passion is ... an eternal sacrifice, and everlastingly effectual to heal; it satisfies the divine justice forever in behalf of all those who rely upon it with firm and unshaken faith.« Yet he clearly taught that men are not, because of the grace of Christ, free to continue in sin. »Wherever there is faith in God, there God is; and wherever God abideth, there a zeal exists urging and impelling men to good works.« D'Aubigne, b. 8, ch. 9

Such was the interest in Zwingli's preaching that the cathedral was filled to overflowing with the crowds that came to listen to him. Little by little, as they could bear it, he opened the truth to his hearers. He was careful not to introduce, at first, points which would startle them and create prejudice. His work was to win their hearts to the teachings of Christ, to soften them by His love, and keep before them His example; and as they should receive the principles of the gospel, their superstitious beliefs and practices would inevitably be overthrown.

Step by step the Reformation advanced in Zurich. In alarm its enemies aroused to active opposition. One year before, the monk of Wittenberg had uttered his No to the pope and the emperor at Worms, and now everything seemed to indicate a similar withstanding of the papal claims at Zurich. Repeated attacks were made upon Zwingli. In the papal cantons, from time to time, disciples of the gospel were brought to the stake, but this was not enough; the teacher of heresy must be silenced. Accordingly the bishop of Constance dispatched three deputies to the Council of Zurich, accusing [179/180]

Zwingli of teaching the people to transgress the laws of the church, thus endangering the peace and good order of society. If the authority of the church were to be set aside, he urged, universal anarchy would result. Zwingli replied that he had been for four years teaching the gospel in Zurich, »which was more quiet and peaceful than any other town in the confederacy.« »Is not, then,« he said, »Christianity the best safeguard of the general security?« Wylie, b. 8, ch. 11

The deputies had admonished the councilors to continue in the church, out of which, they declared, there was no salvation. Zwingli responded: »Let not this accusation move you. The foundation of the church is the same Rock, the same Christ, that gave Peter his name because he confessed Him faithfully. In every nation whosoever believes with all his heart in the Lord Jesus is accepted of God. Here, truly, is the church, out of which no one can be saved.« D'Aubigne, London ed., b. 8, ch. 11 As a result of the conference, one of the bishop's deputies accepted the reformed faith. The council declined to take action against Zwingli, and Rome prepared for a fresh attack. The Reformer, when apprised of the plots of his enemies, exclaimed: »Let them come on; I fear them as the beetling cliff fears the waves that thunder at its feet.« Wylie, b. 8, ch. 11 The efforts of the ecclesiastics only furthered the cause which they sought to overthrow. The truth continued to spread. In Germany its adherents, cast down by Luther's disappearance, took heart again, as they saw the progress of the gospel in Switzerland.

As the Reformation became established in Zurich, its fruits were more fully seen in the suppression of vice and the promotion of order and harmony. »Peace has her habitation in our town,« wrote Zwingli; »no quarrel, no hypocrisy, no envy, no strife. Whence can such union come but from the Lord, and our doctrine, which fills us with the fruits of peace and piety?« Ibid., b. 8, ch. 15

The victories gained by the Reformation stirred the Romanists to still more determined efforts for its overthrow. Seeing how little had been accomplished by persecution in suppressing Luther's work in Germany, they decided to meet the reform with its own weapons. They would hold a disputation with Zwingli, and having the arrangement of matters, they would make sure of victory by choosing, themselves, not only the place of the combat, but the judges that should decide between the disputants. And if they could once get Zwingli into their power, they would take care that he did not escape them. The leader

silenced, the movement could speedily be crushed. This

purpose, however, was carefully concealed. The disputation was appointed to be held at Baden; but Zwingli was not present. The Council of Zurich, suspecting the designs of the papists, and warned by the burning piles kindled in the papal cantons for confessors of the gospel, forbade their pastor to expose himself to this peril. At Zurich he was ready to meet all the partisans that Rome might send; but to go to Baden, where the blood of martyrs for the truth had just been shed, was to go to certain death. Oecolampadius and Haller were chosen to represent the Reformers, while the famous Dr. Eck, supported by a host of learned doctors and prelates, was the champion of Rome.

Though Zwingli was not present at the conference, his influence was felt. The secretaries were all chosen by the papists, and others were forbidden to take notes, on pain of death. Notwithstanding this, Zwingli received daily a faithful account of what was said at Baden. A student in attendance at the disputation made a record each evening of the arguments that day presented. These papers two other students undertook to deliver, with the daily letters of Oecolampadius, to Zwingli at Zurich. The Reformer answered, giving counsel and suggestions. His letters were written by night, and the students returned with them to Baden in the morning. To elude the vigilance of the guard stationed at the city gates, these messengers brought baskets of poultry on their heads, and they were permitted to pass without hindrance.Thus Zwingli maintained the battle with his wily antagonists. He »has labored more,« said Myconius, »by his meditations, his sleepless nights, and the advice which he transmitted to Baden, than he would have done by discussing in person in the midst of his enemies.« D'Aubigne, b. 11, ch. 13

The Romanists, flushed with anticipated triumph, had come to Baden attired in their richest robes and glittering with jewels. They fared luxuriously, their tables spread with the most costly delicacies and the choicest wines. The burden of their ecclesiastical duties was lightened by gaiety and reveling. In marked contrast appeared the Reformers, who were looked upon by the people as little better than a company of beggars, and whose frugal fare kept them but short time at table. Oecolampadius's landlord, taking occasion to watch him in his room, found him always engaged in study or at prayer, and greatly wondering, reported that the heretic was at least »very pious.«

At the conference, »Eck haughtily ascended a pulpit splendidly decorated, while the humble Oecolampadius, meanly clothed, was forced to take his seat in front of his opponent on a rudely carved stool.« Ibid., b. 11, ch. 13 Eck's stentorian voice and unbounded assurance never failed him. His zeal was stimulated by the hope of gold as well as fame; for the defender of the faith was to be rewarded by a handsome fee. When better arguments failed, he had resort to insults, and even to oaths. Oecolampadius, modest and self-distrustful, had shrunk from the combat, and he entered upon it with the solemn avowal: »I acknowledge no other standard of judgment than the word of God.« Ibid., b. 11, ch. 13 Though gentle and courteous in demeanor, he proved himself able and unflinching. While the Romanists, according to their wont, appealed for authority to the customs of the church, the Reformer adhered steadfastly to the Holy Scriptures. »Custom,« he said, »has no force in our Switzerland, unless it be according to the constitution; now, in matters of faith, the Bible is our constitution.« Ibid., b. 11, ch. 13 The contrast between the two disputants was not without effect. The calm, clear reasoning of the Reformer, so gently and modestly presented, appealed to minds that turned in disgust from Eck's boastful and boisterous assumptions.

The discussion continued eighteen days. At its close the papists with great confidence claimed the victory. Most of the deputies sided with Rome, and the Diet pronounced the Reformers vanquished and declared that they, together with Zwingli, their leader, were cut off from the church. But the fruits of the conference revealed on which side the advantage lay. The contest resulted in a strong impetus to the Protestant cause, and it was not long afterward that the important cities of Bern and Basel declared for the Reformation.

John Oekolampad (1482-1531)

John Eck (1486-1543)

Chapter 10

Progress of Reform in Germany

Luther's mysterious disappearance excited consternation throughout all Germany. Inquiries concerning him were heard everywhere. The wildest rumors were circulated, and many believed that he had been murdered. There was great lamentation, not only by his avowed friends, but by thousands who had not openly taken their stand with the Reformation. Many bound themselves by a solemn oath to avenge his death.

The Romish leaders saw with terror to what a pitch had risen the feeling against them. Though at first exultant at the supposed death of Luther, they soon desired to hide from the wrath of the people. His enemies had not been so troubled by his most daring acts while among them as they were at his removal. Those who in their rage had sought to destroy the bold Reformer were filled with fear now that he had become a helpless captive. »The only remaining way of saving ourselves,« said one, »is to light torches, and hunt for Luther through the whole world, to restore him to the nation that is calling for him.« D'Aubigne, b. 9, ch. 1 The edict of the emperor seemed to fall powerless. The papal legates were filled with indignation as they saw that it commanded far less attention than did the fate of Luther.

The tidings that he was safe, though a prisoner, calmed the fears of the people, while it still further aroused their enthusiasm in his favor. His writings were read with greater eagerness than ever before. Increasing numbers joined the cause of the heroic man who had, at such fearful odds, defended the word of God. The Reformation was constantly gaining in strength. The seed which Luther had sown sprang up everywhere. His absence accomplished a work which his presence would have failed to do. Other laborers felt a new responsibility, now that their great leader was removed. With new faith and earnestness they pressed forward to do all in their power, that the work so nobly begun might not be hindered. But Satan was not idle. He now attempted what he has attempted in every other reformatory movement – to deceive and destroy the people by palming off upon them a counterfeit in place of the true work. As there were false Christs in the first century of the Christian church, so there arose false prophets in the sixteenth century.

A few men, deeply affected by the excitement in the religious world, imagined themselves to have received special revelations from Heaven, and claimed to have been divinely commissioned to carry forward to its completion the Reformation which, they declared, had been but feebly begun by Luther. In truth, they were undoing the very work which he had accomplished. They rejected the great principle which was the very foundation of the Reformation – that the word of God is the all-sufficient rule of faith and practice; and for that unerring guide they substituted the changeable, uncertain standard of their own feelings and impressions. By this act of setting aside the great detector of error and falsehood the way was opened for Satan to control minds as best pleased himself.

One of these prophets claimed to have been instructed by the angel Gabriel. A student who united with him forsook his studies, declaring that he had been endowed by God Himself with wisdom to expound His word. Others who were naturally inclined to fanaticism united with them. The proceedings of these enthusiasts created no little excitement. The preaching of Luther had aroused the people everywhere to feel the necessity of reform, and now some really honest persons were misled by the pretensions of the new prophets. The leaders of the movement proceeded to Wittenberg and urged their claims upon Melanchthon and his colaborers. Said they: »We are sent by God to instruct the people. We have held familiar conversations with the Lord; we know what will happen; in a word, we are apostles and prophets, and appeal to Dr. Luther.« Ibid., b. 9, ch. 7

The Reformers were astonished and perplexed. This was such an element as they had never before encountered, and they knew not what course to pursue. Said Melanchthon: »There are indeed extraordinary spirits in these men; but what spirits? ... On the one hand, let us beware of quenching the Spirit of God, and on the other, of being led astray by the spirit of Satan.« Ibid., b. 9, ch. 7 The fruit of the new teaching soon became apparent. The people were led to neglect the Bible or to cast it wholly aside. The schools were thrown into confusion. Students, spurning all restraint, abandoned their studies and withdrew from the university. The men who thought themselves competent to revive and control the work of the Reformation succeeded only in bringing it to the verge of ruin. The Romanists now regained their confidence and exclaimed exultingly: »One last struggle, and all will be ours.« Ibid., b. 9, ch. 7

Luther at the Wartburg, hearing of what had occurred, said with deep concern: »I always expected that Satan would send us this plague.« Ibid., b. 9, ch. 7 He perceived the true character of those pretended prophets and saw the danger that threatened the cause of truth. The opposition of the pope and the emperor had not caused him so great perplexity and distress as he now experienced. From the professed friends of the Reformation had risen its worst enemies. The very truths which had brought him so great joy and consolation were being employed to stir up strife and create confusion in the church.

In the work of reform, Luther had been urged forward by the Spirit of God, and had been carried beyond himself. He had not purposed to take such positions as he did, or to make so radical changes. He had been but the instrument in the hand of Infinite Power. Yet he often trembled for the result of his work. He had once said: »If I knew that my doctrine injured one man, one single man, however lowly and obscure, – which it cannot, for it is the gospel itself, – I would rather die ten times than not retract it.« Ibid., b. 9, ch. 7

And now Wittenberg itself, the very center of the Reformation, was fast falling under the power of fanaticism and lawlessness. This terrible condition had not resulted from the teachings of Luther; but throughout Germany his enemies were charging it upon him. In bitterness of soul he sometimes asked: »Can such, then, be the end of this great work of the Reformation?« Ibid., b. 9, ch. 7 Again, as he wrestled with God in prayer, peace flowed into his heart. »The work is not mine, but Thine own,« he said; »Thou wilt not suffer it to be corrupted by superstition or fanaticism.« But the thought of remaining longer from the conflict in such a crisis, became insupportable. He determined to return to Wittenberg. Without delay he set out on his perilous journey. He was under the ban of the empire. Enemies were at liberty to take his life; friends were forbidden to aid or shelter him. The imperial government was adopting the most stringent measures against his adherents. But he saw that the work of the gospel was imperiled, and in the name of the Lord he went out fearlessly to battle for the truth.

In a letter to the elector, after stating his purpose to leave the Wartburg, Luther said: »Be it known to your highness that

I am going to Wittenberg under a protection far higher than that of princes and electors. I think not of soliciting your highness's support, and far from desiring your protection, I would rather protect you myself. If I knew that your highness could or would protect me, I would not go to Wittenberg at all. There is no sword that can further this cause. God alone must do everything, without the help or concurrence of man. He who has the greatest faith is he who is most able to protect.« Ibid., b. 9, ch. 8

In a second letter, written on the way to Wittenberg, Luther added: »I am ready to incur the displeasure of your highness and the anger of the whole world. Are not the Wittenbergers my sheep? Has not God entrusted them to me? And ought I not, if necessary, to expose myself to death for their sakes? Besides, I fear to see a terrible outbreak in Germany, by which God will punish our nation.« Ibid., b. 9, ch. 7

With great caution and humility, yet with decision and firmness, he entered upon his work. »By the word,« said he, »must we overthrow and destroy what has been set up by violence. I will not make use of force against the superstitious and unbelieving. ... No one must be constrained. Liberty is the very essence of faith.« Ibid., b. 9, ch. 8

It was soon noised through Wittenberg that Luther had returned and that he was to preach. The people flocked from all directions, and the church was filled to overflowing. Ascending the pulpit, he with great wisdom and gentleness instructed, exhorted, and reproved. Touching the course of some who had resorted to violent measures in abolishing the mass, he said: »The mass is a bad thing; God is opposed to it; it ought to be abolished; and I would that throughout the whole world it were replaced by the supper of the gospel. But let no one be torn from it by force. We must leave the matter in God's hands. His word must act, and not we. And why so? you will ask. Because I do not hold men's hearts in my hand, as the potter holds the clay. We have a right to speak: we have not the right to act. Let us preach; the rest belongs unto God. Were I to employ force, what should I gain? Grimace, formality, apings, human ordinances, and hypocrisy. ... But there would be no sincerity of heart, nor faith, nor charity. Where these three are wanting, all is wanting, and I would not give a pear stalk for such a result. ... God does more by His word alone than you and I and all the world by our united strength. God lays hold upon the heart; and when the heart is taken,
 all is won. ... »I will preach, discuss, and write; but I will

constrain none, for faith is a voluntary act. See what I have done. I stood up against the pope, indulgences, and papists, but without violence or tumult. I put forward God's word; I preached and wrote - this was all I did. And yet while I was asleep, ... the word that I had preached overthrew popery, so that neither prince nor emperor has done it so much harm. And yet I did nothing; the word alone did all. If I had wished to appeal to force, the whole of Germany would perhaps have been deluged with blood. But what would have been the result? Ruin and desolation both to body and soul. I therefore kept quiet, and left the word to run through the world alone.« Ibid., b. 9, ch. 8

Day after day, for a whole week, Luther continued to preach to eager crowds. The word of God broke the spell of fanatical excitement. The power of the gospel brought back the misguided people into the way of truth. Luther had no desire to encounter the fanatics whose course had been productive of so great evil. He knew them to be men of unsound judgment and undisciplined passions, who, while claiming to be specially illuminated from heaven, would not endure the slightest contradiction or even the kindest reproof or counsel. Arrogating to themselves supreme authority, they required everyone, without a question, to acknowledge their claims. But, as they demanded an interview with him, he consented to meet them; and so successfully did he expose their pretensions that the impostors at once departed from Wittenberg.

The fanaticism was checked for a time; but several years later it broke out with greater violence and more terrible results. Said Luther, concerning the leaders in this movement: »To them the Holy Scriptures were but a dead letter, and they all began to cry, 'The Spirit! the Spirit!' But most assuredly I will not follow where their spirit leads them. May God of His mercy preserve me from a church in which there are none but saints. I desire to dwell with the humble, the feeble, the sick, who know and feel their sins, and who groan and cry continually to God from the bottom of their hearts to obtain His consolation and support.« Ibid., b. 10, ch. 10

Thomas Munzer, the most active of the fanatics, was a man of considerable ability, which, rightly directed, would have enabled him to do good; but he had not learned the first principles of true religion. »He was possessed with a desire of reforming the world, and forgot, as all enthusiasts do, that the reformation should begin with himself.« Ibid., b. 9, ch. 8 He was ambitious to obtain position and influence, and was unwilling to be second, even to Luther. He declared that the Reformers, in substituting the authority of Scripture for that of the pope, were only establishing a different form of popery. He himself, he claimed, had been divinely commissioned to introduce the true reform. »He who possesses this spirit,« said Munzer, »possesses the true faith, although he should never see the Scriptures in his life.« Ibid., b. 10, ch. 10

The fanatical teachers gave themselves up to be governed by impressions, regarding every thought and impulse as the voice of God; consequently they went to great extremes. Some even burned their Bibles, exclaiming: "The letter killeth, but the Spirit giveth life." Munzer's teaching appealed to men's desire for the marvelous, while it gratified their pride by virtually placing human ideas and opinions above the word of God. His doctrines were received by thousands. He soon denounced all order in public worship, and declared that to obey princes was to attempt to serve both God and Belial. The minds of the people, already beginning to throw off the yoke of the papacy, were also becoming impatient under the restraints of civil authority. Munzer's revolutionary teachings, claiming divine sanction, led them to break away from all control and give the rein to their prejudices and passions. The most terrible scenes of sedition and strife followed, and the fields of Germany were drenched with blood.

The agony of soul which Luther had so long before experienced at Erfurt now pressed upon him with redoubled power as he saw the results of fanaticism charged upon the Reformation. The papist princes declared – and many were ready to credit the statement – that the rebellion was the legitimate fruit of Luther's doctrines. Although this charge was without the slightest foundation, it could not but cause the Reformer great distress. That the cause of truth should be thus disgraced by being ranked with the basest fanaticism, seemed more than he could endure. On the other hand, the leaders in the revolt hated Luther because he had not only opposed their doctrines and denied their claims to divine inspiration, but had pronounced them rebels against the civil authority. In retaliation they denounced him as a base pretender. He seemed to have brought upon himself the enmity of both princes and people.

The Romanists exulted, expecting to witness the speedy downfall of the Reformation; and they blamed Luther, even for the errors which he had been most earnestly endeavoring to correct. The fanatical party, by falsely claiming to have been treated with great injustice, succeeded in gaining the sympathies of a large class of the people, and, as is often the case with those who take the wrong side, they came to be regarded as martyrs. Thus the ones who were exerting every energy in opposition to the Reformation were pitied and lauded as the victims of cruelty and oppression. This was the work of Satan, prompted by the same spirit of rebellion which was first manifested in heaven.

Satan is constantly seeking to deceive men and lead them to call sin righteousness, and righteousness sin. How successful has been his work! How often censure and reproach are cast upon God's faithful servants because they will stand fearlessly in defense of the truth! Men who are but agents of Satan are praised and flattered, and even looked upon as martyrs, while those who should be respected and sustained for their fidelity to God, are left to stand alone, under suspicion and distrust.

Counterfeit holiness, spurious sanctification, is still doing its work of deception. Under various forms it exhibits the same spirit as in the days of Luther, diverting minds from the Scriptures and leading men to follow their own feelings and impressions rather than to yield obedience to the law of God. This is one of Satan's most successful devices to cast reproach upon purity and truth. Fearlessly did Luther defend the gospel from the attacks which came from every quarter. The word of God proved itself a weapon mighty in every conflict. With that word he warred against the usurped authority of the pope, and the rationalistic philosophy of the schoolmen, while he stood firm as a rock against the fanaticism that sought to ally itself with the Reformation.

Each of these opposing elements was in its own way setting aside the Holy Scriptures and exalting human wisdom as the source of religious truth and knowledge. Rationalism idolizes reason and makes this the criterion for religion. Romanism, claiming for her sovereign pontiff an inspiration descended in unbroken line from the apostles, and unchangeable through all time, gives ample opportunity for every species of extravagance and corruption to be concealed under the sanctity of the apostolic commission. The inspiration claimed by Munzer and his associates proceeded from no higher source than the vagaries of the imagination, and its influence was subversive of all authority, human or divine. True Christianity receives the word of God as the great treasure house of inspired truth and the test of all inspiration. Upon his return from the Wartburg, Luther completed his translation of the New Testament, and the gospel was soon after given to the people of Germany in their own language. This translation was received with great joy by all who loved the truth; but it was scornfully rejected by those who chose human traditions and the commandments of men.

The priests were alarmed at the thought that the common people would now be able to discuss with them the precepts of God's word, and that their own ignorance would thus be exposed. The weapons of their carnal reasoning were powerless against the sword of the Spirit. Rome summoned all her authority to prevent the circulation of the Scriptures; but decrees, anathemas, and tortures were alike in vain. The more she condemned and prohibited the Bible, the greater was the anxiety of the people to know what it really taught. All who could read were eager to study the word of God for themselves. They carried it about with them, and read and reread, and could not be satisfied until they had committed large portions to memory. Seeing the favor with which the New Testament was received, Luther immediately began the translation of the Old, and published it in parts as fast as completed. Luther's writings were welcomed alike in city and in hamlet. »What Luther and his friends composed, others circulated. Monks, convinced of the unlawfulness of monastic obligations, desirous of exchanging a long life of slothfulness for one of active exertion, but too ignorant to proclaim the word of God, traveled through the provinces, visiting hamlets and cottages, where they sold the books of Luther and his friends. Germany soon swarmed with these bold colporteurs.« Ibid., b. 9, ch. 11

These writings were studied with deep interest by rich and poor, the learned and the ignorant. At night the teachers of the village schools read them aloud to little groups gathered at the fireside. With every effort some souls would be convicted of the truth and, receiving the word with gladness, would in their turn tell the good news to others.

The words of Inspiration were verified: »The entrance of Thy words giveth light; it giveth understanding unto the simple.« Psalm 119:130 The study of the Scriptures was working a mighty change in the minds and hearts of the people. The papal rule had placed upon its subjects an iron yoke which held them in ignorance and degradation. A superstitious observance of forms had been scrupulously maintained; but in all their service the heart and intellect had had little part. The preaching of Luther, setting forth the plain truths of God's word, and then the word itself, placed in the hands of the common people, had aroused their dormant powers, not only purifying and ennobling the spiritual nature, but imparting new strength and vigor to the intellect.

Persons of all ranks were to be seen with the Bible in their hands, defending the doctrines of the Reformation. The papists who had left the study of the Scriptures to the priests and monks now called upon them to come forward and refute the new teachings. But, ignorant alike of the Scriptures and of the power of God, priests and friars were totally defeated by those whom they had denounced as unlearned and heretical. »Unhappily,« said a Catholic writer, »Luther had persuaded his followers to put no faith in any other oracle than the Holy Scriptures.« D'Aubigne, b. 9, ch. 11 Crowds would gather to hear the truth advocated by men of little education, and even discussed by them with learned and eloquent theologians. The shameful ignorance of these great men was made apparent as their arguments were met by the simple teachings of God's word. Laborers, soldiers, women, and even children, were better acquainted with the Bible teachings than were the priests and learned doctors.

The contrast between the disciples of the gospel and the upholders of popish superstition was no less manifest in the ranks of scholars than among the common people. »Opposed to the old champions of the hierarchy, who had neglected the study of languages and the cultivation of literature, ... were generous-minded youth, devoted to study, investigating Scripture, and familiarizing themselves with the masterpieces of antiquity. Possessing an active mind, an elevated soul, and intrepid heart, these young men soon acquired such knowledge that for a long period none could compete with them. ... Accordingly, when these youthful defenders of the Reformation met the Romish doctors in any assembly, they attacked them with such ease and confidence that these ignorant men hesitated, became embarrassed, and fell into a contempt merited in the eyes of all.« Ibid., b. 9, ch. 11

As the Romish clergy saw their congregations diminishing, they invoked the aid of the magistrates, and by every means in their power endeavored to bring back their hearers. But the people [195/196] had found in the new teachings that which supplied the wants of their souls, and they turned away from those who had so long fed them with the worthless husks of superstitious rites and human traditions.

When persecution was kindled against the teachers of the truth, they gave heed to the words of Christ: »When they persecute you in this city, flee ye into another.« Matthew 10:23 The light penetrated everywhere. The fugitives would find somewhere a hospitable door opened to them, and there abiding, they would preach Christ, sometimes in the church, or, if denied that privilege, in private houses or in the open air. Wherever they could obtain a hearing was a consecrated temple. The truth, proclaimed with such energy and assurance, spread with irresistible power. In vain both ecclesiastical and civil authorities were invoked to crush the heresy. In vain they resorted to imprisonment, torture, fire, and sword. Thousands of believers sealed their faith with their blood, and yet the work went on. Persecution served only to extend the truth, and the fanaticism which Satan endeavored to unite with it resulted in making more clear the contrast between the work of Satan and the work of God.

Luther's studyroom at the Wartburg

Chapter 11

Protest of the Princes

One of the noblest testimonies ever uttered for the Reformation was the Protest offered by the Christian princes of Germany at the Diet of Spires in 1529. The courage, faith, and firmness of those men of God gained for succeeding ages liberty of thought and of conscience. Their Protest gave to the reformed church the name of Protestant; its principles are »the very essence of Protestantism.« D'Aubigne, b. 13, ch. 6

A dark and threatening day had come for the Reformation. Notwithstanding the Edict of Worms, declaring Luther to be an outlaw and forbidding the teaching or belief of his doctrines, religious toleration had thus far prevailed in the empire. God's providence had held in check the forces that opposed the truth. Charles V was bent on crushing the Reformation, but often as he raised his hand to strike he had been forced to turn aside the blow. Again and again the immediate destruction of all who dared to oppose themselves to Rome appeared inevitable; but at the critical moment the armies of the Turk appeared on the eastern frontier, or the king of France, or even the pope himself, jealous of the increasing greatness of the emperor, made war upon him; and thus, amid the strife and tumult of nations, the Reformation had been left to strengthen and extend. At last, however, the papal sovereigns had stifled their feuds, that they might make common cause against the Reformers. The Diet of Spires in 1526 had given each state full liberty in matters of religion until the meeting of a general council; but no sooner had the dangers passed which secured this concession, than the emperor summoned a second Diet to convene at Spires in 1529 for the purpose of crushing heresy. The princes were to be induced, by peaceable means if possible, to side against the Reformation; but if these failed, Charles was prepared to resort to the sword.

The papists were exultant. They appeared at Spires in great numbers, and openly manifested their hostility toward the Reformers and all who favored them. Said Melanchthon: »We are the execration and the sweepings of the world; but Christ will look down on His poor people, and will preserve them.« Ibid., b. 13, ch. 5

The evangelical princes in attendance at the Diet were forbidden even to have the gospel preached in their dwellings. But the people of Spires thirsted for the word of God, and, notwithstanding the prohibition, thousands flocked to the services held in the chapel of the elector of Saxony.

This hastened the crisis. An imperial message announced to the Diet that as the resolution granting liberty of conscience had given rise to great disorders, the emperor required that it be annulled. This arbitrary act excited the indignation and alarm of the evangelical Christians. Said one: »Christ has again fallen into the hands of Caiaphas and Pilate.« The Romanists became more violent. A bigoted papist declared: »The Turks are better than the Lutherans; for the Turks observe fast days, and the Lutherans violate them. If we must choose between the Holy Scriptures of God and the old errors of the church, we should reject the former.« Said Melanchthon: »Every day, in full assembly, Faber casts some new stone at us gospelers.« Ibid., b. 13, ch. 5

Religious toleration had been legally established, and the evangelical states were resolved to oppose the infringement of their rights. Luther, being still under the ban imposed by the Edict of Worms, was not permitted to be present at Spires; but his place was supplied by his colaborers and the princes whom God had raised up to defend His cause in this emergency. The noble Frederick of Saxony, Luther's former protector, had been removed by death; but Duke John, his brother and successor, had joyfully welcomed the Reformation, and while a friend of peace, he displayed great energy and courage in all matters relating to the interests of the faith. The priests demanded that the states which had accepted the Reformation submit implicitly to Romish jurisdiction. The Reformers, on the other hand, claimed the liberty which had previously been granted. They could not consent that Rome should again bring under her control those states that had with so great joy received the word of God.

As a compromise it was finally proposed that where the Reformation had not become established, the Edict of Worms should be rigorously enforced; and that "in those where the people had deviated from it, and where they could not conform to it without danger of revolt, they should at least effect no new reform, they should touch upon no controverted point, they should not oppose the celebration of the mass, they should permit no Roman Catholic to embrace Lutheranism.« Ibid., b. 13, ch. 5 This measure passed the Diet, to the great satisfaction of the popish priests and prelates.

If this edict were enforced, »the Reformation could neither be extended ... where as yet it was unknown, nor be established on solid foundations ... where it already existed.« Ibid., b. 13, ch. 5

Liberty of speech would be prohibited. No conversions would be allowed. And to these restrictions and prohibitions the friends of the Reformation were required at once to submit. The hopes of the world seemed about to be extinguished. »The re-establishment of the Romish hierarchy ... would infallibly bring back the ancient abuses;« and an occasion would readily be found for »completing the destruction of a work already so violently shaken« by fanaticism and dissension. Ibid., b. 13, ch. 5

As the evangelical party met for consultation, one looked to another in blank dismay. From one to another passed the inquiry: »What is to be done?« Mighty issues for the world were at stake. »Shall the chiefs of the Reformation submit, and accept the edict? How easily might the Reformers at this crisis, which was truly a tremendous one, have argued themselves into a wrong course! How many plausible pretexts and fair reasons might they have found for submission! The Lutheran princes were guaranteed the free exercise of their religion. The same boon was extended to all those of their subjects who, prior to the passing of the measure, had embraced the reformed views. Ought not this to content them? How many perils would submission avoid! On what unknown hazards and conflicts would opposition launch them! Who knows what opportunities the future may bring? Let us embrace peace; let us seize the olive branch Rome holds out, and close the wounds of Germany. With arguments like these might the Reformers have justified their adoption of a course which would have assuredly issued in no long time in the overthrow of their cause. »Happily they looked at the principle on which this arrangement was based, and they acted in faith. What was that principle? It was the right of Rome to coerce conscience and forbid free inquiry. But were not themselves and their Protestant subjects to enjoy religious freedom? Yes, as a favor specially stipulated for in the arrangement, but not as a right. As to all outside that arrangement, the great principle of authority was to rule; conscience was out of court; Rome was infallible judge, and must [199/200] be obeyed. The acceptance of the proposed arrangement would have been a virtual admission that religious liberty ought to be confined to reformed Saxony; and as to all the rest of Christendom, free inquiry and the profession of the reformed faith were crimes, and must be visited with the dungeon and the stake. Could they consent to localize religious liberty? to have it proclaimed that the Reformation had made its last convert? had subjugated its last acre? and that wherever Rome bore sway at this hour, there her dominion was to be perpetuated? Could the Reformers have pleaded that they were innocent of the blood of those hundreds and thousands who, in pursuance of this arrangement, would have to yield up their lives in popish lands? This would have been to betray, at that supreme hour, the cause of the gospel and the liberties of Christendom.« Wylie, b. 9, ch. 15 Rather would they »sacrifice everything, even their states, their crowns, and their lives.« D'Aubigne, b. 13, ch. 5

»Let us reject this decree,« said the princes. »In matters of conscience the majority has no power.« The deputies declared: »It is to the decree of 1526 that we are indebted for the peace that the empire enjoys: its abolition would fill Germany with troubles and divisions. The Diet is incompetent to do more than preserve religious liberty until the council meets.« Ibid., b. 13, ch. 5 To protect liberty of conscience is the duty of the state, and this is the limit of its authority in matters of religion. Every secular government that attempts to regulate or enforce religious observances by civil authority is sacrificing the very principle for which the evangelical Christian so nobly struggled.

The papists determined to put down what they termed »daring obstinacy.« They began by endeavoring to cause divisions among the supporters of the Reformation and to intimidate all who had not openly declared in its favor. The representatives of the free cities were at last summoned before the Diet and required to declare whether they would accede to the terms of the proposition. They pleaded for delay, but in vain. When brought to the test, nearly one half their number sided with the Reformers. Those who thus refused to sacrifice liberty of conscience and the right of individual judgment well knew that their position marked them for future criticism, condemnation, and persecution. Said one of the delegates: »We must either deny the word of God, or - be burnt.« Ibid., b. 13, ch. 5

King Ferdinand, the emperor's representative at the Diet, saw

that the decree would cause serious divisions unless

the princes could be induced to accept and sustain it. He therefore tried the art of persuasion, well knowing that to employ force with such men would only render them the more determined. He »begged the princes to accept the decree, assuring them that the emperor would be exceedingly pleased with them.« But these faithful men acknowledged an authority above that of earthly rulers, and they answered calmly: »We will obey the emperor in everything that may contribute to maintain peace and the honor of God.« Ibid., b. 13, ch. 5

In the presence of the Diet the king at last announced to the elector and his friends that the edict »was about to be drawn up in the form of an imperial decree,« and that »their only remaining course was to submit to the majority.« Having thus spoken, he withdrew from the assembly, giving the Reformers no opportunity for deliberation or reply. »To no purpose they sent a deputation entreating the king to return.« To their remonstrances he answered only: »It is a settled affair; submission is all that remains.« Ibid., b. 13, ch. 5

The imperial party were convinced that the Christian princes would adhere to the Holy Scriptures as superior to human doctrines and requirements; and they knew that wherever this principle was accepted, the papacy would eventually be overthrown. But, like thousands since their time, looking only »at the things which are seen,« they flattered themselves that the cause of the emperor and the pope was strong, and that of the Reformers weak. Had the Reformers depended upon human aid alone, they would have been as powerless as the papists supposed. But though weak in numbers, and at variance with Rome, they had their strength. They appealed »from the report of the Diet to the word of God, and from the emperor Charles to Jesus Christ, the King of kings and Lord of lords.« Ibid., b. 13, ch. 6

As Ferdinand had refused to regard their conscientious convictions, the princes decided not to heed his absence, but to bring their Protest before the national council without delay. A solemn declaration was therefore drawn up and presented to the Diet: »We protest by these presents, before God, our only Creator, Preserver, Redeemer, and Saviour, and who will one day be our Judge, as well as before all men and all creatures, that we, for us and for our people, neither consent nor adhere in any manner whatsoever to the proposed decree, in anything that is contrary to God, to His holy word, to our right conscience, to the salvation of our souls.«

»What! we ratify this edict! We assert that when Almighty God calls a man to His knowledge, this man nevertheless cannot receive the knowledge of God!« »There is no sure doctrine but such as is conformable to the word of God. ... The Lord forbids the teaching of any other doctrine. ... The Holy Scriptures ought to be explained by other and clearer texts; ... this Holy Book is, in all things necessary for the Christian, easy of understanding, and calculated to scatter the darkness. We are resolved, with the grace of God, to maintain the pure and exclusive preaching of His only word, such as it is contained in the biblical books of the Old and New Testaments, without adding anything thereto that may be contrary to it. This word is the only truth; it is the sure rule of all doctrine and of all life, and can never fail or deceive us. He who builds on this foundation shall stand against all the powers of hell, while all the human vanities that are set up against it shall fall before the face of God.«

»For this reason we reject the yoke that is imposed on us.« »At the same time we are in expectation that his imperial majesty will behave toward us like a Christian prince who loves God above all things; and we declare ourselves ready to pay unto him, as well as unto you, gracious lords, all the affection and obedience that are our just and legitimate duty.« Ibid., b. 13, ch. 6

A deep impression was made upon the Diet. The majority were filled with amazement and alarm at the boldness of the protesters. The future appeared to them stormy and uncertain. Dissension, strife, and bloodshed seemed inevitable. But the Reformers, assured of the justice of their cause, and relying upon the arm of Omnipotence, were »full of courage and firmness.« »The principles contained in this celebrated Protest ... constitute the very essence of Protestantism. Now this Protest opposes two abuses of man in matters of faith: the first is the intrusion of the civil magistrate, and the second the arbitrary authority of the church. Instead of these abuses, Protestantism sets the power of conscience above the magistrate, and the authority of the word of God above the visible church. In the first place, it rejects the civil power in divine things, and says with the prophets and apostles, 'We must obey God rather than man.' In presence of the crown of Charles the Fifth, it uplifts the crown of Jesus Christ. But it goes farther: it lays down the principle that all human teaching should be subordinate to the oracles of God.« Ibid., b. 13, ch. 6

The protesters had moreover affirmed their right to utter freely their convictions of truth. They would not only believe and obey, but teach what the word of God presents, and they denied the right of priest or magistrate to interfere. The Protest of Spires was a solemn witness against religious intolerance, and an assertion of the right of all men to worship God according to the dictates of their own consciences. The declaration had been made. It was written in the memory of thousands and registered in the books of heaven, where no effort of man could erase it. All evangelical Germany adopted the Protest as the expression of its faith. Everywhere men beheld in this declaration the promise of a new and better era. Said one of the princes to the Protestants of Spires: »May the Almighty, who has given you grace to confess energetically, freely, and fearlessly, preserve you in that Christian firmness until the day of eternity.« Ibid., b. 13, ch. 6

Had the Reformation, after attaining a degree of success, consented to temporize to secure favor with the world, it would have been untrue to God and to itself, and would thus have ensured its own destruction. The experience of these noble Reformers contains a lesson for all succeeding ages. Satan's manner of working against God and His word has not changed; he is still as much opposed to the Scriptures being made the guide of life as in the sixteenth century. In our time there is a wide departure from their doctrines and precepts, and there is need of a return to the great Protestant principle – the Bible, and the Bible only, as the rule of faith and duty. Satan is still working through every means which he can control to destroy religious liberty. The antichristian power which the protesters of Spires rejected is now with renewed vigor seeking to re-establish its lost supremacy. The same unswerving adherence to the word of God manifested at that crisis of the Reformation is the only hope of reform today. There appeared tokens of danger to the Protestants; there were tokens, also, that the divine hand was stretched out to protect the faithful. It was about this time that »Melanchthon hastily conducted through the streets of Spires toward the Rhine his friend Simon Grynaeus, pressing him to cross the river. The latter was astonished at such precipitation. 'An old man of grave and solemn air, but who is unknown to me,' said Melanchthon, 'appeared before me and said, In a minute officers of justice will be sent by Ferdinand to arrest Grynaeus.'«

During the day, Grynaeus had been scandalized at a sermon by Faber, a leading papal doctor; and at the close, remonstrated with him for defending »certain detestable errors.« »Faber dissembled his anger, but immediately after repaired to the king, from whom he had obtained an order against the importunate professor of Heidelberg. Melanchthon doubted not that God had saved his friend by sending one of His holy angels to forewarn him. Motionless on the banks of the Rhine, he waited until the waters of that stream had rescued Grynaeus from his persecutors. 'At last,' cried Melanchthon, as he saw him on the opposite side, 'at last he is torn from the cruel jaws of those who thirst for innocent blood.' When he returned to his house, Melanchthon was informed that officers in search of Grynaeus had ransacked it from top to bottom.« Ibid., b. 13, ch. 6

The Reformation was to be brought into greater prominence before the mighty ones of the earth. The evangelical princes had been denied a hearing by King Ferdinand; but they were to be granted an opportunity to present their cause in the presence of the emperor and the assembled dignitaries of church and state. To quiet the dissensions which disturbed the empire, Charles V, in the year following the Protest of Spires, convoked a diet at Augsburg, over which he announced his intention to preside in person. Thither the Protestant leaders were summoned.

Great dangers threatened the Reformation; but its advocates still trusted their cause with God, and pledged themselves to be firm to the gospel. The elector of Saxony was urged by his councilors not to appear at the Diet. The emperor, they said, required the attendance of the princes in order to draw them into a snare. »Is it not risking everything to go and shut oneself up within the walls of a city with a powerful enemy?« But others nobly declared, »Let the princes only comport themselves with courage, and God's cause is saved.« »God is faithful; He will not abandon us,« said Luther. Ibid., b. 14, ch. 2

The elector set out, with his retinue, for Augsburg. All were acquainted with the dangers that menaced him, and many went forward with gloomy countenance and troubled heart. But Luther, who accompanied them as far as Coburg, revived their sinking faith by singing the hymn, written on that journey, »A strong tower is our God.« Many an anxious foreboding was banished, many a heavy heart lightened, at the sound of the inspiring strains.

The reformed princes had determined upon having a statement of their views in systematic form, with the evidence from the Scriptures, to present before the Diet; and the task of its preparation was committed to Luther, Melanchthon, and their associates. This Confession was accepted by the Protestants as an exposition of their faith, and they assembled to affix their names to the important document. It was a solemn and trying time. The Reformers were solicitous that their cause should not be confounded with political questions; they felt that the Reformation should exercise no other influence than that which proceeds from the word of God. As the Christian princes advanced to sign the Confession, Melanchthon interposed, saying: »It is for the theologians and ministers to propose these things; let us reserve for other matters the authority of the mighty ones of the earth.« »God forbid,« replied John of Saxony, »that you should exclude me. I am resolved to do what is right, without troubling myself about my crown. I desire to confess the Lord. My electoral hat and my ermine are not so precious to me as the cross of Jesus Christ.« Having thus spoken, he wrote down his name. Said another of the princes as he took the pen: »If the honor of my Lord Jesus Christ requires it, I am ready ... to leave my goods and life behind.« »I would rather renounce my subjects and my states, rather quit the country of my fathers staff in hand,« he continued, »than receive any other doctrine than that which is contained in this Confession.« Ibid., b. 14, ch. 6 Such was the faith and daring of those men of God.

The appointed time came to appear before the emperor. Charles V, seated upon his throne, surrounded by the electors and the princes, gave audience to the Protestant Reformers. The confession of their faith was read. In that august assembly the truths of the gospel were clearly set forth, and the errors of the papal church were pointed out. Well has that day been pronounced »the greatest day of the Reformation, and one of the most glorious in the history of Christianity and of mankind.« Ibid., b. 14, ch. 7

But a few years had passed since the monk of Wittenberg stood alone at Worms before the national council. Now in his stead were the noblest and most powerful princes of the empire. Luther had been forbidden to appear at Augsburg, but he had been present by his words and prayers. »I am overjoyed,« he wrote, »that I have lived until this hour, in which Christ has been publicly exalted by such illustrious confessors, and in so glorious an assembly.« [207/208]

Ibid., b. 14, ch. 7 Thus was fulfilled what the Scripture says: »I will speak of Thy testimonies ... before kings.« Psalm 119:46

In the days of Paul the gospel for which he was imprisoned was thus brought before the princes and nobles of the imperial city. So on this occasion, that which the emperor had forbidden to be preached from the pulpit was proclaimed from the palace; what many had regarded as unfit even for servants to listen to was heard with wonder by the masters and lords of the empire. Kings and great men were the auditory, crowned princes were the preachers, and the sermon was the royal truth of God. »Since the apostolic age,« says a writer, »there has never been a greater work or a more magnificent confession.« D'Aubigne, b. 14, ch. 7

»All that the Lutherans have said is true; we cannot deny it,« declared a papist bishop. »Can you refute by sound reasons the Confession made by the elector and his allies?« asked another of Dr. Eck. »With the writings of the apostles and prophets – no!« was the reply; »but with those of the Fathers and of the councils – yes!« »I understand,« responded the questioner. »The Lutherans, according to you, are in Scripture, and we are outside.« Ibid., b. 14, ch. 8 Some of the princes of Germany were won to the reformed faith. The emperor himself declared that the Protestant articles were but the truth. The Confession was translated into many languages and circulated through all Europe, and it has been accepted by millions in succeeding generations as the expression of their faith.

God's faithful servants were not toiling alone. While principalities and powers and wicked spirits in high places were leagued against them, the Lord did not forsake His people. Could their eyes have been opened, they would have seen as marked evidence of divine presence and aid as was granted to a prophet of old. When Elisha's servant pointed his master to the hostile army surrounding them and cutting off all opportunity for escape, the prophet prayed: »Lord, I pray Thee, open his eyes, that he may see.« 2 Kings 6:17 And, lo, the mountain was filled with chariots and horses of fire, the army of heaven stationed to protect the man of God. Thus did angels guard the workers in the cause of the Reformation.

One of the principles most firmly maintained by Luther was that there should be no resort to secular power in support of the Reformation, and no appeal to arms for its defense. He rejoiced that
 the gospel was confessed by princes of the empire;

but when they proposed to unite in a defensive league, he declared that »the doctrine of the gospel should be defended by God alone. ... The less man meddled in the work, the more striking would be God's intervention in its behalf. All the politic precautions suggested were, in his view, attributable to unworthy fear and sinful mistrust.« D'Aubigne, London ed., b. 10, ch. 14

When powerful foes were uniting to overthrow the reformed faith, and thousands of swords seemed about to be unsheathed against it, Luther wrote: »Satan is putting forth his fury; ungodly pontiffs are conspiring; and we are threatened with war. Exhort the people to contend valiantly before the throne of the Lord, by faith and prayer, so that our enemies, vanquished by the Spirit of God, may be constrained to peace. Our chief want, our chief labor, is prayer; let the people know that they are now exposed to the edge of the sword and to the rage of Satan, and let them pray.« D'Aubigne, b. 10, ch. 14

Again, at a later date, referring to the league contemplated by the reformed princes, Luther declared that the only weapon employed in this warfare should be »the sword of the Spirit.« He wrote to the elector of Saxony: »We cannot on our conscience approve the proposed alliance. We would rather die ten times than see our gospel cause one drop of blood to be shed. Our part is to be like lambs of the slaughter. The cross of Christ must be borne. Let your highness be without fear. We shall do more by our prayers than all our enemies by their boastings. Only let not your hands be stained with the blood of your brethren. If the emperor requires us to be given up to his tribunals, we are ready to appear. You cannot defend our faith: each one should believe at his own risk and peril.« Ibid., b. 14, ch. 1

From the secret place of prayer came the power that shook the world in the Great Reformation. There, with holy calmness, the servants of the Lord set their feet upon the rock of His promises. During the struggle at Augsburg, Luther »did not pass a day without devoting three hours at least to prayer, and they were hours selected from those the most favorable to study.« In the privacy of his chamber he was heard to pour out his soul before God in words »full of adoration, fear, and hope, as when one speaks to a friend.« »I know that Thou art our Father and our God,« he said, »and that Thou wilt scatter the persecutors of Thy children; for Thou art Thyself endangered with us. All this matter is Thine, and it is only by Thy constraint that we have put our hands to it. Defend us, then, O Father!« Ibid., b. 14, ch. 6

To Melanchthon, who was crushed under the burden of anxiety and fear, he wrote: »Grace and peace in Christ – in Christ, I say, and not in the world. Amen. I hate with exceeding hatred those extreme cares which consume you. If the cause is unjust, abandon it; if the cause is just, why should we belie the promises of Him who commands us to sleep without fear? ... Christ will not be wanting to the work of justice and truth. He lives, He reigns; what fear, then, can we have?« Ibid., b. 14, ch. 6

God did listen to the cries of His servants. He gave to princes and ministers grace and courage to maintain the truth against the rulers of the darkness of this world. Saith the Lord: »Behold, I lay in Zion a chief cornerstone, elect, precious: and he that believeth on Him shall not be confounded.« 1 Peter 2:6 The Protestant Reformers had built on Christ, and the gates of hell could not prevail against them.

Kaiser Karl V. (1500-1558)

John the Steadfast (1468-1532)

Chapter 12

The French Reformation

The Protest of Spires and the Confession at Augsburg, which marked the triumph of the Reformation in Germany, were followed by years of conflict and darkness. Weakened by divisions among its supporters, and assailed by powerful foes, Protestantism seemed destined to be utterly destroyed. Thousands sealed their testimony with their blood. Civil war broke out; the Protestant cause was betrayed by one of its leading adherents; the noblest of the reformed princes fell into the hands of the emperor and were dragged as captives from town to town. But in the moment of his apparent triumph, the emperor was smitten with defeat. He saw the prey wrested from his grasp, and he was forced at last to grant toleration to the doctrines which it had been the ambition of his life to destroy. He had staked his kingdom, his treasures, and life itself upon the crushing out of the heresy. Now he saw his armies wasted by battle, his treasuries drained, his many kingdoms threatened by revolt, while everywhere the faith which he had vainly endeavored to suppress, was extending. Charles V had been battling against omnipotent power. God had said, »Let there be light,« but the emperor had sought to keep the darkness unbroken. His purposes had failed; and in premature old age, worn out with the long struggle, he abdicated the throne and buried himself in a cloister.

In Switzerland, as in Germany, there came dark days for the Reformation. While many cantons accepted the reformed faith, others clung with blind persistence to the creed of Rome. Their persecution of those who desired to receive the truth finally gave rise to civil war. Zwingli and many who had united with him in reform fell on the bloody field of Cappel. Oecolampadius, overcome by these terrible disasters, soon after died. Rome was triumphant, and in many places seemed about to recover all that she had lost. But He whose counsels are from everlasting had not forsaken His cause or His people. His hand would bring deliverance for them. In other lands He had raised up laborers to carry forward the reform. In

France, before the name of Luther had been heard as a Reformer, the day had already begun to break. One of the first to catch the light was the aged Lefevre, a man of extensive learning, a professor in the University of Paris, and a sincere and zealous papist. In his researches into ancient literature his attention was directed to the Bible, and he introduced its study among his students. Lefevre was an enthusiastic adorer of the saints, and he had undertaken to prepare a history of the saints and martyrs as given in the legends of the church. This was a work which involved great labor; but he had already made considerable progress in it, when, thinking that he might obtain useful assistance from the Bible, he began its study with this object. Here indeed he found saints brought to view, but not such as figured in the Roman calendar. A flood of divine light broke in upon his mind. In amazement and disgust he turned away from his self-appointed task and devoted himself to the word of God. The precious truths which he there discovered he soon began to teach.

In 1512, before either Luther or Zwingli had begun the work of reform, Lefevre wrote: »It is God who gives us, by faith, that righteousness which by grace alone justifies to eternal life.« Wylie, b. 13, ch. 1 Dwelling upon the mysteries of redemption, he exclaimed: »Oh, the unspeakable greatness of that exchange, – the Sinless One is condemned, and he who is guilty goes free; the Blessing bears the curse, and the cursed is brought into blessing; the Life dies, and the dead live; the Glory is whelmed in darkness, and he who knew nothing but confusion of face is clothed with glory.« D'Aubigne, London ed., b. 12, ch. 2

And while teaching that the glory of salvation belongs solely to God, he also declared that the duty of obedience belongs to man. »If thou art a member of Christ's church,« he said, »thou art a member of His body; if thou art of His body, then thou art full of the divine nature. ... Oh, if men could but enter into the understanding of this privilege, how purely, chastely, and holily would they live, and how contemptible, when compared with the glory within them, – that glory which the eye of flesh cannot see, – would they deem all the glory of this world.« Ibid., b. 12, ch. 2 There were some among Lefevre's students who listened eagerly to his words, and who, long after the teacher's voice should be silenced, were to continue to declare the truth. Such was William Farel. The son of pious parents, and educated to accept with implicit faith the teachings of the church, he might, with the apostle Paul, have declared concerning himself: »After the most straitest sect of our religion I lived a Pharisee.« Acts 26:5 A devoted Romanist, he burned with zeal to destroy all who should dare to oppose the church. »I would gnash my teeth like a furious wolf,« he afterward said, referring to this period of his life, »when I heard anyone speaking against the pope.« Wylie, b. 13, ch. 2 He had been untiring in his adoration of the saints, in company with Lefevre making the round of the churches of Paris, worshipping at the altars, and adorning with gifts the holy shrines. But these observances could not bring peace of soul. Conviction of sin fastened upon him, which all the acts of penance that he practiced failed to banish. As to a voice from heaven he listened to the Reformer's words: »Salvation is of grace.« »The Innocent One is condemned, and the criminal is acquitted.« »It is the cross of Christ alone that openeth the gates of heaven, and shutteth the gates of hell.« Ibid., b. 13, ch. 2 Farel joyfully accepted the truth. By a conversion like that of Paul he turned from the bondage of tradition to the liberty of the sons of God. »Instead of the murderous heart of a ravening wolf,« he came back, he says, »quietly like a meek and harmless lamb, having his heart entirely withdrawn from the pope, and given to Jesus Christ.« D'Aubigne, b. 12, ch. 3 While Lefevre continued to spread the light among his students, Farel, as zealous in the cause of Christ as he had been in that of the pope, went forth to declare the truth in public. A dignitary of the church, the bishop of Meaux, soon after united with them. Other teachers who ranked high for their ability and learning joined in proclaiming the gospel, and it won adherents among all classes, from the homes of artisans and peasants to the palace of the king. The sister of Francis I, then the reigning monarch, accepted the reformed faith. The king himself, and the queen mother, appeared for a time to regard it with favor, and with high hopes the Reformers looked forward to the time when France should be won to the gospel.

But their hopes were not to be realized. Trial and persecution awaited the disciples of Christ. This, however, was mercifully veiled from their eyes. A time of peace intervened, that they might gain strength to meet the tempest; and the Reformation made rapid progress. The bishop of Meaux labored zealously in his own diocese to instruct both the clergy and the people. Ignorant and immoral priests were removed, and, so far as possible, replaced by men of learning and piety. The bishop greatly desired that his people might have access to the word of God for themselves, and this was soon accomplished. Lefevre undertook the translation of the New Testament; and at the very time when Luther's German Bible was issuing from the press in Wittenberg, the French New Testament was published at Meaux. The bishop spared no labor or expense to circulate it in his parishes, and soon the peasants of Meaux were in possession of the Holy Scriptures. As travelers perishing from thirst welcome with joy a living water spring, so did these souls receive the message of heaven. The laborers in the field, the artisans in the workshop, cheered their daily toil by talking of the precious truths of the Bible. At evening, instead of resorting to the wine-shops, they assembled in one another's homes to read God's word and join in prayer and praise. A great change was soon manifest in these communities. Though belonging to the humblest class, an unlearned and hard-working peasantry, the reforming, uplifting power of divine grace was seen in their lives. Humble, loving, and holy, they stood as witnesses to what the gospel will accomplish for those who receive it in sincerity.

The light kindled at Meaux shed its beams afar. Every day the number of converts was increasing. The rage of the hierarchy was for a time held in check by the king, who despised the narrow bigotry of the monks; but the papal leaders finally prevailed. Now the stake was set up. The bishop of Meaux, forced to choose between the fire and recantation, accepted the easier path; but notwithstanding the leader's fall, his flock remained steadfast. Many witnessed for the truth amid the flames. By their courage and fidelity at the stake, these humble Christians spoke to thousands who in days of peace had never heard their testimony.

It was not alone the humble and the poor that amid suffering and scorn dared to bear witness for Christ. In the lordly halls of the castle and the palace there were kingly souls by whom truth was valued above wealth or rank or even life. Kingly armor concealed a loftier and more steadfast spirit than did the bishop's robe and miter. Louis de Berquin was of noble birth. A brave and courtly knight, he was devoted to study, polished in manners, and of blameless morals. »He was,« says a writer, »a great follower of the papistical constitutions, and a great hearer of masses and sermons; ... and he crowned all his other virtues by holding Lutheranism in special abhorrence.« But, like so many others, providentially guided to the Bible, he was amazed to find there, »not the doctrines of Rome, but the doctrines of Luther.«

 Wylie, b. 13, ch. 9 Henceforth he gave himself with entire devotion to the cause of the gospel. »The most learned of the nobles of France,« his genius and eloquence, his indomitable courage and heroic zeal, and his influence at court, – for he was a favorite with the king, – caused him to be regarded by many as one destined to be the Reformer of his country. Said Beza: »Berquin would have been a second Luther, had he found in Francis I a second elector.« »He is worse than Luther,« cried the papists. Ibid., b. 13, ch. 9 More dreaded he was indeed by the Romanists of France. They thrust him into prison as a heretic, but he was set at liberty by the king. For years the struggle continued. Francis, wavering between Rome and the Reformation, alternately tolerated and restrained the fierce zeal of the monks. Berquin was three times imprisoned by the papal authorities, only to be released by the monarch, who, in admiration of his genius and his nobility of character, refused to sacrifice him to the malice of the hierarchy.

Berquin was repeatedly warned of the danger that threatened him in France, and urged to follow the steps of those who had found safety in voluntary exile. The timid and time-serving Erasmus, who with all the splendor of his scholarship failed of that moral greatness which holds life and honor subservient to truth, wrote to Berquin: »Ask to be sent as ambassador to some foreign country; go and travel in Germany. You know Beda and such as he – he is a thousand-headed monster, darting venom on every side. Your enemies are named legion. Were your cause better than that of Jesus Christ, they will not let you go till they have miserably destroyed you. Do not trust too much to the king's protection. At all events, do not compromise me with the faculty of theology.« Ibid., b. 13, ch. 9 But as dangers thickened, Berquin's zeal only waxed the stronger. So far from adopting the politic and self-serving counsel of Erasmus, he determined upon still bolder measures. He would not only stand in defense of the truth, but he would attack error. The charge of heresy which the Romanists were seeking to fasten upon him, he would rivet upon them. The most active and bitter of his opponents were the learned doctors and monks of the theological department in the great University of Paris, one of the highest ecclesiastical authorities both in the city and the nation. From the writings of these doctors, Berquin drew twelve propositions which he publicly declared to be »opposed to the Bible, and heretical;« and he appealed to the king to act as judge in the controversy.

The monarch, not loath to bring into contrast the power and acuteness of the opposing champions, and glad of an opportunity of humbling the pride of these haughty monks, bade the Romanists defend their cause by the Bible. This weapon, they well knew, would avail them little; imprisonment, torture, and the stake were arms which they better understood how to wield. Now the tables were turned, and they saw themselves about to fall into the pit into which they had hoped to plunge Berquin. In amazement they looked about them for some way of escape.

»Just at that time an image of the Virgin at the corner of one of the streets, was mutilated.« There was great excitement in the city. Crowds of people flocked to the place, with expressions of mourning and indignation. The king also was deeply moved. Here was an advantage which the monks could turn to good account, and they were quick to improve it. »These are the fruits of the doctrines of Berquin,« they cried. »All is about to be overthrown – religion, the laws, the throne itself – by this Lutheran conspiracy.« Ibid., b. 13, ch. 9

Again Berquin was apprehended. The king withdrew from Paris, and the monks were thus left free to work their will. The Reformer was tried and condemned to die, and lest Francis should even yet interpose to save him, the sentence was executed on the very day it was pronounced. At noon Berquin was conducted to the place of death. An immense throng gathered to witness the event, and there were many who saw with astonishment and misgiving that the victim had been chosen from the best and bravest of the noble families of France. Amazement, indignation, scorn, and bitter hatred darkened the faces of that surging crowd; but upon one face no shadow rested. The martyr's thoughts were far from that scene of tumult; he was conscious only of the presence of his Lord. The wretched tumbrel upon which he rode, the frowning faces of his persecutors, the dreadful death to which he was going – these he heeded not; He who liveth and was dead, and is alive for evermore, and hath the keys of death and of hell, was beside him. Berquin's countenance was radiant with the light and peace of heaven. He had attired himself in goodly raiment, wearing »a cloak of velvet, a doublet of satin and damask, and golden hose.« D'Aubigne, History of the Reform. in Europe in the Time of Calvin, b. 2, ch. 16 He was about to testify to his faith in the presence of the King of kings and the witnessing universe, and no token of mourning should belie his joy.

As the procession moved slowly through the crowded streets, the people marked with wonder the unclouded peace, and joyous triumph, of his look and bearing. »He is,« they said, »like one who sits in a temple, and meditates on holy things.« Wylie, b. 13, ch. 9 At the stake, Berquin endeavored to address a few words to the people; but the monks, fearing the result, began to shout, and the soldiers to clash their arms, and their clamor drowned the martyr's voice. Thus in 1529 the highest literary and ecclesiastical authority of cultured Paris »set the populace of 1793 the base example of stifling on the scaffold the sacred words of the dying.« Ibid., b. 13, ch. 9 Berquin was strangled, and his body was consumed in the flames. The tidings of his death caused sorrow to the friends of the Reformation throughout France. But his example was not lost. »We, too, are ready,« said the witnesses for the truth, »to meet death cheerfully, setting our eyes on the life that is to come.« D'Aubigne, History of the Reform. in Europe in the Time of Calvin, b. 2, ch. 16

During the persecution of Meaux, the teachers of the reformed faith were deprived of their license to preach, and they departed to other fields. Lefevre after a time made his way to Germany. Farel returned to his native town in eastern France, to spread the light in the home of his childhood. Already tidings had been received of what was going on at Meaux, and the truth, which he taught with fearless zeal, found listeners. Soon the authorities were roused to silence him, and he was banished from the city. Though he could no longer labor publicly, he traversed the plains and villages, teaching in private dwellings and in secluded meadows, and finding shelter in the forests and among the rocky caverns which had been his haunts in boyhood. God was preparing him for greater trials. »The crosses, persecutions, and machinations of Satan, of which I was forewarned, have not been wanting,« he said; »they are even much severer than I could have borne of myself; but God is my Father; He has provided and always will provide me the strength which I require.« D'Aubigne, History of the Reform. of the Sixteenth Century, b. 12, ch. 9 As in apostolic days, persecution had »fallen out rather unto the furtherance of the gospel.« Philippians 1:12 Driven from Paris and Meaux, »they that were scattered abroad went everywhere preaching the word.« Acts 8:4 And thus the light found its way into many of the remote provinces of France.

God was still preparing workers to extend His cause. In one of the schools of Paris was a thoughtful, quiet youth, already giving evidence of a powerful and penetrating mind, and no less marked for the blamelessness of his life than for intellectual ardor and religious devotion. His genius and application soon made him the pride of the college, and it was confidently anticipated that John [218/219]

Calvin would become one of the ablest and most honored defenders of the church. But a ray of divine light penetrated even within the walls of scholasticism and superstition by which Calvin was enclosed. He heard of the new doctrines with a shudder, nothing doubting that the heretics deserved the fire to which they were given. Yet all unwittingly he was brought face to face with the heresy and forced to test the power of Romish theology to combat the Protestant teaching.

A cousin of Calvin's, who had joined the Reformers, was in Paris. The two kinsmen often met and discussed together the matters that were disturbing Christendom. »There are but two religions in the world,« said Olivetan, the Protestant. »The one class of religions are those which men have invented, in all of which man saves himself by ceremonies and good works; the other is that one religion which is revealed in the Bible, and which teaches man to look for salvation solely from the free grace of God.« »I will have none of your new doctrines,« exclaimed Calvin; »think you that I have lived in error all my days?« Wylie, b. 13, ch. 7

But thoughts had been awakened in his mind which he could not banish at will. Alone in his chamber he pondered upon his cousin's words. Conviction of sin fastened upon him; he saw himself, without an intercessor, in the presence of a holy and just Judge. The mediation of saints, good works, the ceremonies of the church, all were powerless to atone for sin. He could see before him nothing but the blackness of eternal despair. In vain the doctors of the church endeavored to relieve his woe. Confession, penance, were resorted to in vain; they could not reconcile the soul with God.

While still engaged in these fruitless struggles, Calvin, chancing one day to visit one of the public squares, witnessed there the burning of a heretic. He was filled with wonder at the expression of peace which rested upon the martyr's countenance. Amid the tortures of that dreadful death, and under the more terrible condemnation of the church, he manifested a faith and courage which the young student painfully contrasted with his own despair and darkness, while living in strictest obedience to the church. Upon the Bible, he knew, the heretics rested their faith. He determined to study it, and discover, if he could, the secret of their joy. In the Bible he found Christ. »O Father,« he cried, »His sacrifice has appeased Thy wrath; His blood has washed away my impurities; His cross has borne my curse; His death has atoned for me. We had devised for ourselves many useless follies,

 but Thou hast placed Thy word before me like a torch,

and Thou hast touched my heart, in order that I may hold in abomination all other merits save those of Jesus.« Martyn, vol. 3, ch. 13 Calvin had been educated for the priesthood. When only twelve years of age he had been appointed to the chaplaincy of a small church, and his head had been shorn by the bishop in accordance with the canon of the church. He did not receive consecration, nor did he fulfill the duties of a priest, but he became a member of the clergy, holding the title of his office, and receiving an allowance in consideration thereof.

Now, feeling that he could never become a priest, he turned for a time to the study of law, but finally abandoned this purpose and determined to devote his life to the gospel. But he hesitated to become a public teacher. He was naturally timid, and was burdened with a sense of the weighty responsibility of the position, and he desired still to devote himself to study. The earnest entreaties of his friends, however, at last won his consent. »Wonderful it is,« he said, »that one of so lowly an origin should be exalted to so great a dignity.« Wylie, b. 13, ch. 9

Quietly did Calvin enter upon his work, and his words were as the dew falling to refresh the earth. He had left Paris, and was now in a provincial town under the protection of the princess Margaret, who, loving the gospel, extended her protection to its disciples. Calvin was still a youth, of gentle, unpretentious bearing. His work began with the people at their homes. Surrounded by the members of the household, he read the Bible and opened the truths of salvation. Those who heard the message carried the good news to others, and soon the teacher passed beyond the city to the outlying towns and hamlets. To both the castle and the cabin he found entrance, and he went forward, laying the foundation of churches that were to yield fearless witnesses for the truth. A few months and he was again in Paris. There was unwonted agitation in the circle of learned men and scholars. The study of the ancient languages had led men to the Bible, and many whose hearts were untouched by its truths were eagerly discussing them and even giving battle to the champions of Romanism. Calvin, though an able combatant in the fields of theological controversy, had a higher mission to accomplish than that of these noisy schoolmen. The minds of men were stirred, and now was the time to open to them the truth. While the halls of the universities were filled with the clamor of theological disputation, Calvin was making his way from house to house, opening the Bible to the people, and speaking to them of Christ and Him crucified.

In God's providence, Paris was to receive another invitation to accept the gospel. The call of Lefevre and Farel had been rejected, but again the message was to be heard by all classes in that great capital. The king, influenced by political considerations, had not yet fully sided with Rome against the Reformation. Margaret still clung to the hope that Protestantism was to triumph in France. She resolved that the reformed faith should be preached in Paris. During the absence of the king, she ordered a Protestant minister to preach in the churches of the city. This being forbidden by the papal dignitaries, the princess threw open the palace. An apartment was fitted up as a chapel, and it was announced that every day, at a specified hour, a sermon would be preached, and the people of every rank and station were invited to attend. Crowds flocked to the service. Not only the chapel, but the antechambers and halls were thronged. Thousands every day assembled – nobles, statesmen, lawyers, merchants, and artisans. The king, instead of forbidding the assemblies, ordered that two of the churches of Paris should be opened. Never before had the city been so moved by the word of God. The spirit of life from heaven seemed to be breathed upon the people. Temperance, purity, order, and industry were taking the place of drunkenness, licentiousness, strife, and idleness. But the hierarchy were not idle. The king still refused to interfere to stop the preaching, and they turned to the populace. No means were spared to excite the fears, the prejudices, and the fanaticism of the ignorant and superstitious multitude. Yielding blindly to her false teachers, Paris, like Jerusalem of old, knew not the time of her visitation nor the things which belonged unto her peace. For two years the word of God was preached in the capital; but, while there were many who accepted the gospel, the majority of the people rejected it. Francis had made a show of toleration, merely to serve his own purposes, and the papists succeeded in regaining the ascendancy. Again the churches were closed, and the stake was set up.

Calvin was still in Paris, preparing himself by study, meditation, and prayer for his future labors, and continuing to spread the light. At last, however, suspicion fastened upon him. The authorities determined to bring him to the flames. Regarding himself as secure in his seclusion, he had no thought of danger, when friends came hurrying to his room with the news that officers were on their way to arrest him. At that instant a loud knocking was heard at the outer entrance.

 There was not a moment to be lost. Some of his friends

detained the officers at the door, while others assisted the Reformer to let himself down from a window, and he rapidly made his way to the outskirts of the city. Finding shelter in the cottage of a laborer who was a friend to the reform, he disguised himself in the garments of his host, and, shouldering a hoe, started on his journey. Traveling southward, he again found refuge in the dominions of Margaret. see D'Aubigne, History of the Reform. in Europe in the Time of Calvin, b. 2, ch. 30

Here for a few months he remained, safe under the protection of powerful friends, and engaged as before in study. But his heart was set upon the evangelization of France, and he could not long remain inactive. As soon as the storm had somewhat abated, he sought a new field of labor in Poitiers, where was a university, and where already the new opinions had found favor. Persons of all classes gladly listened to the gospel. There was no public preaching, but in the home of the chief magistrate, in his own lodgings, and sometimes in a public garden, Calvin opened the words of eternal life to those who desired to listen. After a time, as the number of hearers increased, it was thought safer to assemble outside the city. A cave in the side of a deep and narrow gorge, where trees and overhanging rocks made the seclusion still more complete, was chosen as the place of meeting. Little companies, leaving the city by different routes, found their way hither. In this retired spot the Bible was read aloud and explained. Here the Lord's Supper was celebrated for the first time by the Protestants of France. From this little church several faithful evangelists were sent out. Once more Calvin returned to Paris. He could not even yet relinquish the hope that France as a nation would accept the Reformation. But he found almost every door of labor closed. To teach the gospel was to take the direct road to the stake, and he at last determined to depart to Germany. Scarcely had he left France when a storm burst over the Protestants, that, had he remained, must surely have involved him in the general ruin.

The French Reformers, eager to see their country keeping pace with Germany and Switzerland, determined to strike a bold blow against the superstitions of Rome, that should arouse the whole nation. Accordingly placards attacking the mass were in one night posted all over France. Instead of advancing the reform, this zealous but ill-judged movement brought ruin, not only upon its propagators, but upon the friends of the reformed faith throughout France. It gave the Romanists what they had long desired – a pretext [224/225] for demanding the utter destruction of the heretics as agitators dangerous to the stability of the throne and the peace of the nation.

By some secret hand – whether of indiscreet friend or wily foe was never known – one of the placards was attached to the door of the king's private chamber. The monarch was filled with horror. In this paper, superstitions that had received the veneration of ages were attacked with an unsparing hand. And the unexampled boldness of obtruding these plain and startling utterances into the royal presence aroused the wrath of the king. In his amazement he stood for a little time trembling and speechless. Then his rage found utterance in the terrible words: »Let all be seized without distinction who are suspected of Lutheresy. I will exterminate them all.« Ibid., b. 4, ch. 10 The die was cast. The king had determined to throw himself fully on the side of Rome.

Measures were at once taken for the arrest of every Lutheran in Paris. A poor artisan, an adherent of the reformed faith, who had been accustomed to summon the believers to their secret assemblies, was seized and, with the threat of instant death at the stake, was commanded to conduct the papal emissary to the home of every Protestant in the city. He shrank in horror from the base proposal, but at last fear of the flames prevailed, and he consented to become the betrayer of his brethren. Preceded by the host, and surrounded by a train of priests, incense bearers, monks, and soldiers, Morin, the royal detective, with the traitor, slowly and silently passed through the streets of the city. The demonstration was ostensibly in honor of the »holy sacrament,« an act of expiation for the insult put upon the mass by the protesters. But beneath this pageant a deadly purpose was concealed. On arriving opposite the house of a Lutheran, the betrayer made a sign, but no word was uttered. The procession halted, the house was entered, the family were dragged forth and chained, and the terrible company went forward in search of fresh victims. They "spared no house, great or small, not even the colleges of the University of Paris. ... Morin made all the city quake. ... It was a reign of terror.« Ibid., b. 4, ch. 10

The victims were put to death with cruel torture, it being specially ordered that the fire should be lowered in order to prolong their agony. But they died as conquerors. Their constancy was unshaken, their peace unclouded. Their persecutors, powerless to move their inflexible firmness, felt themselves defeated. »The scaffolds were distributed over all the quarters of Paris, and the burnings followed on successive

days, the design being to spread the terror of heresy

by spreading the executions. The advantage, however, in the end, remained with the gospel. All Paris was enabled to see what kind of men the new opinions could produce. There was no pulpit like the martyr's pile. The serene joy that lighted up the faces of these men as they passed along ... to the place of execution, their heroism as they stood amid the bitter flames, their meek forgiveness of injuries, transformed, in instances not a few, anger into pity, and hate into love, and pleaded with resistless eloquence in behalf of the gospel.« Wylie, b. 13, ch. 20

The priests, bent upon keeping the popular fury at its height, circulated the most terrible accusations against the Protestants. They were charged with plotting to massacre the Catholics, to overthrow the government, and to murder the king. Not a shadow of evidence could be produced in support of the allegations. Yet these prophecies of evil were to have a fulfillment; under far different circumstances, however, and from causes of an opposite character. The cruelties that were inflicted upon the innocent Protestants by the Catholics accumulated in a weight of retribution, and in after centuries wrought the very doom they had predicted to be impending, upon the king, his government, and his subjects; but it was brought about by infidels and by the papists themselves. It was not the establishment, but the suppression, of Protestantism, that, three hundred years later, was to bring upon France these dire calamities.

Suspicion, distrust, and terror now pervaded all classes of society. Amid the general alarm it was seen how deep a hold the Lutheran teaching had gained upon the minds of men who stood highest for education, influence, and excellence of character. Positions of trust and honor were suddenly found vacant. Artisans, printers, scholars, professors in the universities, authors, and even courtiers, disappeared. Hundreds fled from Paris, self-constituted exiles from their native land, in many cases thus giving the first intimation that they favored the reformed faith. The papists looked about them in amazement at thought of the unsuspected heretics that had been tolerated among them. Their rage spent itself upon the multitudes of humbler victims who were within their power. The prisons were crowded, and the very air seemed darkened with the smoke of burning piles, kindled for the confessors of the gospel.

Francis I had gloried in being a leader in the great movement for the revival of learning which marked the opening of the sixteenth century. He had delighted to gather at his court men of letters [226/227] from every country. To his love of learning and his contempt for the ignorance and superstition of the monks was due, in part at least, the degree of toleration that had been granted to the reform. But, inspired with zeal to stamp out heresy, this patron of learning issued an edict declaring printing abolished all over France! Francis I presents one among the many examples on record showing that intellectual culture is not a safeguard against religious intolerance and persecution.

France by a solemn and public ceremony was to commit herself fully to the destruction of Protestantism. The priests demanded that the affront offered to High Heaven in the condemnation of the mass be expiated in blood, and that the king, in behalf of his people, publicly give his sanction to the dreadful work.

The 21st of January, 1535, was fixed upon for the awful ceremonial. The superstitious fears and bigoted hatred of the whole nation had been roused. Paris was thronged with the multitudes that from all the surrounding country crowded her streets. The day was to be ushered in by a vast and imposing procession. »The houses along the line of march were hung with mourning drapery, and altars rose at intervals.« Before every door was a lighted torch in honor of the »holy sacrament.« Before daybreak the procession formed at the palace of the king. »First came the banners and crosses of the several parishes; next appeared the citizens, walking two and two, and bearing torches.« The four orders of friars followed, each in its own peculiar dress. Then came a vast collection of famous relics. Following these rode lordly ecclesiastics in their purple and scarlet robes and jeweled adornings, a gorgeous and glittering array.

»The host was carried by the bishop of Paris under a magnificent canopy, ... supported by four princes of the blood. ... After the host walked the king. ... Francis I on that day wore no crown, nor robe of state.« With »head uncovered, his eyes cast on the ground, and in his hand a lighted taper,« the king of France appeared »in the character of a penitent.« Ibid., b. 13, ch. 21 At every altar he bowed down in humiliation, nor for the vices that defiled his soul, nor the innocent blood that stained his hands, but for the deadly sin of his subjects who had dared to condemn the mass. Following him came the queen and the dignitaries of state, also walking two and two, each with a lighted torch.

As a part of the services of the day the monarch himself addressed the high officials of the kingdom in the great hall of the bishop's pal-

ace. With a sorrowful countenance he appeared before

them and in words of moving eloquence bewailed »the crime, the blasphemy, the day of sorrow and disgrace,« that had come upon the nation. And he called upon every loyal subject to aid in the extirpation of the pestilent heresy that threatened France with ruin. »As true, messieurs, as I am your king,« he said, »if I knew one of my own limbs spotted or infected with this detestable rottenness, I would give it you to cut off. ... And further, if I saw one of my children defiled by it, I would not spare him. ... I would deliver him up myself, and would sacrifice him to God.« Tears choked his utterance, and the whole assembly wept, with one accord exclaiming: »We will live and die for the Catholic religion!« D'Aubigne, History of the Reform. in Europe in the Time of Calvin, b. 4, ch. 12

Terrible had become the darkness of the nation that had rejected the light of truth. The grace »that bringeth salvation« had appeared; but France, after beholding its power and holiness, after thousands had been drawn by its divine beauty, after cities and hamlets had been illuminated by its radiance, had turned away, choosing darkness rather than light. They had put from them the heavenly gift when it was offered them. They had called evil good, and good evil, till they had fallen victims to their willful self-deception. Now, though they might actually believe that they were doing God service in persecuting His people, yet their sincerity did not render them guiltless. The light that would have saved them from deception, from staining their souls with bloodguiltiness, they had willfully rejected. A solemn oath to extirpate heresy was taken in the great cathedral where, nearly three centuries later, the Goddess of Reason was to be enthroned by a nation that had forgotten the living God. Again the procession formed, and the representatives of France set out to begin the work which they had sworn to do. »At short distances scaffolds had been erected, on which certain Protestant Christians were to be burned alive, and it was arranged that the fagots should be lighted at the moment the king approached, and that the procession should halt to witness the execution.« Wylie, b. 13, ch. 21 The details of the tortures endured by these witnesses for Christ are too harrowing for recital; but there was no wavering on the part of the victims. On being urged to recant, one answered: »I only believe in what the prophets and the apostles formerly preached, and what all the company of saints believed. My faith has a confidence in God which will resist all the powers of hell.« D'Aubigne, History of the Reform. in Europe in the Time of Calvin, b. 4, ch. 12

Again and again the procession halted at the places of torture. Upon reaching their starting point at the royal palace, the crowd dispersed, and the king and the prelates withdrew, well satisfied with the day's proceedings and congratulating themselves that the work now begun would be continued to the complete destruction of heresy.

The gospel of peace which France had rejected was to be only too surely rooted out, and terrible would be the results. On the 21st of January, 1793, two hundred and fifty-eight years from the very day that fully committed France to the persecution of the Reformers, another procession, with a far different purpose, passed through the streets of Paris. »Again the king was the chief figure; again there were tumult and shouting; again there was heard the cry for more victims; again there were black scaffolds; and again the scenes of the day were closed by horrid executions; Louis XVI, struggling hand to hand with his jailers and executioners, was dragged forward to the block, and there held down by main force till the ax had fallen, and his dissevered head rolled on the scaffold.« Wylie, b. 13, ch. 21 Nor was the king the only victim; near the same spot two thousand and eight hundred human beings perished by the guillotine during the bloody days of the Reign of Terror.

The Reformation had presented to the world an open Bible, unsealing the precepts of the law of God and urging its claims upon the consciences of the people. Infinite Love had unfolded to men the statutes and principles of heaven. God had said: »Keep therefore and do them; for this is your wisdom and your understanding in the sight of the nations, which shall hear all these statutes, and say, Surely this great nation is a wise and understanding people.« Deuteronomy 4:6 When France rejected the gift of heaven, she sowed the seeds of anarchy and ruin; and the inevitable outworking of cause and effect resulted in the Revolution and the Reign of Terror.

Long before the persecution excited by the placards, the bold and ardent Farel had been forced to flee from the land of his birth. He repaired to Switzerland, and by his labors, seconding the work of Zwingli, he helped to turn the scale in favor of the Reformation. His later years were to be spent here, yet he continued to exert a decided influence upon the reform in France. During the first years of his exile, his efforts were especially directed to spreading the gospel in his native country. He spent considerable time in preaching among his countrymen near the frontier, where with tireless vigilance he watched the conflict and aided by his words of encouragement and counsel. With the assistance of other exiles, the writings of the German Reformers were translated into the French language and, together with the French Bible, were printed in large quantities. By colporteurs these works were sold extensively in France. They were furnished to the colporteurs at a low price, and thus the profits of the work enabled them to continue it.

Farel entered upon his work in Switzerland in the humble guise of a schoolmaster. Repairing to a secluded parish, he devoted himself to the instruction of children. Besides the usual branches of learning, he cautiously introduced the truths of the Bible, hoping through the children to reach the parents. There were some who believed, but the priests came forward to stop the work, and the superstitious country people were roused to oppose it. »That cannot be the gospel of Christ,« urged the priest, »seeing the preaching of it does not bring peace, but war.« Wylie, b. 14, ch. 3 Like the first disciples, when persecuted in one city he fled to another. From village to village, from city to city, he went, traveling on foot, enduring hunger, cold, and weariness, and everywhere in peril of his life. He preached in the market places, in the churches, sometimes in the pulpits of the cathedrals. Sometimes he found the church empty of hearers; at times his preaching was interrupted by shouts and jeers; again he was pulled violently out of the pulpit. More than once he was set upon by the rabble and beaten almost to death. Yet he pressed forward. Though often repulsed, with unwearying persistence he returned to the attack; and, one after another, he saw towns and cities which had been strongholds of popery, opening their gates to the gospel. The little parish where he had first labored soon accepted the reformed faith. The cities of Morat and Neuchatel also renounced the Romish rites and removed the idolatrous images from their churches.

Farel had long desired to plant the Protestant standard in Geneva. If this city could be won, it would be a center for the Reformation in France, in Switzerland, and in Italy. With this object before him, he had continued his labors until many of the surrounding towns and hamlets had been gained. Then with a single companion he entered Geneva. But only two sermons was he permitted to preach. The priests, having vainly endeavored to secure his condemnation by the civil authorities, summoned him before an ecclesiastical council, to which they came with arms concealed under their robes, determined to take his life. Outside the hall, a furious mob, with clubs and swords, was gathered to make sure of his death if he should succeed in escaping the council. The presence of magistrates and an armed force, however, saved him. Early next morning he was conducted, with his companion, across the lake to a place of safety. Thus ended his first effort to evangelize Geneva. For the next trial a lowlier instrument was chosen – a young man, so humble in appearance that he was coldly treated even by the professed friends of reform. But what could such a one do where Farel had been rejected? How could one of little courage and experience withstand the tempest before which the strongest and bravest had been forced to flee? »Not by might, nor by power, but by My Spirit, saith the Lord.« Zechariah 4:6 »God hath chosen the weak things of the world to confound the things which are mighty.« »Because the foolishness of God is wiser than men; and the weakness of God is stronger than men.« 1 Corinthians 1:27, 25

Froment began his work as a schoolmaster. The truths which he taught the children at school they repeated at their homes. Soon the parents came to hear the Bible explained, until the schoolroom was filled with attentive listeners. New Testaments and tracts were freely distributed, and they reached many who dared not come openly to listen to the new doctrines. After a time this laborer also was forced to flee; but the truths he taught had taken hold upon the minds of the people. The Reformation had been planted, and it continued to strengthen and extend. The preachers returned, and through their labors the Protestant worship was finally established in Geneva.

John Calvin (1509-1564)

The city had already declared for the Reformation when Calvin, after various wanderings and vicissitudes, entered its gates. Returning from a last visit to his birthplace, he was on his way to Basel, when, finding the direct road occupied by the armies of Charles V, he was forced to take the circuitous route by Geneva. In this visit Farel recognized the hand of God. Though Geneva had accepted the reformed faith, yet a great work remained to be accomplished here. It is not as communities but as individuals that men are converted to God; the work of regeneration must be wrought in the heart and conscience by the power of the Holy Spirit, not by the decrees of councils. While the people of Geneva had cast off the authority of Rome, they were not so ready to renounce the vices that had flourished under her rule. To establish here the pure principles of the gospel and to prepare this people to fill worthily the position to which Providence seemed calling them were not light tasks.

Farel was confident that he had found in Calvin one whom he could unite with himself in this work. In the name of God he solemnly adjured the young evangelist to remain and labor here. Calvin drew back in alarm. Timid and peace-loving, he shrank from contact with the bold, independent, and even violent spirit of the Genevese. The feebleness of his health, together with his studious habits, led him to seek retirement. Believing that by his pen he could best serve the cause of reform, he desired to find a quiet retreat for study, and there, through the press, instruct and build up the churches. But Farel's solemn admonition came to him as a call from Heaven, and he dared not refuse. It seemed to him, he said, "that the hand of God was stretched down from heaven, that it lay hold of him, and fixed him irrevocably to the place he was so impatient to leave.« D'Aubigne, History of the Reform. in Europe in the Time of Calvin, b. 9, ch. 17 At this time great perils surrounded the Protestant cause. The anathemas of the pope thundered against Geneva, and mighty nations threatened it with destruction. How was this little city to resist the powerful hierarchy that had so often forced kings and emperors to submission? How could it stand against the armies of the world's great conquerors?

Throughout Christendom, Protestantism was menaced by formidable foes. The first triumphs of the Reformation past, Rome summoned new forces, hoping to accomplish its destruction. At this time the order of the Jesuits was created, the most cruel, unscrupulous, and powerful of all the champions of popery. Cut off from earthly ties and human interests, dead to the claims of natural affection, reason and conscience wholly silenced, they knew no rule, no tie, but that of their order, and no duty but to extend its power. see Appendix The gospel of Christ had enabled its adherents to meet danger and endure suffering, undismayed by cold, hunger, toil, and poverty, to uphold the banner of truth in face of the rack, the dungeon, and the stake. To combat these forces, Jesuitism inspired its followers with a fanaticism that enabled them to endure like dangers, and to oppose to the power of truth all the weapons of deception. There was no crime too great for them to commit, no deception too base for them to practice, no disguise too difficult for them to assume. Vowed to perpetual poverty and humility, it was their studied aim to secure wealth and power, to be devoted to the overthrow of Protestantism, and the re-establishment of the papal supremacy.

When appearing as members of their order, they wore a garb of sanctity, visiting prisons and hospitals, ministering to the sick and the poor, professing to have renounced the world, and bearing the sacred name of Jesus, who went about doing good. But under this blameless exterior the most criminal and deadly purposes were often concealed. It was a fundamental principle of the order that the end justifies the means. By this code, lying, theft, perjury, assassination, were not only pardonable but commendable, when they served the interests of the church. Under various disguises the Jesuits worked their way into offices of state, climbing up to be the counselors of kings, and shaping the policy of nations. They became servants to act as spies upon their masters. They established colleges for the sons of princes and nobles, and schools for the common people; and the children of Protestant parents were drawn into an observance of popish rites. All the outward pomp and display of the Romish worship was brought to bear to confuse the mind and dazzle and captivate the imagination, and thus the liberty for which the fathers had toiled and bled was betrayed by the sons. The Jesuits rapidly spread themselves over Europe, and wherever they went, there followed a revival of popery.

To give them greater power, a bull was issued re-establishing the inquisition. see Appendix Notwithstanding the general abhorrence with which it was regarded, even in Catholic countries, this terrible tribunal was again set up by popish rulers, and atrocities too terrible to bear the light of day were repeated in its secret dungeons. In many countries, thousands upon thousands of the very flower of the nation, the purest and noblest, the most intellectual and highly educated, pious and devoted pastors, industrious and patriotic citizens, brilliant scholars, talented artists, skillful artisans, were slain or forced to flee to other lands. Such were the means which Rome had invoked to quench the light of the Reformation, to withdraw from men the Bible, and to restore the ignorance and superstition of the Dark Ages. But under God's blessing and the labors of those noble men whom He had raised up to succeed Luther, Protestantism was not overthrown. Not to the favor or arms of princes was it to owe its strength. The smallest countries, the humblest and least powerful

 nations, became its strongholds. It was little Geneva in

John Knox (1514-1572)

Faber Stapulensis (1450-1536)

the midst of mighty foes plotting her destruction; it was Holland on her sandbanks by the northern sea, wrestling against the tyranny of Spain, then the greatest and most opulent of kingdoms; it was bleak, sterile Sweden, that gained victories for the Reformation.

For nearly thirty years Calvin labored at Geneva, first to establish there a church adhering to the morality of the Bible, and then for the advancement of the Reformation throughout Europe. His course as a public leader was not faultless, nor were his doctrines free from error. But he was instrumental in promulgating truths that were of special importance in his time, in maintaining the principles of Protestantism against the fast-returning tide of popery, and in promoting in the reformed churches simplicity and purity of life, in place of the pride and corruption fostered under the Romish teaching.

From Geneva, publications and teachers went out to spread the reformed doctrines. To this point the persecuted of all lands looked for instruction, counsel, and encouragement. The city of Calvin became a refuge for the hunted Reformers of all Western Europe. Fleeing from the awful tempests that continued for centuries, the fugitives came to the gates of Geneva. Starving, wounded, bereft of home and kindred, they were warmly welcomed and tenderly cared for; and finding a home here, they blessed thc city of their adoption by their skill, their learning, and their piety. Many who sought here a refuge returned to their own countries to resist the tyranny of Rome. John Knox, the brave Scotch Reformer, not a few of the English Puritans, the Protestants of Holland and of Spain, and the Huguenots of France carried from Geneva the torch of truth to lighten the darkness of their native lands.

CHAPTER 13

THE NETHERLANDS AND SCANDINAVIA

In The Netherlands the papal tyranny very early called forth resolute protest. Seven hundred years before Luther's time the Roman pontiff was thus fearlessly impeached by two bishops, who, having been sent on an embassy to Rome, had learned the true character of the »holy see«: God »has made His queen and spouse, the church, a noble and everlasting provision for her family, with a dowry that is neither fading nor corruptible, and given her an eternal crown and scepter; ... all which benefits you like a thief intercept. You set up yourself in the temple of God; instead of a pastor, you are become a wolf to the sheep; ... you would make us believe you are a supreme bishop, but you rather behave like a tyrant. ... Whereas you ought to be a servant of servants, as you call yourself, you endeavor to become a lord of lords. ... You bring the commands of God into contempt. ... The Holy Ghost is the builder of all churches as far as the earth extends. ... The city of our God, of which we are the citizens, reaches to all the regions of the heavens; and it is greater than the city, by the holy prophets named Babylon, which pretends to be divine, wins herself to heaven, and brags that her wisdom is immortal; and finally, though without reason, that she never did err, nor ever can.« Gerard Brandt, History of the Reformation in and About the Low Countries 1:6

Others arose from century to century to echo this protest. And those early teachers who, traversing different lands and known by various names, bore the character of the Vaudois missionaries, and spread everywhere the knowledge of the gospel, penetrated to the Netherlands. Their doctrines spread rapidly. The Waldensian Bible they translated in verse into the Dutch language. They declared »that there was great advantage in it; no jests, no fables, no trifles, no deceits, but the words of truth; that indeed there was here and there a hard crust, but that the marrow and sweetness of what was good and holy might be easily discovered in it.« Ibid. 1:14 Thus wrote the friends of the ancient faith, in the twelfth century.

 Now began the Romish persecutions; but in the midst

of fagots and torture the believers continued to multiply, steadfastly declaring that the Bible is the only infallible authority in religion, and that »no man should be coerced to believe, but should be won by preaching.« Martyn 2:87

The teachings of Luther found a congenial soil in the Netherlands, and earnest and faithful men arose to preach the gospel. From one of the provinces of Holland came Menno Simons. Educated a Roman Catholic and ordained to the priesthood, he was wholly ignorant of the Bible, and he would not read it for fear of being beguiled into heresy. When a doubt concerning the doctrine of transubstantiation forced itself upon him, he regarded it as a temptation from Satan, and by prayer and confession sought to free himself from it; but in vain. By mingling in scenes of dissipation he endeavored to silence the accusing voice of conscience; but without avail. After a time he was led to the study of the New Testament, and this, with Luther's writings, caused him to accept the reformed faith. He soon after witnessed in a neighboring village the beheading of a man who was put to death for having been rebaptized. This led him to study the Bible in regard to infant baptism. He could find no evidence for it in the Scriptures, but saw that repentance and faith are everywhere required as the condition of receiving baptism.

Menno withdrew from the Roman Church and devoted his life to teaching the truths which he had received. In both Germany and the Netherlands a class of fanatics had risen, advocating absurd and seditious doctrines, outraging order and decency, and proceeding to violence and insurrection. Menno saw the horrible results to which these movements would inevitably lead, and he strenuously opposed the erroneous teachings and wild schemes of the fanatics. There were many, however, who had been misled by these fanatics, but who had renounced their pernicious doctrines; and there were still remaining many descendants of the ancient Christians, the fruits of the Waldensian teaching. Among these classes Menno labored with great zeal and success. For twenty-five years he traveled, with his wife and children, enduring great hardships and privations, and frequently in peril of his life. He traversed the Netherlands and northern Germany, laboring chiefly among the humbler classes but exerting a widespread influence. Naturally eloquent, though possessing a limited education, he was a man of unwavering integrity, of humble spirit and gentle manners, and of sincere and earnest piety, exemplifying in his own life the precepts which he taught, and he commanded the confidence of the people. His followers were scattered and oppressed. They suffered greatly from being confounded with the fanatical Munsterites. Yet great numbers were converted under his labors.

Nowhere were the reformed doctrines more generally received than in the Netherlands. In few countries did their adherents endure more terrible persecution. In Germany Charles V had banned the Reformation, and he would gladly have brought all its adherents to the stake; but the princes stood up as a barrier against his tyranny. In the Netherlands his power was greater, and persecuting edicts followed each other in quick succession. To read the Bible, to hear or preach it, or even to speak concerning it, was to incur the penalty of death by the stake. To pray to God in secret, to refrain from bowing to an image, or to sing a psalm, was also punishable with death. Even those who should abjure their errors were condemned, if men, to die by the sword; if women, to be buried alive. Thousands perished under the reign of Charles and of Philip II.

At one time a whole family was brought before the inquisitors, charged with remaining away from mass and worshiping at home. On his examination as to their practices in secret the youngest son answered: »We fall on our knees, and pray that God may enlighten our minds and pardon our sins; we pray for our sovereign, that his reign may be prosperous and his life happy; we pray for our magistrates, that God may preserve them.« Wylie, b. 18, ch. 6 Some of the judges were deeply moved, yet the father and one of his sons were condemned to the stake. The rage of the persecutors was equaled by the faith of the martyrs. Not only men but delicate women and young maidens displayed unflinching courage. »Wives would take their stand by their husband's stake, and while he was enduring the fire they would whisper words of solace, or sing psalms to cheer him.« »Young maidens would lie down in their living grave as if they were entering into their chamber of nightly sleep; or go forth to the scaffold and the fire, dressed in their best apparel, as if they were going to their marriage.« Ibid., b. 18, ch. 6 As in the days when paganism sought to destroy the gospel, the blood of the Christians was seed. see Tertullian, Apology, § 50 Persecution served to increase the number of witnesses for the truth. Year after year the monarch, stung to madness by the unconquerable

 determination of the people, urged on his cruel work;

but in vain. Under the noble William of Orange the Revolution at last brought to Holland freedom to worship God.

In the mountains of Piedmont, on the plains of France and the shores of Holland, the progress of the gospel was marked with the blood of its disciples. But in the countries of the North it found a peaceful entrance. Students at Wittenberg, returning to their homes, carried the reformed faith to Scandinavia. The publication of Luther's writings also spread the light. The simple, hardy people of the North turned from the corruption, the pomp, and the superstitions of Rome, to welcome the purity, the simplicity, and the life-giving truths of the Bible.

Tausen, »the Reformer of Denmark,« was a peasant's son. The boy early gave evidence of vigorous intellect; he thirsted for an education; but this was denied him by the circumstances of his parents, and he entered a cloister. Here the purity of his life, together with his diligence and fidelity, won the favor of his superior. Examination showed him to

Burning of Anabaptists in the 16th century

possess talent that promised at some future day good service to the church. It was determined to give him an education at some one of the universities of Germany or the Netherlands. The young student was granted permission to choose a school for himself, with one proviso, that he must not go to Wittenberg. The scholar of the church was not to be endangered by the poison of heresy. So said the friars.

Tausen went to Cologne, which was then, as now, one of the strongholds of Romanism. Here he soon became disgusted with the mysticisms of the schoolmen. About the same time he obtained Luther's writings. He read them with wonder and delight, and greatly desired to enjoy the personal instruction of the Reformer. But to do so he must risk giving offense to his monastic superior and forfeiting his support. His decision was soon made, and erelong he was enrolled as a student at Wittenberg.

On returning to Denmark, he again repaired to his cloister. No one as yet suspected him of Lutheranism; he did not reveal his secret, but endeavored, without exciting the prejudices of his companions, to lead them to a purer faith and a holier life. He opened the Bible, and explained its true meaning, and at last preached Christ to them as the sinner's righteousness and his only hope of salvation. Great was the wrath of the prior, who had built high hopes upon him as a valiant defender of Rome. He was at once removed from his own monastery to another and confined to his cell under strict supervision.

To the terror of his new guardians several of the monks soon declared themselves converts to Protestantism. Through the bars of his cell Tausen had communicated to his companions a knowledge of the truth. Had those Danish fathers been skilled in the church's plan of dealing with heresy, Tausen's voice would never again have been heard; but instead of consigning him to a tomb in some underground dungeon, they expelled him from the monastery. Now they were powerless. A royal edict, just issued, offered protection to the teachers of the new doctrine. Tausen began to preach. The churches were opened to him, and the people thronged to listen. Others also were preaching the word of God. The New Testament, translated into the Danish tongue, was widely circulated. The efforts made by the papists to overthrow the work resulted in extending it, and erelong Denmark declared its acceptance of the reformed faith.

In Sweden, also, young men who had drunk from the well of Wittenberg carried the water of life to their countrymen. Two of the leaders in the Swedish Reformation, Olaf and Laurentius Petri, the sons of a blacksmith of Orebro, studied under Luther and Melanchthon, and the truths which they thus learned they were diligent to teach. Like the great Reformer, Olaf aroused the people by his zeal and eloquence, while Laurentius, like Melanchthon, was learned, thoughtful, and calm. Both were men of ardent piety, of high theological attainments, and of unflinching courage in advancing the truth. Papist opposition was not lacking. The Catholic priest stirred up the ignorant and superstitious people. Olaf Petri was often assailed by the mob, and upon several occasions barely escaped with his life. These Reformers were, however, favored and protected by the king.

Under the rule of the Roman Church the people were sunken in poverty and ground down by oppression. They were destitute of the Scriptures; and having a religion of mere signs and ceremonies, which conveyed no light to the mind, they were returning to the superstitious beliefs and pagan practices of their heathen ancestors. The nation was divided into contending factions, whose perpetual strife increased the misery of all. The king determined upon a reformation in the state and the church, and he welcomed these able assistants in the battle against Rome. In the presence of the monarch and the leading men of Sweden, Olaf Petri with great ability defended the doctrines of the reformed faith against the Romish champions. He declared that the teachings of the Fathers are to be received only when in accordance with the Scriptures; that the essential doctrines of the faith are presented in the Bible in a clear and simple manner, so that all men may understand them. Christ said, »My doctrine is not Mine, but His that sent Me«; John 7:16 and Paul declared that should he preach any other gospel than that which he had received, he would be accursed. Galatians 1:8 »How, then,« said the Reformer, »shall others presume to enact dogmas at their pleasure, and impose them as things necessary to salvation?« Wylie, b. 10, ch. 4 He showed that the decrees of the church are of no authority when in opposition to the commands of God, and maintained the great Protestant principle that »the Bible and the Bible only« is the rule of faith and practice.

This contest, though conducted upon a stage comparatively obscure, serves to show us »the sort of men that formed the rank and file of the army of the Reformers. They were not illiterate, sectarian, noisy controversialists – far from it; they were men who had studied the word of God, and knew well how to wield the weapons with which the armory of the Bible supplied them. In respect of erudition they were ahead of their age. When we confine our attention to such brilliant centers as Wittenberg and Zurich, and to such illustrious names as those of Luther and Melanchthon, of Zwingli and Oecolampadius, we are apt to be told, these were the leaders of the movement, and we should naturally expect in them prodigious power and vast acquisitions; but the subordinates were not like these. Well, we turn to the obscure theater of Sweden, and the humble names of Olaf and Laurentius Petri - from the masters to the disciples – what do we find? ... Scholars and theologians; men who have thoroughly mastered the whole system of gospel truth, and who win an easy victory over the sophists of the schools and the dignitaries of Rome.« Ibid., b. 10, ch. 4

As the result of this disputation the king of Sweden accepted the Protestant faith, and not long afterward the national assembly declared in its favor. The New Testament had been translated by Olaf Petri into the Swedish language, and at the desire of the king the two brothers undertook the translation of the whole Bible. Thus for the first time the people of Sweden received the word of God in their native tongue. It was ordered by the Diet that throughout the kingdom, ministers should explain the Scriptures and that the children in the schools should be taught to read the Bible.

Steadily and surely the darkness of ignorance and superstition was dispelled by the blessed light of the gospel. Freed from Romish oppression, the nation attained to a strength and greatness it had never before reached. Sweden became one of the bulwarks of Protestantism. A century later, at a time of sorest peril, this small and hitherto feeble nation – the only one in Europe that dared lend a helping hand – came to the deliverance of Germany in the terrible struggle of the Thirty Years' War. All Northern Europe seemed about to be brought again under the tyranny of Rome. It was the armies of Sweden that enabled Germany to turn the tide of popish success, to win toleration for the Protestants, - Calvinists as well as Lutherans, - and to restore liberty of conscience to those countries that had accepted the Reformation.

CHAPTER 14

LATER ENGLISH REFORMERS

While Luther was opening a closed Bible to the people of Germany, Tyndale was impelled by the Spirit of God to do the same for England. Wycliffe's Bible had been translated from the Latin text, which contained many errors. It had never been printed, and the cost of manuscript copies was so great that few but wealthy men or nobles could procure it; and, furthermore, being strictly proscribed by the church, it had had a comparatively narrow circulation. In 1516, a year before the appearance of Luther's theses, Erasmus had published his Greek and Latin version of the New Testament. Now for the first time the word of God was printed in the original tongue. In this work many errors of former versions were corrected, and the sense was more clearly rendered. It led many among the educated classes to a better knowledge of the truth, and gave a new impetus to the work of reform. But the common people were still, to a great extent, debarred from God's word. Tyndale was to complete the work of Wycliffe in giving the Bible to his countrymen.

A diligent student and an earnest seeker for truth, he had received the gospel from the Greek Testament of Erasmus. He fearlessly preached his convictions, urging that all doctrines be tested by the Scriptures. To the papist claim that the church had given the Bible, and the church alone could explain it, Tyndale responded: »Do you know who taught the eagles to find their prey? Well, that same God teaches His hungry children to find their Father in His word. Far from having given us the Scriptures, it is you who have hidden them from us; it is you who burn those who teach them, and if you could, you would burn the Scriptures themselves.« D'Aubigne, History of the Reformation of the Sixteenth Century, b. 18, ch. 4

Tyndale's preaching excited great interest; many accepted the truth. But the priests were on the alert, and no sooner had he left the field than they by their threats and misrepresentations endeavored to destroy his work. Too often they succeeded. »What is to be done?« he exclaimed. »While I am sowing in one place, the en- [245/246] emy ravages the field I have just left. I cannot be everywhere. Oh! if Christians possessed the Holy Scriptures in their own tongue, they could of themselves withstand these sophists. Without the Bible it is impossible to establish the laity in the truth.« Ibid., b. 18, ch. 4

A new purpose now took possession of his mind. »It was in the language of Israel,« said he, »that the psalms were sung in the temple of Jehovah; and shall not the gospel speak the language of England among us? ... Ought the church to have less light at noonday than at the dawn? ... Christians must read the New Testament in their mother tongue.« The doctors and teachers of the church disagreed among themselves. Only by the Bible could men arrive at the truth. »One holdeth this doctor, another that. ... Now each of these authors contradicts the other. How then can we distinguish him who says right from him who says wrong? ... How? ... Verily by God's word.« Ibid., b. 18, ch. 4

It was not long after that a learned Catholic doctor, engaging in controversy with him, exclaimed: »We were better to be without God's laws than the pope's.« Tyndale replied: »I defy the pope and all his laws; and if God spare my life, ere many years I will cause a boy that driveth the plow to know more of the Scripture than you do.« Anderson, Annals of the English Bible, p. 19

The purpose which he had begun to cherish, of giving to the people the New Testament Scriptures in their own language, was now confirmed, and he immediately applied himself to the work. Driven from his home by persecution, he went to London, and there for a time pursued his labors undisturbed. But again the violence of the papists forced him to flee. All England seemed closed against him, and he resolved to seek shelter in Germany. Here he began the printing of the English New Testament. Twice the work was stopped; but when forbidden to print in one city, he went to another. At last he made his way to Worms, where, a few years before, Luther had defended the gospel before the Diet. In that ancient city were many friends of the Reformation, and Tyndale there prosecuted his work without further hindrance. Three thousand copies of the New Testament were soon finished, and another edition followed in the same year.

With great earnestness and perseverance he continued his labors. Notwithstanding the English authorities had guarded their ports with the strictest vigilance, the word of God was in various ways secretly conveyed to London and thence circulated throughout the country. The papists attempted to suppress the truth, but in vain. The bishop of Durham at one time bought of a bookseller who was a friend of Tyndale his whole stock of Bibles, for the purpose of destroying them, supposing that this would greatly hinder the work. But, on the contrary, the money thus furnished, purchased material for a new and better edition, which, but for this, could not have been published. When Tyndale was afterward made a prisoner, his liberty was offered him on condition that he would reveal the names of those who had helped him meet the expense of printing his Bibles. He replied that the bishop of Durham had done more than any other person; for by paying a large price for the books left on hand, he had enabled him to go on with good courage.

Tyndale was betrayed into the hands of his enemies, and at one time suffered imprisonment for many months. He finally witnessed for his faith by a martyr's death; but the weapons which he prepared have enabled other soldiers to do battle through all the centuries even to our time. Latimer maintained from the pulpit that the Bible ought to be read in the language of the people. The Author of Holy Scripture, said he, »is God Himself;« and this Scripture partakes of the might and eternity of its Author. »There is no king, emperor, magistrate, and ruler ... but are bound to obey ... His holy word.« »Let us not take any bywalks, but let God's word direct us: let us not walk after ... our forefathers, nor seek not what they did, but what they should have done.« Hugh Latimer, »First Sermon Preached Before King Edward VI.«

Barnes and Frith, the faithful friends of Tyndale, arose to defend the truth. The Ridleys and Cranmer followed. These leaders in the English Reformation were men of learning, and most of them had been highly esteemed for zeal or piety in the Romish communion. Their opposition to the papacy was the result of their knowledge of the errors of the »holy see.« Their acquaintance with the mysteries of Babylon gave greater power to their testimonies against her. »Now I would ask a strange question,« said Latimer. »Who is the most diligent bishop and prelate in all England? ... I see you listening and hearkening that I should name him. ... I will tell you: it is the devil. ... He is never out of his diocese; call for him when you will, he is ever at home; ... he is ever at his plow. ... Ye shall never find him idle, I warrant you. ... Where the devil is resident, ... there away with books, and up with candles; away with Bibles, and up with beads; away with the light of the gospel, and up with the light of candles, yea, at noondays; ... down with Christ's cross, up with purgatory pickpurse; ... away with cloth- [247/248] ing the naked, the poor, and impotent, up with decking of images and gay garnishing of stocks and stones; up with man's traditions and his laws, down with God's traditions and His most holy word. ... O that our prelates would be as diligent to sow the corn of good doctrine, as Satan is to sow cockle and darnel!« Ibid., »Sermon of the Plough.«

The grand principle maintained by these Reformers – the same that had been held by the Waldenses, by Wycliffe, by John Huss, by Luther, Zwingli, and those who united with them – was the infallible authority of the Holy Scriptures as a rule of faith and practice. They denied the right of popes, councils, Fathers, and kings, to control the conscience in matters of religion. The Bible was their authority, and by its teaching they tested all doctrines and all claims. Faith in God and His word sustained these holy men as they yielded up their lives at the stake. »Be of good comfort,« exclaimed Latimer to his fellow martyr as the flames were about to silence their voices, »we shall this day light such a candle, by God's grace, in England, as I trust shall never be put out.« Works of Hugh Latimer 1:8

In Scotland the seeds of truth scattered by Columba and his colaborers had never been wholly destroyed. For hundreds of years after the churches of England submitted to Rome, those of Scotland maintained their freedom. In the twelfth century, however, popery became established here, and in no country did it exercise a more absolute sway. Nowhere was the darkness deeper. Still there came rays of light to pierce the gloom and give promise of the coming day. The Lollards, coming from England with the Bible and the teachings of Wycliffe, did much to preserve the knowledge of the gospel, and every century had its witnesses and martyrs.

With the opening of the Great Reformation came the writings of Luther, and then Tyndale's English New Testament. Unnoticed by the hierarchy, these messengers silently traversed the mountains and valleys, kindling into new life the torch of truth so nearly extinguished in Scotland, and undoing the work which Rome for four centuries of oppression had done. Then the blood of martyrs gave fresh impetus to the movement. The papist leaders, suddenly awakening to the danger that threatened their cause, brought to the stake some of the noblest and most honored of the sons of Scotland. They did but erect a pulpit, from which the words of these dying witnesses were heard throughout the land, thrilling the souls of the people with an undying purpose to

 cast off the shackles of Rome. Hamilton and Wishart,

princely in character as in birth, with a long line of humbler disciples, yielded up their lives at the stake. But from the burning pile of Wishart there came one whom the flames were not to silence, one who under God was to strike the death knell of popery in Scotland.

John Knox had turned away from the traditions and mysticisms of the church, to feed upon the truths of God's word; and the teaching of Wishart had confirmed his determination to forsake the communion of Rome and join himself to the persecuted Reformers.

Urged by his companions to take the office of preacher, he shrank with trembling from its responsibility, and it was only after days of seclusion and painful conflict with himself that he consented. But having once accepted the position, he pressed forward with inflexible determination and undaunted courage as long as life continued. This truehearted Reformer feared not the face of man. The fires of martyrdom, blazing around him, served only to quicken his zeal to greater intensity. With the tyrant's ax held menacingly over his head, he stood his ground, striking sturdy blows on the right hand and on the left to demolish idolatry.

When brought face to face with the queen of Scotland, in whose presence the zeal of many a leader of the Protestants had abated, John Knox bore unswerving witness for the truth. He was not to be won by caresses; he quailed not before threats. The queen charged him with heresy. He had taught the people to receive a religion prohibited by the state, she declared, and had thus transgressed God's command enjoining subjects to obey their princes. Knox answered firmly: »As right religion took neither original strength nor authority from worldly princes, but from the eternal God alone, so are not subjects bound to frame their religion according to the appetites of their princes. For oft it is that princes are the most ignorant of all others in God's true religion. ... If all the seed of Abraham had been of the religion of Pharaoh, whose subjects they long were, I pray you, madam, what religion would there have been in the world? Or if all men in the days of the apostles had been of the religion of the Roman emperors, what religion would there have been upon the face of the earth? ... And so, madam, ye may perceive that subjects are not bound to the religion of their princes, albeit they are commanded to give them obedience.« Said Mary: »Ye interpret the Scriptures in one manner, and they [the Roman Catholic teachers] interpret in another; whom shall I believe, and who shall be judge?« »Ye shall believe God, that plainly speaketh in His word,« answered the Reformer; »and farther than the word teaches you, ye neither shall believe the one nor the other. The word of God is plain in itself; and if there appear any obscurity in one place, the Holy Ghost, which is never contrary to Himself, explains the same more clearly in other places, so that there can remain no doubt but unto such as obstinately remain ignorant.« David Laing, The Collected Works of John Knox, vol. 2, pp. 281, 284

Such were the truths that the fearless Reformer, at the peril of his life, spoke in the ear of royalty. With the same undaunted courage he kept to his purpose, praying and fighting the battles of the Lord, until Scotland was free from popery.

In England the establishment of Protestantism as the national religion diminished, but did not wholly stop, persecution. While many of the doctrines of Rome had been renounced, not a few of its forms were retained. The supremacy of the pope was rejected, but in his place the monarch was enthroned as the head of the church. In the service of the church there was still a wide departure from the purity and simplicity of the gospel. The great principle of religious liberty was not yet understood. Though the horrible cruelties which Rome employed against heresy were resorted to but rarely by Protestant rulers, yet the right of every man to worship God according to the dictates of his own conscience was not acknowledged. All were required to accept the doctrines and observe the forms of worship prescribed by the established church. Dissenters suffered persecution, to a greater or less extent, for hundreds of years.

In the seventeenth century thousands of pastors were expelled from their positions. The people were forbidden, on pain of heavy fines, imprisonment, and banishment, to attend any religious meetings except such as were sanctioned by the church. Those faithful souls who could not refrain from gathering to worship God were compelled to meet in dark alleys, in obscure garrets, and at some seasons in the woods at midnight. In the sheltering depths of the forest, a temple of God's own building, those scattered and persecuted children of the Lord assembled to pour out their souls in prayer and praise. But despite all their precautions, many suffered for their faith. The jails were crowded. Families were broken up. Many were banished to foreign lands. Yet God was with His people, and persecution could not prevail to silence their testimony. Many were

driven across the ocean to America and here laid the

foundations of civil and religious liberty which have been the bulwark and glory of this country.

Again, as in apostolic days, persecution turned out to the furtherance of the gospel. In a loathsome dungeon crowded with profligates and felons, John Bunyan breathed the very atmosphere of heaven; and there he wrote his wonderful allegory of the pilgrim's journey from the land of destruction to the celestial city. For over two hundred years that voice from Bedford jail has spoken with thrilling power to the hearts of men. Bunyan's Pilgrim's Progress and Grace Abounding to the Chief of Sinners have guided many feet into the path of life.

Baxter, Flavel, Alleine, and other men of talent, education, and deep Christian experience stood up in valiant defense of the faith which was once delivered to the saints. The work accomplished by these men, proscribed and outlawed by the rulers of this world, can never perish. Flavel's Fountain of Life and Method of Grace have taught thousands how to commit the keeping of their souls to Christ. Baxter's Reformed Pastor has proved a blessing to many who desire a revival of the work of God, and his Saints' Everlasting Rest has done its work in leading souls to the »rest« that remaineth for the people of God.

A hundred years later, in a day of great spiritual darkness, Whitefield and the Wesleys appeared as light bearers for God. Under the rule of the established church the people of England had lapsed into a state of religious declension hardly to be distinguished from heathenism. Natural religion was the favorite study of the clergy, and included most of their theology. The higher classes sneered at piety, and prided themselves on being above what they called its fanaticism. The lower classes were grossly ignorant and abandoned to vice, while the church had no courage or faith any longer to support the downfallen cause of truth. The great doctrine of justification by faith, so clearly taught by Luther, had been almost wholly lost sight of; and the Romish principle of trusting to good works for salvation, had taken its placc. Whitefield and the Wesleys, who were members of the established church, were sincere seekers for the favor of God, and this they had been taught was to be secured by a virtuous life and an observance of the ordinances of religion.

When Charles Wesley at one time fell ill, and anticipated that death was approaching, he was asked upon what he rested his hope of eternal life. His answer was: »I have used my best [252/253] endeavors to serve God.« As the friend who had put the question seemed not to be fully satisfied with his answer, Wesley thought: »What! are not my endeavors a sufficient ground of hope? Would he rob me of my endeavors? I have nothing else to trust to.« John Whitehead, Life of the Rev. Charles Wesley, p. 102 Such was the dense darkness that had settled down on the church, hiding the atonement, robbing Christ of His glory, and turning the minds of men from their only hope of salvation - the blood of the crucified Redeemer. Wesley and his associates were led to see that true religion is seated in the heart, and that God's law extends to the thoughts as well as to the words and actions. Convinced of the necessity of holiness of heart, as well as correctness of outward deportment, they set out in earnest upon a new life. By the most diligent and prayerful efforts they endeavored to subdue the evils of the natural heart. They lived a life of self-denial, charity, and humiliation, observing with great rigor and exactness every measure which they thought could be helpful to them in obtaining what they most desired – that holiness which could secure the favor of God. But they did not obtain the object which they sought. In vain were their endeavors to free themselves from the condemnation of sin or to break its power. It was the same struggle which Luther had experienced in his cell at Erfurt. It was the same question which had tortured his soul – »How should man be just before God?« Job 9:2

The fires of divine truth, well-nigh extinguished upon the altars of Protestantism, were to be rekindled from the ancient torch handed down the ages by the Bohemian Christians. After the Reformation, Protestantism in Bohemia had been trampled out by the hordes of Rome. All who refused to renounce the truth were forced to flee. Some of these, finding refuge in Saxony, there maintained the ancient faith. It was from the descendants of these Christians that light came to Wesley and his associates.

John and Charles Wesley, after being ordained to the ministry, were sent on a mission to America. On board the ship was a company of Moravians. Violent storms were encountered on the passage, and John Wesley, brought face to face with death, felt that he had not the assurance of peace with God. The Germans, on the contrary, manifested a calmness and trust to which he was a stranger.

»I had long before,« he says, »observed the great seriousness of their behavior. Of their humility they had given a continual proof,
 by performing those servile offices for the other pas-

sengers which none of the English would undertake; for which they desired and would receive no pay, saying it was good for their proud hearts, and their loving Saviour had done more for them. And every day had given them occasion of showing a meekness which no injury could move. If they were pushed, struck, or thrown about, they rose again and went away; but no complaint was found in their mouth. There was now an opportunity of trying whether they were delivered from the spirit of fear, as well as from that of pride, anger, and revenge. In the midst of the psalm wherewith their service began, the sea broke over, split the mainsail in pieces, covered the ship, and poured in between the decks as if the great deep had already swallowed us up. A terrible screaming began among the English. The Germans calmly sang on. I asked one of them afterwards, 'Were you not afraid?' He answered, 'I thank God, no.' I asked, 'But were not your women and children afraid?' He replied mildly, 'No; our women and children are not afraid to die.'« Whitehead, Life of the Rev. John Wesley, p. 10

Upon arriving in Savannah, Wesley for a short time abode with the Moravians, and was deeply impressed with their Christian deportment. Of one of their religious services, in striking contrast to the lifeless formalism of the Church of England, he wrote: »The great simplicity as well as solemnity of the whole almost made me forget the seventeen hundred years between, and imagine myself in one of those assemblies where form and state were not; but Paul, the tentmaker, or Peter, the fisherman, presided; yet with the demonstration of the Spirit and of power.« Ibid., pp. 11,12 On his return to England, Wesley, under the instruction of a Moravian preacher, arrived at a clearer understanding of Bible faith. He was convinced that he must renounce all dependence upon his own works for salvation and must trust wholly to »the Lamb of God, which taketh away the sin of the world.« At a meeting of the Moravian society in London a statement was read from Luther, describing the change which the Spirit of God works in the heart of the believer. As Wesley listened, faith was kindled in his soul. »I felt my heart strangely warmed,« he says. »I felt I did trust in Christ, Christ alone, for salvation: and an assurance was given me, that He had taken away my sins, even mine, and saved me from the law of sin and death.« Ibid., p. 52

Through long years of wearisome and comfortless striving - years of rigorous self-denial, of reproach and humiliation – Wesley had steadfastly adhered to his one purpose of seeking God. [255/256]

Now he had found Him; and he found that the grace which he had toiled to win by prayers and fasts, by almsdeeds and self-abnegation, was a gift, »without money and without price.«

Once established in the faith of Christ, his whole soul burned with the desire to spread everywhere a knowledge of the glorious gospel of God's free grace. »I look upon all the world as my parish,« he said; »in whatever part of it I am, I judge it meet, right, and my bounden duty, to declare unto all that are willing to hear, the glad tidings of salvation.« Ibid., p. 74

He continued his strict and self-denying life, not now as the ground, but the result of faith; not the root, but the fruit of holiness. The grace of God in Christ is the foundation of the Christian's hope, and that grace will be manifested in obedience. Wesley's life was devoted to the preaching of the great truths which he had received – justification through faith in the atoning blood of Christ, and the renewing power of the Holy Spirit upon the heart, bringing forth fruit in a life conformed to the example of Christ.

Whitefield and the Wesleys had been prepared for their work by long and sharp personal convictions of their own lost condition; and that they might be able to endure hardness as good soldiers of Christ, they had been subjected to the fiery ordeal of scorn, derision, and persecution, both in the university and as they were entering the ministry. They and a few others who sympathized with them were contemptuously called Methodists by their ungodly fellow students – a name which is at the present time regarded as honorable by one of the largest denominations in England and America. As members of the Church of England they were strongly attached to her forms of worship, but the Lord had presented before them in His word a higher standard. The Holy Spirit urged them to preach Christ and Him crucified. The power of the Highest attended their labors. Thousands were convicted and truly converted. It was necessary that these sheep be protected from ravening wolves. Wesley had no thought of forming a new denomination, but he organized them under what was called the Methodist Connection.

Mysterious and trying was the opposition which these preachers encountered from the established church; yet God, in His wisdom, had overruled events to cause the reform to begin within the church itself. Had it come wholly from without, it would not have

 penetrated where it was so much needed. But as the

revival preachers were churchmen, and labored within the pale of the church wherever they could find opportunity, the truth had an entrance where the doors would otherwise have remained closed. Some of the clergy were roused from their moral stupor and became zealous preachers in their own parishes. Churches that had been petrified by formalism were quickened into life.

In Wesley's time, as in all ages of the church's history, men of different gifts performed their appointed work. They did not harmonize upon every point of doctrine, but all were moved by the Spirit of God, and united in the absorbing aim to win souls to Christ. The differences between Whitefield and the Wesleys threatened at one time to create alienation; but as they learned meekness in the school of Christ, mutual forbearance and charity reconciled them. They had no time to dispute, while error and iniquity were teeming everywhere, and sinners were going down to ruin.

The servants of God trod a rugged path. Men of influence and learning employed their powers against them. After a time many of the clergy manifested determined hostility, and the doors of the churches were closed against a pure faith and those who proclaimed it. The course of the clergy in denouncing them from the pulpit aroused the elements of darkness, ignorance, and iniquity. Again and again did John Wesley escape death by a miracle of God's mercy. When the rage of the mob was excited against him, and there seemed no way of escape, an angel in human form came to his side, the mob fell back, and the servant of Christ passed in safety from the place of danger.

Of his deliverance from the enraged mob on one of these occasions, Wesley said: »Many endeavored to throw me down while we were going down hill on a slippery path to the town; as well judging that if I was once on the ground, I should hardly rise any more. But I made no stumble at all, nor the least slip, till I was entirely out of their hands. ... Although many strove to lay hold on my collar or clothes, to pull me down, they could not fasten at all: only one got fast hold of the flap of my waistcoat, which was soon left in his hand; the other flap, in the pocket of which was a bank note, was torn but half off. ... A lusty man just behind, struck at me several times, with a large oaken stick; with which if he had struck me once on the back part of my head, it would have saved him all further trouble. But every time, the blow was turned aside, I know not how; for I could not move to the right hand or left. ... Another [257/258] came rushing through the press, and raising his arm to strike, on a sudden let it drop, and only stroked my head, saying, 'What soft hair he has!' ... The very first men whose hearts were turned were the heroes of the town, the captains of the rabble on all occasions, one of them having been a prize fighter at the bear gardens. ... »By how gentle degrees does God prepare us for His will! Two years ago, a piece of brick grazed my shoulders. It was a year after that the stone struck me between the eyes. Last month I received one blow, and this evening two, one before we came into the town, and one after we were gone out; but both were as nothing: for though one man struck me on the breast with all his might, and the other on the mouth with such force that the blood gushed out immediately, I felt no more pain from either of the blows than if they had touched me with a straw.« John Wesley, Works, vol. 3, pp. 297, 298

The Methodists of those early days – people as well as preachers – endured ridicule and persecution, alike from church members and from the openly irreligious who were inflamed by their misrepresentations. They were arraigned before courts of justice – such only in name, for justice was rare in the courts of that time. Often they suffered violence from their persecutors. Mobs went from house to house, destroying furniture and goods, plundering whatever they chose, and brutally abusing men, women, and children. In some instances, public notices were posted, calling upon those who desired to assist in breaking the windows and robbing the houses of the Methodists, to assemble at a given time and place. These open violations of both human and divine law were allowed to pass without a reprimand. A systematic persecution was carried on against a people whose only fault was that of seeking to turn the feet of sinners from the path of destruction to the path of holiness.

Said John Wesley, referring to the charges against himself and his associates: »Some allege that the doctrines of these men are false, erroneous, and enthusiastic; that they are new and unheard-of till of late; that they are Quakerism, fanaticism, popery. This whole pretense has been already cut up by the roots, it having been shown at large that every branch of this doctrine is the plain doctrine of Scripture interpreted by our own church. Therefore it cannot be either false or erroneous, provided the Scripture be true.« »Others allege, 'Their doctrine is too strict; they make the way to heaven too

narrow.' And this is in truth the original objection, (as

it was almost the only one for some time,) and is secretly at the bottom of a thousand more, which appear in various forms. But do they make the way to heaven any narrower than our Lord and His apostles made it? Is their doctrine stricter than that of the Bible? Consider only a few plain texts: 'Thou shalt love the Lord thy God with all thy heart, and with all thy mind, and with all thy soul, and with all thy strength.' 'For every idle word which men shall speak, they shall give an account in the day of judgment.' 'Whether ye eat, or drink, or whatever ye do, do all to the glory of God.'«

»If their doctrine is stricter than this, they are to blame; but you know in your conscience it is not. And who can be one jot less strict without corrupting the word of God? Can any steward of the mysteries of God be found faithful if he change any part of that sacred depositum? No. He can abate nothing, he can soften nothing; he is constrained to declare to all men, 'I may not bring down the Scripture to your taste. You must come up to it, or perish forever.' This is the real ground of that other popular cry concerning 'the uncharitableness of these men.' Uncharitable, are they? In what respect? Do they not feed the hungry and clothe the naked? 'No; that is not the thing: they are not wanting in this: but they are so uncharitable in judging! they think none can be saved but those of their own way.'« Ibid., vol. 3, pp. 152, 153 The spiritual declension which had been manifest in England just before the time of Wesley was in great degree the result of antinomian teaching. Many affirmed that Christ had abolished the moral law and that Christians are therefore under no obligation to observe it; that a believer is freed from the »bondage of good works.« Others, though admitting the perpetuity of the law, declared that it was unnecessary for ministers to exhort the people to obedience of its precepts, since those whom God had elected to salvation would, »by the irresistible impulse of divine grace, be led to the practice of piety and virtue,« while those who were doomed to eternal reprobation »did not have power to obey the divine law.«

Others, also holding that »the elect cannot fall from grace nor forfeit the divine favor,« arrived at the still more hideous conclusion that »the wicked actions they commit are not really sinful, nor to be considered as instances of their violation of the divine law, and that, consequently, they have no occasion either to confess their sins or to break them off by repentance.« McClintock and Strong, Cyclopedia, art. »Antinomians.« Therefore, they declared that even one of the vilest of sins, »considered universally an enormous violation of the divine law, is not a sin in the sight of God,« if committed by one of the elect, »because it is one of the essential and distinctive characteristics of the elect, that they cannot do anything that is either displeasing to God or prohibited by the law.«

These monstrous doctrines are essentially the same as the later teaching of popular educators and theologians – that there is no unchangeable divine law as the standard of right, but that the standard of morality is indicated by society itself, and has constantly been subject to change. All these ideas are inspired by the same master spirit – by him who, even among the sinless inhabitants of heaven, began his work of seeking to break down the righteous restraints of the law of God. The doctrine of the divine decrees, unalterably fixing the character of men, had led many to a virtual rejection of the law of God. Wesley steadfastly opposed the errors of the antinomian teachers and showed that this doctrine which led to antinomianism was contrary to the Scriptures. »The grace of God that bringeth salvation hath appeared to all men.« »This is good and acceptable in the sight of God our Saviour; who will have all men to be saved, and to come unto the knowledge of the truth. For there is one God, and one mediator between God and men, the man Christ Jesus; who gave Himself a ransom for all.« Titus 2:11; 1 Timothy 2:3-6 The Spirit of God is freely bestowed to enable every man to lay hold upon the means of salvation. Thus Christ, »the true Light,« »lighteth every man that cometh into the world.« John 1:9 Men fail of salvation through their own willful refusal of the gift of life.

In answer to the claim that at the death of Christ the precepts of the Decalogue had been abolished with the ceremonial law, Wesley said: »The moral law, contained in the Ten Commandments and enforced by the prophets, He did not take away. It was not the design of His coming to revoke any part of this. This is a law which never can be broken, which 'stands fast as the faithful witness in heaven.' ... This was from the beginning of the world, being 'written not on tables of stone,' but on the hearts of all the children of men, when they came out of the hands of the Creator. And however the letters once wrote by the finger of God are now in a great measure defaced by sin, yet can they not wholly be blotted out, while we have any consciousness of good and evil. Every part of this law must remain in force upon all

 mankind, and in all ages; as not depending either on

time or place, or any other circumstances liable to change, but on the nature of God, and the nature of man, and their unchangeable relation to each other.« »'I am not come to destroy, but to fulfill.' ... Without question, His meaning in this place is (consistently with all that goes before and follows after), – I am come to establish it in its fullness, in spite of all the glosses of men: I am come to place in a full and clear view whatsoever was dark or obscure therein: I am come to declare the true and full import of every part of it; to show the length and breadth, the entire extent, of every commandment contained therein, and the height and depth, the inconceivable purity and spirituality of it in all its branches.« Wesley, sermon 25

Wesley declared the perfect harmony of the law and the gospel. »There is, therefore, the closest connection that can be conceived, between the law and the gospel. On the one hand, the law continually makes way for, and points us to, the gospel; on the other, the gospel continually leads us to a more exact fulfilling of the law. The law, for instance, requires us to love God, to love our neighbor, to be meek, humble, or holy. We feel that we are not sufficient for these things; yea, that 'with man this is impossible;' but we see a promise of God to give us that love, and to make us humble, meek, and holy: we lay hold of this gospel, of these glad tidings; it is done unto us according to our faith; and 'the righteousness of the law is fulfilled in us,' through faith which is in Christ Jesus. ...

»In the highest rank of the enemies of the gospel of Christ,« said Wesley, »are they who openly and explicitly 'judge the law' itself, and 'speak evil of the law;' who teach men to break (to dissolve, to loose, to untie the obligation of) not one only, whether of the least or of the greatest, but all the commandments at a stroke. ... The most surprising of all the circumstances that attend this strong delusion, is that they who are given up to it, really believe that they honor Christ by overthrowing His law, and that they are magnifying His office while they are destroying His doctrine! Yea, they honor Him just as Judas did when he said, 'Hail, Master, and kissed Him.' And He may as justly say to every one of them, 'Betrayest thou the Son of man with a kiss?' It is no other than betraying Him with a kiss, to talk of His blood, and take away His crown; to set light by any part of His law, under pretense of advancing His gospel. Nor indeed can anyone escape this charge, who preaches faith in any such a manner as either directly or indirectly tends to set aside any branch of obedience: who preaches Christ so as to disannul, or weaken in any wise, the least of the commandments of God.« Ibid.

To those who urged that »the preaching of the gospel answers all the ends of the law,« Wesley replied: »This we utterly deny. It does not answer the very first end of the law, namely, the convincing men of sin, the awakening those who are still asleep on the brink of hell.« The apostle Paul declares that »by the law is the knowledge of sin;« »and not until man is convicted of sin, will he truly feel his need of the atoning blood of Christ. ... 'They that be whole,' as our Lord Himself observes, 'need not a physician, but they that are sick.' It is absurd, therefore, to offer a physician to them that are whole, or that at least imagine themselves so to be. You are first to convince them that they are sick; otherwise they will not thank you for your labor. It is equally absurd to offer Christ to them whose heart is whole, having never yet been broken.« Ibid., sermon 35

Thus while preaching the gospel of the grace of God, Wesley, like his Master, sought to »magnify the law, and make it honorable.« Faithfully did he accomplish the work given him of God, and glorious were the results which he was permitted to behold. At the close of his long life of more than fourscore years – above half a century spent in itinerant ministry – his avowed adherents numbered more than half a million souls. But the multitude that through his labors had been lifted from the ruin and degradation of sin to a higher and a purer life, and the number who by his teaching had attained to a deeper and richer experience, will never be known till the whole family of the redeemed shall be gathered into the kingdom of God. His life presents a lesson of priceless worth to every Christian. Would that the faith and humility, the untiring zeal, self-sacrifice, and devotion of this servant of Christ might be reflected in the churches of today!

Chapter 15

The Bible and the French Revolution

In the sixteenth century the Reformation, presenting an open Bible to the people, had sought admission to all the countries of Europe. Some nations welcomed it with gladness, as a messenger of Heaven. In other lands the papacy succeeded to a great extent in preventing its entrance; and the light of Bible knowledge, with its elevating influences, was almost wholly excluded. In one country, though the light found entrance, it was not comprehended by the darkness. For centuries, truth and error struggled for the mastery. At last the evil triumphed, and the truth of Heaven was thrust out. »This is the condemnation, that light is come into the world, and men loved darkness rather than light.« John 3:19 The nation was left to reap the results of the course which she had chosen. The restraint of God's Spirit was removed from a people that had despised the gift of His grace. Evil was permitted to come to maturity. And all the world saw the fruit of willful rejection of the light.

The war against the Bible, carried forward for so many centuries in France, culminated in the scenes of the Revolution. That terrible outbreaking was but the legitimate result of Rome's suppression of the Scriptures. see Appendix It presented the most striking illustration which the world has ever witnessed of the working out of the papal policy – an illustration of the results to which for more than a thousand years the teaching of the Roman Church had been tending.

The suppression of the Scriptures during the period of papal supremacy was foretold by the prophets; and the Revelator points also to the terrible results that were to accrue especially to France from the domination of the »man of sin.« Said the angel of the Lord: »The holy city shall they tread underfoot forty and two months. And I will give power unto My two witnesses, and they shall prophesy a thousand two hundred and threescore days, clothed in sackcloth. ... And when they shall have finished their testimony, the beast that ascendeth out of the bottomless pit shall make war against them, and shall overcome them, and kill them. And their dead bodies shall lie in the street of the great city, which spiritually is called Sodom and Egypt, where also our Lord was crucified. ... And they that dwell upon the earth shall rejoice over them, and make merry, and shall send gifts one to another; because these two prophets tormented them that dwelt on the earth. And after three days and a half the Spirit of life from God entered into them, and they stood upon their feet; and great fear fell upon them which saw them.« Revelation 11:2-11

The periods here mentioned – »forty and two months,« and »a thousand two hundred and threescore days« – are the same, alike representing the time in which the church of Christ was to suffer oppression from Rome. The 1260 years of papal supremacy began in A.D. 538, and would therefore terminate in 1798. see Appendix note for p. 54 At that time a French army entered Rome and made the pope a prisoner, and he died in exile. Though a new pope was soon afterward elected, the papal hierarchy has never since been able to wield the power which it before possessed.

The persecution of the church did not continue throughout the entire period of the 1260 years. God in mercy to His people cut short the time of their fiery trial. In foretelling the »great tribulation« to befall the church, the Saviour said: »Except those days should be shortened, there should no flesh be saved: but for the elect's sake those days shall be shortened.« Matthew 24:22 Through the influence of the Reformation the persecution was brought to an end prior to 1798. Concerning the two witnesses the prophet declares further: »These are the two olive trees, and the two candlesticks standing before the God of the earth.« »Thy word,« said the psalmist, »is a lamp unto my feet, and a light unto my path.« Rev. 11:4; Psalm 119:105 The two witnesses represent the Scriptures of the Old and the New Testament. Both are important testimonies to the origin and perpetuity of the law of God. Both are witnesses also to the plan of salvation. The types, sacrifices, and prophecies of the Old Testament point forward to a Saviour to come. The Gospels and Epistles of the New Testament tell of a Saviour who has come in the exact manner foretold by type and prophecy.

»They shall prophesy a thousand two hundred and three-score days, clothed in sackcloth.« During the greater part of this period, God's witnesses remained in a state of obscurity. The papal power sought to hide from the people the word of truth, and set before them false witnesses to contradict its testimony. see Appendix When the Bible

 was proscribed by religious and secular authority; when

its testimony was perverted, and every effort made that men and demons could invent to turn the minds of the people from it; when those who dared proclaim its sacred truths were hunted, betrayed, tortured, buried in dungeon cells, martyred for their faith, or compelled to flee to mountain fastnesses, and to dens and caves of the earth – then the faithful witnesses prophesied in sackcloth. Yet they continued their testimony throughout the entire period of 1260 years. In the darkest times there were faithful men who loved God's word and were jealous for His honor. To these loyal servants were given wisdom, power, and authority to declare His truth during the whole of this time.

»And if any man will hurt them, fire proceedeth out of their mouth, and devoureth their enemies: and if any man will hurt them, he must in this manner be killed.« Revelation 11:5 Men cannot with impunity trample upon the word of God. The meaning of this fearful denunciation is set forth in the closing chapter of the Revelation: »I testify unto every man that heareth the words of the prophecy of this book, If any man shall add unto these things, God shall add unto him the plagues that are written in this book: and if any man shall take away from the words of the book of this prophecy, God shall take away his part out of the book of life, and out of the holy city, and from the things which are written in this book.« Rev. 22:18,19

Such are the warnings which God has given to guard men against changing in any manner that which He has revealed or commanded. These solemn denunciations apply to all who by their influence lead men to regard lightly the law of God. They should cause those to fear and tremble who flippantly declare it a matter of little consequence whether we obey God's law or not. All who exalt their own opinions above divine revelation, all who would change the plain meaning of Scripture to suit their own convenience, or for the sake of conforming to the world, are taking upon themselves a fearful responsibility. The written word, the law of God, will measure the character of every man and condemn all whom this unerring test shall declare wanting.

»When they shall have finished [are finishing] their testimony.« The period when the two witnesses were to prophesy clothed in sackcloth, ended in 1798. As they were approaching the termination of their work in obscurity, war was to be made upon them by the power represented as »the beast that ascendeth out of the bottomless pit.« In many of the nations of Europe the powers that ruled in church and state had for centuries been controlled by Satan through the medium of the papacy. But here is brought to view a new manifestation of satanic power.

It had been Rome's policy, under a profession of reverence for the Bible, to keep it locked up in an unknown tongue and hidden away from the people. Under her rule the witnesses prophesied »clothed in sackcloth.« But another power – the beast from the bottomless pit - was to arise to make open, avowed war upon the word of God.

»The great city« in whose streets the witnesses are slain, and where their dead bodies lie, is »spiritually« Egypt. Of all nations presented in Bible history, Egypt most boldly denied the existence of the living God and resisted His commands. No monarch ever ventured upon more open and highhanded rebellion against the authority of Heaven than did the king of Egypt. When the message was brought him by Moses, in the name of the Lord, Pharaoh proudly answered: »Who is Jehovah, that I should hearken unto His voice to let Israel go? I know not Jehovah, and moreover I will not let Israel go.« Exodus 5:2, A.R.V. This is atheism, and the nation represented by Egypt would give voice to a similar denial of the claims of the living God and would manifest a like spirit of unbelief and defiance. »The great city« is also compared, »spiritually,« to Sodom. The corruption of Sodom in breaking the law of God was especially manifested in licentiousness. And this sin was also to be a pre-eminent characteristic of the nation that should fulfill the specifications of this scripture. According to the words of the prophet, then, a little before the year 1798 some power of satanic origin and character would rise to make war upon the Bible. And in the land where the testimony of God's two witnesses should thus be silenced, there would be manifest the atheism of the Pharaoh and the licentiousness of Sodom.

This prophecy has received a most exact and striking fulfillment in the history of France. During the Revolution, in 1793, »the world for the first time heard an assembly of men, born and educated in civilization, and assuming the right to govern one of the finest of the European nations, uplift their united voice to deny the most solemn truth which man's soul receives, and renounce unanimously the belief and worship of a Deity.« Sir Walter Scott, Life of Napoleon, vol. 1, ch. 17 »France is the only nation in the world concerning which the authentic record survives, that as a nation she lifted her hand in open rebellion against the Author of the universe. Plenty of blasphemers,

 plenty of infidels, there have been, and still continue to

be, in England, Germany, Spain, and elsewhere; but France stands apart in the world's history as the single state which, by the decree of her Legislative Assembly, pronounced that there was no God, and of which the entire population of the capital, and a vast majority elsewhere, women as well as men, danced and sang with joy in accepting the announcement.« Blackwood's Magazine, Nov. 1870

France presented also the characteristics which especially distinguished Sodom. During the Revolution there was manifest a state of moral debasement and corruption similar to that which brought destruction upon the cities of the plain. And the historian presents together the atheism and the licentiousness of France, as given in the prophecy: "Intimately connected with these laws affecting religion, was that which reduced the union of marriage – the most sacred engagement which human beings can form, and the permanence of which leads most strongly to the consolidation of society – to the state of a mere civil contract of a transitory character, which any two persons might engage in and cast loose at pleasure. ... If fiends had set themselves to work to discover a mode of most effectually destroying whatever is venerable, graceful, or permanent in domestic life, and of obtaining at the same time an assurance that the mischief which it was their object to create should be perpetuated from one generation to another, they could not have invented a more effectual plan that the degradation of marriage. ... Sophie Arnoult, an actress famous for the witty things she said, described the republican marriage as 'the sacrament of adultery.'« Scott, vol. 1, ch. 17 »Where also our Lord was crucified.« This specification of the prophecy was also fulfilled by France. In no land had the spirit of enmity against Christ been more strikingly displayed. In no country had the truth encountered more bitter and cruel opposition. In the persecution which France had visited upon the confessors of the gospel, she had crucified Christ in the person of His disciples.

Century after century the blood of the saints had been shed. While the Waldenses laid down their lives upon the mountains of Piedmont »for the word of God, and for the testimony of Jesus Christ,« similar witness to the truth had been borne by their brethren, the Albigenses of France. In the days of the Reformation its disciples had been put to death with horrible tortures. King and nobles, highborn women and delicate maidens, the pride and chivalry of the nation, had feasted their eyes upon the agonies of the martyrs of Jesus. The brave Huguenots, battling for those rights which the human heart holds most sacred, had poured out their blood on many a hard-fought field. The Protestants were counted as outlaws, a price was set upon their heads, and they were hunted down like wild beasts. The »Church in the Desert,« the few descendants of the ancient Christians that still lingered in France in the eighteenth century, hiding away in the mountains of the south, still cherished the faith of their fathers. As they ventured to meet by night on mountainside or lonely moor, they were chased by dragoons and dragged away to lifelong slavery in the galleys. The purest, the most refined, and the most intelligent of the French were chained, in horrible torture, amidst robbers and assassins. see Wylie, b. 22, ch. 6 Others, more mercifully dealt with, were shot down in cold blood, as, unarmed and helpless, they fell upon their knees in prayer. Hundreds of aged men, defenseless women, and innocent children were left dead upon the earth at their place of meeting. In traversing the mountainside or the forest, where they had been accustomed to assemble, it was not unusual to find »at every four paces, dead bodies dotting the sward, and corpses hanging suspended from the trees.« Their country, laid waste with the sword, the ax, the fagot, »was converted into one vast, gloomy wilderness.« »These atrocities were enacted ... in no dark age, but in the brilliant era of Louis XIV. Science was then cultivated, letters flourished, the divines of the court and of the capital were learned and eloquent men, and greatly affected the graces of meekness and charity.« Ibid., b. 22, ch. 7 But blackest in the black catalogue of crime, most horrible among the fiendish deeds of all the dreadful centuries, was the St. Bartholomew Massacre. The world still recalls with shuddering horror the scenes of that most cowardly and cruel onslaught. The king of France, urged on by Romish priests and prelates, lent his sanction to the dreadful work. A bell, tolling at dead of night, was a signal for the slaughter. Protestants by thousands, sleeping quietly in their homes, trusting to the plighted honor of their king, were dragged forth without a warning and murdered in cold blood.

As Christ was the invisible leader of His people from Egyptian bondage, so was Satan the unseen leader of his subjects in this horrible work of multiplying martyrs. For seven days the massacre was continued in Paris, the first three with inconceivable fury. And it was not confined to the city itself, but by special order of the king

was extended to all the provinces and towns where

Protestants were found. Neither age nor sex was respected. Neither the innocent babe nor the man of gray hairs was spared. Noble and peasant, old and young, mother and child, were cut down together. Throughout France the butchery continued for two months. Seventy thousand of the very flower of the nation perished.

»When the news of the massacre reached Rome, the exultation among the clergy knew no bounds. The cardinal of Lorraine rewarded the messenger with a thousand crowns; the cannon of St. Angelo thundered forth a joyous salute; and bells rang out from every steeple; bonfires turned night into day; and Gregory XIII, attended by the cardinals and other ecclesiastical dignitaries, went in long procession to the church of St. Louis, where the cardinal of Lorraine chanted a Te Deum. ... A medal was struck to commemorate the massacre, and in the Vatican may still be seen three frescoes of Vasari, describing the attack upon the admiral, the king in council plotting the massacre, and the massacre itself. Gregory sent Charles the Golden Rose; and four months after the massacre, ... he listened complacently to the sermon of a French priest, ... who spoke of 'that day so full of happiness and joy, when the most holy father received the news, and went in solemn state to render thanks to God and St. Louis.'« Henry White, The Massacre of St. Bartholomew, ch. 14, par. 34

The same master spirit that urged on the St. Bartholomew Massacre led also in the scenes of the Revolution. Jesus Christ was declared to be an impostor, and the rallying cry of the French infidels was, »Crush the Wretch,« meaning Christ. Heaven-daring blasphemy and abominable wickedness went hand in hand, and the basest of men, the most abandoned monsters of cruelty and vice, were most highly exalted. In all this, supreme homage was paid to Satan; while Christ, in His characteristics of truth, purity, and unselfish love, was crucified.

»The beast that ascendeth out of the bottomless pit shall make war against them, and shall overcome them, and kill them.« The atheistical power that ruled in France during the Revolution and the Reign of Terror, did wage such a war against God and His holy word as the world had never witnessed. The worship of the Deity was abolished by the National Assembly. Bibles were collected and publicly burned with every possible manifestation of scorn. The law of God was trampled underfoot. The institutions of the Bible were abolished. The weekly rest day was set aside, and in its stead every tenth day was devoted to reveling and blasphemy. Baptism and the Communion

Commemorative coins of St. Bartholomew

Massacre of St. Bartholomew (1572)

were prohibited. And announcements posted conspicuously over the burial places declared death to be an eternal sleep.

The fear of God was said to be so far from the beginning of wisdom that it was the beginning of folly. All religious worship was prohibited, except that of liberty and the country. The »constitutional bishop of Paris was brought forward to play the principal part in the most impudent and scandalous farce ever acted in the face of a national representation. ... He was brought forward in full procession, to declare to the Convention that the religion which he had taught so many years was, in every respect, a piece of priestcraft, which had no foundation either in history or sacred truth. He disowned, in solemn and explicit terms, the existence of the Deity to whose worship he had been consecrated, and devoted himself in future to the homage of liberty, equality, virtue, and morality. He then laid on the table his episcopal decorations, and received a fraternal embrace from the president of the Convention. Several apostate priests followed the example of this prelate.« Scott, vol. 1, ch. 17 »And they that dwell upon the earth shall rejoice over them, and make merry, and shall send gifts one to another; because these two prophets tormented them that dwelt on the earth.« Infidel France had silenced the reproving voice of God's two witnesses. The word of truth lay dead in her streets, and those who hated the restrictions and requirements of God's law were jubilant. Men publicly defied the King of heaven. Like the sinners of old, they cried: »How doth God know? and is there knowledge in the Most High?« Psalm 73:11

With blasphemous boldness almost beyond belief, one of the priests of the new order said: »God, if You exist, avenge Your injured name. I bid You defiance! You remain silent; You dare not launch Your thunders. Who after this will believe in Your existence?« Lacretelle, History 11:309; in Sir Archibald Alison, History of Europe, vol. 1, ch. 10 What an echo is this of the Pharaoh's demand: »Who is Jehovah, that I should obey His voice?« »I know not Jehovah!«

»The fool hath said in his heart, There is no God.« Psalm 14:1 And the Lord declares concerning the perverters of the truth: »Their folly shall be manifest unto all.« 2 Timothy 3:9 After France had renounced the worship of the living God, »the high and lofty One that inhabiteth eternity,« it was only a little time till she descended to degrading idolatry, by the worship of the Goddess of Reason, in the person of a profligate woman. And this in the representative assembly of the nation, and by its highest civil and legislative authorities! Says the historian: »One of the ceremonies of this insane time stands unrivaled for absurdity combined with impiety. The doors of the Convention were thrown open to a band of musicians, preceded by whom, the members of the municipal body entered in solemn procession, singing a hymn in praise of liberty, and escorting, as the object of their future worship, a veiled female, whom they termed the Goddess of Reason. Being brought within the bar, she was unveiled with great form, and placed on the right of the president, when she was generally recognized as a dancing girl of the opera. ... To this person, as the fittest representative of that reason whom they worshiped, the National Convention of France rendered public homage.« »This impious and ridiculous mummery had a certain fashion; and the installation of the Goddess of Reason was renewed and imitated throughout the nation, in such places where the inhabitants desired to show themselves equal to all the heights of the Revolution.« Scott, vol. 1, ch. 17 Said the orator who introduced the worship of Reason: »Legislators! Fanaticism has given way to reason. Its bleared eyes could not endure the brilliancy of the light. This day an immense concourse has assembled beneath those gothic vaults, which, for the first time, re-echoed the truth. There the French have celebrated the only true worship, – that of Liberty, that of Reason. There we have formed wishes for the prosperity of the arms of the Republic. There we have abandoned inanimate idols for Reason, for that animated image, the masterpiece of nature.« M.A. Thiers, History of the French Revolution, vol. 2, pp. 370, 371

When the goddess was brought into the Convention, the orator took her by the hand, and turning to the assembly said: »Mortals, cease to tremble before the powerless thunders of a God whom your fears have created. Henceforth acknowledge no divinity but Reason. I offer you its noblest and purest image; if you must have idols, sacrifice only to such as this. ... Fall before the august Senate of Freedom, oh! Veil of Reason!« »The goddess, after being embraced by the president, was mounted on a magnificent car, and conducted, amid an immense crowd, to the cathedral of Notre Dame, to take the place of the Deity. There she was elevated on the high altar, and received the adoration of all present.« Alison, vol. 1, ch. 10

This was followed, not long afterward, by the public burning of the Bible. On one occasion »the Popular Society of the Museum« entered the hall of the municipality, exclaiming, »Vive la Raison!« and carrying on the top of a pole the half-burned remains of several books, among others breviaries, missals, and the Old and New Testaments, which »expiated in a great fire,« said the president, »all the fooleries which they have made the human race commit.« Journal of Paris, 1793, No. 318. Quoted in Buchez-Roux, Collection of Parliamentary History, vol. 30, pp. 200, 201

It was popery that had begun the work which atheism was completing. The policy of Rome had wrought out those conditions, social, political, and religious, that were hurrying France on to ruin. Writers, in referring to the horrors of the Revolution, say that these excesses are to be charged upon the throne and the church. (See Appendix.) In strict justice they are to be charged upon the church. Popery had poisoned the minds of kings against the Reformation, as an enemy to the crown, an element of discord that would be fatal to the peace and harmony of the nation. It was the genius of Rome that by this means inspired the direst cruelty and the most galling oppression which proceeded from the throne.

The spirit of liberty went with the Bible. Wherever the gospel was received, the minds of the people were awakened. They began to cast off the shackles that had held them bondslaves of ignorance, vice, and superstition. They began to think and act as men. Monarchs saw it and trembled for their despotism. Rome was not slow to inflame their jealous fears. Said the pope to the regent of France in 1525: »This mania [Protestantism] will not only confound and destroy religion, but all principalities, nobility, laws, orders, and ranks besides.« G. de Felice, History of the Protestants of France, b. 1, ch. 2, par. 8 A few years later a papal nuncio warned the king: »Sire, be not deceived. The Protestants will upset all civil as well as religious order. ... The throne is in as much danger as the altar. ... The introduction of a new religion must necessarily introduce a new government.« D'Aubigne, History of the Reformation in Europe in the Time of Calvin, b. 2, ch. 36 And theologians appealed to the prejudices of the people by declaring that the Protestant doctrine »entices men away to novelties and folly; it robs the king of the devoted affection of his subjects, and devastates both church and state.« Thus Rome succeeded in arraying France against the Reformation. »It was to uphold the throne, preserve the nobles, and maintain the laws, that the sword of persecution was first unsheathed in France.« Wylie, b. 13, ch. 4

Little did the rulers of the land foresee the results of that fateful policy. The teaching of the Bible would have implanted in the minds and hearts of the people those principles of justice, temperance, truth, equity, and benevolence which are the very cornerstone of a nation's prosperity. »Righteousness exalteth a nation.« Thereby »the throne is established.« Proverbs 14:34; 16:12 »The work of righteousness shall be peace;« and the effect, »quietness and assurance forever.« Isaiah 32:17 He who obeys the divine law will most truly respect and obey the laws of his country. He who fears God will honor the king in the exercise of all just and legitimate authority. But unhappy France prohibited the Bible and banned its disciples. Century after century, men of principle and integrity, men of intellectual acuteness and moral strength, who had the courage to avow their convictions and the faith to suffer for the truth - for centuries these men toiled as slaves in the galleys, perished at the stake, or rotted in dungeon cells. Thousands upon thousands found safety in flight; and this continued for two hundred and fifty years after the opening of the Reformation.

»Scarcely was there a generation of Frenchmen during the long period that did not witness the disciples of the gospel fleeing before the insane fury of the persecutor, and carrying with them the intelligence, the arts, the industry, the order, in which, as a rule, they pre-eminently excelled, to enrich the lands in which they found an asy- [277/278] lum. And in proportion as they replenished other countries with these good gifts, did they empty their own of them. If all that was now driven away had been retained in France; if, during these three hundred years, the industrial skill of the exiles had been cultivating her soil; if, during these three hundred years, their artistic bent had been improving her manufactures; if, during these three hundred years, their creative genius and analytic power had been enriching her literature and cultivating her science; if their wisdom had been guiding her councils, their bravery fighting her battles, their equity framing her laws, and the religion of the Bible strengthening the intellect and governing the conscience of her people, what a glory would at this day have encompassed France! What a great, prosperous, and happy country – a pattern to the nations – would she have been! »But a blind and inexorable bigotry chased from her soil every teacher of virtue, every champion of order, every honest defender of the throne; it said to the men who would have made their country a 'renown and glory' in the earth, Choose which you will have, a stake or exile. At last the ruin of the state was complete; there remained no more conscience to be proscribed; no more religion to be dragged to the stake; no more patriotism to be chased into banishment.« Wylie, b. 13, ch. 20 And the Revolution, with all its horrors, was the dire result.

»With the flight of the Huguenots a general decline settled upon France. Flourishing manufacturing cities fell into decay; fertile districts returned to their native wildness; intellectual dullness and moral declension succeeded a period of unwonted progress. Paris became one vast almshouse, and it is estimated that, at the breaking out of the Revolution, two hundred thousand paupers claimed charity from the hands of the king. The Jesuits alone flourished in the decaying nation, and ruled with dreadful tyranny over churches and schools, the prisons and the galleys.« The gospel would have brought to France the solution of those political and social problems that baffled the skill of her clergy, her king, and her legislators, and finally plunged the nation into anarchy and ruin. But under the domination of Rome the people had lost the Saviour's blessed lessons of self-sacrifice and unselfish love. They had been led away from the practice of self-denial for the good of others. The rich had found no rebuke for their oppression of the poor, the poor no help for their servitude and degradation. The selfishness of the wealthy and powerful grew more and more apparent and oppressive. For centuries the greed and profligacy of the noble resulted in grinding extortion toward the peasant. The rich wronged the poor, and the poor hated the rich.

In many provinces the estates were held by the nobles, and the laboring classes were only tenants; they were at the mercy of their landlords and were forced to submit to their exorbitant demands. The burden of supporting both the church and the state fell upon the middle and lower classes, who were heavily taxed by the civil authorities and by the clergy. »The pleasure of the nobles was considered the supreme law; the farmers and the peasants might starve, for aught their oppressors cared. ... The people were compelled at every turn to consult the exclusive interest of the landlord. The lives of the agricultural laborers were lives of incessant work and unrelieved misery; their complaints, if they ever dared to complain, were treated with insolent contempt. The courts of justice would always listen to a noble as against a peasant; bribes were notoriously accepted by the judges; and the merest caprice of the aristocracy had the force of law, by virtue of this system of universal corruption. Of the taxes wrung from the commonalty, by the secular magnates on the one hand, and the clergy on the other, not half ever found its way into the royal or episcopal treasury; the rest was squandered in profligate self-indulgence. And the men who thus impoverished their fellow subjects were themselves exempt from taxation, and entitled by law or custom to all the appointments of the state. The privileged classes numbered a hundred and fifty thousand, and for their gratification millions were condemned to hopeless and degrading lives.« see Appendix

The court was given up to luxury and profligacy. There was little confidence existing between the people and the rulers. Suspicion fastened upon all the measures of the government as designing and selfish. For more than half a century before the time of the Revolution the throne was occupied by Louis XV, who, even in those evil times, was distinguished as an indolent, frivolous, and sensual monarch. With a depraved and cruel aristocracy and an impoverished and ignorant lower class, the state financially embarrassed and the people exasperated, it needed no prophet's eye to foresee a terrible impending outbreak. To the warnings of his counselors the king was accustomed to reply: »Try to make things go on as long as I am likely to live; after my death it may be as it will.« It was in vain that the necessity of reform was urged. He saw the evils, but had neither the courage nor the power to meet them. The doom awaiting France was but too truly pictured in his indolent and selfish answer, »After me, the deluge!« By working upon the jealousy of the kings and the ruling classes, Rome had influenced them to keep the people in bondage, well knowing that the state would thus be weakened, and purposing by this means to fasten both rulers and people in her thrall. With farsighted policy she perceived that in order to enslave men effectually, the shackles must be bound upon their souls; that the surest way to prevent them from escaping their bondage was to render them incapable of freedom. A thousandfold more terrible than the physical suffering which resulted from her policy, was the moral degradation. Deprived of the Bible, and abandoned to the teachings of bigotry and selfishness, the people were shrouded in ignorance and superstition, and sunken in vice, so that they were wholly unfitted for self-government. But the outworking of all this was widely different from what Rome had purposed. Instead of holding the masses in a blind submission to her dogmas, her work resulted in making them infidels and revolutionists. Romanism they despised as priestcraft. They beheld the clergy as a party to their oppression. The only god they knew was the god of Rome; her teaching was their only religion. They regarded her greed and cruelty as the legitimate fruit of the Bible, and they would have none of it.

Rome had misrepresented the character of God and perverted His requirements, and now men rejected both the Bible and its Author. She had required a blind faith in her dogmas, under the pretended sanction of the Scriptures. In the reaction, Voltaire and his associates cast aside God's word altogether and spread everywhere the poison of infidelity. Rome had ground down the people under her iron heel; and now the masses, degraded and brutalized, in their recoil from her tyranny, cast off all restraint. Enraged at the glittering cheat to which they had so long paid homage, they rejected truth and falsehood together; and mistaking license for liberty, the slaves of vice exulted in their imagined freedom.

At the opening of the Revolution, by a concession of the king, the people were granted a representation exceeding that of the nobles and the clergy combined. Thus the balance of power was in their hands; but they were not prepared to use it with wisdom and moderation. Eager to redress the wrongs they had suffered, they determined to undertake the reconstruction of society. An outraged populace, whose minds were filled with bitter and long-treasured memories of wrong, resolved to revolutionize the state of misery that had grown unbearable and to avenge themselves upon those whom they regarded as the authors of their sufferings. The oppressed wrought out the lesson they had learned under tyranny and became the oppressors of those who had oppressed them. Unhappy France reaped in blood the harvest she had sown. Terrible were the results of her submission to the controlling power of Rome. Where France, under the influence of Romanism, had set up the first stake at the opening of the Reformation, there the Revolution set up its first guillotine. On the very spot where the first martyrs to the Protestant faith were burned in the sixteenth century, the first victims were guillotined in the eighteenth. In repelling the gospel, which would have brought her healing, France had opened the door to infidelity and ruin. When the restraints of God's law were cast aside, it was found that the laws of man were inadequate to hold in check the powerful tides of human passion; and the nation swept on to revolt and anarchy. The war against the Bible inaugurated an era which stands in the world's history as the Reign of Terror. Peace and happiness were banished from the homes and hearts of men. No one was secure. He who triumphed today was suspected, condemned, tomorrow. Violence and lust held undisputed sway.

King, clergy, and nobles were compelled to submit to the atrocities of an excited and maddened people. Their thirst for vengeance was only stimulated by the execution of the king; and those who had decreed his death soon followed him to the scaffold. A general slaughter of all suspected of hostility to the Revolution was determined. The prisons were crowded, at one time containing more than two hundred thousand captives. The cities of the kingdom were filled with scenes of horror. One party of revolutionists was against another party, and France became a vast field for contending masses, swayed by the fury of their passions. »In Paris one tumult succeeded another, and the citizens were divided into a medley of factions, that seemed intent on nothing but mutual extermination.« And to add to the general misery, the nation became involved in a prolonged and devastating war with the great powers of Europe. »The country was nearly bankrupt, the armies were clamoring for arrears of pay, the Parisians were starving, the provinces were laid waste by brigands, and civilization was almost extinguished in anarchy and license.«

All too well the people had learned the lessons of cruelty and torture which Rome had so diligently taught. A day of retribution at last had come. It was not now the disciples of Jesus that were thrust into dungeons and dragged to the stake. Long ago these had perished or been driven into exile. Unsparing Rome now felt the deadly power of those whom she had trained to delight in deeds of blood. »The example of persecution which the clergy of France had exhibited for so many ages, was now retorted upon them with signal vigor. The scaffolds ran red with the blood of the priests. The galleys and the prisons, once crowded with Huguenots, were now filled with their persecutors. Chained to the bench and toiling at the oar, the Roman Catholic clergy experienced all those woes which their church had so freely inflicted on the gentle heretics.« see Appendix »Then came those days when the most barbarous of all codes was administered by the most barbarous of all tribunals; when no man could greet his neighbors or say his prayers ... without danger of committing a capital crime; when spies lurked in every corner; when the guillotine was long and hard at work every morning; when the jails were filled as close as the holds of a slave ship; when the gutters ran foaming with blood into the Seine. ... While the daily wagonloads of victims were carried to their doom through the streets of Paris, the proconsuls, whom the sovereign committee had sent forth to the departments, reveled in an extravagance of cruelty unknown even in the capital. The knife of the deadly machine rose and fell too slow for their work of slaughter. Long rows of captives were mowed down with grapeshot. Holes were made in the bottom of crowded barges. Lyons was turned into a desert. At Arras even the cruel mercy of a speedy death was denied to the prisoners. All down the Loire, from Saumur to the sea, great flocks of crows and kites feasted on naked corpses, twined together in hideous embraces. No mercy was shown to sex or age. The number of young lads and of girls of seventeen who were murdered by that execrable government, is to be reckoned by hundreds. Babies torn from the breast were tossed from pike to pike along the Jacobin ranks.« see Appendix In the short space of ten years, multitudes of human beings perished.

All this was as Satan would have it. This was what for ages he had been working to secure. His policy is deception from first to last, and his steadfast purpose is to bring woe and wretchedness upon men, to deface and defile the workmanship of God, to mar the divine purposes of benevolence and love, and thus cause grief in heaven. Then by his deceptive arts he blinds the minds of men, and leads them to throw back the blame of his work upon God, as if all this misery were

 the result of the Creator's plan. In like manner, when

those who have been degraded and brutalized through his cruel power achieve their freedom, he urges them on to excesses and atrocities. Then this picture of unbridled license is pointed out by tyrants and oppressors as an illustration of the results of liberty. When error in one garb has been detected, Satan only masks it in a different disguise, and multitudes receive it as eagerly as at the first. When the people found Romanism to be a deception, and he could not through this agency lead them to transgression of God's law, he urged them to regard all religion as a cheat, and the Bible as a fable; and, casting aside the divine statutes, they gave themselves up to unbridled iniquity.

The fatal error which wrought such woe for the inhabitants of France was the ignoring of this one great truth: that true freedom lies within the proscriptions of the law of God. »O that thou hadst hearkened to My commandments! then had thy peace been as a river, and thy righteousness as the waves of the sea.« »There is no peace, saith the Lord, unto the wicked.« »But whoso hearkeneth unto Me shall dwell safely, and shall be quiet from fear of evil.« Isaiah 48:18, 22; Proverbs 1:33 Atheists, infidels, and apostates oppose and denounce God's law; but the results of their influence prove that the well-being of man is bound up with his obedience of the divine statutes. Those who will not read the lesson from the book of God are bidden to read it in the history of nations. When Satan wrought through the Roman Church to lead men away from obedience, his agency was concealed, and his work was so disguised that the degradation and misery which resulted were not seen to be the fruit of transgression. And his power was so far counteracted by the working of the Spirit of God that his purposes were prevented from reaching their full fruition. The people did not trace the effect to its cause and discover the source of their miseries. But in the Revolution the law of God was openly set aside by the National Council. And in the Reign of Terror which followed, the working of cause and effect could be seen by all.

When France publicly rejected God and set aside the Bible, wicked men and spirits of darkness exulted in their attainment of the object so long desired – a kingdom free from the restraints of the law of God. Because sentence against an evil work was not speedily executed, therefore the heart of the sons of men was »fully set in them to do evil.« Ecclesiastes 8:11 But the transgression of a just and righteous law must inevitably result in misery and ruin. Though not visited at once with judgments, the wickedness of men was nevertheless surely working out their doom. Centuries of apostasy and crime had been treasuring up wrath against the day of retribution; and when their iniquity was full, the despisers of God learned too late that it is a fearful thing to have worn out the divine patience. The restraining Spirit of God, which imposes a check upon the cruel power of Satan, was in a great measure removed, and he whose only delight is the wretchedness of men was permitted to work his will. Those who had chosen the service of rebellion were left to reap its fruits until the land was filled with crimes too horrible for pen to trace. From devastated provinces and ruined cities a terrible cry was heard – a cry of bitterest anguish. France was shaken as if by an earthquake. Religion, law, social order, the family, the state, and the church – all were smitten down by the impious hand that had been lifted against the law of God. Truly spoke the wise man: »The wicked shall fall by his own wickedness.« »Though a sinner do evil a hundred times, and his days be prolonged, yet surely I know that it shall be well with them that fear God, which fear before Him: but it shall not be well with the wicked.« Proverbs 11:5; Ecclesiastes 8:12-13 »They hated knowledge, and did not choose the fear of the Lord;" "therefore shall they eat of the fruit of their own way, and be filled with their own devices.« Proverbs 1:29, 31

God's faithful witnesses, slain by the blasphemous power that »ascendeth out of the bottomless pit,« were not long to remain silent. »After three days and a half the Spirit of life from God entered into them, and they stood upon their feet; and great fear fell upon them which saw them.« Rev. 11:11 It was in 1793 that the decrees which abolished the Christian religion and set aside the Bible passed the French Assembly. Three years and a half later a resolution rescinding these decrees, thus granting toleration to the Scriptures, was adopted by the same body. The world stood aghast at the enormity of guilt which had resulted from a rejection of the Sacred Oracles, and men recognized the necessity of faith in God and His word as the foundation of virtue and morality. Saith the Lord: »Whom hast thou reproached and blasphemed? and against whom hast thou exalted thy voice, and lifted up thine eyes on high? even against the Holy One of Israel,« Isaiah 37:23

»Therefore, behold, I will cause them to know, this once will I cause them to know My hand and My might; and they shall know that My name is Jehovah.« Jeremiah 16:21, A.R.V. Concerning the two witnesses the prophet declares further: »And they heard a great voice from heaven

 saying unto them, Come up hither. And they ascended

up to heaven in a cloud; and their enemies beheld them.« Revelation 11:12 Since France made war upon God's two witnesses, they have been honored as never before. In 1804 the British and Foreign Bible Society was organized. This was followed by similar organizations, with numerous branches, upon the continent of Europe. In 1816 the American Bible Society was founded. When the British Society was formed, the Bible had been printed and circulated in fifty tongues. It has since been translated into many hundreds of languages and dialects. see Appendix For the fifty years preceding 1792, little attention was given to the work of foreign missions. No new societies were formed, and there were but few churches that made any effort for the spread of Christianity in heathen lands. But toward the close of the eighteenth century a great change took place. Men became dissatisfied with the results of rationalism and realized the necessity of divine revelation and experimental religion. From this time the work of foreign missions attained an unprecedented growth. see Appendix

The improvements in printing have given an impetus to the work of circulating the Bible. The increased facilities for communication between different countries, the breaking down of ancient barriers of prejudice and national exclusiveness, and the loss of secular power by the pontiff of Rome have opened the way for the entrance of the word of God. For some years the Bible has been sold without restraint in the streets of Rome, and it has now been carried to every part of the habitable globe. The infidel Voltaire once boastingly said: »I am weary of hearing people repeat that twelve men established the Christian religion. I will prove that one man may suffice to overthrow it.« Generations have passed since his death. Millions have joined in the war upon the Bible. But it is so far from being destroyed, that where there were a hundred in Voltaire's time, there are now ten thousand, yes, a hundred thousand copies of the book of God. In the words of an early Reformer concerning the Christian church, »The Bible is an anvil that has worn out many hammers.« Saith the Lord: »No weapon that is formed against thee shall prosper; and every tongue that shall rise against thee in judgment thou shalt condemn.« Isaiah 54:17

»The word of our God shall stand forever.« »All His commandments are sure. They stand fast for ever and ever, and are done in truth and uprightness.« Isaiah 40:8; Psalm 111:7, 8 Whatever is built upon the authority of man will be overthrown; but that which is founded upon the rock of God's immutable word shall stand forever.

CHAPTER 16

THE PILGRIM FATHERS

The English Reformers, while renouncing the doctrines of Romanism, had retained many of its forms. Thus though the authority and the creed of Rome were rejected, not a few of her customs and ceremonies were incorporated into the worship of the Church of England. It was claimed that these things were not matters of conscience; that though they were not commanded in Scripture, and hence were nonessential, yet not being forbidden, they were not intrinsically evil. Their observance tended to narrow the gulf which separated the reformed churches from Rome, and it was urged that they would promote the acceptance of the Protestant faith by Romanists.

To the conservative and compromising, these arguments seemed conclusive. But there was another class that did not so judge. The fact that these customs »tended to bridge over the chasm between Rome and the Reformation«, Martyn, vol. 5, p. 22 was in their view a conclusive argument against retaining them. They looked upon them as badges of the slavery from which they had been delivered and to which they had no disposition to return. They reasoned that God has in His word established the regulations governing His worship, and that men are not at liberty to add to these or to detract from them. The very beginning of the great apostasy was in seeking to supplement the authority of God by that of the church. Rome began by enjoining what God had not forbidden, and she ended by forbidding what He had explicitly enjoined. Many earnestly desired to return to the purity and simplicity which characterized the primitive church. They regarded many of the established customs of the English Church as monuments of idolatry, and they could not in conscience unite in her worship. But the church, being supported by the civil authority, would permit no dissent from her forms. Attendance upon her service was required by law, and unauthorized assemblies for religious worship were prohibited, under penalty of imprisonment, exile, and death.

At the opening of the seventeenth century the monarch who had just ascended the throne of England declared his determination to make the Puritans »conform, or ... harry them out of the land, or else worse.« George Bancroft, History of the United States of America, pt. 1, ch. 12, par. 6 Hunted, persecuted, and imprisoned, they could discern in the future no promise of better days, and many yielded to the conviction that for such as would serve God according to the dictates of their conscience, »England was ceasing forever to be a habitable place.« J. G. Palfrey, History of New England, ch. 3, par. 43 Some at last determined to seek refuge in Holland. Difficulties, losses, and imprisonment were encountered. Their purposes were thwarted, and they were betrayed into the hands of their enemies. But steadfast perseverance finally conquered, and they found shelter on the friendly shores of the Dutch Republic.

In their flight they had left their houses, their goods, and their means of livelihood. They were strangers in a strange land, among a people of different language and customs. They were forced to resort to new and untried occupations to earn their bread. Middle-aged men, who had spent their lives in tilling the soil, had now to learn mechanical trades. But they cheerfully accepted the situation and lost no time in idleness or repining. Though often pinched with poverty, they thanked God for the blessings which were still granted them and found their joy in unmolested spiritual communion. »They knew they were pilgrims, and looked not much on those things, but lifted up their eyes to heaven, their dearest country, and quieted their spirits.« Bancroft, pt. 1, ch. 12, par. 15

In the midst of exile and hardship their love and faith waxed strong. They trusted the Lord's promises, and He did not fail them in time of need. His angels were by their side, to encourage and support them. And when God's hand seemed pointing them across the sea, to a land where they might found for themselves a state, and leave to their children the precious heritage of religious liberty, they went forward, without shrinking, in the path of providence. God had permitted trials to come upon His people to prepare them for the accomplishment of His gracious purpose toward them. The church had been brought low, that she might be exalted. God was about to display His power in her behalf, to give to the world another evidence that He will not forsake those who trust in Him. He had overruled events to cause the wrath of Satan and the plots of evil men to advance His glory and to bring His people to a place of security. Persecution and exile were opening the way to freedom.

When first constrained to separate from the English Church, the Puritans had joined themselves together by a solemn covenant, as the Lord's free people, »to walk together in all His ways made known or to be made known to them.« J. Brown, The Pilgrim Fathers, p. 74 Here was the true spirit of reform, the vital principle of Protestantism. It was with this purpose that the Pilgrims departed from Holland to find a home in the New World. John Robinson, their pastor, who was providentially prevented from accompanying them, in his farewell address to the exiles said: »Brethren, we are now erelong to part asunder, and the Lord knoweth whether I shall live ever to see your faces more. But whether the Lord hath appointed it or not, I charge you before God and His blessed angels to follow me no farther than I have followed Christ. If God should reveal anything to you by any other instrument of His, be as ready to receive it as ever you were to receive any truth of my ministry; for I am very confident the Lord hath more truth and light yet to break forth out of His holy word.« Martyn 5:70

»For my part, I cannot sufficiently bewail the condition of the reformed churches, who are come to a period in religion, and will go at present no farther than the instruments of their reformation. The Lutherans cannot be drawn to go beyond what Luther saw; ... and the Calvinists, you see, stick fast where they were left by that great man of God, who yet saw not all things. This is a misery much to be lamented; for though they were burning and shining lights in their time, yet they penetrated not into the whole counsel of God, but were they now living, would be as willing to embrace further light as that which they first received.« D. Neal, History of the Puritans 1:269

»Remember your church covenant, in which you have agreed to walk in all the ways of the Lord, made or to be made known unto you. Remember your promise and covenant with God and with one another, to receive whatever light and truth shall be made known to you from His written word; but withal, take heed, I beseech you, what you receive for truth, and compare it and weigh it with other scriptures of truth before you accept it; for it is not possible the Christian world should come so lately out of such thick antichristian darkness, and that full perfection of knowledge should break forth at once.« Martyn, vol. 5, pp. 70, 71

It was the desire for liberty of conscience that inspired the Pilgrims to brave the perils of the long journey across the sea, to endure the hardships and dangers of the wilderness, and with God's blessing to lay, on the shores of America, the foundation of a mighty nation. Yet honest and God-fearing as they were, the Pilgrims did not yet comprehend the great principle of religious liberty. The freedom which they sacrificed so much to secure for themselves, they were not equally ready to grant to others. »Very few, even of the foremost thinkers and moralists of the seventeenth century, had any just conception of that grand principle, the outgrowth of the New Testament, which acknowledges God as the sole judge of human faith.« Ibid. 5, p. 297

The doctrine that God has committed to the church the right to control the conscience, and to define and punish heresy, is one of the most deeply rooted of papal errors. While the Reformers rejected the creed of Rome, they were not entirely free from her spirit of intolerance. The dense darkness in which, through the long ages of her rule, popery had enveloped all Christendom, had not even yet been wholly dissipated. Said one of the leading ministers in the colony of Massachusetts Bay: »It was toleration that made the world antichristian; and the church never took harm by the punishment of heretics.« Ibid., vol. 5, p. 335 The regulation was adopted by the colonists that only church members should have a voice in the civil government. A kind of state church was formed, all the people being required to contribute to the support of the clergy, and the magistrates being authorized to suppress heresy. Thus the secular power was in the hands of the church. It was not long before these measures led to the inevitable result – persecution.

Eleven years after the planting of the first colony, Roger Williams came to the New World. Like the early Pilgrims he came to enjoy religious freedom; but, unlike them, he saw – what so few in his time had yet seen – that this freedom was the inalienable right of all, whatever might be their creed. He was an earnest seeker for truth, with Robinson holding it impossible that all the light from God's word had yet been received. Williams »was the first person in modern Christendom to establish civil government on the doctrine of the liberty of conscience, the equality of opinions before the law.« Bancroft, pt. 1, ch. 15, par. 16 He declared it to be the duty of the magistrate to restrain crime, but never to control the conscience. »The public or the magistrates may decide,« he said, »what is due from man to man; but when they attempt to prescribe a man's duties to God, they are out of place, and there can be no safety; for it is clear that if the magistrate has the power, he may decree one set of opinions or beliefs today and another tomorrow; as has been done in England by different kings and queens, and by different popes and councils in the Roman Church; so that belief would become a heap of confusion.« Martyn, vol. 5, p. 340

Attendance at the services of the established church was required under a penalty of fine or imprisonment. "Williams reprobated the law; the worst statute in the English code was that which did but enforce attendance upon the parish church. To compel men to unite with those of a different creed, he regarded as an open violation of their natural rights; to drag to public worship the irreligious and the unwilling, seemed only like requiring hypocrisy. ... 'No one should be bound to worship, or,' he added, 'to maintain a worship, against his own consent.' 'What!' exclaimed his antagonists, amazed at his tenets, 'is not the laborer worthy of his hire?' 'Yes,' replied he, 'from them that hire him.'« Bancroft, pt. 1, ch. 15, par. 2

Roger Williams was respected and beloved as a faithful minister, a man of rare gifts, of unbending integrity and true benevolence; yet his steadfast denial of the right of civil magistrates to authority over the church, and his demand for religious liberty, could not be tolerated. The application of this new doctrine, it was urged, would »subvert the fundamental state and government of the country.« Ibid., pt. 1, ch. 15, par. 10 He was sentenced to banishment from the colonies, and, finally, to avoid arrest, he was forced to flee, amid the cold and storms of winter, into the unbroken forest. »For fourteen weeks,« he says, »I was sorely tossed in a bitter season, not knowing what bread or bed did mean.« But »the ravens fed me in the wilderness,« and a hollow tree often served him for a shelter. Martyn, vol. 5, pp. 349, 350 Thus he continued his painful flight through the snow and the trackless forest, until he found refuge with an Indian tribe whose confidence and affection he had won while endeavoring to teach them the truths of the gospel.

Making his way at last, after months of change and wandering, to the shores of Narragansett Bay, he there laid the foundation of the first state of modern times that in the fullest sense recognized the right of religious freedom. The fundamental principle of Roger Williams's colony was »that every man should have liberty to worship God according to the light of his own conscience.« Ibid., vol. 5, p. 354

 His little state, Rhode Island, became the asylum of

the oppressed, and it increased and prospered until its foundation principles – civil and religious liberty – became the cornerstones of the American Republic.

In that grand old document which our forefathers set forth as their bill of rights – the Declaration of Independence – they declared: »We hold these truths to be self-evident, that all men are created equal; that they are endowed by their Creator with certain unalienable rights; that among these are life, liberty, and the pursuit of happiness.« And the Constitution guarantees, in the most explicit terms, the inviolability of conscience: »No religious test shall ever be required as a qualification to any office or public trust under the United States.« »Congress shall make no law respecting an establishment of religion, or prohibiting the free exercise thereof.«

»The framers of the Constitution recognized the eternal principle that man's relation with his God is above human legislation, and his rights of conscience inalienable. Reasoning was not necessary to establish this truth; we are conscious of it in our own bosoms. It is this consciousness which, in defiance of human laws, has sustained so many martyrs in tortures and flames. They felt that their duty to God was superior to human enactments, and that man could exercise no authority over their consciences. It is an inborn principle which nothing can eradicate.« Congressional documents (U.S.A.), serial No. 200, document No. 271

As the tidings spread through the countries of Europe, of a land where every man might enjoy the fruit of his own labor and obey the convictions of his own conscience, thousands flocked to the shores of the New World. Colonies rapidly multiplied. »Massachusetts, by special law, offered free welcome and aid, at the public cost, to Christians of any nationality who might fly beyond the Atlantic 'to escape from wars or famine, or the oppression of their persecutors.' Thus the fugitive and the downtrodden were, by statute, made the guests of the commonwealth.« Martyn, vol. 5, p. 417 In twenty years from the first landing at Plymouth, as many thousand Pilgrims were settled in New England.

To secure the object which they sought, »they were content to earn a bare subsistence by a life of frugality and toil. They asked nothing from the soil but the reasonable returns of their own labor. No golden vision threw a deceitful halo around their path. ... They were content with the slow but steady progress of their social polity. They patiently endured the privations of the wilderness, watering the tree of liberty with their tears, and with the sweat of their brow, till it took deep root in the land.«

The Bible was held as the foundation of faith, the source of wisdom, and the charter of liberty. Its principles were diligently taught in the home, in the school, and in the church, and its fruits were manifest in thrift, intelligence, purity, and temperance. One might be for years a dweller in the Puritan settlement, »and not see a drunkard, or hear an oath, or meet a beggar.« Bancroft, pt. 1, ch. 19, par. 25 It was demonstrated that the principles of the Bible are the surest safeguards of national greatness. The feeble and isolated colonies grew to a confederation of powerful states, and the world marked with wonder the peace and prosperity of »a church without a pope, and a state without a king.«

But continually increasing numbers were attracted to the shores of America, actuated by motives widely different from those of the first Pilgrims. Though the primitive faith and purity exerted a widespread and molding power, yet its influence became less and less as the numbers increased of those who sought only worldly advantage.

The regulation adopted by the early colonists, of permitting only members of the church to vote or to hold office in the civil government, led to most pernicious results. This measure had been accepted as a means of preserving the purity of the state, but it resulted in the corruption of the church. A profession of religion being the condition of suffrage and officeholding, many, actuated solely by motives of worldly policy, united with the church without a change of heart. Thus the churches came to consist, to a considerable extent, of unconverted persons; and even in the ministry were those who not only held errors of doctrine, but who were ignorant of the renewing power of the Holy Spirit. Thus again was demonstrated the evil results, so often witnessed in the history of the church from the days of Constantine to the present, of attempting to build up the church by the aid of the state, of appealing to the secular power in support of the gospel of Him who declared: »My kingdom is not of this world.« John 18:36 The union of the church with the state, be the degree never so slight, while it may appear to bring the world nearer to the church, does in reality but bring the church nearer to the world.

The great principle so nobly advocated by Robinson and Roger Williams, that truth is progressive, that Christians should stand ready to accept all the light which may shine from

God's holy word, was lost sight of by their descendants. The Protestant churches of America, – and those of Europe as well, – so highly favored in receiving the blessings of the Reformation, failed to press forward in the path of reform. Though a few faithful men arose, from time to time, to proclaim new truth and expose long-cherished error, the majority, like the Jews in Christ's day or the papists in the time of Luther, were content to believe as their fathers had believed and to live as they had lived. Therefore religion again degenerated into formalism; and errors and superstitions which would have been cast aside had the church continued to walk in the light of God's word, were retained and cherished. Thus the spirit inspired by the Refor-

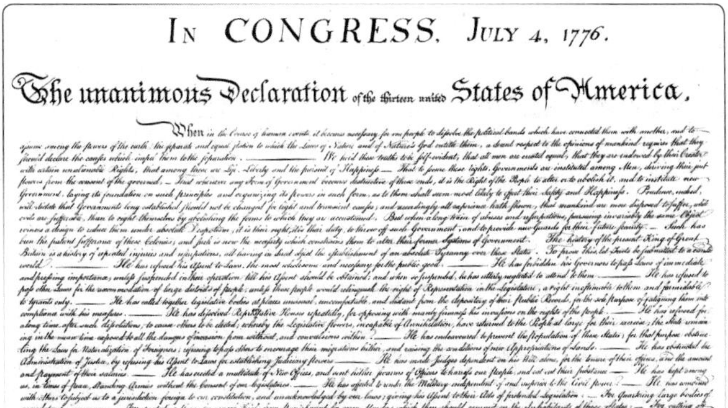
IN CONGRESS, JULY 4, 1776.

The unanimous Declaration of the thirteen united States of America,

Constitution / Declaration of Independence in America

mation gradually died out, until there was almost as great need of reform in the Protestant churches as in the Roman Church in the time of Luther. There was the same worldliness and spiritual stupor, a similar reverence for the opinions of men, and substitution of human theories for the teachings of God's word.

The wide circulation of the Bible in the early part of the nineteenth century, and the great light thus shed upon the world, was not followed by a corresponding advance in knowledge of revealed truth, or in experimental religion. Satan could not, as in former ages, keep God's word from the people; it had been placed within the reach of all; but in order still to accomplish his object, he led many to value it but lightly. Men neglected to search the Scriptures, and thus they continued to accept false interpretations, and to cherish doctrines which had no foundation in the Bible.

Seeing the failure of his efforts to crush out the truth by persecution, Satan had again resorted to the plan of compromise which led to the great apostasy and the formation of the Church of Rome. He had induced Christians to ally themselves, not now with pagans, but with those who, by their devotion to the things of this world, had proved themselves to be as truly idolaters as were the worshipers of graven images. And the results of this union were no less pernicious now than in former ages; pride and extravagance were fostered under the guise of religion, and the churches became corrupted. Satan continued to pervert the doctrines of the Bible, and traditions that were to ruin millions were taking deep root. The church was upholding and defending these traditions, instead of contending for »the faith which was once delivered unto the saints.« Thus were degraded the principles for which the Reformers had done and suffered so much.

CHAPTER 17

HERALDS OF THE MORNING

One of the most solemn and yet most glorious truths revealed in the Bible is that of Christ's second coming to complete the great work of redemption. To God's pilgrim people, so long left to sojourn in »the region and shadow of death,« a precious, joy-inspiring hope is given in the promise of His appearing, who is »the resurrection and the life,« to »bring home again His banished.« The doctrine of the second advent is the very keynote of the Sacred Scriptures. From the day when the first pair turned their sorrowing steps from Eden, the children of faith have waited the coming of the Promised One to break the destroyer's power and bring them again to the lost Paradise. Holy men of old looked forward to the advent of the Messiah in glory, as the consummation of their hope. Enoch, only the seventh in descent from them that dwelt in Eden, he who for three centuries on earth walked with his God, was permitted to behold from afar the coming of the Deliverer. »Behold,« he declared, »the Lord cometh with ten thousands of His saints, to execute judgment upon all.« Jude 14, 15 The patriarch Job in the night of his affliction exclaimed with unshaken trust: »I know that my Redeemer liveth, and that He shall stand at the latter day upon the earth: ... in my flesh shall I see God: whom I shall see for myself, and mine eyes shall behold, and not another.« Job 19:25-27

The coming of Christ to usher in the reign of righteousness has inspired the most sublime and impassioned utterances of the sacred writers. The poets and prophets of the Bible have dwelt upon it in words glowing with celestial fire. The psalmist sang of the power and majesty of Israel's King: »Out of Zion, the perfection of beauty, God hath shined. Our God shall come, and shall not keep silence. ... He shall call to the heavens from above, and to the earth, that He may judge His people.« Psalm 50:2-4 »Let the heavens rejoice, and let the earth be glad ... before the Lord: for He cometh, for He cometh to judge the earth: He shall judge the world with righteousness, and the people with His truth.« Psalm 96:11-13 Said the prophet Isaiah: »Awake and sing, ye that dwell in dust: for thy dew is as the dew of herbs, and the earth shall cast out the dead.« »Thy dead men shall live, together with my dead body shall they arise.« »He will swallow up death in victory; and the Lord God will wipe away tears from off all faces; and the rebuke of His people shall He take away from off all the earth: for the Lord hath spoken it. And it shall be said in that day, Lo, this is our God; we have waited for Him, and He will save us: this is the Lord; we have waited for Him, we will be glad and rejoice in His salvation.« Isaiah 26:19; 25:8, 9

And Habakkuk, rapt in holy vision, beheld His appearing. »God came from Teman, and the Holy One from Mount Paran. His glory covered the heavens, and the earth was full of His praise. And His brightness was as the light.« »He stood, and measured the earth: He beheld, and drove asunder the nations; and the everlasting mountains were scattered, the perpetual hill did bow: His ways are everlasting.« »Thou didst ride upon Thine horses and Thy chariots of salvation.« »The mountains saw Thee, and they trembled: ... the deep uttered his voice, and lifted up his hands on high. The sun and moon stood still in their habitation: at the light of Thine arrows they went, and at the shining of Thy glittering spear.« »Thou wentest forth for the salvation of Thy people, even for salvation with Thine anointed.« Habakkuk 3:3,4,6,8,10,11,13

When the Saviour was about to be separated from His disciples, He comforted them in their sorrow with the assurance that He would come again: »Let not your heart be troubled. ... In My Father's house are many mansions. ... I go to prepare a place for you. And if I go and prepare a place for you, I will come again, and receive you unto Myself.« John 14:1-3 »The Son of man shall come in His glory, and all the holy angels with Him.« »Then shall He sit upon the throne of His glory: and before Him shall be gathered all nations.« Matthew 25:31-32

The angels who lingered upon Olivet after Christ's ascension repeated to the disciples the promise of His return: »This same Jesus, which is taken up from you into heaven, shall so come in like manner as ye have seen Him go into heaven.« Acts 1:11 And the apostle Paul, speaking by the Spirit of Inspiration, testified: »The Lord Himself shall descend from heaven with a shout, with the voice of the Archangel, and with the trump of God.« 1 Thessalonians 4:16 Says the prophet of Patmos: »Behold, He cometh with clouds; and every eye shall see Him.« Revelation 1:7 About His coming cluster the glories of that »restitution of all things, which God hath spoken by the mouth of all His holy prophets since the world began.« Acts 3:21 Then the long-continued rule of evil shall be broken; »the kingdoms of this world« will become »the kingdoms of our Lord, and of His Christ; and He shall reign for ever and ever.« Revelation 11:15 »The glory of the Lord shall be revealed, and all flesh shall see it together.« »The Lord God will cause righteousness and praise to spring forth before all the nations.« He shall be »for a crown of glory, and for a diadem of beauty, unto the residue of His people.« Isaiah 40:5; 61:11; Isaiah 28:5

It is then that the peaceful and long-desired kingdom of the Messiah shall be established under the whole heaven. »The Lord shall comfort Zion: He will comfort all her waste places; and He will make her wilderness like Eden, and her desert like the garden of the Lord.« »The glory of Lebanon shall be given unto it, the excellency of Carmel and Sharon.« »Thou shalt no more be termed Forsaken; neither shall thy land any more be termed Desolate: but thou shalt be called My Delight, and thy land Beulah.« »As the bridegroom rejoiceth over the bride, so shall thy God rejoice over thee.« Isaiah 51:3; 35:2; 62:4, 5, margin

The coming of the Lord has been in all ages the hope of His true followers. The Saviour's parting promise upon Olivet, that He would come again, lighted up the future for His disciples, filling their hearts with joy and hope that sorrow could not quench nor trials dim. Amid suffering and persecution, the »appearing of the great God and our Saviour Jesus Christ« was the »blessed hope.« When the Thessalonian Christians were filled with grief as they buried their loved ones, who had hoped to live to witness the coming of the Lord, Paul, their teacher, pointed them to the resurrection, to take place at the Saviour's advent. Then the dead in Christ should rise, and together with the living be caught up to meet the Lord in the air. »And so,« he said, »shall we ever be with the Lord. Wherefore comfort one another with these words.« 1.Thess. 4:16-18 On rocky Patmos the beloved disciple hears the promise, »Surely I come quickly,« and his longing response voices the prayer of the church in all her pilgrimage, »Even so, come, Lord Jesus.« Rev. 22:20 From the dungeon, the stake, the scaffold, where saints and martyrs witnessed for the truth, comes down the centuries the utterance of their faith and hope. Being »assured of His personal resurrection, and consequently of their own at His coming, for this cause,« says one of these Christians, »they despised death, and were found to be above it.« Daniel T. Taylor, The Reign of Christ on Earth: or, The Voice of the Church in All Ages, p. 33 They were willing to go down to the grave, that they might »rise free.« Ibid., p. 54 They looked for the »Lord to come from heaven in the clouds with the glory of His Father,« »bringing to the just the times of the kingdom.« The Waldenses cherished the same faith. Ibid., pp. 129-132 Wycliffe looked forward to the Redeemer's appearing as the hope of the church. Ibid., pp. 132-134

Luther declared: »I persuade myself verily, that the day of judgment will not be absent full three hundred years. God will not, cannot, suffer this wicked world much longer.« »The great day is drawing near in which the kingdom of abominations shall be overthrown.« Ibid., p. 158,134 »This aged world is not far from its end,« said Melanchthon. Calvin bids Christians »not to hesitate, ardently desiring the day of Christ's coming as of all events most auspicious;« and declares that »the whole family of the faithful will keep in view that day.« »We must hunger after Christ, we must seek, contemplate,« he says, »till the dawning of that great day, when our Lord will fully manifest the glory of His kingdom.« Ibid., pp. 158,134 »Has not the Lord Jesus carried up our flesh into heaven?« said Knox, the Scotch Reformer, »and shall He not return? We know that He shall return, and that with expedition.« Ridley and Latimer, who laid down their lives for the truth, looked in faith for the Lord's coming. Ridley wrote: "The world without doubt – this I do believe, and therefore I say it – draws to an end. Let us with John, the servant of God, cry in our hearts unto our Saviour Christ, Come, Lord Jesus, come.« Ibid., pp. 151,145

»The thoughts of the coming of the Lord,« said Baxter, »are most sweet and joyful to me.« Richard Baxter, Works, vol. 17, p. 555 »It is the work of faith and the character of His saints to love His appearing and to look for that blessed hope.« »If death be the last enemy to be destroyed at the resurrection, we may learn how earnestly believers should long and pray for the second coming of Christ, when this full and final conquest shall be made.« Ibid., vol. 17, p. 500 »This is the day that all believers should long, and hope, and wait for, as being the accomplishment of all the work of their redemption, and all the desires and endeavors of their souls.« »Hasten, O Lord, this blessed day!« Ibid., vol. 17, pp. 182, 183 Such was the hope of the apostolic church, of the »church in the wilderness,« and of the Reformers.

Prophecy not only foretells the manner and object of Christ's coming, but presents tokens by which men are to know when it is near. Said Jesus: »There shall be signs in the sun, and in the moon, and in the stars.« Luke 21:25 »The sun shall be darkened, and the moon shall not give her light, and the stars of heaven shall fall, and the powers that are in heaven shall be shaken.

And then shall they see the Son of man coming in the clouds with great power and glory.« Mark 13:24-26 The revelator thus describes the first of the signs to precede the second advent: »There was a great earthquake; and the sun became black as sackcloth of hair, and the moon became as blood.« Revelation 6:12

These signs were witnessed before the opening of the nineteenth century. In fulfillment of this prophecy there occurred, in the year 1755, the most terrible earthquake that has ever been recorded. Though commonly known as the earthquake of Lisbon, it extended to the greater part of Europe, Africa, and America. It was felt in Greenland, in the West Indies, in the island of Madeira, in Norway and Sweden, Great Britain and Ireland. It pervaded an extent of not less than four million square miles. In Africa the shock was almost as severe as in Europe. A great part of Algiers was destroyed; and a short distance from Morocco, a village containing eight or ten thousand inhabitants was swallowed up. A vast wave swept over the coast of Spain and Africa engulfing cities and causing great destruction. It was in Spain and Portugal that the shock manifested its extreme violence. At Cadiz the inflowing wave was said to be sixty feet high. Mountains, »some of the largest in Portugal, were impetuously shaken, as it were, from their very foundations, and some of them opened at their summits, which were split and rent in a wonderful manner, huge masses of them being thrown down into the adjacent valleys. Flames are related to have issued from these mountains.« Sir Charles Lyell, Principles of Geology, p. 495

At Lisbon »a sound of thunder was heard underground, and immediately afterwards a violent shock threw down the greater part of that city. In the course of about six minutes sixty thousand persons perished. The sea first retired, and laid the bar dry; it then rolled in, rising fifty feet or more above its ordinary level.« »Among other extraordinary events related to have occurred at Lisbon during the catastrophe, was the subsidence of a new quay, built entirely of marble, at an immense expense. A great concourse of people had collected there for safety, as a spot where they might be beyond the reach of falling ruins; but suddenly the quay sank down with all the people on it, and not one of the dead bodies ever floated to the surface.« Ibid., p. 495 »The shock« of the earthquake »was instantly followed by the fall of every church and convent, almost all the large public buildings, and more than one fourth of the houses. In [304/305] about two hours after the shock, fires broke out in different quarters, and raged with such violence for the space of nearly three days, that the city was completely desolated. The earthquake happened on a holyday, when the churches and convents were full of people, very few of whom escaped.« Encyclopedia Americana, art. »Lisbon,« note (ed. 1831) »The terror of the people was beyond description. Nobody wept; it was beyond tears. They ran hither and thither, delirious with horror and astonishment, beating their faces and breasts, crying, 'Misericordia! the world's at an end!' Mothers forgot their children, and ran about loaded with crucifixed images. Unfortunately, many ran to the churches for protection; but in vain was the sacrament exposed; in vain did the poor creatures embrace the altars; images, priests, and people were buried in one common ruin.« It has been estimated that ninety thousand persons lost their lives on that fatal day.

Twenty-five years later appeared the next sign mentioned in the prophecy – the darkening of the sun and moon. What rendered this more striking was the fact that the time of its fulfillment had been definitely pointed out. In the Saviour's conversation with His disciples upon Olivet, after describing the long period of trial for the church, – the 1260 years of papal persecution, concerning which He had promised that the tribulation should be shortened, – He thus mentioned certain events to precede His coming, and fixed the time when the first of these should be witnessed: »In those days, after that tribulation, the sun shall be darkened, and the moon shall not give her light.« Mark 13:24 The 1260 days, or years, terminated in 1798. A quarter of a century earlier, persecution had almost wholly ceased. Following this

Earthquake at Lisbon in 1755

persecution, according to the words of Christ, the sun was to be darkened. On the 19th of May, 1780, this prophecy was fulfilled. »Almost, if not altogether alone, as the most mysterious and as yet unexplained phenomenon of its kind, ... stands the dark day of May 19, 1780, – a most unaccountable darkening of the whole visible heavens and atmosphere in New England.« R. M. Devens, Our First Century, p. 89

An eyewitness living in Massachusetts describes the event as follows: »In the morning the sun rose clear, but was soon overcast. The clouds became lowery, and from them, black and ominous, as they soon appeared, lightning flashed, thunder rolled, and a little rain fell. Toward nine o'clock, the clouds became thinner, and assumed a brassy or coppery appearance, and earth, rocks, trees, buildings, water, and persons were changed by this strange, unearthly light. A few minutes later, a heavy black cloud spread over the entire sky except a narrow rim at the horizon, and it was as dark as it usually is at nine o'clock on a summer evening. ... »Fear, anxiety, and awe gradually filled the minds of the people. Women stood at the door, looking out upon the dark landscape; men returned from their labor in the fields; the carpenter left his tools, the blacksmith his forge, the tradesman his counter. Schools were dismissed, and tremblingly the children fled homeward. Travelers put up at the nearest farmhouse. 'What is coming?' queried every lip and heart. It seemed as if a hurricane was about to dash across the land, or as if it was the day of the consummation of all things.«

»Candles were used; and hearth fires shone as brightly as on a moonless evening in autumn. ... Fowls retired to their roosts and went to sleep, cattle gathered at the pasture bars and lowed, frogs peeped, birds sang their evening songs, and bats flew about. But the human knew that night had not come. ... Dr. Nathanael Whittaker, pastor of the Tabernacle church in Salem, held religious services in the meeting-house, and preached a sermon in which he maintained that the darkness was supernatural. Congregations came together in many other places. The texts for the extemporaneous sermons were invariably those that seemed to indicate that the darkness was consonant with Scriptural prophecy. ... The darkness was most dense shortly after eleven o'clock.« The Essex Antiquarian, April, 1899, vol. 3, No. 4, pp. 53, 54

»In most parts of the country it was so great in the daytime, that the people could not tell the hour by either watch or clock, nor dine, nor manage their domestic business, without the light of candles. ... The extent of this darkness was extraordinary. It was observed as far east as Falmouth. To the westward it reached to the farthest part of Connecticut, and to Albany. To the southward, it was observed along the seacoasts; and to the north as far as the American settlements extend.« William Gordon, History of the Rise, Progress, and Establishment of the Independence of the U.S.A., vol. 3, p. 57

The intense darkness of the day was succeeded, an hour or two before evening, by a partially clear sky, and the sun appeared, though it was still obscured by the black, heavy mist. »After sundown, the clouds came again overhead, and it grew dark very fast.« »Nor was the darkness of the night less uncommon and terrifying than that of the day; notwithstanding there was almost a full moon, no object was discernible but by the help of some artificial light, which, when seen from the neighboring houses and other places at a distance, appeared through a kind of Egyptian darkness which seemed almost impervious to the rays.« Isaiah Thomas, Massachusetts Spy; or, American Oracle of Liberty, vol. 10, No. 472 (May 25, 1780) Said an eyewitness of the scene: »I could not help conceiving at the time, that if every luminous body in the universe had been shrouded in impenetrable shades, or struck out of existence, the darkness could not have been more complete.« Letter by Dr. Samuel Tenney, of Exeter, New Hampshire, December, 1785 (in Massachusetts Historical Society Collections, 1792, 1st series, vol. 1, p. 97) Though at nine o'clock that night the moon rose to the full, »it had not the least effect to dispel the deathlike shadows.« After midnight the darkness disappeared, and the moon, when first visible, had the appearance of blood.

May 19, 1780, stands in history as »The Dark Day.« Since the time of Moses no period of darkness of equal density, extent, and duration, has ever been recorded. The description of this event, as given by eyewitnesses, is but an echo of the words of the Lord, recorded by the prophet Joel, twenty-five hundred years previous to their fulfillment: »The sun shall be turned into darkness, and the moon into blood, before the great and terrible day of the Lord come.« Joel 2:31 Christ had bidden His people watch for the signs of His advent and rejoice as they should behold the tokens of their coming King. »When these things begin to come to pass,« He said, »then look up, and lift up your heads; for your redemption draweth nigh.« He pointed His followers to the budding trees of spring, and said: »When they now shoot forth, ye see and know of your own selves that summer is now nigh at hand. So likewise ye, when ye see these things come to pass, know ye that the kingdom of God is nigh at hand.« Luke 21:28, 30, 31

But as the spirit of humility and devotion in the church had given place to pride and formalism, love for Christ and faith in His coming had grown cold. Absorbed in worldliness and pleasure seeking, the professed people of God were blinded to the Saviour's instructions concerning the signs of His appearing. The doctrine of the second advent had been neglected; the scriptures relating to it were obscured by misinterpretation, until it was, to a great extent, ignored and forgotten. Especially was this the case in the churches of America. The freedom and comfort enjoyed by all classes of society, the ambitious desire for wealth and luxury, begetting an absorbing devotion to money-making, the eager rush for popularity and power, which seemed to be within the reach of all, led men to center their interests and hopes on the things of this life, and to put far in the future that solemn day when the present order of things should pass away. When the Saviour pointed out to His followers the signs of His return, He foretold the state of backsliding that would exist just prior to His second advent. There would be, as in the days of Noah, the activity and stir of worldly business and pleasure seeking – buying, selling, planting, building, marrying, and giving in marriage – with forgetfulness of God and the future life. For those living at this time, Christ's admonition is: »Take heed to yourselves, lest at any time your hearts be overcharged with surfeiting, and drunkenness, and cares of this life, and so that day come upon you unawares.« »Watch ye therefore, and pray always, that ye may be accounted worthy to escape all these things that shall come to pass, and to stand before the Son of man.« Luke 21:34, 36

The condition of the church at this time is pointed out in the Saviour's words in the Revelation: »Thou hast a name that thou livest, and art dead.« And to those who refuse to arouse from their careless security, the solemn warning is addressed: »If therefore thou shalt not watch, I will come on thee as a thief, and thou shalt not know what hour I will come upon thee.« Revelation 3:1, 3

It was needful that men should be awakened to their danger; that they should be roused to prepare for the solemn events connected with the close of probation. The prophet of God declares: »The day of the Lord is great and very terrible; and who can abide it?« Who shall stand when He appeareth who is »of purer eyes than to behold evil,« and cannot »look on iniquity«? Joel 2:11; Habakkuk 1:13 To them that cry, »My God, we know Thee,« yet have transgressed His covenant, and hastened after another god, hiding iniquity in their hearts, and loving the paths of unrighteousness – to these the day of the Lord is »darkness, and not light, even very dark, and no brightness in it.« Hosea 8:2, 1; Psalm 16:4; Amos 5:20 »It shall come to pass at that time,« saith the Lord, »that I will search Jerusalem with candles, and punish the men that are settled on their lees: that say in their heart, The Lord will not do good, neither will He do evil.« Zephaniah 1:12 »I will punish the world for their evil, and the wicked for their iniquity; and I will cause the arrogancy of the proud to cease, and will lay low the haughtiness of the terrible.« Isaiah 13:11 »Neither their silver nor their gold shall be able to deliver them;« »their goods shall become a booty, and their houses a desolation.« Zephaniah 1:18, 13

The prophet Jeremiah, looking forward to this fearful time, exclaimed: »I am pained at my very heart. ... I cannot hold my peace, because thou hast heard, O my soul, the sound of the trumpet, the alarm of war. Destruction upon destruction is cried.« Jeremiah 4:19, 20 »That day is a day of wrath, a day of trouble and distress, a day of wasteness and desolation, a day of darkness and gloominess, a day of clouds and thick darkness, a day of the trumpet and alarm.« Zephaniah 1:15-16 »Behold, the day of the Lord cometh, ... to lay the land desolate: and He shall destroy the sinners thereof out of it.« Isaiah 13:9

In view of that great day the word of God, in the most solemn and impressive language, calls upon His people to arouse from their spiritual lethargy and to seek His face with repentance and humiliation: »Blow ye the trumpet in Zion, and sound an alarm in My holy mountain: let all the inhabitants of the land tremble: for the day of the Lord cometh, for it is nigh at hand.« »Sanctify a fast, call a solemn assembly: gather the people, sanctify the congregation, assemble the elders, gather the children: ... let the bridegroom go forth of his chamber, and the bride out of her closet. Let the priests, the ministers of the Lord, weep between the porch and the altar.« »Turn ye even to Me with all your heart, and with fasting, and with weeping, and with mourning: and rend your heart, and not your garments, and turn unto the Lord your God: for He is gracious and merciful, slow to anger, and of great kindness.« Joel 2:1, 15-17, 12-13

To prepare a people to stand in the day of God, a great work of reform was to be accomplished. God saw that many of His professed people were not building for eternity, and in His mercy He was about to send a message of warning to arouse them from their stupor and lead them to make ready for the coming of the Lord.

This warning is brought to view in Revelation 14. Here is a threefold message represented as proclaimed by heavenly beings and immediately followed by the coming of the Son of man to reap »the harvest of the earth.« The first of these warnings announces the approaching judgment. The prophet beheld an angel flying »in the midst of heaven, having the everlasting gospel to preach unto them that dwell on the earth, and to every nation, and kindred, and tongue, and people, saying with a loud voice, Fear God, and give glory to Him; for the hour of His judgment is come: and worship Him that made heaven, and earth, and the sea, and the fountains of waters.« Rev. 14:6-7

This message is declared to be a part of »the everlasting gospel.« The work of preaching the gospel has not been committed to angels, but has been entrusted to men. Holy angels have been employed in directing this work, they have in charge the great movements for the salvation of men; but the actual proclamation of the gospel is performed by the servants of Christ upon the earth. Faithful men, who were obedient to the promptings of God's Spirit and the teachings of His word, were to proclaim this warning to the world. They were those who had taken heed to the »sure word of prophecy,« the »light that shineth in a dark place, until the day dawn, and the daystar arise.« 2 Peter 1:19 They had been seeking the knowledge of God more than all hid treasures, counting it »better than the merchandise of silver, and the gain thereof than fine gold.« Proverbs 3:14 And the Lord revealed to them the great things of the kingdom. »The secret of the Lord is with them that fear Him; and He will show them His covenant.« Psalm 25:14

It was not the scholarly theologians who had an understanding of this truth, and engaged in its proclamation. Had these been faithful watchmen, diligently and prayerfully searching the Scriptures, they would have known the time of night; the prophecies would have opened to them the events about to take place. But they did not occupy this position, and the message was given by humbler men. Said Jesus: »Walk while ye have the light, lest darkness come upon you.« John 12:35 Those who turn away from the light which God has given, or who neglect to seek it when it is within their reach, are left in darkness. But the Saviour declares: »He that followeth Me shall not walk in darkness, but shall have the light of life.« John 8:12 Whoever is with singleness of purpose seeking to do God's will, earnestly heeding the light already given, will receive greater light; to that soul some star of heavenly radiance will be sent to guide him into all truth. At the time of Christ's first advent the priests and scribes of the Holy City, to whom were entrusted the oracles of God, might have discerned the signs of the times and proclaimed the coming of the Promised One. The prophecy of Micah designated His birthplace; Daniel specified the time of His advent. Micah 5:2; Daniel 9:25 God committed these prophecies to the Jewish leaders; they were without excuse if they did not know and declare to the people that the Messiah's coming was at hand. Their ignorance was the result of sinful neglect. The Jews were building monuments for the slain prophets of God, while by their deference to the great men of earth they were paying homage to the servants of Satan. Absorbed in their ambitious strife for place and power among men, they lost sight of the divine honors proffered them by the King of heaven.

With profound and reverent interest the elders of Israel should have been studying the place, the time, the circumstances, of the greatest event in the world's history – the coming of the Son of God to accomplish the redemption of man. All the people should have been watching and waiting that they might be among the first to welcome the world's Redeemer. But, lo, at Bethlehem two weary travelers from the hills of Nazareth traverse the whole length of the narrow street to the eastern extremity of the town, vainly seeking a place of rest and shelter for the night. No doors are open to receive them. In a wretched hovel prepared for cattle, they at last find refuge, and there the Saviour of the world is born.

Heavenly angels had seen the glory which the Son of God shared with the Father before the world was, and they had looked forward with intense interest to His appearing on earth as an event fraught with the greatest joy to all people. Angels were appointed to carry the glad tidings to those who were prepared to receive it and who would joyfully make it known to the inhabitants of the earth. Christ had stooped to take upon Himself man's nature; He was to bear an infinite weight of woe as He should make His soul an offering for sin; yet angels desired that even in His humiliation the Son of the Highest might appear before men with a dignity and glory befitting His character. Would the great men of earth assemble at Israel's capital to greet His coming? Would legions of angels present Him to the expectant company?

An angel visits the earth to see who are prepared to welcome Jesus. But he can discern no tokens of expectancy. He hears no voice of
 praise and triumph that the period of Messiah's com-

ing is at hand. The angel hovers for a time over the chosen city and the temple where the divine presence has been manifested for ages; but even here is the same indifference. The priests, in their pomp and pride, are offering polluted sacrifices in the temple. The Pharisees are with loud voices addressing the people or making boastful prayers at the corners of the streets. In the palaces of kings, in the assemblies of philosophers, in the schools of the rabbis, all are alike unmindful of the wondrous fact which has filled all heaven with joy and praise – that the Redeemer of men is about to appear upon the earth.

There is no evidence that Christ is expected, and no preparation for the Prince of life. In amazement the celestial messenger is about to return to heaven with the shameful tidings, when he discovers a group of shepherds who are watching their flocks by night, and, as they gaze into the starry heavens, are contemplating the prophecy of a Messiah to come to earth, and longing for the advent of the world's Redeemer. Here is a company that is prepared to receive the heavenly message. And suddenly the angel of the Lord appears, declaring the good tidings of great joy. Celestial glory floods all the plain, an innumerable company of angels is revealed, and as if the joy were too great for one messenger to bring from heaven, a multitude of voices break forth in the anthem which all the nations of the saved shall one day sing: »Glory to God in the highest, and on earth peace, good will toward men.« Luke 2:14 Oh, what a lesson is this wonderful story of Bethlehem! How it rebukes our unbelief, our pride and self-sufficiency. How it warns us to beware, lest by our criminal indifference we also fail to discern the signs of the times, and therefore know not the day of our visitation.

It was not alone upon the hills of Judea, not among the lowly shepherds only, that angels found the watchers for Messiah's coming. In the land of the heathen also were those that looked for Him; they were wise men, rich and noble, the philosophers of the East. Students of nature, the Magi had seen God in His handiwork. From the Hebrew Scriptures they had learned of the Star to arise out of Jacob, and with eager desire they awaited His coming, who should be not only the »Consolation of Israel,« but a »Light to lighten the Gentiles,« and »for salvation unto the ends of the earth.« Luke 2:25, 32; Acts 13:47 They were seekers for light, and light from the throne of God illumined the path for their feet. While the priests and rabbis of Jerusalem, the appointed guardians and expounders of the truth, were shrouded in darkness, the Heaven-sent star guided these Gentile strangers to the birthplace of the newborn King. It is »unto them that look for Him« that Christ is to »appear the second time without sin unto salvation.« Hebrews 9:28 Like the tidings of the Saviour's birth, the message of the second advent was not committed to the religious leaders of the people. They had failed to preserve their connection with God, and had refused light from heaven; therefore they were not of the number described by the apostle Paul: »But ye, brethren, are not in darkness, that that day should overtake you as a thief. Ye are all the children of light, and the children of the day: we are not of the night, nor of darkness.« 1 Thessalonians 5:4-5

The watchmen upon the walls of Zion should have been the first to catch the tidings of the Saviour's advent, the first to lift their voices to proclaim Him near, the first to warn the people to prepare for His coming. But they were at ease, dreaming of peace and safety, while the people were asleep in their sins. Jesus saw His church, like the barren fig tree, covered with pretentious leaves, yet destitute of precious fruit. There was a boastful observance of the forms of religion, while the spirit of true humility, penitence, and faith - which alone could render the service acceptable to God – was lacking. Instead of the graces of the Spirit there were manifested pride, formalism, vainglory, selfishness, oppression. A backsliding church closed their eyes to the signs of the times. God did not forsake them, or suffer His faithfulness to fail; but they departed from Him, and separated themselves from His love. As they refused to comply with the conditions, His promises were not fulfilled to them.

Such is the sure result of neglect to appreciate and improve the light and privileges which God bestows. Unless the church will follow on in His opening providence, accepting every ray of light, performing every duty which may be revealed, religion will inevitably degenerate into the observance of forms, and the spirit of vital godliness will disappear. This truth has been repeatedly illustrated in the history of the church. God requires of His people works of faith and obedience corresponding to the blessings and privileges bestowed. Obedience requires a sacrifice and involves a cross; and this is why so many of the professed followers of Christ refused to receive the light from heaven, and, like the Jews of old, knew not the time of their visitation. Luke 19:44 Because of their pride and unbelief the Lord passed them by and revealed His truth to those who, like the shepherds of Bethlehem and the Eastern Magi, had given heed to all the light they had received.

Chapter 18

An American Reformer

An Upright, honest-hearted farmer, who had been led to doubt the divine authority of the Scriptures, yet who sincerely desired to know the truth, was the man specially chosen of God to lead out in the proclamation of Christ's second coming. Like many other reformers, William Miller had in early life battled with poverty and had thus learned the great lessons of energy and self-denial. The members of the family from which he sprang were characterized by an independent, liberty-loving spirit, by capability of endurance, and ardent patriotism – traits which were also prominent in his character. His father was a captain in the army of the Revolution, and to the sacrifices which he made in the struggles and sufferings of that stormy period may be traced the straitened circumstances of Miller's early life.

He had a sound physical constitution, and even in childhood gave evidence of more than ordinary intellectual strength. As he grew older, this became more marked. His mind was active and well developed, and he had a keen thirst for knowledge. Though he did not enjoy the advantages of a collegiate education, his love of study and a habit of careful thought and close criticism rendered him a man of sound judgment and comprehensive views. He possessed an irreproachable moral character and an enviable reputation, being generally esteemed for integrity, thrift, and benevolence. By dint of energy and application he early acquired a competence, though his habits of study were still maintained. He filled various civil and military offices with credit, and the avenues to wealth and honor seemed wide open to him. His mother was a woman of sterling piety, and in childhood, he had been subject to religious impressions. In early manhood, however, he was thrown into the society of deists, whose influence was the stronger from the fact that they were mostly good citizens and men of humane and benevolent disposition. Living, as they did, in the midst of Christian institutions, their characters had been to some extent molded by their surroundings.

For the excellencies which won them respect and confidence they were indebted to the Bible; and yet these good gifts were so perverted as to exert an influence against the word of God. By association with these men, Miller was led to adopt their sentiments. The current interpretations of Scripture presented difficulties which seemed to him insurmountable; yet his new belief, while setting aside the Bible, offered nothing better to take its place, and he remained far from satisfied. He continued to hold these views, however, for about twelve years. But at the age of thirty-four the Holy Spirit impressed his heart with a sense of his condition as a sinner. He found in his former belief no assurance of happiness beyond the grave. The future was dark and gloomy. Referring afterward to his feelings at this time, he said: »Annihilation was a cold and chilling thought, and accountability was sure destruction to all. The heavens were as brass over my head, and the earth as iron under my feet. Eternity – what was it? And death – why was it? The more I reasoned, the further I was from demonstration. The more I thought, the more scattered were my conclusions. I tried to stop thinking, but my thoughts would not be controlled. I was truly wretched, but did not understand the cause. I murmured and complained, but knew not of whom. I knew that there was a wrong, but knew not how or where to find the right. I mourned, but without hope.«

In this state he continued for some months. »Suddenly,« he says, »the character of a Saviour was vividly impressed upon my mind. It seemed that there might be a being so good and compassionate as to himself atone for our transgressions, and thereby save us from suffering the penalty of sin. I immediately felt how lovely such a being must be, and imagined that I could cast myself into the arms of, and trust in the mercy of, such a one. But the question arose, How can it be proved that such a being does exist? Aside from the Bible, I found that I could get no evidence of the existence of such a Saviour, or even of a future state. ... »I saw that the Bible did bring to view just such a Saviour as I needed; and I was perplexed to find how an uninspired book should develop principles so perfectly adapted to the wants of a fallen world. I was constrained to admit that the Scriptures must be a revelation from God. They became my delight; and in Jesus I found a friend. The Saviour became to me the chiefest among ten thousand; and the Scriptures, which before

 were dark and contradictory, now became the lamp to

my feet and light to my path. My mind became settled and satisfied. I found the Lord God to be a Rock in the midst of the ocean of life. The Bible now became my chief study, and I can truly say, I searched it with great delight. I found the half was never told me. I wondered why I had not seen its beauty and glory before, and marveled that I could have ever rejected it. I found everything revealed that my heart could desire, and a remedy for every disease of the soul. I lost all taste for other reading, and applied my heart to get wisdom from God.« S. Bliss, Memoirs of Wm. Miller, pp. 65-67

Miller publicly professed his faith in the religion which he had despised. But his infidel associates were not slow to bring forward all those arguments which he himself had often urged against the divine authority of the Scriptures. He was not then prepared to answer them; but he reasoned that if the Bible is a revelation from God, it must be consistent with itself; and that as it was given for man's instruction, it must be adapted to his understanding. He determined to study the Scriptures for himself, and ascertain if every apparent contradiction could not be harmonized.

Endeavoring to lay aside all preconceived opinions, and dispensing with commentaries, he compared scripture with scripture by the aid of the marginal references and the concordance. He pursued his study in a regular and methodical manner; beginning with Genesis, and reading verse by verse, he proceeded no faster than the meaning of the several passages so unfolded as to leave him free from all embarrassment. When he found anything obscure, it was his custom to compare it with every other text which seemed to have any reference to the matter under consideration. Every word was permitted to have its proper bearing upon the subject of the text, and if his view of it harmonized with every collateral passage, it ceased to be a difficulty. Thus whenever he met with a passage hard to be understood he found an explanation in some other portion of the Scriptures. As he studied with earnest prayer for divine enlightenment, that which had before appeared dark to his understanding was made clear. He experienced the truth of the psalmist's words: »The entrance of Thy words giveth light; it giveth understanding unto the simple.« Psalm 119:130

With intense interest he studied the books of Daniel and the Revelation, employing the same principles of interpretation as in the other scriptures, and found, to his great joy, that the prophetic symbols could be understood. He saw that the proph- [319/320] ecies, so far as they had been fulfilled, had been fulfilled literally; that all the various figures, metaphors, parables, similitudes, etc., were either explained in their immediate connection, or the terms in which they were expressed were defined in other scriptures, and when thus explained, were to be literally understood. »I was thus satisfied,« he says, »that the Bible is a system of revealed truths, so clearly and simply given that the wayfaring man, though a fool, need not err therein.« Bliss, p. 70 Link after link of the chain of truth rewarded his efforts, as step by step he traced down the great lines of prophecy. Angels of heaven were guiding his mind and opening the Scriptures to his understanding.

Taking the manner in which the prophecies had been fulfilled in the past as a criterion by which to judge of the fulfillment of those which were still future, he became satisfied that the popular view of the spiritual reign of Christ – a temporal millennium before the end of the world - was not sustained by the word of God. This doctrine, pointing to a thousand years of righteousness and peace before the personal coming of the Lord, put far off the terrors of the day of God. But, pleasing though it may be, it is contrary to the teachings of Christ and His apostles, who declared that the wheat and the tares and to grow together until the harvest, the end of the world; that »evil men and seducers shall wax worse and worse;« that »in the last days perilous times shall come;« and that the kingdom of darkness shall continue until the advent of the Lord and shall be consumed with the spirit of His mouth and be destroyed with the brightness of His coming. Matthew 13:30, 38-41; 2 Timothy 3:13, 1; 2 Thessalonians 2:8

The doctrine of the world's conversion and the spiritual reign of Christ was not held by the apostolic church. It was not generally accepted by Christians until about the beginning of the eighteenth century. Like every other error, its results were evil. It taught men to look far in the future for the coming of the Lord and prevented them from giving heed to the signs heralding His approach. It induced a feeling of confidence and security that was not well founded and led many to neglect the preparation necessary in order to meet their Lord.

Miller found the literal, personal coming of Christ to be plainly taught in the Scriptures. Says Paul: »The Lord Himself shall descend from heaven with a shout, with the voice of the Archangel, and with the trump of God.« 1 Thess. 4:16 And the Saviour declares: »They shall

 see the Son of man coming in the clouds of heaven with

power and great glory.« »For as the lightning cometh out of the east, and shineth even unto the west; so shall also the coming of the Son of man be.« Matthew 24:30, 27 He is to be accompanied by all the hosts of heaven. »The Son of man shall come in His glory, and all the holy angels with Him.« Mt. 25:31 »And He shall send His angels with a great sound of a trumpet, and they shall gather together His elect.« Matthew 24:31

At His coming the righteous dead will be raised, and the righteous living will be changed. »We shall not all sleep,« says Paul, »but we shall all be changed, in a moment, in the twinkling of an eye, at the last trump: for the trumpet shall sound, and the dead shall be raised incorruptible, and we shall be changed. For this corruptible must put on incorruption, and this mortal must put on immortality.« 1 Corinthians 15:51-53 And in his letter to the Thessalonians, after describing the coming of the Lord, he says: »The dead in Christ shall rise first: then we which are alive and remain shall be caught up together with them in the clouds, to meet the Lord in the air: and so shall we ever be with the Lord.« 1 Thessalonians 4:16-17

Not until the personal advent of Christ can His people receive the kingdom. The Saviour said: »When the Son of man shall come in His glory, and all the holy angels with Him, then shall He sit upon the throne of His glory: and before Him shall be gathered all nations: and He shall separate them one from another, as a shepherd divideth his sheep from the goats: and He shall set the sheep on His right hand, but the goats on the left. Then shall the King say unto them on His right hand, Come, ye blessed of My Father, inherit the kingdom prepared for you from the foundation of the world.« Matthew 25:31-34

We have seen by the scriptures just given that when the Son of man comes, the dead are raised incorruptible and the living are changed. By this great change they are prepared to receive the kingdom; for Paul says: »Flesh and blood cannot inherit the kingdom of God; neither doth corruption inherit incorruption.« 1 Corinthians 15:50 Man in his present state is mortal, corruptible; but the kingdom of God will be incorruptible, enduring forever. Therefore man in his present state cannot enter into the kingdom of God. But when Jesus comes, He confers immortality upon His people; and then He calls them to inherit the kingdom of which they have hitherto been only heirs.

These and other scriptures clearly proved to Miller's mind that the events which were generally expected to take place before the coming of Christ, such as the universal reign of peace and the setting up of the kingdom of God upon the earth, were to be subsequent to the second advent. Furthermore, all the signs of the times and the condition of the world corresponded to the prophetic description of the last days. He was forced to the conclusion, from the study of Scripture alone, that the period allotted for the continuance of the earth in its present state was about to close.

»Another kind of evidence that vitally affected my mind,« he says, »was the chronology of the Scriptures. ... I found that predicted events, which had been fulfilled in the past, often occurred within a given time. The one hundred and twenty years to the flood; Genesis 6:3 the seven days that were to precede it, with forty days of predicted rain; Genesis 7:4 the four hundred years of the sojourn of Abraham's seed; Genesis 15:13 the three days of the butler's and baker's dreams; Genesis 40:12-20 the seven years of Pharaoh's; Genesis 41:28-54 the forty years in the wilderness; Numbers 14:34 the three and a half years of famine; 1 Kings 17:1; see Luke 4:25 ... the seventy years' captivity; Jeremiah 25:11 Nebuchadnezzar's seven times; Daniel 4:13-16 and the seven weeks, threescore and two weeks, and the one week, making seventy weeks, determined upon the Jews Daniel 9:24.27 – the events limited by these times were all once only a matter of prophecy, and were fulfilled in accordance with the predictions.« Bliss, pp. 74, 75

When, therefore, he found, in his study of the Bible, various chronological periods that, according to his understanding of them, extended to the second coming of Christ, he could not but regard them as the »times before appointed,« which God had revealed unto His servants. »The secret things,« says Moses, »belong unto the Lord our God: but those things which are revealed belong unto us and to our children forever;« and the Lord declares by the prophet Amos, that He »will do nothing, but He revealeth His secret unto His servants the prophets.« Deuteronomy 29:29; Amos 3:7 The students of God's word may, then, confidently expect to find the most stupendous event to take place in human history clearly pointed out in the Scriptures of truth.

»As I was fully convinced,« says Miller, »that all Scripture given by inspiration of God is profitable; 2 Timothy 3:16 that it came not at any time by the will of man, but was written as holy men were moved by the Holy Ghost, 2 Peter 1:21 and was written 'for our learning, that we through patience and comfort of the Scriptures might have hope', Romans 15:4 I could but regard the chronological portions of the Bible

as being as much a portion of the word of God, and as

much entitled to our serious consideration, as any other portion of the Scriptures. I therefore felt that in endeavoring to comprehend what God had in His mercy seen fit to reveal to us, I had no right to pass over the prophetic periods.« Bliss, p. 75 The prophecy which seemed most clearly to reveal the time of the second advent was that of Daniel 8:14: »Unto two thousand and three hundred days; then shall the sanctuary be cleansed.« Following his rule of making Scripture its own interpreter, Miller learned that a day in symbolic prophecy represents a year Numbers 14:34; Ezekiel 4:6 he saw that the period of 2300 prophetic days, or literal years, would extend far beyond the close of the Jewish dispensation, hence it could not refer to the sanctuary of that dispensation. Miller accepted the generally received view that in the Christian age the earth is the sanctuary, and he therefore understood that the cleansing of the sanctuary foretold in Daniel 8:14 represented the purification of the earth by fire at the second coming of Christ. If, then, the correct starting point could be found for the 2300 days, he concluded that the time of the second advent could be readily ascertained. Thus would be revealed the time of that great consummation, the time when the present state, with »all its pride and power, pomp and vanity, wickedness and oppression, would come to an end;« when the curse would be »removed from off the earth, death be destroyed, reward be given to the servants of God, the prophets and saints, and them who fear His name, and those be destroyed that destroy the earth.« Bliss, p. 76

With a new and deeper earnestness, Miller continued the examination of the prophecies, whole nights as well as days being devoted to the study of what now appeared of such stupendous importance and all-absorbing interest. In the eighth chapter of Daniel he could find no clue to the starting point of the 2300 days; the angel Gabriel, though commanded to make Daniel understand the vision, gave him only a partial explanation. As the terrible persecution to befall the church was unfolded to the prophet's vision, physical strength gave way. He could endure no more, and the angel left him for a time. Daniel »fainted, and was sick certain days.« »And I was astonished at the vision,« he says, »but none understood it.«

Yet God had bidden His messenger: »Make this man to understand the vision.« That commission must be fulfilled. In obedience to it, the angel, some time afterward, returned to Daniel, saying: »I am now come forth to give thee skill and understanding;« »therefore understand the matter, and consider the vision.« Daniel 8:27, 16; 9:22, 23, 25-27 There was one important point in the vision of chapter 8 which had been left unexplained, namely, that relating to time – the period of the 2300 days; therefore the angel, in resuming his explanation, dwells chiefly upon the subject of time:

»Seventy weeks are determined upon thy people and upon thy Holy City. ... Know therefore and understand, that from the going forth of the commandment to restore and to build Jerusalem unto the Messiah the Prince shall be seven weeks, and threescore and two weeks: the street shall be built again, and the wall, even in troublous times. And after threescore and two weeks shall Messiah be cut off, but not for Himself. ... And He shall confirm the covenant with many for one week: and in the midst of the week He shall cause the sacrifice and the oblation to cease.«

The angel had been sent to Daniel for the express purpose of explaining to him the point which he had failed to understand in the vision of the eighth chapter, the statement relative to time – »unto two thousand and three hundred days; then shall the sanctuary be cleansed.« After bidding Daniel »understand the matter, and consider the vision,« the very first words of the angel are: »Seventy weeks are determined upon thy people and upon thy Holy City.« The word here translated »determined« literally signifies »cut off.« Seventy weeks, representing 490 years, are declared by the angel to be cut off, as specially pertaining to the Jews. But from what were they cut off? As the 2300 days was the only period of time mentioned in chapter 8, it must be the period from which the seventy weeks were cut off; the seventy weeks must therefore be a part of the 2300 days, and the two periods must begin together. The seventy weeks were declared by the angel to date from the going forth of the commandment to restore and build Jerusalem. If the date of this commandment could be found, then the starting point for the great period of the 2300 days would be ascertained.

In the seventh chapter of Ezra the decree is found. Verses 12-26 In its completest form it was issued by Artaxerxes, king of Persia, 457 B.C. But in Ezra 6:14 the house of the Lord at Jerusalem is said to have been built »according to the commandment [»decree,« margin] of Cyrus, and Darius, and Artaxerxes king of Persia.« These three kings, in originating, reaffirming, and completing the decree, brought it to

the perfection required by the prophecy to mark the

beginning of the 2300 years. Taking 457 B.C., the time when the decree was completed, as the date of the commandment, every specification of the prophecy concerning the seventy weeks was seen to have been fulfilled.

»From the going forth of the commandment to restore and to build Jerusalem unto the Messiah the Prince shall be seven weeks, and threescore and two weeks« – namely, sixty-nine weeks, or 483 years. The decree of Artaxerxes went into effect in the autumn of 457 B.C. From this date, 483 years extend to the autumn of A.D. 27. see Appendix At that time this prophecy was fulfilled. The word »Messiah« signifies »the Anointed One.« In the autumn of A.D. 27 Christ was baptized by John and received the anointing of the Spirit. The apostle Peter testifies that »God anointed Jesus of Nazareth with the Holy Ghost and with power.« Acts 10:38 And the Saviour Himself declared: »The Spirit of the Lord is upon Me, because He hath anointed Me to preach the gospel to the poor.« Luke 4:18 After His baptism He went into Galilee, »preaching the gospel of the kingdom of God, and saying, The time is fulfilled.« Mark 1:14-15

»And He shall confirm the covenant with many for one week.« The »week« here brought to view is the last one of the seventy; it is the last seven years of the period allotted especially to the Jews. During this time, extending from A.D. 27 to A.D. 34, Christ, at first in person and afterward by His disciples, extended the gospel invitation especially to the Jews. As the apostles went forth with the good tidings of the kingdom, the Saviour's direction was: »Go not into the way of the Gentiles, and into any city of the Samaritans enter ye not: but go rather to the lost sheep of the house of Israel.« Matthew 10:5-6

»In the midst of the week He shall cause the sacrifice and the oblation to cease.« In A.D. 31, three and a half years after His baptism, our Lord was crucified. With the great sacrifice offered upon Calvary, ended that system of offerings which for four thousand years had pointed forward to the Lamb of God. Type had met antitype, and all the sacrifices and oblations of the ceremonial system were there to cease. The seventy weeks, or 490 years, especially allotted to the Jews, ended, as we have seen, in A.D. 34. At that time, through the action of the Jewish Sanhedrin, the nation sealed its rejection of the gospel by the martyrdom of Stephen and the persecution of the followers of Christ. Then the message of salvation, no longer restricted to the chosen people, was given to the world. The disciples, forced by persecution to flee from Jerusalem, »went everywhere preaching the word.« »Philip went down to the city of Samaria, and preached Christ unto them.« Peter, divinely guided, opened the gospel to the centurion of Caesarea, the God-fearing Cornelius; and the ardent Paul, won to the faith of Christ, was commissioned to carry the glad tidings »far hence unto the Gentiles.« Acts 8:4, 5; 22:21 Thus far every specification of the prophecies is strikingly fulfilled, and the beginning of the seventy weeks is fixed beyond question at 457 B.C., and their expiration in A.D. 34. From this data there is no difficulty in finding the termination of the 2300 days. The seventy weeks – 490 days – having been cut off from the 2300, there were 1810 days remaining. After the end of 490 days, the 1810 days were still to be fulfilled. From A.D. 34, 1810 years extend to 1844. Consequently the 2300 days of Daniel 8:14 terminate in 1844. At the expiration of this great prophetic period, upon the testimony of the angel of God, »the sanctuary shall be cleansed.« Thus the time of the cleansing of the sanctuary – which was almost universally believed to take place at the second advent – was definitely pointed out.

Miller and his associates at first believed that the 2300 days would terminate in the spring of 1844, whereas the prophecy points to the autumn of that year. see Appendix The misapprehension of this point brought disappointment and perplexity to those who had fixed upon the earlier date as the time of the Lord's coming. But this did not in the least affect the strength of the argument showing that the 2300 days terminated in the year 1844, and that the great event represented by the cleansing of the sanctuary must then take place. Entering upon the study of the Scriptures as he had done, in order to prove that they were a revelation from God, Miller had not, at the outset, the slightest expectation of reaching the conclusion at which he had now arrived. He himself could hardly credit the results of his investigation. But the Scripture evidence was too clear and forcible to be set aside.

He had devoted two years to the study of the Bible, when, in 1818, he reached the solemn conviction that in about twenty-five years Christ would appear for the redemption of His people. »I need not speak,« says Miller, »of the joy that filled my heart in view of the delightful prospect, nor of the ardent longings of my soul for a participation in the joys of the redeemed. The Bible was now to me a new book. It was indeed a feast of reason; all that was dark, mystical, or obscure to me in its teachings, had been dissipated from my mind before the clear light that now dawned from its sacred pages; and, oh, how bright and glorious the truth appeared! All the contradictions and inconsistencies I had before found in the word were gone; and although there were many portions of which I was not satisfied I had a full understanding, yet so much light had emanated from it to the illumination of my before darkened mind, that I felt a delight in studying the Scripture which I had not before supposed could be derived from its teachings.« Bliss, pp. 76, 77

»With the solemn conviction that such momentous events were predicted in the Scriptures to be fulfilled in so short a space of time, the question came home to me with mighty power regarding my duty to the world, in view of the evidence that had affected my own mind.« Ibid., p. 81 He could not but feel that it was his duty to impart to others the light which he had received. He expected to encounter opposition from the ungodly, but was confident that all Christians would rejoice in the hope of meeting the Saviour whom they professed to love. His only fear was that in their great joy at the prospect of glorious deliverance, so soon to be consummated, many would receive the doctrine without sufficiently examining the Scriptures in demonstration of its truth. He therefore hesitated to present it, lest he should be in error and be the means of misleading others. He was thus led to review the evidences in support of the conclusions at which he had arrived, and to consider carefully every difficulty which presented itself to his mind. He found that objections vanished before the light of God's word, as mist before the rays of the sun. Five years spent thus left him fully convinced of the correctness of his position.

And now the duty of making known to others what he believed to be so clearly taught in the Scriptures, urged itself with new force upon him. »When I was about my business,« he said, »it was continually ringing in my ears, 'Go and tell the world of their danger.' This text was constantly occurring to me: 'When I say unto the wicked, O wicked man, thou shalt surely die; if thou dost not speak to warn the wicked from his way, that wicked man shall die in his iniquity; but his blood will I require at thine hand. Nevertheless, if thou warn the wicked of his way to turn from it; if he do not turn from his way, he shall die in his iniquity; but thou hast delivered thy soul.« Ezekiel 33:8-9 I felt that if the wicked could be effectually warned, multitudes of them would repent; and that if they were not warned, their blood might be required at my hand.« Bliss, p. 92 He began to present his views in private as he had opportunity, praying that some minister might feel their force and devote himself to their promulgation. But he could not banish the conviction that he had a personal duty to perform in giving the warning. The words were ever recurring to his mind: »Go and tell it to the world; their blood will I require at thy hand.« For nine years he waited, the burden still pressing upon his soul, until in 1831 he for the first time publicly gave the reasons of his faith. As Elisha was called from following his oxen in the field, to receive the mantle of consecration to the prophetic office, so was William Miller called to leave his plow and open to the people the mysteries of the kingdom of God. With trembling he entered upon his work, leading his hearers down, step by step, through the prophetic periods to the second appearing of Christ. With every effort he gained strength and courage as he saw the widespread interest excited by his words.

It was only at the solicitation of his brethren, in whose words he heard the call of God, that Miller consented to present his views in public. He was now fifty years of age, unaccustomed to public speaking, and burdened with a sense of unfitness for the work before him. But from the first his labors were blessed in a remarkable manner to the salvation of souls. His first lecture was followed by a religious awakening in which thirteen entire families, with the exception of two persons, were converted. He was immediately urged to speak in other places, and in nearly every place his labor resulted in a revival of the work of God. Sinners were converted, Christians were roused to greater consecration, and deists and infidels were led to acknowledge the truth of the Bible and the Christian religion. The testimony of those among whom he labored was: »A class of minds are reached by him not within the influence of other men.« Ibid., p.138 His preaching was calculated to arouse the public mind to the great things of religion and to check the growing worldliness and sensuality of the age.

In nearly every town there were scores, in some, hundreds, converted as a result of his preaching. In many places Protestant churches of nearly all denominations were thrown open to him, and the invitations to labor usually came from the ministers of the several congregations. It was his invariable rule not to labor in any place to which he had not been invited, yet he soon found himself

 unable to comply with half the requests that poured in

upon him. Many who did not accept his views as to the exact time of the second advent were convinced of the certainty and nearness of Christ's coming and their need of preparation. In some of the large cities his work produced a marked impression. Liquor dealers abandoned the traffic and turned their shops into meeting rooms; gambling dens were broken up; infidels, deists, Universalists, and even the most abandoned profligates were reformed, some of whom had not entered a house of worship for years. Prayer meetings were established by the various denominations, in different quarters, at almost every hour, businessmen assembling at midday for prayer and praise. There was no extravagant excitement, but an almost universal solemnity on the minds of the people. His work, like that of the early Reformers, tended rather to convince the understanding and arouse the conscience than merely to excite the emotions.

In 1833 Miller received a license to preach, from the Baptist Church, of which he was a member. A large number of the ministers of his denomination also approved his work, and it was with their formal sanction that he continued his labors. He traveled and preached unceasingly, though his personal labors were confined principally to the New England and Middle States. For several years his expenses were met wholly from his own private purse, and he never afterward received enough to meet the expense of travel to the places where he was invited. Thus his public labors, so far from being a pecuniary benefit, were a heavy tax upon his property, which gradually diminished during this period of his life. He was the father of a large family, but as they were all frugal and industrious, his farm sufficed for their maintenance as well as his own.

In 1833, two years after Miller began to present in public the evidences of Christ's soon coming, the last of the signs appeared which were promised by the Saviour as tokens of His second advent. Said Jesus: »The stars shall fall from heaven.« Matthew 24:29 And John in the Revelation declared, as he beheld in vision the scenes that should herald the day of God: »The stars of heaven fell unto the earth, even as a fig tree casteth her untimely figs, when she is shaken of a mighty wind.« Revelation 6:13 This prophecy received a striking and impressive fulfillment in the great meteoric shower of November 13, 1833. That was the most extensive and wonderful display of falling stars which has ever been recorded; »the whole firmament, over all the United States, being then, for hours, in fiery commotion! No [332/333] celestial phenomenon has ever occurred in this country, since its first settlement, which was viewed with such intense admiration by one class in the community, or with so much dread and alarm by another.« »Its sublimity and awful beauty still linger in many minds. ... Never did rain fall much thicker than the meteors fell toward the earth; east, west, north, and south, it was the same. In a word, the whole heavens seemed in motion. ... The display, as described in Professor Silliman's Journal, was seen all over North America. ... From two o'clock until broad daylight, the sky being perfectly serene and cloudless, an incessant play of dazzlingly brilliant luminosities was kept up in the whole heavens.« R. M. Devens, American Progress; or, The Great Events of the Greatest Century, ch. 28, pars. 1-5

»No language, indeed, can come up to the splendor of that magnificent display; ... no one who did not witness it can form an adequate conception of its glory. It seemed as if the whole starry heavens had congregated at one point near the zenith, and were simultaneously shooting forth, with the velocity of lightning, to every part of the horizon; and yet they were not exhausted – thousands swiftly followed in the tracks of thousands, as if created for the occasion.« F. Reed, in the Christian Advocate and Journal, Dec. 13, 1833

»A more correct picture of a fig tree casting its figs when blown by a mighty wind, it was not possible to behold.« »The Old Countryman,« Portland Evening Advertiser, November 26, 1833

In the New York Journal of Commerce of November 14, 1833, appeared a long article regarding this wonderful phenomenon, containing this statement: »No philosopher or scholar has told or recorded an event, I suppose, like that of yesterday morning. A prophet eighteen hundred years ago foretold it exactly, if we will be at the trouble of understanding stars falling to mean falling stars, ... in the only sense in which it is possible to be literally true.«

Thus was displayed the last of those signs of His coming, concerning which Jesus bade His disciples: »When ye shall see all these things, know that it is near, even at the doors.« Matthew 24:33 After these signs, John beheld, as the great event next impending, the heavens departing as a scroll, while the earth quaked, mountains and islands removed out of their places, and the wicked in terror sought to flee from the presence of the Son of man. Revelation 6:12-17 Many who witnessed the falling of the stars, looked upon it as a herald of the coming judgment, »an awful type, a sure forerunner, a merciful sign, of that great and dreadful day.« – »The Old Countryman,« Portland Evening Advertiser, Nov. 26, 1833 Thus the attention of the people was directed to the fulfillment of prophecy, and many were led to give heed to the warning of the second advent.

In the year 1840 another remarkable fulfillment of prophecy excited widespread interest. Two years before, Josiah Litch, one of the leading ministers preaching the second advent, published an exposition of Revelation 9, predicting the fall of the Ottoman Empire. According to his calculations, this power was to be overthrown »in A.D. 1840, sometime in the month of August;« and only a few days previous to its accomplishment he wrote: »Allowing the first period, 150 years, to have been exactly fulfilled before Deacozes ascended the throne by permission of the Turks, and that the 391 years, fifteen days, commenced at the close of the first period, it will end on the 11th of August, 1840, when the Ottoman power in Constantinople may be expected to be broken. And this, I believe, will be found to be the case.« Josiah Litch, in Signs of the Times, and Expositor of Prophecy, Aug. 1, 1840

At the very time specified, Turkey, through her ambassadors, accepted the protection of the allied powers of Europe, and thus placed herself under the control of Christian nations. The event exactly fulfilled the prediction. see Appendix When it became known, multitudes were convinced of the correctness of the principles of prophetic interpretation adopted by Miller and his associates, and a wonderful impetus was given to the advent movement. Men of learning and position united with Miller, both in preaching and in publishing his views, and from 1840 to 1844 the work rapidly extended.

William Miller possessed strong mental powers, disciplined by thought and study; and he added to these the wisdom of heaven by connecting himself with the Source of wisdom. He was a man of sterling worth, who could not but command respect and esteem wherever integrity of character and moral excellence were valued. Uniting true kindness of heart with Christian humility and the power of self-control, he was attentive and affable to all, ready to listen to the opinions of others and to weigh their arguments. Without passion or excitement he tested all theories and doctrines by the word of God, and his sound reasoning and thorough knowledge of the Scriptures enabled him to refute error and expose falsehood.

Yet he did not prosecute his work without bitter opposition. As with earlier Reformers, the truths which he presented were not received with favor by popular religious teachers. As these could not maintain their position by the Scriptures, they were driven to resort to the sayings and doctrines of men, to the traditions of the Fathers. But the word of God was the only testimony accepted by the preachers of the advent truth. »The Bible, and the Bible only,« was their watchword. The lack of Scripture argument on the part of their opponents was supplied by ridicule and scoffing. Time, means, and talents were employed in maligning those whose only offense was that they looked with joy for the return of their Lord and were striving to live holy lives and to exhort others to prepare for His appearing. Earnest were the efforts put forth to draw away the minds of the people from the subject of the second advent. It was made to appear a sin, something of which men should be ashamed, to study the prophecies which relate to the coming of Christ and the end of the world. Thus the popular ministry undermined faith in the word of God. Their teaching made men infidels, and many took license to walk after their own ungodly lusts. Then the authors of the evil charged it all upon Adventists.

While drawing crowded houses of intelligent and attentive hearers, Miller's name was seldom mentioned by the religious press except by way of ridicule or denunciation. The careless and ungodly emboldened by the position of religious teachers, resorted to opprobrious epithets,

William Miller (1782-1849)

Miller's prophetic map

to base and blasphemous witticisms, in their efforts to heap contumely upon him and his work. The gray-headed man who had left a comfortable home to travel at his own expense from city to city, from town to town, toiling unceasingly to bear to the world the solemn warning of the judgment near, was sneeringly denounced as a fanatic, a liar, a speculating knave. The ridicule, falsehood, and abuse heaped upon him called forth indignant remonstrance, even from the secular press. »To treat a subject of such overwhelming majesty and fearful consequences,« with lightness and ribaldry was declared by worldly men to be »not merely to sport with the feelings of its propagators and advocates,« but »to make a jest of the day of judgment, to scoff at the Deity Himself, and contemn the terrors of His judgment bar.« Bliss, p. 183 The instigator of all evil sought not only to counteract the effect of the advent message, but to destroy the messenger himself.

Miller made a practical application of Scripture truth to the hearts of his hearers, reproving their sins and disturbing their self-satisfaction, and his plain and cutting words aroused their enmity. The opposition manifested by church members toward his message emboldened the baser classes to go to greater lengths; and enemies plotted to take his life as he should leave the place of meeting. But holy angels were in the throng, and one of these, in the form of a man, took the arm of this servant of the Lord and led him in safety from the angry mob. His work was not yet done, and Satan and his emissaries were disappointed in their purpose. Despite all opposition, the interest in the advent movement had continued to increase. From scores and hundreds, the congregations had grown to as many thousands. Large accessions had been made to the various churches, but after a time the spirit of opposition was manifested even against these converts, and the churches began to take disciplinary steps with those who had embraced Miller's views. This action called forth a response from his pen, in an address to Christians of all denominations, urging that if his doctrines were false, he should be shown his error from the Scriptures.

»What have we believed,« he said, »that we have not been commanded to believe by the word of God, which you yourselves allow is the rule, and only rule, of our faith and practice? What have we done that should call down such virulent denunciations against us from pulpit and press, and give you just cause to exclude us [Adventists] from your churches and fellowship?« »If we are wrong, pray show us wherein consists our wrong. Show us from the word of God that we are in error; we have had ridicule enough; that can never convince us that we are in the wrong; the word of God alone can change our views. Our conclusions have been formed deliberately and prayerfully, as we have seen the evidence in the Scriptures.« Ibid., pp. 250, 252

From age to age the warnings which God has sent to the world by His servants have been received with like incredulity and unbelief. When the iniquity of the antediluvians moved Him to bring a flood of waters upon the earth, He first made known to them His purpose, that they might have opportunity to turn from their evil ways. For a hundred and twenty years was sounded in their ears the warning to repent, lest the wrath of God be manifested in their destruction. But the message seemed to them an idle tale, and they believed it not. Emboldened in their wickedness they mocked the messenger of God, made light of his entreaties, and even accused him of presumption. How dare one man stand up against all the great men of the earth? If Noah's message were true, why did not all the world see it and believe it? One man's assertion against the wisdom of thousands! They would not credit the warning, nor would they seek shelter in the ark.

Scoffers pointed to the things of nature, – to the unvarying succession of the seasons, to the blue skies that had never poured out rain, to the green fields refreshed by the soft dews of night, – and they cried out: »Doth he not speak parables?« In contempt they declared the preacher of righteousness to be a wild enthusiast; and they went on, more eager in their pursuit of pleasure, more intent upon their evil ways, than before. But their unbelief did not hinder the predicted event. God bore long with their wickedness, giving them ample opportunity for repentance; but at the appointed time His judgments were visited upon the rejecters of His mercy.

Christ declares that there will exist similar unbelief concerning His second coming. As the people of Noah's day »knew not until the Flood came, and took them all away; so,« in the words of our Saviour, »shall also the coming of the Son of man be.« Matthew 24:39 When the professed people of God are uniting with the world, living as they live, and joining with them in forbidden pleasures; when the luxury of the world becomes the luxury of the church; when the marriage bells are chiming, and all are looking forward to many years of worldly prosperity – then, suddenly as the lightning flashes from the heavens, will come the end of their bright visions and delusive hopes. As God sent His servant to warn the world of the coming Flood, so He sent chosen messengers to make known the nearness of the final judgment. And as Noah's contemporaries laughed to scorn the predictions of the preacher of righteousness, so in Miller's day many, even of the professed people of God, scoffed at the words of warning.

And why were the doctrine and preaching of Christ's second coming so unwelcome to the churches? While to the wicked the advent of the Lord brings woe and desolation, to the righteous it is fraught with joy and hope. This great truth had been the consolation of God's faithful ones through all the ages; why had it become, like its Author, »a stone of stumbling« and »a rock of offense« to His professed people? It was our Lord Himself who promised His disciples: »If I go and prepare a place for you, I will come again, and receive you unto Myself.« John 14:3 It was the compassionate Saviour, who, anticipating the loneliness and sorrow of His followers, commissioned angels to comfort them with the assurance that He would come again in person, even as He went into heaven. As the disciples stood gazing intently upward to catch the last glimpse of Him whom they loved, their attention was arrested by the words: »Ye men of Galilee, why stand ye gazing up into heaven? this same Jesus, which is taken up from you into heaven, shall so come in like manner as ye have seen Him go into heaven.« Acts 1:11 Hope was kindled afresh by the angels' message. The disciples »returned to Jerusalem with great joy: and were continually in the temple, praising and blessing God.« Luke 24:52-53 They were not rejoicing because Jesus had been separated from them and they were left to struggle with the trials and temptations of the world, but because of the angels' assurance that He would come again.

The proclamation of Christ's coming should now be, as when made by the angels to the shepherds of Bethlehem, good tidings of great joy. Those who really love the Saviour cannot but hail with gladness the announcement founded upon the word of God that He in whom their hopes of eternal life are centered is coming again, not to be insulted, despised, and rejected, as at His first advent, but in power and glory, to redeem His people. It is those who do not love the Saviour that desire Him to remain away, and there can be no more conclusive evidence that the churches have departed from God than the irritation and animosity excited by this

Heaven-sent message. Those who accepted the advent doctrine were roused to the necessity of repentance and humiliation before God. Many had long been halting between Christ and the world; now they felt that it was time to take a stand. »The things of eternity assumed to them an unwonted reality. Heaven was brought near, and they felt themselves guilty before God.« Bliss, p. 146 Christians were quickened to new spiritual life. They were made to feel that time was short, that what they had to do for their fellow men must be done quickly. Earth receded, eternity seemed to open before them, and the soul, with all that pertained to its immortal weal or woe, was felt to eclipse every temporal object. The Spirit of God rested upon them and gave power to their earnest appeals to their brethren, as well as to sinners, to prepare for the day of God. The silent testimony of their daily life was a constant rebuke to formal and unconsecrated church members. These did not wish to be disturbed in their pursuit of pleasure, their devotion to money-making, and their ambition for worldly honor. Hence the enmity and opposition excited against the advent faith and those who proclaimed it.

As the arguments from the prophetic periods were found to be impregnable, opposers endeavored to discourage investigation of the subject by teaching that the prophecies were sealed. Thus Protestants followed in the steps of Romanists. While the papal church withholds the Bible see Appendix from the people, Protestant churches claimed that an important part of the Sacred Word – and that the part which brings to view truths specially applicable to our time – could not be understood.

Ministers and people declared that the prophecies of Daniel and the Revelation were incomprehensible mysteries. But Christ directed His disciples to the words of the prophet Daniel concerning events to take place in their time, and said: »Whoso readeth, let him understand.« Matthew 24:15 And the assertion that the Revelation is a mystery, not to be understood, is contradicted by the very title of the book: »The Revelation of Jesus Christ, which God gave unto Him, to show unto His servants things which must shortly come to pass. ... Blessed is he that readeth, and they that hear the words of this prophecy, and keep those things which are written therein: for the time is at hand.« Revelation 1:1-3

Says the prophet: »Blessed is he that readeth« – there are those who will not read; the blessing is not for them. »And they that hear« – there are some, also, who refuse to hear anything concerning the prophecies; the blessing is not for this class. »And keep those things which are written therein« – many refuse to heed the warnings and instructions contained in the Revelation; none of these can claim the blessing promised. All who ridicule the subjects of the prophecy and mock at the symbols here solemnly given, all who refuse to reform their lives and to prepare for the coming of the Son of man, will be unblessed.

In view of the testimony of Inspiration, how dare men teach that the Revelation is a mystery beyond the reach of human understanding? It is a mystery revealed, a book opened. The study of the Revelation directs the mind to the prophecies of Daniel, and both present most important instruction, given of God to men, concerning events to take place at the close of this world's history. To John were opened scenes of deep and thrilling interest in the experience of the church. He saw the position, dangers, conflicts, and final deliverance of the people of God. He records the closing messages which are to ripen the harvest of the earth, either as sheaves for the heavenly garner or as fagots for the fires of destruction. Subjects of vast importance were revealed to him, especially for the last church, that those who should turn from error to truth might be instructed concerning the perils and conflicts before them. None need be in darkness in regard to what is coming upon the earth.

Why, then, this widespread ignorance concerning an important part of Holy Writ? Why this general reluctance to investigate its teachings? It is the result of a studied effort of the prince of darkness to conceal from men that which reveals his deceptions. For this reason, Christ the Revelator, foreseeing the warfare that would be waged against the study of the Revelation, pronounced a blessing upon all who should read, hear, and observe the words of the prophecy.

Chapter 19

Light Through Darkness

The work of God in the earth presents, from age to age, a striking similarity in every great reformation or religious movement. The principles of God's dealing with men are ever the same. The important movements of the present have their parallel in those of the past, and the experience of the church in former ages has lessons of great value for our own time.

No truth is more clearly taught in the Bible than that God by His Holy Spirit especially directs His servants on earth in the great movements for the carrying forward of the work of salvation. Men are instruments in the hand of God, employed by Him to accomplish His purposes of grace and mercy. Each has his part to act; to each is granted a measure of light, adapted to the necessities of his time, and sufficient to enable him to perform the work which God has given him to do. But no man, however honored of Heaven, has ever attained to a full understanding of the great plan of redemption, or even to a perfect appreciation of the divine purpose in the work for his own time. Men do not fully understand what God would accomplish by the work which He gives them to do; they do not comprehend, in all its bearings, the message which they utter in His name. »Canst thou by searching find out God? canst thou find out the Almighty unto perfection?« »My thoughts are not your thoughts, neither are your ways My ways, saith the Lord. For as the heavens are higher than the earth, so are My ways higher than your ways, and My thoughts than your thoughts.« »I am God, and there is none like Me, declaring the end from the beginning, and from ancient times the things that are not yet done.« Job 11:7; Isaiah 55:8-9; 46:9-10

Even the prophets who were favored with the special illumination of the Spirit did not fully comprehend the import of the revelations committed to them. The meaning was to be unfolded from age to age, as the people of God should need the instruction therein contained. Peter, writing of the salvation brought to light through the gospel, says: Of this salvation »the prophets have inquired and searched diligently, who prophesied of the grace that should come unto you: searching what, or what manner of time the Spirit of Christ which was in them did signify, when it testified beforehand the sufferings of Christ, and the glory that should follow. Unto whom it was revealed, that not unto themselves, but unto us they did minister.« 1 Peter 1:10-12

Yet while it was not given to the prophets to understand fully the things revealed to them, they earnestly sought to obtain all the light which God had been pleased to make manifest. They »inquired and searched diligently,« »searching what, or what manner of time the Spirit of Christ which was in them did signify.« What a lesson to the people of God in the Christian age, for whose benefit these prophecies were given to His servants! »Unto whom it was revealed, that not unto themselves, but unto us they did minister.« Witness those holy men of God as they »inquired and searched diligently« concerning revelations given them for generations that were yet unborn. Contrast their holy zeal with the listless unconcern with which the favored ones of later ages treat this gift of Heaven. What a rebuke to the ease-loving, worldloving indifference which is content to declare that the prophecies cannot be understood!

Though the finite minds of men are inadequate to enter into the counsels of the Infinite One, or to understand fully the working out of His purposes, yet often it is because of some error or neglect on their own part that they so dimly comprehend the messages of Heaven. Not infrequently the minds of the people, and even of God's servants, are so blinded by human opinions, the traditions and false teaching of men, that they are able only partially to grasp the great things which He has revealed in His word. Thus it was with the disciples of Christ, even when the Saviour was with them in person. Their minds had become imbued with the popular conception of the Messiah as a temporal prince, who was to exalt Israel to the throne of the universal empire, and they could not understand the meaning of His words foretelling His sufferings and death.

Christ Himself had sent them forth with the message: »The time is fulfilled, and the kingdom of God is at hand: repent ye, and believe the gospel.« Mark 1:15 That message was based on the prophecy of Daniel 9. The sixty-nine weeks were declared by the angel to extend to »the Messiah the Prince,« and with high hopes and joyful anticipations the disciples looked forward to the establishment of Messiah's kingdom at Jerusalem to rule over the whole earth. They preached the message which Christ had committed to them, though they themselves misapprehended its meaning. While their announcement was founded on Daniel 9:25, they did not see, in the next verse of the same chapter, that Messiah was to be cut off. From their very birth their hearts had been set upon the anticipated glory of an earthly empire, and this blinded their understanding alike to the specifications of the prophecy and to the words of Christ.

They performed their duty in presenting to the Jewish nation the invitation of mercy, and then, at the very time when they expected to see their Lord ascend the throne of David, they beheld Him seized as a malefactor, scourged, derided, and condemned, and lifted up on the cross of Calvary. What despair and anguish wrung the hearts of those disciples during the days while their Lord was sleeping in the tomb!

Christ had come at the exact time and in the manner foretold by prophecy. The testimony of Scripture had been fulfilled in every detail of His ministry. He had preached the message of salvation, and »His word was with power.« The hearts of His hearers had witnessed that it was of Heaven. The word and the Spirit of God attested the divine commission of His Son. The disciples still clung with undying affection to their beloved Master. And yet their minds were shrouded in uncertainty and doubt. In their anguish they did not then recall the words of Christ pointing forward to His suffering and death. If Jesus of Nazareth had been the true Messiah, would they have been thus plunged in grief and disappointment? This was the question that tortured their souls while the Saviour lay in His sepulcher during the hopeless hours of that Sabbath which intervened between His death and His resurrection.

Though the night of sorrow gathered dark about these followers of Jesus, yet were they not forsaken. Saith the prophet: »When I sit in darkness, the Lord shall be a light unto me. ... He will bring me forth to the light, and I shall behold His righteousness.« »Yea, the darkness hideth not from Thee; but the night shineth as the day: the darkness and the light are both alike to Thee.« God hath spoken: »Unto the upright there ariseth light in the darkness.« »I will bring the blind by a way that they knew not; I will lead them in paths that they have not known: I will make darkness light before them, and crooked things straight. These things will I do unto them, and not forsake them.« Micah 7:8-9; Psalm 139:12; 112:4; Isaiah 42:16

The announcement which had been made by the disciples in the name of the Lord was in every particular correct, and the events to which it pointed were even then taking place. »The time is fulfilled, the kingdom of God is at hand,« had been their message. At the expiration of »the time« – the sixty-nine weeks of Daniel 9, which were to extend to the Messiah, »the Anointed One« – Christ had received the anointing of the Spirit after His baptism by John in Jordan. And the »kingdom of God« which they had declared to be at hand was established by the death of Christ. This kingdom was not, as they had been taught to believe, an earthly empire. Nor was it that future, immortal kingdom which shall be set up when »the kingdom and dominion, and the greatness of the kingdom under the whole heaven, shall be given to the people of the saints of the Most High;« that everlasting kingdom, in which »all dominions shall serve and obey Him.« Daniel 7:27 As used in the Bible, the expression »kingdom of God« is employed to designate both the kingdom of grace and the kingdom of glory. The kingdom of grace is brought to view by Paul in the Epistle to the Hebrews. After pointing to Christ, the compassionate intercessor who is »touched with the feeling of our infirmities,« the apostle says: »Let us therefore come boldly unto the throne of grace, that we may obtain mercy, and find grace.« Hebrews 4:15, 16 The throne of grace represents the kingdom of grace; for the existence of a throne implies the existence of a kingdom. In many of His parables Christ uses the expression »the kingdom of heaven« to designate the work of divine grace upon the hearts of men.

So the throne of glory represents the kingdom of glory; and this kingdom is referred to in the Saviour's words: »When the Son of man shall come in His glory, and all the holy angels with Him, then shall He sit upon the throne of His glory: and before Him shall be gathered all nations.« Matthew 25:31-32 This kingdom is yet future. It is not to be set up until the second advent of Christ.

The kingdom of grace was instituted immediately after the fall of man, when a plan was devised for the redemption of the guilty race. It then existed in the purpose and by the promise of God; and through faith, men could become its subjects. Yet it was not actually established until the death of Christ. Even after entering upon His earthly mission, the Saviour, wearied with the stubbornness and ingratitude of men, might have drawn back from the sacrifice of Calvary. In Gethsemane the cup of woe trembled in

His hand. He might even then have wiped the blood-sweat from His brow and have left the guilty race to perish in their iniquity. Had He done this, there could have been no redemption for fallen men. But when the Saviour yielded up His life, and with His expiring breath cried out, »It is finished,« then the fulfillment of the plan of redemption was assured. The promise of salvation made to the sinful pair in Eden was ratified. The kingdom of grace, which had before existed by the promise of God, was then established.

Thus the death of Christ – the very event which the disciples had looked upon as the final destruction of their hope – was that which made it forever sure. While it had brought them a cruel disappointment, it was the climax of proof that their belief had been correct. The event that had filled them with mourning and despair was that which opened the door of hope to every child of Adam, and in which centered the future life and eternal happiness of all God's faithful ones in all the ages.

Purposes of infinite mercy were reaching their fulfillment, even through the disappointment of the disciples. While their hearts had been won by the divine grace and power of His teaching, who »spake as never man spake,« yet intermingled with the pure gold of their love for Jesus, was the base alloy of worldly pride and selfish ambitions. Even in the Passover chamber, at that solemn hour when their Master was already entering the shadow of Gethsemane, there was »a strife among them, which of them should be accounted the greatest.« Luke 22:24 Their vision was filled with the throne, the crown, and the glory, while just before them lay the shame and agony of the garden, the judgment hall, the cross of Calvary. It was their pride of heart, their thirst for worldly glory, that had led them to cling so tenaciously to the false teaching of their time, and to pass unheeded the Saviour's words showing the true nature of His kingdom, and pointing forward to His agony and death. And these errors resulted in the trial – sharp but needful – which was permitted for their correction. Though the disciples had mistaken the meaning of their message, and had failed to realize their expectations, yet they had preached the warning given them of God, and the Lord would reward their faith and honor their obedience. To them was to be entrusted the work of heralding to all nations the glorious gospel of their risen Lord. It was to prepare them for this work that the experience which seemed to

 them so bitter had been permitted. After His resurrection Jesus appeared to His disciples on the way to Emmaus, and, »beginning at Moses and all the prophets, He expounded unto them in all the Scriptures the things concerning Himself.« Luke 24:27 The hearts of the disciples were stirred. Faith was kindled. They were »begotten again into a lively hope« even before Jesus revealed Himself to them. It was His purpose to enlighten their understanding and to fasten their faith upon the »sure word of prophecy.« He wished the truth to take firm root in their minds, not merely because it was supported by His personal testimony, but because of the unquestionable evidence presented by the symbols and shadows of the typical law, and by the prophecies of the Old Testament. It was needful for the followers of Christ to have an intelligent faith, not only in their own behalf, but that they might carry the knowledge of Christ to the world. And as the very first step in imparting this knowledge, Jesus directed the disciples to »Moses and all the prophets.« Such was the testimony given by the risen Saviour to the value and importance of the Old Testament Scriptures.

What a change was wrought in the hearts of the disciples as they looked once more on the loved countenance of their Master! Luke 24:32 In a more complete and perfect sense than ever before they had »found Him, of whom Moses in the law, and the prophets, did write.« The uncertainty, the anguish, the despair, gave place to perfect assurance, to unclouded faith. What marvel that after His ascension they »were continually in the temple, praising and blessing God.« The people, knowing only of the Saviour's ignominious death, looked to see in their faces the expression of sorrow, confusion, and defeat; but they saw there gladness and triumph. What a preparation these disciples had received for the work before them! They had passed through the deepest trial which it was possible for them to experience, and had seen how, when to human vision all was lost, the word of God had been triumphantly accomplished. Henceforward what could daunt their faith or chill the ardor of their love? In the keenest sorrow they had »strong consolation,« a hope which was as »an anchor of the soul, both sure and steadfast.« Hebrews 6:18-19 They had been witness to the wisdom and power of God, and they were »persuaded, that neither death, nor life, nor angels, nor principalities, nor powers, nor things present, nor things to come, nor height, nor depth, nor any other creature,« would be able to separate them from »the love of God, which [349/350] is in Christ Jesus our Lord.« »In all these things,« they said, »we are more than conquerors through Him that loved us.« Romans 8:38,39,37 »The word of the Lord endureth forever.« 1 Peter 1:25 And »who is he that condemneth? It is Christ that died, yea rather, that is risen again, who is even at the right hand of God, who also maketh intercession for us.« Romans 8:34 Saith the Lord: »My people shall never be ashamed.« Joel.2:26 »Weeping may endure for a night, but joy cometh in the morning.« Psalm 30:5 When on His resurrection day these disciples met the Saviour, and their hearts burned within them as they listened to His words; when they looked upon the head and hands and feet that had been bruised for them; when, before His ascension, Jesus led them out as far as Bethany, and lifting up His hands in blessing, bade them, »Go ye into all the world, and preach the gospel,« adding, »Lo, I am with you alway« Mark 16:15; Matthew 28:20 when on the Day of Pentecost the promised Comforter descended and the power from on high was given and the souls of the believers thrilled with the conscious presence of their ascended Lord – then, even though, like His, their pathway led through sacrifice and martyrdom, would they have exchanged the ministry of the gospel of His grace, with the »crown of righteousness« to be received at His coming, for the glory of an earthly throne, which had been the hope of their earlier discipleship? He who is »able to do exceeding abundantly above all that we ask or think,« had granted them, with the fellowship of His sufferings, the communion of His joy – the joy of »bringing many sons unto glory,« joy unspeakable, an »eternal weight of glory,« to which, says Paul, »our light affliction, which is but for a moment,« is »not worthy to be compared.«

The experience of the disciples who preached the »gospel of the kingdom« at the first advent of Christ, had its counterpart in the experience of those who proclaimed the message of His second advent. As the disciples went out preaching, »The time is fulfilled, the kingdom of God is at hand,« so Miller and his associates proclaimed that the longest and last prophetic period brought to view in the Bible was about to expire, that the judgment was at hand, and the everlasting kingdom was to be ushered in. The preaching of the disciples in regard to time was based on the seventy weeks of Daniel 9. The message given by Miller and his associates announced the termination of the 2300 days of Daniel 8:14, of which the seventy weeks form a part.

The preaching of each was based upon the fulfillment of a different portion of the same great prophetic period. Like the first disciples, William Miller and his associates did not, themselves, fully comprehend the import of the message which they bore. Errors that had been long established in the church prevented them from arriving at a correct interpretation of an important point in the prophecy. Therefore, though they proclaimed the message which God had committed to them to be given to the world, yet through a misapprehension of its meaning they suffered disappointment. In explaining Daniel 8:14, »Unto two thousand and three hundred days; then shall the sanctuary be cleansed,« Miller, as has been stated, adopted the generally received view that the earth is the sanctuary, and he believed that the cleansing of the sanctuary represented the purification of the earth by fire at the coming of the Lord. When, therefore, he found that the close of the 2300 days was definitely foretold, he concluded that this revealed the time of the second advent. His error resulted from accepting the popular view as to what constitutes the sanctuary.

In the typical system, which was a shadow of the sacrifice and priesthood of Christ, the cleansing of the sanctuary was the last service performed by the high priest in the yearly round of ministration. It was the closing work of the atonement – a removal or putting away of sin from Israel. It prefigured the closing work in the ministration of our High Priest in heaven, in the removal or blotting out of the sins of His people, which are registered in the heavenly records. This service involves a work of investigation, a work of judgment; and it immediately precedes the coming of Christ in the clouds of heaven with power and great glory; for when He comes, every case has been decided. Says Jesus: »My reward is with Me, to give every man according as his work shall be.« Revelation 22:12 It is this work of judgment, immediately preceding the second advent, that is announced in the first angel's message of Revelation 14:7: »Fear God, and give glory to Him; for the hour of His judgment is come.«

Those who proclaimed this warning gave the right message at the right time. But as the early disciples declared, »The time is fulfilled, and the kingdom of God is at hand,« based on the prophecy of Daniel 9, while they failed to perceive that the death of the Messiah was foretold in the same scripture, so Miller and his associates preached the message based on Daniel 8:14 and Revelation

14:7, and failed to see that there were still other messages brought to view in Revelation 14, which were also to be given before the advent of the Lord. As the disciples were mistaken in regard to the kingdom to be set up at the end of the seventy weeks, so Adventists were mistaken in regard to the event to take place at the expiration of the 2300 days. In both cases there was an acceptance of, or rather an adherence to, popular errors that blinded the mind to the truth. Both classes fulfilled the will of God in delivering the message which He desired to be given, and both, through their own misapprehension of their message, suffered disappointment.

Yet God accomplished His own beneficent purpose in permitting the warning of the judgment to be given just as it was. The great day was at hand, and in His providence the people were brought to the test of a definite time, in order to reveal to them what was in their hearts. The message was designed for the testing and purification of the church. They were to be led to see whether their affections were set upon this world or upon Christ and heaven. They professed to love the Saviour; now they were to prove their love. Were they ready to renounce their worldly hopes and ambitions, and welcome with joy the advent of their Lord? The message was designed to enable them to discern their true spiritual state; it was sent in mercy to arouse them to seek the Lord with repentance and humiliation.

The disappointment also, though the result of their own misapprehension of the message which they gave, was to be overruled for good. It would test the hearts of those who had professed to receive the warning. In the face of their disappointment would they rashly give up their experience and cast away their confidence in God's word? or would they, in prayer and humility, seek to discern where they had failed to comprehend the significance of the prophecy? How many had moved from fear, or from impulse and excitement? How many were halfhearted and unbelieving? Multitudes professed to love the appearing of the Lord. When called to endure the scoffs and reproach of the world, and the test of delay and disappointment, would they renounce the faith? Because they did not immediately understand the dealings of God with them, would they cast aside truths sustained by the clearest testimony of His word?

This test would reveal the strength of those who with real faith had obeyed what they believed to be the teaching of the word and

the Spirit of God. It would teach them, as only such an

experience could, the danger of accepting the theories and interpretations of men, instead of making the Bible its own interpreter. To the children of faith the perplexity and sorrow resulting from their error would work the needed correction. They would be led to a closer

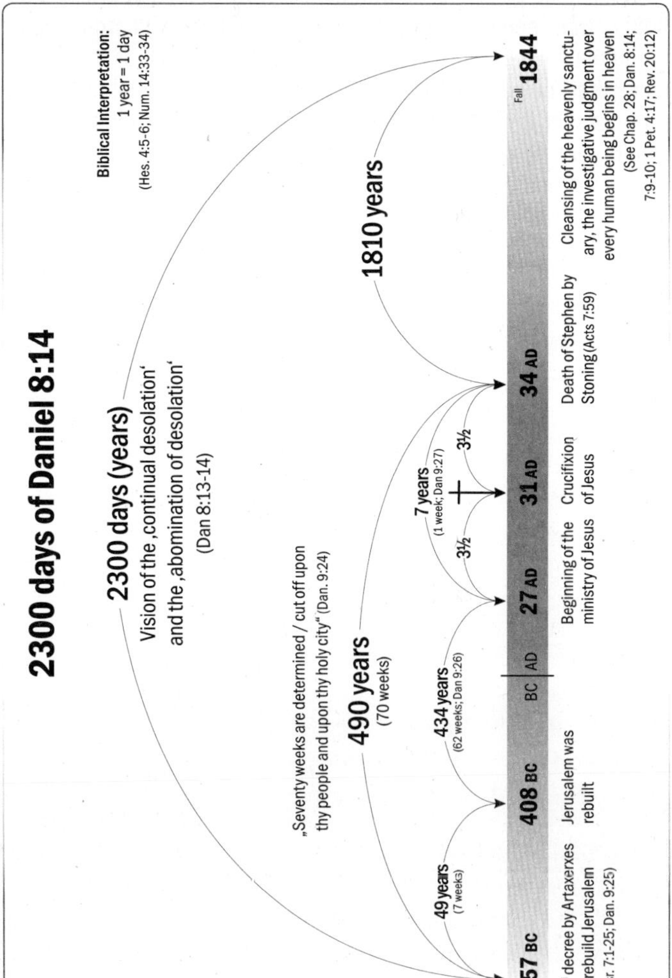

study of the prophetic word. They would be taught to examine more carefully the foundation of their faith, and to reject everything, however widely accepted by the Christian world, that was not founded upon the Scriptures of truth.

With these believers, as with the first disciples, that which in the hour of trial seemed dark to their understanding would afterward be made plain. When they should see the »end of the Lord« they would know that, notwithstanding the trial resulting from their errors, His purposes of love toward them had been steadily fulfilling. They would learn by a blessed experience that He is “very pitiful, and of tender mercy;« that all His paths »are mercy and truth unto such as keep His covenant and His testimonies.«

Chapter 20

A Great Religious Awakening

A Great religious awakening under the proclamation of Christ's soon coming is foretold in the prophecy of the first angel's message of Revelation 14. An angel is seen flying »in the midst of heaven, having the everlasting gospel to preach unto them that dwell on the earth, and to every nation, and kindred, and tongue, and people.« »With a loud voice« he proclaims the message: »Fear God, and give glory to Him; for the hour of His judgment is come: and worship Him that made heaven, and earth, and the sea, and the fountains of waters.« Verses 6-7

The fact that an angel is said to be the herald of this warning is significant. By the purity, the glory, and the power of the heavenly messenger, divine wisdom has been pleased to represent the exalted character of the work to be accomplished by the message and the power and glory that were to attend it. And the angel's flight »in the midst of heaven,« the »loud voice« with which the warning is uttered, and its promulgation to all »that dwell on the earth,« – »to every nation, and kindred, and tongue, and people,« – give evidence of the rapidity and world-wide extent of the movement.

The message itself sheds light as to the time when this movement is to take place. It is declared to be a part of the »everlasting gospel;« and it announces the opening of the judgment. The message of salvation has been preached in all ages; but this message is a part of the gospel which could be proclaimed only in the last days, for only then would it be true that the hour of judgment had come. The prophecies present a succession of events leading down to the opening of the judgment. This is especially true of the book of Daniel. But that part of his prophecy which related to the last days, Daniel was bidden to close up and seal »to the time of the end.« Not till we reach this time could a message concerning the judgment be proclaimed, based on the fulfillment of these prophecies. But at the time of the end, says the prophet, »many shall run to and fro, and knowledge shall be increased.« Daniel 12:4

The apostle Paul warned the church not to look for the coming of Christ in his day. »That day shall not come,« he says, »except there come a falling away first, and that man of sin be revealed.« 2 Thessalonians 2:3 Not till after the great apostasy, and the long period of the reign of the »man of sin,« can we look for the advent of our Lord. The »man of sin,« which is also styled »the mystery of iniquity,« »the son of perdition,« and »that wicked,« represents the papacy, which, as foretold in prophecy, was to maintain its supremacy for 1260 years. This period ended in 1798. The coming of Christ could not take place before that time. Paul covers with his caution the whole of the Christian dispensation down to the year 1798. It is this side of that time that the message of Christ's second coming is to be proclaimed.

No such message has ever been given in past ages. Paul, as we have seen, did not preach it; he pointed his brethren into the then far-distant future for the coming of the Lord. The Reformers did not proclaim it. Martin Luther placed the judgment about three hundred years in the future from his day. But since 1798 the book of Daniel has been unsealed, knowledge of the prophecies has increased, and many have proclaimed the solemn message of the judgment near.

Like the great Reformation of the sixteenth century, the advent movement appeared in different countries of Christendom at the same time. In both Europe and America men of faith and prayer were led to the study of the prophecies, and, tracing down the inspired record, they saw convincing evidence that the end of all things was at hand. In different lands there were isolated bodies of Christians who, solely by the study of the Scriptures, arrived at the belief that the Saviour's advent was near.

In 1821, three years after Miller had arrived at his exposition of the prophecies pointing to the time of the judgment, Dr. Joseph Wolff, »the missionary to the world,« began to proclaim the Lord's soon coming. Wolff was born in Germany, of Hebrew parentage, his father being a Jewish rabbi. While very young he was convinced of the truth of the Christian religion. Of an active, inquiring mind, he had been an eager listener to the conversations that took place in his father's house as devout Hebrews daily assembled to recount the hopes and anticipations of their people, the glory of the coming Messiah, and the restoration of Israel. One day hearing Jesus of Nazareth mentioned, the boy inquired who He was. »A Jew of the greatest talent,« was the an-

swer; »but as He pretended to be the Messiah, the Jewish tribunal sentenced Him to death.« »Why,« rejoined the questioner, »is Jerusalem destroyed, and why are we in captivity?« »Alas, alas!« answered his father, »because the Jews murdered the prophets.« The thought was at once suggested to the child: »Perhaps Jesus was also a prophet, and the Jews killed Him when He was innocent.« Travels and Adventures of the Rev. Joseph Wolff, vol. 1, p. 6 So strong was this feeling that, though forbidden to enter a Christian church, he would often linger outside to listen to the preaching.

When only seven years old he was boasting to an aged Christian neighbor of the future triumph of Israel at the advent of the Messiah, when the old man said kindly: »Dear boy, I will tell you who the real Messiah was: He was Jesus of Nazareth, ... whom your ancestors have crucified, as they did the prophets of old. Go home and read the fifty-third chapter of Isaiah, and you will be convinced that Jesus Christ is the Son of God.« Ibid., vol. 1, p. 7 Conviction at once fastened upon him. He went home and read the scripture, wondering to see how perfectly it had been fulfilled in Jesus of Nazareth. Were the words of the Christian true? The boy asked of his father an explanation of the prophecy, but was met with a silence so stern that he never again dared to refer to the subject. This, however, only increased his desire to know more of the Christian religion.

The knowledge he sought was studiously kept from him in his Jewish home; but, when only eleven years old, he left his father's house and went out into the world to gain for himself an education, to choose his religion and his lifework. He found a home for a time with kinsmen, but was soon driven from them as an apostate, and alone and penniless he had to make his own way among strangers. He went from place to place, studying diligently and maintaining himself by teaching Hebrew. Through the influence of a Catholic instructor he was led to accept the Romish faith and formed the purpose of becoming a missionary to his own people. With this object he went, a few years later, to pursue his studies in the College of the Propaganda at Rome. Here his habit of independent thought and candid speech brought upon him the imputation of heresy. He openly attacked the abuses of the church and urged the necessity of reform. Though at first treated with special favor by the papal dignitaries, he was after a time removed from Rome. Under the surveillance of the church he went from place to place, until it became evident that he could never be brought to submit to the bondage of Romanism. He was declared to be incorrigible and was left at liberty to go where he pleased. He now made his way to England and, professing the Protestant faith, united with the English Church. After two years' study he set out, in 1821, upon his mission.

While Wolff accepted the great truth of Christ's first advent as »a Man of Sorrows, and acquainted with grief,« he saw that the prophecies bring to view with equal clearness His second advent with power and glory. And while he sought to lead his people to Jesus of Nazareth as the Promised One, and to point them to His first coming in humiliation as a sacrifice for the sins of men, he taught them also of His second coming as a king and deliverer.

»Jesus of Nazareth, the true Messiah,« he said, »whose hands and feet were pierced, who was brought like a lamb to the slaughter, who was the Man of Sorrows and acquainted with grief, who after the scepter was taken from Judah, and the legislative power from between his feet, came the first time; shall come the second time in the clouds of heaven, and with the trump of the Archangel« Joseph Wolff, Researches and Missionary Labors, p. 62 »and shall stand upon the Mount of Olives; and that dominion, once consigned to Adam over the creation, and forfeited by him, Genesis 1:26; 3:17 shall be given to Jesus. He shall be king over all the earth. The groanings and lamentations of the creation shall cease, but songs of praises and thanksgivings shall be heard. ... When Jesus comes in the glory of His Father, with the holy angels, ... the dead believers shall rise first. 1 Thessalonians 4:16; 1 Corinthians 15:32 This is what we Christians call the first resurrection. Then the animal kingdom shall change its nature.« Isaiah 11:6-9 and be subdued unto Jesus. Psalm 8 Universal peace shall prevail.« Journal of the Rev. Joseph Wolff, pp. 378, 379 »The Lord again shall look down upon the earth, and say, 'Behold, it is very good.'« Ibid., p. 294

Wolff believed the coming of the Lord to be at hand, his interpretation of the prophetic periods placing the great consummation within a very few years of the time pointed out by Miller. To those who urged from the scripture, »Of that day and hour knoweth no man,« that men are to know nothing concerning the nearness of the advent, Wolff replied: »Did our Lord say that that day and hour should never be known? Did He not give us signs of the times, in order that we may know at least the approach of His coming, as one knows the approach of the summer by the fig tree putting forth its leaves? Matthew 24:32 Are

 we never to know that period, whilst He Himself exhorteth us not only to read Daniel the prophet, but to understand it? and in that very Daniel, where it is said that the words were shut up to the time of the end (which was the case in his time), and that 'many shall run to and fro' (a Hebrew expression for observing and thinking upon the time), 'and knowledge' (regarding that time) 'shall be increased.' Daniel 12:4 Besides this, our Lord does not intend to say by this, that the approach of the time shall not be known, but that the exact 'day and hour knoweth no man.' Enough, He does say, shall be known by the signs of the times, to induce us to prepare for His coming, as Noah prepared the ark.« Wolff, Researches and Missionary Labors, pp. 404, 405

Concerning the popular system of interpreting, or misinterpreting, the Scriptures, Wolff wrote: »The greater part of the Christian church have swerved from the plain sense of Scripture, and have turned to the phantomizing system of the Buddhists, who believe that the future happiness of mankind will consist in moving about in the air, and suppose that when they are reading Jews they must understand Gentiles; and when they read Jerusalem, they must understand the church; and if it is said earth, it means sky; and for coming of the Lord they must understand the progress of the missionary societies; and going up to the mountain of the Lord's house, signifies a grand class meeting of Methodists.« Journal of the Rev. Joseph Wolff, p. 96

During the 25 years from 1821 to 1845, Wolff traveled extensively: in Africa, visiting Egypt and Abyssinia; in Asia, traversing Palestine, Syria, Persia, Bokhara, and India. He also visited the United States, on the journey thither preaching on the island of Saint Helena. He arrived in New York in August, 1837; and, after speaking in that city, he preached in Philadelphia and Baltimore, and finally proceeded to Washington. Here, he says, »on a motion brought forward by the ex-President, John Quincy Adams, in one of the houses of Congress, the House unanimously granted to me the use of the Congress Hall for a lecture, which I delivered on a Saturday, honored with the presence of all the members of Congress, and also of the bishop of Virginia, and of the clergy and citizens of Washington. The same honor was granted to me by the members of the government of New Jersey and Pennsylvania, in whose presence I delivered lectures on my researches in Asia, and also on the personal reign of Jesus Christ.« Ibid., pp. 398, 399

Dr. Wolff traveled in the most barbarous countries without the protection of any European authority, enduring many hardships and surrounded with countless perils. He was bastinadoed and starved, sold as a slave, and three times condemned to death. He was beset by robbers, and sometimes nearly perished from thirst. Once he was stripped of all that he possessed and left to travel hundreds of miles on foot through the mountains, the snow beating in his face and his naked feet benumbed by contact with the frozen ground.

When warned against going unarmed among savage and hostile tribes, he declared himself »provided with arms« – »prayer, zeal for Christ, and confidence in His help.« »I am also,« he said, »provided with the love of God and my neighbor in my heart, and the Bible is in my hand.« W.H.D. Adams, In Perils Oft, p. 192 The Bible in Hebrew and English he carried with him wherever he went. Of one of his later journeys he says: »I ... kept the Bible open in my hand. I felt my power was in the Book, and that its might would sustain me.« Ibid., p. 201

Thus he persevered in his labors until the message of the judgment had been carried to a large part of the habitable globe. Among Jews, Turks, Parsees, Hindus, and many other nationalities and races he distributed the word of God in these various tongues and everywhere heralded the approaching reign of the Messiah.

In his travels in Bokhara he found the doctrine of the Lord's soon coming held by a remote and isolated people. The Arabs of Yemen, he says, »are in possession of a book called Seera, which gives notice of the second coming of Christ and His reign in glory; and they expect great events to take place in the year 1840.« Journal of the Rev. Joseph Wolff, p. 377 »In Yemen ... I spent six days with the children of Rechab. They drink no wine, plant no vineyard, sow no seed, and live in tents, and remember good old Jonadab, the son of Rechab; and I found in their company children of Israel, of the tribe of Dan, ... who expect, with the children of Rechab, the speedy arrival of the Messiah in the clouds of heaven.« Ibid., p. 389 A similar belief was found by another missionary to exist in Tatary. A Tatar priest put the question to the missionary as to when Christ would come the second time. When the missionary answered that he knew nothing about it, the priest seemed greatly surprised at such ignorance in one who professed to be a Bible teacher, and stated his own belief, founded on prophecy, that Christ would come about 1844.

As early as 1826 the advent message began to be preached in England. The movement here did not take so definite a form as in America; the exact time of the advent was not so generally taught, but the great truth of Christ's soon coming in power and glory was extensively proclaimed. And this not among the dissenters and nonconformists only. Mourant Brock, an English writer, states that about seven hundred ministers of the Church of England were engaged in preaching »this gospel of the kingdom.« The message pointing to 1844 as the time of the Lord's coming was also given in Great Britain. Advent publications from the United States were widely circulated. Books and journals were republished in England. And in 1842 Robert Winter, an Englishman by birth, who had received the advent faith in America, returned to his native country to herald the coming of the Lord. Many united with him in the work, and the message of the judgment was proclaimed in various parts of England.

In South America, in the midst of barbarism and priest-craft, Lacunza, a Spaniard and a Jesuit, found his way to the Scriptures and thus received the truth of Christ's speedy return. Impelled to give the warning, yet desiring to escape the censures of Rome, he published his views under the assumed name of »Rabbi Ben-Ezra,« representing himself as a converted Jew. Lacunza lived in the eighteenth century, but it was about 1825 that his book, having found its way to London, was translated into the English language. Its publication served to deepen the interest already awakening in England in the subject of the second advent.

In Germany the doctrine had been taught in the eighteenth century by Bengel, a minister in the Lutheran Church and a celebrated Biblical scholar and critic. Upon completing his education, Bengel had »devoted himself to the study of theology, to which the grave and religious tone of his mind, deepened by his early training and discipline, naturally inclined him. Like other young men of thoughtful character, before and since, he had to struggle with doubts and difficulties of a religious nature, and he alludes, with much feeling, to the 'many arrows which pierced his poor heart, and made his youth hard to bear.'«

Becoming a member of the consistory of Wurttemberg, he advocated the cause of religious liberty. »While maintaining the rights and privileges of the church, he was an advocate for all reasonable freedom being accorded to those who felt themselves bound, on grounds of conscience, to withdraw from her communion.« Encyclopaedia Britannica, 9th ed., art. »Bengel.« The good effects of this policy are still felt in his native province.

It was while preparing a sermon from Revelation 21 for advent Sunday that the light of Christ's second coming broke in upon Bengel's mind. The prophecies of the Revelation unfolded to his understanding as never before. Overwhelmed with a sense of the stupendous importance and surpassing glory of the scenes presented by the prophet, he was forced to turn for a time from the contemplation of the subject. In the pulpit it again presented itself to him with all its vividness and power. From that time he devoted himself to the study of the prophecies, especially those of the Apocalypse, and soon arrived at the belief that they pointed to the coming of Christ as near. The date which he fixed upon as the time of the second advent was within a very few years of that afterward held by Miller.

Bengel's writings have been spread throughout Christendom. His views of prophecy were quite generally received in his own state of Wurttemberg, and to some extent in other parts of Germany. The movement continued after his death, and the advent message was heard in Germany at the same time that it was attracting attention in other lands. At an early date some of the believers went to Russia and there formed colonies, and the faith of Christ's soon coming is still held by the German churches of that country.

The light shone also in France and Switzerland. At Geneva where Farel and Calvin had spread the truth of the Reformation, Gaussen preached the message of the second advent. While a student at school, Gaussen had encountered that spirit of rationalism which pervaded all Europe during the latter part of the eighteenth and the opening of the nineteenth century; and when he entered the ministry he was not only ignorant of true faith, but inclined to skepticism. In his youth he had become interested in the study of prophecy. After reading Rollin's Ancient History, his attention was called to the second chapter of Daniel, and he was struck with the wonderful exactness with which the prophecy had been fulfilled, as seen in the historian's record. Here was a testimony to the inspiration of the Scriptures, which served as an anchor to him amid the perils of later years. He could not rest satisfied with the teachings of rationalism, and in studying the Bible and searching for clearer light he was, after a time, led to a positive faith. As he pursued his investigation of the prophecies he arrived at the belief that the coming of the Lord was at hand. Impressed with the solemnity and importance of this great truth, he

 desired to bring it before the people; but the popular

belief that the prophecies of Daniel are mysteries and cannot be understood was a serious obstacle in his way. He finally determined – as Farel had done before him in evangelizing Geneva – to begin with the children, through whom he hoped to interest the parents.

»I desire this to be understood,« he afterward said, speaking of his object in this undertaking, »it is not because of its small importance, but on the contrary because of its great value, that I wished to present it in this familiar form, and that I addressed it to the children. I desired to be heard, and I feared that I would not be if I addressed myself to the grown people first.« »I determined therefore to go to the youngest. I gather an audience of children; if the group enlarges, if it is seen that they listen, are pleased, interested, that they understand and explain the subject, I am sure to have a second circle soon, and in their turn, grown people will see that it is worth their while to sit down and study. When this is done, the cause is gained.« L. Gaussen, Daniel the Prophet, vol. 2, Preface

The effort was successful. As he addressed the children, older persons came to listen. The galleries of his church were filled with attentive hearers. Among them were men of rank and learning, and strangers and foreigners visiting Geneva; and thus the message was carried to other parts. Encouraged by this success, Gaussen published his lessons, with the hope of promoting the study of the prophetic books in the churches of the French-speaking people. »To publish instruction given to the children,« says Gaussen, »is to say to adults, who too often neglect such books under the false pretense that they are obscure, 'How can they be obscure, since your children understand them?'« »I had a great desire,« he adds, »to render a knowledge of the prophecies popular in our flocks, if possible.« »There is no study, indeed, which it seems to me answers the needs of the time better.« »It is by this that we are to prepare for the tribulation near at hand, and watch and wait for Jesus Christ.«

Though one of the most distinguished and beloved of preachers in the French language, Gaussen was after a time suspended from the ministry, his principal offense being that instead of the church's catechism, a tame and rationalistic manual, almost destitute of positive faith, he had used the Bible in giving instruction to the youth. He afterward became teacher in a theological school, while on Sunday he continued his work as catechist, addressing the children and instructing them in the Scriptures. His works on prophecy also excited much interest. From the professor's chair, through the press, and in his favorite occupation as teacher of children he continued for many years to exert an extensive influence and was instrumental in calling the attention of many to the study of the prophecies which showed that the coming of the Lord was near.

In Scandinavia also the advent message was proclaimed, and a widespread interest was kindled. Many were roused from their careless security to confess and forsake their sins, and seek pardon in the name of Christ. But the clergy of the state church opposed the movement, and through their influence some who preached the message were thrown into prison. In many places where the preachers of the Lord's soon coming were thus silenced, God was pleased to send the message, in a miraculous manner, through little children. As they were under age, the law of the state could not restrain them, and they were permitted to speak unmolested.

The movement was chiefly among the lower class, and it was in the humble dwellings of the laborers that the people assembled to hear the warning. The child-preachers themselves were mostly poor cottagers. Some of them were not more than six or eight years of age; and while their lives testified that they loved the Saviour, and were trying to live in obedience to God's holy requirements, they ordinarily manifested only the intelligence and ability usually seen in children of that age.

When standing before the people, however, it was evident that they were moved by an influence beyond their own natural gifts. Tone and manner changed, and with solemn power they gave the warning of the judgment, employing the very words of Scripture: »Fear God, and give glory to Him; for the hour of His judgment is come.« They reproved the sins of the people, not only condemning immorality and vice, but rebuking worldliness and backsliding, and warning their hearers to make haste to flee from the wrath to come. The people heard with trembling. The convicting Spirit of God spoke to their hearts. Many were led to search the Scriptures with new and deeper interest, the intemperate and immoral were reformed, others abandoned their dishonest practices, and a work was done so marked that even ministers of the state church were forced to acknowledge that the hand of God was in the movement.

It was God's will that the tidings of the Saviour's coming should be given in the Scandinavian countries; and when the voices of His servants were silenced, He put His Spirit upon the children, that the work might be accomplished. When Jesus drew near to Jerusalem attended by the rejoicing multitudes that, with shouts of triumph and the waving of palm branches, heralded Him as the Son of David, the jealous Pharisees called upon Him to silence them; but Jesus answered that all this was in fulfillment of prophecy, and if these should hold their peace, the very stones would cry out. The people, intimidated by the threats of the priests and rulers, ceased their joyful proclamation as they entered the gates of Jerusalem; but the children in the temple courts afterward took up the refrain, and, waving their branches of palm, they cried: »Hosanna to the Son of David!« Matthew 21:8-16

When the Pharisees, sorely displeased, said unto Him, »Hearest Thou what these say?« Jesus answered, »Yea; have ye never read, Out of the mouth of babes and sucklings Thou hast perfected praise?« As God wrought through children at the time of Christ's first advent, so He wrought through them in giving the message of His second advent. God's word must be fulfilled, that the proclamation of the Saviour's coming should be given to all peoples, tongues, and nations.

To William Miller and his colaborers it was given to preach the warning in America. This country became the center of the great advent movement. It was here that the prophecy of the first angel's message had its most direct fulfillment. The writings of Miller and his associates were carried to distant lands. Wherever missionaries had penetrated in all the world, were sent the glad tidings of Christ's speedy return. Far and wide spread the message of the everlasting gospel: »Fear God, and give glory to Him; for the hour of His judgment is come.«

The testimony of the prophecies which seemed to point to the coming of Christ in the spring of 1844 took deep hold of the minds of the people. As the message went from state to state, there was everywhere awakened widespread interest. Many were convinced that the arguments from the prophetic periods were correct, and, sacrificing their pride of opinion, they joyfully received the truth. Some ministers laid aside their sectarian views and feelings, left their salaries and their churches, and united in proclaiming the coming of Jesus. There were comparatively few ministers, however, who would accept this message; therefore it was largely committed to humble laymen. Farmers left their fields, mechanics their tools, traders their merchandise, professional men their positions; and yet the number of workers was small in comparison with the work to be accomplished. The condition of an ungodly church and a world lying in wickedness, burdened the souls of the true watchmen, and they willingly endured toil, privation, and suffering, that they might call men to repentance unto salvation. Though opposed by Satan, the work went steadily forward, and the advent truth was accepted by many thousands.

Everywhere the searching testimony was heard, warning sinners, both worldlings and church members, to flee from the wrath to come. Like John the Baptist, the forerunner of Christ, the preachers laid the ax at the root of the tree and urged all to bring forth fruit meet for repentance. Their stirring appeals were in marked contrast to the assurances of peace and safety that were heard from popular pulpits; and wherever the message was given, it moved the people. The simple, direct testimony of the Scriptures, set home by the power of the Holy Spirit, brought a weight of conviction which few were able wholly to resist. Professors of religion were roused from their false security. They saw their backslidings, their worldliness and unbelief, their pride and selfishness. Many sought the Lord with repentance and humiliation. The affections that had so long clung to earthly things they now fixed upon heaven. The Spirit of God rested upon them, and with hearts softened and subdued they joined to sound the cry: »Fear God, and give glory to Him; for the hour of His judgment is come.«

Sinners inquired with weeping: »What must I do to be saved?« Those whose lives had been marked with dishonesty were anxious to make restitution. All who found peace in Christ longed to see others share the blessing. The hearts of parents were turned to their children, and the hearts of children to their parents. The barriers of pride and reserve were swept away. Heartfelt confessions were made, and the members of the household labored for the salvation of those who were nearest and dearest. Often was heard the sound of earnest intercession. Everywhere were souls in deep anguish pleading with God. Many wrestled all night in prayer for the assurance that their own sins were pardoned, or for the conversion of their relatives or neighbors.

All classes flocked to the Adventist meetings. Rich and poor, high and low, were, from various causes, anxious to hear for themselves the doctrine of the second advent. The Lord held the spirit of opposition in check while His servants explained the reasons of their faith. Sometimes the instrument was feeble; but the Spirit of God gave power to His truth. The presence of holy angels was felt in these assemblies, and many were daily added to the believers. As the evidences of Christ's soon coming were repeated, vast crowds listened in breathless silence to the solemn words. Heaven and earth seemed to approach each other. The power of God was felt upon old and young and middle-aged. Men sought their homes with praises upon their lips, and the glad sound rang out upon the still night air. None who attended those meetings can ever forget those scenes of deepest interest.

The proclamation of a definite time for Christ's coming called forth great opposition from many of all classes, from the minister in the pulpit down to the most reckless, Heaven-daring sinner. The words of prophecy were fulfilled: »There shall come in the last days scoffers, walking after their own lusts, and saying, Where is the promise of His coming? for since the fathers fell asleep, all things continue as they were from the beginning of the creation.« 2 Peter 3:3-4 Many who professed to love the Saviour, declared that they had no opposition to the doctrine of the second advent; they merely objected to the definite time. But God's all-seeing eye read their hearts. They did not wish to hear of Christ's coming to judge the world in righteousness. They had been unfaithful servants, their works would not bear the inspection of the heart-searching God, and they feared to meet their Lord. Like the Jews at the time of Christ's first advent they were not prepared to welcome Jesus. They not only refused to listen to the plain arguments from the Bible, but ridiculed those who were looking for the Lord. Satan and his angels exulted, and flung the taunt in the face of Christ and holy angels that His professed people had so little love for Him that they did not desire His appearing.

»No man knoweth the day nor the hour« was the argument most often brought forward by rejecters of the advent faith. The scripture is: »Of that day and hour knoweth no man, no not the angels of heaven, but My Father only.« Matthew 24:36 A clear and harmonious explanation of this text was given by those who were looking for the Lord, and the wrong use made of it by their opponents was clearly shown. The words were spoken by Christ in that memorable conversation with His disciples upon Olivet after He had for the last time departed from the temple. The disciples had asked the question: »What shall be the sign of Thy coming, and of the end of the world?« Jesus gave them signs, and said: »When ye shall see all these things, know that it is near, even at the doors.« Verses 3, 33 One saying of the Saviour must not be made to destroy another. Though no man knoweth the day nor the hour of His coming, we are instructed and required to know when it is near. We are further taught that to disregard His warning, and refuse or neglect to know when His advent is near, will be as fatal for us as it was for those who lived in the days of Noah not to know when the flood was coming. And the parable in the same chapter, contrasting the faithful and the unfaithful servant, and giving the doom of him who said in his heart, »My Lord delayeth His coming,« shows in what light Christ will regard and reward those whom He finds watching, and teaching His coming, and those denying it. »Watch therefore,« He says. »Blessed is that servant, whom his Lord when He cometh shall find so doing.« Verses 42, 46 »If therefore thou shalt not watch, I will come on thee as a thief, and thou shalt not know what hour I will come upon thee.« Revelation 3:3

Paul speaks of a class to whom the Lord's appearing will come unawares. »The day of the Lord so cometh as a thief in the night. For when they shall say, Peace and safety; then sudden destruction cometh upon them, ... and they shall not escape.« But he adds, to those who have given heed to the Saviour's warning: »Ye, brethren, are not in darkness, that that day should overtake you as a thief. Ye are all the children of light, and the children of the day: we are not of the night, nor of darkness.« 1 Thessalonians 5:2-5

Thus it was shown that Scripture gives no warrant for men to remain in ignorance concerning the nearness of Christ's coming. But those who desired only an excuse to reject the truth closed their ears to this explanation, and the words »No man knoweth the day nor the hour« continued to be echoed by the bold scoffer and even by the professed minister of Christ. As the people were roused, and began to inquire the way of salvation, religious teachers stepped in between them and the truth, seeking to quiet their fears by falsely interpreting the word of God. Unfaithful watchmen united in the work of the great deceiver, crying, Peace, peace, when God had not spoken peace. Like the Pharisees in Christ's day, many refused to enter the kingdom of heaven themselves, and those who were entering in they hindered.
 The blood of these souls will be required at their hand.

The most humble and devoted in the churches were usually the first to receive the message. Those who studied the Bible for themselves could not but see the unscriptural character of the popular views of prophecy; and wherever the people were not controlled by the influence of the clergy, wherever they would search the word of God for themselves, the advent doctrine needed only to be compared with the Scriptures to establish its divine authority.

Many were persecuted by their unbelieving brethren. In order to retain their position in the church, some consented to be silent in regard to their hope; but others felt that loyalty to God forbade them thus to hide the truths which He had committed to their trust. Not a few were cut off from the fellowship of the church for no other reason than expressing their belief in the coming of Christ. Very precious to those who bore this trial of their faith were the words of the prophet: »Your brethren that hated you, that cast you out for My name's sake, said, Let the Lord be glorified: but He shall appear to your joy, and they shall be ashamed.« Isaiah 66:5 Angels of God were watching with the deepest interest the result of the warning. When there was a general rejection of the message by the churches, angels turned away in sadness. But there were many who had not yet been tested in regard to the advent truth. Many were misled by husbands, wives, parents, or children, and were made to believe it a sin even to listen to such heresies as were taught by the Adventists. Angels were bidden to keep faithful watch over these souls, for another light was yet to shine upon them from the throne of God.

With unspeakable desire those who had received the message watched for the coming of their Saviour. The time when they expected to meet Him was at hand. They approached this hour with a calm solemnity. They rested in sweet communion with God, and earnest of the peace that was to be theirs in the bright hereafter. None who experienced this hope and trust can forget those precious hours of waiting. For some weeks preceding the time, worldly business was for the most part laid aside. The sincere believers carefully examined every thought and emotion of their hearts as if upon their deathbeds and in a few hours to close their eyes upon earthly scenes. There was no making of »ascension robes«; see Appendix but all felt the need of internal evidence that they were prepared to meet the Saviour; their white robes were purity of soul – characters cleansed from sin by the atoning blood of Christ. Would that there were still with the professed people of God the same spirit of heart searching, the same earnest, determined faith. Had they continued thus to humble themselves before the Lord and press their petitions at the mercy seat they would be in possession of a far richer experience than they now have. There is too little prayer, too little real conviction of sin, and the lack of living faith leaves many destitute of the grace so richly provided by our Redeemer.

God designed to prove His people. His hand covered a mistake in the reckoning of the prophetic periods. Adventists did not discover the error, nor was it discovered by the most learned of their opponents. The latter said: »Your reckoning of the prophetic periods is correct. Some great event is about to take place; but it is not what Mr. Miller predicts; it is the conversion of the world, and not the second advent of Christ.« see Appendix

The time of expectation passed, and Christ did not appear for the deliverance of His people. Those who with sincere faith and love had looked for their Saviour, experienced a bitter disappointment. Yet the purposes of God were being accomplished; He was testing the hearts of those who professed to be waiting for His appearing. There were among them many who had been actuated by no higher motive than fear. Their profession of faith had not affected their hearts or their lives. When the expected event failed to take place, these persons declared that they were not disappointed; they had never believed that Christ would come. They were among the first to ridicule the sorrow of the true believers.

But Jesus and all the heavenly host looked with love and sympathy upon the tried and faithful yet disappointed ones. Could the veil separating the visible world have been swept back, angels would have been seen drawing near to these steadfast souls and shielding them from the shafts of Satan.

Chapter 21

A Warning Rejected

In preaching the doctrine of the second advent, William Miller and his associates had labored with the sole purpose of arousing men to a preparation for the judgment. They had sought to awaken professors of religion to the true hope of the church and to their need of a deeper Christian experience, and they labored also to awaken the unconverted to the duty of immediate repentance and conversion to God. »They made no attempt to convert men to a sect or party in religion. Hence they labored among all parties and sects, without interfering with their organization or discipline.«

»In all my labors,« said Miller, »I never had the desire or thought to establish any separate interest from that of existing denominations, or to benefit one at the expense of another. I thought to benefit all. Supposing that all Christians would rejoice in the prospect of Christ's coming, and that those who could not see as I did would not love any the less those who should embrace this doctrine, I did not conceive there would ever be any necessity for separate meetings. My whole object was a desire to convert souls to God, to notify the world of a coming judgment, and to induce my fellow men to make that preparation of heart which will enable them to meet their God in peace. The great majority of those who were converted under my labors united with the various existing churches.« Bliss, p. 328

As his work tended to build up the churches, it was for a time regarded with favor. But as ministers and religious leaders decided against the advent doctrine and desired to suppress all agitation of the subject, they not only opposed it from the pulpit, but denied their members the privilege of attending preaching upon the second advent, or even of speaking of their hope in the social meetings of the church. Thus the believers found themselves in a position of great trial and perplexity. They loved their churches and were loath to separate from them; but as they saw the testimony of God's word suppressed and their right to investigate the prophecies denied they felt that loyalty to God forbade them to submit. Those [375/376] who sought to shut out the testimony of God's word they could not regard as constituting the church of Christ, »the pillar and ground of the truth.« Hence they felt themselves justified in separating from their former connection. In the summer of 1844 about fifty thousand withdrew from the churches.

About this time a marked change was apparent in most of the churches throughout the United States. There had been for many years a gradual but steadily increasing conformity to worldly practices and customs, and a corresponding decline in real spiritual life; but in that year there were evidences of a sudden and marked declension in nearly all the churches of the land. While none seemed able to suggest the cause, the fact itself was widely noted and commented upon by both the press and the pulpit.

At a meeting of the presbytery of Philadelphia, Mr. Barnes, author of a commentary widely used and pastor of one of the leading churches in that city, "stated that he had been in the ministry for twenty years, and never, till the last Communion, had he administered the ordinance without receiving more or less into the church. But now there are no awakenings, no conversions, not much apparent growth in grace in professors, and none come to his study to converse about the salvation of their souls. With the increase of business, and the brightening prospects of commerce and manufacture, there is an increase of worldly-mindedness. Thus it is with all the denominations.« Congregational Journal, May 23, 1844

In the month of February of the same year, Professor Finney of Oberlin College said: »We have had the fact before our minds, that, in general, the Protestant churches of our country, as such, were either apathetic or hostile to nearly all the moral reforms of the age. There are partial exceptions, yet not enough to render the fact otherwise than general. We have also another corroborated fact: the almost universal absence of revival influence in the churches. The spiritual apathy is almost all-pervading, and is fearfully deep; so the religious press of the whole land testifies. ... Very extensively, church members are becoming devotees of fashion, – join hands with the ungodly in parties of pleasure, in dancing, in festivities, etc. ... But we need not expand this painful subject. Suffice it that the evidence thickens and rolls heavily upon us, to show that the churches generally are becoming sadly degenerate. They have gone very far from the Lord, and He has withdrawn Himself from them.«

And a writer in the Religious Telescope testified: »We have never witnessed such a general declension of religion as at the present. Truly, the church should awake, and search into the cause of this affliction; for as an affliction everyone that loves Zion must view it. When we call to mind how 'few and far between' cases of true conversion are, and the almost unparalleled impertinence and hardness of sinners, we almost involuntarily exclaim, 'Has God forgotten to be gracious? or, Is the door of mercy closed?'«

Such a condition never exists without cause in the church itself. The spiritual darkness which falls upon nations, upon churches and individuals, is due, not to an arbitrary withdrawal of the succors of divine grace on the part of God, but to neglect or rejection of divine light on the part of men. A striking illustration of this truth is presented in the history of the Jewish people in the time of Christ. By their devotion to the world and forgetfulness of God and His word, their understanding had become darkened, their hearts earthly and sensual. Thus they were in ignorance concerning Messiah's advent, and in their pride and unbelief they rejected the Redeemer. God did not even then cut off the Jewish nation from a knowledge of, or a participation in, the blessings of salvation. But those who rejected the truth lost all desire for the gift of Heaven. They had »put darkness for light, and light for darkness,« until the light which was in them became darkness; and how great was that darkness!

It suits the policy of Satan that men should retain the forms of religion if but the spirit of vital godliness is lacking. After their rejection of the gospel, the Jews continued zealously to maintain their ancient rites, they rigorously preserved their national exclusiveness, while they themselves could not but admit that the presence of God was no longer manifest among them. The prophecy of Daniel pointed so unmistakably to the time of Messiah's coming, and so directly foretold His death, that they discouraged its study, and finally the rabbis pronounced a curse on all who should attempt a computation of the time. In blindness and impenitence the people of Israel during succeeding centuries have stood, indifferent to the gracious offers of salvation, unmindful of the blessings of the gospel, a solemn and fearful warning of the danger of rejecting light from heaven.

Wherever the cause exists, the same results will follow. He who deliberately stifles his convictions of duty because it interferes with his inclinations will finally lose the power to distinguish between truth and error. The understanding becomes darkened, the conscience callous, the heart hardened, and the soul is separated from God. Where the message of divine truth is spurned or slighted, there the church will be enshrouded in darkness; faith and love grow cold, and estrangement and dissension enter. Church members center their interests and energies in worldly pursuits, and sinners become hardened in their impenitence.

The first angel's message of Revelation 14, announcing the hour of God's judgment and calling upon men to fear and worship Him, was designed to separate the professed people of God from the corrupting influences of the world and to arouse them to see their true condition of worldliness and backsliding. In this message, God has sent to the church a warning, which, had it been accepted, would have corrected the evils that were shutting them away from Him. Had they received the message from heaven, humbling their hearts before the Lord and seeking in sincerity a preparation to stand in His presence, the Spirit and power of God would have been manifested among them. The church would again have reached that blessed state of unity, faith, and love which existed in apostolic days, when the believers »were of one heart and of one soul,« and »spake the word of God with boldness,« when »the Lord added to the church daily such as should be saved.« Acts 4:32, 31; 2:4 If God's professed people would receive the light as it shines upon them from His word, they would reach that unity for which Christ prayed, that which the apostle describes, »the unity of the Spirit in the bond of peace.« »There is,« he says, »one body, and one Spirit, even as ye are called in one hope of your calling; one Lord, one faith, one baptism.« Ephesians 4:3-5

Such were the blessed results experienced by those who accepted the advent message. They came from different denominations, and their denominational barriers were hurled to the ground; conflicting creeds were shivered to atoms; the unscriptural hope of a temporal millennium was abandoned, false views of the second advent were corrected, pride and conformity to the world were swept away; wrongs were made right; hearts were united in the sweetest fellowship, and love and joy reigned supreme. If this doctrine did this for the few who did receive it, it would have done the same for all if all had received it.

But the churches generally did not accept the warning. Their ministers, who, as watchmen »unto the house of Israel,«

should have been the first to discern the tokens of Jesus' coming, had failed to learn the truth either from the testimony of the prophets or from the signs of the times. As worldly hopes and ambitions filled the heart, love for God and faith in His word had grown cold; and when the advent doctrine was presented, it only aroused their prejudice and unbelief. The fact that the message was, to a great extent, preached by laymen, was urged as an instrument against it. As of old, the plain testimony of God's word was met with the inquiry: »Have any of the rulers or of the Pharisees believed?« And finding how difficult a task it was to refute the arguments drawn from the prophetic periods, many discouraged the study of the prophecies, teaching that the prophetic books were sealed and were not to be understood. Multitudes, trusting implicitly to their pastors, refused to listen to the warning; and others, though convinced of the truth, dared not confess it, lest they should be »put out of the synagogue.« The message which God had sent for the testing and purification of the church revealed all too surely how great was the number who had set their affections on this world rather than upon Christ. The ties which bound them to earth were stronger than the attractions heavenward. They chose to listen to the voice of worldly wisdom and turned away from the heart-searching message of truth.

In refusing the warning of the first angel, they rejected the means which Heaven had provided for their restoration. They spurned the gracious messenger that would have corrected the evils which separated them from God, and with greater eagerness they turned to seek the friendship of the world. Here was the cause of that fearful condition of worldliness, backsliding, and spiritual death which existed in the churches in 1844.

In Revelation 14 the first angel is followed by a second proclaiming: »Babylon is fallen, is fallen, that great city, because she made all nations drink of the wine of the wrath of her fornication.« Revelation 14:8 The term »Babylon« is derived from »Babel,« and signifies confusion. It is employed in Scripture to designate the various forms of false or apostate religion. In Revelation 17 Babylon is represented as a woman – a figure which is used in the Bible as the symbol of a church, a virtuous woman representing a pure church, a vile woman an apostate church.

In the Bible the sacred and enduring character of the relation that exists between Christ and His church is represented by [380/381] the union of marriage. The Lord has joined His people to Himself by a solemn covenant, He promising to be their God, and they pledging themselves to be His and His alone. He declares: »I will betroth thee unto Me forever; yea, I will betroth thee unto Me in righteousness, and in judgment, and in loving-kindness, and in mercies.« Hosea 2:19 And, again: »I am married unto you.« Jeremiah 3:14 And Paul employs the same figure in the New Testament when he says: »I have espoused you to one husband, that I may present you as a chaste virgin to Christ.« 2 Corinthians 11:2

The unfaithfulness of the church to Christ in permitting her confidence and affection to be turned from Him, and allowing the love of worldly things to occupy the soul, is likened to the violation of the marriage vow. The sin of Israel in departing from the Lord is presented under this figure; and the wonderful love of God which they thus despised is touchingly portrayed: »I sware unto thee, and entered into a covenant with thee, saith the Lord God, and thou becamest Mine.« »And thou wast exceeding beautiful and thou didst prosper into a kingdom. And thy renown went forth among the heathen for thy beauty: for it was perfect through My comeliness, which I had put upon thee. ... But thou didst trust in thine own beauty, and playedst the harlot because of thy renown.« »As a wife treacherously departeth from her husband, so have ye dealt treacherously with Me, O house of Israel, saith the Lord;« »as a wife that committeth adultery, which taketh strangers instead of her husband!« Ezekiel 16:8, 13-15, 32; Jeremiah 3:20

In the New Testament, language very similar is addressed to professed Christians who seek the friendship of the world above the favor of God. Says the apostle James: »Ye adulterers and adulteresses, know ye not that the friendship of the world is enmity with God? whosoever therefore will be a friend of the world is the enemy of God.«

The woman (Babylon) of Revelation 17 is described as »arrayed in purple and scarlet color, and decked with gold and precious stones and pearls, having a golden cup in her hand full of abominations and filthiness: ... and upon her forehead was a name written, Mystery, Babylon the Great, the mother of harlots.« Says the prophet: »I saw the woman drunk with the blood of the saints, and with the blood of the martyrs of Jesus.« Babylon is further declared to be »that great city, which reigneth over the kings of the earth.« Revelation 17:4-6, 18 The power that for so many centuries maintained despotic

sway over the monarchs of Christendom is Rome. The

purple and scarlet color, the gold and precious stones and pearls, vividly picture the magnificence and more than kingly pomp affected by the haughty see of Rome. And no other power could be so truly declared »drunken with the blood of the saints« as that church which has so cruelly persecuted the followers of Christ. Babylon is also charged with the sin of unlawful connection with »the kings of the earth.« It was by departure from the Lord, and alliance with the heathen, that the Jewish church became a harlot; and Rome, corrupting herself in like manner by seeking the support of worldly powers, receives a like condemnation.

Babylon is said to be »the mother of harlots.« By her daughters must be symbolized churches that cling to her doctrines and traditions, and follow her example of sacrificing the truth and the approval of God, in order to form an unlawful alliance with the world. The message of Revelation 14, announcing the fall of Babylon must apply to religious bodies that were once pure and have become corrupt. Since this message follows the warning of the judgment, it must be given in the last days; therefore it cannot refer to the Roman Church alone, for that church has been in a fallen condition for many centuries. Furthermore, in the eighteenth chapter of the Revelation the people of God are called upon to come out of Babylon.

According to this scripture, many of God's people must still be in Babylon. And in what religious bodies are the greater part of the followers of Christ now to be found? Without doubt, in the various churches professing the Protestant faith. At the time of their rise these churches took a noble stand for God and the truth, and His blessing was with them. Even the unbelieving world was constrained to acknowledge the beneficent results that followed an acceptance of the principles of the gospel. In the words of the prophet to Israel: »Thy renown went forth among the heathen for thy beauty: for it was perfect through My comeliness, which I had put upon thee, saith the Lord God.« But they fell by the same desire which was the curse and ruin of Israel – the desire of imitating the practices and courting the friendship of the ungodly. »Thou didst trust in thine own beauty, and playedst the harlot because of thy renown.« Ezekiel 16:14-15

Many of the Protestant churches are following Rome's example of iniquitous connection with »the kings of the earth« – the state churches, by their relation to secular governments; and other denominations, by seeking the favor of the world. And the term »Babylon« – confusion – may be appropriately applied to these bodies, all professing to derive their doctrines from the Bible, yet divided into almost innumerable sects, with widely conflicting creeds and theories. Besides a sinful union with the world, the churches that separated from Rome present other of her characteristics. A Roman Catholic work argues that »if the Church of Rome were ever guilty of idolatry in relation to the saints, her daughter, the Church of England, stands guilty of the same, which has ten churches dedicated to Mary for one dedicated to Christ.« Richard Challoner, The Catholic Christian Instructed, Preface, pp. 21, 22

And Dr. Hopkins, in »A Treatise on the Millennium,« declares: »There is no reason to consider the antichristian spirit and practices to be confined to that which is now called the Church of Rome. The Protestant churches have much of antichrist in them, and are far from being wholly reformed from ... corruptions and wickedness.« Samuel Hopkins, Works, vol. 2, p. 328 Concerning the separation of the Presbyterian Church from Rome, Dr. Guthrie writes: »Three hundred years ago, our church, with an open Bible on her banner, and this motto, 'Search the Scriptures,' on her scroll, marched out from the gates of Rome.« Then he asks the significant question: »Did they come clean out of Babylon?« Thomas Guthrie, The Gospel in Ezekiel, p. 237

»The Church of England,« says Spurgeon, »seems to be eaten through and through with sacramentarianism; but nonconformity appears to be almost as badly riddled with philosophical infidelity. Those of whom we thought better things are turning aside one by one from the fundamentals of the faith. Through and through, I believe, the very heart of England is honeycombed with a damnable infidelity which dares still go into the pulpit and call itself Christian.«

What was the origin of the great apostasy? How did the church first depart from the simplicity of the gospel? By conforming to the practices of paganism, to facilitate the acceptance of Christianity by the heathen. The apostle Paul declared, even in his day, »The mystery of iniquity doth already work.« 2 Thessalonians 2:7 During the lives of the apostles the church remained comparatively pure. But »toward the latter end of the second century most of the churches assumed a new form; the first simplicity disappeared, and insensibly, as the old disciples retired to their graves, their children, along with new converts, ... came forward and new-modeled the cause.« Robert Robinson, Ecclesiastical Researches, ch. 6, par. 17, p. 51 To secure converts, the exalted standard of the Christian faith was lowered, and as the result »a pagan flood, flowing into the church, carried with it its customs, practices, and idols.« Gavazzi, Lectures, p. 278 As the Christian religion secured the favor and support of secular rulers, it was nominally accepted by multitudes; but while in appearance Christians, many »remained in substance pagans, especially worshiping in secret their idols.« Ibid., p. 278

Has not the same process been repeated in nearly every church calling itself Protestant? As the founders, those who possessed the true spirit of reform, pass away, their descendants come forward and »new-model the cause.« While blindly clinging to the creed of their fathers and refusing to accept any truth in advance of what they saw, the children of the reformers depart widely from their example of humility, self-denial, and renunciation of the world. Thus »the first simplicity disappears.« A worldly flood, flowing into the church, carries »with it its customs, practices, and idols.«

Alas, to what a fearful extent is that friendship of the world which is »enmity with God,« now cherished among the professed followers of Christ! How widely have the popular churches throughout Christendom departed from the Bible standard of humility, self-denial, simplicity, and godliness!

Said John Wesley, in speaking of the right use of money: »Do not waste any part of so precious a talent, merely in gratifying the desire of the eye, by superfluous or expensive apparel, or by needless ornaments. Waste no part of it in curiously adorning your houses; in superfluous or expensive furniture; in costly pictures, painting, gilding. ... Lay out nothing to gratify the pride of life, to gain the admiration or praise of men. ... 'So long as thou doest well unto thyself, men will speak good of thee.' So long as thou art 'clothed in purple and fine linen,' and farest 'sumptuously every day,' no doubt many will applaud thy elegance of taste, thy generosity and hospitality. But do not buy their applause so dear. Rather be content with the honor that cometh from God.« Wesley, Works, Sermon 50, »The Use of Money.« But in many churches of our time such teaching is disregarded.

A profession of religion has become popular with the world. Rulers, politicians, lawyers, doctors, merchants, join the church as a means of securing the respect and confidence of society, and advancing their own worldly interests. Thus they seek to cover all their unrighteous transactions under a profession of Christianity. The various religious bodies, re-enforced by the wealth and influence of these baptized worldlings, make a still higher bid for popularity and patronage. Splendid churches, embellished in the most extravagant manner, are erected on popular avenues. The worshipers array themselves in costly and fashionable attire. A high salary is paid for a talented minister to entertain and attract the people. His sermons must not touch popular sins, but be made smooth and pleasing for fashionable ears. Thus fashionable sinners are enrolled on the church records, and fashionable sins are concealed under a pretense of godliness.

Commenting on the present attitude of professed Christians toward the world, a leading secular journal says: »Insensibly the church has yielded to the spirit of the age, and adapted its forms of worship to modern wants.« »All things, indeed, that help to make religion attractive, the church now employs as its instruments.« And a writer in the New York Independent speaks thus concerning Methodism as it is: »The line of separation between the godly and the irreligious fades out into a kind of penumbra, and zealous men on both sides are toiling to obliterate all difference between their modes of action and enjoyment.« »The popularity of religion tends vastly to increase the number of those who would secure its benefits without squarely meeting its duties.« Says Howard Crosby: »It is a matter of deep concern that we find Christ's church so little fulfilling the designs of its Lord. Just as the ancient Jews let a familiar intercourse with the idolatrous nations steal away their hearts from God, ... so the church of Jesus now is, by its false partnerships with an unbelieving world, giving up the divine methods of its true life, and yielding itself to the pernicious, though often plausible, habits of a Christless society, using the arguments and reaching the conclusions which are foreign to the revelation of God, and directly antagonistic to all growth in grace.«
The Healthy Christian: An Appeal to the Church, pp. 141, 142

In this tide of worldliness and pleasure seeking, self-denial and selfsacrifice for Christ's sake are almost wholly lost. »Some of the men and women now in active life in our churches were educated, when children, to make sacrifices in order to be able to give or do something for Christ.« But »if funds are wanted now, ... nobody must be called on to give. Oh, no! have a fair, tableau, mock trial, antiquarian supper, or something to eat – anything to amuse the people.«

Governor Washburn of Wisconsin in his annual message, January 9, 1873, declared: »Some law seems to be required to break up the schools where gamblers are made. These are everywhere. Even the church (unwittingly, no doubt) is sometimes found doing the work of the devil. Gift concerts, gift enterprises and raffles, sometimes in aid of religious or charitable objects, but often for less worthy purposes, lotteries, prize packages, etc., are all devices to obtain money without value received. Nothing is so demoralizing or intoxicating, particularly to the young, as the acquisition of money or property without labor. Respectable people engaging in these chance enterprises, and easing their consciences with the reflection that the money is to go to a good object, it is not strange that the youth of the state should so often fall into the habits which the excitement of games of hazard is almost certain to engender.«

The spirit of worldly conformity is invading the churches throughout Christendom. Robert Atkins, in a sermon preached in London, draws a dark picture of the spiritual declension that prevails in England: »The truly righteous are diminished from the earth, and no man layeth it to heart. The professors of religion of the present day, in every church, are lovers of the world, conformers to the world, lovers of creature comfort, and aspirers after respectability. They are called to suffer with Christ, but they shrink from even reproach. ... Apostasy, apostasy, apostasy, is engraven on the very front of every church; and did they know it, and did they feel it, there might be hope; but, alas! they cry, 'We are rich, and increased in goods, and stand in need of nothing.'« Second Advent Library, tract No. 39

The great sin charged against Babylon is that she »made all nations drink of the wine of the wrath of her fornication.« This cup of intoxication which she presents to the world represents the false doctrines that she has accepted as the result of her unlawful connection with the great ones of the earth. Friendship with the world corrupts her faith, and in her turn she exerts a corrupting influence upon the world by teaching doctrines which are opposed to the plainest statements of Holy Writ.

Rome withheld the Bible from the people and required all men to accept her teachings in its place. It was the work of the Reformation to restore to men the word of God; but is it not too true that in the churches of our time men are taught to rest their faith upon their creed and the teachings of their church rather than on the Scriptures? Said Charles Beecher, speaking of the Protestant churches: »They shrink from any rude word against creeds with the same sensitiveness with which those holy fathers would have shrunk from a rude word against the rising veneration of saints and martyrs which they were fostering. ... The Protestant evangelical denominations have so tied up one another's hands, and their own, that, between them all, a man cannot become a preacher at all, anywhere, without accepting some book besides the Bible. ... There is nothing imaginary in the statement that the creed power is now beginning to prohibit the Bible as really as Rome did, though in a subtler way.« Sermon on »The Bible a Sufficient Creed,« delivered at Fort Wayne, Indiana, Feb. 22, 1846

When faithful teachers expound the word of God, there arise men of learning, ministers professing to understand the Scriptures, who denounce sound doctrine as heresy, and thus turn away inquirers after truth. Were it not that the world is hopelessly intoxicated with the wine of Babylon, multitudes would be convicted and converted by the plain, cutting truths of the word of God. But religious faith appears so confused and discordant that the people know not what to believe as truth. The sin of the world's impenitence lies at the door of the church.

The second angel's message of Revelation 14 was first preached in the summer of 1844, and it then had a more direct application to the churches of the United States, where the warning of the judgment had been most widely proclaimed and most generally rejected, and where the declension in the churches had been most rapid. But the message of the second angel did not reach its complete fulfillment in 1844. The churches then experienced a moral fall, in consequence of their refusal of the light of the advent message; but that fall was not complete. As they have continued to reject the special truths for this time they have fallen lower and lower. Not yet, however, can it be said that »Babylon is fallen,... because she made all nations drink of the wine of the wrath of her fornication.« She has not yet made all nations do this. The spirit of world conforming and indifference to the testing truths for our time exists and has been gaining ground in churches of the Protestant faith in all the countries of Christendom; and these churches are included in the solemn and terrible denunciation of the second angel. But the work of apostasy has not yet reached its culmination.

The Bible declares that before the coming of the Lord, Satan will work »with all power and signs and lying wonders, and with all
 deceivableness of unrighteousness;« and they that

»received not the love of the truth, that they might be saved,« will be left to receive »strong delusion, that they should believe a lie.« 2 Thessalonians 2:9-11 Not until this condition shall be reached, and the union of the church with the world shall be fully accomplished throughout Christendom, will the fall of Babylon be complete. The change is a progressive one, and the perfect fulfillment of Revelation 14:8 is yet future.

Notwithstanding the spiritual darkness and alienation from God that exist in the churches which constitute Babylon, the great body of Christ's true followers are still to be found in their communion. There are many of these who have never seen the special truths for this time. Not a few are dissatisfied with their present condition and are longing for clearer light. They look in vain for the image of Christ in the churches with which they are connected. As these bodies depart further and further from the truth, and ally themselves more closely with the world, the difference between the two classes will widen, and it will finally result in separation. The time will come when those who love God supremely can no longer remain in connection with such as are »lovers of pleasures more than lovers of God; having a form of godliness, but denying the power thereof.«

Revelation 18 points to the time when, as the result of rejecting the threefold warning of Revelation 14:6-12, the church will have fully reached the condition foretold by the second angel, and the people of God still in Babylon will be called upon to separate from her communion. This message is the last that will ever be given to the world; and it will accomplish its work. When those that »believed not the truth, but had pleasure in unrighteousness« 2 Thessalonians 2:12, shall be left to receive strong delusion and to believe a lie, then the light of truth will shine upon all whose hearts are open to receive it, and all the children of the Lord that remain in Babylon will heed the call: »Come out of her, My people« Revelation 18:4

Chapter 22

Prophecies Fulfilled

When the time passed at which the Lord's coming was first expected, – in the spring of 1844, – those who had looked in faith for His appearing were for a season involved in doubt and uncertainty. While the world regarded them as having been utterly defeated and proved to have been cherishing a delusion, their source of consolation was still the word of God. Many continued to search the Scriptures, examining anew the evidences of their faith and carefully studying the prophecies to obtain further light. The Bible testimony in support of their position seemed clear and conclusive. Signs which could not be mistaken pointed to the coming of Christ as near. The special blessing of the Lord, both in the conversion of sinners and the revival of spiritual life among Christians, had testified that the message was of Heaven. And though the believers could not explain their disappointment, they felt assured that God had led them in their past experience. Interwoven with prophecies which they had regarded as applying to the time of the second advent was instruction specially adapted to their state of uncertainty and suspense, and encouraging them to wait patiently in the faith that what was now dark to their understanding would in due time be made plain.

Among these prophecies was that of Habakkuk 2:1-4: »I will stand upon my watch, and set me upon the tower, and will watch to see what He will say unto me, and what I shall answer when I am reproved. And the Lord answered me, and said, Write the vision, and make it plain upon tables, that he may run that readeth it. For the vision is yet for an appointed time, but at the end it shall speak, and not lie: though it tarry, wait for it; because it will surely come, it will not tarry. Behold, his soul which is lifted up is not upright in him: but the just shall live by his faith.«

As early as 1842 the direction given in this prophecy to »write the vision, and make it plain upon tables, that he may run that readeth it,« had suggested to Charles Fitch the preparation of a prophetic chart to illustrate the visions of Daniel and the Revelation. The publication of this chart was regarded as a fulfillment of the command given by Habakkuk. No one, however, then noticed that an apparent delay in the accomplishment of the vision – a tarrying time – is presented in the same prophecy. After the disappointment, this scripture appeared very significant: »The vision is yet for an appointed time, but at the end it shall speak, and not lie: though it tarry, wait for it; because it will surely come, it will not tarry. ... The just shall live by his faith.«

A portion of Ezekiel's prophecy also was a source of strength and comfort to believers: »The word of the Lord came unto me, saying, Son of man, what is that proverb that ye have in the land of Israel, saying, The days are prolonged, and every vision faileth? Tell them therefore, Thus saith the Lord God. ... The days are at hand, and the effect of every vision. ... I will speak, and the word that I shall speak shall come to pass; it shall be no more prolonged.« »They of the house of Israel say, The vision that he seeth is for many days to come, and he prophesieth of the times that are far off. Therefore say unto them, Thus saith the Lord God; There shall none of My words be prolonged any more, but the word which I have spoken shall be done.« Ezekiel 12:21-25, 27, 28

The waiting ones rejoiced, believing that He who knows the end from the beginning had looked down through the ages and, foreseeing their disappointment, had given them words of courage and hope. Had it not been for such portions of Scripture, admonishing them to wait with patience and to hold fast their confidence in God's word, their faith would have failed in that trying hour.

The parable of the ten virgins of Matthew 25 also illustrates the experience of the Adventist people. In Matthew 24 in answer to the question of His disciples concerning the sign of His coming and of the end of the world, Christ had pointed out some of the most important events in the history of the world and of the church from His first to His second advent; namely, the destruction of Jerusalem, the great tribulation of the church under the pagan and papal persecutions, the darkening of the sun and moon, and the falling of the stars. After this He spoke of His coming in His kingdom, and related the parable describing the two classes of servants who look for His appearing. Chapter 25 opens with the words: »Then shall the kingdom of heaven be likened unto ten virgins.« Here is brought to view the church living in the last days, the same that is pointed out in the close of chapter 24. In this parable their experience is illustrated by the incidents of an Eastern marriage. »Then shall the kingdom of heaven be likened unto ten virgins, which took their lamps, and went forth to meet the bridegroom. And five of them were wise, and five were foolish. They that were foolish took their lamps, and took no oil with them: but the wise took oil in their vessels with their lamps. While the bridegroom tarried, they all slumbered and slept. And at midnight there was a cry made, Behold, the bridegroom cometh; go ye out to meet him.«

The coming of Christ, as announced by the first angel's message, was understood to be represented by the coming of the bridegroom. The widespread reformation under the proclamation of His soon coming, answered to the going forth of the virgins. In this parable, as in that of, Matthew 24 two classes are represented. All had taken their lamps, the Bible, and by its light had gone forth to meet the Bridegroom. But while »they that were foolish took their lamps, and took no oil with them,« »the wise took oil in their vessels with their lamps.« The latter class had received the grace of God, the regenerating, enlightening power of the Holy Spirit, which renders His word a lamp to the feet and a light to the path. In the fear of God they had studied the Scriptures to learn the truth, and had earnestly sought for purity of heart and life. These had a personal experience, a faith in God and in His word, which could not be overthrown by disappointment and delay. Others »took their lamps, and took no oil with them.« They had moved from impulse. Their fears had been excited by the solemn message, but they had depended upon the faith of their brethren, satisfied with the flickering light of good emotions, without a thorough understanding of the truth or a genuine work of grace in the heart. These had gone forth to meet the Lord, full of hope in the prospect of immediate reward; but they were not prepared for delay and disappointment. When trials came, their faith failed, and their lights burned dim.

»While the bridegroom tarried, they all slumbered and slept.« By the tarrying of the bridegroom is represented the passing of the time when the Lord was expected, the disappointment, and the seeming delay. In this time of uncertainty, the interest of the superficial and halfhearted soon began to waver, and their efforts to relax; but those whose faith was based on a personal knowledge of the Bible had a rock beneath their feet, which the waves of disappointment could not wash away. »They all slumbered and slept;« one class in unconcern and abandonment of their faith, the other class patiently waiting till clearer light should be given. Yet in the night of trial the latter seemed to lose, to some extent, their zeal and devotion. The halfhearted and superficial could no longer lean upon the faith of their brethren. Each must stand or fall for himself. About this time, fanaticism began to appear. Some who had pro-fessed to be zealous believers in the message rejected the word of God as the one infallible guide and, claiming to be led by the Spirit, gave themselves up to the control of their own feelings, impressions, and imaginations. There were some who manifested a blind and bigoted zeal, denouncing all who would not sanction their course. Their fanatical ideas and exercises met with no sympathy from the great body of Adventists; yet they served to bring reproach upon the cause of truth.

Satan was seeking by this means to oppose and destroy the work of God. The people had been greatly stirred by the advent movement, thousands of sinners had been converted, and faithful men were giving themselves to the work of proclaiming the truth, even in the tarrying time. The prince of evil was losing his subjects; and in order to bring reproach upon the cause of God, he sought to deceive some who professed the faith and to drive them to extremes. Then his agents stood ready to seize upon every error, every failure, every unbecoming act, and hold it up before the people in the most exaggerated light, to render Adventists and their faith odious. Thus the greater the number whom he could crowd in to make a profession of faith in the second advent while his power controlled their hearts, the greater advantage would he gain by calling attention to them as representatives of the whole body of believers.

Satan is »the accuser of the brethren,« and it is his spirit that inspires men to watch for the errors and defects of the Lord's people, and to hold them up to notice, while their good deeds are passed by without a mention. He is always active when God is at work for the salvation of souls. When the sons of God come to present themselves before the Lord, Satan comes also among them. In every revival he is ready to bring in those who are unsanctified in heart and unbalanced in mind. When these have accepted some points of truth, and gained a place with believers, he works through them to introduce theories that will deceive the unwary. No man is proved to be a true Christian because he is found in company with the children of God, even in the house of worship and around the table of the Lord. Satan is frequently there upon the most solemn occasions in the form of those whom he can use as his agents. The prince of evil contests every inch of ground over which God's people advance in their journey toward the heavenly city. In all the history of the church no reformation has been carried forward without encountering serious obstacles. Thus it was in Paul's day. Wherever the apostle raised up a church, there were some who professed to receive the faith, but who brought in heresies, that, if received, would eventually crowd out the love of the truth. Luther also suffered great perplexity and distress from the course of fanatical persons who claimed that God had spoken directly through them, and who therefore set their own ideas and opinions above the testimony of the Scriptures. Many who were lacking in faith and experience, but who had considerable self-sufficiency, and who loved to hear and tell some new thing, were beguiled by the pretensions of the new teachers, and they joined the agents of Satan in their work of tearing down what God had moved Luther to build up. And the Wesleys, and others who blessed the world by their influence and their faith, encountered at every step the wiles of Satan in pushing overzealous, unbalanced, and unsanctified ones into fanaticism of every grade.

William Miller had no sympathy with those influences that led to fanaticism. He declared, with Luther, that every spirit should be tested by the word of God. »The devil,« said Miller, »has great power over the minds of some at the present day. And how shall we know what manner of spirit they are of? The Bible answers: 'By their fruits ye shall know them.'... There are many spirits gone out into the world; and we are commanded to try the spirits. The spirit that does not cause us to live soberly, righteously, and godly, in this present world, is not the Spirit of Christ. I am more and more convinced that Satan has much to do in these wild movements. ... Many among us who pretend to be wholly sanctified, are following the traditions of men, and apparently are as ignorant of truth as others who make no such pretensions.« Bliss, pp. 236, 237 »The spirit of error will lead us from the truth; and the Spirit of God will lead us into truth. But, say you, a man may be in an error, and think he has the truth. What then? We answer, The Spirit and word agree. If a man judges himself by the word of God, and finds a perfect harmony through the whole word, then he must believe he has the

 truth; but if he finds the spirit by which he is led does not harmonize with the whole tenor of God's law or Book, then let him walk carefully, lest he be caught in the snare of the devil.« The Advent Herald and Signs of the Times Reporter,January 15, 1845 »I have often obtained more evidence of inward piety from a kindling eye, a wet cheek, and a choked utterance, than from all the noise of Christendom.« Bliss, p. 282

In the days of the Reformation its enemies charged all the evils of fanaticism upon the very ones who were laboring most earnestly against it. A similar course was pursued by the opposers of the advent movement. And not content with misrepresenting and exaggerating the errors of extremists and fanatics, they circulated unfavorable reports that had not the slightest semblance of truth. These persons were actuated by prejudice and hatred. Their peace was disturbed by the proclamation of Christ at the door. They feared it might be true, yet hoped it was not, and this was the secret of their warfare against Adventists and their faith.

The fact that a few fanatics worked their way into the ranks of Adventists is no more reason to decide that the movement was not of God than was the presence of fanatics and deceivers in the church in Paul's or Luther's day a sufficient excuse for condemning their work. Let the people of God arouse out of sleep and begin in earnest the work of repentance and reformation; let them search the Scriptures to learn the truth as it is in Jesus; let them make an entire consecration to God, and evidence will not be wanting that Satan is still active and vigilant. With all possible deception he will manifest his power, calling to his aid all the fallen angels of his realm.

It was not the proclamation of the second advent that caused fanaticism and division. These appeared in the summer of 1844, when Adventists were in a state of doubt and perplexity concerning their real position. The preaching of the first angel's message and of the »midnight cry« tended directly to repress fanaticism and dissension. Those who participated in these solemn movements were in harmony; their hearts were filled with love for one another and for Jesus, whom they expected soon to see. The one faith, the one blessed hope, lifted them above the control of any human influence, and proved a shield against the assaults of Satan.

»While the bridegroom tarried, they all slumbered and slept. And at midnight there was a cry made, Behold, the bridegroom cometh; go ye out to meet him. Then all those virgins arose, and trimmed their lamps.« Matthew 25:5-7 In the summer of 1844, midway between the time when it had been first thought that the 2300 days would end, and the autumn of the same year, to which it was afterward found that they extended, the message was proclaimed in the very words of Scripture: »Behold, the Bridegroom cometh!«

That which led to this movement was the discovery that the decree of Artaxerxes for the restoration of Jerusalem, which formed the starting point for the period of the 2300 days, went into effect in the autumn of the year 457 B.C., and not at the beginning of the year, as had been formerly believed. Reckoning from the autumn of 457, the 2300 years terminate in the autumn of 1844. see Appendix note for p. 329

Arguments drawn from the Old Testament types also pointed to the autumn as the time when the event represented by the »cleansing of the sanctuary« must take place. This was made very clear as attention was given to the manner in which the types relating to the first advent of Christ had been fulfilled.

The slaying of the Passover lamb was a shadow of the death of Christ. Says Paul: »Christ our Passover is sacrificed for us.« 1 Corinthians 5:7 The sheaf of first fruits, which at the time of the Passover was waved before the Lord, was typical of the resurrection of Christ. Paul says, in speaking of the resurrection of the Lord and of all His people: »Christ the first fruits; afterward they that are Christ's at His coming.« 1 Corinthians 15:23 Like the wave sheaf, which was the first ripe grain gathered before the harvest, Christ is the first fruits of that immortal harvest of redeemed ones that at the future resurrection shall be gathered into the garner of God.

These types were fulfilled, not only as to the event, but as to the time. On the fourteenth day of the first Jewish month, the very day and month on which for fifteen long centuries the Passover lamb had been slain, Christ, having eaten the Passover with His disciples, instituted that feast which was to commemorate His own death as »the Lamb of God, which taketh away the sin of the world.« That same night He was taken by wicked hands to be crucified and slain. And as the antitype of the wave sheaf our Lord was raised from the dead on the third day, »the first fruits of them that slept,« a sample of all the resurrected just, whose »vile body« shall be changed, and »fashioned like unto His glorious body.« Verse 20; Philippians 3:21

In like manner the types which relate to the second advent must be fulfilled at the time pointed out in the symbolic service. Under the Mosaic system the cleansing of the sanctuary, or the great Day of Atonement, occurred on the tenth day of the seventh Jewish month, Leviticus 16:29-34 when the high priest, having made an atonement for all Israel, and thus removed their sins from the sanctuary, came forth and blessed the people. So it was believed that Christ, our great High Priest, would appear to purify the earth by the destruction of sin and sinners, and to bless His waiting people with immortality. The tenth day of the seventh month, the great Day of Atonement, the time of the cleansing of the sanctuary, which in the year 1844 fell upon the twenty-second of October, was regarded as the time of the Lord's coming. This was in harmony with the proofs already presented that the 2300 days would terminate in the autumn, and the conclusion seemed irresistible.

In the parable of Matthew 25 the time of waiting and slumber is followed by the coming of the bridegroom. This was in accordance with the arguments just presented, both from prophecy and from the types. They carried strong conviction of their truthfulness; and the »midnight cry« was heralded by thousands of believers.

Like a tidal wave the movement swept over the land. From city to city, from village to village, and into remote country places it went, until the waiting people of God were fully aroused. Fanaticism disappeared before this proclamation like early frost before the rising sun. Believers saw their doubt and perplexity removed, and hope and courage animated their hearts. The work was free from those extremes which are ever manifested when there is human excitement without the controlling influence of the word and Spirit of God. It was similar in character to those seasons of humiliation and returning unto the Lord which among ancient Israel followed messages of reproof from His servants. It bore the characteristics that mark the work of God in every age. There was little ecstatic joy, but rather deep searching of heart, confession of sin, and forsaking of the world. A preparation to meet the Lord was the burden of agonizing spirits. There was persevering prayer and unreserved consecration to God.

Said Miller in describing that work: »There is no great expression of joy: that is, as it were, suppressed for a future occasion, when all heaven and earth will rejoice together with joy unspeakable and full of glory. There is no shouting: that, too, is reserved for the shout from heaven. The singers are silent: they are waiting to join the angelic hosts, the choir from heaven. ... There is no clashing of sentiments: all are of one heart and of one mind.« Bliss, pp. 270, 271

Another who participated in the movement testified: »It produced everywhere the most deep searching of heart and humiliation of soul before the God of high heaven. It caused a weaning of affections from the things of this world, a healing of controversies and animosities, a confession of wrongs, a breaking down before God, and penitent, brokenhearted supplications to Him for pardon and acceptance. It caused self-abasement and prostration of soul, such as we never before witnessed. As God by Joel commanded, when the great day of God should be at hand, it produced a rending of hearts and not of garments, and a turning unto the Lord with fasting, and weeping, and mourning. As God said by Zechariah, a spirit of grace and supplication was poured out upon His children; they looked to Him whom they had pierced, there was a great mourning in the land, ... and those who were looking for the Lord afflicted their souls before Him.« Bliss, in Advent Shield and Review, vol. I, p. 271 (January, 1845)

Of all the great religious movements since the days of the apostles, none have been more free from human imperfection and the wiles of Satan than was that of the autumn of 1844. Even now, after the lapse of many years, all who shared in that movement and who have stood firm upon the platform of truth still feel the holy influence of that blessed work and bear witness that it was of God.

At the call, »The Bridegroom cometh; go ye out to meet Him,« the waiting ones »arose and trimmed their lamps;« they studied the word of God with an intensity of interest before unknown. Angels were sent from heaven to arouse those who had become discouraged and prepare them to receive the message. The work did not stand in the wisdom and learning of men, but in the power of God. It was not the most talented, but the most humble and devoted, who were the first to hear and obey the call. Farmers left their crops standing in the fields, mechanics laid down their tools, and with tears and rejoicing went out to give the warning. Those who had formerly led in the cause were among the last to join in this movement. The churches in general closed their doors against this message, and a large company of those who received it withdrew from their connection. In the providence of God this proclamation united with the second angel's message and gave power to that work.

The message, »Behold, the Bridegroom cometh!« was not so much a matter of argument, though the Scripture proof was clear and conclusive. There went with it an impelling power that moved the soul. There was no doubt, no questioning. Upon the occasion of Christ's triumphal entry into Jerusalem the people who were assembled from all parts of the land to keep the feast flocked to the Mount of Olives, and as they joined the throng that were escorting Jesus they caught the inspiration of the hour and helped to swell the shout: »Blessed is He that cometh in the name of the Lord!« Matthew 21:9 In like manner did unbelievers who flocked to the Adventist meetings - some from curiosity, some merely to ridicule – feel the convincing power attending the message: »Behold, the Bridegroom cometh!«

At that time there was faith that brought answers to prayer – faith that had respect to the recompense of reward. Like showers of rain upon the thirsty earth, the Spirit of grace descended upon the earnest seekers. Those who expected soon to stand face to face with their Redeemer felt a solemn joy that was unutterable. The softening, subduing power of the Holy Spirit melted the heart as His blessing was bestowed in rich measure upon the faithful, believing ones.

Carefully and solemnly those who received the message came up to the time when they hoped to meet their Lord. Every morning they felt that it was their first duty to secure the evidence of their acceptance with God. Their hearts were closely united, and they prayed much with and for one another. They often met together in secluded places to commune with God, and the voice of intercession ascended to heaven from the fields and groves. The assurance of the Saviour's approval was more necessary to them than their daily food; and if a cloud darkened their minds, they did not rest until it was swept away. As they felt the witness of pardoning grace, they longed to behold Him whom their souls loved.

But again they were destined to disappointment. The time of expectation passed, and their Saviour did not appear. With unwavering confidence they had looked forward to His coming, and now they felt as did Mary when, coming to the Saviour's tomb and finding it empty, she exclaimed with weeping: »They have taken away my Lord, and I know not where they have laid Him.« John 20:13

A feeling of awe, a fear that the message might be true, had for a time served as a restraint upon the unbelieving world. After the passing of the time this did not at once disappear; at first they dared not triumph over the disappointed ones; but as no tokens of God's wrath were seen, they recovered from their fears and resumed their reproach and ridicule. A large class who had professed to believe in the Lord's soon coming, renounced their faith. Some who had been very confident were so deeply wounded in their pride that they felt like fleeing from the world. Like Jonah, they complained of God, and chose death rather than life. Those who had based their faith upon the opinions of others, and not upon the word of God, were now as ready again to change their views. The scoffers won the weak and cowardly to their ranks, and all these united in declaring that there could be no more fears or expectations now. The time had passed, the Lord had not come, and the world might remain the same for thousands of years.

The earnest, sincere believers had given up all for Christ and had shared His presence as never before. They had, as they believed, given their last warning to the world; and, expecting soon to be received into the society of their divine Master and the heavenly angels, they had, to a great extent, withdrawn from the society of those who did not receive the message. With intense desire they had prayed: »Come, Lord Jesus, and come quickly.« But He had not come. And now to take up again the heavy burden of life's cares and perplexities, and to endure the taunts and sneers of a scoffing world, was a terrible trial of faith and patience.

Yet this disappointment was not so great as was that experienced by the disciples at the time of Christ's first advent. When Jesus rode triumphantly into Jerusalem, His followers believed that He was about to ascend the throne of David and deliver Israel from her oppressors. With high hopes and joyful anticipations they vied with one another in showing honor to their King. Many spread their outer garments as a carpet in His path, or strewed before Him the leafy branches of the palm. In their enthusiastic joy they united in the glad acclaim: »Hosanna to the Son of David!« When the Pharisees, disturbed and angered by this outburst of rejoicing, wished Jesus to rebuke His disciples, He replied: »If these should hold their peace, the stones would immediately cry out.« Luke 19:40 Prophecy must be fulfilled. The disciples were accomplishing the purpose of God; yet they were doomed to a bitter disappointment. But a few days had passed ere they witnessed the Saviour's agonizing death, and laid Him in the tomb. Their expectations had not been realized in a single particular, and their hopes died with Jesus. Not till their Lord had come forth

 triumphant from the grave could they perceive that all

had been foretold by prophecy, and »that Christ must needs have suffered, and risen again from the dead.« Acts 17:3 Five hundred years before, the Lord had declared by the prophet Zechariah: »Rejoice greatly, O daughter of Zion; shout, O daughter of Jerusalem: behold, thy King cometh unto thee: He is just, and having salvation; lowly, and riding upon an ass, and upon a colt the foal of an ass.« Zechariah 9:9 Had the disciples realized that Christ was going to judgment and to death, they could not have fulfilled this prophecy.

In like manner Miller and his associates fulfilled prophecy and gave a message which Inspiration had foretold should be given to the world, but which they could not have given had they fully understood the prophecies pointing out their disappointment, and presenting another message to be preached to all nations before the Lord should come. The first and second angels' messages were given at the right time and accomplished the work which God designed to accomplish by them.

The world had been looking on, expecting that if the time passed and Christ did not appear, the whole system of Adventism would be given up. But while many, under strong temptation, yielded their faith, there were some who stood firm. The fruits of the advent movement, the spirit of humility and heart searching, of renouncing of the world and reformation of life, which had attended the work, testified that it was of God. They dared not deny that the power of the Holy Spirit had witnessed to the preaching of the second advent, and they could detect no error in their reckoning of the prophetic periods. The ablest of their opponents had not succeeded in overthrowing their system of prophetic interpretation. They could not consent, without Bible evidence, to renounce positions which had been reached through earnest, prayerful study of the Scriptures, by minds enlightened by the Spirit of God and hearts burning with its living power; positions which had withstood the most searching criticisms and the most bitter opposition of popular religious teachers and worldly-wise men, and which had stood firm against the combined forces of learning and eloquence, and the taunts and revilings alike of the honorable and the base.

True, there had been a failure as to the expected event, but even this could not shake their faith in the word of God. When Jonah proclaimed in the streets of Nineveh that within forty days the city would be overthrown, the Lord accepted the humiliation of the

Ninevites and extended their period of probation; yet the message of Jonah was sent of God, and Nineveh was tested according to His will. Adventists believed that in like manner God had led them to give the warning of the judgment. »It has,« they declared, »tested the hearts of all who heard it, and awakened a love for the Lord's appearing; or it has called forth a hatred, more or less perceivable, but known to God, of His coming. It has drawn a line, ... so that those who will examine their own hearts, may know on which side of it they would have been found, had the Lord then come – whether they would have exclaimed, 'Lo! this is our God, we have waited for Him, and He will save us;' or whether they would have called to the rocks and mountains to fall on them to hide them from the face of Him that sitteth on the throne, and from the wrath of the Lamb. God thus, as we believe, has tested His people, has tried their faith, has proved them, and seen whether they would shrink, in the hour of trial, from the position in which He might see fit to place them; and whether they would relinquish this world and rely with implicit confidence in the word of God.«

The Advent Herald and Signs of the Times Reporter, vol. 8, No. 14 (Nov 13, 1844)

The feelings of those who still believed that God had led them in their past experience are expressed in the words of William Miller: »Were I to live my life over again, with the same evidence that I then had, to be honest with God and man I should have to do as I have done.« »I hope that I have cleansed my garments from the blood of souls. I feel that, as far as it was in my power, I have freed myself from all guilt in their condemnation.« »Although I have been twice disappointed,« wrote this man of God, »I am not yet cast down or discouraged. ... My hope in the coming of Christ is as strong as ever. I have done only what, after years of solemn consideration, I felt it my solemn duty to do. If I have erred, it has been on the side of charity, love to my fellow men, and conviction of duty to God.« »One thing I do know, I have preached nothing but what I believed; and God has been with me; His power has been manifested in the work, and much good has been effected.« »Many thousands, to all human appearance, have been made to study the Scriptures by the preaching of the time; and by that means, through faith and the sprinkling of the blood of Christ, have been reconciled to God.« Bliss, pp. 256, 255, 277, 280, 281 »I have never courted the smiles of the proud, nor quailed when the world frowned. I shall not now purchase their favor, nor

 shall I go beyond duty to tempt their hate. I shall never

seek my life at their hands, nor shrink, I hope, from losing it, if God in His good providence so orders.« J. White, Life of Wm. Miller, p. 315

God did not forsake His people; His Spirit still abode with those who did not rashly deny the light which they had received, and denounce the advent movement. In the Epistle to the Hebrews are words of encouragement and warning for the tried, waiting ones at this crisis: »Cast not away therefore your confidence, which hath great recompense of reward. For ye have need of patience, that, after ye have done the will of God, ye might receive the promise. For yet a little while, and He that shall come will come, and will not tarry. Now the just shall live by faith: but if any man draw back, My soul shall have no pleasure in him. But we are not of them who draw back unto perdition; but of them that believe to the saving of the soul.« Hebr. 10:35-39 That this admonition is addressed to the church in the last days is evident from the words pointing to the nearness of the Lord's coming: »For yet a little while, and He that shall come will come and will not tarry.«

And it is plainly implied that there would be a seeming delay and that the Lord would appear to tarry. The instruction here given is especially adapted to the experience of Adventists at this time. The people here addressed were in danger of making shipwreck of faith. They had done the will of God in following the guidance of His Spirit and His word; yet they could not understand His purpose in their past experience, nor could they discern the pathway before them, and they were tempted to doubt whether God had indeed been leading them. At this time the words were applicable: »Now the just shall live by faith.« As the bright light of the »midnight cry« had shone upon their pathway, and they had seen the prophecies unsealed and the rapidly fulfilling signs telling that the coming of Christ was near, they had walked, as it were, by sight. But now, bowed down by disappointed hopes, they could stand only by faith in God and in His word. The scoffing world were saying: »You have been deceived. Give up your faith, and say that the advent movement was of Satan.« But God's word declared: »If any man draw back, My soul shall have no pleasure in him.« To renounce their faith now, and deny the power of the Holy Spirit which had attended the message, would be drawing back toward perdition. They were encouraged to steadfastness by the words of Paul: »Cast not away therefore your confidence;« »ye have need of patience,« »for yet a little while, and He that shall come will come, and will not tarry.« Their only safe course was to cherish the light which they had already received of God, hold fast to His promises, and continue to search the Scriptures, and patiently wait and watch to receive further light.

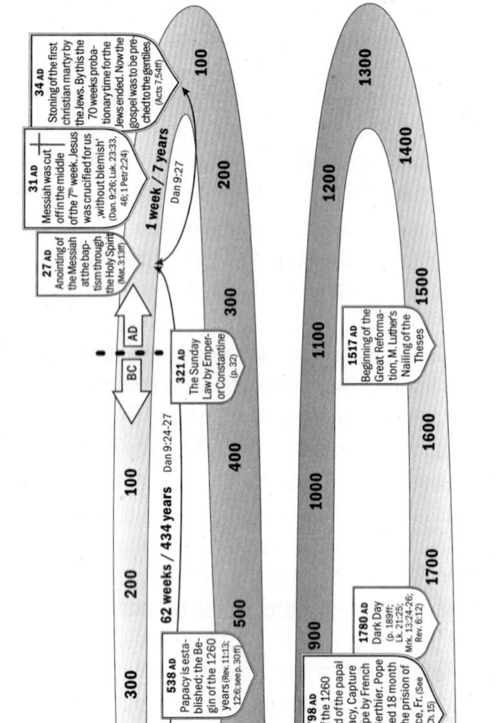

It takes 457 years BC and 1843 AD, to come up to 2300 years. If Artaxerxes had given the decree at the beginning of the year 457 BC, the 2300 year-days would have reached unto the end of 1843. But this decree was issued not until the Fall of 457 BC, so that the 2300 years ended in Fall of 1844 BC.

Chapter 23

What ist the Sanctuary?

The scripture which above all others had been both the foundation and the central pillar of the advent faith was the declaration: »Unto two thousand and three hundred days; then shall the sanctuary be cleansed.« Daniel 8:14 These had been familiar words to all believers in the Lord's soon coming. By the lips of thousands was this prophecy repeated as the watchword of their faith. All felt that upon the events therein foretold depended their brightest expectations and most cherished hopes. These prophetic days had been shown to terminate in the autumn of 1844. In common with the rest of the Christian world, Adventists then held that the earth, or some portion of it, was the sanctuary. They understood that the cleansing of the sanctuary was the purification of the earth by the fires of the last great day, and that this would take place at the second advent. Hence the conclusion that Christ would return to the earth in 1844.

But the appointed time had passed, and the Lord had not appeared. The believers knew that God's word could not fail; their interpretation of the prophecy must be at fault; but where was the mistake? Many rashly cut the knot of difficulty by denying that the 2300 days ended in 1844. No reason could be given for this except that Christ had not come at the time they expected Him. They argued that if the prophetic days had ended in 1844, Christ would then have returned to cleanse the sanctuary by the purification of the earth by fire; and that since He had not come, the days could not have ended.

To accept this conclusion was to renounce the former reckoning of the prophetic periods. The 2300 days had been found to begin when the commandment of Artaxerxes for the restoration and building of Jerusalem went into effect, in the autumn of 457 B.C. Taking this as the starting point, there was perfect harmony in the application of all the events foretold in the explanation of that period in Daniel 9:25-27. Sixty-nine weeks, the first 483 of the 2300 years, were to reach to the Messiah, the Anointed One; and Christ's baptism and anointing by the Holy Spirit, A.D. 27, exactly fulfilled the specification. In the midst of the seventieth week, Messiah was to be cut off. Three and a half years after His baptism, Christ was crucified, in the spring of A.D. 31. The seventy weeks, or 490 years, were to pertain especially to the Jews. At the expiration of this period the nation sealed its rejection of Christ by the persecution of His disciples, and the apostles turned to the Gentiles, A.D. 34. The first 490 years of the 2300 having then ended, 1810 years would remain. From A.D. 34, 1810 years extend to 1844. »Then,« said the angel, »shall the sanctuary be cleansed.« All the preceding specifications of the prophecy had been unquestionably fulfilled at the time appointed.

With this reckoning, all was clear and harmonious, except that it was not seen that any event answering to the cleansing of the sanctuary had taken place in 1844. To deny that the days ended at that time was to involve the whole question in confusion, and to renounce positions which had been established by unmistakable fulfillments of prophecy.

But God had led His people in the great advent movement; His power and glory had attended the work, and He would not permit it to end in darkness and disappointment, to be reproached as a false and fanatical excitement. He would not leave His word involved in doubt and uncertainty. Though many abandoned their former reckoning of the prophetic periods and denied the correctness of the movement based thereon, others were unwilling to renounce points of faith and experience that were sustained by the Scriptures and by the witness of the Spirit of God. They believed that they had adopted sound principles of interpretation in their study of the prophecies, and that it was their duty to hold fast the truths already gained, and to continue the same course of Biblical research. With earnest prayer they reviewed their position and studied the Scriptures to discover their mistake. As they could see no error in their reckoning of the prophetic periods, they were led to examine more closely the subject of the sanctuary. In their investigation they learned that there is no Scripture evidence sustaining the popular view that the earth is the sanctuary; but they found in the Bible a full explanation of the subject of the sanctuary, its nature, location, and services; the testimony of the sacred writers being so clear and ample as to place the matter beyond all question. The apostle Paul, in the Epistle to the Hebrews, says: »Then verily the first covenant had also ordinances of divine service, and a worldly sanctuary. For there was a tabernacle made; the first, wherein was the candlestick, and the table, and the shewbread; which is called the sanctuary. And after the second veil, the tabernacle which is called the holiest of all; which had the golden censer, and the ark of the covenant overlaid round about with gold, wherein was the golden pot that had manna, and Aaron's rod that budded, and the tables of the covenant; and over it the cherubims of glory shadowing the mercy seat.« Hebrews 9:1-5

The sanctuary to which Paul here refers was the tabernacle built by Moses at the command of God as the earthly dwelling place of the Most High. »Let them make Me a sanctuary; that I may dwell among them«, Exodus 25:8 was the direction given to Moses while in the mount with God. The Israelites were journeying through the wilderness, and the tabernacle was so constructed that it could be removed from place to place; yet it was a structure of great magnificence. Its walls consisted of upright boards heavily plated with gold and set in sockets of silver, while the roof was formed of a series of curtains, or coverings, the outer of skins, the innermost of fine linen beautifully wrought with figures of cherubim. Besides the outer court, which contained the altar of burnt offering, the tabernacle itself consisted of two apartments called the holy and the most holy place, separated by a rich and beautiful curtain, or veil; a similar veil closed the entrance to the first apartment.

In the holy place was the candlestick, on the south, with its seven lamps giving light to the sanctuary both by day and by night; on the north stood the table of shewbread; and before the veil separating the holy from the most holy was the golden altar of incense, from which the cloud of fragrance, with the prayers of Israel, was daily ascending before God. In the most holy place stood the ark, a chest of precious wood overlaid with gold, the depository of the two tables of stone upon which God had inscribed the law of Ten Commandments. Above the ark, and forming the cover to the sacred chest, was the mercy seat, a magnificent piece of workmanship, surmounted by two cherubim, one at each end, and all wrought of solid gold. In this apartment the divine presence was manifested in the cloud of glory between the cherubim.

After the settlement of the Hebrews in Canaan, the tabernacle was replaced by the temple of Solomon, which, though a permanent structure and upon a larger scale, observed the same proportions, and was similarly furnished. In this form the sanctuary existed – except while it lay in ruins in Daniel's time – until its destruction by the Romans, in A.D. 70. This is the only sanctuary that ever existed on the earth, of which the Bible gives any information. This was declared by Paul to be the sanctuary of the first covenant. But has the new covenant no sanctuary?

Turning again to the book of Hebrews, the seekers for truth found that the existence of a second, or new-covenant sanctuary, was implied in the words of Paul already quoted: »Then verily the first covenant had also ordinances of divine service, and a worldly sanctuary.« And the use of the word »also« intimates that Paul has before made mention of this sanctuary. Turning back to the beginning of the previous chapter, they read: »Now of the things which we have spoken this is the sum: We have such an High Priest, who is set on the right hand of the throne of the Majesty in the heavens; a Minister of the sanctuary, and of the true tabernacle, which the Lord pitched, and not man.« Hebrews 8:1-2 Here is revealed the sanctuary of the new covenant. The sanctuary of the first covenant was pitched by man, built by Moses; this is pitched by the Lord, not by man. In that sanctuary the earthly priests performed their service; in this, Christ, our great High Priest, ministers at God's right hand. One sanctuary was on earth, the other is in heaven.

Further, the tabernacle built by Moses was made after a pattern. The Lord directed him: »According to all that I show thee, after the pattern of the tabernacle, and the pattern of all the instruments thereof, even so shall ye make it.« And again the charge was given, »Look that thou make them after their pattern, which was showed thee in the mount.« Exodus 25:9, 40 And Paul says that the first tabernacle »was a figure for the time then present, in which were offered both gifts and sacrifices;« that its holy places were »patterns of things in the heavens;« that the priests who offered gifts according to the law served »unto the example and shadow of heavenly things,« and that »Christ is not entered into the holy places made with hands, which are the figures of the true; but into heaven itself, now to appear in the presence of God for us.« Hebrews 9:9, 23; 8:5; 9:24

The sanctuary in heaven, in which Jesus ministers in our behalf, is the great original, of which the sanctuary built by Moses was a copy. God placed His Spirit upon the builders of the earthly sanctuary. The artistic skill displayed in its construction was a manifestation of divine wisdom. The walls had the appearance of massive gold, reflecting in every direction the light of the seven lamps of the golden candlestick. The table of shewbread and the altar of incense glittered like burnished gold. The gorgeous curtain which formed the ceiling, inwrought with figures of angels in blue and purple and scarlet, added to the beauty of the scene. And beyond the second veil was the holy Shekinah, the visible manifestation of God's glory, before which none but the high priest could enter and live.

The matchless splendor of the earthly tabernacle reflected to human vision the glories of that heavenly temple where Christ our forerunner ministers for us before the throne of God. The abiding place of the King of kings, where thousand thousands minister unto Him, and ten thousand times ten thousand stand before Him; Daniel 7:10 that temple, filled with the glory of the eternal throne, where seraphim, its shining guardians, veil their faces in adoration, could find, in the most magnificent structure ever reared by human hands, but a faint reflection of its vastness and glory. Yet important truths concerning the heavenly sanctuary and the great work there carried forward for man's redemption were taught by the earthly sanctuary and its services.

The holy places of the sanctuary in heaven are represented by the two apartments in the sanctuary on earth. As in vision the apostle John was granted a view of the temple of God in heaven, he beheld there »seven lamps of fire burning before the throne.« Revelation 4:5 He saw an angel »having a golden censer; and there was given unto him much incense, that he should offer it with the prayers of all saints upon the golden altar which was before the throne.« Revelation 8:3 Here the prophet was permitted to behold the first apartment of the sanctuary in heaven; and he saw there the »seven lamps of fire« and »the golden altar,« represented by the golden candlestick and the altar of incense in the sanctuary on earth. Again, »the temple of God was opened« Revelation 11:19 and he looked within the inner veil, upon the holy of holies. Here he beheld »the ark of His testament,« represented by the sacred chest constructed by Moses to contain the law of God. Thus those who were studying the subject found indisputable proof of the existence of a sanctuary in heaven. Moses made the earthly sanctuary after a pattern which was shown him. Paul teaches that that pattern was the true sanctuary which is in heaven. And John testifies that he saw it in heaven.

In the temple in heaven, the dwelling place of God, His throne is established in righteousness and judgment. In the most holy place is His law, the great rule of right by which all mankind are tested. The ark that enshrines the tables of the law is covered with the mercy seat, before which Christ pleads His blood in the sinner's behalf. Thus is represented the union of justice and mercy in the plan of human redemption. This union infinite wisdom alone could devise and infinite power accomplish; it is a union that fills all heaven with wonder and adoration. The cherubim of the earthly sanctuary, looking reverently down upon the mercy seat, represent the interest with which the heavenly host contemplate the work of redemption.

This is the mystery of mercy into which angels desire to look – that God can be just while He justifies the repenting sinner and renews His intercourse with the fallen race; that Christ could stoop to raise unnumbered multitudes from the abyss of ruin and clothe them with the spotless garments of His own righteousness to unite with angels who have never fallen and to dwell forever in the presence of God.

The work of Christ as man's intercessor is presented in that beautiful prophecy of Zechariah concerning Him »whose name is the Branch.« Says the prophet: »He shall build the temple of the Lord; and He shall bear the glory, and shall sit and rule upon His [the Father's] throne; and He shall be a priest upon His throne: and the counsel of peace shall be between Them both.« Zechariah 6:12-13

»He shall build the temple of the Lord.« By His sacrifice and mediation Christ is both the foundation and the builder of the church of God. The apostle Paul points to Him as »the chief Cornerstone; in whom all the building fitly framed together groweth into an holy temple in the Lord: in whom ye also,« he says, »are builded together for an habitation of God through the Spirit.« Ephesians 2:20-22 »He shall bear the glory.« To Christ belongs the glory of redemption for the fallen race. Through the eternal ages, the song of the ransomed ones will be: »Unto Him that loved us, and washed us from our sins in His own blood, ... to Him be glory and dominion for ever and ever.« Revelation 1:5-6

He »shall sit and rule upon His throne; and He shall be a priest upon His throne.« Not now »upon the throne of His glory;« the kingdom of glory has not yet been ushered in. Not until His work as a mediator shall be ended will God »give unto Him the throne of His father David,« a kingdom of which »there shall be no end.« Luke 1:32-33 As a priest, Christ is now set down with the Father in His throne. Revelation 3:21 Upon the throne with the eternal, self-existent One is He who »hath borne our griefs, and carried our sorrows,« who »was in all points tempted like as we are, yet without sin,« that He might be »able to succor them that are tempted.« »If any man sin, we have an advocate with the Father.« Isaiah 53:4; Hebrews 4:15; 2:18; 1 John 2:1 His intercession is that of a pierced and broken body, of a spotless life. The wounded hands, the pierced side, the marred feet, plead for fallen man, whose redemption was purchased at such infinite cost. »And the counsel of peace shall be between Them both.« The love of the Father, no less than of the Son, is the fountain of salvation for the lost race. Said Jesus to His disciples before He went away: »I say not unto you, that I will pray the Father for you: for the Father Himself loveth you.« John 16:26-27 God was »in Christ, reconciling the world unto Himself.« 2 Corinthians 5:19 And in the ministration in the sanctuary above, »the counsel of peace shall be between Them both.« »God so loved the world, that He gave His only-begotten Son, that whosoever believeth in Him should not perish, but have everlasting life.« John 3:16

The question, What is the sanctuary? is clearly answered in the Scriptures. The term »sanctuary,« as used in the Bible, refers, first, to the tabernacle built by Moses, as a pattern of heavenly things; and, secondly, to the »true tabernacle« in heaven, to which the earthly sanctuary pointed. At the death of Christ the typical service ended. The »true tabernacle« in heaven is the sanctuary of the new covenant. And as the prophecy of Daniel 8:14 is fulfilled in this dispensation, the sanctuary to which it refers must be the sanctuary of the new covenant. At the termination of the 2300 days, in 1844, there had been no sanctuary on earth for many centuries. Thus the prophecy, »Unto two thousand and three hundred days; then shall the sanctuary be cleansed,« unquestionably points to the sanctuary in heaven.

But the most important question remains to be answered: What is the cleansing of the sanctuary? That there was such a service in connection with the earthly sanctuary is stated in the Old Testament Scriptures. But can there be anything in heaven to be cleansed? In Hebrews 9 the cleansing of both the earthly and the heavenly sanctuary is plainly taught. »Almost all things are by the law purged with blood; and without shedding of blood is no remission. It was therefore necessary that the patterns of things in the heavens should be purified with these [the blood of animals]; but the heavenly things themselves with better sacrifices than these« Hebrews 9:22-23 even the precious blood of Christ.

The cleansing, both in the typical and in the real service, must be accomplished with blood: in the former, with the blood of animals; in the latter, with the blood of Christ. Paul states, as the reason why this cleansing must be performed with blood, that without shedding of blood is no remission. Remission, or putting away of sin, is the work to be accomplished. But how could there be sin connected with the sanctuary, either in heaven or upon the earth? This may be learned by reference to the symbolic service; for the priests who officiated on earth, served »unto the example and shadow of heavenly things.« Hebr. 8:5

The ministration of the earthly sanctuary consisted of two divisions; the priests ministered daily in the holy place, while once a year the high priest performed a special work of atonement in the most holy, for the cleansing of the sanctuary. Day by day the repentant sinner brought his offering to the door of the tabernacle and, placing his hand upon the victim's head, confessed his sins, thus in figure transferring them from himself to the innocent sacrifice. The animal was then slain. »Without shedding of blood,« says the apostle, there is no remission of sin. »The life of the flesh is in the blood.« Leviticus 17:11 The broken law of God demanded the life of the transgressor. The blood, representing the forfeited life of the sinner, whose guilt the victim bore, was carried by the priest into the holy place and sprinkled before the veil, behind which was the ark containing the law that the sinner had transgressed. By this ceremony the sin was, through the blood, transferred in figure to the sanctuary. In some cases the blood was not taken into the holy place; but the flesh was then to be eaten by the priest, as Moses directed the sons of Aaron, saying: »God hath given it you to bear the iniquity of the congregation.« Leviticus 10:17 Both ceremonies alike symbolized the transfer of the sin from the penitent to the sanctuary.

Such was the work that went on, day by day, throughout the year. The sins of Israel were thus transferred to the sanctuary, and a special work became necessary for their removal. God commanded that an atonement be made for each of the sacred apartments. »He shall make an atonement for the holy place, because of the uncleanness of the children of Israel, and because of their transgressions in all their sins: and so shall he do for the tabernacle of the congregation, that remaineth among them in the midst of their uncleanness.« An atonement was also to be made for the altar, to »cleanse it, and hallow it from the uncleanness of the children of Israel.« Lev. 16:16, 19

Once a year, on the great Day of Atonement, the priest entered the most holy place for the cleansing of the sanctuary. The work there performed completed the yearly round of ministration. On the Day of Atonement two kids of the goats were brought to the door of the tabernacle, and lots were cast upon them, »one lot for the Lord, and the other lot for the scapegoat.« Verse 8 The goat upon which fell the lot for the Lord was to be slain as a sin offering for the people. And the priest was to bring his blood within the veil and sprinkle it upon the mercy seat and before the mercy seat. The blood was also to be sprinkled upon the altar of incense that was before the veil.

»And Aaron shall lay both his hands upon the head of the live goat, and confess over him all the iniquities of the children of Israel, and all their transgressions in all their sins, putting them upon the head of the goat, and shall send him away by the hand of a fit man into the wilderness: and the goat shall bear upon him all their iniquities unto a land not inhabited.« Verses 21-22 The scapegoat came no more into the camp of Israel, and the man who led him away was required to wash himself and his clothing with water before returning to the camp.

The whole ceremony was designed to impress the Israelites with the holiness of God and His abhorrence of sin; and, further, to show them that they could not come in contact with sin without becoming polluted. Every man was required to afflict his soul while this work of atonement was going forward. All business was to be laid aside, and the whole congregation of Israel were to spend the day in solemn humiliation before God, with prayer, fasting, and deep searching of heart.

Important truths concerning the atonement are taught by the typical service. A substitute was accepted in the sinner's stead; but the sin was not canceled by the blood of the victim. A means was thus provided by which it was transferred to the sanctuary. By the offering of blood the sinner acknowledged the authority of the law, confessed his guilt in transgression, and expressed his desire for pardon through faith in a Redeemer to come; but he was not yet entirely released from the condemnation of the law. On the Day of Atonement the high priest, having taken an offering from the congregation, went into the most holy place with the blood of this offering, and sprinkled it upon the mercy seat, directly over the law, to make satisfaction for its claims. Then, in his character of mediator, he took the sins upon himself and bore them from the sanctuary. Placing his hands upon the head of the scapegoat, he confessed over him all these sins, thus in figure transferring them from himself to the goat. The goat then bore them away, and they were regarded as forever separated from the people. Such was the service performed »unto the example and shadow of heavenly things.« And what was done in type in the ministration of the earthly sanctuary is done in reality in the ministration of the heavenly sanctuary. After His ascension our Saviour began His work as our high priest. Says Paul: »Christ is not entered into the holy places made with hands, which are the figures of the true; but into heaven itself, now to appear in the presence of God for us.« Hebrews 9:24

The ministration of the priest throughout the year in the first apartment of the sanctuary, "within the veil" which formed the door and separated the holy place from the outer court, represents the work of ministration upon which Christ entered at His ascension. It was the work of the priest in the daily ministration to present before God the blood of the sin offering, also the incense which ascended with the prayers of Israel. So did Christ plead His blood before the Father in behalf of sinners, and present before Him also, with the precious fragrance of His own righteousness, the prayers of penitent believers. Such was the work of ministration in the first apartment of the sanctuary in heaven.

Thither the faith of Christ's disciples followed Him as He ascended from their sight. Here their hopes centered, »which hope we have,« said Paul, »as an anchor of the soul, both sure and steadfast, and which entereth into that within the veil; whither the forerunner is for us entered, even Jesus, made an high priest forever.« »Neither by the blood of goats and calves, but by His own blood He entered in once into the holy place, having obtained eternal redemption for us.« Hebrews 6:19-20; 9:12

For eighteen centuries this work of ministration continued in the first apartment of the sanctuary. The blood of Christ, pleaded in behalf of penitent believers, secured their pardon and acceptance with the Father, yet their sins still remained upon the books of record. As in the typical service there was a work of atonement at the close of the year, so before Christ's work for the redemption of men is completed there is a work of atonement for the removal of sin from the sanctuary. This is the service which began when the

2300 days ended. At that time, as foretold by Daniel the prophet, our High Priest entered the most holy, to perform the last division of His solemn work – to cleanse the sanctuary.

As anciently the sins of the people were by faith placed upon the sin offering and through its blood transferred, in figure, to the earthly sanctuary, so in the new covenant the sins of the repentant are by faith placed upon Christ and transferred, in fact, to the heavenly sanctuary. And as the typical cleansing of the earthly was accomplished by the removal of the sins by which it had been polluted, so the actual cleansing of the heavenly is to be accomplished by the removal, or blotting out, of the sins which are there recorded. But before this can be accomplished, there must be an examination of the books of record to determine who, through repentance of sin and faith in Christ, are entitled to the benefits of His atonement. The cleansing of the sanctuary therefore involves a work of investigation – a work of judgment. This work must be performed prior to the coming of Christ to redeem His people; for when He comes, His reward is with Him to give to every man according to his works. Revelation 22:12

Thus those who followed in the light of the prophetic word saw that, instead of coming to the earth at the termination of the 2300 days in 1844, Christ then entered the most holy place of the heavenly sanctuary to perform the closing work of atonement preparatory to His coming.

It was seen, also, that while the sin offering pointed to Christ as a sacrifice, and the high priest represented Christ as a mediator, the scapegoat typified Satan, the author of sin, upon whom the sins of the truly penitent will finally be placed. When the high priest, by virtue of the blood of the sin offering, removed the sins from the sanctuary, he placed them upon the scapegoat. When Christ, by virtue of His own blood, removes the sins of His people from the heavenly sanctuary at the close of His ministration, He will place them upon Satan, who, in the execution of the judgment, must bear the final penalty. The scapegoat was sent away into a land not inhabited, never to come again into the congregation of Israel. So will Satan be forever banished from the presence of God and His people, and he will be blotted from existence in the final destruction of sin and sinners.

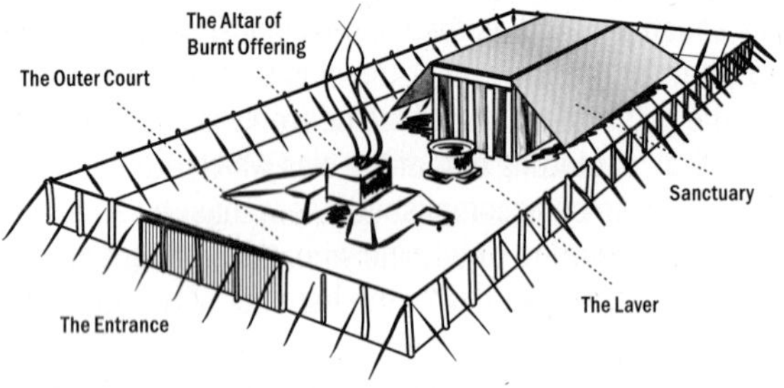
The Altar of
Burnt Offering
The Outer Court
Sanctuary
The Laver
The Entrance

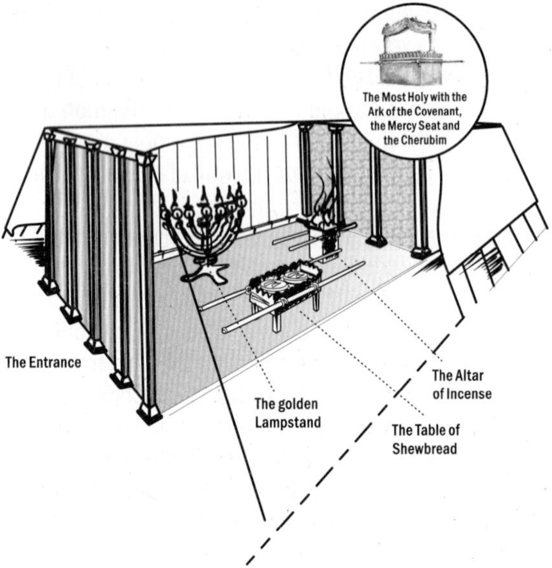
The Most Holy with the
Ark of the Covenant,
the Mercy Seat and
the Cherubim
The Entrance
The Altar
of Incense
The golden
Lampstand
The Table of
Shewbread

Chapter 24

In the Holy of Holies

The subject of the sanctuary was the key which unlocked the mystery of the disappointment of 1844. It opened to view a complete system of truth, connected and harmonious, showing that God's hand had directed the great advent movement and revealing present duty as it brought to light the position and work of His people. As the disciples of Jesus after the terrible night of their anguish and disappointment were »glad when they saw the Lord,« so did those now rejoice who had looked in faith for His second coming. They had expected Him to appear in glory to give reward to His servants. As their hopes were disappointed, they had lost sight of Jesus, and with Mary at the sepulcher they cried: »They have taken away my Lord, and I know not where they have laid Him.« Now in the holy of holies they again beheld Him, their compassionate High Priest, soon to appear as their king and deliverer. Light from the sanctuary illumined the past, the present, and the future. They knew that God had led them by His unerring providence. Though, like the first disciples, they themselves had failed to understand the message which they bore, yet it had been in every respect correct. In proclaiming it they had fulfilled the purpose of God, and their labor had not been in vain in the Lord. Begotten »again unto a lively hope,« they rejoiced »with joy unspeakable and full of glory.«

Both the prophecy of Daniel 8:14 »Unto two thousand and three hundred days; then shall the sanctuary be cleansed,« and the first angel's message, »Fear God, and give glory to Him; for the hour of His judgment is come,« pointed to Christ's ministration in the most holy place, to the investigative judgment, and not to the coming of Christ for the redemption of His people and the destruction of the wicked. The mistake had not been in the reckoning of the prophetic periods, but in the event to take place at the end of the 2300 days. Through this error the believers had suffered disappointment, yet all that was foretold by the prophecy, and all that they had any Scripture warrant to expect, had been accomplished. At the very time when they were lamenting the failure of their hopes, the event had taken place which was foretold by the message, and which must be fulfilled before the Lord could appear to give reward to His servants.

Christ had come, not to the earth, as they expected, but, as foreshadowed in the type, to the most holy place of the temple of God in heaven. He is represented by the prophet Daniel as coming at this time to the Ancient of Days: »I saw in the night visions, and, behold, one like the Son of man came with the clouds of heaven, and came« – not to the earth, but – »to the Ancient of Days, and they brought Him near before Him.« Daniel 7:13

This coming is foretold also by the prophet Malachi: “The Lord, whom ye seek, shall suddenly come to His temple, even the Messenger of the covenant, whom ye delight in: behold, He shall come, saith the Lord of hosts.« Malachi 3:1 The coming of the Lord to His temple was sudden, unexpected, to His people. They were not looking for Him there. They expected Him to come to earth, »in flaming fire taking vengeance on them that know not God, and that obey not the gospel.« 2 Thessalonians 1:8

But the people were not yet ready to meet their Lord. There was still a work of preparation to be accomplished for them. Light was to be given, directing their minds to the temple of God in heaven; and as they should by faith follow their High Priest in His ministration there, new duties would be revealed. Another message of warning and instruction was to be given to the church.

Says the prophet: »Who may abide the day of His coming? and who shall stand when He appeareth? for He is like a refiner's fire, and like fullers' soap: and He shall sit as a refiner and purifier of silver: and He shall purify the sons of Levi, and purge them as gold and silver, that they may offer unto the Lord an offering in righteousness.« Malachi 3:2-3 Those who are living upon the earth when the intercession of Christ shall cease in the sanctuary above are to stand in the sight of a holy God without a mediator. Their robes must be spotless, their characters must be purified from sin by the blood of sprinkling. Through the grace of God and their own diligent effort they must be conquerors in the battle with evil. While the investigative judgment is going forward in heaven, while the sins of penitent believers are being removed from the sanctuary, there is to be a special work of purification, of putting away of sin, among

God's people upon earth. This work is more clearly

presented in the messages of Revelation 14. When this work shall have been accomplished, the followers of Christ will be ready for His appearing. »Then shall the offering of Judah and Jerusalem be pleasant unto the Lord, as in the days of old, and as in former years.« Malachi 3:4 Then the church which our Lord at His coming is to receive to Himself will be a »glorious church, not having spot, or wrinkle, or any such thing.« Ephesians 5:27 Then she will look »forth as the morning, fair as the moon, clear as the sun, and terrible as an army with banners.« Song of Solomon 6:10

Besides the coming of the Lord to His temple, Malachi also foretells His second advent, His coming for the execution of the judgment, in these words: »And I will come near to you to judgment; and I will be a swift witness against the sorcerers, and against the adulterers, and against false swearers, and against those that oppress the hireling in his wages, the widow, and the fatherless, and that turn aside the stranger from his right, and fear not Me, saith the Lord of hosts.« Malachi 3:5 Jude refers to the same scene when he says, »Behold, the Lord cometh with ten thousands of His saints, to execute judgment upon all, and to convince all that are ungodly among them of all their ungodly deeds.« Jude 14-15 This coming, and the coming of the Lord to His temple, are distinct and separate events. The coming of Christ as our high priest to the most holy place, for the cleansing of the sanctuary, brought to view in Daniel 8:14; the coming of the Son of man to the Ancient of Days, as presented in Daniel 7:13; and the coming of the Lord to His temple, foretold by Malachi, are descriptions of the same event; and this is also represented by the coming of the bridegroom to the marriage, described by Christ in the parable of the ten virgins, of Matthew 25.

In the summer and autumn of 1844 the proclamation, »Behold, the Bridegroom cometh,« was given. The two classes represented by the wise and foolish virgins were then developed – one class who looked with joy to the Lord's appearing, and who had been diligently preparing to meet Him; another class that, influenced by fear and acting from impulse, had been satisfied with a theory of the truth, but were destitute of the grace of God. In the parable, when the bridegroom came, »they that were ready went in with him to the marriage.« The coming of the bridegroom, here brought to view, takes place before the marriage. The marriage represents the reception by Christ of His kingdom. The Holy City, the New Jerusalem, which is the capital and representative of the kingdom, is called »the bride, the Lamb's wife.« Said the angel to John: »Come hither, I will show thee the bride, the Lamb's wife.« »He carried me away in the spirit,« says the prophet, »and showed me that great city, the holy Jerusalem, descending out of heaven from God.« Revelation 21:9, 10 Clearly, then, the bride represents the Holy City, and the virgins that go out to meet the bridegroom are a symbol of the church. In the Revelation the people of God are said to be the guests at the marriage supper. Revelation 19:9 If guests, they cannot be represented also as the bride. Christ, as stated by the prophet Daniel, will receive from the Ancient of Days in heaven, »dominion, and glory, and a kingdom;« He will receive the New Jerusalem, the capital of His kingdom, "prepared as a bride adorned for her husband.« Daniel 7:14; Revelation 21:2 Having received the kingdom, He will come in His glory, as King of kings and Lord of lords, for the redemption of His people, who are to »sit down with Abraham, and Isaac, and Jacob,« at His table in His kingdom, Matthew 8:11; Luke 22:30 to partake of the marriage supper of the Lamb.

The proclamation, »Behold, the Bridegroom cometh,« in the summer of 1844, led thousands to expect the immediate advent of the Lord. At the appointed time the Bridegroom came, not to the earth, as the people expected, but to the Ancient of Days in heaven, to the marriage, the reception of His kingdom. »They that were ready went in with Him to the marriage: and the door was shut.« They were not to be present in person at the marriage; for it takes place in heaven, while they are upon the earth. The followers of Christ are to »wait for their Lord, when He will return from the wedding.« Luke 12:36 But they are to understand His work, and to follow Him by faith as He goes in before God. It is in this sense that they are said to go in to the marriage.

In the parable it was those that had oil in their vessels with their lamps that went in to the marriage. Those who, with a knowledge of the truth from the Scriptures, had also the Spirit and grace of God, and who, in the night of their bitter trial, had patiently waited, searching the Bible for clearer light – these saw the truth concerning the sanctuary in heaven and the Saviour's change in ministration, and by faith they followed Him in His work in the sanctuary above. And all who through the testimony of the Scriptures accept the same truths, following Christ by faith as He enters in before God to perform the last work of mediation, and at its close to receive His kingdom – all

these are represented as going in to the marriage. In

the parable of Matthew 22 the same figure of the marriage is introduced, and the investigative judgment is clearly represented as taking place before the marriage. Previous to the wedding the king comes in to see the guests, to see if all are attired in the wedding garment, the spotless robe of character washed and made white in the blood of the Lamb. Matthew 22:11; Revelation 7:14 He who is found wanting is cast out, but all who upon examination are seen to have the wedding garment on are accepted of God and accounted worthy of a share in His kingdom and a seat upon His throne. This work of examination of character, of determining who are prepared for the kingdom of God, is that of the investigative judgment, the closing of work in the sanctuary above.

When the work of investigation shall be ended, when the cases of those who in all ages have professed to be followers of Christ have been examined and decided, then, and not till then, probation will close, and the door of mercy will be shut. Thus in the one short sentence, »They that were ready went in with Him to the marriage: and the door was shut,« we are carried down through the Saviour's final ministration, to the time when the great work for man's salvation shall be completed.

In the service of the earthly sanctuary, which, as we have seen, is a figure of the service in the heavenly, when the high priest on the Day of Atonement entered the most holy place, the ministration in the first apartment ceased. God commanded: »There shall be no man in the tabernacle of the congregation when he goeth in to make an atonement in the holy place, until he comes out.« Leviticus 16:17 So when Christ entered the holy of holies to perform the closing work of the atonement, He ceased His ministration in the first apartment. But when the ministration in the first apartment ended, the ministration in the second apartment began. When in the typical service the high priest left the holy on the Day of Atonement, he went in before God to present the blood of the sin offering in behalf of all Israel who truly repented of their sins. So Christ had only completed one part of His work as our intercessor, to enter upon another portion of the work, and He still pleaded His blood before the Father in behalf of sinners.

This subject was not understood by Adventists in 1844. After the passing of the time when the Saviour was expected, they still believed His coming to be near; they held that they had reached an important crisis and that the work of Christ as man's intercessor before God had ceased. It appeared to them to be taught in the Bible that man's probation would close a short time before the actual coming of the Lord in the clouds of heaven. This seemed evident from those scriptures which point to a time when men will seek, knock, and cry at the door of mercy, and it will not be opened. And it was a question with them whether the date to which they had looked for the coming of Christ might not rather mark the beginning of this period which was immediately to precede His coming. Having given the warning of the judgment near, they felt that their work for the world was done, and they lost their burden of soul for the salvation of sinners, while the bold and blasphemous scoffing of the ungodly seemed to them another evidence that the Spirit of God had been withdrawn from the rejecters of His mercy. All this confirmed them in the belief that probation had ended, or, as they then expressed it, »the door of mercy was shut.«

But clearer light came with the investigation of the sanctuary question. They now saw that they were correct in believing that the end of the 2300 days in 1844 marked an important crisis. But while it was true that that door of hope and mercy by which men had for eighteen hundred years found access to God, was closed, another door was opened, and forgiveness of sins was offered to men through the intercession of Christ in the most holy. One part of His ministration had closed, only to give place to another. There was still an »open door« to the heavenly sanctuary, where Christ was ministering in the sinner's behalf.

Now was seen the application of those words of Christ in the Revelation, addressed to the church at this very time: »These things saith He that is holy, He that is true, He that hath the key of David, He that openeth, and no man shutteth; and shutteth, and no man openeth; I know thy works: behold, I have set before thee an open door, and no man can shut it.« Revelation 3:7-8

It is those who by faith follow Jesus in the great work of the atonement who receive the benefits of His mediation in their behalf, while those who reject the light which brings to view this work of ministration are not benefited thereby. The Jews who rejected the light given at Christ's first advent, and refused to believe on Him as the Saviour of the world, could not receive pardon through Him. When Jesus at His ascension entered by His own blood into the heavenly sanctuary to shed upon His disciples the blessings of His mediation, the Jews were left in total darkness to continue their useless sacrifices and offerings. The ministration of types and shadows had ceased. That door by which men had formerly found access to God was no longer open. The Jews had refused to seek Him in the only way whereby He could then be found, through the ministration in the sanctuary in heaven. Therefore they found no communion with God. To them the door was shut. They had no knowledge of Christ as the true sacrifice and the only mediator before God; hence they could not receive the benefits of His mediation.

The condition of the unbelieving Jews illustrates the condition of the careless and unbelieving among professed Christians, who are willingly ignorant of the work of our merciful High Priest. In the typical service, when the high priest entered the most holy place, all Israel were required to gather about the sanctuary and in the most solemn manner humble their souls before God, that they might receive the pardon of their sins and not be cut off from the congregation. How much more essential in this antitypical Day of Atonement that we understand the work of our High Priest and know what duties are required of us.

Men cannot with impunity reject the warning which God in mercy sends them. A message was sent from heaven to the world in Noah's day, and their salvation depended upon the manner in which they treated that message. Because they rejected the warning, the Spirit of God was withdrawn from the sinful race, and they perished in the waters of the Flood. In the time of Abraham, mercy ceased to plead with the guilty inhabitants of Sodom, and all but Lot with his wife and two daughters were consumed by the fire sent down from heaven. So in the days of Christ. The Son of God declared to the unbelieving Jews of that generation: »Your house is left unto you desolate.« Matthew 23:38 Looking down to the last days, the same Infinite Power declares, concerning those who "received not the love of the truth, that they might be saved«: »For this cause God shall send them strong delusion, that they should believe a lie: that they all might be damned who believed not the truth, but had pleasure in unrighteousness.« 2 Thessalonians 2:10-12 As they reject the teachings of His word, God withdraws His Spirit and leaves them to the deceptions which they love. But Christ still intercedes in man's behalf, and light will be given to those who seek it. Though this was not at first understood by Adventists, it was afterward made plain as the Scriptures which define their true position began to open before them.

The passing of the time in 1844 was followed by a period of great trial to those who still held the advent faith. Their only relief, so far as ascertaining their true position was concerned, was the light which directed their minds to the sanctuary above. Some renounced their faith in their former reckoning of the prophetic periods and ascribed to human or satanic agencies the powerful influence of the Holy Spirit which had attended the advent movement. Another class firmly held that the Lord had led them in their past experience; and as they waited and watched and prayed to know the will of God they saw that their great High Priest had entered upon another work of ministration, and, following Him by faith, they were led to see also the closing work of the church. They had a clearer understanding of the first and second angels' messages, and were prepared to receive and give to the world the solemn warning of the third angel of Revelation 14.

Christ's Ministry in the Heavenly Sanctuary

Chapter 25

God's Law Immutable

»The temple of God was opened in heaven, and there was seen in His temple the ark of His testament.« Revelation 11:19 The ark of God's testament is in the holy of holies, the second apartment of the sanctuary. In the ministration of the earthly tabernacle, which served »unto the example and shadow of heavenly things,« this apartment was opened only upon the great Day of Atonement for the cleansing of the sanctuary. Therefore the announcement that the temple of God was opened in heaven and the ark of His testament was seen points to the opening of the most holy place of the heavenly sanctuary in 1844 as Christ entered there to perform the closing work of the atonement. Those who by faith followed their great High Priest as He entered upon His ministry in the most holy place, beheld the ark of His testament. As they had studied the subject of the sanctuary they had come to understand the Saviour's change of ministration, and they saw that He was now officiating before the ark of God, pleading His blood in behalf of sinners.

The ark in the tabernacle on earth contained the two tables of stone, upon which were inscribed the precepts of the law of God. The ark was merely a receptacle for the tables of the law, and the presence of these divine precepts gave to it its value and sacredness. When the temple of God was opened in heaven, the ark of His testament was seen. Within the holy of holies, in the sanctuary in heaven, the divine law is sacredly enshrined – the law that was spoken by God Himself amid the thunders of Sinai and written with His own finger on the tables of stone.

The law of God in the sanctuary in heaven is the great original, of which the precepts inscribed upon the tables of stone and recorded by Moses in the Pentateuch were an unerring transcript. Those who arrived at an understanding of this important point were thus led to see the sacred, unchanging character of the divine law. They saw, as never before, the force of the Saviour's words: »Till heaven and earth pass, one jot or one tittle shall in no wise pass from the law.« Matthew 5:18 The law of God, being a revelation of His will, a transcript of His character, must forever endure, »as a faithful witness in heaven.« Not one command has been annulled; not a jot or tittle has been changed. Says the psalmist: »Forever, O Lord, Thy word is settled in heaven.« »All His commandments are sure. They stand fast for ever and ever.« Psalm 119:89; 111:7-8

In the very bosom of the Decalogue is the fourth commandment, as it was first proclaimed: »Remember the Sabbath day, to keep it holy. Six days shalt thou labor, and do all thy work: but the seventh day is the Sabbath of the Lord thy God: in it thou shalt not do any work, thou, nor thy son, nor thy daughter, thy manservant, nor thy maidservant, nor thy cattle, nor thy stranger that is within thy gates: for in six days the Lord made heaven and earth, the sea, and all that in them is, and rested the seventh day: wherefore the Lord blessed the Sabbath day, and hallowed it.« Exodus 20:8-11

The Spirit of God impressed the hearts of those students of His word. The conviction was urged upon them that they had ignorantly transgressed this precept by disregarding the Creator's rest day. They began to examine the reasons for observing the first day of the week instead of the day which God had sanctified. They could find no evidence in the Scriptures that the fourth commandment had been abolished, or that the Sabbath had been changed; the blessing which first hallowed the seventh day had never been removed. They had been honestly seeking to know and to do God's will; now, as they saw themselves transgressors of His law, sorrow filled their hearts, and they manifested their loyalty to God by keeping His Sabbath holy.

Many and earnest were the efforts made to overthrow their faith. None could fail to see that if the earthly sanctuary was a figure or pattern of the heavenly, the law deposited in the ark on earth was an exact transcript of the law in the ark in heaven; and that an acceptance of the truth concerning the heavenly sanctuary involved an acknowledgment of the claims of God's law and the obligation of the Sabbath of the fourth commandment. Here was the secret of the bitter and determined opposition to the harmonious exposition of the Scriptures that revealed the ministration of Christ in the heavenly sanctuary. Men sought to close the door which God had opened, and to open the door which He had closed. But »He that openeth, and

no man shutteth; and shutteth, and no man openeth,«

had declared: »Behold, I have set before thee an open door, and no man can shut it.« Revelation 3:7-8 Christ had opened the door, or ministration, of the most holy place, light was shining from that open door of the sanctuary in heaven, and the fourth commandment was shown to be included in the law which is there enshrined; what God had established, no man could overthrow.

Those who had accepted the light concerning the mediation of Christ and the perpetuity of the law of God found that these were the truths presented in Revelation 14. The messages of this chapter constitute a threefold warning see Appendix which is to prepare the inhabitants of the earth for the Lord's second coming. The announcement, »The hour of His judgment is come,« points to the closing work of Christ's ministration for the salvation of men. It heralds a truth which must be proclaimed until the Saviour's intercession shall cease and He shall return to the earth to take His people to Himself. The work of judgment which began in 1844 must continue until the cases of all are decided, both of the living and the dead; hence it will extend to the close of human probation. That men may be prepared to stand in the judgment, the message commands them to »fear God, and give glory to Him,« »and worship Him that made heaven, and earth, and the sea, and the fountains of waters.« The result of an acceptance of these messages is given in the word: »Here are they that keep the commandments of God, and the faith of Jesus.« In order to be prepared for the judgment, it is necessary that men should keep the law of God. That law will be the standard of character in the judgment. The apostle Paul declares: »As many as have sinned in the law shall be judged by the law, ... in the day when God shall judge the secrets of men by Jesus Christ.« And he says that »the doers of the law shall be justified.« Romans 2:12-16 Faith is essential in order to the keeping of the law of God; for »without faith it is impossible to please Him.« And »whatsoever is not of faith is sin.« Hebrews 11:6; Romans 14:23

By the first angel, men are called upon to »fear God, and give glory to Him« and to worship Him as the Creator of the heavens and the earth. In order to do this, they must obey His law. Says the wise man: »Fear God, and keep His commandments: for this is the whole duty of man.« Ecclesiastes 12:13 Without obedience to His commandments no worship can be pleasing to God. »This is the love of God, that we keep His commandments.« »He that turneth away his ear from hearing the law, even his prayer shall be abomination.« 1 John 5:3;

Proverbs 28:9 The duty to worship God is based upon the fact that He is the Creator and that to Him all other beings owe their existence. And wherever, in the Bible, His claim to reverence and worship, above the gods of the heathen, is presented, there is cited the evidence of His creative power. »All the gods of the nations are idols: but the Lord made the heavens.« Psalm 96:5 »To whom then will ye liken Me, or shall I be equal? saith the Holy One. Lift up your eyes on high, and behold who hath created these things.« »Thus saith the Lord that created the heavens; God Himself that formed the earth and made it: ... I am the Lord; and there is none else.« Isaiah 40:25-26; 45:18 Says the psalmist: »Know ye that the Lord He is God: it is He that hath made us, and not we ourselves.« »O come, let us worship and bow down: let us kneel before the Lord our Maker.« Psalm 100:3; 95:6 And the holy beings who worship God in heaven state, as the reason why their homage is due to Him: »Thou art worthy, O Lord, to receive glory and honor and power: for Thou hast created all things.« Revelation 4:11

In Revelation 14, men are called upon to worship the Creator; and the prophecy brings to view a class that, as the result of the threefold message, are keeping the commandments of God. One of these commandments points directly to God as the Creator. The fourth precept declares: »The seventh day is the Sabbath of the Lord thy God: ... for in six days the Lord made heaven and earth, the sea, and all that in them is, and rested the seventh day: wherefore the Lord blessed the Sabbath day, and hallowed it.« Exodus 20:10-11 Concerning the Sabbath, the Lord says, further, that it is »a sign, ... that ye may know that I am the Lord your God.« Ezekiel 20:20 And the reason given is: »For in six days the Lord made heaven and earth, and on the seventh day He rested, and was refreshed.« Exodus 31:17

»The importance of the Sabbath as the memorial of creation is that it keeps ever present the true reason why worship is due to God« – because He is the Creator, and we are His creatures. »The Sabbath therefore lies at the very foundation of divine worship, for it teaches this great truth in the most impressive manner, and no other institution does this. The true ground of divine worship, not of that on the seventh day merely, but of all worship, is found in the distinction between the Creator and His creatures. This great fact can never become obsolete, and must never be forgotten.« J. N. Andrews, History of the Sabbath, chapter 27 It was to keep this truth ever before the minds of men,

 that God instituted the Sabbath in Eden; and so long

as the fact that He is our Creator continues to be a reason why we should worship Him, so long the Sabbath will continue as its sign and memorial. Had the Sabbath been universally kept, man's thoughts and affections would have been led to the Creator as the object of reverence and worship, and there would never have been an idolater, an atheist, or an infidel. The keeping of the Sabbath is a sign of loyalty to the true God, »Him that made heaven, and earth, and the sea, and the fountains of waters.« It follows that the message which commands men to worship God and keep His commandments will especially call upon them to keep the fourth commandment.

In contrast to those who keep the commandments of God and have the faith of Jesus, the third angel points to another class, against whose errors a solemn and fearful warning is uttered: »If any man worship the beast and his image, and receive his mark in his forehead, or in his hand, the same shall drink of the wine of the wrath of God.« Revelation 14:9-10 A correct interpretation of the symbols employed is necessary to an understanding of this message. What is represented by the beast, the image, the mark?

The line of prophecy in which these symbols are found begins with Revelation 12, with the dragon that sought to destroy Christ at His birth. The dragon is said to be Satan; Revelation 12:9 he it was that moved upon Herod to put the Saviour to death. But the chief agent of Satan in making war upon Christ and His people during the first centuries of the Christian Era was the Roman Empire, in which paganism was the prevailing religion. Thus while the dragon, primarily, represents Satan, it is, in a secondary sense, a symbol of pagan Rome.

In chapter 13 verses 1-10 is described another beast, »like unto a leopard,« to which the dragon gave »his power, and his seat, and great authority.« This symbol, as most Protestants have believed, represents the papacy, which succeeded to the power and seat and authority once held by the ancient Roman empire. Of the leopardlike beast it is declared: »There was given unto him a mouth speaking great things and blasphemies. ... And he opened his mouth in blasphemy against God, to blaspheme His name, and His tabernacle, and them that dwell in heaven. And it was given unto him to make war with the saints, and to overcome them: and power was given him over all kindreds, and tongues, and nations.« This prophecy, which is nearly identical with the description of the little horn of Daniel 7, unquestionably points to the papacy. »Power was given unto him to continue forty and two months.« And, says the prophet, »I saw one of his heads as it were wounded to death.« And again: »He that leadeth into captivity shall go into captivity: he that killeth with the sword must be killed with the sword.« The forty and two months are the same as the »time and times and the dividing of time,« three years and a half, or 1260 days, of Daniel 7 the time during which the papal power was to oppress God's people. This period, as stated in preceding chapters, began with the supremacy of the papacy, A.D. 538, and terminated in 1798. At that time the pope was made captive by the French army, the papal power received its deadly wound, and the prediction was fulfilled, »He that leadeth into captivity shall go into captivity.«

At this point another symbol is introduced. Says the prophet: »I beheld another beast coming up out of the earth; and he had two horns like a lamb.« Verse 11 Both the appearance of this beast and the manner of its rise indicate that the nation which it represents is unlike those presented under the preceding symbols. The great kingdoms that have ruled the world were presented to the prophet Daniel as beasts of prey, rising when »the four winds of the heaven strove upon the great sea.« Daniel 7:2 In Revelation 17 an angel explained that waters represent »peoples, and multitudes, and nations, and tongues.« Rev. 17:15 Winds are a symbol of strife. The four winds of heaven striving upon the great sea represent the terrible scenes of conquest and revolution by which kingdoms have attained to power.

But the beast with lamblike horns was seen »coming up out of the earth.« Instead of overthrowing other powers to establish itself, the nation thus represented must arise in territory previously unoccupied and grow up gradually and peacefully. It could not, then, arise among the crowded and struggling nationalities of the Old World – that turbulent sea of »peoples, and multitudes, and nations, and tongues.« It must be sought in the Western Continent.

What nation of the New World was in 1798 rising into power, giving promise of strength and greatness, and attracting the attention of the world? The application of the symbol admits of no question. One nation, and only one, meets the specifications of this prophecy; it points unmistakably to the United States of America. Again and again the thought, almost the exact words, of the sacred writer has been unconsciously employed by the orator and the historian in describing the rise and growth of this nation. The beast was seen »coming up out of the earth;« and, according to the translators, the word here rendered »coming up« literally signifies »to grow or spring up as a plant.« And, as we have seen, the nation must arise in territory previously unoccupied. A prominent writer, describing the rise of the United States, speaks of »the mystery of her coming forth from vacancy,« and says: »Like a silent seed we grew into empire.« G. A. Townsend, The New World Compared With the Old, p. 462 A European journal in 1850 spoke of the United States as a wonderful empire, which was »emerging,« and »amid the silence of the earth daily adding to its power and pride.« The Dublin Nation.

Edward Everett, in an oration on the Pilgrim founders of this nation, said: »Did they look for a retired spot, inoffensive for its obscurity, and safe in its remoteness, where the little church of Leyden might enjoy the freedom of conscience? Behold the mighty regions over which, in peaceful conquest, ... they have borne the banners of the cross!« Speech delivered at Plymouth, Massachusetts, Dec. 22, 1824, p. 11

»And he had two horns like a lamb.« The lamblike horns indicate youth, innocence, and gentleness, fitly representing the character of the United States when presented to the prophet as »coming up« in 1798. Among the Christian exiles who first fled to America and sought an asylum from royal oppression and priestly intolerance were many who determined to establish a government upon the broad foundation of civil and religious liberty. Their views found place in the Declaration of Independence, which sets forth the great truth that »all men are created equal« and endowed with the inalienable right to »life, liberty, and the pursuit of happiness.« And the Constitution guarantees to the people the right of self-government, providing that representatives elected by the popular vote shall enact and administer the laws. Freedom of religious faith was also granted, every man being permitted to worship God according to the dictates of his conscience. Republicanism and Protestantism became the fundamental principles of the nation. These principles are the secret of its power and prosperity. The oppressed and downtrodden throughout Christendom have turned to this land with interest and hope. Millions have sought its shores, and the United States has risen to a place among the most powerful nations of the earth.

But the beast with lamblike horns »spake as a dragon. And he exerciseth all the power of the first beast before him, and causeth the earth and them which dwell therein to worship the first [440/441] beast, whose deadly wound was healed; ... saying to them that dwell on the earth, that they should make an image to the beast, which had the wound by a sword, and did live.« Revelation 13:11-14 The lamblike horns and dragon voice of the symbol point to a striking contradiction between the professions and the practice of the nation thus represented. The »speaking« of the nation is the action of its legislative and judicial authorities. By such action it will give the lie to those liberal and peaceful principles which it has put forth as the foundation of its policy. The prediction that it will speak »as a dragon« and exercise »all the power of the first beast« plainly foretells a development of the spirit of intolerance and persecution that was manifested by the nations represented by the dragon and the leopardlike beast. And the statement that the beast with two horns »causeth the earth and them which dwell therein to worship the first beast« indicates that the authority of this nation is to be exercised in enforcing some observance which shall be an act of homage to the papacy.

Such action would be directly contrary to the principles of this government, to the genius of its free institutions, to the direct and solemn avowals of the Declaration of Independence, and to the Constitution. The founders of the nation wisely sought to guard against the employment of secular power on the part of the church, with its inevitable result – intolerance and persecution. The Constitution provides that »Congress shall make no law respecting an establishment of religion, or prohibiting the free exercise thereof,« and that »no religious test shall ever be required as a qualification to any office or public trust under the United States.« Only in flagrant violation of these safeguards to the nation's liberty, can any religious observance be enforced by civil authority. But the inconsistency of such action is no greater than is represented in the symbol. It is the beast with lamblike horns – in profession pure, gentle, and harmless – that speaks as a dragon. »Saying to them that dwell on the earth, that they should make an image to the beast.« Here is clearly presented a form of government in which the legislative power rests with the people, a most striking evidence that the United States is the nation denoted in the prophecy.

But what is the »image to the beast«? and how is it to be formed? The image is made by the two-horned beast, and is an image to the beast. It is also called an image of the beast. Then to learn what the image is like and how it is to be formed we must study the charac-
 teristics of the beast itself – the papacy. When the

early church became corrupted by departing from the simplicity of the gospel and accepting heathen rites and customs, she lost the Spirit and power of God; and in order to control the consciences of the people, she sought the support of the secular power. The result was the papacy, a church that controlled the power of the state and employed it to further her own ends, especially for the punishment of »heresy.« In order for the United States to form an image of the beast, the religious power must so control the civil government that the authority of the state will also be employed by the church to accomplish her own ends.

Whenever the church has obtained secular power, she has employed it to punish dissent from her doctrines. Protestant churches that have followed in the steps of Rome by forming alliance with worldly powers have manifested a similar desire to restrict liberty of conscience. An example of this is given in the long-continued persecution of dissenters by the Church of England. During the sixteenth and seventeenth centuries, thousands of nonconformist ministers were forced to flee from their churches, and many, both of pastors and people, were subjected to fine, imprisonment, torture, and martyrdom. It was apostasy that led the early church to seek the aid of the civil government, and this prepared the way for the development of the papacy – the beast. Said Paul: »There« shall »come a falling away, ... and that man of sin be revealed.« 2 Thess. 2:3 So apostasy in the church will prepare the way for the image to the beast.

The Bible declares that before the coming of the Lord there will exist a state of religious declension similar to that in the first centuries. »In the last days perilous times shall come. For men shall be lovers of their own selves, covetous, boasters, proud, blasphemers, disobedient to parents, unthankful, unholy, without natural affection, trucebreakers, false accusers, incontinent, fierce, despisers of those that are good, traitors, heady, high-minded, lovers of pleasures more than lovers of God; having a form of godliness, but denying the power thereof.« 2 Timothy 3:1-5 »Now the Spirit speaketh expressly, that in the latter times some shall depart from the faith, giving heed to seducing spirits, and doctrines of devils.« 1 Timothy 4:1 Satan will work »with all power and signs and lying wonders, and with all deceivableness of unrighteousness.« And all that »received not the love of the truth, that they might be saved,« will be left to accept »strong delusion, that they should believe a lie.« 2 Thessalonians 2:9-11

When this state of ungodliness shall be reached, the same results will follow as in the first centuries. The wide diversity of belief in the Protestant churches is regarded by many as decisive proof that no effort to secure a forced uniformity can ever be made. But there has been for years, in churches of the Protestant faith, a strong and growing sentiment in favor of a union based upon common points of doctrine. To secure such a union, the discussion of subjects upon which all were not agreed – however important they might be from a Bible standpoint – must necessarily be waived.

Charles Beecher, in a sermon in the year 1846, declared that the ministry of »the evangelical Protestant denominations« is »not only formed all the way up under a tremendous pressure of merely human fear, but they live, and move, and breathe in a state of things radically corrupt, and appealing every hour to every baser element of their nature to hush up the truth, and bow the knee to the power of apostasy. Was not this the way things went with Rome? Are we not living her life over again? And what do we see just ahead? Another general council! A world's convention! Evangelical alliance, and universal creed!« Sermon on »The Bible a Sufficient Creed,« delivered at Fort Wayne, Indiana, Feb. 22, 1846 When this shall be gained, then, in the effort to secure complete uniformity, it will be only a step to the resort to force.

When the leading churches of the United States, uniting upon such points of doctrine as are held by them in common, shall influence the state to enforce their decrees and to sustain their institutions, then Protestant America will have formed an image of the Roman hierarchy, and the infliction of civil penalties upon dissenters will inevitably result. The beast with two horns »causeth [commands] all, both small and great, rich and poor, free and bond, to receive a mark in their right hand, or in their foreheads: and that no man might buy or sell, save he that had the mark, or the name of the beast, or the number of his name.« Revelation 13:16-17

The third angel's warning is: »If any man worship the beast and his image, and receive his mark in his forehead, or in his hand, the same shall drink of the wine of the wrath of God.« »The beast« mentioned in this message, whose worship is enforced by the two-horned beast, is the first, or leopardlike beast of Revelation 13 – the papacy. The »image to the beast« represents that form of apostate Protestantism which will be developed when the Protestant churches shall seek the aid of the civil power for the enforcement of their dogmas. The »mark of the beast« still remains to be defined. After the warning against the worship of the beast and his image the prophecy declares: »Here are they that keep the commandments of God, and the faith of Jesus.« Since those who keep God's commandments are thus placed in contrast with those that worship the beast and his image and receive his mark, it follows that the keeping of God's law, on the one hand, and its violation, on the other, will make the distinction between the worshipers of God and the worshipers of the beast.

The special characteristic of the beast, and therefore of his image, is the breaking of God's commandments. Says Daniel, of the little horn, the papacy: »He shall think to change times and the law.« Daniel 7:25, R.V. And Paul styled the same power the »man of sin,« who was to exalt himself above God. One prophecy is a complement of the other. Only by changing God's law could the papacy exalt itself above God; whoever should understandingly keep the law as thus changed would be giving supreme honor to that power by which the change was made. Such an act of obedience to papal laws would be a mark of allegiance to the pope in the place of God.

The papacy has attempted to change the law of God. The second commandment, forbidding image worship, has been dropped from the law, and the fourth commandment has been so changed as to authorize the observance of the first instead of the seventh day as the Sabbath. But papists urge, as a reason for omitting the second commandment, that it is unnecessary, being included in the first, and that they are giving the law exactly as God designed it to be understood. This cannot be the change foretold by the prophet. An intentional, deliberate change is presented: »He shall think to change the times and the law.« The change in the fourth commandment exactly fulfills the prophecy. For this the only authority claimed is that of the church. Here the papal power openly sets itself above God.

While the worshipers of God will be especially distinguished by their regard for the fourth commandment, – since this is the sign of His creative power and the witness to His claim upon man's reverence and homage, – the worshipers of the beast will be distinguished by their efforts to tear down the Creator's memorial, to exalt the institution of Rome. It was in behalf of the Sunday that popery first asserted its arrogant claims; see Appendix and its first resort to the power of the state was to compel the observance of Sunday as »the Lord's day.« But the Bible points to the seventh day, and not to the first, as the Lord's day. Said Christ: »The Son of man is Lord also of the Sabbath.« The fourth commandment declares: »The seventh day is the Sabbath of the Lord.« And by the prophet Isaiah the Lord designates it: »My holy day.« Mark 2:28; Isaiah 58:13

The claim so often put forth that Christ changed the Sabbath is disproved by His own words. In His Sermon on the Mount He said: »Think not that I am come to destroy the law, or the prophets: I am not come to destroy, but to fulfill. For verily I say unto you, Till heaven and earth pass, one jot or one tittle shall in no wise pass from the law, till all be fulfilled. Whosoever therefore shall break one of these least commandments, and shall teach men so, he shall be called the least in the kingdom of heaven: but whosoever shall do and teach them, the same shall be called great in the kingdom of heaven,« Matthew 5:17-19

It is a fact generally admitted by Protestants that the Scriptures give no authority for the change of the Sabbath. This is plainly stated in publications issued by the American Tract Society and the American Sunday School Union. One of these works acknowledges »the complete silence of the New Testament so far as any explicit command for the Sabbath [Sunday, the first day of the week] or definite rules for its observance are concerned.« George Elliott, The Abiding Sabbath, p. 184

Another says: »Up to the time of Christ's death, no change had been made in the day;« and, »so far as the record shows, they [the apostles] did not ... give any explicit command enjoining the abandonment of the seventh-day Sabbath, and its observance on the first day of the week.« A. E. Waffle, The Lord's Day, pp. 186-188

Roman Catholics acknowledge that the change of the Sabbath was made by their church, and declare that Protestants by observing the Sunday are recognizing her power. In the Catholic Catechism of Christian Religion, in answer to a question as to the day to be observed in obedience to the fourth commandment, this statement is made: »During the old law, Saturday was the day sanctified; but the church, instructed by Jesus Christ, and directed by the Spirit of God, has substituted Sunday for Saturday; so now we sanctify the first, not the seventh day. Sunday means, and now is, the day of the Lord.«

As the sign of the authority of the Catholic Church, papist writers cite »the very act of changing the Sabbath into Sunday, which Protestants allow of; ... because by keeping Sunday, they acknowledge the church's power to ordain feasts, and to command them under sin.« Henry Tuberville, An Abridgment of the Christian Doctrine, p. 58

What then is the change of the Sabbath, but the sign, or mark, of the authority of the Roman Church – »the mark of the beast«?

The Roman Church has not relinquished her claim to supremacy; and when the world and the Protestant churches accept a sabbath of her creating, while they reject the Bible Sabbath, they virtually admit this assumption. They may claim the authority of tradition and of the Fathers for the change; but in so doing they ignore the very principle which separates them from Rome – that »the Bible, and the Bible only, is the religion of Protestants.« The papist can see that they are deceiving themselves, willingly closing their eyes to the facts in the case. As the movement for Sunday enforcement gains favor, he rejoices, feeling assured that it will eventually bring the whole Protestant world under the banner of Rome.

Romanists declare that »the observance of Sunday by the Protestants is an homage they pay, in spite of themselves, to the authority of the [Catholic] Church.« Mgr. Segur, Plain Talk About the Protestantism of Today, p. 213 The enforcement of Sundaykeeping on the part of Protestant churches is an enforcement of the worship of the papacy – of the beast. Those who, understanding the claims of the fourth commandment, choose to observe the false instead of the true Sabbath are thereby paying homage to that power by which alone it is commanded. But in the very act of enforcing a religious duty by secular power, the churches would themselves form an image to the beast; hence the enforcement of Sundaykeeping in the United States would be an enforcement of the worship of the beast and his image.

But Christians of past generations observed the Sunday, supposing that in so doing they were keeping the Bible Sabbath; and there are now true Christians in every church, not excepting the Roman Catholic communion, who honestly believe that Sunday is the Sabbath of divine appointment. God accepts their sincerity of purpose and their integrity before Him. But when Sunday observance shall be enforced by law, and the world shall be enlightened concerning the obligation of the true Sabbath, then whoever shall transgress the command of God, to obey a precept which has no higher authority than that of Rome, will thereby honor popery above God. He is paying homage to Rome and to the power which enforces the institution ordained by Rome. He is worshiping the beast and his image. As men then reject the institution which God has declared to be the sign of His authority, and honor in its stead that which

CATHOLIC CATECHISM http://www.vatican.va/archive/ccc_css/archive/catechism/command.htm		THE TEN COMMANDMENTS As it is written in the Holy Bible (Exodus 20:1-17) KING JAMES VERSION 1955
1. I am the LORD your God: you shall not have strange Gods before me.		**1.** I am the LORD thy God, which have brought thee out of the land of Egypt, out of the house of bondage.
2. You shall not take the name of the LORD your God in vain.	REMOVED	**2.** Thou shalt have no other gods before me. Thou shalt not make unto thee any graven image, or any likeness of any thing that is in heaven above, or that is in the earth beneath, or that is in the water under the earth: Thou shalt not bow down thyself to them, nor serve them: for I the LORD thy God am a jealous God, visiting the iniquity of the fathers upon the children unto the third and fourth generation of them that hate me; And showing mercy unto thousands of them that love me, and keep my commandments.
3. Remember to keep holy the LORD'S Day.	REPLACED	**3.** Thou shalt not take the name of the LORD thy God in vain; for the LORD will not hold him guiltless that taketh his name in vain.
4. Honor your father and your mother.	CHANGED	**4.** **Remember the sabbath day, to keep it holy. 9 Six days shalt thou labour, and do all thy work: 10 But the seventh day is the sabbath of the LORD thy God: in it thou shalt not do any work, thou, nor thy son, nor thy daughter, thy manservant, nor thy maidservant, nor thy cattle, nor thy stranger that is within thy gates: 11 For in six days the LORD made heaven and earth, the sea, and all that in them is, and rested the seventh day: wherefore the LORD blessed the sabbath day, and hallowed it.**
5. You shall not kill.		**5.** Honour thy father and thy mother: that thy days may be long upon the land which the LORD thy God giveth thee.
6. You shall not commit adultery.		**6.** Thou shalt not kill.
7. You shall not steal.		**7.** Thou shalt not commit adultery.
8. You shall not bear false witness against your neighbor.		**8.** Thou shalt not steal.
9. You shall not covet your neighbor's wife.	DIVIDED	**9.** Thou shalt not bear false witness against thy neighbour.
10. You shall not covet your neighbor's goods.		**10.** Thou shalt not covet thy neighbour's house, thou shalt not covet thy neighbour's wife, nor his manservant, nor his maidservant, nor his ox, nor his as, nor any thing that is thy neighbour's.

Against the Text in the Bible is in catholic catechism the 2. Command totally removed. Here for is the 10. Command in 9. and 10. Command divided. The 4. Command is changed and counts as the 3. Command

Comparison of the Ten Commandments of the Catholic Church, with God's commandments

Rome has chosen as the token of her supremacy, they will thereby accept the sign of allegiance to Rome – »the mark of the beast.« And it is not until the issue is thus plainly set before the people, and they are brought to choose between the commandments of God and the commandments of men, that those who continue in transgression will receive »the mark of the beast.«

The most fearful threatening ever addressed to mortals is contained in the third angel's message. That must be a terrible sin which calls down the wrath of God unmingled with mercy. Men are not to be left in darkness concerning this important matter; the warning against this sin is to be given to the world before the visitation of God's judgments, that all may know why they are to be inflicted, and have opportunity to escape them. Prophecy declares that the first angel would make his announcement to »every nation, and kindred, and tongue, and people.« The warning of the third angel, which forms a part of the same threefold message, is to be no less widespread. It is represented in the prophecy as being proclaimed with a loud voice, by an angel flying in the midst of heaven; and it will command the attention of the world.

In the issue of the contest all Christendom will be divided into two great classes – those who keep the commandments of God and the faith of Jesus, and those who worship the beast and his image and receive his mark. Although church and state will unite their power to compel »all, both small and great, rich and poor, free and bond« Revelation 13:16 to receive »the mark of the beast,« yet the people of God will not receive it. The prophet of Patmos beholds »them that had gotten the victory over the beast, and over his image, and over his mark, and over the number of his name, stand on the sea of glass, having the harps of God« and singing the song of Moses and the Lamb. Revelation 15:2-3

Chapter 26

A Work of Reform

The work of Sabbath reform to be accomplished in the last days is foretold in the prophecy of Isaiah: »Thus saith the Lord, Keep ye judgment, and do justice: for My salvation is near to come, and My righteousness to be revealed. Blessed is the man that doeth this, and the son of man that layeth hold on it; that keepeth the Sabbath from polluting it, and keepeth his hand from doing any evil.« »The sons of the stranger, that join themselves to the Lord, to serve Him, and to love the name of the Lord, to be His servants, everyone that keepeth the Sabbath from polluting it, and taketh hold of My covenant; even them will I bring to My holy mountain, and make them joyful in My house of prayer.« Isaiah 56:1, 2, 6, 7

These words apply in the Christian age, as shown by the context: »The Lord God which gathereth the outcasts of Israel saith, Yet will I gather others to him, beside those that are gathered unto him.« Verse 8 Here is foreshadowed the gathering in of the Gentiles by the gospel. And upon those who then honor the Sabbath, a blessing is pronounced. Thus the obligation of the fourth commandment extends past the crucifixion, resurrection, and ascension of Christ, to the time when His servants should preach to all nations the message of glad tidings.

The Lord commands by the same prophet: »Bind up the testimony, seal the law among My disciples.« Isaiah 8:16 The seal of God's law is found in the fourth commandment. This only, of all the ten, brings to view both the name and the title of the Lawgiver. It declares Him to be the Creator of the heavens and the earth, and thus shows His claim to reverence and worship above all others. Aside from this precept, there is nothing in the Decalogue to show by whose authority the law is given. When the Sabbath was changed by the papal power, the seal was taken from the law. The disciples of Jesus are called upon to restore it by exalting the Sabbath of the fourth commandment to its rightful position as the Creator's memorial and the sign of His authority.

»To the law and to the testimony.« While conflicting doctrines and theories abound, the law of God is the one unerring rule by which all opinions, doctrines, and theories are to be tested. Says the prophet: »If they speak not according to this word, it is because there is no light in them.« Verse 20

Again, the command is given: »Cry aloud, spare not, lift up thy voice like a trumpet, and show My people their transgression, and the house of Jacob their sins.« It is not the wicked world, but those whom the Lord designates as »my people,« that are to be reproved for their transgressions. He declares further: »Yet they seek Me daily, and delight to know My ways, as a nation that did righteousness, and forsook not the ordinance of their God.« Isaiah 58:1, 2 Here is brought to view a class who think themselves righteous and appear to manifest great interest in the service of God; but the stern and solemn rebuke of the Searcher of hearts proves them to be trampling upon the divine precepts.

The prophet thus points out the ordinance which has been forsaken: »Thou shalt raise up the foundations of many generations; and thou shalt be called, The repairer of the breach, The restorer of paths to dwell in. If thou turn away thy foot from the Sabbath, from doing thy pleasure on My holy day; and call the Sabbath a delight, the holy of the Lord, honorable; and shalt honor Him, not doing thine own ways, nor finding thine own pleasure, nor speaking thine own words: then shalt thou delight thyself in the Lord.« Verses 12-14 This prophecy also applies in our time. The breach was made in the law of God when the Sabbath was changed by the Roman power. But the time has come for that divine institution to be restored. The breach is to be repaired and the foundation of many generations to be raised up.

Hallowed by the Creator's rest and blessing, the Sabbath was kept by Adam in his innocence in holy Eden; by Adam, fallen yet repentant, when he was driven from his happy estate. It was kept by all the patriarchs, from Abel to righteous Noah, to Abraham, to Jacob. When the chosen people were in bondage in Egypt, many, in the midst of prevailing idolatry, lost their knowledge of God's law; but when the Lord delivered Israel, He proclaimed His law in awful grandeur to the assembled multitude, that they might know His will and fear and obey Him forever.

From that day to the present the knowledge of God's law has
 been preserved in the earth, and the Sabbath of the

fourth commandment has been kept. Though the »man of sin« succeeded in trampling underfoot God's holy day, yet even in the period of his supremacy there were, hidden in secret places, faithful souls who paid it honor. Since the Reformation, there have been some in every generation to maintain its observance. Though often in the midst of reproach and persecution, a constant testimony has been borne to the perpetuity of the law of God and the sacred obligation of the creation Sabbath.

These truths, as presented in Revelation 14 in connection with »the everlasting gospel,« will distinguish the church of Christ at the time of His appearing. For as the result of the threefold message it is announced: »Here are they that keep the commandments of God, and the faith of Jesus.« And this message is the last to be given before the coming of the Lord. Immediately following its proclamation the Son of man is seen by the prophet, coming in glory to reap the harvest of the earth. Those who received the light concerning the sanctuary and the immutability of the law of God were filled with joy and wonder as they saw the beauty and harmony of the system of truth that opened to their understanding. They desired that the light which appeared to them so precious might be imparted to all Christians; and they could not but believe that it would be joyfully accepted. But truths that would place them at variance with the world were not welcome to many who claimed to be followers of Christ. Obedience to the fourth commandment required a sacrifice from which the majority drew back.

As the claims of the Sabbath were presented, many reasoned from the worldling's standpoint. Said they: »We have always kept Sunday, our fathers kept it, and many good and pious men have died happy while keeping it. If they were right, so are we. The keeping of this new Sabbath would throw us out of harmony with the world, and we would have no influence over them. What can a little company keeping the seventh day hope to accomplish against all the world who are keeping Sunday?« It was by similar arguments that the Jews endeavored to justify their rejection of Christ. Their fathers had been accepted of God in presenting the sacrificial offerings, and why could not the children find salvation in pursuing the same course? So, in the time of Luther, papists reasoned that true Christians had died in the Catholic faith, and therefore that religion was sufficient for salvation. Such reasoning would prove an effectual barrier to all advancement in religious faith or practice.

Many urged that Sundaykeeping had been an established doctrine and a widespread custom of the church for many centuries. Against this argument it was shown that the Sabbath and its observance were more ancient and widespread, even as old as the world itself, and bearing the sanction both of angels and of God. When the foundations of the earth were laid, when the morning stars sang together, and all the sons of God shouted for joy, then was laid the foundation of the Sabbath. Job 38:6-7; Genesis 2:1-3 Well may this institution demand our reverence; it was ordained by no human authority and rests upon no human traditions; it was established by the Ancient of Days and commanded by His eternal word.

As the attention of the people was called to the subject of Sabbath reform, popular ministers perverted the word of God, placing such interpretations upon its testimony as would best quiet inquiring minds. And those who did not search the Scriptures for themselves were content to accept conclusions that were in accordance with their desires. By argument, sophistry, the traditions of the Fathers, and the authority of the church, many endeavored to overthrow the truth. Its advocates were driven to their Bibles to defend the validity of the fourth commandment. Humble men, armed with the word of truth alone, withstood the attacks of men of learning, who, with surprise and anger, found their eloquent sophistry powerless against the simple, straightforward reasoning of men who were versed in the Scriptures rather than in the subtleties of the schools.

In the absence of Bible testimony in their favor, many with unwearying persistence urged – forgetting how the same reasoning had been employed against Christ and His apostles: »Why do not our great men understand this Sabbath question? But few believe as you do. It cannot be that you are right and that all the men of learning in the world are wrong.«

To refute such arguments it was needful only to cite the teachings of the Scriptures and the history of the Lord's dealings with His people in all ages. God works through those who hear and obey His voice, those who will, if need be, speak unpalatable truths, those who do not fear to reprove popular sins. The reason why He does not oftener choose men of learning and high position to lead out in reform movements is that they trust to their creeds, theories, and theological systems, and feel no need to be taught of God.

 Only those who have a personal connection with the

Source of wisdom are able to understand or explain the Scriptures. Men who have little of the learning of the schools are sometimes called to declare the truth, not because they are unlearned, but because they are not too self-sufficient to be taught of God. They learn in the school of Christ, and their humility and obedience make them great. In committing to them a knowledge of His truth, God confers upon them an honor, in comparison with which earthly honor and human greatness sink into insignificance.

The majority of Adventists rejected the truths concerning the sanctuary and the law of God, and many also renounced their faith in the advent movement and adopted unsound and conflicting views of the prophecies which applied to that work. Some were led into the error of repeatedly fixing upon a definite time for the coming of Christ. The light which was now shining on the subject of the sanctuary should have shown them that no prophetic period extends to the second advent; that the exact time of this advent is not foretold. But, turning from the light, they continued to set time after time for the Lord to come, and as often they were disappointed.

When the Thessalonian church received erroneous views concerning the coming of Christ, the apostle Paul counseled them to test their hopes and anticipations carefully by the word of God. He cited them to prophecies revealing the events to take place before Christ should come, and showed that they had no ground to expect Him in their day. »Let no man deceive you by any means«, 2 Thessalonians 2:3 are his words of warning. Should they indulge expectations that were not sanctioned by the Scriptures, they would be led to a mistaken course of action; disappointment would expose them to the derision of unbelievers, and they would be in danger of yielding to discouragement and would be tempted to doubt the truths essential for their salvation. The apostle's admonition to the Thessalonians contains an important lesson for those who live in the last days. Many Adventists have felt that unless they could fix their faith upon a definite time for the Lord's coming, they could not be zealous and diligent in the work of preparation. But as their hopes are again and again excited, only to be destroyed, their faith receives such a shock that it becomes well-nigh impossible for them to be impressed by the great truths of prophecy.

The preaching of a definite time for the judgment, in the giving of the first message, was ordered by God. The computation of the prophetic periods on which that message was based, placing the close of the 2300 days in the autumn of 1844, stands without impeachment. The repeated efforts to find new dates for the beginning and close of the prophetic periods, and the unsound reasoning necessary to sustain these positions, not only lead minds away from the present truth, but throw contempt upon all efforts to explain the prophecies. The more frequently a definite time is set for the second advent, and the more widely it is taught, the better it suits the purposes of Satan. After the time has passed, he excites ridicule and contempt of its advocates, and thus casts reproach upon the great advent movement of 1843 and 1844. Those who persist in this error will at last fix upon a date too far in the future for the coming of Christ. Thus they will be led to rest in a false security, and many will not be undeceived until it is too late.

The history of ancient Israel is a striking illustration of the past experience of the Adventist body. God led His people in the advent movement, even as He led the children of Israel from Egypt. In the great disappointment their faith was tested as was that of the Hebrews at the Red Sea. Had they still trusted to the guiding hand that had been with them in their past experience, they would have seen the salvation of God. If all who had labored unitedly in the work in 1844, had received the third angel's message and proclaimed it in the power of the Holy Spirit, the Lord would have wrought mightily with their efforts. A flood of light would have been shed upon the world. Years ago the inhabitants of the earth would have been warned, the closing work completed, and Christ would have come for the redemption of His people. It was not the will of God that Israel should wander forty years in the wilderness; He desired to lead them directly to the land of Canaan and establish them there, a holy, happy people. But »they could not enter in because of unbelief.« Hebrews 3:19 Because of their backsliding and apostasy they perished in the desert, and others were raised up to enter the Promised Land. In like manner, it was not the will of God that the coming of Christ should be so long delayed and His people should remain so many years in this world of sin and sorrow. But unbelief separated them from God. As they refused to do the work which He had appointed them, others were raised up to proclaim the message. In mercy to the world, Jesus delays His coming, that sinners may have an opportunity to hear the warning and find in Him a shelter before the wrath of God shall be poured out.

Now as in former ages, the presentation of a truth that reproves the sins and errors of the times will excite opposition. »Everyone that doeth evil hateth the light, neither cometh to the light, lest his deeds should be reproved.« John 3:20 As men see that they cannot maintain their position by the Scriptures, many determine to maintain it at all hazards, and with a malicious spirit they assail the character and motives of those who stand in defense of unpopular truth. It is the same policy which has been pursued in all ages. Elijah was declared to be a troubler in Israel, Jeremiah a traitor, Paul a polluter of the temple. From that day to this, those who would be loyal to truth have been denounced as seditious, heretical, or schismatic. Multitudes who are too unbelieving to accept the sure word of prophecy will receive with unquestioning credulity an accusation against those who dare to reprove fashionable sins. This spirit will increase more and more. And the Bible plainly teaches that a time is approaching when the laws of the state will so conflict with the law of God that whosoever would obey all the divine precepts must brave reproach and punishment as an evildoer. In view of this, what is the duty of the messenger of truth? Shall he conclude that the truth ought not to be presented, since often its only effect is to arouse men to evade or resist its claims? No; he has no more reason for withholding the testimony of God's word, because it excites opposition, than had earlier Reformers. The confession of faith made by saints and martyrs was recorded for the benefit of succeeding generations. Those living examples of holiness and steadfast integrity have come down to inspire courage in those who are now called to stand as witnesses for God. They received grace and truth, not for themselves alone, but that, through them, the knowledge of God might enlighten the earth. Has God given light to His servants in this generation? Then they should let it shine forth to the world.

Anciently the Lord declared to one who spoke in His name: »The house of Israel will not hearken unto thee; for they will not hearken unto Me.« Nevertheless He said: »Thou shalt speak My words unto them, whether they will hear, or whether they will forbear.« Ezekiel 3:7; 2:7 To the servant of God at this time is the command addressed: »Lift up thy voice like a trumpet, and show My people their transgression, and the house of Jacob their sins.«

So far as his opportunities extend, everyone who has received the light of truth is under the same solemn and fearful responsibility as was the prophet of Israel, to whom the word of the Lord came, saying: »Son of man, I have set thee a watchman unto the house of Israel; therefore thou shalt hear the word at My mouth, and warn them from Me. When I say unto the wicked, O wicked man, thou shalt surely die; if thou dost not speak to warn the wicked from his way, that wicked man shall die in his iniquity; but his blood will I require at thine hand. Nevertheless, if thou warn the wicked of his way to turn from it; if he do not turn from his way, he shall die in his iniquity; but thou hast delivered thy soul.« Ezekiel 33:7-9

The great obstacle both to the acceptance and to the promulgation of truth is the fact that it involves inconvenience and reproach. This is the only argument against the truth which its advocates have never been able to refute. But this does not deter the true followers of Christ. These do not wait for truth to become popular. Being convinced of their duty, they deliberately accept the cross, with the apostle Paul counting that »our light affliction, which is but for a moment, worketh for us a far more exceeding and eternal weight of glory;« with one of old, »esteeming the reproach of Christ greater riches than the treasures in Egypt.« 2 Corinthians 4:17; Hebrews 11:26

Whatever may be their profession, it is only those who are world servers at heart that act from policy rather than principle in religious things. We should choose the right because it is right, and leave consequences with God. To men of principle, faith, and daring, the world is indebted for its great reforms. By such men the work of reform for this time must be carried forward.

Thus saith the Lord: »Hearken unto Me, ye that know righteousness, the people in whose heart is My law; fear ye not the reproach of men, neither be ye afraid of their revilings. For the moth shall eat them up like a garment, and the worm shall eat them like wool: but My righteousness shall be forever, and My salvation from generation to generation.« Isaiah 51:7-8

CHAPTER 27

MODERN REVIVALS

Wherever the word of God has been faithfully preached, results have followed that attested its divine origin. The Spirit of God accompanied the message of His servants, and the word was with power. Sinners felt their consciences quickened. The »light which lighteth every man that cometh into the world« illumined the secret chambers of their souls, and the hidden things of darkness were made manifest. Deep conviction took hold upon their minds and hearts. They were convinced of sin and of righteousness and of judgment to come. They had a sense of the righteousness of Jehovah and felt the terror of appearing, in their guilt and uncleanness, before the Searcher of hearts. In anguish they cried out: »Who shall deliver me from the body of this death?« As the cross of Calvary, with its infinite sacrifice for the sins of men, was revealed, they saw that nothing but the merits of Christ could suffice to atone for their transgressions; this alone could reconcile man to God. With faith and humility they accepted the Lamb of God, that taketh away the sin of the world. Through the blood of Jesus they had »remission of sins that are past.«

These souls brought forth fruit meet for repentance. They believed and were baptized, and rose to walk in newness of life – new creatures in Christ Jesus; not to fashion themselves according to the former lusts, but by the faith of the Son of God to follow in His steps, to reflect His character, and to purify themselves even as He is pure. The things they once hated they now loved, and the things they once loved they hated. The proud and self-assertive became meek and lowly of heart. The vain and supercilious became serious and unobtrusive. The profane became reverent, the drunken sober, and the profligate pure. The vain fashions of the world were laid aside. Christians sought not the »outward adorning of plaiting the hair, and of wearing of gold, or of putting on of apparel; but ... the hidden man of the heart, in that which is not corruptible, even the ornament of a meek and quiet spirit, which is in the sight of God of great price.« 1 Peter 3:3-4 Revivals brought deep heart-searching and humility. They were characterized by solemn, earnest appeals to the sinner, by yearning compassion for the purchase of the blood of Christ. Men and women prayed and wrestled with God for the salvation of souls. The fruits of such revivals were seen in souls who shrank not at self-denial and sacrifice, but rejoiced that they were counted worthy to suffer reproach and trial for the sake of Christ. Men beheld a transformation in the lives of those who had professed the name of Jesus. The community was benefited by their influence. They gathered with Christ, and sowed to the Spirit, to reap life everlasting.

It could be said of them: »Ye sorrowed to repentance.« »For godly sorrow worketh repentance to salvation not to be repented of: but the sorrow of the world worketh death. For behold this selfsame thing, that ye sorrowed after a godly sort, what carefulness it wrought in you, yea, what clearing of yourselves, yea, what indignation, yea, what fear, yea, what vehement desire, yea, what zeal, yea, what revenge! In all things ye have approved yourselves to be clear in this matter.« 2 Corinthians 7:9-11 This is the result of the work of the Spirit of God. There is no evidence of genuine repentance unless it works reformation. If he restore the pledge, give again that he had robbed, confess his sins, and love God and his fellow men, the sinner may be sure that he has found peace with God. Such were the effects that in former years followed seasons of religious awakening. Judged by their fruits, they were known to be blessed of God in the salvation of men and the uplifting of humanity.

But many of the revivals of modern times have presented a marked contrast to those manifestations of divine grace which in earlier days followed the labors of God's servants. It is true that a widespread interest is kindled, many profess conversion, and there are large accessions to the churches; nevertheless the results are not such as to warrant the belief that there has been a corresponding increase of real spiritual life. The light which flames up for a time soon dies out, leaving the darkness more dense than before.

Popular revivals are too often carried by appeals to the imagination, by exciting the emotions, by gratifying the love for what is new and startling. Converts thus gained have little desire to listen to Bible truth, little interest in the testimony of prophets and apostles. Unless a religious service has something of a sensational character, it has no attractions for them. A message which appeals to un-

impassioned reason awakens no response. The plain

warnings of God's word, relating directly to their eternal interests, are unheeded.

With every truly converted soul the relation to God and to eternal things will be the great topic of life. But where, in the popular churches of today, is the spirit of consecration to God? The converts do not renounce their pride and love of the world. They are no more willing to deny self, to take up the cross, and follow the meek and lowly Jesus, than before their conversion. Religion has become the sport of infidels and skeptics because so many who bear its name are ignorant of its principles. The power of godliness has well-nigh departed from many of the churches. Picnics, church theatricals, church fairs, fine houses, personal display, have banished thoughts of God. Lands and goods and worldly occupations engross the mind, and things of eternal interest receive hardly a passing notice.

Notwithstanding the widespread declension of faith and piety, there are true followers of Christ in these churches. Before the final visitation of God's judgments upon the earth there will be among the people of the Lord such a revival of primitive godliness as has not been witnessed since apostolic times. The Spirit and power of God will be poured out upon His children. At that time many will separate themselves from those churches in which the love of this world has supplanted love for God and His word. Many, both of ministers and people, will gladly accept those great truths which God has caused to be proclaimed at this time to prepare a people for the Lord's second coming. The enemy of souls desires to hinder this work; and before the time for such a movement shall come, he will endeavor to prevent it by introducing a counterfeit. In those churches which he can bring under his deceptive power he will make it appear that God's special blessing is poured out; there will be manifest what is thought to be great religious interest. Multitudes will exult that God is working marvelously for them, when the work is that of another spirit. Under a religious guise, Satan will seek to extend his influence over the Christian world.

In many of the revivals which have occurred during the last half century, the same influences have been at work, to a greater or less degree, that will be manifest in the more extensive movements of the future. There is an emotional excitement, a mingling of the true with the false, that is well adapted to mislead. Yet none need be deceived. In the light of God's word it is not difficult to determine [463/464] the nature of these movements. Wherever men neglect the testimony of the Bible, turning away from those plain, soul-testing truths which require self-denial and renunciation of the world, there we may be sure that God's blessing is not bestowed. And by the rule which Christ Himself has given, »Ye shall know them by their fruits«, Matthew 7:16 it is evident that these movements are not the work of the Spirit of God.

In the truths of His word, God has given to men a revelation of Himself; and to all who accept them they are a shield against the deceptions of Satan. It is a neglect of these truths that has opened the door to the evils which are now becoming so widespread in the religious world. The nature and the importance of the law of God have been, to a great extent, lost sight of. A wrong conception of the character, the perpetuity, and the obligation of the divine law has led to errors in relation to conversion and sanctification, and has resulted in lowering the standard of piety in the church. Here is to be found the secret of the lack of the Spirit and power of God in the revivals of our time.

There are, in the various denominations, men eminent for their piety, by whom this fact is acknowledged and deplored. Professor Edwards A. Park, in setting forth the current religious perils, ably says: »One source of danger is the neglect of the pulpit to enforce the divine law. In former days the pulpit was an echo of the voice of conscience. ... Our most illustrious preachers gave a wonderful majesty to their discourses by following the example of the Master, and giving prominence to the law, its precepts, and its threatenings. They repeated the two great maxims, that the law is a transcript of the divine perfections, and that a man who does not love the law does not love the gospel; for the law, as well as the gospel, is a mirror reflecting the true character of God. This peril leads to another, that of underrating the evil of sin, the extent of it, the demerit of it. In proportion to the rightfulness of the commandment is the wrongfulness of disobeying it. ... »Affiliated to the dangers already named is the danger of underestimating the justice of God. The tendency of the modern pulpit is to strain out the divine justice from the divine benevolence, to sink benevolence into a sentiment rather than exalt it into a principle. The new theological prism puts asunder what God has joined together. Is the divine law a good or an evil? It is a good. Then justice is good; for it is a disposition to execute the law. From the habit of underrating the divine law and justice, the extent and demerit of human disobedience, men easily slide into the habit of underestimating the grace which has provided an atonement for sin.« Thus the gospel loses its value and importance in the minds of men, and soon they are ready practically to cast aside the Bible itself.

Many religious teachers assert that Christ by His death abolished the law, and men are henceforth free from its requirements. There are some who represent it as a grievous yoke, and in contrast to the bondage of the law they present the liberty to be enjoyed under the gospel. But not so did prophets and apostles regard the holy law of God. Said David: »I will walk at liberty: for I seek Thy precepts.« Psalm 119:45 The apostle James, who wrote after the death of Christ, refers to the Decalogue as »the royal law« and »the perfect law of liberty.« James 2:8; 1:25 And the revelator, half a century after the crucifixion, pronounces a blessing upon them »that do His commandments, that they may have right to the tree of life, and may enter in through the gates into the city.« Revelation 22:14

The claim that Christ by His death abolished His Father's law is without foundation. Had it been possible for the law to be changed or set aside, then Christ need not have died to save man from the penalty of sin. The death of Christ, so far from abolishing the law, proves that it is immutable. The Son of God came to »magnify the law, and make it honorable.« Isaiah 42:21 He said: »Think not that I am come to destroy the law;« »till heaven and earth pass, one jot or one tittle shall in no wise pass from the law.« Matthew 5:17, 18 And concerning Himself He declares: »I delight to do Thy will, O my God: yea, Thy law is within My heart.« Psalm 40:8

The law of God, from its very nature, is unchangeable. It is a revelation of the will and the character of its Author. God is love, and His law is love. Its two great principles are love to God and love to man. »Love is the fulfilling of the law.« Romans 13:10 The character of God is righteousness and truth; such is the nature of His law. Says the psalmist: »Thy law is the truth:« »all Thy commandments are righteousness.« Psalm 119:142, 172 And the apostle Paul declares: »The law is holy, and the commandment holy, and just, and good.« Romans 7:12 Such a law, being an expression of the mind and will of God, must be as enduring as its Author.

It is the work of conversion and sanctification to reconcile men to God by bringing them into accord with the principles of His law. In the beginning, man was created in the image of God. He was in perfect harmony with the nature and the law of God; the principles of righteousness were written upon his heart. But sin alienated him from his Maker. He no longer reflected the divine image. His heart was at war with the principles of God's law. »The carnal mind is enmity against God: for it is not subject to the law of God, neither indeed can be.« Romans 8:7 But »God so loved the world, that He gave His only-begotten Son,« that man might be reconciled to God. Through the merits of Christ he can be restored to harmony with his Maker. His heart must be renewed by divine grace; he must have a new life from above. This change is the new birth, without which, says Jesus, »he cannot see the kingdom of God.« The first step in reconciliation to God is the conviction of sin. »Sin is the transgression of the law.« »By the law is the knowledge of sin.« 1 John 3:4; Romans 3:20 In order to see his guilt, the sinner must test his character by God's great standard of righteousness. It is a mirror which shows the perfection of a righteous character and enables him to discern the defects in his own.

The law reveals to man his sins, but it provides no remedy. While it promises life to the obedient, it declares that death is the portion of the transgressor. The gospel of Christ alone can free him from the condemnation or the defilement of sin. He must exercise repentance toward God, whose law has been transgressed; and faith in Christ, his atoning sacrifice. Thus he obtains »remission of sins that are past« and becomes a partaker of the divine nature. He is a child of God, having received the spirit of adoption, whereby he cries: »Abba, Father!«

Is he now free to transgress God's law? Says Paul: »Do we then make void the law through faith? God forbid: yea, we establish the law.« »How shall we, that are dead to sin, live any longer therein?« And John declares: »This is the love of God, that we keep His commandments: and His commandments are not grievous.« Romans 3:31; 6:2; 1 John 5:3 In the new birth the heart is brought into harmony with God, as it is brought into accord with His law. When this mighty change has taken place in the sinner, he has passed from death unto life, from sin unto holiness, from transgression and rebellion to obedience and loyalty. The old life of alienation from God has ended; the new life of reconciliation, of faith and love, has begun. Then »the righteousness of the law« will »be fulfilled in us, who walk not after the flesh, but after the Spirit.« Romans 8:4 And the language of the soul will be: »O how love I Thy law! it is my meditation all the day.« Psalm 119:97

»The law of the Lord is perfect, converting the soul.« Psalm 19:7 Without the law, men have no just conception of the purity and holiness of God or of their own guilt and uncleanness. They have no true conviction of sin and feel no need of repentance. Not seeing their lost condition as violators of God's law, they do not realize their need of the atoning blood of Christ. The hope of salvation is accepted without a radical change of heart or reformation of life. Thus superficial conversions abound, and multitudes are joined to the church who have never been united to Christ.

Erroneous theories of sanctification, also, springing from neglect or rejection of the divine law, have a prominent place in the religious movements of the day. These theories are both false in doctrine and dangerous in practical results; and the fact that they are so generally finding favor, renders it doubly essential that all have a clear understanding of what the Scriptures teach upon this point. True sanctification is a Bible doctrine. The apostle Paul, in his letter to the Thessalonian church, declares: »This is the will of God, even your sanctification.« And he prays: »The very God of peace sanctify you wholly.« 1 Thessalonians 4:3; 5:23

The Bible clearly teaches what sanctification is and how it is to be attained. The Saviour prayed for His disciples: »Sanctify them through Thy truth: Thy word is truth.« John 17:17 And Paul teaches that believers are to be »sanctified by the Holy Ghost.« Romans 15:16 What is the work of the Holy Spirit? Jesus told His disciples: »When He, the Spirit of truth, is come, He will guide you into all truth.« John 16:13 And the psalmist says: »Thy law is the truth.« By the word and the Spirit of God are opened to men the great principles of righteousness embodied in His law. And since the law of God is »holy, and just, and good,« a transcript of the divine perfection, it follows that a character formed by obedience to that law will be holy. Christ is a perfect example of such a character. He says: »I have kept My Father's commandments.« »I do always those things that please Him.« John 15:10; 8:29 The followers of Christ are to become like Him – by the grace of God to form characters in harmony with the principles of His holy law. This is Bible sanctification.

This work can be accomplished only through faith in Christ, by the power of the indwelling Spirit of God. Paul admonishes believers: »Work out your own salvation with fear and trembling. For it is God which worketh in you both to will and to do of His good pleasure.« Philippians 2:12-13 The Christian will feel the promptings of sin, but he will maintain a constant warfare against it. Here is where Christ's help is needed. Human weakness becomes united to divine strength, and faith exclaims: »Thanks be to God, which giveth us the victory through our Lord Jesus Christ.« 1 Corinthians 15:57

The Scriptures plainly show that the work of sanctification is progressive. When in conversion the sinner finds peace with God through the blood of the atonement, the Christian life has but just begun. Now he is to »go on unto perfection;« to grow up »unto the measure of the stature of the fullness of Christ.« Says the apostle Paul: »This one thing I do, forgetting those things which are behind, and reaching forth unto those things which are before, I press toward the mark for the prize of the high calling of God in Christ Jesus.« Philippians 3:13-14 And Peter sets before us the steps by which Bible sanctification is to be attained: »Giving all diligence, add to your faith virtue; and to virtue knowledge; and to knowledge temperance; and to temperance patience; and to patience godliness; and to godliness brotherly kindness; and to brotherly kindness charity. ... If ye do these things, ye shall never fall.« 2 Peter 1:5-10

Those who experience the sanctification of the Bible will manifest a spirit of humility. Like Moses, they have had a view of the awful majesty of holiness, and they see their own unworthiness in contrast with the purity and exalted perfection of the Infinite One.

The prophet Daniel was an example of true sanctification. His long life was filled up with noble service for his Master. He was a man »greatly beloved« Daniel 10:11 of Heaven. Yet instead of claiming to be pure and holy, this honored prophet identified himself with the really sinful of Israel as he pleaded before God in behalf of his people: »We do not present our supplications before Thee for our righteousness, but for Thy great mercies.« »We have sinned, we have done wickedly.« He declares: »I was speaking, and praying, and confessing my sin and the sin of my people.« And when at a later time the Son of God appeared, to give him instruction, Daniel says: »My comeliness was turned in me into corruption, and I retained no strength.« Daniel 9:18, 15, 20; 10:8

When Job heard the voice of the Lord out of the whirlwind, he exclaimed: »I abhor myself, and repent in dust and ashes.« Job 42:6 It was when Isaiah saw the glory of the Lord, and heard the cherubim
 crying, »Holy, holy, holy, is the Lord of hosts,« that he

cried out, »Woe is me! for I am undone.« Isaiah 6:3, 5 Paul, after he was caught up into the third heaven and heard things which it was not possible for a man to utter, speaks of himself as »less than the least of all saints.«, 2 Corinthians 12:2-4 margin; Ephesians 3:8 It was the beloved John, who leaned on Jesus' breast and beheld His glory, that fell as one dead before the feet of the angel. Revelation 1:17 There can be no self-exaltation, no boastful claim to freedom from sin, on the part of those who walk in the shadow of Calvary's cross. They feel that it was their sin which caused the agony that broke the heart of the Son of God, and this thought will lead them to self-abasement. Those who live nearest to Jesus discern most clearly the frailty and sinfulness of humanity, and their only hope is in the merit of a crucified and risen Saviour.

The sanctification now gaining prominence in the religious world carries with it a spirit of self-exaltation and a disregard for the law of God that mark it as foreign to the religion of the Bible. Its advocates teach that sanctification is an instantaneous work, by which, through faith alone, they attain to perfect holiness. »Only believe,« say they, »and the blessing is yours.« No further effort on the part of the receiver is supposed to be required. At the same time they deny the authority of the law of God, urging that they are released from obligation to keep the commandments. But is it possible for men to be holy, in accord with the will and character of God, without coming into harmony with the principles which are an expression of His nature and will, and which show what is well pleasing to Him?

The desire for an easy religion that requires no striving, no selfdenial, no divorce from the follies of the world, has made the doctrine of faith, and faith only, a popular doctrine; but what saith the word of God? Says the apostle James: »What doth it profit, my brethren, though a man say he hath faith, and have not works? can faith save him? ... Wilt thou know, O vain man, that faith without works is dead? Was not Abraham our father justified by works, when he had offered Isaac his son upon the altar? Seest thou how faith wrought with his works, and by works was faith made perfect? ... Ye see then how that by works a man is justified, and not by faith only.« James 2:14-24

The testimony of the word of God is against this ensnaring doctrine of faith without works. It is not faith that claims the favor of Heaven without complying with the conditions upon which mercy is to be granted, it is presumption; for genuine faith has its foundation in the promises and provisions of the Scriptures. Let none deceive themselves with the belief that they can become holy while willfully violating one of God's requirements. The commission of a known sin silences the witnessing voice of the Spirit and separates the soul from God. »Sin is the transgression of the law.« And »whosoever sinneth [transgresseth the law] hath not seen Him, neither known Him.« 1 John 3:6 Though John in his epistles dwells so fully upon love, yet he does not hesitate to reveal the true character of that class who claim to be sanctified while living in transgression of the law of God. »He that saith, I know Him, and keepeth not His commandments, is a liar, and the truth is not in him. But whoso keepeth His word, in him verily is the love of God perfected.« 1 John 2:4, 5 Here is the test of every man's profession. We cannot accord holiness to any man without bringing him to the measurement of God's only standard of holiness in heaven and in earth. If men feel no weight of the moral law, if they belittle and make light of God's precepts, if they break one of the least of these commandments, and teach men so, they shall be of no esteem in the sight of Heaven, and we may know that their claims are without foundation.

And the claim to be without sin is, in itself, evidence that he who makes this claim is far from holy. It is because he has no true conception of the infinite purity and holiness of God or of what they must become who shall be in harmony with His character; because he has no true conception of the purity and exalted loveliness of Jesus, and the malignity and evil of sin, that man can regard himself as holy. The greater the distance between himself and Christ, and the more inadequate his conceptions of the divine character and requirements, the more righteous he appears in his own eyes.

The sanctification set forth in the Scriptures embraces the entire being – spirit, soul, and body. Paul prayed for the Thessalonians that their »whole spirit and soul and body be preserved blameless unto the coming of our Lord Jesus Christ.« 1 Thessalonians 5:23 Again he writes to believers: »I beseech you therefore, brethren, by the mercies of God, that ye present your bodies a living sacrifice, holy, acceptable unto God.« Romans 12:1 In the time of ancient Israel every offering brought as a sacrifice to God was carefully examined. If any defect was discovered in the animal presented, it was refused; for God had commanded that the offering be »without blemish.«

 So Christians are bidden to present their bodies, »a

living sacrifice, holy, acceptable unto God.« In order to do this, all their powers must be preserved in the best possible condition. Every practice that weakens physical or mental strength unfits man for the service of his Creator. And will God be pleased with anything less than the best we can offer? Said Christ: »Thou shalt love the Lord thy God with all thy heart.« Those who do love God with all the heart will desire to give Him the best service of their life, and they will be constantly seeking to bring every power of their being into harmony with the laws that will promote their ability to do His will. They will not, by the indulgence of appetite or passion, enfeeble or defile the offering which they present to their heavenly Father.

Peter says: »Abstain from fleshly lusts, which war against the soul.« 1.Peter 2:11 Every sinful gratification tends to benumb the faculties and deaden the mental and spiritual perceptions, and the word or the Spirit of God can make but a feeble impression upon the heart. Paul writes to the Corinthians: »Let us cleanse ourselves from all filthiness of the flesh and spirit, perfecting holiness in the fear of God.« 2 Corinthians 7:1 And with the fruits of the Spirit – »love, joy, peace, long-suffering, gentleness, goodness, faith, meekness« – he classes »temperance.« Galatians 5:22-23

Notwithstanding these inspired declarations, how many professed Christians are enfeebling their powers in the pursuit of gain or the worship of fashion; how many are debasing their godlike manhood by gluttony, by wine drinking, by forbidden pleasure. And the church, instead of rebuking, too often encourages the evil by appealing to appetite, to desire for gain or love of pleasure, to replenish her treasury, which love for Christ is too feeble to supply. Were Jesus to enter the churches of today and behold the feasting and unholy traffic there conducted in the name of religion, would He not drive out those desecrators, as He banished the money-changers from the temple?

The apostle James declares that the wisdom from above is »first pure.« Had he encountered those who take the precious name of Jesus upon lips defiled by tobacco, those whose breath and person are contaminated by its foul odor, and who pollute the air of heaven and force all about them to inhale the poison – had the apostle come in contact with a practice so opposed to the purity of the gospel, would he not have denounced it as »earthly, sensual, devilish«? Slaves of tobacco, claiming the blessing of entire sanctification, [474/475] talk of their hope of heaven; but God's word plainly declares that »there shall in no wise enter into it anything that defileth.« Revelation 21:27 »Know ye not that your body is the temple of the Holy Ghost which is in you, which ye have of God, and ye are not your own? for ye are bought with a price: therefore glorify God in your body, and in your spirit, which are God's.« 1 Corinthians 6:19-20 He whose body is the temple of the Holy Spirit will not be enslaved by a pernicious habit. His powers belong to Christ, who has bought him with the price of blood. His property is the Lord's. How could he be guiltless in squandering this entrusted capital? Professed Christians yearly expend an immense sum upon useless and pernicious indulgences, while souls are perishing for the word of life. God is robbed in tithes and offerings, while they consume upon the altar of destroying lust more than they give to relieve the poor or for the support of the gospel. If all who profess to be followers of Christ were truly sanctified, their means, instead of being spent for needless and even hurtful indulgences, would be turned into the Lord's treasury, and Christians would set an example of temperance, self-denial, and self-sacrifice. Then they would be the light of the world.

The world is given up to self-indulgence. »The lust of the flesh, and the lust of the eyes, and the pride of life« control the masses of the people. But Christ's followers have a holier calling. »Come out from among them, and be ye separate, saith the Lord, and touch not the unclean.« In the light of God's word we are justified in declaring that sanctification cannot be genuine which does not work this utter renunciation of the sinful pursuits and gratifications of the world.

To those who comply with the conditions, »Come out from among them, and be ye separate, ... and touch not the unclean,« God's promise is, »I will receive you, and will be a Father unto you, and ye shall be My sons and daughters, saith the Lord Almighty.« 2 Corinthians 6:17-18 It is the privilege and the duty of every Christian to have a rich and abundant experience in the things of God. »I am the light of the world,« said Jesus. »He that followeth Me shall not walk in darkness, but shall have the light of life.« John 8:12 »The path of the just is as the shining light, that shineth more and more unto the perfect day.« Proverbs 4:18 Every step of faith and obedience brings the soul into closer connection with the Light of the world, in whom there »is no darkness at all.« The bright beams of the Sun of Righteousness shine upon

 the servants of God, and they are to reflect His rays. As

the stars tell us that there is a great light in heaven with whose glory they are made bright, so Christians are to make it manifest that there is a God on the throne of the universe whose character is worthy of praise and imitation. The graces of His Spirit, the purity and holiness of His character, will be manifest in His witnesses.

Paul in his letter to the Colossians sets forth the rich blessings granted to the children of God. He says: We »do not cease to pray for you, and to desire that ye might be filled with the knowledge of His will in all wisdom and spiritual understanding; that ye might walk worthy of the Lord unto all pleasing, being fruitful in every good work, and increasing in the knowledge of God; strengthened with all might, according to His glorious power, unto all patience and long-suffering with joyfulness.« Colossians 1:9-11

Again he writes of his desire that the brethren at Ephesus might come to understand the height of the Christian's privilege. He opens before them, in the most comprehensive language, the marvelous power and knowledge that they might possess as sons and daughters of the Most High. It was theirs »to be strengthened with might by His Spirit in the inner man,« to be »rooted and grounded in love,« to »comprehend with all saints what is the breadth, and length, and depth, and height; and to know the love of Christ, which passeth knowledge.« But the prayer of the apostle reaches the climax of privilege when he prays that »ye might be filled with all the fullness of God.« Ephesians 3:16-19

Here are revealed the heights of attainment that we may reach through faith in the promises of our heavenly Father, when we fulfill His requirements. Through the merits of Christ we have access to the throne of Infinite Power. »He that spared not His own Son, but delivered Him up for us all, how shall He not with Him also freely give us all things?« Romans 8:32 The Father gave His Spirit without measure to His Son, and we also may partake of its fullness. Jesus says, »If ye then, being evil, know how to give good gifts unto your children: how much more shall your heavenly Father give the Holy Spirit to them that ask Him?« Luke 11:13 »If ye shall ask anything in My name, I will do it.« »Ask, and ye shall receive, that your joy may be full.« John 14:14; 16:24

While the Christian's life will be characterized by humility, it should not be marked with sadness and self-depreciation. It is the privilege of everyone so to live that God will approve and bless him. It is not the will of our heavenly Father that we should be ever under condemnation and darkness. There is no evidence of true humility in going with the head bowed down and the heart filled with thoughts of self. We may go to Jesus and be cleansed, and stand before the law without shame and remorse. »There is therefore now no condemnation to them which are in Christ Jesus, who walk not after the flesh, but after the Spirit.« Romans 8:1

Through Jesus the fallen sons of Adam become »sons of God.« »Both He that sanctifieth and they who are sanctified are all of one: for which cause He is not ashamed to call them brethren.« Hebrews 2:11 The Christian's life should be one of faith, of victory, and joy in God. "Whatsoever is born of God overcometh the world: and this is the victory that overcometh the world, even our faith.« 1 John 5:4 Truly spoke God's servant Nehemiah: »The joy of the Lord is your strength.« Nehemiah 8:10 And Paul says: »Rejoice in the Lord alway: and again I say, Rejoice.« »Rejoice evermore. Pray without ceasing. In everything give thanks: for this is the will of God in Christ Jesus concerning you.« Philippians 4:4; 1.Thessalonians 5:16-18

Such are the fruits of Bible conversion and sanctification; and it is because the great principles of righteousness set forth in the law of God are so indifferently regarded by the Christian world that these fruits are so rarely witnessed. This is why there is manifest so little of that deep, abiding work of the Spirit of God which marked revivals in former years. It is by beholding that we become changed. And as those sacred precepts in which God has opened to men the perfection and holiness of His character are neglected, and the minds of the people are attracted to human teachings and theories, what marvel that there has followed a decline of living piety in the church. Saith the Lord: »They have forsaken Me the fountain of living waters, and hewed them out cisterns, broken cisterns, that can hold no water.« Jer. 2:13

»Blessed is the man that walketh not in the counsel of the ungodly. ... But his delight is in the law of the Lord; and in His law doth he meditate day and night. And he shall be like a tree planted by the rivers of water, that bringeth forth his fruit in his season; his leaf also shall not wither; and whatsoever he doeth shall prosper.« Psalm 1:1-3 It is only as the law of God is restored to its rightful position that there can be a revival of primitive faith and godliness among His professed people. »Thus saith the Lord, Stand ye in the ways, and see, and ask for the old paths, where is the good way, and walk therein, and ye shall find rest for your souls.« Jeremiah 6:16

Chapter 28

Facing Life's Record

»I beheld,« says the prophet Daniel, »till thrones were placed, and One that was Ancient of Days did sit: His raiment was white as snow, and the hair of His head like pure wool; His throne was fiery flames, and the wheels thereof burning fire. A fiery stream issued and came forth from before Him: thousand thousands ministered unto Him, and ten thousand times ten thousand stood before Him: the judgment was set, and the books were opened.« Daniel 7:9, 10, R.V.

Thus was presented to the prophet's vision the great and solemn day when the characters and the lives of men should pass in review before the Judge of all the earth, and to every man should be rendered »according to his works.« The Ancient of Days is God the Father. Says the psalmist: »Before the mountains were brought forth, or ever Thou hadst formed the earth and the world, even from everlasting to everlasting, Thou art God.« Psalm 90:2 It is He, the source of all being, and the fountain of all law, that is to preside in the judgment. And holy angels as ministers and witnesses, in number »ten thousand times ten thousand, and thousands of thousands,« attend this great tribunal.

»And, behold, one like the Son of man came with the clouds of heaven, and came to the Ancient of Days, and they brought Him near before Him. And there was given Him dominion, and glory, and a kingdom, that all people, nations, and languages, should serve Him: His dominion is an everlasting dominion, which shall not pass away.« Daniel 7:13-14 The coming of Christ here described is not His second coming to the earth. He comes to the Ancient of Days in heaven to receive dominion and glory and a kingdom, which will be given Him at the close of His work as a mediator. It is this coming, and not His second advent to the earth, that was foretold in prophecy to take place at the termination of the 2300 days in 1844. Attended by heavenly angels, our great High Priest enters the holy of holies and there appears in the presence of God to engage in the last acts of His ministration in behalf of man – to perform the work of investigative judgment and to make an atonement for all who are shown to be entitled to its benefits. In the typical service only those who had come before God with confession and repentance, and whose sins, through the blood of the sin offering, were transferred to the sanctuary, had a part in the service of the Day of Atonement. So in the great day of final atonement and investigative judgment the only cases considered are those of the professed people of God. The judgment of the wicked is a distinct and separate work, and takes place at a later period. »Judgment must begin at the house of God: and if it first begin at us, what shall the end be of them that obey not the gospel?« 1 Peter 4:17

The books of record in heaven, in which the names and the deeds of men are registered, are to determine the decisions of the judgment. Says the prophet Daniel: »The judgment was set, and the books were opened.« The revelator, describing the same scene, adds: »Another book was opened, which is the book of life: and the dead were judged out of those things which were written in the books, according to their works.« Rev. 20:12 The book of life contains the names of all who have ever entered the service of God. Jesus bade His disciples: »Rejoice, because your names are written in heaven.« Luke 10:20 Paul speaks of his faithful fellow workers, »whose names are in the book of life.« Philippians 4:3 Daniel, looking down to »a time of trouble, such as never was,« declares that God's people shall be delivered, »everyone that shall be found written in the book.« And the revelator says that those only shall enter the city of God whose names »are written in the Lamb's book of life.« Daniel 12:1; Revelation 21:27

»A book of remembrance« is written before God, in which are recorded the good deeds of »them that feared the Lord, and that thought upon His name.« Malachi 3:16 Their words of faith, their acts of love, are registered in heaven. Nehemiah refers to this when he says: »Remember me, O my God, ... and wipe not out my good deeds that I have done for the house of my God.« Nehemiah 13:14 In the book of God's remembrance every deed of righteousness is immortalized. There every temptation resisted, every evil overcome, every word of tender pity expressed, is faithfully chronicled. And every act of sacrifice, every suffering and sorrow endured for Christ's sake, is recorded. Says the psalmist: »Thou tellest my wanderings: put Thou my tears into Thy bottle: are they not in Thy book?« Psalm 56:8 There is a record also of the sins of men. »For God shall bring every work into judgment, with every secret thing, whether it be good, or whether it be evil.« »Every idle word that men shall speak, they shall give account thereof in the day of judgment.« Says the Saviour: »By thy words thou shalt be justified, and by thy words thou shalt be condemned.« Ecclesiastes 12:14; Matthew 12:36-37 The secret purposes and motives appear in the unerring register; for God »will bring to light the hidden things of darkness, and will make manifest the counsels of the hearts.« 1 Corinthians 4:5 »Behold, it is written before Me, ... your iniquities, and the iniquities of your fathers together, saith the Lord.« Isaiah 65:6-7

Every man's work passes in review before God and is registered for faithfulness or unfaithfulness. Opposite each name in the books of heaven is entered with terrible exactness every wrong word, every selfish act, every unfulfilled duty, and every secret sin, with every artful dissembling. Heaven-sent warnings or reproofs neglected, wasted moments, unimproved opportunities, the influence exerted for good or for evil, with its far-reaching results, all are chronicled by the recording angel.

The law of God is the standard by which the characters and the lives of men will be tested in the judgment. Says the wise man: »Fear God, and keep His commandments: for this is the whole duty of man. For God shall bring every work into judgment.« Ecclesiastes 12:13-14 The apostle James admonishes his brethren: »So speak ye, and so do, as they that shall be judged by the law of liberty.« James 2:12

Those who in the judgment are »accounted worthy« will have a part in the resurrection of the just. Jesus said: »They which shall be accounted worthy to obtain that world, and the resurrection from the dead, ... are equal unto the angels; and are the children of God, being the children of the resurrection.« Luke 20:35-36 And again He declares that »they that have done good« shall come forth »unto the resurrection of life.« John 5:29 The righteous dead will not be raised until after the judgment at which they are accounted worthy of »the resurrection of life.« Hence they will not be present in person at the tribunal when their records are examined and their cases decided. Jesus will appear as their advocate, to plead in their behalf before God. »If any man sin, we have an advocate with the Father, Jesus Christ the righteous.« 1 John 2:1 »For Christ is not entered into the holy places made with hands, which are the figures of the true; but into heaven itself, now to appear in the presence of God for us.« »Wherefore He is able also to save them to the uttermost that come unto God by Him, seeing He ever liveth to make intercession for them.« Hebrews 9:24; 7:25

As the books of record are opened in the judgment, the lives of all who have believed on Jesus come in review before God. Beginning with those who first lived upon the earth, our Advocate presents the cases of each successive generation, and closes with the living. Every name is mentioned, every case closely investigated. Names are accepted, names rejected. When any have sins remaining upon the books of record, unrepented of and unforgiven, their names will be blotted out of the book of life, and the record of their good deeds will be erased from the book of God's remembrance. The Lord declared to Moses: »Whosoever hath sinned against Me, him will I blot out of My book.« Exodus 32:33 And says the prophet Ezekiel: »When the righteous turneth away from his righteousness, and committeth iniquity, ... all his righteousness that he hath done shall not be mentioned.« Ezekiel 18:24

All who have truly repented of sin, and by faith claimed the blood of Christ as their atoning sacrifice, have had pardon entered against their names in the books of heaven; as they have become partakers of the righteousness of Christ, and their characters are found to be in harmony with the law of God, their sins will be blotted out, and they themselves will be accounted worthy of eternal life. The Lord declares, by the prophet Isaiah: »I, even I, am He that blotteth out thy transgressions for Mine own sake, and will not remember thy sins.« Isaiah 43:25 Said Jesus: »He that overcometh, the same shall be clothed in white raiment; and I will not blot out his name out of the book of life, but I will confess his name before My Father, and before His angels.« »Whosoever therefore shall confess Me before men, him will I confess also before My Father which is in heaven. But whosoever shall deny Me before men, him will I also deny before My Father which is in heaven.« Revelation 3:5; Matthew 10:32-33

The deepest interest manifested among men in the decisions of earthly tribunals but faintly represents the interest evinced in the heavenly courts when the names entered in the book of life come up in review before the Judge of all the earth. The divine Intercessor presents the plea that all who have overcome through faith in His blood be forgiven their transgressions, that they be restored to their Eden home, and crowned as joint heirs with Himself to »the first dominion.« Micah 4:8 Satan in his efforts to deceive and tempt our race had thought to frustrate the divine plan in man's creation; but Christ

now asks that this plan be carried into effect as if man

had never fallen. He asks for His people not only pardon and justification, full and complete, but a share in His glory and a seat upon His throne. While Jesus is pleading for the subjects of His grace, Satan accuses them before God as transgressors. The great deceiver has sought to lead them into skepticism, to cause them to lose confidence in God, to separate themselves from His love, and to break His law. Now he points to the record of their lives, to the defects of character, the unlikeness to Christ, which has dishonored their Redeemer, to all the sins that he has tempted them to commit, and because of these he claims them as his subjects.

Jesus does not excuse their sins, but shows their penitence and faith, and, claiming for them forgiveness, He lifts His wounded hands before the Father and the holy angels, saying: I know them by name. I have graven them on the palms of My hands. »The sacrifices of God are a broken spirit: a broken and a contrite heart, O God, Thou wilt not despise.« Psalm 51:17 And to the accuser of His people He declares: »The Lord rebuke thee, O Satan; even the Lord that hath chosen Jerusalem rebuke thee: is not this a brand plucked out of the fire?« Zechariah 3:2 Christ will clothe His faithful ones with His own righteousness, that He may present them to His Father »a glorious church, not having spot, or wrinkle, or any such thing.« Eph. 5:27 Their names stand enrolled in the book of life, and concerning them it is written: "They shall walk with Me in white: for they are worthy.« Revelation 3:4

Thus will be realized the complete fulfillment of the new-covenant promise: »I will forgive their iniquity, and I will remember their sin no more.« »In those days, and in that time, saith the Lord, the iniquity of Israel shall be sought for, and there shall be none; and the sins of Judah, and they shall not be found.« Jeremiah 31:34; 50:20 »In that day shall the branch of the Lord be beautiful and glorious, and the fruit of the earth shall be excellent and comely for them that are escaped of Israel. And it shall come to pass, that he that is left in Zion, and he that remaineth in Jerusalem, shall be called holy, even everyone that is written among the living in Jerusalem.« Isaiah 4:2-3

The work of the investigative judgment and the blotting out of sins is to be accomplished before the second advent of the Lord. Since the dead are to be judged out of the things written in the books, it is impossible that the sins of men should be blotted out until after the judgment at which their cases are to be investigated. But the apostle Peter distinctly states that the sins of believers will be blotted out »when the times of refreshing shall come from the presence of the Lord; and He shall send Jesus Christ.« Acts 3:19-20 When the investigative judgment closes, Christ will come, and His reward will be with Him to give to every man as his work shall be. In the typical service the high priest, having made the atonement for Israel, came forth and blessed the congregation. So Christ, at the close of His work as mediator, will appear, »without sin unto salvation«, Hebrews 9:28 to bless His waiting people with eternal life. As the priest, in removing the sins from the sanctuary, confessed them upon the head of the scapegoat, so Christ will place all these sins upon Satan, the originator and instigator of sin. The scapegoat, bearing the sins of Israel, was sent away »unto a land not inhabited«; Leviticus 16:22 so Satan, bearing the guilt of all the sins which he has caused God's people to commit, will be for a thousand years confined to the earth, which will then be desolate, without inhabitant, and he will at last suffer the full penalty of sin in the fires that shall destroy all the wicked. Thus the great plan of redemption will reach its accomplishment in the final eradication of sin and the deliverance of all who have been willing to renounce evil. At the time appointed for the judgment – the close of the 2300 days, in 1844 – began the work of investigation and blotting out of sins. All who have ever taken upon themselves the name of Christ must pass its searching scrutiny. Both the living and the dead are to be judged »out of those things which were written in the books, according to their works.«

Sins that have not been repented of and forsaken will not be pardoned and blotted out of the books of record, but will stand to witness against the sinner in the day of God. He may have committed his evil deeds in the light of day or in the darkness of night; but they were open and manifest before Him with whom we have to do. Angels of God witnessed each sin and registered it in the unerring records. Sin may be concealed, denied, covered up from father, mother, wife, children, and associates; no one but the guilty actors may cherish the least suspicion of the wrong; but it is laid bare before the intelligences of heaven. The darkness of the darkest night, the secrecy of all deceptive arts, is not sufficient to veil one thought from the knowledge of the Eternal. God has an exact record of every unjust account and every unfair dealing. He is not deceived by appearances of piety. He makes no mistakes in His estimation of character. Men may be deceived by those who are corrupt in heart, but God pierces all disguises and reads the inner life. How solemn is the thought! Day after day, passing into eternity, bears its burden of records for the books of heaven. Words once spoken, deeds once done, can never be recalled. Angels have registered both the good and the evil. The mightiest conqueror upon the earth cannot call back the record of even a single day. Our acts, our words, even our most secret motives, all have their weight in deciding our destiny for weal or woe. Though they may be forgotten by us, they will bear their testimony to justify or condemn.

As the features of the countenance are reproduced with unerring accuracy on the polished plate of the artist, so the character is faithfully delineated in the books above. Yet how little solicitude is felt concerning that record which is to meet the gaze of heavenly beings. Could the veil which separates the visible from the invisible world be swept back, and the children of men behold an angel recording every word and deed, which they must meet again in the judgment, how many words that are daily uttered would remain unspoken, how many deeds would remain undone.

In the judgment the use made of every talent will be scrutinized. How have we employed the capital lent us of Heaven? Will the Lord at His coming receive His own with usury? Have we improved the powers entrusted us, in hand and heart and brain, to the glory of God and the blessing of the world? How have we used our time, our pen, our voice, our money, our influence? What have we done for Christ, in the person of the poor, the afflicted, the orphan, or the widow?

God has made us the depositaries of His holy word; what have we done with the light and truth given us to make men wise unto salvation? No value is attached to a mere profession of faith in Christ; only the love which is shown by works is counted genuine. Yet it is love alone which in the sight of Heaven makes any act of value. Whatever is done from love, however small it may appear in the estimation of men, is accepted and rewarded of God.

The hidden selfishness of men stands revealed in the books of heaven. There is the record of unfulfilled duties to their fellow men, of forgetfulness of the Saviour's claims. There they will see how often were given to Satan the time, thought, and strength that belonged to Christ. Sad is the record which angels bear to heaven. Intelligent beings, professed followers of Christ, are absorbed in the acquirement of worldly possessions or the enjoyment of earthly plea- [486/487] sures. Money, time, and strength are sacrificed for display and self-indulgence; but few are the moments devoted to prayer, to the searching of the Scriptures, to humiliation of soul and confession of sin.

Satan invents unnumbered schemes to occupy our minds, that they may not dwell upon the very work with which we ought to be best acquainted. The archdeceiver hates the great truths that bring to view an atoning sacrifice and an all-powerful mediator. He knows that with him everything depends on his diverting minds from Jesus and His truth. Those who would share the benefits of the Saviour's mediation should permit nothing to interfere with their duty to perfect holiness in the fear of God. The precious hours, instead of being given to pleasure, to display, or to gain seeking, should be devoted to an earnest, prayerful study of the word of truth. The subject of the sanctuary and the investigative judgment should be clearly understood by the people of God. All need a knowledge for themselves of the position and work of their great High Priest. Otherwise it will be impossible for them to exercise the faith which is essential at this time or to occupy the position which God designs them to fill. Every individual has a soul to save or to lose. Each has a case pending at the bar of God. Each must meet the great Judge face to face. How important, then, that every mind contemplate often the solemn scene when the judgment shall sit and the books shall be opened, when, with Daniel, every individual must stand in his lot, at the end of the days.

All who have received the light upon these subjects are to bear testimony of the great truths which God has committed to them. The sanctuary in heaven is the very center of Christ's work in behalf of men. It concerns every soul living upon the earth. It opens to view the plan of redemption, bringing us down to the very close of time and revealing the triumphant issue of the contest between righteousness and sin. It is of the utmost importance that all should thoroughly investigate these subjects and be able to give an answer to everyone that asketh them a reason of the hope that is in them.

The intercession of Christ in man's behalf in the sanctuary above is as essential to the plan of salvation as was His death upon the cross. By His death He began that work which after His resurrection He ascended to complete in heaven. We must by faith enter within the veil, »whither the forerunner is for us entered.« Hebrews 6:20 There the light from the cross of Calvary is reflected. There we may gain a

 clearer insight into the mysteries of redemption. The

salvation of man is accomplished at an infinite expense to heaven; the sacrifice made is equal to the broadest demands of the broken law of God. Jesus has opened the way to the Father's throne, and through His mediation the sincere desire of all who come to Him in faith may be presented before God. »He that covereth his sins shall not prosper: but whoso confesseth and forsaketh them shall have mercy.« Proverbs 28:13 If those who hide and excuse their faults could see how Satan exults over them, how he taunts Christ and holy angels with their course, they would make haste to confess their sins and to put them away. Through defects in the character, Satan works to gain control of the whole mind, and he knows that if these defects are cherished, he will succeed. Therefore he is constantly seeking to deceive the followers of Christ with his fatal sophistry that it is impossible for them to overcome. But Jesus pleads in their behalf His wounded hands, His bruised body; and He declares to all who would follow Him: »My grace is sufficient for thee.« 2 Corinthians 12:9 »Take My yoke upon you, and learn of Me; for I am meek and lowly in heart: and ye shall find rest unto your souls. For My yoke is easy, and My burden is light.« Matthew 11:29, 30 Let none, then, regard their defects as incurable. God will give faith and grace to overcome them.

We are now living in the great day of atonement. In the typical service, while the high priest was making the atonement for Israel, all were required to afflict their souls by repentance of sin and humiliation before the Lord, lest they be cut off from among the people. In like manner, all who would have their names retained in the book of life should now, in the few remaining days of their probation, afflict their souls before God by sorrow for sin and true repentance. There must be deep, faithful searching of heart. The light, frivolous spirit indulged by so many professed Christians must be put away. There is earnest warfare before all who would subdue the evil tendencies that strive for the mastery. The work of preparation is an individual work. We are not saved in groups. The purity and devotion of one will not offset the want of these qualities in another. Though all nations are to pass in judgment before God, yet He will examine the case of each individual with as close and searching scrutiny as if there were not another being upon the earth. Everyone must be tested and found without spot or wrinkle or any such thing.

Solemn are the scenes connected with the closing work of the atonement. Momentous are the interests involved therein. The judgment is now passing in the sanctuary above. For many years this work has been in progress. Soon – none know how soon – it will pass to the cases of the living. In the awful presence of God our lives are to come up in review. At this time above all others it behooves every soul to heed the Saviour's admonition: »Watch and pray: for ye know not when the time is.« Mark 13:33 »If therefore thou shalt not watch, I will come on thee as a thief, and thou shalt not know what hour I will come upon thee.« Rev. 3:3

»MENE, MENE, TEKEL UPHARSIN« Daniel 5, 22-28

When the work of the investigative judgment closes, the destiny of all will have been decided for life or death. Probation is ended a short time before the appearing of the Lord in the clouds of heaven. Christ in the Revelation, looking forward to that time, declares: »He that is unjust, let him be unjust still: and he which is filthy, let him be filthy still: and he that is righteous let him be righteous still: and he that is holy, let him be holy still. And, behold, I come quickly; and My reward is with Me, to give every man according as his work shall be.« Revelation 22:11-12

The righteous and the wicked will still be living upon the earth in their mortal state – men will be planting and building, eating and drinking, all unconscious that the final, irrevocable decision has been pronounced in the sanctuary above. Before the Flood, after Noah entered the ark, God shut him in and shut the ungodly out; but for seven days the people, knowing not that their doom was fixed, continued their careless, pleasure-loving life and mocked the warnings of impending judgment. »So,« says the Saviour, »shall also the coming of the Son of man be.« Matthew 24:39

Silently, unnoticed as the midnight thief, will come the decisive hour which marks the fixing of every man's destiny, the final withdrawal of mercy's offer to guilty men. »Watch ye therefore: ... lest coming suddenly He find you sleeping.« Mark 13:35-36 Perilous is the condition of those who, growing weary of their watch, turn to the attractions of the world. While the man of business is absorbed in the pursuit of gain, while the pleasure lover is seeking indulgence, while the daughter of fashion is arranging her adornments – it may be in that hour the Judge of all the earth will pronounce the sentence: »Thou art weighed in the balances, and art found wanting.« Daniel 5:27

CHAPTER 29

THE ORIGIN OF EVIL

To many minds the origin of sin and the reason for its existence are a source of great perplexity. They see the work of evil, with its terrible results of woe and desolation, and they question how all this can exist under the sovereignty of One who is infinite in wisdom, in power, and in love. Here is a mystery of which they find no explanation. And in their uncertainty and doubt they are blinded to truths plainly revealed in God's word and essential to salvation. There are those who, in their inquiries concerning the existence of sin, endeavor to search into that which God has never revealed; hence they find no solution of their difficulties; and such as are actuated by a disposition to doubt and cavil seize upon this as an excuse for rejecting the words of Holy Writ. Others, however, fail of a satisfactory understanding of the great problem of evil, from the fact that tradition and misinterpretation have obscured the teaching of the Bible concerning the character of God, the nature of His government, and the principles of His dealing with sin.

It is impossible to explain the origin of sin so as to give a reason for its existence. Yet enough may be understood concerning both the origin and the final disposition of sin to make fully manifest the justice and benevolence of God in all His dealings with evil. Nothing is more plainly taught in Scripture than that God was in no wise responsible for the entrance of sin; that there was no arbitrary withdrawal of divine grace, no deficiency in the divine government, that gave occasion for the uprising of rebellion. Sin is an intruder, for whose presence no reason can be given. It is mysterious, unaccountable; to excuse it is to defend it. Could excuse for it be found, or cause be shown for its existence, it would cease to be sin. Our only definition of sin is that given in the word of God; it is »the transgression of the law;« it is the outworking of a principle at war with the great law of love which is the foundation of the divine government.

Before the entrance of evil there was peace and joy throughout the universe. All was in perfect harmony with the Creator's will. Love for God was supreme, love for one another impartial. Christ the Word, the Only Begotten of God, was one with the eternal Father, – one in nature, in character, and in purpose, – the only being in all the universe that could enter into all the counsels and purposes of God. By Christ the Father wrought in the creation of all heavenly beings. »By Him were all things created, that are in heaven, ... whether they be thrones, or dominions, or principalities, or powers«; Colossians 1:16 and to Christ, equally with the Father, all heaven gave allegiance.

The law of love being the foundation of the government of God, the happiness of all created beings depended upon their perfect accord with its great principles of righteousness. God desires from all His creatures the service of love – homage that springs from an intelligent appreciation of His character. He takes no pleasure in a forced allegiance, and to all He grants freedom of will, that they may render Him voluntary service. But there was one that chose to pervert this freedom. Sin originated with him who, next to Christ, had been most honored of God and who stood highest in power and glory among the inhabitants of heaven.

Before his fall, Lucifer was first of the covering cherubs, holy and undefiled. »Thus saith the Lord God; Thou sealest up the sum, full of wisdom, and perfect in beauty. Thou hast been in Eden the garden of God; every precious stone was thy covering. ... Thou art the anointed cherub that covereth; and I have set thee so: thou wast upon the holy mountain of God; thou hast walked up and down in the midst of the stones of fire. Thou wast perfect in thy ways from the day that thou wast created, till iniquity was found in thee.« Ezekiel 28:12-15

Lucifer might have remained in favor with God, beloved and honored by all the angelic host, exercising his noble powers to bless others and to glorify his Maker. But, says the prophet, »Thine heart was lifted up because of thy beauty, thou hast corrupted thy wisdom by reason of thy brightness.« Verse 17 Little by little, Lucifer came to indulge a desire for self-exaltation. »Thou hast set thine heart as the heart of God.« »Thou hast said, ... I will exalt my throne above the stars of God: I will sit also upon the mount of the congregation. ... I will ascend above the heights of the clouds; I will be like the Most High.« Verse 6; Isaiah 14:13-14

Instead of seeking to make God supreme in the affections and allegiance of His creatures, it was Lucifer's endeavor to win their service and homage to himself. And coveting the honor which the infinite Father had bestowed upon His Son, this prince of angels aspired to power which it was the prerogative of Christ alone to wield. All heaven had rejoiced to reflect the Creator's glory and to show forth His praise. And while God was thus honored, all had been peace and gladness. But a note of discord now marred the celestial harmonies. The service and exaltation of self, contrary to the Creator's plan, awakened forebodings of evil in minds to whom God's glory was supreme. The heavenly councils pleaded with Lucifer. The Son of God presented before him the greatness, the goodness, and the justice of the Creator, and the sacred, unchanging nature of His law. God Himself had established the order of heaven; and in departing from it, Lucifer would dishonor his Maker, and bring ruin upon himself. But the warning, given in infinite love and mercy, only aroused a spirit of resistance. Lucifer allowed jealousy of Christ to prevail, and he became the more determined.

Pride in his own glory nourished the desire for supremacy. The high honors conferred upon Lucifer were not appreciated as the gift of God and called forth no gratitude to the Creator. He gloried in his brightness and exaltation, and aspired to be equal with God. He was beloved and reverenced by the heavenly host. Angels delighted to execute his commands, and he was clothed with wisdom and glory above them all. Yet the Son of God was the acknowledged Sovereign of heaven, one in power and authority with the Father. In all the councils of God, Christ was a participant, while Lucifer was not permitted thus to enter into the divine purposes. »Why,« questioned this mighty angel, »should Christ have the supremacy? Why is He thus honored above Lucifer?«

Leaving his place in the immediate presence of God, Lucifer went forth to diffuse the spirit of discontent among the angels. Working with mysterious secrecy, and for a time concealing his real purpose under an appearance of reverence for God, he endeavored to excite dissatisfaction concerning the laws that governed heavenly beings, intimating that they imposed an unnecessary restraint. Since their natures were holy, he urged that the angels should obey the dictates of their own will. He sought to create sympathy for himself by representing that God had dealt unjustly with him in bestowing supreme honor upon Christ. He claimed that in aspiring to greater power and

 honor he was not aiming at self-exaltation, but was

seeking to secure liberty for all the inhabitants of heaven, that by this means they might attain to a higher state of existence.

God in His great mercy bore long with Lucifer. He was not immediately degraded from his exalted station when he first indulged the spirit of discontent, nor even when he began to present his false claims before the loyal angels. Long was he retained in heaven. Again and again he was offered pardon on condition of repentance and submission. Such efforts as only infinite love and wisdom could devise were made to convince him of his error. The spirit of discontent had never before been known in heaven. Lucifer himself did not at first see whither he was drifting; he did not understand the real nature of his feelings. But as his dissatisfaction was proved to be without cause, Lucifer was convinced that he was in the wrong, that the divine claims were just, and that he ought to acknowledge them as such before all heaven. Had he done this, he might have saved himself and many angels. He had not at this time fully cast off his allegiance to God. Though he had forsaken his position as covering cherub, yet if he had been willing to return to God, acknowledging the Creator's wisdom, and satisfied to fill the place appointed him in God's great plan, he would have been reinstated in his office. But pride forbade him to submit. He persistently defended his own course, maintained that he had no need of repentance, and fully committed himself, in the great controversy, against his Maker.

All the powers of his master mind were now bent to the work of deception, to secure the sympathy of the angels that had been under his command. Even the fact that Christ had warned and counseled him was perverted to serve his traitorous designs. To those whose loving trust bound them most closely to him, Satan had represented that he was wrongly judged, that his position was not respected, and that his liberty was to be abridged. From misrepresentation of the words of Christ he passed to prevarication and direct falsehood, accusing the Son of God of a design to humiliate him before the inhabitants of heaven. He sought also to make a false issue between himself and the loyal angels. All whom he could not subvert and bring fully to his side he accused of indifference to the interests of heavenly beings.

The very work which he himself was doing he charged upon those who remained true to God. And to sustain his charge of God's injustice toward him, he resorted to misrepresentation of the words and acts of the Creator. It was his policy to perplex the angels with subtle arguments concerning the purposes of God. Everything that was simple he shrouded in mystery, and by artful perversion cast doubt upon the plainest statements of Jehovah. His high position, in such close connection with the divine administration, gave greater force to his representations, and many were induced to unite with him in rebellion against Heaven's authority.

God in His wisdom permitted Satan to carry forward his work, until the spirit of disaffection ripened into active revolt. It was necessary for his plans to be fully developed, that their true nature and tendency might be seen by all. Lucifer, as the anointed cherub, had been highly exalted; he was greatly loved by the heavenly beings, and his influence over them was strong. God's government included not only the inhabitants of heaven, but of all the worlds that He had created; and Satan thought that if he could carry the angels of heaven with him in rebellion, he could carry also the other worlds. He had artfully presented his side of the question, employing sophistry and fraud to secure his objects. His power to deceive was very great, and by disguising himself in a cloak of falsehood he had gained an advantage. Even the loyal angels could not fully discern his character or see to what his work was leading.

Satan had been so highly honored, and all his acts were so clothed with mystery, that it was difficult to disclose to the angels the true nature of his work. Until fully developed, sin would not appear the evil thing it was. Heretofore it had had no place in the universe of God, and holy beings had no conception of its nature and malignity. They could not discern the terrible consequences that would result from setting aside the divine law. Satan had, at first, concealed his work under a specious profession of loyalty to God. He claimed to be seeking to promote the honor of God, the stability of His government, and the good of all the inhabitants of heaven. While instilling discontent into the minds of the angels under him, he had artfully made it appear that he was seeking to remove dissatisfaction. When he urged that changes be made in the order and laws of God's government, it was under the pretense that these were necessary in order to preserve harmony in heaven.

In His dealing with sin, God could employ only righteousness and truth. Satan could use what God could not – flattery and deceit. He had sought to falsify the word of God and had misrepresented His plan of government before the angels, claiming that God was not just in laying laws and rules upon the inhabitants of heaven; that in requiring submission and obedience from His creatures, He was seeking merely the exaltation of Himself. Therefore it must be demonstrated before the inhabitants of heaven, as well as of all the worlds, that God's government was just, His law perfect. Satan had made it appear that he himself was seeking to promote the good of the universe. The true character of the usurper, and his real object, must be understood by all. He must have time to manifest himself by his wicked works.

The discord which his own course had caused in heaven, Satan charged upon the law and government of God. All evil he declared to be the result of the divine administration. He claimed that it was his own object to improve upon the statutes of Jehovah. Therefore it was necessary that he should demonstrate the nature of his claims, and show the working out of his proposed changes in the divine law. His own work must condemn him. Satan had claimed from the first that he was not in rebellion. The whole universe must see the deceiver unmasked.

Even when it was decided that he could no longer remain in heaven, Infinite Wisdom did not destroy Satan. Since the service of love can alone be acceptable to God, the allegiance of His creatures must rest upon a conviction of His justice and benevolence. The inhabitants of heaven and of other worlds, being unprepared to comprehend the nature or consequences of sin, could not then have seen the justice and mercy of God in the destruction of Satan. Had he been immediately blotted from existence, they would have served God from fear rather than from love. The influence of the deceiver would not have been fully destroyed, nor would the spirit of rebellion have been utterly eradicated. Evil must be permitted to come to maturity. For the good of the entire universe through ceaseless ages Satan must more fully develop his principles, that his charges against the divine government might be seen in their true light by all created beings, that the justice and mercy of God and the immutability of His law might forever be placed beyond all question.

Satan's rebellion was to be a lesson to the universe through all coming ages, a perpetual testimony to the nature and terrible results of sin. The working out of Satan's rule, its effects upon both men and angels, would show what must be the fruit of [498/499] setting aside the divine authority. It would testify that with the existence of God's government and His law is bound up the well-being of all the creatures He has made. Thus the history of this terrible experiment of rebellion was to be a perpetual safeguard to all holy intelligences, to prevent them from being deceived as to the nature of transgression, to save them from committing sin and suffering its punishments.

To the very close of the controversy in heaven the great usurper continued to justify himself. When it was announced that with all his sympathizers he must be expelled from the abodes of bliss, then the rebel leader boldly avowed his contempt for the Creator's law. He reiterated his claim that angels needed no control, but should be left to follow their own will, which would ever guide them right. He denounced the divine statutes as a restriction of their liberty and declared that it was his purpose to secure the abolition of law; that, freed from this restraint, the hosts of heaven might enter upon a more exalted, more glorious state of existence. With one accord, Satan and his host threw the blame of their rebellion wholly upon Christ, declaring that if they had not been reproved, they would never have rebelled. Thus stubborn and defiant in their disloyalty, seeking vainly to overthrow the government of God, yet blasphemously claiming to be themselves the innocent victims of oppressive power, the archrebel and all his sympathizers were at last banished from heaven.

The same spirit that prompted rebellion in heaven still inspires rebellion on earth. Satan has continued with men the same policy which he pursued with the angels. His spirit now reigns in the children of disobedience. Like him they seek to break down the restraints of the law of God and promise men liberty through transgression of its precepts. Reproof of sin still arouses the spirit of hatred and resistance. When God's messages of warning are brought home to the conscience, Satan leads men to justify themselves and to seek the sympathy of others in their course of sin. Instead of correcting their errors, they excite indignation against the reprover, as if he were the sole cause of difficulty. From the days of righteous Abel to our own time such is the spirit which has been displayed toward those who dare to condemn sin. By the same misrepresentation of the character of God as he had practiced in heaven,

 causing Him to be regarded as severe and tyrannical,

Satan induced man to sin. And having succeeded thus far, he declared that God's unjust restrictions had led to man's fall, as they had led to his own rebellion. But the Eternal One Himself proclaims His character: »The Lord God, merciful and gracious, long-suffering, and abundant in goodness and truth, keeping mercy for thousands, forgiving iniquity and transgression and sin, and that will by no means clear the guilty.« Exodus 34:6-7

In the banishment of Satan from heaven, God declared His justice and maintained the honor of His throne. But when man had sinned through yielding to the deceptions of this apostate spirit, God gave an evidence of His love by yielding up His only-begotten Son to die for the fallen race. In the atonement the character of God is revealed. The mighty argument of the cross demonstrates to the whole universe that the course of sin which Lucifer had chosen was in no wise chargeable upon the government of God.

In the contest between Christ and Satan, during the Saviour's earthly ministry, the character of the great deceiver was unmasked. Nothing could so effectually have uprooted Satan from the affections of the heavenly angels and the whole loyal universe as did his cruel warfare upon the world's Redeemer. The daring blasphemy of his demand that Christ should pay him homage, his presumptuous boldness in bearing Him to the mountain summit and the pinnacle of the temple, the malicious intent betrayed in urging Him to cast Himself down from the dizzy height, the unsleeping malice that hunted Him from place to place, inspiring the hearts of priests and people to reject His love, and at the last to cry, »Crucify Him! crucify Him!« – all this excited the amazement and indignation of the universe.

It was Satan that prompted the world's rejection of Christ. The prince of evil exerted all his power and cunning to destroy Jesus; for he saw that the Saviour's mercy and love, His compassion and pitying tenderness, were representing to the world the character of God. Satan contested every claim put forth by the Son of God and employed men as his agents to fill the Saviour's life with suffering and sorrow. The sophistry and falsehood by which he had sought to hinder the work of Jesus, the hatred manifested through the children of disobedience, his cruel accusations against Him whose life was one of unexampled goodness, all sprang from deep-seated revenge. The pent-up fires of envy and malice, hatred and revenge, burst forth on Calvary against the Son of God, while all heaven gazed upon the scene in silent horror. When the great sacrifice had been consummated, Christ ascended on high, refusing the adoration of angels until He had presented the request: »I will that they also, whom Thou hast given Me, be with Me where I am.« John 17:24 Then with inexpressible love and power came forth the answer from the Father's throne: »Let all the angels of God worship Him.« Hebrews 1:6 Not a stain rested upon Jesus. His humiliation ended, His sacrifice completed, there was given unto Him a name that is above every name.

Now the guilt of Satan stood forth without excuse. He had revealed his true character as a liar and a murderer. It was seen that the very same spirit with which he ruled the children of men, who were under his power, he would have manifested had he been permitted to control the inhabitants of heaven. He had claimed that the transgression of God's law would bring liberty and exaltation; but it was seen to result in bondage and degradation.

Satan's lying charges against the divine character and government appeared in their true light. He had accused God of seeking merely the exaltation of Himself in requiring submission and obedience from His creatures, and had declared that, while the Creator exacted selfdenial from all others, He Himself practiced no self-denial and made no sacrifice. Now it was seen that for the salvation of a fallen and sinful race, the Ruler of the universe had made the greatest sacrifice which love could make; for »God was in Christ, reconciling the world unto Himself.« 2 Corinthians 5:19 It was seen, also, that while Lucifer had opened the door for the entrance of sin by his desire for honor and supremacy, Christ had, in order to destroy sin, humbled Himself and become obedient unto death.

God had manifested His abhorrence of the principles of rebellion. All heaven saw His justice revealed, both in the condemnation of Satan and in the redemption of man. Lucifer had declared that if the law of God was changeless, and its penalty could not be remitted, every transgressor must be forever debarred from the Creator's favor. He had claimed that the sinful race were placed beyond redemption and were therefore his rightful prey. But the death of Christ was an argument in man's behalf that could not be overthrown. The penalty of the law fell upon Him who was equal with God, and man was free to accept the righteousness of Christ and by a life of penitence and humiliation to triumph, as the Son of God had triumphed, over the power of Satan. Thus God is just and yet the justifier of all who believe in Jesus.

But it was not merely to accomplish the redemption of man that Christ came to the earth to suffer and to die. He came to »magnify the law« and to »make it honorable.« Not alone that the inhabitants of this world might regard the law as it should be regarded; but it was to demonstrate to all the worlds of the universe that God's law is unchangeable. Could its claims have been set aside, then the Son of God need not have yielded up His life to atone for its transgression. The death of Christ proves it immutable. And the sacrifice to which infinite love impelled the Father and the Son, that sinners might be redeemed, demonstrates to all the universe – what nothing less than this plan of atonement could have sufficed to do – that justice and mercy are the foundation of the law and government of God. In the final execution of the judgment it will be seen that no cause for sin exists. When the Judge of all the earth shall demand of Satan, »Why hast thou rebelled against Me, and robbed Me of the subjects of My kingdom?« the originator of evil can render no excuse. Every mouth will be stopped, and all the hosts of rebellion will be speechless.

The cross of Calvary, while it declares the law immutable, proclaims to the universe that the wages of sin is death. In the Saviour's expiring cry, »It is finished,« the death knell of Satan was rung. The great controversy which had been so long in progress was then decided, and the final eradication of evil was made certain. The Son of God passed through the portals of the tomb, that »through death He might destroy him that had the power of death, that is, the devil.« Hebrews 2:14 Lucifer's desire for self-exaltation had led him to say: »I will exalt my throne above the stars of God: ... I will be like the Most High.« God declares: »I will bring thee to ashes upon the earth, ... and never shalt thou be any more.« Isaiah 14:13-14; Ezekiel 28:18-19 When »the day cometh, that shall burn as an oven; ... all the proud, yea, and all that do wickedly, shall be stubble: and the day that cometh shall burn them up, saith the Lord of hosts, that it shall leave them neither root nor branch.« Malachi 4:1

The whole universe will have become witnesses to the nature and results of sin. And its utter extermination, which in the beginning would have brought fear to angels and dishonor to God, will now vindicate His love and establish His honor before the [504/505] universe of beings who delight to do His will, and in whose heart is His law. Never will evil again be manifest. Says the word of God: »Affliction shall not rise up the second time.« Nahum 1:9 The law of God, which Satan has reproached as the yoke of bondage, will be honored as the law of liberty. A tested and proved creation will never again be turned from allegiance to Him whose character has been fully manifested before them as fathomless love and infinite wisdom.

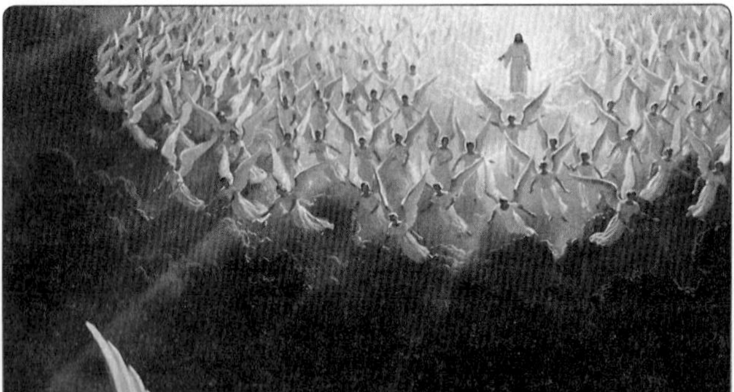

Satan and his Angels were cast out of Heaven (Revelation 12, 7-12)

CHAPTER 30

ENMITY BETWEEN MAN AND SATAN

I will put enmity between thee and the woman, and between thy seed and her seed; it shall bruise thy head, and thou shalt bruise his heel.« Genesis 3:15 The divine sentence pronounced against Satan after the fall of man was also a prophecy, embracing all the ages to the close of time and foreshadowing the great conflict to engage all the races of men who should live upon the earth.

God declares: »I will put enmity.« This enmity is not naturally entertained. When man transgressed the divine law, his nature became evil, and he was in harmony, and not at variance, with Satan. There exists naturally no enmity between sinful man and the originator of sin. Both became evil through apostasy. The apostate is never at rest, except as he obtains sympathy and support by inducing others to follow his example.

For this reason fallen angels and wicked men unite in desperate companionship. Had not God specially interposed, Satan and man would have entered into an alliance against Heaven; and instead of cherishing enmity against Satan, the whole human family would have been united in opposition to God.

Satan tempted man to sin, as he had caused angels to rebel, that he might thus secure co-operation in his warfare against Heaven. There was no dissension between himself and the fallen angels as regards their hatred of Christ; while on all other points there was discord, they were firmly united in opposing the authority of the Ruler of the universe. But when Satan heard the declaration that enmity should exist between himself and the woman, and between his seed and her seed, he knew that his efforts to deprave human nature would be interrupted; that by some means man was to be enabled to resist his power.

Satan's enmity against the human race is kindled because, through Christ, they are the objects of God's love and mercy. He desires to thwart the divine plan for man's redemption, to cast dishonor upon God, by defacing and defiling His handiwork; he would cause grief in heaven and fill the earth with woe and desolation. And he points to all this evil as the result of God's work in creating man.

It is the grace that Christ implants in the soul which creates in man enmity against Satan. Without this converting grace and renewing power, man would continue the captive of Satan, a servant ever ready to do his bidding. But the new principle in the soul creates conflict where hitherto had been peace. The power which Christ imparts enables man to resist the tyrant and usurper. Whoever is seen to abhor sin instead of loving it, whoever resists and conquers those passions that have held sway within, displays the operation of a principle wholly from above.

The antagonism that exists between the spirit of Christ and the spirit of Satan was most strikingly displayed in the world's reception of Jesus. It was not so much because He appeared without worldly wealth, pomp, or grandeur that the Jews were led to reject Him. They saw that He possessed power which would more than compensate for the lack of these outward advantages. But the purity and holiness of Christ called forth against Him the hatred of the ungodly. His life of self-denial and sinless devotion was a perpetual reproof to a proud, sensual people. It was this that evoked enmity against the Son of God. Satan and evil angels joined with evil men. All the energies of apostasy conspired against the Champion of truth.

The same enmity is manifested toward Christ's followers as was manifested toward their Master. Whoever sees the repulsive character of sin, and in strength from above resists temptation, will assuredly arouse the wrath of Satan and his subjects. Hatred of the pure principles of truth, and reproach and persecution of its advocates, will exist as long as sin and sinners remain. The followers of Christ and the servants of Satan cannot harmonize. The offense of the cross has not ceased. »All that will live godly in Christ Jesus shall suffer persecution.« 2 Timothy 3:12

Satan's agents are constantly working under his direction to establish his authority and build up his kingdom in opposition to the government of God. To this end they seek to deceive Christ's followers and allure them from their allegiance. Like their leader, they misconstrue and pervert the Scriptures to accomplish their object. As Satan endeavored to cast reproach upon God, so do his agents
 seek to malign God's people. The spirit which put

Christ to death moves the wicked to destroy His followers. All this is foreshadowed in that first prophecy: »I will put enmity between thee and the woman, and between thy seed and her seed.« And this will continue to the close of time.

Satan summons all his forces and throws his whole power into the combat. Why is it that he meets with no greater resistance? Why are the soldiers of Christ so sleepy and indifferent? Because they have so little real connection with Christ; because they are so destitute of His Spirit. Sin is not to them repulsive and abhorrent, as it was to their Master. They do not meet it, as did Christ, with decisive and determined resistance. They do not realize the exceeding evil and malignity of sin, and they are blinded both to the character and the power of the prince of darkness. There is little enmity against Satan and his works, because there is so great ignorance concerning his power and malice, and the vast extent of his warfare against Christ and His church. Multitudes are deluded here. They do not know that their enemy is a mighty general who controls the minds of evil angels, and that with well-matured plans and skillful movements he is warring against Christ to prevent the salvation of souls. Among professed Christians, and even among ministers of the gospel, there is heard scarcely a reference to Satan, except perhaps an incidental mention in the pulpit. They overlook the evidences of his continual activity and success; they neglect the many warnings of his subtlety; they seem to ignore his very existence.

While men are ignorant of his devices, this vigilant foe is upon their track every moment. He is intruding his presence in every department of the household, in every street of our cities, in the churches, in the national councils, in the courts of justice, perplexing, deceiving, seducing, everywhere ruining the souls and bodies of men, women, and children, breaking up families, sowing hatred, emulation, strife, sedition, murder. And the Christian world seem to regard these things as though God had appointed them and they must exist.

Satan is continually seeking to overcome the people of God by breaking down the barriers which separate them from the world. Ancient Israel were enticed into sin when they ventured into forbidden association with the heathen. In a similar manner are modern Israel led astray. »The God of this world hath blinded the minds of them which believe not, lest the light of the glorious gospel [507/508] of Christ, who is the image of God, should shine unto them.« 2 Corinthians 4:4 All who are not decided followers of Christ are servants of Satan. In the unregenerate heart there is love of sin and a disposition to cherish and excuse it. In the renewed heart there is hatred of sin and determined resistance against it. When Christians choose the society of the ungodly and unbelieving, they expose themselves to temptation. Satan conceals himself from view and stealthily draws his deceptive covering over their eyes. They cannot see that such company is calculated to do them harm; and while all the time assimilating to the world in character, words, and actions, they are becoming more and more blinded.

Conformity to worldly customs converts the church to the world; it never converts the world to Christ. Familiarity with sin will inevitably cause it to appear less repulsive. He who chooses to associate with the servants of Satan will soon cease to fear their master. When in the way of duty we are brought into trial, as was Daniel in the king's court, we may be sure that God will protect us; but if we place ourselves under temptation we shall fall sooner or later.

The tempter often works most successfully through those who are least suspected of being under his control. The possessors of talent and education are admired and honored, as if these qualities could atone for the absence of the fear of God or entitle men to His favor. Talent and culture, considered in themselves, are gifts of God; but when these are made to supply the place of piety, when, instead of bringing the soul nearer to God, they lead away from Him, then they become a curse and a snare. The opinion prevails with many that all which appears like courtesy or refinement must, in some sense, pertain to Christ. Never was there a greater mistake. These qualities should grace the character of every Christian, for they would exert a powerful influence in favor of true religion; but they must be consecrated to God, or they also are a power for evil. Many a man of cultured intellect and pleasant manners, who would not stoop to what is commonly regarded as an immoral act, is but a polished instrument in the hands of Satan. The insidious, deceptive character of his influence and example renders him a more dangerous enemy to the cause of Christ than are those who are ignorant and uncultured.

By earnest prayer and dependence upon God, Solomon obtained the wisdom which excited the wonder and admiration of the world. But when he turned from the Source of his strength, and went forward relying upon himself, he fell a prey to temptation. Then the marvelous powers bestowed on this wisest of kings only rendered him a more effective agent of the adversary of souls.

While Satan is constantly seeking to blind their minds to the fact, let Christians never forget that they »wrestle not against flesh and blood, but against principalities, against powers, against the rulers of the darkness of this world, against wicked spirits in high places.« Ephesians 6:12, margin The inspired warning is sounding down the centuries to our time: »Be sober, be vigilant; because your adversary the devil, as a roaring lion, walketh about, seeking whom he may devour.« 1 Peter 5:8 »Put on the whole armor of God, that ye may be able to stand against the wiles of the devil.« Ephesians 6:11

From the days of Adam to our own time, our great enemy has been exercising his power to oppress and destroy. He is now preparing for his last campaign against the church. All who seek to follow Jesus will be brought into conflict with this relentless foe. The more nearly the Christian imitates the divine Pattern, the more surely will he make himself a mark for the attacks of Satan. All who are actively engaged in the cause of God, seeking to unveil the deceptions of the evil one and to present Christ before the people, will be able to join in the testimony of Paul, in which he speaks of serving the Lord with all humility of mind, with many tears and temptations.

Satan assailed Christ with his fiercest and most subtle temptations, but he was repulsed in every conflict. Those battles were fought in our behalf; those victories make it possible for us to conquer. Christ will give strength to all who seek it. No man without his own consent can be overcome by Satan. The tempter has no power to control the will or to force the soul to sin. He may distress, but he cannot contaminate. He can cause agony, but not defilement. The fact that Christ has conquered should inspire His followers with courage to fight manfully the battle against sin and Satan.

Chapter 31

Agency of Evil Spirits

The connection of the visible with the invisible world, the ministration of angels of God, and the agency of evil spirits, are plainly revealed in the Scriptures, and inseparably interwoven with human history. There is a growing tendency to disbelief in the existence of evil spirits, while the holy angels that »minister for them who shall be heirs of salvation« Hebrews 1:14 are regarded by many as spirits of the dead. But the Scriptures not only teach the existence of angels, both good and evil, but present unquestionable proof that these are not disembodied spirits of dead men.

Before the creation of man, angels were in existence; for when the foundations of the earth were laid, »the morning stars sang together, and all the sons of God shouted for joy.« Job 38:7 After the fall of man, angels were sent to guard the tree of life, and this before a human being had died. Angels are in nature superior to men, for the psalmist says that man was made »a little lower than the angels.« Psalm 8:5

We are informed in Scripture as to the number, and the power and glory, of the heavenly beings, of their connection with the government of God, and also of their relation to the work of redemption. »The Lord hath prepared His throne in the heavens; and His kingdom ruleth over all.« And, says the prophet, »I heard the voice of many angels round about the throne.« In the presence chamber of the King of kings they wait – »angels, that excel in strength,« »ministers of His, that do His pleasure,« »hearkening unto the voice of His word.« Psalm 103:19-21; Revelation 5:11 Ten thousand times ten thousand and thousands of thousands, were the heavenly messengers beheld by the prophet Daniel. The apostle Paul declared them »an innumerable company.« Daniel 7:10; Hebrews 12:22 As God's messengers they go forth, like »the appearance of a flash of lightning,« Ezekiel 1:14 so dazzling their glory, and so swift their flight. The angel that appeared at the Saviour's tomb, his countenance »like lightning, and his raiment white as snow,« caused the keepers for fear of him to quake, and

they »became as dead men.« Matthew 28:3-4 When Sennacherib, the haughty Assyrian, reproached and blasphemed God, and threatened Israel with destruction, »it came to pass that night, that the angel of the Lord went out, and smote in the camp of the Assyrians an hundred fourscore and five thousand.« There were »cut off all the mighty men of valor, and the leaders and captains,« from the army of Sennacherib. »So he returned with shame of face to his own land.« 2 Kings 19:35; 2 Chronicles 32:21

Angels are sent on missions of mercy to the children of God. To Abraham, with promises of blessing; to the gates of Sodom, to rescue righteous Lot from its fiery doom; to Elijah, as he was about to perish from weariness and hunger in the desert; to Elisha, with chariots and horses of fire surrounding the little town where he was shut in by his foes; to Daniel, while seeking divine wisdom in the court of a heathen king, or abandoned to become the lions' prey; to Peter, doomed to death in Herod's dungeon; to the prisoners at Philippi; to Paul and his companions in the night of tempest on the sea; to open the mind of Cornelius to receive the gospel; to dispatch Peter with the message of salvation to the Gentile stranger – thus holy angels have, in all ages, ministered to God's people.

A guardian angel is appointed to every follower of Christ. These heavenly watchers shield the righteous from the power of the wicked one. This Satan himself recognized when he said: »Doth Job fear God for nought? Hast not Thou made an hedge about him, and about his house, and about all that he hath on every side?« Job 1:9-10 The agency by which God protects His people is presented in the words of the psalmist: »The angel of the Lord encampeth round about them that fear Him, and delivereth them.« Psalm 34:7 Said the Saviour, speaking of those that believe in Him: »Take heed that ye despise not one of these little ones; for I say unto you, That in heaven their angels do always behold the face of My Father.« Matthew 18:10 The angels appointed to minister to the children of God have at all times access to His presence.

Thus God's people, exposed to the deceptive power and unsleeping malice of the prince of darkness, and in conflict with all the forces of evil, are assured of the unceasing guardianship of heavenly angels. Nor is such assurance given without need. If God has granted to His children promise of grace and protection, it is because there are mighty agencies of evil to be met – agencies numerous, determined, and untiring, of whose malignity and power none can safely be ignorant or unheeding.

Evil spirits, in the beginning created sinless, were equal in nature, power, and glory with the holy beings that are now God's messengers. But fallen through sin, they are leagued together for the dishonor of God and the destruction of men. United with Satan in his rebellion, and with him cast out from heaven, they have, through all succeeding ages, co-operated with him in his warfare against the divine authority. We are told in Scripture of their confederacy and government, of their various orders, of their intelligence and subtlety, and of their malicious designs against the peace and happiness of men.

Old Testament history presents occasional mention of their existence and agency; but it was during the time when Christ was upon the earth that evil spirits manifested their power in the most striking manner. Christ had come to enter upon the plan devised for man's redemption, and Satan determined to assert his right to control the world. He had succeeded in establishing idolatry in every part of the earth except the land of Palestine. To the only land that had not fully yielded to the tempter's sway, Christ came to shed upon the people the light of heaven. Here two rival powers claimed supremacy. Jesus was stretching out His arms of love, inviting all who would to find pardon and peace in Him. The hosts of darkness saw that they did not possess unlimited control, and they understood that if Christ's mission should be successful, their rule was soon to end. Satan raged like a chained lion and defiantly exhibited his power over the bodies as well as the souls of men.

The fact that men have been possessed with demons, is clearly stated in the New Testament. The persons thus afflicted were not merely suffering with disease from natural causes. Christ had perfect understanding of that with which He was dealing, and He recognized the direct presence and agency of evil spirits.

A striking example of their number, power, and malignity, and also of the power and mercy of Christ, is given in the Scripture account of the healing of the demoniacs at Gadara. Those wretched maniacs, spurning all restraint, writhing, foaming, raging, were filling the air with their cries, doing violence to themselves, and endangering all who should approach them. Their bleeding and disfigured bodies and distracted minds presented a spectacle well pleasing to the prince of darkness. One of the demons controlling the sufferers declared: »My name is Legion: for we are many.« Mark 5:9 In the Roman army a legion consisted of from three to five thousand men. Satan's hosts also are marshaled in companies, and the single company to which these demons belonged numbered no less than a legion.

At the command of Jesus the evil spirits departed from their victims, leaving them calmly sitting at the Saviour's feet, subdued, intelligent, and gentle. But the demons were permitted to sweep a herd of swine into the sea; and to the dwellers of Gadara the loss of these outweighed the blessings which Christ had bestowed, and the divine Healer was entreated to depart. This was the result which Satan designed to secure. By casting the blame of their loss upon Jesus, he aroused the selfish fears of the people and prevented them from listening to His words. Satan is constantly accusing Christians as the cause of loss, misfortune, and suffering, instead of allowing the reproach to fall where it belongs – upon himself and his agents.

But the purposes of Christ were not thwarted. He allowed the evil spirits to destroy the herd of swine as a rebuke to those Jews who were raising these unclean beasts for the sake of gain. Had not Christ restrained the demons, they would have plunged into the sea, not only the swine, but also their keepers and owners. The preservation of both the keepers and the owners was due alone to His power, mercifully exercised for their deliverance. Furthermore, this event was permitted to take place that the disciples might witness the cruel power of Satan upon both man and beast. The Saviour desired His followers to have a knowledge of the foe whom they were to meet, that they might not be deceived and overcome by his devices. It was also His will that the people of that region should behold His power to break the bondage of Satan and release his captives. And though Jesus Himself departed, the men so marvelously delivered, remained to declare the mercy of their Benefactor.

Other instances of a similar nature are recorded in the Scriptures. The daughter of the Syrophoenician woman was grievously vexed with a devil, whom Jesus cast out by His word. Mark 7:26-30

»One possessed with a devil, blind, and dumb«; Matthew 12:22 a youth who had a dumb spirit, that ofttimes »cast him into the fire, and into the waters, to destroy him«; Mark 9:17-27 the maniac who, tormented by »a spirit of an unclean devil« Luke 4:33-36 disturbed the Sabbath quiet of the synagogue at Capernaum – all were healed by the compassionate Saviour. In nearly every instance, Christ addressed the demon as an intelligent entity, commanding him to come out of his victim and to torment him no more. The worshipers at Capernaum, beholding His mighty power, »were all amazed, and spake among themselves, saying, What a word is this! for with authority and power He commandeth the unclean spirits, and they come out.« Luke 4:36

Those possessed with devils are usually represented as being in a condition of great suffering; yet there were exceptions to this rule. For the sake of obtaining supernatural power, some welcomed the satanic influence. These of course had no conflict with the demons. Of this class were those who possessed the spirit of divination, – Simon Magus, Elymas the sorcerer, and the damsel who followed Paul and Silas at Philippi. None are in greater danger from the influence of evil spirits than those who, notwithstanding the direct and

King Saul and the Witch of Endor (1 Samuel 28.7 to 25)

ample testimony of the Scriptures, deny the existence and agency of the devil and his angels. So long as we are ignorant of their wiles, they have almost inconceivable advantage; many give heed to their suggestions while they suppose themselves to be following the dictates of their own wisdom. This is why, as we approach the close of time, when Satan is to work with greatest power to deceive and destroy, he spreads everywhere the belief that he does not exist. It is his policy to conceal himself and his manner of working.

There is nothing that the great deceiver fears so much as that we shall become acquainted with his devices. The better to disguise his real character and purposes, he has caused himself to be so represented as to excite no stronger emotion than ridicule or contempt. He is well pleased to be painted as a ludicrous or loathsome object, misshapen, half animal and half human. He is pleased to hear his name used in sport and mockery by those who think themselves intelligent and well informed. It is because he has masked himself with consummate skill that the question is so widely asked: "Does such a being really exist?" It is an evidence of his success that theories giving the lie to the plainest testimony of the Scriptures are so generally received in the religious world. And it is because Satan can most readily control the minds of those who are unconscious of his influence, that the word of God gives us so many examples of his malignant work, unveiling before us his secret forces, and thus placing us on our guard against his assaults.

The power and malice of Satan and his host might justly alarm us were it not that we may find shelter and deliverance in the superior power of our Redeemer. We carefully secure our houses with bolts and locks to protect our property and our lives from evil men; but we seldom think of the evil angels who are constantly seeking access to us, and against whose attacks we have, in our own strength, no method of defense. If permitted, they can distract our minds, disorder and torment our bodies, destroy our possessions and our lives. Their only delight is in misery and destruction. Fearful is the condition of those who resist the divine claims and yield to Satan's temptations, until God gives them up to the control of evil spirits. But those who follow Christ are ever safe under His watchcare. Angels that excel in strength are sent from heaven to protect them. The wicked one cannot break through the guard which God has stationed about His people.

Chapter 32

Snares of Satan

The great controversy between Christ and Satan, that has been carried forward for nearly six thousand years, is soon to close; and the wicked one redoubles his efforts to defeat the work of Christ in man's behalf and to fasten souls in his snares. To hold the people in darkness and impenitence till the Saviour's mediation is ended, and there is no longer a sacrifice for sin, is the object which he seeks to accomplish.

When there is no special effort made to resist his power, when indifference prevails in the church and the world, Satan is not concerned; for he is in no danger of losing those whom he is leading captive at his will. But when the attention is called to eternal things, and souls are inquiring, »What must I do to be saved?« he is on the ground, seeking to match his power against the power of Christ and to counteract the influence of the Holy Spirit.

The Scriptures declare that upon one occasion, when the angels of God came to present themselves before the Lord, Satan came also among them, Job 1:6 not to bow before the Eternal King, but to further his own malicious designs against the righteous. With the same object he is in attendance when men assemble for the worship of God. Though hidden from sight, he is working with all diligence to control the minds of the worshipers. Like a skillful general he lays his plans beforehand. As he sees the messenger of God searching the Scriptures, he takes note of the subject to be presented to the people. Then he employs all his cunning and shrewdness so to control circumstances that the message may not reach those whom he is deceiving on that very point. The one who most needs the warning will be urged into some business transaction which requires his presence, or will by some other means be prevented from hearing the words that might prove to him a savor of life unto life.

Again, Satan sees the Lord's servants burdened because of the spiritual darkness that enshrouds the people. He hears their earnest prayers for divine grace and power to break the spell of indifference, carelessness, and indolence. Then with renewed zeal he plies his arts. He tempts men to the indulgence of appetite or to some other form of self-gratification, and thus benumbs their sensibilities so that they fail to hear the very things which they most need to learn.

Satan well knows that all whom he can lead to neglect prayer and the searching of the Scriptures, will be overcome by his attacks. Therefore he invents every possible device to engross the mind. There has ever been a class professing godliness, who, instead of following on to know the truth, make it their religion to seek some fault of character or error of faith in those with whom they do not agree. Such are Satan's right-hand helpers. Accusers of the brethren are not few, and they are always active when God is at work and His servants are rendering Him true homage. They will put a false coloring upon the words and acts of those who love and obey the truth. They will represent the most earnest, zealous, self-denying servants of Christ as deceived or deceivers. It is their work to misrepresent the motives of every true and noble deed, to circulate insinuations, and arouse suspicion in the minds of the inexperienced. In every conceivable manner they will seek to cause that which is pure and righteous to be regarded as foul and deceptive.

But none need be deceived concerning them. It may be readily seen whose children they are, whose example they follow, and whose work they do. »Ye shall know them by their fruits.« Matthew 7:16 Their course resembles that of Satan, the envenomed slanderer, »the accuser of our brethren.« Revelation 12:10

The great deceiver has many agents ready to present any and every kind of error to ensnare souls – heresies prepared to suit the varied tastes and capacities of those whom he would ruin. It is his plan to bring into the church insincere, unregenerate elements that will encourage doubt and unbelief, and hinder all who desire to see the work of God advance and to advance with it. Many who have no real faith in God or in His word assent to some principles of truth and pass as Christians, and thus they are enabled to introduce their errors as Scriptural doctrines.

The position that it is of no consequence what men believe is one of Satan's most successful deceptions. He knows that the truth, received in the love of it, sanctifies the soul of the receiver; therefore he is constantly seeking to substitute false theories, fables, another gospel. From the beginning the servants of God have contended against false teachers, not merely as vicious men, but as inculcators of falsehoods that were fatal to the soul. Elijah, Jeremiah, Paul, firmly and fearlessly opposed those who were turning men from the word of God. That liberality which regards a correct religious faith as unimportant found no favor with these holy defenders of the truth.

The vague and fanciful interpretations of Scripture, and the many conflicting theories concerning religious faith, that are found in the Christian world are the work of our great adversary to confuse minds so that they shall not discern the truth. And the discord and division which exist among the churches of Christendom are in a great measure due to the prevailing custom of wresting the Scriptures to support a favorite theory. Instead of carefully studying God's word with humility of heart to obtain a knowledge of His will, many seek only to discover something odd or original. In order to sustain erroneous doctrines or unchristian practices, some will seize upon passages of Scripture separated from the context, perhaps quoting half of a single verse as proving their point, when the remaining portion would show the meaning to be quite the opposite. With the cunning of the serpent they entrench themselves behind disconnected utterances construed to suit their carnal desires. Thus do many willfully pervert the word of God. Others, who have an active imagination, seize upon the figures and symbols of Holy Writ, interpret them to suit their fancy, with little regard to the testimony of Scripture as its own interpreter, and then they present their vagaries as the teachings of the Bible. Whenever the study of the Scriptures is entered upon without a prayerful, humble, teachable spirit, the plainest and simplest as well as the most difficult passages will be wrested from their true meaning. The papal leaders select such portions of Scripture as best serve their purpose, interpret to suit themselves, and then present these to the people, while they deny them the privilege of studying the Bible and understanding its sacred truths for themselves. The whole Bible should be given to the people just as it reads. It would be better for them not to have Bible instruction at all than to have the teaching of the Scriptures thus grossly misrepresented.

The Bible was designed to be a guide to all who wish to become acquainted with the will of their Maker. God gave to men the sure word of prophecy; angels and even Christ Himself came to make known to Daniel and John the things that must shortly come to pass.

 Those important matters that concern our salvation

were not left involved in mystery. They were not revealed in such a way as to perplex and mislead the honest seeker after truth. Said the Lord by the prophet Habakkuk: »Write the vision, and make it plain, ... that he may run that readeth it.« Habakkuk 2:2 The word of God is plain to all who study it with a prayerful heart. Every truly honest soul will come to the light of truth. »Light is sown for the righteous.« Psalm 97:11 And no church can advance in holiness unless its members are earnestly seeking for truth as for hid treasure.

By the cry, Liberality, men are blinded to the devices of their adversary, while he is all the time working steadily for the accomplishment of his object. As he succeeds in supplanting the Bible by human speculations, the law of God is set aside, and the churches are under the bondage of sin while they claim to be free.

To many, scientific research has become a curse. God has permitted a flood of light to be poured upon the world in discoveries in science and art; but even the greatest minds, if not guided by the word of God in their research, become bewildered in their attempts to investigate the relations of science and revelation.

Human knowledge of both material and spiritual things is partial and imperfect; therefore many are unable to harmonize their views of science with Scripture statements. Many accept mere theories and speculations as scientific facts, and they think that God's word is to be tested by the teachings of »science falsely so called.« 1 Timothy 6:20 The Creator and His works are beyond their comprehension; and because they cannot explain these by natural laws, Bible history is regarded as unreliable. Those who doubt the reliability of the records of the Old and New Testaments too often go a step further and doubt the existence of God and attribute infinite power to nature. Having let go their anchor, they are left to beat about upon the rocks of infidelity.

Thus many err from the faith and are seduced by the devil. Men have endeavored to be wiser than their Creator; human philosophy has attempted to search out and explain mysteries which will never be revealed through the eternal ages. If men would but search and understand what God had made known of Himself and His purposes, they would obtain such a view of the glory, majesty, and power of Jehovah that they would realize their own littleness and would be content with that which has been revealed for themselves and their children.

It is a masterpiece of Satan's deceptions to keep the minds of men searching and conjecturing in regard to that which God has not made known and which He does not intend that we shall understand. It was thus that Lucifer lost his place in heaven. He became dissatisfied because all the secrets of God's purposes were not confided to him, and he entirely disregarded that which was revealed concerning his own work in the lofty position assigned him. By arousing the same discontent in the angels under his command, he caused their fall. Now he seeks to imbue the minds of men with the same spirit and to lead them also to disregard the direct commands of God.

Those who are unwilling to accept the plain, cutting truths of the Bible are continually seeking for pleasing fables that will quiet the conscience. The less spiritual, self-denying, and humiliating the doctrines presented, the greater the favor with which they are received. These persons degrade the intellectual powers to serve their carnal desires. Too wise in their own conceit to search the Scriptures with contrition of soul and earnest prayer for divine guidance, they have no shield from delusion. Satan is ready to supply the heart's desire, and he palms off his deceptions in the place of truth. It was thus that the papacy gained its power over the minds of men; and by rejection of the truth because it involves a cross, Protestants are following the same path. All who neglect the word of God to study convenience and policy, that they may not be at variance with the world, will be left to receive damnable heresy for religious truth. Every conceivable form of error will be accepted by those who willfully reject the truth. He who looks with horror upon one deception will readily receive another. The apostle Paul, speaking of a class who »received not the love of the truth, that they might be saved,« declares: »For this cause God shall send them strong delusion, that they should believe a lie: that they all might be damned who believed not the truth, but had pleasure in unrighteousness.« 2 Thessalonians 2:10-12 With such a warning before us it behooves us to be on our guard as to what doctrines we receive.

Among the most successful agencies of the great deceiver are the delusive teachings and lying wonders of spiritualism. Disguised as an angel of light, he spreads his nets where least suspected. If men would but study the Book of God with earnest prayer that they might understand it, they would not be left in darkness to receive false doctrines. But as they reject the truth they fall a prey to deception.

Another dangerous error is the doctrine that denies the deity of Christ, claiming that He had no existence before His advent to this world. This theory is received with favor by a large class who profess to believe the Bible; yet it directly contradicts the plainest statements of our Saviour concerning His relationship with the Father, His divine character, and His pre-existence. It cannot be entertained without the most unwarranted wresting of the Scriptures. It not only lowers man's conceptions of the work of redemption, but undermines faith in the Bible as a revelation from God. While this renders it the more dangerous, it makes it also harder to meet. If men reject the testimony of the inspired Scriptures concerning the deity of Christ, it is in vain to argue the point with them; for no argument, however conclusive, could convince them. »The natural man receiveth not the things of the Spirit of God: for they are foolishness unto him: neither can he know them, because they are spiritually discerned.« 1 Corinthians 2:14 None who hold this error can have a true conception of the character or the mission of Christ, or of the great plan of God for man's redemption.

Still another subtle and mischievous error is the fast-spreading belief that Satan has no existence as a personal being; that the name is used in Scripture merely to represent men's evil thoughts and desires. The teaching so widely echoed from popular pulpits, that the second advent of Christ is His coming to each individual at death, is a device to divert the minds of men from His personal coming in the clouds of heaven. For years Satan has thus been saying, »Behold, He is in the secret chambers«; Matthew 24:23-26 and many souls have been lost by accepting this deception.

Again, worldly wisdom teaches that prayer is not essential. Men of science claim that there can be no real answer to prayer; that this would be a violation of law, a miracle, and that miracles have no existence. The universe, say they, is governed by fixed laws, and God Himself does nothing contrary to these laws. Thus they represent God as bound by His own laws – as if the operation of divine laws could exclude divine freedom. Such teaching is opposed to the testimony of the Scriptures. Were not miracles wrought by Christ and His apostles? The same compassionate Saviour lives today, and He is as willing to listen to the prayer of faith as when He walked visibly among men. The natural cooperates with the supernatural. It is a part of God's plan to grant us, in answer to the prayer of faith, that which He would not bestow did we not thus ask. Innumerable are the erroneous doctrines and fanciful ideas that are obtaining among the churches of Christendom. It is impossible to estimate the evil results of removing one of the landmarks fixed by the word of God. Few who venture to do this stop with the rejection of a single truth. The majority continue to set aside one after another of the principles of truth, until they become actual infidels.

The errors of popular theology have driven many a soul to skepticism who might otherwise have been a believer in the Scriptures. It is impossible for him to accept doctrines which outrage his sense of justice, mercy, and benevolence; and since these are represented as the teaching of the Bible, he refuses to receive it as the word of God.

And this is the object which Satan seeks to accomplish. There is nothing that he desires more than to destroy confidence in God and in His word. Satan stands at the head of the great army of doubters, and he works to the utmost of his power to beguile souls into his ranks. It is becoming fashionable to doubt. There is a large class by whom the word of God is looked upon with distrust for the same reason as was its Author – because it reproves and condemns sin. Those who are unwilling to obey its requirements endeavor to overthrow its authority. They read the Bible, or listen to its teachings as presented from the sacred desk, merely to find fault with the Scriptures or with the sermon. Not a few become infidels in order to justify or excuse themselves in neglect of duty. Others adopt skeptical principles from pride and indolence. Too ease-loving to distinguish themselves by accomplishing anything worthy of honor, which requires effort and self-denial, they aim to secure a reputation for superior wisdom by criticizing the Bible. There is much which the finite mind, unenlightened by divine wisdom, is powerless to comprehend; and thus they find occasion to criticize. There are many who seem to feel that it is a virtue to stand on the side of unbelief, skepticism, and infidelity. But underneath an appearance of candor it will be found that such persons are actuated by self-confidence and pride. Many delight in finding something in the Scriptures to puzzle the minds of others. Some at first criticize and reason on the wrong side, from a mere love of controversy. They do not realize that they are thus entangling themselves in the snare of the fowler. But having openly expressed unbelief, they feel that they must maintain their position. Thus they unite with the ungodly and close to themselves the gates of Paradise.

God has given in His word sufficient evidence of its divine character. The great truths which concern our redemption are clearly presented. By the aid of the Holy Spirit, which is promised to all who seek it in sincerity, every man may understand these truths for himself. God has granted to men a strong foundation upon which to rest their faith. Yet the finite minds of men are inadequate fully to comprehend the plans and purposes of the Infinite One. We can never by searching find out God. We must not attempt to lift with presumptuous hand the curtain behind which He veils His majesty. The apostle exclaims: »How unsearchable are His judgments, and His ways past finding out!« Romans 11:33 We can so far comprehend His dealings with us, and the motives by which He is actuated, that we may discern boundless love and mercy united to infinite power. Our Father in heaven orders everything in wisdom and righteousness, and we are not to be dissatisfied and distrustful, but to bow in reverent submission.

He will reveal to us as much of His purposes as it is for our good to know, and beyond that we must trust the Hand that is omnipotent, the Heart that is full of love. While God has given ample evidence for faith, He will never remove all excuse for unbelief. All who look for hooks to hang their doubts upon will find them. And those who refuse to accept and obey God's word until every objection has been removed, and there is no longer an opportunity for doubt, will never come to the light. Distrust of God is the natural outgrowth of the unrenewed heart, which is at enmity with Him. But faith is inspired by the Holy Spirit, and it will flourish only as it is cherished. No man can become strong in faith without a determined effort. Unbelief strengthens as it is encouraged; and if men, instead of dwelling upon the evidences which God has given to sustain their faith, permit themselves to question and cavil, they will find their doubts constantly becoming more confirmed. But those who doubt God's promises and distrust the assurance of His grace are dishonoring Him; and their influence, instead of drawing others to Christ, tends to repel them from Him. They are unproductive trees, that spread their dark branches far and wide, shutting away the sunlight from other plants, and causing them to droop and die under the chilling shadow. The lifework of these persons will appear as a never-ceasing witness against them. They are sowing seeds of doubt and skepticism that will yield an unfailing harvest.

There is but one course for those to pursue who honestly desire to be freed from doubts. Instead of questioning and caviling concerning that which they do not understand, let them give heed to the light which already shines upon them, and they will receive greater light. Let them do every duty which has been made plain to their understanding, and they will be enabled to understand and perform those of which they are now in doubt. Satan can present a counterfeit so closely resembling the truth that it deceives those who are willing to be deceived, who desire to shun the self-denial and sacrifice demanded by the truth; but it is impossible for him to hold under his power one soul who honestly desires, at whatever cost, to know the truth. Christ is the truth and the »Light, which lighteth every man that cometh into the world.« John 1:9 The Spirit of truth has been sent to guide men into all truth. And upon the authority of the Son of God it is declared: »Seek, and ye shall find.« »If any man will do His will, he shall know of the doctrine.« Matthew 7:7; John 7:17

The followers of Christ know little of the plots which Satan and his hosts are forming against them. But He who sitteth in the heavens will overrule all these devices for the accomplishment of His deep designs. The Lord permits His people to be subjected to the fiery ordeal of temptation, not because He takes pleasure in their distress and affliction, but because this process is essential to their final victory. He could not, consistently with His own glory, shield them from temptation; for the very object of the trial is to prepare them to resist all the allurements of evil.

Neither wicked men nor devils can hinder the work of God, or shut out His presence from His people, if they will, with subdued, contrite hearts, confess and put away their sins, and in faith claim His promises. Every temptation, every opposing influence, whether open or secret, may be successfully resisted, »not by might, nor by power, but by My Spirit, saith the Lord of hosts.« Zechariah 4:6

»The eyes of the Lord are over the righteous, and His ears are open unto their prayers. ... And who is he that will harm you, if ye be followers of that which is good?« 1 Peter 3:12-13 When Balaam, allured by the promise of rich rewards, practiced enchantments against Israel, and by sacrifices to the Lord sought to invoke a curse upon His people, the Spirit of God forbade the evil which he longed to pronounce, and Balaam was forced to exclaim: »How shall I curse,

whom God hath not cursed? or how shall I defy, whom

the Lord hath not defied?« »Let me die the death of the righteous, and let my last end be like his!« When sacrifice had again been offered, the ungodly prophet declared: »Behold, I have received commandment to bless: and He hath blessed; and I cannot reverse it. He hath not beheld iniquity in Jacob, neither hath He seen perverseness in Israel: the Lord his God is with him, and the shout of a King is among them.« »Surely there is no enchantment against Jacob, neither is there any divination against Israel: according to this time it shall be said of Jacob and of Israel, What hath God wrought!« Yet a third time altars were erected, and again Balaam essayed to secure a curse. But from the unwilling lips of the prophet, the Spirit of God declared the prosperity of His chosen, and rebuked the folly and malice of their foes: »Blessed is he that blesseth thee, and cursed is he that curseth thee.« Numbers 23:8, 10, 20, 21, 23; 24:9

The people of Israel were at this time loyal to God; and so long as they continued in obedience to His law, no power in earth or hell could prevail against them. But the curse which Balaam had not been permitted to pronounce against God's people, he finally succeeded in bringing upon them by seducing them into sin. When they transgressed God's commandments, then they separated themselves from Him, and they were left to feel the power of the destroyer.

Satan is well aware that the weakest soul who abides in Christ is more than a match for the hosts of darkness, and that, should he reveal himself openly, he would be met and resisted. Therefore he seeks to draw away the soldiers of the cross from their strong fortification, while he lies in ambush with his forces, ready to destroy all who venture upon his ground. Only in humble reliance upon God, and obedience to all His commandments, can we be secure.

No man is safe for a day or an hour without prayer. Especially should we entreat the Lord for wisdom to understand His word. Here are revealed the wiles of the tempter and the means by which he may be successfully resisted. Satan is an expert in quoting Scripture, placing his own interpretation upon passages, by which he hopes to cause us to stumble. We should study the Bible with humility of heart, never losing sight of our dependence upon God. While we must constantly guard against the devices of Satan, we should pray in faith continually: »Lead us not into temptation.«

Chapter 33

The First Great Deception

With the earliest history of man, Satan began his efforts to deceive our race. He who had incited rebellion in heaven desired to bring the inhabitants of the earth to unite with him in his warfare against the government of God. Adam and Eve had been perfectly happy in obedience to the law of God, and this fact was a constant testimony against the claim which Satan had urged in heaven, that God's law was oppressive and opposed to the good of His creatures. And furthermore, Satan's envy was excited as he looked upon the beautiful home prepared for the sinless pair. He determined to cause their fall, that, having separated them from God and brought them under his own power, he might gain possession of the earth and here establish his kingdom in opposition to the Most High.

Had Satan revealed himself in his real character, he would have been repulsed at once, for Adam and Eve had been warned against this dangerous foe; but he worked in the dark, concealing his purpose, that he might more effectually accomplish his object. Employing as his medium the serpent, then a creature of fascinating appearance, he addressed himself to Eve: »Hath God said, Ye shall not eat of every tree of the garden?« Genesis 3:1 Had Eve refrained from entering into argument with the tempter, she would have been safe; but she ventured to parley with him and fell a victim to his wiles. It is thus that many are still overcome. They doubt and argue concerning the requirements of God; and instead of obeying the divine commands, they accept human theories, which but disguise the devices of Satan.

»The woman said unto the serpent, We may eat of the fruit of the trees of the garden: but of the fruit of the tree which is in the midst of the garden, God hath said, Ye shall not eat of it, neither shall ye touch it, lest ye die. And the serpent said unto the woman, Ye shall not surely die: for God doth know that in the day ye eat thereof, then your eyes shall be opened, and ye shall be as gods, knowing good and evil.« Verses 2-5 He declared that they would become like God, possessing greater wisdom than before and being capable of a higher state of existence. Eve yielded to temptation; and through her influence, Adam was led into sin. They accepted the words of the serpent, that God did not mean what He said; they distrusted their Creator and imagined that He was restricting their liberty and that they might obtain great wisdom and exaltation by transgressing His law.

But what did Adam, after his sin, find to be the meaning of the words, »In the day that thou eatest thereof thou shalt surely die«? Did he find them to mean, as Satan had led him to believe, that he was to be ushered into a more exalted state of existence? Then indeed there was great good to be gained by transgression, and Satan was proved to be a benefactor of the race. But Adam did not find this to be the meaning of the divine sentence. God declared that as a penalty for his sin, man should return to the ground whence he was taken: »Dust thou art, and unto dust shalt thou return.« Verse 19 The words of Satan, »Your eyes shall be opened,« proved to be true in this sense only: After Adam and Eve had disobeyed God, their eyes were opened to discern their folly; they did know evil, and they tasted the bitter fruit of transgression.

In the midst of Eden grew the tree of life, whose fruit had the power of perpetuating life. Had Adam remained obedient to God, he would have continued to enjoy free access to this tree and would have lived forever. But when he sinned he was cut off from partaking of the tree of life, and he became subject to death. The divine sentence, »Dust thou art, and unto dust shalt thou return,« points to the utter extinction of life.

Immortality, promised to man on condition of obedience, had been forfeited by transgression. Adam could not transmit to his posterity that which he did not possess; and there could have been no hope for the fallen race had not God, by the sacrifice of His Son, brought immortality within their reach. While »death passed upon all men, for that all have sinned,« Christ »hath brought life and immortality to light through the gospel.« Romans 5:12; 2 Timothy 1:10 And only through Christ can immortality be obtained. Said Jesus: »He that believeth on the Son hath everlasting life: and he that believeth not the Son shall not see life.« John 3:36 Every man may come into possession of this priceless blessing if he will comply with the conditions. All »who by patient continuance in well-doing seek for glory and honor and immortality,« will receive »eternal life.« Romans 2:7

The only one who promised Adam life in disobedience was the great deceiver. And the declaration of the serpent to Eve in Eden – »Ye shall not surely die« – was the first sermon ever preached upon the immortality of the soul. Yet this declaration, resting solely upon the authority of Satan, is echoed from the pulpits of Christendom and is received by the majority of mankind as readily as it was received by our first parents. The divine sentence, »The soul that sinneth, it shall die«, Ezekiel 18:20 is made to mean: The soul that sinneth, it shall not die, but live eternally. We cannot but wonder at the strange infatuation which renders men so credulous concerning the words of Satan and so unbelieving in regard to the words of God. Had man after his fall been allowed free access to the tree of life, he would have lived forever, and thus sin would have been immortalized. But cherubim and a flaming sword kept »the way of the tree of life«, Genesis 3:24 and not one of the family of Adam has been permitted to pass that barrier and partake of the life-giving fruit. Therefore there is not an immortal sinner.

But after the Fall, Satan bade his angels make a special effort to inculcate the belief in man's natural immortality; and having induced the people to receive this error, they were to lead them on to conclude that the sinner would live in eternal misery. Now the prince of darkness, working through his agents, represents God as a revengeful tyrant, declaring that He plunges into hell all those who do not please Him, and causes them ever to feel His wrath; and that while they suffer unutterable anguish and writhe in the eternal flames, their Creator looks down upon them with satisfaction.

Thus the archfiend clothes with his own attributes the Creator and Benefactor of mankind. Cruelty is satanic. God is love; and all that He created was pure, holy, and lovely, until sin was brought in by the first great rebel. Satan himself is the enemy who tempts man to sin, and then destroys him if he can; and when he has made sure of his victim, then he exults in the ruin he has wrought. If permitted, he would sweep the entire race into his net. Were it not for the interposition of divine power, not one son or daughter of Adam would escape. Satan is seeking to overcome men today, as he overcame our first parents, by shaking their confidence in their Creator and leading them to doubt the wisdom of His government and the justice of His laws. Satan and his emissaries represent God as even worse than themselves, in

 order to justify their own malignity and rebellion. The

great deceiver endeavors to shift his own horrible cruelty of character upon our heavenly Father, that he may cause himself to appear as one greatly wronged by his expulsion from heaven because he would not submit to so unjust a governor. He presents before the world the liberty which they may enjoy under his mild sway, in contrast with the bondage imposed by the stern decrees of Jehovah. Thus he succeeds in luring souls away from their allegiance to God.

How repugnant to every emotion of love and mercy, and even to our sense of justice, is the doctrine that the wicked dead are tormented with fire and brimstone in an eternally burning hell; that for the sins of a brief earthly life they are to suffer torture as long as God shall live. Yet this doctrine has been widely taught and is still embodied in many of the creeds of Christendom. Said a learned doctor of divinity: »The sight of hell torments will exalt the happiness of the saints forever. When they see others who are of the same nature and born under the same circumstances, plunged in such misery, and they so distinguished, it will make them sensible of how happy they are.« Another used these words: »While the decree of reprobation is eternally executing on the vessels of wrath, the smoke of their torment will be eternally ascending in view of the vessels of mercy, who, instead of taking the part of these miserable objects, will say, Amen, Alleluia! praise ye the Lord!«

Where, in the pages of God's word, is such teaching to be found? Will the redeemed in heaven be lost to all emotions of pity and compassion, and even to feelings of common humanity? Are these to be exchanged for the indifference of the stoic or the cruelty of the savage? No, no; such is not the teaching of the Book of God. Those who present the views expressed in the quotations given above may be learned and even honest men, but they are deluded by the sophistry of Satan. He leads them to misconstrue strong expressions of Scripture, giving to the language the coloring of bitterness and malignity which pertains to himself, but not to our Creator. »As I live, saith the Lord God, I have no pleasure in the death of the wicked; but that the wicked turn from his way and live: turn ye, turn ye from your evil ways; for why will ye die?« Ezekiel 33:11

What would be gained to God should we admit that He delights in witnessing unceasing tortures; that He is regaled with the groans and shrieks and imprecations of the suffering creatures whom He holds in the flames of hell? Can these horrid sounds [535/536] be music in the ear of Infinite Love? It is urged that the infliction of endless misery upon the wicked would show God's hatred of sin as an evil which is ruinous to the peace and order of the universe. Oh, dreadful blasphemy! As if God's hatred of sin is the reason why it is perpetuated. For, according to the teachings of these theologians, continued torture without hope of mercy maddens its wretched victims, and as they pour out their rage in curses and blasphemy, they are forever augmenting their load of guilt. God's glory is not enhanced by thus perpetuating continually increasing sin through ceaseless ages.

It is beyond the power of the human mind to estimate the evil which has been wrought by the heresy of eternal torment. The religion of the Bible, full of love and goodness, and abounding in compassion, is darkened by superstition and clothed with terror. When we consider in what false colors Satan has painted the character of God, can we wonder that our merciful Creator is feared, dreaded, and even hated? The appalling views of God which have spread over the world from the teachings of the pulpit have made thousands, yes, millions, of skeptics and infidels.

The theory of eternal torment is one of the false doctrines that constitute the wine of the abomination of Babylon, of which she makes all nations drink. Revelation 14:8; 17:2 That ministers of Christ should have accepted this heresy and proclaimed it from the sacred desk is indeed a mystery. They received it from Rome, as they received the false sabbath. True, it has been taught by great and good men; but the light on this subject had not come to them as it has come to us. They were responsible only for the light which shone in their time; we are accountable for that which shines in our day. If we turn from the testimony of God's word, and accept false doctrines because our fathers taught them, we fall under the condemnation pronounced upon Babylon; we are drinking of the wine of her abomination.

A large class to whom the doctrine of eternal torment is revolting are driven to the opposite error. They see that the Scriptures represent God as a being of love and compassion, and they cannot believe that He will consign His creatures to the fires of an eternally burning hell. But holding that the soul is naturally immortal, they see no alternative but to conclude that all mankind will finally be saved. Many

regard the threatenings of the Bible as designed merely

to frighten men into obedience, and not to be literally fulfilled. Thus the sinner can live in selfish pleasure, disregarding the requirements of God, and yet expect to be finally received into His favor. Such a doctrine, presuming upon God's mercy, but ignoring His justice, pleases the carnal heart and emboldens the wicked in their iniquity. To show how believers in universal salvation wrest the Scriptures to sustain their soul-destroying dogmas, it is needful only to cite their own utterances. At the funeral of an irreligious young man, who had been killed instantly by an accident, a Universalist minister selected as his text the Scripture statement concerning David: »He was comforted concerning Amnon, seeing he was dead.« 2 Samuel 13:39

»I am frequently asked,« said the speaker, »what will be the fate of those who leave the world in sin, die, perhaps, in a state of inebriation, die with the scarlet stains of crime unwashed from their robes, or die as this young man died, having never made a profession or enjoyed an experience of religion. We are content with the Scriptures; their answer shall solve the awful problem. Amnon was exceedingly sinful; he was unrepentant, he was made drunk, and while drunk was killed. David was a prophet of God; he must have known whether it would be ill or well for Amnon in the world to come. What were the expressions of his heart? 'The soul of King David longed to go forth unto Absalom: for he was comforted concerning Amnon, seeing he was dead.'« Verse 39

»And what is the inference to be deduced from this language? Is it not that endless suffering formed no part of his religious belief? So we conceive; and here we discover a triumphant argument in support of the more pleasing, more enlightened, more benevolent hypothesis of ultimate universal purity and peace. He was comforted, seeing his son was dead. And why so? Because by the eye of prophecy he could look forward into the glorious future and see that son far removed from all temptations, released from the bondage and purified from the corruptions of sin, and after being made sufficiently holy and enlightened, admitted to the assembly of ascended and rejoicing spirits. His only comfort was that, in being removed from the present state of sin and suffering, his beloved son had gone where the loftiest breathings of the Holy Spirit would be shed upon his darkened soul, where his mind would be unfolded to the wisdom of heaven and the sweet raptures of immortal love, and thus prepared with a sanctified nature to enjoy the rest and society of the heavenly inheritance. In these thoughts we would be understood to believe that the salvation of heaven depends upon nothing which we can do in this life; neither upon a present change of heart, nor upon present belief, or a present profession of religion.« Thus does the professed minister of Christ reiterate the falsehood uttered by the serpent in Eden: »Ye shall not surely die.« »In the day ye eat thereof, then your eyes shall be opened, and ye shall be as gods.« He declares that the vilest of sinners – the murderer, the thief, and the adulterer – will after death be prepared to enter into immortal bliss.

And from what does this perverter of the Scriptures draw his conclusions? From a single sentence expressing David's submission to the dispensation of Providence. His soul »longed to go forth unto Absalom; for he was comforted concerning Amnon, seeing he was dead.« The poignancy of his grief having been softened by time, his thoughts turned from the dead to the living son, self-banished through fear of the just punishment of his crime. And this is the evidence that the incestuous, drunken Amnon was at death immediately transported to the abodes of bliss, there to be purified and prepared for the companionship of sinless angels! A pleasing fable indeed, well suited to gratify the carnal heart! This is Satan's own doctrine, and it does his work effectually. Should we be surprised that, with such instruction, wickedness abounds?

The course pursued by this one false teacher illustrates that of many others. A few words of Scripture are separated from the context, which would in many cases show their meaning to be exactly opposite to the interpretation put upon them; and such disjointed passages are perverted and used in proof of doctrines that have no foundation in the word of God. The testimony cited as evidence that the drunken Amnon is in heaven is a mere inference directly contradicted by the plain and positive statement of the Scriptures that no drunkard shall inherit the kingdom of God. 1 Corinthians 6:10 It is thus that doubters, unbelievers, and skeptics turn the truth into a lie. And multitudes have been deceived by their sophistry and rocked to sleep in the cradle of carnal security. If it were true that the souls of all men passed directly to heaven at the hour of dissolution, then we might well covet death rather than life. Many have been led by this belief to put an end to their existence. When overwhelmed with
 trouble, perplexity, and disappointment, it seems an

easy thing to break the brittle thread of life and soar away into the bliss of the eternal world.

God has given in His word decisive evidence that He will punish the transgressors of His law. Those who flatter themselves that He is too merciful to execute justice upon the sinner, have only to look to the cross of Calvary. The death of the spotless Son of God testifies that »the wages of sin is death,« that every violation of God's law must receive its just retribution. Christ the sinless became sin for man. He bore the guilt of transgression, and the hiding of His Father's face, until His heart was broken and His life crushed out. All this sacrifice was made that sinners might be redeemed. In no other way could man be freed from the penalty of sin. And every soul that refuses to become a partaker of the atonement provided at such a cost must bear in his own person the guilt and punishment of transgression.

Let us consider what the Bible teaches further concerning the ungodly and unrepentant, whom the Universalist places in heaven as holy, happy angels. »I will give unto him that is athirst of the fountain of the water of life freely.« Revelation 21:6 This promise is only to those that thirst. None but those who feel their need of the water of life, and seek it at the loss of all things else, will be supplied. »He that overcometh shall inherit all things; and I will be his God, and he shall be My son.« Verse 7 Here, also, conditions are specified. In order to inherit all things, we must resist and overcome sin.

The Lord declares by the prophet Isaiah: »Say ye to the righteous, that it shall be well with him.« »Woe unto the wicked! it shall be ill with him: for the reward of his hands shall be given him.« Isaiah 3:10-11 »Though a sinner do evil an hundred times,« says the wise man, »and his days be prolonged, yet surely I know that it shall be well with them that fear God, which fear before Him: but it shall not be well with the wicked.« Ecclesiastes 8:12-13 And Paul testifies that the sinner is treasuring up unto himself »wrath against the day of wrath and revelation of the righteous judgment of God; who will render to every man according to his deeds;« »tribulation and anguish upon every soul of man that doeth evil.« Romans 2:5, 6, 9

»No fornicator, nor unclean person, nor covetous man, who is an idolater, hath any inheritance in the kingdom of Christ and God.« Ephesians 5:5, A.R.V. »Follow peace with all men, and holiness, without which no man shall see the Lord.« Hebrews 12:14 »Blessed are they that do His commandments, that they may have right to the tree of life, and may enter in through the gates into the city. For without are dogs, and sorcerers, and whoremongers, and murderers, and idolaters, and whosoever loveth and maketh a lie.« Rev. 22:14-15

God has given to men a declaration of His character and of His method of dealing with sin. »The Lord God, merciful and gracious, long-suffering and abundant in goodness and truth, keeping mercy for thousands, forgiving iniquity and transgression and sin, and that will by no means clear the guilty.« Exodus 34:6-7 »All the wicked will He destroy.« »The transgressors shall be destroyed together: the end of the wicked shall be cut off.« Psalm 145:20; 37:38 The power and authority of the divine government will be employed to put down rebellion; yet all the manifestations of retributive justice will be perfectly consistent with the character of God as a merciful, long-suffering, benevolent being.

God does not force the will or judgment of any. He takes no pleasure in a slavish obedience. He desires that the creatures of His hands shall love Him because He is worthy of love. He would have them obey Him because they have an intelligent appreciation of His wisdom, justice, and benevolence. And all who have a just conception of these qualities will love Him because they are drawn toward Him in admiration of His attributes.

The principles of kindness, mercy, and love, taught and exemplified by our Saviour, are a transcript of the will and character of God. Christ declared that He taught nothing except that which He had received from His Father. The principles of the divine government are in perfect harmony with the Saviour's precept, »Love your enemies.« God executes justice upon the wicked, for the good of the universe, and even for the good of those upon whom His judgments are visited. He would make them happy if He could do so in accordance with the laws of His government and the justice of His character. He surrounds them with the tokens of His love, He grants them a knowledge of His law, and follows them with the offers of His mercy; but they despise His love, make void His law, and reject His mercy. While constantly receiving His gifts, they dishonor the Giver; they hate God because they know that He abhors their sins. The Lord bears long with their perversity; but the decisive hour will come at last, when their destiny is to be decided. Will He then chain these rebels to His side? Will He force them to do His will?

Those who have chosen Satan as their leader and have been controlled by his power are not prepared to enter the presence of God. Pride, deception, licentiousness, cruelty, have become fixed in their characters. Can they enter heaven to dwell forever with those whom they despised and hated on earth? Truth will never be agreeable to a liar; meekness will not satisfy self-esteem and pride; purity is not acceptable to the corrupt; disinterested love does not appear attractive to the selfish. What source of enjoyment could heaven offer to those who are wholly absorbed in earthly and selfish interests? Could those whose lives have been spent in rebellion against God be suddenly transported to heaven and witness the high, the holy state of perfection that ever exists there, - every soul filled with love, every countenance beaming with joy, enrapturing music in melodious strains rising in honor of God and the Lamb, and ceaseless streams of light flowing upon the redeemed from the face of Him who sitteth upon the throne, - could those whose hearts are filled with hatred of God, of truth and holiness, mingle with the heavenly throng and join their songs of praise? Could they endure the glory of God and the Lamb? No, no; years of probation were granted them, that they might form characters for heaven; but they have never trained the mind to love purity; they have never learned the language of heaven, and now it is too late. A life of rebellion against God has unfitted them for heaven. Its purity, holiness, and peace would be torture to them; the glory of God would be a consuming fire. They would long to flee from that holy place. They would welcome destruction, that they might be hidden from the face of Him who died to redeem them. The destiny of the wicked is fixed by their own choice. Their exclusion from heaven is voluntary with themselves, and just and merciful on the part of God.

Like the waters of the Flood the fires of the great day declare God's verdict that the wicked are incurable. They have no disposition to submit to divine authority. Their will has been exercised in revolt; and when life is ended, it is too late to turn the current of their thoughts in the opposite direction, too late to turn from transgression to obedience, from hatred to love. In sparing the life of Cain the murderer, God gave the world an example of what would be the result of permitting the sinner to live to continue a course of unbridled iniquity. Through the influence of Cain's teaching and example, multitudes of his descendants were led into sin, until »the wickedness of man was great in the earth« and »every imagination of the thoughts of [543/544] his heart was only evil continually.« »The earth also was corrupt before God, and the earth was filled with violence.« Genesis 6:5, 11

In mercy to the world, God blotted out its wicked inhabitants in Noah's time. In mercy He destroyed the corrupt dwellers in Sodom. Through the deceptive power of Satan the workers of iniquity obtain sympathy and admiration, and are thus constantly leading others to rebellion. It was so in Cain's and in Noah's day, and in the time of Abraham and Lot; it is so in our time. It is in mercy to the universe that God will finally destroy the rejecters of His grace. »The wages of sin is death; but the gift of God is eternal life through Jesus Christ our Lord.« Romans 6:23

While life is the inheritance of the righteous, death is the portion of the wicked. Moses declared to Israel: »I have set before thee this day life and good, and death and evil.« Deuteronomy 30:15 The death referred to in these scriptures is not that pronounced upon Adam, for all mankind suffer the penalty of his transgression. It is »the second death« that is placed in contrast with everlasting life.

In consequence of Adam's sin, death passed upon the whole human race. All alike go down into the grave. And through the provisions of the plan of salvation, all are to be brought forth from their graves. »There shall be a resurrection of the dead, both of the just and unjust;« »for as in Adam all die, even so in Christ shall all be made alive.« Acts 24:15; 1 Corinthians 15:22 But a distinction is made between the two classes that are brought forth. »All that are in the graves shall hear His voice, and shall come forth; they that have done good, unto the resurrection of life; and they that have done evil, unto the resurrection of damnation.« John 5:28-29 They who have been »accounted worthy« of the resurrection of life are »blessed and holy.« »On such the second death hath no power.« Revelation 20:6 But those who have not, through repentance and faith, secured pardon, must receive the penalty of transgression – »the wages of sin.« They suffer punishment varying in duration and intensity, »according to their works,« but finally ending in the second death. Since it is impossible for God, consistently with His justice and mercy, to save the sinner in his sins, He deprives him of the existence which his transgressions have forfeited and of which he has proved himself unworthy. Says an inspired writer: »Yet a little while, and the wicked shall not be: yea, thou shalt diligently consider his place, and it

shall not be.« And another declares: »They shall be as

though they had not been.« Psalm 37:10; Obadiah 16 Covered with infamy, they sink into hopeless, eternal oblivion.

Thus will be made an end of sin, with all the woe and ruin which have resulted from it. Says the psalmist: »Thou hast destroyed the wicked, Thou hast put out their name forever and ever. O thou enemy, destructions are come to a perpetual end.« Psalm 9:5, 6 John, in the Revelation, looking forward to the eternal state, hears a universal anthem of praise undisturbed by one note of discord. Every creature in heaven and earth was heard ascribing glory to God. Revelation 5:13 There will then be no lost souls to blaspheme God as they writhe in never-ending torment; no wretched beings in hell will mingle their shrieks with the songs of the saved. Upon the fundamental error of natural immortality rests the doctrine of consciousness in death – a doctrine, like eternal torment, opposed to the teachings of the Scriptures, to the dictates of reason, and to our feelings of humanity. According to the popular belief, the redeemed in heaven are acquainted with all that takes place on the earth and especially with the lives of the friends whom they have left behind.

But how could it be a source of happiness to the dead to know the troubles of the living, to witness the sins committed by their own loved ones, and to see them enduring all the sorrows, disappointments, and anguish of life? How much of heaven's bliss would be enjoyed by those who were hovering over their friends on earth? And how utterly revolting is the belief that as soon as the breath leaves the body the soul of the impenitent is consigned to the flames of hell! To what depths of anguish must those be plunged who see their friends passing to the grave unprepared, to enter upon an eternity of woe and sin! Many have been driven to insanity by this harrowing thought.

What say the Scriptures concerning these things? David declares that man is not conscious in death. »His breath goeth forth, he returneth to his earth; in that very day his thoughts perish.« Psalm 146:4 Solomon bears the same testimony: »The living know that they shall die: but the dead know not anything.« »Their love, and their hatred, and their envy, is now perished; neither have they any more a portion forever in anything that is done under the sun.« »There is no work, nor device, nor knowledge, nor wisdom, in the grave, whither thou goest.« Ecclesiastes 9:5, 6, 10

When, in answer to his prayer, Hezekiah's life was prolonged fifteen years, the grateful king rendered to God a tribute of praise for His great mercy. In this song he tells the reason why he thus rejoices: »The grave cannot praise Thee, death cannot celebrate Thee: they that go down into the pit cannot hope for Thy truth. The living, the living, he shall praise Thee, as I do this day.« Isaiah 38:18-19 Popular theology represents the righteous dead as in heaven, entered into bliss and praising God with an immortal tongue; but Hezekiah could see no such glorious prospect in death. With his words agrees the testimony of the psalmist: »In death there is no remembrance of Thee: in the grave who shall give Thee thanks?« »The dead praise not the Lord, neither any that go down into silence.« Psalm 6:5; 115:17

Peter on the Day of Pentecost declared that the patriarch David »is both dead and buried, and his sepulcher is with us unto this day.« »For David is not ascended into the heavens.« Acts 2:29, 34 The fact that David remains in the grave until the resurrection proves that the righteous do not go to heaven at death. It is only through the resurrection, and by virtue of the fact that Christ has risen, that David can at last sit at the right hand of God.

And said Paul: »If the dead rise not, then is not Christ raised: and if Christ be not raised, your faith is vain; ye are yet in your sins. Then they also which are fallen asleep in Christ are perished.« 1 Corinthians 15:16-18 If for four thousand years the righteous had gone directly to heaven at death, how could Paul have said that if there is no resurrection, »they also which are fallen asleep in Christ are perished«? No resurrection would be necessary. The martyr Tyndale, referring to the state of the dead, declared: »I confess openly, that I am not persuaded that they be already in the full glory that Christ is in, or the elect angels of God are in. Neither is it any article of my faith; for if it were so, I see not but then the preaching of the resurrection of the flesh were a thing in vain.« William Tyndale, Preface to New Testament (ed. 1534). Reprinted in British Reformers - Tindal, Frith, Barnes, p. 349

It is an undeniable fact that the hope of immortal blessedness at death has led to a widespread neglect of the Bible doctrine of the resurrection. This tendency was remarked by Dr. Adam Clarke, who said: »The doctrine of the resurrection appears to have been thought of much more consequence among the primitive Christians than it is now! How is this? The apostles were continually insisting on it, and exciting the followers of God to diligence, obedience, and cheerfulness through it. And their successors in the present day seldom mention it! So apostles preached, and so primitive

Christians believed; so we preach, and so our hearers believe. There is not a doctrine in the gospel on which more stress is laid; and there is not a doctrine in the present system of preaching which is treated with more neglect!« Commentary, remarks on 1.Corinthians 15, par. 3

This has continued until the glorious truth of the resurrection has been almost wholly obscured and lost sight of by the Christian world. Thus a leading religious writer, commenting on the words of Paul in 1 Thessalonians 4:13-18, says:«For all practical purposes of comfort the doctrine of the blessed immortality of the righteous takes the place for us of any doubtful doctrine of the Lord's second coming. At our death the Lord comes for us. That is what we are to wait and watch for. The dead are already passed into glory. They do not wait for the trump for their judgment and blessedness.«

But when about to leave His disciples, Jesus did not tell them that they would soon come to Him. »I go to prepare a place for you,« He said. »And if I go and prepare a place for you, I will come again, and receive you unto Myself.« John 14:2-3 And Paul tells us, further, that »the Lord Himself shall descend from heaven with a shout, with the voice of the Archangel, and with the trump of God: and the dead in Christ shall rise first: then we which are alive and remain shall be caught up together with them in the clouds, to meet the Lord in the air: and so shall we ever be with the Lord.« And he adds: »Comfort one another with these words.« 1 Thessalonians 4:16-18 How wide the contrast between these words of comfort and those of the Universalist minister previously quoted! The latter consoled the bereaved friends with the assurance that, however sinful the dead might have been, when he breathed out his life here he was to be received among the angels. Paul points his brethren to the future coming of the Lord, when the fetters of the tomb shall be broken, and the »dead in Christ« shall be raised to eternal life.

Before any can enter the mansions of the blessed, their cases must be investigated, and their characters and their deeds must pass in review before God. All are to be judged according to the things written in the books and to be rewarded as their works have been. This judgment does not take place at death. Mark the words of Paul: »He hath appointed a day, in the which He will judge the world in righteousness by that Man whom He hath ordained; whereof He hath given assurance unto all men, in that He hath raised Him from the dead.« Acts 17:31 Here the apostle plainly stated that a specified time, then future, had been fixed upon for the judgment of the world.

Jude refers to the same period: »The angels which kept not their first estate, but left their own habitation, He hath reserved in everlasting chains under darkness unto the judgment of the great day.« And, again, he quotes the words of Enoch: »Behold, the Lord cometh with ten thousands of His saints, to execute judgment upon all.« Jude 6, 14-15 John declares that he »saw the dead, small and great, stand before God; and the books were opened: ... and the dead were judged out of those things which were written in the books.« Revelation 20:12

But if the dead are already enjoying the bliss of heaven or writhing in the flames of hell, what need of a future judgment? The teachings of God's word on these important points are neither obscure nor contradictory; they may be understood by common minds. But what candid mind can see either wisdom or justice in the current theory? Will the righteous, after the investigation of their cases at the judgment, receive the commendation, »Well done, thou good and faithful servant: ... enter thou into the joy of thy Lord,« when they have been dwelling in His presence, perhaps for long ages? Are the wicked summoned from the place of torment to receive sentence from the Judge of all the earth: »Depart from Me, ye cursed, into everlasting fire«? Matthew 25:21, 41

Oh, solemn mockery! shameful impeachment of the wisdom and justice of God!

The theory of the immortality of the soul was one of those false doctrines that Rome, borrowing from paganism, incorporated into the religion of Christendom. Martin Luther classed it with the »monstrous fables that form part of the Roman dunghill of decretals.« E. Petavel, The Problem of Immortality, p. 255 Commenting on the words of Solomon in Ecclesiastes, that the dead know not anything, the Reformer says: "Another place proving that the dead have no ... feeling. There is, saith he, no duty, no science, no knowledge, no wisdom there. Solomon judgeth that the dead are asleep, and feel nothing at all. For the dead lie there, accounting neither days nor years, but when they are awaked, they shall seem to have slept scarce one minute.« Martin Luther, Exposition of Solomon's Booke Called Ecclesiastes, p. 152

Nowhere in the Sacred Scriptures is found the statement that
 the righteous go to their reward or the wicked to their

punishment at death. The patriarchs and prophets have left no such assurance. Christ and His apostles have given no hint of it. The Bible clearly teaches that the dead do not go immediately to heaven. They are represented as sleeping until the resurrection. 1 Thessalonians 4:14; Job 14:10-12 In the very day when the silver cord is loosed and the golden bowl broken, Ecclesiastes 12:6 man's thoughts perish. They that go down to the grave are in silence. They know no more of anything that is done under the sun. Job 14:21 Blessed rest for the weary righteous! Time, be it long or short, is but a moment to them. They sleep; they are awakened by the trump of God to a glorious immortality. »For the trumpet shall sound, and the dead shall be raised incorruptible. ... So when this corruptible shall have put on incorruption, and this mortal shall have put on immortality, then shall be brought to pass the saying that is written, Death is swallowed up in victory.« 1 Corinthians 15:52-54 As they are called forth from their deep slumber they begin to think just where they ceased. The last sensation was the pang of death; the last thought, that they were falling beneath the power of the grave. When they arise from the tomb, their first glad thought will be echoed in the triumphal shout: »O death, where is thy sting? O grave, where is thy victory?« Verse 55

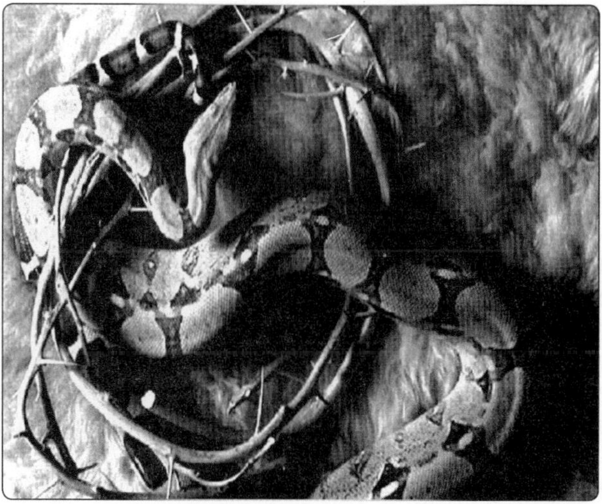

Chapter 34

Can Our Dead Speak to Us?

The ministration of holy angels, as presented in the Scriptures, is a truth most comforting and precious to every follower of Christ. But the Bible teaching upon this point has been obscured and perverted by the errors of popular theology. The doctrine of natural immortality, first borrowed from the pagan philosophy, and in the darkness of the great apostasy incorporated into the Christian faith, has supplanted the truth, so plainly taught in Scripture, that »the dead know not anything.« Multitudes have come to believe that it is spirits of the dead who are the »ministering spirits, sent forth to minister for them who shall be heirs of salvation.« And this notwithstanding the testimony of Scripture to the existence of heavenly angels, and their connection with the history of man, before the death of a human being.

The doctrine of man's consciousness in death, especially the belief that spirits of the dead return to minister to the living, has prepared the way for modern spiritualism. If the dead are admitted to the presence of God and holy angels, and privileged with knowledge far exceeding what they before possessed, why should they not return to the earth to enlighten and instruct the living? If, as taught by popular theologians, spirits of the dead are hovering about their friends on earth, why should they not be permitted to communicate with them, to warn them against evil, or to comfort them in sorrow? How can those who believe in man's consciousness in death reject what comes to them as divine light communicated by glorified spirits? Here is a channel regarded as sacred, through which Satan works for the accomplishment of his purposes. The fallen angels who do his bidding appear as messengers from the spirit world. While professing to bring the living into communication with the dead, the prince of evil exercises his bewitching influence upon their minds.

He has power to bring before men the appearance of their departed friends. The counterfeit is perfect; the familiar look, the words,
 the tone, are reproduced with marvelous distinctness.

Many are comforted with the assurance that their loved ones are enjoying the bliss of heaven, and without suspicion of danger, they give ear »to seducing spirits, and doctrines of devils.«

When they have been led to believe that the dead actually return to communicate with them, Satan causes those to appear who went into the grave unprepared. They claim to be happy in heaven and even to occupy exalted positions there, and thus the error is widely taught that no difference is made between the righteous and the wicked. The pretended visitants from the world of spirits sometimes utter cautions and warnings which prove to be correct. Then, as confidence is gained, they present doctrines that directly undermine faith in the Scriptures. With an appearance of deep interest in the well-being of their friends on earth, they insinuate the most dangerous errors. The fact that they state some truths, and are able at times to foretell future events, gives to their statements an appearance of reliability; and their false teachings are accepted by the multitudes as readily, and believed as implicitly, as if they were the most sacred truths of the Bible. The law of God is set aside, the Spirit of grace despised, the blood of the covenant counted an unholy thing. The spirits deny the deity of Christ and place even the Creator on a level with themselves. Thus under a new disguise the great rebel still carries on his warfare against God, begun in heaven and for nearly six thousand years continued upon the earth.

Many endeavor to account for spiritual manifestations by attributing them wholly to fraud and sleight of hand on the part of the medium. But while it is true that the results of trickery have often been palmed off as genuine manifestations, there have been, also, marked exhibitions of supernatural power. The mysterious rapping with which modern spiritualism began was not the result of human trickery or cunning, but was the direct work of evil angels, who thus introduced one of the most successful of soul-destroying delusions. Many will be ensnared through the belief that spiritualism is a merely human imposture; when brought face to face with manifestations which they cannot but regard as supernatural, they will be deceived, and will be led to accept them as the great power of God.

These persons overlook the testimony of the Scriptures concerning the wonders wrought by Satan and his agents. It was by satanic aid that Pharaoh's magicians were enabled to counterfeit the work of God. Paul testifies that before the second advent of

Christ there will be similar manifestations of satanic power. The coming of the Lord is to be preceded by »the working of Satan with all power and signs and lying wonders, and with all deceivableness of unrighteousness.« 2 Thessalonians 2:9-10 And the apostle John, describing the miracleworking power that will be manifested in the last days, declares: »He doeth great wonders, so that he maketh fire come down from heaven on the earth in the sight of men, and deceiveth them that dwell on the earth by the means of those miracles which he had power to do.« Revelation 13:13-14 No mere impostures are here foretold. Men are deceived by the miracles which Satan's agents have power to do, not which they pretend to do.

The prince of darkness, who has so long bent the powers of his mastermind to the work of deception, skillfully adapts his temptations to men of all classes and conditions. To persons of culture and refinement he presents spiritualism in its more refined and intellectual aspects, and thus succeeds in drawing many into his snare. The wisdom which spiritualism imparts is that described by the apostle James, which »descendeth not from above, but is earthly, sensual, devilish.« James 3:15 This, however, the great deceiver conceals when concealment will best suit his purpose.

He who could appear clothed with the brightness of the heavenly seraphs before Christ in the wilderness of temptation, comes to men in the most attractive manner as an angel of light. He appeals to the reason by the presentation of elevating themes; he delights the fancy with enrapturing scenes; and he enlists the affections by his eloquent portrayals of love and charity. He excites the imagination to lofty flights, leading men to take so great pride in their own wisdom that in their hearts they despise the Eternal One. That mighty being who could take the world's Redeemer to an exceedingly high mountain and bring before Him all the kingdoms of the earth and the glory of them, will present his temptations to men in a manner to pervert the senses of all who are not shielded by divine power. Satan beguiles men now as he beguiled Eve in Eden by flattery, by kindling a desire to obtain forbidden knowledge, by exciting ambition for self-exaltation. It was cherishing these evils that caused his fall, and through them he aims to compass the ruin of men. »Ye shall be as gods,« he declares, »knowing good and evil.« Genesis 3:5 Spiritualism teaches »that man is the creature of progression; that it is his destiny from his birth to

 progress, even to eternity, toward the Godhead.« And

again: »Each mind will judge itself and not another.« »The judgment will be right, because it is the judgment of self. ... The throne is within you.« Said a spiritualistic teacher, as the »spiritual consciousness« awoke within him: »My fellow men, all were unfallen demigods.« And another declares: »Any just and perfect being is Christ.«

Thus, in place of the righteousness and perfection of the infinite God, the true object of adoration; in place of the perfect righteousness of His law, the true standard of human attainment, Satan has substituted the sinful, erring nature of man himself as the only object of adoration, the only rule of judgment, or standard of character. This is progress, not upward, but downward.

It is a law both of the intellectual and the spiritual nature that by beholding we become changed. The mind gradually adapts itself to the subjects upon which it is allowed to dwell. It becomes assimilated to that which it is accustomed to love and reverence. Man will never rise higher than his standard of purity or goodness or truth. If self is his loftiest ideal, he will never attain to anything more exalted. Rather, he will constantly sink lower and lower. The grace of God alone has power to exalt man. Left to himself, his course must inevitably be downward.

To the self-indulgent, the pleasure-loving, the sensual, spiritualism presents itself under a less subtle disguise than to the more refined and intellectual; in its grosser forms they find that which is in harmony with their inclinations. Satan studies every indication of the frailty of human nature, he marks the sins which each individual is inclined to commit, and then he takes care that opportunities shall not be wanting to gratify the tendency to evil. He tempts men to excess in that which is in itself lawful, causing them, through intemperance, to weaken physical, mental, and moral power. He has destroyed and is destroying thousands through the indulgence of the passions, thus brutalizing the entire nature of man. And to complete his work, he declares, through the spirits that »true knowledge places man above all law;« that »whatever is, is right;« that »God doth not condemn;« and that »all sins which are committed are innocent.« When the people are thus led to believe that desire is the highest law, that liberty is license, and that man is accountable only to himself, who can wonder that corruption and depravity teem on every hand? Multitudes eagerly accept teachings that leave them at liberty to obey the promptings of the carnal heart. The reins of self-control are laid upon the neck of lust, the powers of mind and soul are made subject to the animal propensities, and Satan exultingly sweeps into his net thousands who profess to be followers of Christ. But none need be deceived by the lying claims of spiritualism. God has given the world sufficient light to enable them to discover the snare. As already shown, the theory which forms the very foundation of spiritualism is at war with the plainest statements of Scripture. The Bible declares that the dead know not anything, that their thoughts have perished; they have no part in anything that is done under the sun; they know nothing of the joys or sorrows of those who were dearest to them on earth.

Furthermore, God has expressly forbidden all pretended communication with departed spirits. In the days of the Hebrews there was a class of people who claimed, as do the spiritualists of today, to hold communication with the dead. But the »familiar spirits,« as these visitants from other worlds were called, are declared by the Bible to be »the spirits of devils.« Compare Numbers 25:1-3; Psalm 106:28; 1 Corinthians 10:20; Revelation 16:14 The work of dealing with familiar spirits was pronounced an abomination to the Lord, and was solemnly forbidden under penalty of death. Leviticus 19:31; 20:27 The very name of witchcraft is now held in contempt. The claim that men can hold intercourse with evil spirits is regarded as a fable of the Dark Ages. But spiritualism, which numbers its converts by hundreds of thousands, yea, by millions, which has made its way into scientific circles, which has invaded churches, and has found favor in legislative bodies, and even in the courts of kings – this mammoth deception is but a revival, in a new disguise, of the witchcraft condemned and prohibited of old. If there were no other evidence of the real character of spiritualism, it should be enough for the Christian that the spirits make no difference between righteousness and sin, between the noblest and purest of the apostles of Christ and the most corrupt of the servants of Satan. By representing the basest of men as in heaven, and highly exalted there, Satan says to the world: »No matter how wicked you are; no matter whether you believe or disbelieve God and the Bible. Live as you please; heaven is your home.« The spiritualist teachers virtually declare: »Everyone that doeth evil is good in the sight of the Lord, and He delighteth in them; or, Where is the God of judgment?« Malachi 2:17 Saith the word of God: »Woe unto them that call evil good, and good evil; that put darkness for light, and light for darkness.« Isaiah 5:20

The apostles, as personated by these lying spirits, are made to contradict what they wrote at the dictation of the Holy Spirit when on earth. They deny the divine origin of the Bible, and thus tear away the foundation of the Christian's hope and put out the light that reveals the way to heaven. Satan is making the world believe that the Bible is a mere fiction, or at least a book suited to the infancy of the race, but now to be lightly regarded, or cast aside as obsolete. And to take the place of the word of God he holds out spiritual manifestations. Here is a channel wholly under his control; by this means he can make the world believe what he will. The Book that is to judge him and his followers he puts in the shade, just where he wants it; the Saviour of the world he makes to be no more than a common man. And as the Roman guard that watched the tomb of Jesus spread the lying report which the priests and elders put into their mouths to disprove His resurrection, so do the believers in spiritual manifestations try to make it appear that there is nothing miraculous in the circumstances of our Saviour's life. After thus seeking to put Jesus in the background, they call attention to their own miracles, declaring that these far exceed the works of Christ.

It is true that spiritualism is now changing its form and, veiling some of its more objectionable features, is assuming a Christian guise. But its utterances from the platform and the press have been before the public for many years, and in these its real character stands revealed. These teachings cannot be denied or hidden.

Even in its present form, so far from being more worthy of toleration than formerly, it is really a more dangerous, because a more subtle, deception. While it formerly denounced Christ and the Bible, it now professes to accept both. But the Bible is interpreted in a manner that is pleasing to the unrenewed heart, while its solemn and vital truths are made of no effect. Love is dwelt upon as the chief attribute of God, but it is degraded to a weak sentimentalism, making little distinction between good and evil. God's justice, His denunciations of sin, the requirements of His holy law, are all kept out of sight. The people are taught to regard the Decalogue as a dead letter. Pleasing, bewitching fables captivate the senses and lead men to reject the Bible as the foundation of their faith. Christ is as verily denied as before; but Satan has so blinded the eyes of the people that the deception is not discerned. There are few who have any just conception of the deceptive power of spiritualism and the danger of coming [557/558] under its influence. Many tamper with it merely to gratify their curiosity. They have no real faith in it and would be filled with horror at the thought of yielding themselves to the spirits' control. But they venture upon the forbidden ground, and the mighty destroyer exercises his power upon them against their will. Let them once be induced to submit their minds to his direction, and he holds them captive. It is impossible, in their own strength, to break away from the bewitching, alluring spell. Nothing but the power of God, granted in answer to the earnest prayer of faith, can deliver these ensnared souls.

All who indulge sinful traits of character, or willfully cherish a known sin, are inviting the temptations of Satan. They separate themselves from God and from the watchcare of His angels; as the evil one presents his deceptions, they are without defense and fall an easy prey. Those who thus place themselves in his power little realize where their course will end. Having achieved their overthrow, the tempter will employ them as his agents to lure others to ruin.

Says the prophet Isaiah: »When they shall say unto you, Seek unto them that have familiar spirits, and unto wizards that peep, and that mutter: should not a people seek unto their God? for the living to the dead? To the law and to the testimony: if they speak not according to this word, it is because there is no light in them.« Isaiah 8:19-20 If men had been willing to receive the truth so plainly stated in the Scriptures concerning the nature of man and the state of the dead, they would see in the claims and manifestations of spiritualism the working of Satan with power and signs and lying wonders. But rather than yield the liberty so agreeable to the carnal heart, and renounce the sins which they love, multitudes close their eyes to the light and walk straight on, regardless of warnings, while Satan weaves his snares about them, and they become his prey. »Because they received not the love of the truth, that they might be saved,« therefore »God shall send them strong delusion, that they should believe a lie.« 2 Thessalonians 2:10-11

Those who oppose the teachings of spiritualism are assailing, not men alone, but Satan and his angels. They have entered upon a contest against principalities and powers and wicked spirits in high places. Satan will not yield one inch of ground except as he is driven back by the power of heavenly messengers. The people of God should be able to meet him, as did our Saviour, with the words: »It is written.« Satan can quote Scripture now as in the days of Christ, and he will pervert its teachings to sustain his delusions. Those who would stand in this time of peril must understand for themselves the testimony of the Scriptures. Many will be confronted by the spirits of devils personating beloved relatives or friends and declaring the most dangerous heresies. These visitants will appeal to our tenderest sympathies and will work miracles to sustain their pretensions. We must be prepared to withstand them with the Bible truth that the dead know not anything and that they who thus appear are the spirits of devils.

Just before us is »the hour of temptation, which shall come upon all the world, to try them that dwell upon the earth.« Revelation 3:10 All whose faith is not firmly established upon the word of God will be deceived and overcome. Satan »works with all deceivableness of unrighteousness« to gain control of the children of men, and his deceptions will continually increase. But he can gain his object only as men voluntarily yield to his temptations. Those who are earnestly seeking a knowledge of the truth and are striving to purify their souls through obedience, thus doing what they can to prepare for the conflict, will find, in the God of truth, a sure defense. »Because thou hast kept the word of My patience, I also will keep thee«, Verse 10 is the Saviour's promise. He would sooner send every angel out of heaven to protect His people than leave one soul that trusts in Him to be overcome by Satan.

The prophet Isaiah brings to view the fearful deception which will come upon the wicked, causing them to count themselves secure from the judgments of God: »We have made a covenant with death, and with hell are we at agreement; when the overflowing scourge shall pass through, it shall not come unto us: for we have made lies our refuge, and under falsehood have we hid ourselves.« Isaiah 28:15 In the class here described are included those who in their stubborn impenitence comfort themselves with the assurance that there is to be no punishment for the sinner; that all mankind, it matters not how corrupt, are to be exalted to heaven, to become as the angels of God. But still more emphatically are those making a covenant wlth death and an agreement with hell, who renounce the truths which Heaven has provided as a defense for the righteous in the day of trouble, and accept the refuge of lies offered by Satan in its stead – the delusive pretensions of spiritualism.

Marvelous beyond expression is the blindness of the people of this generation. Thousands reject the word of God as [560/561] unworthy of belief and with eager confidence receive the deceptions of Satan. Skeptics and scoffers denounce the bigotry of those who contend for the faith of prophets and apostles, and they divert themselves by holding up to ridicule the solemn declarations of the Scriptures concerning Christ and the plan of salvation, and the retribution to be visited upon the rejecters of the truth. They affect great pity for minds so narrow, weak, and superstitious as to acknowledge

the claims of God and obey the requirements of His law. They manifest as much assurance as if, indeed, they had made a covenant with death and an agreement with hell – as if they had erected an impassable, impenetrable barrier between themselves and the vengeance of God.

Nothing can arouse their fears. So fully have they yielded to the tempter, so closely are they united with him, and so thoroughly imbued with his spirit, that they have no power and no inclination to break away from his snare.

Satan has long been preparing for his final effort to deceive the world. The foundation of his work was laid by the assurance given to Eve in Eden: »Ye shall not surely die.« »In the day ye eat thereof, then your eyes shall be opened, and ye shall be as gods, knowing good and evil.« Genesis 3:4-5 Little by little he has prepared the way for his masterpiece of deception in the development of spiritualism. He has not yet reached the full accomplishment of his designs; but it will be reached in the last remnant of time. Says the prophet: »I saw three unclean spirits like frogs; ... they are the spirits of devils, working miracles, which go forth unto the kings of the earth and of the whole world, to gather them to the battle of that great day of God Almighty.« Revelation 16:13-14 Except those who are kept by the power of God, through faith in His word, the whole world will be swept into the ranks of this delusion. The people are fast being lulled to a fatal security, to be awakened only by the outpouring of the wrath of God.

Saith the Lord God: »Judgment also will I lay to the line, and righteousness to the plummet: and the hail shall sweep away the refuge of lies, and the waters shall overflow the hiding place. And your covenant with death shall be disannulled, and your agreement with hell shall not stand; when the overflowing scourge shall pass through, then ye shall be trodden down by it.« Isaiah 28:17-18

Chapter 35

Liberty of Conscience Threatened

Romanism is now regarded by Protestants with far greater favor than in former years. In those countries where Catholicism is not in the ascendancy, and the papists are taking a conciliatory course in order to gain influence, there is an increasing indifference concerning the doctrines that separate the reformed churches from the papal hierarchy; the opinion is gaining ground that, after all, we do not differ so widely upon vital points as has been supposed, and that a little concession on our part will bring us into a better understanding with Rome. The time was when Protestants placed a high value upon the liberty of conscience which had been so dearly purchased. They taught their children to abhor popery and held that to seek harmony with Rome would be disloyalty to God. But how widely different are the sentiments now expressed!

The defenders of the papacy declare that the church has been maligned, and the Protestant world are inclined to accept the statement. Many urge that it is unjust to judge the church of today by the abominations and absurdities that marked her reign during the centuries of ignorance and darkness. They excuse her horrible cruelty as the result of the barbarism of the times and plead that the influence of modern civilization has changed her sentiments. Have these persons forgotten the claim of infallibility put forth for eight hundred years by this haughty power? So far from being relinquished, this claim was affirmed in the nineteenth century with greater positiveness than ever before. As Rome asserts that the »church never erred; nor will it, according to the Scriptures, ever err« John L. von Mosheim, Institutes of Ecclesiastical History, book 3, century II, part 2, chapter 2, section 9, note 17 how can she renounce the principles which governed her course in past ages?

The papal church will never relinquish her claim to infallibility. All that she has done in her persecution of those who reject her dogmas she holds to be right; and would she not repeat the same acts, should the opportunity be presented? Let the restraints now imposed by

 secular governments be removed and Rome be reinstated in her former power, and there would speedily be a revival of her tyranny and persecution. A well-known writer speaks thus of the attitude of the papal hierarchy as regards freedom of conscience, and of the perils which especially threaten the United States from the success of her policy: »There are many who are disposed to attribute any fear of Roman Catholicism in the United States to bigotry or childishness. Such see nothing in the character and attitude of Romanism that is hostile to our free institutions, or find nothing portentous in its growth. Let us, then, first compare some of the fundamental principles of our government with those of the Catholic Church.

»The Constitution of the United States guarantees liberty of conscience. Nothing is dearer or more fundamental. Pope Pius IX, in his Encyclical Letter of Aug. 15, 1854, said: 'The absurd and erroneous doctrines or ravings in defense of liberty of conscience are a most pestilential error – a pest, of all others, most to be dreaded in a state.' The same pope, in his Encyclical Letter of Dec. 8, 1864, anathematized 'those who assert the liberty of conscience and of religious worship,' also 'all such as maintain that the church may not employ force.'«

»The pacific tone of Rome in the United States does not imply a change of heart. She is tolerant where she is helpless. Says Bishop O'Connor: 'Religious liberty is merely endured until the opposite can be carried into effect without peril to the Catholic world.'... The archbishop of St. Louis once said: 'Heresy and unbelief are crimes; and in Christian countries, as in Italy and Spain, for instance, where all the people are Catholics, and where the Catholic religion is an essential part of the law of the land, they are punished as other crimes.'...«

»Every cardinal, archbishop, and bishop in the Catholic Church takes an oath of allegiance to the pope, in which occur the following words: 'Heretics, schismatics, and rebels to our said lord (the pope), or his aforesaid successors, I will to my utmost persecute and oppose.'« Josiah Strong, Our Country, ch. 5, pars. 2-4; see Appendix for Corrected References

It is true that there are real Christians in the Roman Catholic communion. Thousands In that church are serving God according to the best light they have. They are not allowed access to His word, and therefore they do not discern the truth. Publ. in 1888 + 1911; see App. They have never seen the contrast between a living heart service and a round of mere forms and ceremonies. God looks with pitying tenderness upon these souls, educated as they are in a faith that is delusive and unsatisfying. He will cause rays of light to penetrate the dense darkness that surrounds them. He will reveal to them the truth as it is in Jesus, and many will yet take their position with His people.

But Romanism as a system is no more in harmony with the gospel of Christ now than at any former period in her history. The Protestant churches are in great darkness, or they would discern the signs of the times. The Roman Church is far-reaching in her plans and modes of operation. She is employing every device to extend her influence and increase her power in preparation for a fierce and determined conflict to regain control of the world, to re-establish persecution, and to undo all that Protestantism has done. Catholicism is gaining ground upon every side. See the increasing number of her churches and chapels in Protestant countries. Look at the popularity of her colleges and seminaries in America, so widely patronized by Protestants. Look at the growth of ritualism in England and the frequent defections to the ranks of the Catholics. These things should awaken the anxiety of all who prize the pure principles of the gospel.

Protestants have tampered with and patronized popery; they have made compromises and concessions which papists themselves are surprised to see and fail to understand. Men are closing their eyes to the real character of Romanism and the dangers to be apprehended from her supremacy. The people need to be aroused to resist the advances of this most dangerous foe to civil and religious liberty. Many Protestants suppose that the Catholic religion is unattractive and that its worship is a dull, meaningless round of ceremony. Here they mistake. While Romanism is based upon deception, it is not a coarse and clumsy imposture. The religious service of the Roman Church is a most impressive ceremonial. Its gorgeous display and solemn rites fascinate the senses of the people and silence the voice of reason and of conscience. The eye is charmed. Magnificent churches, imposing processions, golden altars, jeweled shrines, choice paintings, and exquisite sculpture appeal to the love of beauty. The ear also is captivated. The music is unsurpassed. The rich notes of the deep-toned organ, blending with the melody of many voices as it swells through the lofty domes and pillared aisles of her grand cathedrals, cannot fail to impress the mind with awe and reverence.

This outward splendor, pomp, and ceremony, that only mocks the longings of the sin-sick soul, is an evidence of inward corruption. The religion of Christ needs not such attractions to recommend it. In the

 light shining from the cross, true Christianity appears

so pure and lovely that no external decorations can enhance its true worth. It is the beauty of holiness, a meek and quiet spirit, which is of value with God. Brilliancy of style is not necessarily an index of pure, elevated thought. High conceptions of art, delicate refinement of taste, often exist in minds that are earthly and sensual. They are often employed by Satan to lead men to forget the necessities of the soul, to lose sight of the future, immortal life, to turn away from their infinite Helper, and to live for this world alone.

A religion of externals is attractive to the unrenewed heart. The pomp and ceremony of the Catholic worship has a seductive, bewitching power, by which many are deceived; and they come to look upon the Roman Church as the very gate of heaven. None but those who have planted their feet firmly upon the foundation of truth, and whose hearts are renewed by the Spirit of God, are proof against her influence. Thousands who have not an experimental knowledge of Christ will be led to accept the forms of godliness without the power. Such a religion is just what the multitudes desire.

The church's claim to the right to pardon leads the Romanist to feel at liberty to sin; and the ordinance of confession, without which her pardon is not granted, tends also to give license to evil. He who kneels before fallen man, and opens in confession the secret thoughts and imaginations of his heart, is debasing his manhood and degrading every noble instinct of his soul. In unfolding the sins of his life to a priest, – an erring, sinful mortal, and too often corrupted with wine and licentiousness, –his standard of character is lowered, and he is defiled in consequence. His thought of God is degraded to the likeness of fallen humanity, for the priest stands as a representative of God. This degrading confession of man to man is the secret spring from which has flowed much of the evil that is defiling the world and fitting it for the final destruction. Yet to him who loves self-indulgence, it is more pleasing to confess to a fellow mortal than to open the soul to God. It is more palatable to human nature to do penance than to renounce sin; it is easier to mortify the flesh by sackcloth and nettles and galling chains than to crucify fleshly lusts. Heavy is the yoke which the carnal heart is willing to bear rather than bow to the yoke of Christ. There is a striking similarity between the Church of Rome and the Jewish Church at the time of Christ's first advent. While the Jews secretly trampled upon every principle of the law of God, they were outwardly rigorous in the observance of its precepts, loading it down with exactions and traditions that made obedience painful and burdensome. As the Jews professed to revere the law, so do Romanists claim to reverence the cross. They exalt the symbol of Christ's sufferings, while in their lives they deny Him whom it represents.

Papists place crosses upon their churches, upon their altars, and upon their garments. Everywhere is seen the insignia of the cross. Everywhere it is outwardly honored and exalted. But the teachings of Christ are buried beneath a mass of senseless traditions, false interpretations, and rigorous exactions. The Saviour's words concerning the bigoted Jews, apply with still greater force to the leaders of the Roman Catholic Church: »They bind heavy burdens and grievous to be borne, and lay them on men's shoulders; but they themselves will not move them with one of their fingers.« Matthew 23:4 Conscientious souls are kept in constant terror fearing the wrath of an offended God, while many of the dignitaries of the church are living in luxury and sensual pleasure.

The worship of images and relics, the invocation of saints, and the exaltation of the pope are devices of Satan to attract the minds of the people from God and from His Son. To accomplish their ruin, he endeavors to turn their attention from Him through whom alone they can find salvation. He will direct them to any object that can be substituted for the One who has said: »Come unto Me, all ye that labor and are heavy-laden, and I will give you rest.« Matthew 11:28 It is Satan's constant effort to misrepresent the character of God, the nature of sin, and the real issues at stake in the great controversy. His sophistry lessens the obligation of the divine law and gives men license to sin. At the same time he causes them to cherish false conceptions of God so that they regard Him with fear and hate rather than with love. The cruelty inherent in his own character is attributed to the Creator; it is embodied in systems of religion and expressed in modes of worship. Thus the minds of men are blinded, and Satan secures them as his agents to war against God. By perverted conceptions of the divine attributes, heathen nations were led to believe human sacrifices necessary to secure the favor of Deity; and horrible cruelties have been perpetrated under the various forms of idolatry.

The Roman Catholic Church, uniting the forms of paganism and Christianity, and, like paganism, misrepresenting the character of God, has resorted to practices no less cruel and revolting. In the

days of Rome's supremacy there were instruments of

torture to compel assent to her doctrines. There was the stake for those who would not concede to her claims. There were massacres on a scale that will never be known until revealed in the judgment. Dignitaries of the church studied, under Satan their master, to invent means to cause the greatest possible torture and not end the life of the victim. In many cases the infernal process was repeated to the utmost limit of human endurance, until nature gave up the struggle, and the sufferer hailed death as a sweet release.

Such was the fate of Rome's opponents. For her adherents she had the discipline of the scourge, of famishing hunger, of bodily austerities in every conceivable, heart-sickening form. To secure the favor of Heaven, penitents violated the laws of God by violating the laws of nature. They were taught to sunder the ties which He has formed to bless and gladden man's earthly sojourn. The churchyard contains millions of victims who spent their lives in vain endeavors to subdue their natural affections, to repress, as offensive to God, every thought and feeling of sympathy with their fellow creatures.

If we desire to understand the determined cruelty of Satan, manifested for hundreds of years, not among those who never heard of God, but in the very heart and throughout the extent of Christendom, we have only to look at the history of Romanism. Through this mammoth system of deception the prince of evil achieves his purpose of bringing dishonor to God and wretchedness to man. And as we see how he succeeds in disguising himself and accomplishing his work through the leaders of the church, we may better understand why he has so great antipathy to the Bible. If that Book is read, the mercy and love of God will be revealed; it will be seen that He lays upon men none of these heavy burdens. All that He asks is a broken and contrite heart, a humble, obedient spirit.

Christ gives no example in His life for men and women to shut themselves in monasteries in order to become fitted for heaven. He has never taught that love and sympathy must be repressed. The Saviour's heart overflowed with love. The nearer man approaches to moral perfection, the keener are his sensibilities, the more acute is his perception of sin, and the deeper his sympathy for the afflicted. The pope claims to be the vicar of Christ; but how does his character bear comparison with that of our Saviour? Was Christ ever known to consign men to the prison or the rack because they did not pay Him homage as the King of heaven? Was His voice heard condemning to death those who did not accept Him? When He was slighted by the people of a Samaritan village, the apostle John was filled with indignation, and inquired: »Lord, wilt Thou that we command fire to come down from heaven, and consume them, even as Elias did?« Jesus looked with pity upon His disciple, and rebuked his harsh spirit, saying: »The Son of man is not come to destroy men's lives, but to save them.« Luke 9:54, 56 How different from the spirit manifested by Christ is that of His professed vicar.

The Roman Church now presents a fair front to the world, covering with apologies her record of horrible cruelties. She has clothed herself in Christlike garments; but she is unchanged. Every principle of the papacy that existed in past ages exists today. The doctrines devised in the darkest ages are still held. Let none deceive themselves. The papacy that Protestants are now so ready to honor is the same that ruled the world in the days of the Reformation, when men of God stood up, at the peril of their lives, to expose her iniquity. She possesses the same pride and arrogant assumption that lorded it over kings and princes, and claimed the prerogatives of God. Her spirit is no less cruel and despotic now than when she crushed out human liberty and slew the saints of the Most High. The papacy is just what prophecy declared that she would be, the apostasy of the latter times. 2 Thess. 2:3-4 It is a part of her policy to assume the character which will best accomplish her purpose; but beneath the variable appearance of the chameleon she conceals the invariable venom of the serpent. »Faith ought not to be kept with heretics, nor persons suspected of heresy«, Lenfant, volume 1, p. 516 she declares. Shall this power, whose record for a thousand years is written in the blood of the saints, be now acknowledged as a part of the church of Christ?

It is not without reason that the claim has been put forth in Protestant countries that Catholicism differs less widely from Protestantism than in former times. There has been a change; but the change is not in the papacy. Catholicism indeed resembles much of the Protestantism that now exists, because Protestantism has so greatly degenerated since the days of the Reformers. As the Protestant churches have been seeking the favor of the world, false charity has blinded their eyes. They do not see but that it is right to believe good of all evil, and as the inevitable result they will finally believe evil of all good. Instead of standing in defense of the faith once delivered to the saints, they are now, as it were, apologizing to Rome for their uncharitable opinion of her, begging pardon for their bigotry. A large class, even of those who look upon Romanism with no favor, apprehend little danger from her power and influence. Many urge that the intellectual and moral darkness prevailing during the Middle Ages favored the spread of her dogmas, superstitions, and oppression, and that the greater intelligence of modern times, the general diffusion of knowledge, and the increasing liberality in matters of religion forbid a revival of intolerance and tyranny. The very thought that such a state of things will exist in this enlightened age is ridiculed. It is true that great light, intellectual, moral, and religious, is shining upon this generation. In the open pages of God's Holy Word, light from heaven has been shed upon the world. But it should be remembered that the greater the light bestowed, the greater the darkness of those who pervert and reject it.

A prayerful study of the Bible would show Protestants the real character of the papacy and would cause them to abhor and to shun it; but many are so wise in their own conceit that they feel no need of humbly seeking God that they may be led into the truth. Although priding themselves on their enlightenment, they are ignorant both of the Scriptures and of the power of God. They must have some means of quieting their consciences, and they seek that which is least spiritual and humiliating. What they desire is a method of forgetting God which shall pass as a method of remembering Him. The papacy is well adapted to meet the wants of all these. It is prepared for two classes of mankind, embracing nearly the whole world - those who would be saved by their merits, and those who would be saved in their sins. Here is the secret of its power.

A day of great intellectual darkness has been shown to be favorable to the success of the papacy. It will yet be demonstrated that a day of great intellectual light is equally favorable for its success. In past ages, when men were without God's word and without the knowledge of the truth, their eyes were blindfolded, and thousands were ensnared, not seeing the net spread for their feet. In this generation there are many whose eyes become dazzled by the glare of human speculations, "science falsely so called;" they discern not the net, and walk into it as readily as if blindfolded. God designed that man's intellectual powers should be held as a gift from his Maker and should be employed in the service of truth and righteousness; but when pride and ambition are cherished, and men exalt their own theories above the word of God, then intelligence can accomplish greater harm than ignorance. Thus the false science of the present day, which undermines faith in the Bible, will prove as successful in preparing the way for the acceptance of the papacy, with its pleasing forms, as did the withholding of knowledge in opening the way for its aggrandizement in the Dark Ages.

In the movements now in progress in the United States to secure for the institutions and usages of the church the support of the state, Protestants are following in the steps of papists. Nay, more, they are opening the door for the papacy to regain in Protestant America the supremacy which she has lost in the Old World. And that which gives greater significance to this movement is the fact that the principal object contemplated is the enforcement of Sunday observance - a custom which originated with Rome, and which she claims as the sign of her authority. It is the spirit of the papacy – the spirit of conformity to worldly customs, the veneration for human traditions above the commandments of God – that is permeating the Protestant churches and leading them on to do the same work of Sunday exaltation which the papacy has done before them.

If the reader would understand the agencies to be employed in the soon-coming contest, he has but to trace the record of the means which Rome employed for the same object in ages past. If he would know how papists and Protestants united will deal with those who reject their dogmas, let him see the spirit which Rome manifested toward the Sabbath and its defenders.

Royal edicts, general councils, and church ordinances sustained by secular power were the steps by which the pagan festival attained its position of honor in the Christian world. The first public measure enforcing Sunday observance was the law enacted by Constantine. A.D. 321; see Appendix note for p. 53 This edict required townspeople to rest on »the venerable day of the sun,« but permitted countrymen to continue their agricultural pursuits. Though virtually a heathen statute, it was enforced by the emperor after his nominal acceptance of Christianity.

The royal mandate not proving a sufficient substitute for divine authority, Eusebius, a bishop who sought the favor of princes, and who was the special friend and flatterer of Constantine, advanced the claim that Christ had transferred the Sabbath to Sunday. Not a single

 testimony of the Scriptures was produced in proof of

the new doctrine. Eusebius himself unwittingly acknowledges its falsity and points to the real authors of the change. »All things,« he says, »whatever that it was duty to do on the Sabbath, these we have transferred to the Lord's Day.« Robert Cox, Sabbath Laws and Sabbath Duties, p. 538 But the Sunday argument, groundless as it was, served to embolden men in trampling upon the Sabbath of the Lord. All who desired to be honored by the world accepted the popular festival.

As the papacy became firmly established, the work of Sunday exaltation was continued. For a time the people engaged in agricultural labor when not attending church, and the seventh day was still regarded as the Sabbath. But steadily a change was effected. Those in holy office were forbidden to pass judgment in any civil controversy on the Sunday. Soon after, all persons, of whatever rank, were commanded to refrain from common labor on pain of a fine for freemen and stripes in the case of servants. Later it was decreed that rich men should be punished with the loss of half of their estates; and finally, that if still obstinate they should be made slaves. The lower classes were to suffer perpetual banishment. Miracles also were called into requisition. Among other wonders it was reported that as a husbandman who was about to plow his field on Sunday cleaned his plow with an iron, the iron stuck fast in his hand, and for two years he carried it about with him, "to his exceeding great pain and shame.« Francis West, Historical and Practical Discourse on the Lord's Day, p. 174

Later the pope gave directions that the parish priest should admonish the violators of Sunday and wish them to go to church and say their prayers, lest they bring some great calamity on themselves and neighbors. An ecclesiastical council brought forward the argument, since so widely employed, even by Protestants, that because persons had been struck by lightning while laboring on Sunday, it must be the Sabbath. »It is apparent,« said the prelates, »how high the displeasure of God was upon their neglect of this day.« An appeal was then made that priests and ministers, kings and princes, and all faithful people »use their utmost endeavors and care that the day be restored to its honor, and, for the credit of Christianity, more devoutly observed for the time to come.« Thomas Morer, Discourse in Six Dialogues on the Name, Notion, and Observation of the Lord's Day, p. 271

The decrees of councils proving insufficient, the secular authorities were besought to issue an edict that would strike terror to the hearts of the people and force them to refrain from labor on the [574/575]

Sunday. At a synod held in Rome, all previous decisions were reaffirmed with greater force and solemnity. They were also incorporated into the ecclesiastical law and enforced by the civil authorities throughout nearly all Christendom. see Heylyn, History of the Sabbath, pt. 2, ch. 5, sec. 7

Still the absence of Scriptural authority for Sundaykeeping occasioned no little embarrassment. The people questioned the right of their teachers to set aside the positive declaration of Jehovah, »The seventh day is the Sabbath of the Lord thy God,« in order to honor the day of the sun. To supply the lack of Bible testimony, other expedients were necessary. A zealous advocate of Sunday, who about the close of the twelfth century visited the churches of England, was resisted by faithful witnesses for the truth; and so fruitless were his efforts that he departed from the country for a season and cast about him for some means to enforce his teachings. When he returned, the lack was supplied, and in his after labors he met with greater success. He brought with him a roll purporting to be from God Himself, which contained the needed command for Sunday observance, with awful threats to terrify the disobedient. This precious document – as base a counterfeit as the institution it supported – was said to have fallen from heaven and to have been found in Jerusalem, upon the altar of St. Simeon, in Golgotha. But, in fact, the pontifical palace at Rome was the source whence it proceeded. Frauds and forgeries to advance the power and prosperity of the church have in all ages been esteemed lawful by the papal hierarchy.

The roll forbade labor from the ninth hour, three o'clock, on Saturday afternoon, till sunrise on Monday; and its authority was declared to be confirmed by many miracles. It was reported that persons laboring beyond the appointed hour were stricken with paralysis. A Miller who attempted to grind his corn, saw, instead of flour, a torrent of blood come forth, and the mill wheel stood still, notwithstanding the strong rush of water. A woman who placed dough in the oven found it raw when taken out, though the oven was very hot. Another who had dough prepared for baking at the ninth hour, but determined to set it aside till Monday, found, the next day, that it had been made into loaves and baked by divine power. A man who baked bread after the ninth hour on Saturday found, when he broke it the next morning, that blood started therefrom. By such absurd and superstitious fabrications did the advocates of Sunday endeavor to establish its sacredness. see Roger de Hoveden, Annals, vol. 2, pp. 526-530

In Scotland, as in England, a greater regard for Sunday was secured by uniting with it a portion of the ancient Sabbath. But the time required to be kept holy varied. An edict from the king of Scotland declared that »Saturday from twelve at noon ought to be accounted holy,« and that no man, from that time till Monday morning, should engage in worldly business. Morer, pp. 290, 291 But notwithstanding all the efforts to establish Sunday sacredness, papists themselves publicly confessed the divine authority of the Sabbath and the human origin of the institution by which it had been supplanted. In the sixteenth century a papal council plainly declared: »Let all Christians remember that the seventh day was consecrated by God, and hath been received and observed, not only by the Jews, but by all others who pretend to worship God; though we Christians have changed their Sabbath into the Lord's Day.« Ibid., p. 281, 282 Those who were tampering with the divine law were not ignorant of the character of their work. They were deliberately setting themselves above God.

A striking illustration of Rome's policy toward those who disagree with her was given in the long and bloody persecution of the Waldenses, some of whom were observers of the Sabbath. Others suffered in a similar manner for their fidelity to the fourth commandment. The history of the churches of Ethiopia and Abyssinia is especially significant. Amid the gloom of the Dark Ages, the Christians of Central Africa were lost sight of and forgotten by the world, and for many centuries they enjoyed freedom in the exercise of their faith. But at last Rome learned of their existence, and the emperor of Abyssinia was soon beguiled into an acknowledgment of the pope as the vicar of Christ. Other concessions followed. An edict was issued forbidding the observance of the Sabbath under the severest penalties. see Michael Geddes, Church History of Ethiopia, p. 311, 312 But papal tyranny soon became a yoke so galling that the Abyssinians determined to break it from their necks. After a terrible struggle the Romanists were banished from their dominions, and the ancient faith was restored. The churches rejoiced in their freedom, and they never forgot the lesson they had learned concerning the deception, the fanaticism, and the despotic power of Rome. Within their solitary realm they were content to remain, unknown to the rest of Christendom.

The churches of Africa held the Sabbath as it was held by the papal church before her complete apostasy. While they kept the seventh day in obedience to the commandment of God, they abstained from labor on the Sunday in conformity to the custom of the church. Upon obtaining supreme power, Rome had trampled upon the Sabbath of God to exalt her own; but the churches of Africa, hidden for nearly a thousand years, did not share in this apostasy. When brought under the sway of Rome, they were forced to set aside the true and exalt the false sabbath; but no sooner had they regained their independence than they returned to obedience to the fourth commandment. see Appendix These records of the past clearly reveal the enmity of Rome toward the true Sabbath and its defenders, and the means which she employs to honor the institution of her creating. The word of God teaches that these scenes are to be repeated as Roman Catholics and Protestants shall unite for the exaltation of the Sunday.

The prophecy of Revelation 13 declares that the power represented by the beast with lamblike horns shall cause »the earth and them which dwell therein« to worship the papacy – there symbolized by the beast »like unto a leopard.« The beast with two horns is also to say »to them that dwell on the earth, that they should make an image to the beast;« and, furthermore, it is to command all, »both small and great, rich and poor, free and bond,« to receive the mark of the beast. Revelation 13:11-16 It has been shown that the United States is the power represented by the beast with lamblike horns, and that this prophecy will be fulfilled when the United States shall enforce Sunday observance, which Rome claims as the special acknowledgment of her supremacy. But in this homage to the papacy the United States will not be alone. The influence of Rome in the countries that once acknowledged her dominion is still far from being destroyed. And prophecy foretells a restoration of her power. »I saw one of his heads as it were wounded to death; and his deadly wound was healed: and all the world wondered after the beast.« Verse 3

The infliction of the deadly wound points to the downfall of the papacy in 1798. After this, says the prophet, »his deadly wound was healed: and all the world wondered after the beast.« Paul states plainly that the »man of sin« will continue until the second advent. 2 Thessalonians 2:3-8 To the very close of time he will carry forward the work of deception. And the revelator declares, also referring to the papacy: »All that dwell upon the earth shall worship him, whose names are not written in the book of life.« Revelation 13:8 In both the Old and the New World, the papacy will receive homage in the honor paid to the Sunday institution, that rests solely upon the authority of the Roman Church. Since the middle of the nineteenth century, students of prophecy in the United States have presented this testimony to the world. In the events now taking place is seen a rapid advance toward the fulfillment of the prediction. With Protestant teachers there is the same claim of divine authority for Sundaykeeping, and the same lack of Scriptural evidence, as with the papal leaders who fabricated miracles to supply the place of a command from God. The assertion that God's judgments are visited upon men for their violation of the Sunday-sabbath, will be repeated; already it is beginning to be urged. And a movement to enforce Sunday observance is fast gaining ground.

Marvelous in her shrewdness and cunning is the Roman Church. She can read what is to be. She bides her time, seeing that the Protestant churches are paying her homage in their acceptance of the false sabbath and that they are preparing to enforce it by the very means which she herself employed in bygone days. Those who reject the light of truth will yet seek the aid of this self-styled infallible power to exalt an institution that originated with her. How readily she will come to the help of Protestants in this work it is not difficult to conjecture. Who understands better than the papal leaders how to deal with those who are disobedient to the church? The Roman Catholic Church, with all its ramifications throughout the world, forms one vast organization under the control, and designed to serve the interests, of the papal see. Its millions of communicants, in every country on the globe, are instructed to hold themselves as bound in allegiance to the pope. Whatever their nationality or their government, they are to regard the authority of the church as above all other. Though they may take the oath pledging their loyalty to the state, yet back of this lies the vow of obedience to Rome, absolving them from every pledge inimical to her interests.

History testifies of her artful and persistent efforts to insinuate herself into the affairs of nations; and having gained a foothold, to further her own aims, even at the ruin of princes and people. In the year 1204, Pope Innocent III extracted from Peter II, king of Arragon, the following extraordinary oath: »I, Peter, king of Arragonians, profess and promise to be ever faithful and obedient to my lord, Pope Innocent, to his Catholic successors, and the Roman Church, and faithfully to preserve my kingdom in his obedience, defending the Catholic faith, and persecuting heretical pravity.« John Dowling, The History of Romanism, b. 5, ch. 6, sec. 55 This is in harmony with the claims regarding the power of the Roman pontiff »that it is lawful for him to depose emperors« and »that he can absolve subjects from their allegiance to unrighteous rulers.« Mosheim, b. 3, cent. 11, pt. 2, ch. 2, sec. 9, note 17. See Appendix note for p. 447

And let it be remembered, it is the boast of Rome that she never changes. The principles of Gregory VII and Innocent III are still the principles of the Roman Catholic Church. And had she but the power, she would put them in practice with as much vigor now as in past centuries. Protestants little know what they are doing when they propose to accept the aid of Rome in the work of Sunday exaltation. While they are bent upon the accomplishment of their purpose, Rome is aiming to re-establish her power, to recover her lost supremacy. Let the principle once be established in the United States that the church may employ or control the power of the state; that religious observances may be enforced by secular laws; in short, that the authority of church and state is to dominate the conscience, and the triumph of Rome in this country is assured.

God's word has given warning of the impending danger; let this be unheeded, and the Protestant world will learn what the purposes of Rome really are, only when it is too late to escape the snare. She is silently growing into power. Her doctrines are exerting their influence in legislative halls, in the churches, and in the hearts of men. She is piling up her lofty and massive structures in the secret recesses of which her former persecutions will be repeated. Stealthily and unsuspectedly she is strengthening her forces to further her own ends when the time shall come for her to strike. All that she desires is vantage ground, and this is already being given her. We shall soon see and shall feel what the purpose of the Roman element is. Whoever shall believe and obey the word of God will thereby incur reproach and persecution.

Vatican, the Center of the Catholic Church in Rome

CHAPTER 36

THE IMPENDING CONFLICT

From the very beginning of the great controversy in heaven it has been Satan's purpose to overthrow the law of God. It was to accomplish this that he entered upon his rebellion against the Creator, and though he was cast out of heaven he has continued the same warfare upon the earth. To deceive men, and thus lead them to transgress God's law, is the object which he has steadfastly pursued. Whether this be accomplished by casting aside the law altogether, or by rejecting one of its precepts, the result will be ultimately the same. He that offends »in one point,« manifests contempt for the whole law; his influence and example are on the side of transgression; he becomes »guilty of all.« James 2:10

In seeking to cast contempt upon the divine statutes, Satan has perverted the doctrines of the Bible, and errors have thus become incorporated into the faith of thousands who profess to believe the Scriptures. The last great conflict between truth and error is but the final struggle of the long-standing controversy concerning the law of God. Upon this battle we are now entering – a battle between the laws of men and the precepts of Jehovah, between the religion of the Bible and the religion of fable and tradition.

The agencies which will unite against truth and righteousness in this contest are now actively at work. God's holy word, which has been handed down to us at such a cost of suffering and blood, is but little valued. The Bible is within the reach of all, but there are few who really accept it as the guide of life. Infidelity prevails to an alarming extent, not in the world merely, but in the church. Many have come to deny doctrines which are the very pillars of the Christian faith. The great facts of creation as presented by the inspired writers, the fall of man, the atonement, and the perpetuity of the law of God, are practically rejected, either wholly or in part, by a large share of the professedly Christian world. Thousands who pride themselves upon their wisdom and independence regard it as an evidence of weakness to place implicit confidence in [582/583] the Bible; they think it a proof of superior talent and learning to cavil at the Scriptures and to spiritualize and explain away their most important truths. Many ministers are teaching their people, and many professors and teachers are instructing their students, that the law of God has been changed or abrogated; and those who regard its requirements as still valid, to be literally obeyed, are thought to be deserving only of ridicule or contempt.

In rejecting the truth, men reject its Author. In trampling upon the law of God, they deny the authority of the Law-giver. It is as easy to make an idol of false doctrines and theories as to fashion an idol of wood or stone. By misrepresenting the attributes of God, Satan leads men to conceive of Him in a false character. With many, a philosophical idol is enthroned in the place of Jehovah; while the living God, as He is revealed in His word, in Christ, and in the works of creation, is worshiped by but few. Thousands deify nature while they deny the God of nature. Though in a different form, idolatry exists in the Christian world today as verily as it existed among ancient Israel in the days of Elijah. The God of many professedly wise men, of philosophers, poets, politicians, journalists – the God of polished fashionable circles, of many colleges and universities, even of some theological institutions - is little better than Baal, the sun-god of Phoenicia.

No error accepted by the Christian world strikes more boldly against the authority of Heaven, none is more directly opposed to the dictates of reason, none is more pernicious in its results, than the modern doctrine, so rapidly gaining ground, that God's law is no longer binding upon men. Every nation has its laws, which command respect and obedience; no government could exist without them; and can it be conceived that the Creator of the heavens and the earth has no law to govern the beings He has made? Suppose that prominent ministers were publicly to teach that the statutes which govern their land and protect the rights of its citizens were not obligatory – that they restricted the liberties of the people, and therefore ought not to be obeyed; how long would such men be tolerated in the pulpit? But is it a graver offense to disregard the laws of states and nations than to trample upon those divine precepts which are the foundation of all government? It would be far more consistent for nations to abolish their statutes, and permit the people to do as they please, than for the Ruler of the universe to annul His law, and leave the world without a standard to condemn the guilty or justify the obedient. Would we know the result of making void the law of God? The experiment has been tried. Terrible were the scenes enacted in France when atheism became the controlling power. It was then demonstrated to the world that to throw off the restraints which God has imposed is to accept the rule of the cruelest of tyrants. When the standard of righteousness is set aside, the way is open for the prince of evil to establish his power in the earth.

Wherever the divine precepts are rejected, sin ceases to appear sinful or righteousness desirable. Those who refuse to submit to the government of God are wholly unfitted to govern themselves. Through their pernicious teachings the spirit of insubordination is implanted in the hearts of children and youth, who are naturally impatient of control; and a lawless, licentious state of society results. While scoffing at the credulity of those who obey the requirements of God, the multitudes eagerly accept the delusions of Satan. They give the rein to lust and practice the sins which have called down judgments upon the heathen.

Those who teach the people to regard lightly the commandments of God sow disobedience to reap disobedience. Let the restraint imposed by the divine law be wholly cast aside, and human laws would soon be disregarded. Because God forbids dishonest practices, coveting, lying, and defrauding, men are ready to trample upon His statutes as a hindrance to their worldly prosperity; but the results of banishing these precepts would be such as they do not anticipate. If the law were not binding, why should any fear to transgress? Property would no longer be safe. Men would obtain their neighbor's possessions by violence, and the strongest would become richest. Life itself would not be respected. The marriage vow would no longer stand as a sacred bulwark to protect the family. He who had the power, would, if he desired, take his neighbor's wife by violence. The fifth commandment would be set aside with the fourth. Children would not shrink from taking the life of their parents if by so doing they could obtain the desire of their corrupt hearts. The civilized world would become a horde of robbers and assassins; and peace, rest, and happiness would be banished from the earth.

Already the doctrine that men are released from obedience to God's requirements has weakened the force of moral obligation and opened the floodgates of iniquity upon the world. Lawlessness, dissipation, and corruption are sweeping in upon us like an overwhelming tide. In the family, Satan is at work. His banner waves, even in professedly Christian households. There is envy, evil surmising, hypocrisy, estrangement, emulation, strife, betrayal of sacred trusts, indulgence of lust. The whole system of religious principles and doctrines, which should form the foundation and framework of social life, seems to be a tottering mass, ready to fall to ruin. The vilest of criminals, when thrown into prison for their offenses, are often made the recipients of gifts and attentions as if they had attained an enviable distinction. Great publicity is given to their character and crimes. The press publishes the revolting details of vice, thus initiating others into the practice of fraud, robbery, and murder; and Satan exults in the success of his hellish schemes. The infatuation of vice, the wanton taking of life, the terrible increase of intemperance and iniquity of every order and degree, should arouse all who fear God, to inquire what can be done to stay the tide of evil.

Courts of justice are corrupt. Rulers are actuated by desire for gain and love of sensual pleasure. Intemperance has beclouded the faculties of many so that Satan has almost complete control of them. Jurists are perverted, bribed, deluded. Drunkenness and revelry, passion, envy, dishonesty of every sort, are represented among those who administer the laws. »Justice standeth afar off: for truth is fallen in the street, and equity cannot enter.« Isaiah 59:14

The iniquity and spiritual darkness that prevailed under the supremacy of Rome were the inevitable result of her suppression of the Scriptures; but where is to be found the cause of the widespread infidelity, the rejection of the law of God, and the consequent corruption, under the full blaze of gospel light in an age of religious freedom? Now that Satan can no longer keep the world under his control by withholding the Scriptures, he resorts to other means to accomplish the same object. To destroy faith in the Bible serves his purpose as well as to destroy the Bible itself. By introducing the belief that God's law is not binding, he as effectually leads men to transgress as if they were wholly ignorant of its precepts. And now, as in former ages, he has worked through the church to further his designs. The religious organizations of the day have refused to listen to unpopular truths plainly brought to view in the Scriptures, and in combating them they have adopted interpretations and taken positions which have sown broadcast the seeds of skepticism. Clinging to the papal error of

natural immortality and man's consciousness in death,

they have rejected the only defense against the delusions of spiritualism. The doctrine of eternal torment has led many to disbelieve the Bible. And as the claims of the fourth commandment are urged upon the people, it is found that the observance of the seventh-day Sabbath is enjoined; and as the only way to free themselves from a duty which they are unwilling to perform, many popular teachers declare that the law of God is no longer binding. Thus they cast away the law and the Sabbath together. As the work of Sabbath reform extends, this rejection of the divine law to avoid the claims of the fourth commandment will become well-nigh universal. The teachings of religious leaders have opened the door to infidelity, to spiritualism, and to contempt for God's holy law; and upon these leaders rests a fearful responsibility for the iniquity that exists in the Christian world.

Yet this very class put forth the claim that the fast-spreading corruption is largely attributable to the desecration of the so-called »Christian sabbath,« and that the enforcement of Sunday observance would greatly improve the morals of society. This claim is especially urged in America, where the doctrine of the true Sabbath has been most widely preached. Here the temperance work, one of the most prominent and important of moral reforms, is often combined with the Sunday movement, and the advocates of the latter represent themselves as laboring to promote the highest interest of society; and those who refuse to unite with them are denounced as the enemies of temperance and reform. But the fact that a movement to establish error is connected with a work which is in itself good, is not an argument in favor of the error. We may disguise poison by mingling it with wholesome food, but we do not change its nature. On the contrary, it is rendered more dangerous, as it is more likely to be taken unawares. It is one of Satan's devices to combine with falsehood just enough truth to give it plausibility. The leaders of the Sunday movement may advocate reforms which the people need, principles which are in harmony with the Bible; yet while there is with these a requirement which is contrary to God's law, His servants cannot unite with them. Nothing can justify them in setting aside the commandments of God for the precepts of men.

Through the two great errors, the immortality of the soul and Sunday sacredness, Satan will bring the people under his deceptions. While the former lays the foundation of spiritualism, the latter creates a bond of sympathy with Rome. The Protestants of the United States will be foremost in stretching their hands across the gulf to grasp the hand of spiritualism; they will reach over the abyss to clasp hands with the Roman power; and under the influence of this threefold union, this country will follow in the steps of Rome in trampling on the rights of conscience. As spiritualism more closely imitates the nominal Christianity of the day, it has greater power to deceive and ensnare. Satan himself is converted, after the modern order of things. He will appear in the character of an angel of light. Through the agency of spiritualism, miracles will be wrought, the sick will be healed, and many undeniable wonders will be performed. And as the spirits will profess faith in the Bible, and manifest respect for the institutions of the church, their work will be accepted as a manifestation of divine power.

The line of distinction between professed Christians and the ungodly is now hardly distinguishable. Church members love what the world loves and are ready to join with them, and Satan determines to unite them in one body and thus strengthen his cause by sweeping all into the ranks of spiritualism. Papists, who boast of miracles as a certain sign of the true church, will be readily deceived by this wonder-working power; and Protestants, having cast away the shield of truth, will also be deluded. Papists, Protestants, and worldlings will alike accept the form of godliness without the power, and they will see in this union a grand movement for the conversion of the world and the ushering in of the long-expected millennium. Through spiritualism, Satan appears as a benefactor of the race, healing the diseases of the people, and professing to present a new and more exalted system of religious faith; but at the same time he works as a destroyer. His temptations are leading multitudes to ruin. Intemperance dethrones reason; sensual indulgence, strife, and bloodshed follow. Satan delights in war, for it excites the worst passions of the soul and then sweeps into eternity its victims steeped in vice and blood. It is his object to incite the nations to war against one another, for he can thus divert the minds of the people from the work of preparation to stand in the day of God.

Satan works through the elements also to garner his harvest of unprepared souls. He has studied the secrets of the laboratories of nature, and he uses all his power to control the elements as far as God allows. When he was suffered to afflict Job, how quickly flocks and

 herds, servants, houses, children, were swept away,

one trouble succeeding another as in a moment. It is God that shields His creatures and hedges them in from the power of the destroyer. But the Christian world have shown contempt for the law of Jehovah; and the Lord will do just what He has declared that He would – He will withdraw His blessings from the earth and remove His protecting care from those who are rebelling against His law and teaching and forcing others to do the same. Satan has control of all whom God does not especially guard. He will favor and prosper some in order to further his own designs, and he will bring trouble upon others and lead men to believe that it is God who is afflicting them.

While appearing to the children of men as a great physician who can heal all their maladies, he will bring disease and disaster, until populous cities are reduced to ruin and desolation. Even now he is at work. In accidents and calamities by sea and by land, in great conflagrations, in fierce tornadoes and terrific hailstorms, in tempests, floods, cyclones, tidal waves, and earthquakes, in every place and in a thousand forms, Satan is exercising his power. He sweeps away the ripening harvest, and famine and distress follow. He imparts to the air a deadly taint, and thousands perish by the pestilence. These visitations are to become more and more frequent and disastrous. Destruction will be upon both man and beast. »The earth mourneth and fadeth away,« »the haughty people ... do languish. The earth also is defiled under the inhabitants thereof; because they have transgressed the laws, changed the ordinance, broken the everlasting covenant.« Isaiah 24:4-5 And then the great deceiver will persuade men that those who serve God are causing these evils. The class that have provoked the displeasure of Heaven will charge all their troubles upon those whose obedience to God's commandments is a perpetual reproof to transgressors. It will be declared that men are offending God by the violation of the Sunday sabbath; that this sin has brought calamities which will not cease until Sunday observance shall be strictly enforced; and that those who present the claims of the fourth commandment, thus destroying reverence for Sunday, are troublers of the people, preventing their restoration to divine favor and temporal prosperity.

Thus the accusation urged of old against the servant of God will be repeated and upon grounds equally well established: »And it came to pass, when Ahab saw Elijah, that Ahab said unto him, Art thou he that troubleth Israel? And he answered, I have [589/590] not troubled Israel; but thou, and thy father's house, in that ye have forsaken the commandments of the Lord, and thou hast followed Baalim.« 1 Kings 18:17-18 As the wrath of the people shall be excited by false charges, they will pursue a course toward God's ambassadors very similar to that which apostate Israel pursued toward Elijah. The miracle-working power manifested through spiritualism will exert its influence against those who choose to obey God rather than men. Communications from the spirits will declare that God has sent them to convince the rejecters of Sunday of their error, affirming that the laws of the land should be obeyed as the law of God. They will lament the great wickedness in the world and second the testimony of religious teachers that the degraded state of morals is caused by the desecration of Sunday. Great will be the indignation excited against all who refuse to accept their testimony.

The Ecumenical Unity at the Expense of the Truth

Satan's policy in this final conflict with God's people is the same that he employed in the opening of the great controversy in heaven. He professed to be seeking to promote the stability of the divine government, while secretly bending every effort to secure its overthrow. And the very work which he was thus endeavoring to accomplish he charged upon the loyal angels. The same policy of deception has marked the history of the Roman Church. It has professed to act as the vicegerent of Heaven, while seeking to exalt itself above God and to change His law. Under the rule of Rome, those who suffered death for their fidelity to the gospel were denounced as evildoers; they were declared to be in league with Satan; and every possible means was employed to cover them with reproach, to cause them to appear in the eyes of the people and even to themselves as the vilest of criminals. So it will be now. While Satan seeks to destroy those who honor God's law, he will cause them to be accused as lawbreakers, as men who are dishonoring God and bringing judgments upon the world. God never forces the will or the conscience; but Satan's constant resort – to gain control of those whom he cannot otherwise seduce – is compulsion by cruelty. Through fear or force he endeavors to rule the conscience and to secure homage to himself. To accomplish this, he works through both religious and secular authorities, moving them to the enforcement of human laws in defiance of the law of God.

Those who honor the Bible Sabbath will be denounced as enemies of law and order, as breaking down the moral restraints of society, causing anarchy and corruption, and calling down the judgments of God upon the earth. Their conscientious scruples will be pronounced obstinacy, stubbornness, and contempt of authority. They will be accused of disaffection toward the government. Ministers who deny the obligation of the divine law will present from the pulpit the duty of yielding obedience to the civil authorities as ordained of God. In legislative halls and courts of justice, commandment keepers will be misrepresented and condemned. A false coloring will be given to their words; the worst construction will be put upon their motives.

As the Protestant churches reject the clear, Scriptural arguments in defense of God's law, they will long to silence those whose faith they cannot overthrow by the Bible. Though they blind their own eyes to the fact, they are now adopting a course which will lead to the persecution of those who conscientiously refuse to do [591/592] what the rest of the Christian world are doing, and acknowledge the claims of the papal sabbath.

The dignitaries of church and state will unite to bribe, persuade, or compel all classes to honor the Sunday. The lack of divine authority will be supplied by oppressive enactments. Political corruption is destroying love of justice and regard for truth; and even in free America, rulers and legislators, in order to secure public favor, will yield to the popular demand for a law enforcing Sunday observance. Liberty of conscience, which has cost so great a sacrifice, will no longer be respected. In the soon-coming conflict we shall see exemplified the prophet's words: »The dragon was wroth with the woman, and went to make war with the remnant of her seed, which keep the commandments of God, and have the testimony of Jesus Christ.« Revelation 12:17

Chapter 37

The Scriptures a Safeguard

To the law and to the testimony: if they speak not according to this word, it is because there is no light in them.« Isaiah 8:20

The people of God are directed to the Scriptures as their safeguard against the influence of false teachers and the delusive power of spirits of darkness. Satan employs every possible device to prevent men from obtaining a knowledge of the Bible; for its plain utterances reveal his deceptions. At every revival of God's work the prince of evil is aroused to more intense activity; he is now putting forth his utmost efforts for a final struggle against Christ and His followers. The last great delusion is soon to open before us. Antichrist is to perform his marvelous works in our sight. So closely will the counterfeit resemble the true that it will be impossible to distinguish between them except by the Holy Scriptures. By their testimony every statement and every miracle must be tested.

Those who endeavor to obey all the commandments of God will be opposed and derided. They can stand only in God. In order to endure the trial before them, they must understand the will of God as revealed in His word; they can honor Him only as they have a right conception of His character, government, and purposes, and act in accordance with them. None but those who have fortified the mind with the truths of the Bible will stand through the last great conflict. To every soul will come the searching test: Shall I obey God rather than men? The decisive hour is even now at hand. Are our feet planted on the rock of God's immutable word? Are we prepared to stand firm in defense of the commandments of God and the faith of Jesus?

Before His crucifixion the Saviour explained to His disciples that He was to be put to death and to rise again from the tomb, and angels were present to impress His words on minds and hearts. But the disciples were looking for temporal deliverance from the Roman yoke, and they could not tolerate the thought that He in whom all their hopes centered should suffer an ignominious death. The words which they needed to remember were banished from their minds; and when the time of trial came, it found them unprepared. The death of Jesus as fully destroyed their hopes as if He had not forewarned them. So in the prophecies the future is opened before us as plainly as it was opened to the disciples by the words of Christ. The events connected with the close of probation and the work of preparation for the time of trouble, are clearly presented. But multitudes have no more understanding of these important truths than if they had never been revealed. Satan watches to catch away every impression that would make them wise unto salvation, and the time of trouble will find them unready.

When God sends to men warnings so important that they are represented as proclaimed by holy angels flying in the midst of heaven, He requires every person endowed with reasoning powers to heed the message. The fearful judgments denounced against the worship of the beast and his image, Revelation 14:9-11 should lead all to a diligent study of the prophecies to learn what the mark of the beast is, and how they are to avoid receiving it. But the masses of the people turn away their ears from hearing the truth and are turned unto fables. The apostle Paul declared, looking down to the last days: »The time will come when they will not endure sound doctrine.« 2 Timothy 4:3 That time has fully come. The multitudes do not want Bible truth, because it interferes with the desires of the sinful, world-loving heart; and Satan supplies the deceptions which they love.

But God will have a people upon the earth to maintain the Bible, and the Bible only, as the standard of all doctrines and the basis of all reforms. The opinions of learned men, the deductions of science, the creeds or decisions of ecclesiastical councils, as numerous and discordant as are the churches which they represent, the voice of the majority – not one nor all of these should be regarded as evidence for or against any point of religious faith. Before accepting any doctrine or precept, we should demand a plain »Thus saith the Lord« in its support. Satan is constantly endeavoring to attract attention to man in the place of God. He leads the people to look to bishops, to pastors, to professors of theology, as their guides, instead of searching the Scriptures to learn their duty for themselves. Then, by controlling the minds of these leaders, he can influence the multitudes according to his will.

When Christ came to speak the words of life, the common people
 heard Him gladly; and many, even of the priests and rul-

ers, believed on Him. But the chief of the priesthood and the leading men of the nation were determined to condemn and repudiate His teachings. Though they were baffled in all their efforts to find accusations against Him, though they could not but feel the influence of the divine power and wisdom attending His words, yet they incased themselves in prejudice; they rejected the clearest evidence of His Messiahship, lest they should be forced to become His disciples. These opponents of Jesus were men whom the people had been taught from infancy to reverence, to whose authority they had been accustomed implicitly to bow. »How is it,« they asked, »that our rulers and learned scribes do not believe on Jesus? Would not these pious men receive Him if He were the Christ?« It was the influence of such teachers that led the Jewish nation to reject their Redeemer.

The spirit which actuated those priests and rulers is still manifested by many who make a high profession of piety. They refuse to examine the testimony of the Scriptures concerning the special truths for this time. They point to their own numbers, wealth, and popularity, and look with contempt upon the advocates of truth as few, poor, and unpopular, having a faith that separates them from the world.

Christ foresaw that the undue assumption of authority indulged by the scribes and Pharisees would not cease with the dispersion of the Jews. He had a prophetic view of the work of exalting human authority to rule the conscience, which has been so terrible a curse to the church in all ages. And His fearful denunciations of the scribes and Pharisees, and His warnings to the people not to follow these blind leaders, were placed on record as an admonition to future generations.

The Roman Church reserves to the clergy the right to interpret the Scriptures. On the ground that ecclesiastics alone are competent to explain God's word, it is withheld from the common people. see appendix note for p. 340 Though the Reformation gave the Scriptures to all, yet the selfsame principle which was maintained by Rome prevents multitudes in Protestant churches from searching the Bible for themselves. They are taught to accept its teachings as interpreted by the church; and there are thousands who dare receive nothing, however plainly revealed in Scripture, that is contrary to their creed or the established teaching of their church.

Notwithstanding the Bible is full of warnings against false teachers, many are ready thus to commit the keeping of their souls to the clergy. There are today thousands of professors of religion who can give no other reason for points of faith which they hold than that they were so instructed by their religious leaders. They pass by the Saviour's teachings almost unnoticed, and place implicit confidence in the words of the ministers. But are ministers infallible? How can we trust our souls to their guidance unless we know from God's word that they are light bearers? A lack of moral courage to step aside from the beaten track of the world leads many to follow in the steps of learned men; and by their reluctance to investigate for themselves, they are becoming hopelessly fastened in the chains of error. They see that the truth for this time is plainly brought to view in the Bible; and they feel the power of the Holy Spirit attending its proclamation; yet they allow the opposition of the clergy to turn them from the light. Though reason and conscience are convinced, these deluded souls dare not think differently from the minister; and their individual judgment, their eternal interests, are sacrificed to the unbelief, the pride and prejudice, of another.

Many are the ways by which Satan works through human influence to bind his captives. He secures multitudes to himself by attaching them by the silken cords of affection to those who are enemies of the cross of Christ. Whatever this attachment may be, parental, filial, conjugal, or social, the effect is the same; the opposers of truth exert their power to control the conscience, and the souls held under their sway have not sufficient courage or independence to obey their own convictions of duty. The truth and the glory of God are inseparable; it is impossible for us, with the Bible within our reach, to honor God by erroneous opinions. Many claim that it matters not what one believes, if his life is only right. But the life is molded by the faith. If light and truth is within our reach, and we neglect to improve the privilege of hearing and seeing it, we virtually reject it; we are choosing darkness rather than light.

»There is a way that seemeth right unto a man, but the end thereof are the ways of death.« Proverbs 16:25 Ignorance is no excuse for error or sin, when there is every opportunity to know the will of God. A man is traveling and comes to a place where there are several roads and a guideboard indicating where each one leads. If he disregards the guideboard, and takes whichever road seems to him to be right, he may be ever so sincere, but will in all probability find himself on the wrong road.

God has given us His word that we may become acquainted with its teachings and know for ourselves what He requires of us. When the lawyer came to Jesus with the inquiry, »What shall I do to inherit eternal life?« the Saviour referred him to the Scriptures, saying: »What is written in the law? how readest thou?« Ignorance will not excuse young or old, nor release them from the punishment due for the transgression of God's law; because there is in their hands a faithful presentation of that law and of its principles and claims. It is not enough to have good intentions; it is not enough to do what a man thinks is right or what the minister tells him is right. His soul's salvation is at stake, and he should search the Scriptures for himself. However strong may be his convictions, however confident he may be that the minister knows what is truth, this is not his foundation. He has a chart pointing out every waymark on the heavenward journey, and he ought not to guess at anything.

It is the first and highest duty of every rational being to learn from the Scriptures what is truth, and then to walk in the light and encourage others to follow his example. We should day by day study the Bible diligently, weighing every thought and comparing scripture with scripture. With divine help we are to form our opinions for ourselves as we are to answer for ourselves before God.

The truths most plainly revealed in the Bible have been involved in doubt and darkness by learned men, who, with a pretense of great wisdom, teach that the Scriptures have a mystical, a secret, spiritual meaning not apparent in the language employed. These men are false teachers. It was to such a class that Jesus declared: »Ye know not the Scriptures, neither the power of God.« Mark 12:24 The language of the Bible should be explained according to its obvious meaning, unless a symbol or figure is employed. Christ has given the promise: »If any man will do His will, he shall know of the doctrine.« John 7:17 If men would but take the Bible as it reads, if there were no false teachers to mislead and confuse their minds, a work would be accomplished that would make angels glad and that would bring into the fold of Christ thousands upon thousands who are now wandering in error.

We should exert all the powers of the mind in the study of the Scriptures and should task the understanding to comprehend, as far as mortals can, the deep things of God; yet we must not forget that the docility and submission of a child is the true spirit of the learner. Scriptural difficulties can never be mastered by the same methods that are employed in grappling with philosophical problems. We should not engage in the study of the Bible with that self-reliance with which so many enter the domains of science, but with a prayerful dependence upon God and a sincere desire to learn His will. We must come with a humble and teachable spirit to obtain knowledge from the great I AM. Otherwise, evil angels will so blind our minds and harden our hearts that we shall not be impressed by the truth.

Many a portion of Scripture which learned men pronounce a mystery, or pass over as unimportant, is full of comfort and instruction to him who has been taught in the school of Christ. One reason why many theologians have no clearer understanding of God's word is, they close their eyes to truths which they do not wish to practice. An understanding of Bible truth depends not so much on the power of intellect brought to the search as on the singleness of purpose, the earnest longing after righteousness.

The Bible should never be studied without prayer. The Holy Spirit alone can cause us to feel the importance of those things easy to be understood, or prevent us from wresting truths difficult of comprehension. It is the office of heavenly angels to prepare the heart so to comprehend God's word that we shall be charmed with its beauty, admonished by its warnings, or animated and strengthened by its promises. We should make the psalmist's petition our own: »Open Thou mine eyes, that I may behold wondrous things out of Thy law.« Psalm 119:18 Temptations often appear irresistible because, through neglect of prayer and the study of the Bible, the tempted one cannot readily remember God's promises and meet Satan with the Scripture weapons. But angels are round about those who are willing to be taught in divine things; and in the time of great necessity they will bring to their remembrance the very truths which are needed. Thus »when the enemy shall come in like a flood, the Spirit of the Lord shall lift up a standard against him.« Isaiah 59:19

Jesus promised His disciples: »The Comforter, which is the Holy Ghost, whom the Father will send in My name, He shall teach you all things, and bring all things to your remembrance, whatsoever I have said unto you.« John 14:26 But the teachings of Christ must previously have been stored in the mind in order for the Spirit of God to bring them to our remembrance in the time of peril.

»Thy word have I hid in mine heart,« said David, »that I might not sin against Thee.« Psalm 119:11

All who value their eternal interests should be on their guard against the inroads of skepticism. The very pillars of truth will be assailed. It is impossible to keep beyond the reach of the sarcasms and sophisms, the insidious and pestilent teachings, of modern infidelity. Satan adapts his temptations to all classes. He assails the illiterate with a jest or sneer, while he meets the educated with scientific objections and philosophical reasoning, alike calculated to excite distrust or contempt of the Scriptures. Even youth of little experience presume to insinuate doubts concerning the fundamental principles of Christianity. And this youthful infidelity, shallow as it is, has its influence. Many are thus led to jest at the faith of their fathers and to do despite to the Spirit of grace. Hebrews 10:29 Many a life that promised to be an honor to God and a blessing to the world has been blighted by the foul breath of infidelity. All who trust to the boastful decisions of human reason and imagine that they can explain divine mysteries and arrive at truth unaided by the wisdom of God are entangled in the snare of Satan.

We are living in the most solemn period of this world's history. The destiny of earth's teeming multitudes is about to be decided. Our own future well-being and also the salvation of other souls depend upon the course which we now pursue. We need to be guided by the Spirit of truth. Every follower of Christ should earnestly inquire: »Lord, what wilt Thou have me to do?« We need to humble ourselves before the Lord, with fasting and prayer, and to meditate much upon His word, especially upon the scenes of the judgment. We should now seek a deep and living experience in the things of God. We have not a moment to lose. Events of vital importance are taking place around us; we are on Satan's enchanted ground. Sleep not, sentinels of God; the foe is lurking near, ready at any moment, should you become lax and drowsy, to spring upon you and make you his prey.

Many are deceived as to their true condition before God. They congratulate themselves upon the wrong acts which they do not commit, and forget to enumerate the good and noble deeds which God requires of them, but which they have neglected to perform. It is not enough that they are trees in the garden of God. They are to answer His expectation by bearing fruit. He holds them accountable for their failure to accomplish all the good which they could have done, through His grace strengthening them. In the books of heaven they are registered as cumberers of the ground. Yet the case of even this class is not utterly hopeless. With those who have slighted God's mercy and abused His grace, the heart of long-suffering love yet pleads. »Wherefore He saith, Awake thou that sleepest, and arise from the dead, and Christ shall give thee light. See then that ye walk circumspectly, ... redeeming the time, because the days are evil.« Ephesians 5:14-16

When the testing time shall come, those who have made God's word their rule of life will be revealed. In summer there is no noticeable difference between evergreens and other trees; but when the blasts of winter come, the evergreens remain unchanged, while other trees are stripped of their foliage. So the falsehearted professor may not now be distinguished from the real Christian, but the time is just upon us when the difference will be apparent. Let opposition arise, let bigotry and intolerance again bear sway, let persecution be kindled, and the halfhearted and hypocritical will waver and yield the faith; but the true Christian will stand firm as a rock, his faith stronger, his hope brighter, than in days of prosperity.

Says the psalmist: »Thy testimonies are my meditation.« »Through Thy precepts I get understanding: therefore I hate every false way.« Psalm 119:99, 104 »Happy is the man that findeth wisdom.« »He shall be as a tree planted by the waters, and that spreadeth out her roots by the river, and shall not see when heat cometh, but her leaf shall be green; and shall not be careful in the year of drought, neither shall cease from yielding fruit.« Proverbs 3:13; Jeremiah 17:8

Chapter 38

The Final Warning

»I saw another angel come down from heaven, having great power; and the earth was lightened with his glory. And he cried mightily with a strong voice, saying, Babylon the great is fallen, is fallen, and is become the habitation of devils, and the hold of every foul spirit, and a cage of every unclean and hateful bird.« »And I heard another voice from heaven, saying, Come out of her, My people, that ye be not partakers of her sins, and that ye receive not of her plagues.« Revelation 18:1, 2, 4

This scripture points forward to a time when the announcement of the fall of Babylon, as made by the second angel of Revelation 14 verse 8, is to be repeated, with the additional mention of the corruptions which have been entering the various organizations that constitute Babylon, since that message was first given, in the summer of 1844. A terrible condition of the religious world is here described. With every rejection of truth the minds of the people will become darker, their hearts more stubborn, until they are entrenched in an infidel hardihood. In defiance of the warnings which God has given, they will continue to trample upon one of the precepts of the Decalogue, until they are led to persecute those who hold it sacred. Christ is set at nought in the contempt placed upon His word and His people. As the teachings of spiritualism are accepted by the churches, the restraint imposed upon the carnal heart is removed, and the profession of religion will become a cloak to conceal the basest iniquity. A belief in spiritual manifestations opens the door to seducing spirits and doctrines of devils, and thus the influence of evil angels will be felt in the churches. Of Babylon, at the time brought to view in this prophecy, it is declared: »Her sins have reached unto heaven, and God hath remembered her iniquities.« Rev. 18:5 She has filled up the measure of her guilt, and destruction is about to fall upon her.

But God still has a people in Babylon; and before the visitation of His judgments these faithful ones must be called out, that they partake not of her sins and »receive not of her plagues.«

Hence the movement symbolized by the angel coming down from heaven, lightening the earth with his glory and crying mightily with a strong voice, announcing the sins of Babylon. In connection with his message the call is heard: »Come out of her, My people.« These announcements, uniting with the third angel's message, constitute the final warning to be given to the inhabitants of the earth.

Fearful is the issue to which the world is to be brought. The powers of earth, uniting to war against the commandments of God, will decree that »all, both small and great, rich and poor, free and bond«, Revelation 13:16 shall conform to the customs of the church by the observance of the false sabbath. All who refuse compliance will be visited with civil penalties, and it will finally be declared that they are deserving of death. On the other hand, the law of God enjoining the Creator's rest day demands obedience and threatens wrath against all who transgress its precepts.

With the issue thus clearly brought before him, whoever shall trample upon God's law to obey a human enactment receives the mark of the beast; he accepts the sign of allegiance to the power which he chooses to obey instead of God. The warning from heaven is: »If any man worship the beast and his image, and receive his mark in his forehead, or in his hand, the same shall drink of the wine of the wrath of God, which is poured out without mixture into the cup of His indignation.« Revelation 14:9-10

But not one is made to suffer the wrath of God until the truth has been brought home to his mind and conscience, and has been rejected. There are many who have never had an opportunity to hear the special truths for this time. The obligation of the fourth commandment has never been set before them in its true light. He who reads every heart and tries every motive will leave none who desire a knowledge of the truth, to be deceived as to the issues of the controversy. The decree is not to be urged upon the people blindly. Everyone is to have sufficient light to make his decision intelligently.

The Sabbath will be the great test of loyalty, for it is the point of truth especially controverted. When the final test shall be brought to bear upon men, then the line of distinction will be drawn between those who serve God and those who serve Him not. While the observance of the false sabbath in compliance with the law of the state, contrary to the fourth commandment, will be an avowal of

 allegiance to a power that is in opposition to God,

the keeping of the true Sabbath, in obedience to God's law, is an evidence of loyalty to the Creator. While one class, by accepting the sign of submission to earthly powers, receive the mark of the beast, the other choosing the token of allegiance to divine authority, receive the seal of God.

Heretofore those who presented the truths of the third angel's message have often been regarded as mere alarmists. Their predictions that religious intolerance would gain control in the United States, that church and state would unite to persecute those who keep the commandments of God, have been pronounced groundless and absurd. It has been confidently declared that this land could never become other than what it has been – the defender of religious freedom. But as the question of enforcing Sunday observance is widely agitated, the event so long doubted and disbelieved is seen to be approaching, and the third message will produce an effect which it could not have had before.

In every generation God has sent His servants to rebuke sin, both in the world and in the church. But the people desire smooth things spoken to them, and the pure, unvarnished truth is not acceptable. Many reformers, in entering upon their work, determined to exercise great prudence in attacking the sins of the church and the nation. They hoped, by the example of a pure Christian life, to lead the people back to the doctrines of the Bible. But the Spirit of God came upon them as it came upon Elijah, moving him to rebuke the sins of a wicked king and an apostate people; they could not refrain from preaching the plain utterances of the Bible – doctrines which they had been reluctant to present. They were impelled to zealously declare the truth and the danger which threatened souls. The words which the Lord gave them they uttered, fearless of consequences, and the people were compelled to hear the warning.

Thus the message of the third angel will be proclaimed. As the time comes for it to be given with greatest power, the Lord will work through humble instruments, leading the minds of those who consecrate themselves to His service. The laborers will be qualified rather by the unction of His Spirit than by the training of literary institutions. Men of faith and prayer will be constrained to go forth with holy zeal, declaring the words which God gives them. The sins of Babylon will be laid open. The fearful results of enforcing the observances of the church by civil authority, the inroads of spiritualism, the stealthy but rapid progress of the papal power – all will be unmasked. By these solemn warnings the people will be stirred. Thousands upon thousands will listen who have never heard words like these. In amazement they hear the testimony that Babylon is the church, fallen because of her errors and sins, because of her rejection of the truth sent to her from heaven. As the people go to their former teachers with the eager inquiry, Are these things so? the ministers present fables, prophesy smooth things, to soothe their fears and quiet the awakened conscience. But since many refuse to be satisfied with the mere authority of men and demand a plain »Thus saith the Lord,« the popular ministry, like the Pharisees of old, filled with anger as their authority is questioned, will denounce the message as of Satan and stir up the sin-loving multitudes to revile and persecute those who proclaim it.

As the controversy extends into new fields and the minds of the people are called to God's downtrodden law, Satan is astir. The power attending the message will only madden those who oppose it. The clergy will put forth almost superhuman efforts to shut away the light lest it should shine upon their flocks. By every means at their command they will endeavor to suppress the discussion of these vital questions. The church appeals to the strong arm of civil power, and, in this work, papists and Protestants unite. As the movement for Sunday enforcement becomes more bold and decided, the law will be invoked against commandment keepers. They will be threatened with fines and imprisonment, and some will be offered positions of influence, and other rewards and advantages, as inducements to renounce their faith. But their steadfast answer is: »Show us from the word of God our error« – the same plea that was made by Luther under similar circumstances. Those who are arraigned before the courts make a strong vindication of the truth, and some who hear them are led to take their stand to keep all the commandments of God. Thus light will be brought before thousands who otherwise would know nothing of these truths.

Conscientious obedience to the word of God will be treated as rebellion. Blinded by Satan, the parent will exercise harshness and severity toward the believing child; the master or mistress will oppress the commandment-keeping servant. Affection will be alienated; children will be disinherited and driven from home.

 The words of Paul will be literally fulfilled: »All that will live godly in Christ Jesus shall suffer persecution.« 2 Timothy 3:12 As the defenders of truth refuse to honor the Sunday-sabbath, some of them will be thrust into prison, some will be exiled, some will be treated as slaves. To human wisdom all this now seems impossible; but as the restraining Spirit of God shall be withdrawn from men, and they shall be under the control of Satan, who hates the divine precepts, there will be strange developments. The heart can be very cruel when God's fear and love are removed.

As the storm approaches, a large class who have professed faith in the third angel's message, but have not been sanctified through obedience to the truth, abandon their position and join the ranks of the opposition. By uniting with the world and partaking of its spirit, they have come to view matters in nearly the same light; and when the test is brought, they are prepared to choose the easy, popular side. Men of talent and pleasing address, who once rejoiced in the truth, employ their powers to deceive and mislead souls. They become the most bitter enemies of their former brethren. When Sabbathkeepers are brought before the courts to answer for their faith, these apostates are the most efficient agents of Satan to misrepresent and accuse them, and by false reports and insinuations to stir up the rulers against them.

In this time of persecution the faith of the Lord's servants will be tried. They have faithfully given the warning, looking to God and to His word alone. God's Spirit, moving upon their hearts, has constrained them to speak. Stimulated with holy zeal, and with the divine impulse strong upon them, they entered upon the performance of their duties without coldly calculating the consequences of speaking to the people the word which the Lord had given them. They have not consulted their temporal interests, nor sought to preserve their reputation or their lives. Yet when the storm of opposition and reproach bursts upon them, some, overwhelmed with consternation, will be ready to exclaim: »Had we foreseen the consequences of our words, we would have held our peace.« They are hedged in with difficulties. Satan assails them with fierce temptations. The work which they have undertaken seems far beyond their ability to accomplish. They are threatened with destruction. The enthusiasm which animated them is gone; yet they cannot turn back. Then, feeling their utter helplessness, they flee to the Mighty One for strength. They remember that the words which they have spoken were not theirs, but His who bade them give the warning. God put the truth into their hearts, and they could not forbear to proclaim it.

The same trials have been experienced by men of God in ages past. Wycliffe, Huss, Luther, Tyndale, Baxter, Wesley, urged that all doctrines be brought to the test of the Bible and declared that they would renounce everything which it condemned. Against these men persecution raged with relentless fury; yet they ceased not to declare the truth. Different periods in the history of the church have each been marked by the development of some special truth, adapted to the necessities of God's people at that time. Every new truth has made its way against hatred and opposition; those who were blessed with its light were tempted and tried. The Lord gives a special truth for the people in an emergency. Who dare refuse to publish it? He commands His servants to present the last invitation of mercy to the world. They cannot remain silent, except at the peril of their souls. Christ's ambassadors have nothing to do with consequences. They must perform their duty and leave results with God.

As the opposition rises to a fiercer height, the servants of God are again perplexed; for it seems to them that they have brought the crisis. But conscience and the word of God assure them that their course is right; and although the trials continue, they are strengthened to bear them. The contest grows closer and sharper, but their faith and courage rise with the emergency. Their testimony is: "We dare not tamper with God's word, dividing His holy law; calling one portion essential and another nonessential, to gain the favor of the world. The Lord whom we serve is able to deliver us. Christ has conquered the powers of earth; and shall we be afraid of a world already conquered?"

Persecution in its varied forms is the development of a principle which will exist as long as Satan exists and Christianity has vital power. No man can serve God without enlisting against himself the opposition of the hosts of darkness. Evil angels will assail him, alarmed that his influence is taking the prey from their hands. Evil men, rebuked by his example, will unite with them in seeking to separate him from God by alluring temptations. When these do not succeed, then a compelling power is employed to force the conscience.

But so long as Jesus remains man's intercessor in the sanctuary above, the restraining influence of the Holy Spirit is felt by rulers and people. It still controls to some extent the laws of the land. Were it not for these laws, the condition of the world would be much worse than it now is. While many of our rulers are active agents of Satan, God also has His agents among the leading men of the nation. The enemy moves upon his servants to propose measures that would greatly impede the work of God; but statesmen who fear the Lord are influenced by holy angels to oppose such propositions with unanswerable arguments. Thus a few men will hold in check a powerful current of evil. The opposition of the enemies of truth will be restrained that the third angel's message may do its work. When the final warning shall be given, it will arrest the attention of these leading men through whom the Lord is now working, and some of them will accept it, and will stand with the people of God through the time of trouble.

The angel who unites in the proclamation of the third angel's message is to lighten the whole earth with his glory. A work of world-wide extent and unwonted power is here foretold. The advent movement of 1840-44 was a glorious manifestation of the power of God; the first angel's message was carried to every missionary station in the world, and in some countries there was the greatest religious interest which has been witnessed in any land since the Reformation of the sixteenth century; but these are to be exceeded by the mighty movement under the last warning of the third angel.

The work will be similar to that of the Day of Pentecost. As the »former rain« was given, in the outpouring of the Holy Spirit at the opening of the gospel, to cause the upspringing of the precious seed, so the »latter rain« will be given at its close for the ripening of the harvest. »Then shall we know, if we follow on to know the Lord: His going forth is prepared as the morning; and He shall come unto us as the rain, as the latter and former rain unto the earth.« Hosea 6:3 »Be glad then, ye children of Zion, and rejoice in the Lord your God: for He hath given you the former rain moderately, and He will cause to come down for you the rain, the former rain, and the latter rain.« Joel 2:23 »In the last days, saith God, I will pour out of My Spirit upon all flesh.« »And it shall come to pass, that whosoever shall call on the name of the Lord shall be saved.« Acts 2:17, 21

The great work of the gospel is not to close with less manifestation of the power of God than marked its opening. The prophecies which were fulfilled in the outpouring of the former rain at the opening of the gospel are again to be fulfilled in the latter rain at its close. Here are »the times of refreshing« to which the apostle Peter looked forward when he said: »Repent ye therefore, and be converted, that your sins may be blotted out, when the times of refreshing shall come from the presence of the Lord; and He shall send Jesus.« Acts 3:19-20

Servants of God, with their faces lighted up and shining with holy consecration, will hasten from place to place to proclaim the message from heaven. By thousands of voices, all over the earth, the warning will be given. Miracles will be wrought, the sick will be healed, and signs and wonders will follow the believers. Satan also works, with lying wonders, even bringing down fire from heaven in the sight of men. Revelation 13:13 Thus the inhabitants of the earth will be brought to take their stand.

The message will be carried not so much by argument as by the deep conviction of the Spirit of God. The arguments have been presented. The seed has been sown, and now it will spring up and bear fruit. The publications distributed by missionary workers have exerted their influence, yet many whose minds were impressed have been prevented from fully comprehending the truth or from yielding obedience. Now the rays of light penetrate everywhere, the truth is seen in its clearness, and the honest children of God sever the bands which have held them. Family connections, church relations, are powerless to stay them now. Truth is more precious than all besides. Notwithstanding the agencies combined against the truth, a large number take their stand upon the Lord's side.

Chapter 39

The Time of Trouble

»At that time shall Michael stand up, the great Prince which standeth for the children of thy people: and there shall be a time of trouble, such as never was since there was a nation even to that same time: and at that time thy people shall be delivered, everyone that shall be found written in the book.« Daniel 12:1

When the third angel's message closes, mercy no longer pleads for the guilty inhabitants of the earth. The people of God have accomplished their work. They have received »the latter rain,« »the refreshing from the presence of the Lord,« and they are prepared for the trying hour before them. Angels are hastening to and fro in heaven. An angel returning from the earth announces that his work is done; the final test has been brought upon the world, and all who have proved themselves loyal to the divine precepts have received »the seal of the living God.« Then Jesus ceases His intercession in the sanctuary above. He lifts His hands and with a loud voice says, »It is done;« and all the angelic host lay off their crowns as He makes the solemn announcement: »He that is unjust, let him be unjust still: and he which is filthy, let him be filthy still: and he that is righteous, let him be righteous still: and he that is holy, let him be holy still.« Revelation 22:11 Every case has been decided for life or death. Christ has made the atonement for His people and blotted out their sins. The number of His subjects is made up; »the kingdom and dominion, and the greatness of the kingdom under the whole heaven,« is about to be given to the heirs of salvation, and Jesus is to reign as King of kings and Lord of lords.

When He leaves the sanctuary, darkness covers the inhabitants of the earth. In that fearful time the righteous must live in the sight of a holy God without an intercessor. The restraint which has been upon the wicked is removed, and Satan has entire control of the finally impenitent. God's long-suffering has ended. The world has rejected His mercy, despised His love, and trampled upon His law. The wicked have passed the boundary of their probation; the Spirit of God, persistently resisted, has been at last withdrawn. Unsheltered by divine grace, they have no protection from the wicked one. Satan will then plunge the inhabitants of the earth into one great, final trouble. As the angels of God cease to hold in check the fierce winds of human passion, all the elements of strife will be let loose. The whole world will be involved in ruin more terrible than that which came upon Jerusalem of old.

A single angel destroyed all the first-born of the Egyptians and filled the land with mourning. When David offended against God by numbering the people, one angel caused that terrible destruction by which his sin was punished. The same destructive power exercised by holy angels when God commands, will be exercised by evil angels when He permits. There are forces now ready, and only waiting the divine permission, to spread desolation everywhere.

Those who honor the law of God have been accused of bringing judgments upon the world, and they will be regarded as the cause of the fearful convulsions of nature and the strife and bloodshed among men that are filling the earth with woe. The power attending the last warning has enraged the wicked; their anger is kindled against all who have received the message, and Satan will excite to still greater intensity the spirit of hatred and persecution.

When God's presence was finally withdrawn from the Jewish nation, priests and people knew it not. Though under the control of Satan, and swayed by the most horrible and malignant passions, they still regarded themselves as the chosen of God. The ministration in the temple continued; sacrifices were offered upon its polluted altars, and daily the divine blessing was invoked upon a people guilty of the blood of God's dear Son and seeking to slay His ministers and apostles. So when the irrevocable decision of the sanctuary has been pronounced and the destiny of the world has been forever fixed, the inhabitants of the earth will know it not. The forms of religion will be continued by a people from whom the Spirit of God has been finally withdrawn; and the satanic zeal with which the prince of evil will inspire them for the accomplishment of his malignant designs, will bear the semblance of zeal for God.

As the Sabbath has become the special point of controversy throughout Christendom, and religious and secular authorities have combined to enforce the observance of the Sunday, the persistent

refusal of a small minority to yield to the popular demand will make them objects of universal execration. It will be urged that the few who stand in opposition to an institution of the church and a law of the state ought not to be tolerated; that it is better for them to suffer than for whole nations to be thrown into confusion and lawlessness. The same argument many centuries ago was brought against Christ by the »rulers of the people.« »It is expedient for us,« said the wily Caiaphas, »that one man should die for the people, and that the whole nation perish not.« John 11:50 This argument will appear conclusive; and a decree will finally be issued against those who hallow the Sabbath of the fourth commandment, denouncing them as deserving of the severest punishment and giving the people liberty, after a certain time, to put them to death. Romanism in the Old World and apostate Protestantism in the New will pursue a similar course toward those who honor all the divine precepts.

The people of God will then be plunged into those scenes of affliction and distress described by the prophet as the time of Jacob's trouble. »Thus saith the Lord: We have heard a voice of trembling, of fear, and not of peace. ... All faces are turned into paleness. Alas! for that day is great, so that none is like it: it is even the time of Jacob's trouble; but he shall be saved out of it.« Jeremiah 30:5-7

Jacob's night of anguish, when he wrestled in prayer for deliverance from the hand of Esau, Genesis 32:24-30 represents the experience of God's people in the time of trouble. Because of the deception practiced to secure his father's blessing, intended for Esau, Jacob had fled for his life, alarmed by his brother's deadly threats. After remaining for many years an exile, he had set out, at God's command, to return with his wives and children, his flocks and herds, to his native country. On reaching the borders of the land, he was filled with terror by the tidings of Esau's approach at the head of a band of warriors, doubtless bent upon revenge. Jacob's company, unarmed and defenseless, seemed about to fall helpless victims of violence and slaughter. And to the burden of anxiety and fear was added the crushing weight of self-reproach, for it was his own sin that had brought this danger. His only hope was in the mercy of God; his only defense must be prayer. Yet he leaves nothing undone on his own part to atone for the wrong to his brother and to avert the threatened danger. So should the followers of Christ, as they approach the time of trouble, make every exertion to place themselves in a proper light before the people, to disarm prejudice, and to avert the danger which threatens liberty of conscience.

Having sent his family away, that they may not witness his distress, Jacob remains alone to intercede with God. He confesses his sin and gratefully acknowledges the mercy of God toward him while with deep humiliation he pleads the covenant made with his fathers and the promises to himself in the night vision at Bethel and in the land of his exile. The crisis in his life has come; everything is at stake. In the darkness and solitude he continues praying and humbling himself before God. Suddenly a hand is laid upon his shoulder. He thinks that an enemy is seeking his life, and with all the energy of despair he wrestles with his assailant. As the day begins to break, the stranger puts forth his superhuman power; at his touch the strong man seems paralyzed, and he falls, a helpless, weeping suppliant, upon the neck of his mysterious antagonist. Jacob knows now that it is the Angel of the covenant with whom he has been in conflict. Though disabled and suffering the keenest pain, he does not relinquish his purpose. Long has he endured perplexity, remorse, and trouble for his sin; now he must have the assurance that it is pardoned. The divine visitant seems about to depart; but Jacob clings to Him, pleading for a blessing. The Angel urges, »Let Me go, for the day breaketh;« but the patriarch exclaims, »I will not let Thee go, except Thou bless me.« What confidence, what firmness and perseverance, are here displayed! Had this been a boastful, presumptuous claim, Jacob would have been instantly destroyed; but his was the assurance of one who confesses his weakness and unworthiness, yet trusts the mercy of a covenant-keeping God.

»He had power over the Angel, and prevailed.« Hosea 12:4 Through humiliation, repentance, and self-surrender, this sinful, erring mortal prevailed with the Majesty of heaven. He had fastened his trembling grasp upon the promises of God, and the heart of Infinite Love could not turn away the sinner's plea. As an evidence of his triumph and an encouragement to others to imitate his example, his name was changed from one which was a reminder of his sin, to one that commemorated his victory. And the fact that Jacob had prevailed with God was an assurance that he would prevail with men. He no longer feared to encounter his brother's anger, for the Lord was his defense.

Satan had accused Jacob before the angels of God, claiming the right to destroy him because of his sin; he had moved upon Esau to march against him; and during the patriarch's long night of wrestling, Satan endeavored to force upon him a sense of his guilt in order to discourage him and break his hold upon God. Jacob was driven almost to despair; but he knew that without help from heaven he must perish. He had sincerely repented of his great sin, and he appealed to the mercy of God. He would not be turned from his purpose, but held fast the Angel and urged his petition with earnest, agonizing cries until he prevailed.

As Satan influenced Esau to march against Jacob, so he will stir up the wicked to destroy God's people in the time of trouble. And as he accused Jacob, he will urge his accusations against the people of God. He numbers the world as his subjects; but the little company who keep the commandments of God are resisting his supremacy. If he could blot them from the earth, his triumph would be complete. He sees that holy angels are guarding them, and he infers that their sins have been pardoned; but he does not know that their cases have been decided in the sanctuary above. He has an accurate knowledge of the sins which he has tempted them to commit, and he presents these before God in the most exaggerated light, representing this people to be just as deserving as himself of exclusion from the favor of God. He declares that the Lord cannot in justice forgive their sins and yet destroy him and his angels. He claims them as his prey and demands that they be given into his hands to destroy.

As Satan accuses the people of God on account of their sins, the Lord permits him to try them to the uttermost. Their confidence in God, their faith and firmness, will be severely tested. As they review the past, their hopes sink; for in their whole lives they can see little good. They are fully conscious of their weakness and unworthiness. Satan endeavors to terrify them with the thought that their cases are hopeless, that the stain of their defilement will never be washed away. He hopes so to destroy their faith that they will yield to his temptations and turn from their allegiance to God.

Though God's people will be surrounded by enemies who are bent upon their destruction, yet the anguish which they suffer is not a dread of persecution for the truth's sake; they fear that every sin has not been repented of, and that through some fault in themselves they will fail to realize the fulfillment of the Saviour's promise: I »will keep thee from the hour of temptation, which shall come upon all the world.« Revelation 3:10 If they could have the assurance of pardon they would not shrink from torture or death; but should they prove unworthy, and lose their lives because of their own defects of character, then God's holy name would be reproached.

On every hand they hear the plottings of treason and see the active working of rebellion; and there is aroused within them an intense desire, an earnest yearning of soul, that this great apostasy may be terminated and the wickedness of the wicked may come to an end. But while they plead with God to stay the work of rebellion, it is with a keen sense of self-reproach that they themselves have no more power to resist and urge back the mighty tide of evil. They feel that had they always employed all their ability in the service of Christ, going forward from strength to strength, Satan's forces would have less power to prevail against them.

They afflict their souls before God, pointing to their past repentance of their many sins, and pleading the Saviour's promise: »Let him take hold of My strength, that he may make peace with Me; and he shall make peace with Me.« Isaiah 27:5 Their faith does not fail because their prayers are not immediately answered. Though suffering the keenest anxiety, terror, and distress, they do not cease their intercessions. They lay hold of the strength of God as Jacob laid hold of the Angel; and the language of their souls is: »I will not let Thee go, except Thou bless me.«

Had not Jacob previously repented of his sin in obtaining the birthright by fraud, God would not have heard his prayer and mercifully preserved his life. So, in the time of trouble, if the people of God had unconfessed sins to appear before them while tortured with fear and anguish, they would be overwhelmed; despair would cut off their faith, and they could not have confidence to plead with God for deliverance. But while they have a deep sense of their unworthiness, they have no concealed wrongs to reveal. Their sins have gone beforehand to judgment and have been blotted out, and they cannot bring them to remembrance.

Satan leads many to believe that God will overlook their unfaithfulness in the minor affairs of life; but the Lord shows in His dealings with Jacob that He will in no wise sanction or tolerate evil. All who endeavor to excuse or conceal their sins, and permit them to remain upon the books of heaven, unconfessed and unforgiven, will be overcome by Satan. The more exalted their profession and the more hon-
 orable the position which they hold, the more grievous

is their course in the sight of God and the more sure the triumph of their great adversary. Those who delay a preparation for the day of God cannot obtain it in the time of trouble or at any subsequent time. The case of all such is hopeless. Those professed Christians who come up to that last fearful conflict unprepared will, in their despair, confess their sins in words of burning anguish, while the wicked exult over their distress. These confessions are of the same character as was that of Esau or of Judas. Those who make them, lament the result of transgression, but not its guilt. They feel no true contrition, no abhorrence of evil. They acknowledge their sin, through fear of punishment; but, like Pharaoh of old, they would return to their defiance of Heaven should the judgments be removed.

Jacob's history is also an assurance that God will not cast off those who have been deceived and tempted and betrayed into sin, but who have returned unto Him with true repentance. While Satan seeks to destroy this class, God will send His angels to comfort and protect them in the time of peril. The assaults of Satan are fierce and determined, his delusions are terrible; but the Lord's eye is upon His people, and His ear listens to their cries. Their affliction is great, the flames of the furnace seem about to consume them; but the Refiner will bring them forth as gold tried in the fire. God's love for His children during the period of their severest trial is as strong and tender as in the days of their sunniest prosperity; but it is needful for them to be placed in the furnace of fire; their earthliness must be consumed, that the image of Christ may be perfectly reflected.

The season of distress and anguish before us will require a faith that can endure weariness, delay, and hunger – a faith that will not faint though severely tried. The period of probation is granted to all to prepare for that time. Jacob prevailed because he was persevering and determined. His victory is an evidence of the power of importunate prayer. All who will lay hold of God's promises, as he did, and be as earnest and persevering as he was, will succeed as he succeeded. Those who are unwilling to deny self, to agonize before God, to pray long and earnestly for His blessing, will not obtain it. Wrestling with God – how few know what it is! How few have ever had their souls drawn out after God with intensity of desire until every power is on the stretch. When waves of despair which no language can express sweep over the suppliant, how few cling with unyielding faith to the promises of God.

Those who exercise but little faith now, are in the greatest danger of falling under the power of satanic delusions and the decree to compel the conscience. And even if they endure the test they will be plunged into deeper distress and anguish in the time of trouble, because they have never made it a habit to trust in God. The lessons of faith which they have neglected they will be forced to learn under a terrible pressure of discouragement.

We should now acquaint ourselves with God by proving His promises. Angels record every prayer that is earnest and sincere. We should rather dispense with selfish gratifications than neglect communion with God. The deepest poverty, the greatest self-denial, with His approval, is better than riches, honors, ease, and friendship without it. We must take time to pray. If we allow our minds to be absorbed by worldly interests, the Lord may give us time by removing from us our idols of gold, of houses, or of fertile lands.

The young would not be seduced into sin if they would refuse to enter any path save that upon which they could ask God's blessing. If the messengers who bear the last solemn warning to the world would pray for the blessing of God, not in a cold, listless, lazy manner, but fervently and in faith, as did Jacob, they would find many places where they could say: »I have seen God face to face, and my life is preserved.« Genesis 32:30 They would be accounted of heaven as princes, having power to prevail with God and with men.

The »time of trouble, such as never was,« is soon to open upon us; and we shall need an experience which we do not now possess and which many are too indolent to obtain. It is often the case that trouble is greater in anticipation than in reality; but this is not true of the crisis before us. The most vivid presentation cannot reach the magnitude of the ordeal. In that time of trial, every soul must stand for himself before God. »Though Noah, Daniel, and Job« were in the land, »as I live, saith the Lord God, they shall deliver neither son nor daughter; they shall but deliver their own souls by their righteousness.« Ezekiel 14:20

Now, while our great High Priest is making the atonement for us, we should seek to become perfect in Christ. Not even by a thought could our Saviour be brought to yield to the power of temptation. Satan finds in human hearts some point where he can gain a foothold; some sinful desire is cherished, by means of which his temptations assert their power. But Christ declared of Himself: »The prince of this world cometh, and hath nothing in Me.« John 14:30 Satan could find nothing in the Son of God that would enable him to gain the victory. He had kept His Father's commandments, and there was no sin in Him that Satan could use to his advantage. This is the condition in which those must be found who shall stand in the time of trouble.

It is in this life that we are to separate sin from us, through faith in the atoning blood of Christ. Our precious Saviour invites us to join ourselves to Him, to unite our weakness to His strength, our ignorance to His wisdom, our unworthiness to His merits. God's providence is the school in which we are to learn the meekness and lowliness of Jesus. The Lord is ever setting before us, not the way we would choose, which seems easier and pleasanter to us, but the true aims of life. It rests with us to co-operate with the agencies which Heaven employs in the work of conforming our characters to the divine model. None can neglect or defer this work but at the most fearful peril to their souls.

The apostle John in vision heard a loud voice in heaven exclaiming: »Woe to the inhabiters of the earth and of the sea! for the devil is come down unto you, having great wrath, because he knoweth that he hath but a short time.« Revelation 12:12 Fearful are the scenes which call forth this exclamation from the heavenly voice. The wrath of Satan increases as his time grows short, and his work of deceit and destruction will reach its culmination in the time of trouble.

Fearful sights of a supernatural character will soon be revealed in the heavens, in token of the power of miracle-working demons. The spirits of devils will go forth to the kings of the earth and to the whole world, to fasten them in deception, and urge them on to unite with Satan in his last struggle against the government of heaven. By these agencies, rulers and subjects will be alike deceived. Persons will arise pretending to be Christ Himself, and claiming the title and worship which belong to the world's Redeemer. They will perform wonderful miracles of healing and will profess to have revelations from heaven contradicting the testimony of the Scriptures.

As the crowning act in the great drama of deception, Satan himself will personate Christ. The church has long professed to look to the Saviour's advent as the consummation of her hopes. Now the great deceiver will make it appear that Christ has come. In different parts of the earth, Satan will manifest himself among [623/624] men as a majestic being of dazzling brightness, resembling the description of the Son of God given by John in the Revelation. Revelation 1:13-15 The glory that surrounds him is unsurpassed by anything that mortal eyes have yet beheld. The shout of triumph rings out upon the air: »Christ has come! Christ has come!« The people prostrate themselves in adoration before him, while he lifts up his hands and pronounces a blessing upon them, as Christ blessed His disciples when He was upon the earth. His voice is soft and subdued, yet full of melody. In gentle, compassionate tones he presents some of the same gracious, heavenly truths which the Saviour uttered; he heals the diseases of the people, and then, in his assumed character of Christ, he claims to have changed the Sabbath to Sunday, and commands all to hallow the day which he has blessed. He declares that those who persist in keeping holy the seventh day are blaspheming his name by refusing to listen to his angels sent to them with light and truth. This is the strong, almost overmastering delusion. Like the Samaritans who were deceived by Simon Magus, the multitudes, from the least to the greatest, give heed to these sorceries, saying: This is »the great power of God.« Acts 8:10

But the people of God will not be misled. The teachings of this false Christ are not in accordance with the Scriptures. His blessing is pronounced upon the worshipers of the beast and his image, the very class upon whom the Bible declares that God's unmingled wrath shall be poured out.

And, furthermore, Satan is not permitted to counterfeit the manner of Christ's advent. The Saviour has warned His people against deception upon this point, and has clearly foretold the manner of His second coming. »There shall arise false Christs, and false prophets, and shall show great signs and wonders; insomuch that, if it were possible, they shall deceive the very elect. ... Wherefore if they shall say unto you, Behold, He is in the desert; go not forth; behold, He is in the secret chambers; believe it not. For as the lightning cometh out of the east, and shineth even unto the west; so shall also the coming of the Son of man be.« Matthew 24:24-27, 31; 25:31; Revelation 1:7; 1 Thess. 4:16-17 This coming there is no possibility of counterfeiting. It will be universally known – witnessed by the whole world.

Only those who have been diligent students of the Scriptures and who have received the love of the truth will be shielded from the powerful delusion that takes the world captive. By the Bible testimony these will detect the deceiver in his disguise. To all the testing time will come. By the sifting of temptation the genuine Christian will be revealed. Are the people of God now so firmly established upon His word that they would not yield to the evidence of their senses? Would they, in such a crisis, cling to the Bible and the Bible only? Satan will, if possible, prevent them from obtaining a preparation to stand in that day. He will so arrange affairs as to hedge up their way, entangle them with earthly treasures, cause them to carry a heavy, wearisome burden, that their hearts may be overcharged with the cares of this life and the day of trial may come upon them as a thief.

As the decree issued by the various rulers of Christendom against commandment keepers shall withdraw the protection of government and abandon them to those who desire their destruction, the people of God will flee from the cities and villages and associate together in companies, dwelling in the most desolate and solitary places. Many will find refuge in the strongholds of the mountains. Like the Christians of the Piedmont valleys, they will make the high places of the earth their sanctuaries and will thank God for »the munitions of rocks.« Isaiah 33:16 But many of all nations and of all classes, high and low, rich and poor, black and white, will be cast into the most unjust and cruel bondage. The beloved of God pass weary days, bound in chains, shut in by prison bars, sentenced to be slain, some apparently left to die of starvation in dark and loathsome dungeons. No human ear is open to hear their moans; no human hand is ready to lend them help.

Will the Lord forget His people in this trying hour? Did He forget faithful Noah when judgments were visited upon the antediluvian world? Did He forget Lot when the fire came down from heaven to consume the cities of the plain?

Did He forget Joseph surrounded by idolaters in Egypt? Did He forget Elijah when the oath of Jezebel threatened him with the fate of the prophets of Baal? Did He forget Jeremiah in the dark and dismal pit of his prison house? Did He forget the three worthies in the fiery furnace? or Daniel in the den of lions?

»Zion said, The Lord hath forsaken me, and my Lord hath forgotten me. Can a woman forget her sucking child, that she should not have compassion on the son of her womb? yea, they may forget, yet will I not forget thee. Behold, I have graven thee upon [626/627] the palms of My hands.« Isaiah 49:14-16 The Lord of hosts has said: »He that toucheth you toucheth the apple of His eye.« Zechariah 2:8

Though enemies may thrust them into prison, yet dungeon walls cannot cut off the communication between their souls and Christ. One who sees their every weakness, who is acquainted with every trial, is above all earthly powers; and angels will come to them in lonely cells, bringing light and peace from heaven. The prison will be as a palace; for the rich in faith dwell there, and the gloomy walls will be lighted up with heavenly light as when Paul and Silas prayed and sang praises at midnight in the Philippian dungeon.

God's judgments will be visited upon those who are seeking to oppress and destroy His people. His long forbearance with the wicked emboldens men in transgression, but their punishment is nonetheless certain and terrible because it is long delayed. »The Lord shall rise up as in Mount Perazim, He shall be wroth as in the valley of Gibeon, that He may do His work, His strange work; and bring to pass His act, His strange act.« Isaiah 28:21 To our merciful God the act of punishment is a strange act. »As I live, saith the Lord God, I have no pleasure in the death of the wicked.« Ezekiel 33:11 The Lord is »merciful and gracious, long-suffering, and abundant in goodness and truth, ... forgiving iniquity and transgression and sin.« Yet He will »by no means clear the guilty.« »The Lord is slow to anger, and great in power, and will not at all acquit the wicked.« Exodus 34:6-7; Nahum 1:3 By terrible things in righteousness He will vindicate the authority of His downtrodden law. The severity of the retribution awaiting the transgressor may be judged by the Lord's reluctance to execute justice. The nation with which He bears long, and which He will not smite until it has filled up the measure of its iniquity in God's account, will finally drink the cup of wrath unmixed with mercy.

When Christ ceases His intercession in the sanctuary, the unmingled wrath threatened against those who worship the beast and his image and receive his mark, Revelation 14:9-10 will be poured out.

The plagues upon Egypt when God was about to deliver Israel were similar in character to those more terrible and extensive judgments which are to fall upon the world just before the final deliverance of God's people. Says the revelator, in describing those terrific scourges: »There fell a noisome and grievous sore upon the men which had the mark of the beast, and upon them which worshiped his image.« The sea »became as the blood of a dead man: and every living soul died in the sea.« And »the rivers and fountains of waters ... became blood.« Terrible as these inflictions are, God's justice stands fully vindicated. The angel of God declares: »Thou art righteous, O Lord, ... because Thou hast judged thus. For they have shed the blood of saints and prophets, and Thou hast given them blood to drink; for they are worthy.« Revelation 16:2-6 By condemning the people of God to death, they have as truly incurred the guilt of their blood as if it had been shed by their hands. In like manner Christ declared the Jews of His time guilty of all the blood of holy men which had been shed since the days of Abel; for they possessed the same spirit and were seeking to do the same work with these murderers of the prophets.

In the plague that follows, power is given to the sun »to scorch men with fire. And men were scorched with great heat.« Verses 8, 9 The prophets thus describe the condition of the earth at this fearful time: »The land mourneth; ... because the harvest of the field is perished. ... All the trees of the field are withered: because joy is withered away from the sons of men.« »The seed is rotten under their clods, the garners are laid desolate. ... How do the beasts groan! the herds of cattle are perplexed, because they have no pasture. ... The rivers of water are dried up, and the fire hath devoured the pastures of the wilderness.« »The songs of the temple shall be howlings in that day, saith the Lord God: there shall be many dead bodies in every place; they shall cast them forth with silence.« Joel 1:10-12, 17-20; Amos 8:3 These plagues are not universal, or the inhabitants of the earth would be wholly cut off. Yet they will be the most awful scourges that have ever been known to mortals. All the judgments upon men, prior to the close of probation, have been mingled with mercy. The pleading blood of Christ has shielded the sinner from receiving the full measure of his guilt; but in the final judgment, wrath is poured out unmixed with mercy. In that day, multitudes will desire the shelter of God's mercy which they have so long despised. »Behold, the days come, saith the Lord God, that I will send a famine in the land, not a famine of bread, nor a thirst for water, but of hearing the words of the Lord: and they shall wander from sea to sea, and from the north even to the east, they shall run to and fro to seek the word of the Lord, and shall not find it.« Amos 8:11-12

The people of God will not be free from suffering; but while persecuted and distressed, while they endure privation and suffer for want of food they will not be left to perish. That God who cared for Elijah will not pass by one of His self-sacrificing children. He who numbers the hairs of their head will care for them, and in time of famine they shall be satisfied. While the wicked are dying from hunger and pestilence, angels will shield the righteous and supply their wants. To him that »walketh righteously« is the promise: »Bread shall be given him; his waters shall be sure.« »When the poor and needy seek water, and there is none, and their tongue faileth for thirst, I the Lord will hear them, I the God of Israel will not forsake them.« Isaiah 33:15-16; 41:17

»Although the fig tree shall not blossom, neither shall fruit be in the vines; the labor of the olive shall fail, and the fields shall yield no meat; the flock shall be cut off from the fold, and there shall be no herd in the stalls;« yet shall they that fear Him »rejoice in the Lord« and joy in the God of their salvation. Habakkuk 3:17-18 »The Lord is thy keeper: the Lord is thy shade upon thy right hand. The sun shall not smite thee by day, nor the moon by night. The Lord shall preserve thee from all evil: He shall preserve thy soul.« »He shall deliver thee from the snare of the fowler, and from the noisome pestilence. He shall cover thee with His feathers, and under His wings shalt thou trust: His truth shall be thy shield and buckler. Thou shalt not be afraid for the terror by night; nor for the arrow that flieth by day; nor for the pestilence that walketh in darkness; nor for the destruction that wasteth at noonday. A thousand shall fall at thy side, and ten thousand at thy right hand; but it shall not come nigh thee. Only with thine eyes shalt thou behold and see the reward of the wicked. Because thou hast made the Lord, which is my refuge, even the Most High, thy habitation; there shall no evil befall thee, neither shall any plague come nigh thy dwelling.« Psalm 121:5-7; 91:3-10

Yet to human sight it will appear that the people of God must soon seal their testimony with their blood as did the martyrs before them. They themselves begin to fear that the Lord has left them to fall by the hand of their enemies. It is a time of fearful agony. Day and night they cry unto God for deliverance. The wicked exult, and the jeering cry is heard: »Where now is your faith? Why does not God deliver you out of our hands if you are indeed His people?« But the waiting ones remember Jesus dying upon Calvary's cross and the chief priests and rulers shouting in mockery: »He saved others; Himself He cannot save. If He be the King of Israel, let Him now come down from the cross, and we will believe Him.« Matthew 27:42 Like Jacob, all are wrestling with God. Their countenances express their internal struggle. Paleness sits upon every face. Yet they cease not their earnest intercession. Could men see with heavenly vision, they would behold companies of angels that excel in strength stationed about those who have kept the word of Christ's patience.

With sympathizing tenderness, angels have witnessed their distress and have heard their prayers. They are waiting the word of their Commander to snatch them from their peril. But they must wait yet a little longer. The people of God must drink of the cup and be baptized with the baptism. The very delay, so painful to them, is the best answer to their petitions. As they endeavor to wait trustingly for the Lord to work they are led to exercise faith, hope, and patience, which have been too little exercised during their religious experience. Yet for the elect's sake the time of trouble will be shortened. »Shall not God avenge His own elect, which cry day and night unto Him? ... I tell you that He will avenge them speedily.« Luke 18:7-8 The end will come more quickly than men expect. The wheat will be gathered and bound in sheaves for the garner of God; the tares will be bound as fagots for the fires of destruction.

The heavenly sentinels, faithful to their trust, continue their watch. Though a general decree has fixed the time when commandment keepers may be put to death, their enemies will in some cases anticipate the decree, and before the time specified, will endeavor to take their lives. But none can pass the mighty guardians stationed about every faithful soul. Some are assailed in their flight from the cities and villages; but the swords raised against them break and fall powerless as a straw. Others are defended by angels in the form of men of war.

In all ages, God has wrought through holy angels for the succor and deliverance of His people. Celestial beings have taken an active part in the affairs of men. They have appeared clothed in garments that shone as the lightning; they have come as men in the garb of wayfarers. Angels have appeared in human form to men of God. They have rested, as if weary, under the oaks at noon. They have accepted the hospitalities of human homes. They have acted as guides to benighted travelers. They have, with their own hands, kindled the fires at the altar. They have opened prison doors and set free the servants of the Lord. Clothed with the panoply of heaven, they came to roll away the stone from the Saviour's tomb.

In the form of men, angels are often in the assemblies of the righteous; and they visit the assemblies of the wicked, as they went to Sodom, to make a record of their deeds, to determine whether they have passed the boundary of God's forbearance. The Lord delights in mercy; and for the sake of a few who really serve Him, He restrains calamities and prolongs the tranquillity of multitudes. Little do sinners against God realize that they are indebted for their own lives to the faithful few whom they delight to ridicule and oppress.

Though the rulers of this world know it not, yet often in their councils angels have been spokesmen. Human eyes have looked upon them; human ears have listened to their appeals; human lips have opposed their suggestions and ridiculed their counsels; human hands have met them with insult and abuse. In the council hall and the court of justice these heavenly messengers have shown an intimate acquaintance with human history; they have proved themselves better able to plead the cause of the oppressed than were their ablest and most eloquent defenders. They have defeated purposes and arrested evils that would have greatly retarded the work of God and would have caused great suffering to His people. In the hour of peril and distress »the angel of the Lord encampeth round about them that fear Him, and delivereth them.« Psalm 34:7

With earnest longing, God's people await the tokens of their coming King. As the watchmen are accosted, »What of the night?« the answer is given unfalteringly, »'The morning cometh, and also the night.' Isaiah 21:11-12 Light is gleaming upon the clouds above the mountaintops. Soon there will be a revealing of His glory. The Sun of Righteousness is about to shine forth. The morning and the night are both at hand – the opening of endless day to the righteous, the settling down of eternal night to the wicked.«

As the wrestling ones urge their petitions before God, the veil separating them from the unseen seems almost withdrawn. The heavens glow with the dawning of eternal day, and like the melody of angel songs the words fall upon the ear: »Stand fast to your allegiance. Help is coming.« Christ, the almighty Victor, holds out to His weary soldiers a crown of immortal glory; and His voice comes from the gates ajar: »Lo, I am with you. Be not afraid. I am acquainted with all your
 sorrows; I have borne your griefs. You are not warring

against untried enemies. I have fought the battle in your behalf, and in My name you are more than conquerors.«

The precious Saviour will send help just when we need it. The way to heaven is consecrated by His footprints. Every thorn that wounds our feet has wounded His. Every cross that we are called to bear He has borne before us. The Lord permits conflicts, to prepare the soul for peace. The time of trouble is a fearful ordeal for God's people; but it is the time for every true believer to look up, and by faith he may see the bow of promise encircling him. »The redeemed of the Lord shall return, and come with singing unto Zion; and everlasting joy shall be upon their head: they shall obtain gladness and joy; and sorrow and mourning shall flee away. I, even I, am He that comforteth you: who art thou, that thou shouldest be afraid of a man that shall die, and of the son of man which shall be made as grass; and forgettest the Lord thy Maker; ... and hast feared continually every day because of the fury of the oppressor, as if he were ready to destroy? and where is the fury of the oppressor? The captive exile hasteneth that he may be loosed, and that he should not die in the pit, nor that his bread should fail. But I am the Lord thy God, that divided the sea, whose waves roared: The Lord of hosts is His name. And I have put My words in thy mouth, and I have covered thee in the shadow of Mine hand.« Isaiah 51:11-16

»Therefore hear now this, thou afflicted, and drunken, but not with wine: Thus saith thy Lord the Lord, and thy God that pleadeth the cause of His people, Behold, I have taken out of thine hand the cup of trembling, even the dregs of the cup of My fury; thou shalt no more drink it again: but I will put it into the hand of them that afflict thee; which have said to thy soul, Bow down, that we may go over: and thou hast laid thy body as the ground, and as the street, to them that went over.« Verses 21-23 The eye of God, looking down the ages, was fixed upon the crisis which His people are to meet, when earthly powers shall be arrayed against them. Like the captive exile, they will be in fear of death by starvation or by violence. But the Holy One who divided the Red Sea before Israel, will manifest His mighty power and turn their captivity. »They shall be Mine, saith the Lord of hosts, in that day when I make up My jewels; and I will spare them, as a man spareth his own son that serveth him.« Malachi 3:17 If the blood of Christ's faithful witnesses were shed at this time, it would not, like the blood of the martyrs, be as seed sown to [634/635] yield a harvest for God. Their fidelity would not be a testimony to convince others of the truth; for the obdurate heart has beaten back the waves of mercy until they return no more. If the righteous were now left to fall a prey to their enemies, it would be a triumph for the prince of darkness. Says the psalmist: »In the time of trouble He shall hide me in His pavilion: in the secret of His tabernacle shall He hide me.« Psalm 27:5 Christ has spoken: »Come, My people, enter thou into thy chambers, and shut thy doors about thee: hide thyself as it were for a little moment, until the indignation be overpast. For, behold, the Lord cometh out of His place to punish the inhabitants of the earth for their iniquity.« Isaiah 26:20-21 Glorious will be the deliverance of those who have patiently waited for His coming and whose names are written in the book of life.

CHAPTER 40

GOD'S PEOPLE DELIVERED

When the protection of human laws shall be withdrawn from those who honor the law of God, there will be, in different lands, a simultaneous movement for their destruction. As the time appointed in the decree draws near, the people will conspire to root out the hated sect. It will be determined to strike in one night a decisive blow, which shall utterly silence the voice of dissent and reproof.

The people of God – some in prison cells, some hidden in solitary retreats in the forests and the mountains – still plead for divine protection, while in every quarter companies of armed men, urged on by hosts of evil angels, are preparing for the work of death. It is now, in the hour of utmost extremity, that the God of Israel will interpose for the deliverance of His chosen. Saith the Lord; »Ye shall have a song, as in the night when a holy solemnity is kept; and gladness of heart, as when one goeth ... to come into the mountain of the Lord, to the Mighty One of Israel. And the Lord shall cause His glorious voice to be heard, and shall show the lighting down of His arm, with the indignation of His anger, and with the flame of a devouring fire, with scattering, and tempest, and hailstones.« Isaiah 30:29-30

With shouts of triumph, jeering, and imprecation, throngs of evil men are about to rush upon their prey, when, lo, a dense blackness, deeper than the darkness of the night, falls upon the earth. Then a rainbow, shining with the glory from the throne of God, spans the heavens and seems to encircle each praying company. The angry multitudes are suddenly arrested. Their mocking cries die away. The objects of their murderous rage are forgotten. With fearful forebodings they gaze upon the symbol of God's covenant and long to be shielded from its overpowering brightness.

By the people of God a voice, clear and melodious, is heard, saying, »Look up,« and lifting their eyes to the heavens, they behold the bow of promise. The black, angry clouds that covered the firmament are parted, and like Stephen they look up steadfastly into heaven and see the glory of God and the Son of man seated upon His throne. In His divine form they discern the marks of His humiliation; and from His lips they hear the request presented before His Father and the holy angels: »I will that they also, whom Thou hast given Me, be with Me where I am.« John 17:24 Again a voice, musical and triumphant, is heard, saying: »They come! they come! holy, harmless, and undefiled. They have kept the word of My patience; they shall walk among the angels;« and the pale, quivering lips of those who have held fast their faith utter a shout of victory.

It is at midnight that God manifests His power for the deliverance of His people. The sun appears, shining in its strength. Signs and wonders follow in quick succession. The wicked look with terror and amazement upon the scene, while the righteous behold with solemn joy the tokens of their deliverance. Everything in nature seems turned out of its course. The streams cease to flow. Dark, heavy clouds come up and clash against each other. In the midst of the angry heavens is one clear space of indescribable glory, whence comes the voice of God like the sound of many waters, saying: »It is done.« Revelation 16:17

That voice shakes the heavens and the earth. There is a mighty earthquake, »such as was not since men were upon the earth, so mighty an earthquake, and so great.« Verses 17-18 The firmament appears to open and shut. The glory from the throne of God seems flashing through. The mountains shake like a reed in the wind, and ragged rocks are scattered on every side. There is a roar as of a coming tempest. The sea is lashed into fury. There is heard the shriek of a hurricane like the voice of demons upon a mission of destruction. The whole earth heaves and swells like the waves of the sea. Its surface is breaking up. Its very foundations seem to be giving way. Mountain chains are sinking. Inhabited islands disappear. The seaports that have become like Sodom for wickedness are swallowed up by the angry waters. Babylon the great has come in remembrance before God, »to give unto her the cup of the wine of the »a talent,« are doing their work of destruction. Verses 19, 21 The proudest cities of the earth are laid low. The lordly palaces, upon which the world's great men have lavished their wealth in order to glorify themselves, are crumbling to ruin before their eyes. Prison walls are rent asunder, and God's people, who have been held in bondage for their faith, are set free.

Graves are opened, and »many of them that sleep in the dust of the earth ... awake, some to everlasting life, and some to shame and everlasting contempt.« Daniel 12:2 All who have died in the faith of the third angel's message come forth from the tomb glorified, to hear God's covenant of peace with those who have kept His law. »They also which pierced Him«, Revelation 1:7 those that mocked and derided Christ's dying agonies, and the most violent opposers of His truth and His people, are raised to behold Him in His glory and to see the honor placed upon the loyal and obedient.

Thick clouds still cover the sky; yet the sun now and then breaks through, appearing like the avenging eye of Jehovah. Fierce lightnings leap from the heavens, enveloping the earth in a sheet of flame. Above the terrific roar of thunder, voices, mysterious and awful, declare the doom of the wicked. The words spoken are not comprehended by all; but they are distinctly understood by the false teachers. Those who a little before were so reckless, so boastful and defiant, so exultant in their cruelty to God's commandment-keeping people, are now overwhelmed with consternation and shuddering in fear. Their wails are heard above the sound of the elements. Demons acknowledge the deity of Christ and tremble before His power, while men are supplicating for mercy and groveling in abject terror.

Said the prophets of old, as they beheld in holy vision the day of God: »Howl ye; for the day of the Lord is at hand; it shall come as a destruction from the Almighty.« Isaiah 13:6 »Enter into the rock, and hide thee in the dust, for fear of the Lord, and for the glory of His majesty. The lofty looks of man shall be humbled, and the haughtiness of men shall be bowed down, and the Lord alone shall be exalted in that day. For the day of the Lord of hosts shall be upon everyone that is proud and lofty, and upon everyone that is lifted up; and he shall be brought low.« »In that day a man shall cast the idols of his silver, and the idols of his gold, which they made each one for himself to worship, to the moles and to the bats; to go into the clefts of the rocks, and into the tops of the ragged rocks, for fear of the Lord, and for the glory of His majesty, when He ariseth to shake terribly the earth.« Isaiah 2:10-12, 20, 21, margin

Through a rift in the clouds there beams a star whose brilliancy is increased fourfold in contrast with the darkness. It speaks hope and joy to the faithful, but severity and wrath to the transgressors of God's law. Those who have sacrificed all for Christ are now secure, hidden as in the secret of the Lord's pavilion. They have been tested, and before the world and the despisers of truth they have evinced their fidelity to Him who died for them. A marvelous change has come over those who have held fast their integrity in the very face of death. They have been suddenly delivered from the dark and terrible tyranny of men transformed to demons. Their faces, so lately pale, anxious, and haggard, are now aglow with wonder, faith, and love. Their voices rise in triumphant song: »God is our refuge and strength, a very present help in trouble. Therefore will not we fear, though the earth be removed, and though the mountains be carried into the midst of the sea; though the waters thereof roar and be troubled, though the mountains shake with the swelling thereof.« Psalm 46:1-3

While these words of holy trust ascend to God, the clouds sweep back, and the starry heavens are seen, unspeakably glorious in contrast with the black and angry firmament on either side. The glory of the celestial city streams from the gates ajar. Then there appears against the sky a hand holding two tables of stone folded together. Says the prophet: »The heavens shall declare His righteousness: for God is judge Himself.« Psalm 50:6 That holy law, God's righteousness, that amid thunder and flame was proclaimed from Sinai as the guide of life, is now revealed to men as the rule of judgment. The hand opens the tables, and there are seen the precepts of the Decalogue, traced as with a pen of fire. The words are so plain that all can read them. Memory is aroused, the darkness of superstition and heresy is swept from every mind, and God's ten words, brief, comprehensive, and authoritative, are presented to the view of all the inhabitants of the earth.

It is impossible to describe the horror and despair of those who have trampled upon God's holy requirements. The Lord gave them His law; they might have compared their characters with it and learned their defects while there was yet opportunity for repentance and reform; but in order to secure the favor of the world, they set aside its precepts and taught others to transgress. They have endeavored to compel God's people to profane His Sabbath. Now they are condemned by that law which they have despised. With awful distinctness they see that they are without excuse. They chose whom they would serve and worship. »Then shall ye return, and discern between the righteous and the wicked, between him that serveth God and him that serveth Him not.« Malachi 3:18 The enemies of God's law, from the ministers down to the least among them, have a new conception of truth and duty. Too late they see that the Sabbath of the fourth commandment is the seal of the living God. Too late they see the true nature of their spurious sabbath and the sandy foundation upon which they have been building. They find that they have been fighting against God. Religious teachers have led souls to perdition while professing to guide them to the gates of Paradise. Not until the day of final accounts will it be known how great is the responsibility of men in holy office and how terrible are the results of their unfaithfulness. Only in eternity can we rightly estimate the loss of a single soul. Fearful will be the doom of him to whom God shall say: Depart, thou wicked servant.

The voice of God is heard from heaven, declaring the day and hour of Jesus' coming, and delivering the everlasting covenant to His people. Like peals of loudest thunder His words roll through the earth. The Israel of God stand listening, with their eyes fixed upward. Their countenances are lighted up with His glory, and shine as did the face of Moses when he came down from Sinai. The wicked cannot look upon them. And when the blessing is pronounced on those who have honored God by keeping His Sabbath holy, there is a mighty shout of victory.

Soon there appears in the east a small black cloud, about half the size of a man's hand. It is the cloud which surrounds the Saviour and which seems in the distance to be shrouded in darkness. The people of God know this to be the sign of the Son of man. In solemn silence they gaze upon it as it draws nearer the earth, becoming lighter and more glorious, until it is a great white cloud, its base a glory like consuming fire, and above it the rainbow of the covenant. Jesus rides forth as a mighty conqueror. Not now a »Man of Sorrows,« to drink the bitter cup of shame and woe, He comes, victor in heaven and earth, to judge the living and the dead. »Faithful and True,« »in righteousness He doth judge and make war.« And »the armies which were in heaven« Revelation 19:11, 14 follow Him. With anthems of celestial melody the holy angels, a vast, unnumbered throng, attend Him on His way. The firmament seems filled with radiant forms – »ten thousand times ten thousand, and thousands of thousands.« No human pen can portray the scene; no mortal mind is adequate to conceive its splendor. »His glory covered the heavens, and the earth was full of His praise. And His brightness was as the light.« Habakkuk 3:3-4 As the living cloud comes still nearer, every eye beholds the Prince of life. No crown of thorns now mars that sacred head; but a diadem of glory rests on His holy brow. His countenance outshines the dazzling brightness of the noonday sun. »And He hath on His vesture and on His thigh a name written, King of kings, and Lord of lords.« Revelation 19:16

Before His presence »all faces are turned into paleness;« upon the rejecters of God's mercy falls the terror of eternal despair. »The heart melteth, and the knees smite together, ... and the faces of them all gather blackness.« Jeremiah 30:6; Nahum 2:10 The righteous cry with trembling: »Who shall be able to stand?« The angels' song is hushed, and there is a period of awful silence. Then the voice of Jesus is heard, saying: »My grace is sufficient for you.« The faces of the righteous are lighted up, and joy fills every heart. And the angels strike a note higher and sing again as they draw still nearer to the earth.

The King of kings descends upon the cloud, wrapped in flaming fire. The heavens are rolled together as a scroll, the earth trembles before Him, and every mountain and island is moved out of its place. "Our God shall come, and shall not keep silence: a fire shall devour before Him, and it shall be very tempestuous round about Him. He shall call to the heavens from above, and to the earth, that He may judge His people.« Psalm 50:3-4 »And the kings of the earth, and the great men, and the rich men, and the chief captains, and the mighty men, and every bondman, and every freeman, hid themselves in the dens and in the rocks of the mountains; and said to the mountains and rocks, Fall on us, and hide us from the face of Him that sitteth on the throne, and from the wrath of the Lamb: for the great day of His wrath is come; and who shall be able to stand?« Revelation 6:15-17

The derisive jests have ceased. Lying lips are hushed into silence. The clash of arms, the tumult of battle, »with confused noise, and garments rolled in blood«, Isaiah 9:5 is stilled. Nought now is heard but the voice of prayer and the sound of weeping and lamentation. The cry bursts forth from lips so lately scoffing: »The great day of His wrath is come; and who shall be able to stand?" The wicked pray to be buried beneath the rocks of the mountains rather than meet the face of Him whom they have despised and rejected.

That voice which penetrates the ear of the dead, they know. How often have its plaintive, tender tones called them to repentance. How often has it been heard in the touching entreaties of a friend, a brother, a Redeemer. To the rejecters of His grace no other could be so full of condemnation, so burdened with denunciation, as that voice which has so long pleaded: »Turn ye, turn ye from your evil ways; for why will ye die?« Ezekiel 33:11 Oh, that it were to them the voice of a stranger! Says Jesus: »I have called, and ye refused; I have stretched out My hand, and no man regarded; but ye have set at nought all My counsel, and would none of My reproof.« Proverbs 1:24,25 That voice awakens memories which they would fain blot out – warnings despised, invitations refused, privileges slighted.

There are those who mocked Christ in His humiliation. With thrilling power come to their minds the Sufferer's words, when, adjured by the high priest, He solemnly declared: »Hereafter shall ye see the Son of man sitting on the right hand of power, and coming in the clouds of heaven.« Matthew 26:64 Now they behold Him in His glory, and they are yet to see Him sitting on the right hand of power.

Those who derided His claim to be the Son of God are speechless now. There is the haughty Herod who jeered at His royal title and bade the mocking soldiers crown Him king. There are the very men who with impious hands placed upon His form the purple robe, upon His sacred brow the thorny crown, and in His unresisting hand the mimic scepter, and bowed before Him in blasphemous mockery. The men who smote and spit upon the Prince of life now turn from His piercing gaze and seek to flee from the overpowering glory of His presence. Those who drove the nails through His hands and feet, the soldier who pierced His side, behold these marks with terror and remorse. With awful distinctness do priests and rulers recall the events of Calvary. With shuddering horror they remember how, wagging their heads in satanic exultation, they exclaimed: »He saved others; Himself He cannot save. If He be the King of Israel, let Him now come down from the cross, and we will believe Him. He trusted in God; let Him deliver Him now, if He will have Him.« Matthew 27:42-43

Vividly they recall the Saviour's parable of the husbandmen who refused to render to their lord the fruit of the vineyard, who abused his servants and slew his son. They remember, too, the sentence which they themselves pronounced: The lord of the vineyard »will miserably destroy those wicked men.« In the sin and punishment of those unfaithful men the priests and elders see their own course and their own just doom. And now there rises a cry of mortal agony. Louder than the shout, »Crucify Him, crucify Him,« which rang through the streets of Jerusalem, swells the awful, despairing wail, »He is the

Son of God! He is the true Messiah!« They seek to flee from the presence of the King of kings. In the deep caverns of the earth, rent asunder by the warring of the elements, they vainly attempt to hide.

In the lives of all who reject truth there are moments when conscience awakens, when memory presents the torturing recollection of a life of hypocrisy and the soul is harassed with vain regrets. But what are these compared with the remorse of that day when »fear cometh as desolation,« when »destruction cometh as a whirlwind«! Proverbs 1:27 Those who would have destroyed Christ and His faithful people now witness the glory which rests upon them. In the midst of their terror they hear the voices of the saints in joyful strains exclaiming: »Lo, this is our God; we have waited for Him, and He will save us.« Isaiah 25:9

Amid the reeling of the earth, the flash of lightning, and the roar of thunder, the voice of the Son of God calls forth the sleeping saints. He looks upon the graves of the righteous, then, raising His hands to heaven, He cries: »Awake, awake, awake, ye that sleep in the dust, and arise!« Throughout the length and breadth of the earth the dead shall hear that voice, and they that hear shall live. And the whole earth shall ring with the tread of the exceeding great army of every nation, kindred, tongue, and people. From the prison house of death they come, clothed with immortal glory, crying: »O death, where is thy sting? O grave, where is thy victory?« 1 Cor. 15:55 And the living righteous and the risen saints unite their voices in a long, glad shout of victory.

All come forth from their graves the same in stature as when they entered the tomb. Adam, who stands among the risen throng, is of lofty height and majestic form, in stature but little below the Son of God. He presents a marked contrast to the people of later generations; in this one respect is shown the great degeneracy of the race. But all arise with the freshness and vigor of eternal youth. In the beginning, man was created in the likeness of God, not only in character, but in form and feature. Sin defaced and almost obliterated the divine image; but Christ came to restore that which had been lost. He will change our vile bodies and fashion them like unto His glorious body. The mortal, corruptible form, devoid of comeliness, once polluted with sin, becomes perfect, beautiful, and immortal. All blemishes and deformities are left in the grave. Restored to the tree of life in the long-lost Eden, the redeemed will »grow up« Malachi 4:2 to the full stature of the race in its primeval glory. The last lingering traces of the curse of sin will be removed, and

Christ's faithful ones will appear in »the beauty of the Lord our God,« in mind and soul and body reflecting the perfect image of their Lord. Oh, wonderful redemption! long talked of, long hoped for, contemplated with eager anticipation, but never fully understood.

The living righteous are changed »in a moment, in the twinkling of an eye.« At the voice of God they were glorified; now they are made immortal and with the risen saints are caught up to meet their Lord in the air. Angels »gather together His elect from the four winds, from one end of heaven to the other.« Little children are borne by holy angels to their mothers' arms. Friends long separated by death are united, nevermore to part, and with songs of gladness ascend together to the City of God.

On each side of the cloudy chariot are wings, and beneath it are living wheels; and as the chariot rolls upward, the wheels cry, »Holy,« and the wings, as they move, cry, »Holy,« and the retinue of angels cry, »Holy, holy, holy, Lord God Almighty.« And the redeemed shout, »Alleluia!« as the chariot moves onward toward the New Jerusalem.

Before entering the City of God, the Saviour bestows upon His followers the emblems of victory and invests them with the insignia of their royal state. The glittering ranks are drawn up in the form of a hollow square about their King, whose form rises in majesty high above saint and angel, whose countenance beams upon them full of benignant love. Throughout the unnumbered host of the redeemed every glance is fixed upon Him, every eye beholds His glory whose »visage was so marred more than any man, and His form more than the sons of men.« Upon the heads of the overcomers, Jesus with His own right hand places the crown of glory. For each there is a crown, bearing his own »new name« Revelation 2:17 and the inscription, »Holiness to the Lord.« In every hand are placed the victor's palm and the shining harp. Then, as the commanding angels strike the note, every hand sweeps the harp strings with skillful touch, awaking sweet music in rich, melodious strains. Rapture unutterable thrills every heart, and each voice is raised in grateful praise: »Unto Him that loved us, and washed us from our sins in His own blood, and hath made us kings and priests unto God and His Father; to Him be glory and dominion for ever and ever.« Revelation 1:5-6 Before the ransomed throng is the Holy City. Jesus opens wide the pearly gates, and the nations that have kept the truth enter in. There they behold the Paradise of God, the home of Adam in his innocency. Then that voice, richer than any music that ever fell on mortal ear, is heard, saying: »Your conflict is ended.« »Come, ye blessed of My Father, inherit the kingdom prepared for you from the foundation of the world.«

Now is fulfilled the Saviour's prayer for His disciples: »Iwill that they also, whom Thou hast given Me, be with Me where I am.« »Faultless before the presence of His glory with exceeding joy«, Jude 24 Christ presents to the Father the purchase of His blood, declaring: »Here am I, and the children whom Thou hast given Me.« »Those that Thou gavest Me I have kept.« Oh, the wonders of redeeming love! the rapture of that hour when the infinite Father, looking upon the ransomed, shall behold His image, sin's discord banished, its blight removed, and the human once more in harmony with the divine!

With unutterable love, Jesus welcomes His faithful ones to the joy of their Lord. The Saviour's joy is in seeing, in the kingdom of glory, the souls that have been saved by His agony and humiliation. And the redeemed will be sharers in His joy, as they behold, among the blessed, those who have been won to Christ through their prayers, their labors, and their loving sacrifice. As they gather about the great white throne, gladness unspeakable will fill their hearts, when they behold those whom they have won for Christ, and see that one has gained others, and these still others, all brought into the haven of rest, there to lay their crowns at Jesus' feet and praise Him through the endless cycles of eternity.

As the ransomed ones are welcomed to the City of God, there rings out upon the air an exultant cry of adoration. The two Adams are about to meet. The Son of God is standing with outstretched arms to receive the father of our race – the being whom He created, who sinned against his Maker, and for whose sin the marks of the crucifixion are borne upon the Saviour's form. As Adam discerns the prints of the cruel nails, he does not fall upon the bosom of his Lord, but in humiliation casts himself at His feet, crying: »Worthy, worthy is the Lamb that was slain!« Tenderly the Saviour lifts him up and bids him look once more upon the Eden home from which he has so long been exiled. After his expulsion from Eden, Adam's life on earth was filled with sorrow. Every dying leaf, every victim of sacrifice, every blight upon the fair face of nature, every stain upon man's purity, was a fresh reminder of his sin. Terrible was the agony of remorse as he beheld iniquity abounding, and, in answer to his warnings, met the reproaches

 cast upon himself as the cause of sin. With patient humility he bore, for nearly a thousand years, the penalty of transgression. Faithfully did he repent of his sin and trust in the merits of the promised Saviour, and he died in the hope of a resurrection. The Son of God redeemed man's failure and fall; and now, through the work of the atonement, Adam is reinstated in his first dominion.

Transported with joy, he beholds the trees that were once his delight – the very trees whose fruit he himself had gathered in the days of his innocence and joy. He sees the vines that his own hands have trained, the very flowers that he once loved to care for. His mind grasps the reality of the scene; he comprehends that this is indeed Eden restored, more lovely now than when he was banished from it. The Saviour leads him to the tree of life and plucks the glorious fruit and bids him eat. He looks about him and beholds a multitude of his family redeemed, standing in the Paradise of God. Then he casts his glittering crown at the feet of Jesus and, falling upon His breast, embraces the Redeemer. He touches the golden harp, and the vaults of heaven echo the triumphant song: »Worthy, worthy, worthy is the Lamb that was slain, and lives again!« The family of Adam take up the strain and cast their crowns at the Saviour's feet as they bow before Him in adoration. This reunion is witnessed by the angels who wept at the fall of Adam and rejoiced when Jesus, after His resurrection, ascended to heaven, having opened the grave for all who should believe on His name. Now they behold the work of redemption accomplished, and they unite their voices in the song of praise.

Upon the crystal sea before the throne, that sea of glass as it were mingled with fire, – so resplendent is it with the glory of God, – are gathered the company that have »gotten the victory over the beast, and over his image, and over his mark, and over the number of his name.« With the Lamb upon Mount Zion, »having the harps of God,« they stand, the hundred and forty and four thousand that were redeemed from among men; and there is heard, as the sound of many waters, and as the sound of a great thunder, »the voice of harpers harping with their harps.« And they sing »a new song« before the throne, a song which no man can learn save the hundred and forty and four thousand. It is the song of Moses and the Lamb – a song of deliverance. None but the hundred and forty-four thousand can learn that song; for it is the song of their experience – an experience such as no other company have ever had. "These are they which follow the Lamb whithersoever He goeth. »These, having been translated from the earth, from among the living, are counted as »the first fruits unto God and to the Lamb.« Revelation 15:2-3; 14:1-5 »These are they which came out of great tribulation; they have passed through the time of trouble such as never was since there was a nation; they have endured the anguish of the time of Jacob's trouble; they have stood without an intercessor through the final outpouring of God's judgments. But they have been delivered, for they have »washed their robes, and made them white in the blood of the Lamb.« »In their mouth was found no guile: for they are without fault« before God. »Therefore are they before the throne of God, and serve Him day and night in His temple: and He that sitteth on the throne shall dwell among them.« They have seen the earth wasted with famine and pestilence, the sun having power to scorch men with great heat, and they themselves have endured suffering, hunger, and thirst. But »they shall hunger no more, neither thirst any more; neither shall the sun light on them, nor any heat. For the Lamb which is in the midst of the throne shall feed them, and shall lead them unto living fountains of waters: and God shall wipe away all tears from their eyes.« Revelation 7:14-17

In all ages the Saviour's chosen have been educated and disciplined in the school of trial. They walked in narrow paths on earth; they were purified in the furnace of affliction. For Jesus' sake they endured opposition, hatred, calumny. They followed Him through conflicts sore; they endured self-denial and experienced bitter disappointments.

By their own painful experience they learned the evil of sin, its power, its guilt, its woe; and they look upon it with abhorrence. A sense of the infinite sacrifice made for its cure humbles them in their own sight and fills their hearts with gratitude and praise which those who have never fallen cannot appreciate. They love much because they have been forgiven much. Having been partakers of Christ's sufferings, they are fitted to be partakers with Him of His glory.

The heirs of God have come from garrets, from hovels, from dungeons, from scaffolds, from mountains, from deserts, from the caves of the earth, from the caverns of the sea. On earth they were »destitute, afflicted, tormented.« Millions went down to the grave loaded with infamy because they steadfastly refused to yield to the deceptive claims of Satan. By human tribunals they were adjudged

 the vilest of criminals. But now »God is judge Himself.«

Psalm 50:6 Now the decisions of earth are reversed. "The rebuke of His people shall He take away.« Isaiah 25:8 »They shall call them, The holy people, The redeemed of the Lord." He hath appointed »to give unto them beauty for ashes, the oil of joy for mourning, the garment of praise for the spirit of heaviness.« Isaiah 62:12; 61:3

They are no longer feeble, afflicted, scattered, and oppressed. Henceforth they are to be ever with the Lord. They stand before the throne clad in richer robes than the most honored of the earth have ever worn. They are crowned with diadems more glorious than were ever placed upon the brow of earthly monarchs. The days of pain and weeping are forever ended. The King of glory has wiped the tears from all faces; every cause of grief has been removed. Amid the waving of palm branches they pour forth a song of praise, clear, sweet, and harmonious; every voice takes up the strain, until the anthem swells through the vaults of heaven: »Salvation to our God which sitteth upon the throne, and unto the Lamb.« And all the inhabitants of heaven respond in the ascription: »Amen: Blessing, and glory, and wisdom, and thanksgiving, and honor, and power, and might, be unto our God for ever and ever.« Revelation 7:10, 12

In this life we can only begin to understand the wonderful theme of redemption. With our finite comprehension we may consider most earnestly the shame and the glory, the life and the death, the justice and the mercy, that meet in the cross; yet with the utmost stretch of our mental powers we fail to grasp its full significance. The length and the breadth, the depth and the height, of redeeming love are but dimly comprehended. The plan of redemption will not be fully understood, even when the ransomed see as they are seen and know as they are known; but through the eternal ages new truth will continually unfold to the wondering and delighted mind. Though the griefs and pains and temptations of earth are ended and the cause removed, the people of God will ever have a distinct, intelligent knowledge of what their salvation has cost.

The cross of Christ will be the science and the song of the redeemed through all eternity. In Christ glorified they will behold Christ crucified. Never will it be forgotten that He whose power created and upheld the unnumbered worlds through the vast realms of space, the Beloved of God, the Majesty of heaven, He whom cherub and shining seraph delighted to adore – humbled Himself to uplift fallen man; that He bore the guilt and shame of sin, and the hiding of His Father's face, till the woes of a lost world broke His heart and crushed out His life on Calvary's cross. That the Maker of all worlds, the Arbiter of all destinies, should lay aside His glory and humiliate Himself from love to man will ever excite the wonder and adoration of the universe. As the nations of the saved look upon their Redeemer and behold the eternal glory of the Father shining in His countenance; as they behold His throne, which is from everlasting to everlasting, and know that His kingdom is to have no end, they break forth in rapturous song: »Worthy, worthy is the Lamb that was slain, and hath redeemed us to God by His own most precious blood!«

The mystery of the cross explains all other mysteries. In the light that streams from Calvary the attributes of God which had filled us with fear and awe appear beautiful and attractive. Mercy, tenderness, and parental love are seen to blend with holiness, justice, and power. While we behold the majesty of His throne, high and lifted up, we see His character in its gracious manifestations, and comprehend, as never before, the significance of that endearing title, »Our Father.«

It will be seen that He who is infinite in wisdom could devise no plan for our salvation except the sacrifice of His Son. The compensation for this sacrifice is the joy of peopling the earth with ransomed beings, holy, happy, and immortal. The result of the Saviour's conflict with the powers of darkness is joy to the redeemed, redounding to the glory of God throughout eternity. And such is the value of the soul that the Father is satisfied with the price paid; and Christ Himself, beholding the fruits of His great sacrifice, is satisfied.

Chapter 41

Desolation of the Earth

»Her sins have reached unto heaven, and God hath remembered her iniquities.... In the cup which she hath filled fill to her double. How much she hath glorified herself, and lived deliciously, so much torment and sorrow give her: for she saith in her heart, I sit a queen, and am no widow, and shall see no sorrow. Therefore shall her plagues come in one day, death, and mourning, and famine; and she shall be utterly burned with fire: for strong is the Lord God who judgeth her. And the kings of the earth, who have committed fornication and lived deliciously with her, shall bewail her, and lament for her, ... saying, Alas, alas that great city Babylon, that mighty city! for in one hour is thy judgment come.« Revelation 18:5-10

»The merchants of the earth,« that have »waxed rich through the abundance of her delicacies,« »shall stand afar off for the fear of her torment, weeping and wailing, and saying, Alas, alas that great city, that was clothed in fine linen, and purple, and scarlet, and decked with gold, and precious stones, and pearls! For in one hour so great riches is come to nought.« Revelation 18:11, 3, 15-17

Such are the judgments that fall upon Babylon in the day of the visitation of God's wrath. She has filled up the measure of her iniquity; her time has come; she is ripe for destruction.

When the voice of God turns the captivity of His people, there is a terrible awakening of those who have lost all in the great conflict of life. While probation continued they were blinded by Satan's deceptions, and they justified their course of sin. The rich prided themselves upon their superiority to those who were less favored; but they had obtained their riches by violation of the law of God. They had neglected to feed the hungry, to clothe the naked, to deal justly, and to love mercy. They had sought to exalt themselves and to obtain the homage of their fellow creatures. Now they are stripped of all that made them great and are left destitute and defenseless. They look with terror upon the destruction of the idols which they preferred before their Maker. They have sold their souls for earthly riches and enjoyments, and have not sought to become rich toward God. The result is, their lives are a failure; their pleasures are now turned to gall, their treasures to corruption. The gain of a lifetime is swept away in a moment. The rich bemoan the destruction of their grand houses, the scattering of their gold and silver. But their lamentations are silenced by the fear that they themselves are to perish with their idols.

The wicked are filled with regret, not because of their sinful neglect of God and their fellow men, but because God has conquered. They lament that the result is what it is; but they do not repent of their wickedness. They would leave no means untried to conquer if they could. The world see the very class whom they have mocked and derided, and desired to exterminate, pass unharmed through pestilence, tempest, and earthquake. He who is to the transgressors of His law a devouring fire, is to His people a safe pavilion.

The minister who has sacrificed truth to gain the favor of men now discerns the character and influence of his teachings. It is apparent that the omniscient eye was following him as he stood in the desk, as he walked the streets, as he mingled with men in the various scenes of life. Every emotion of the soul, every line written, every word uttered, every act that led men to rest in a refuge of falsehood, has been scattering seed; and now, in the wretched, lost souls around him, he beholds the harvest. Saith the Lord: »They have healed the hurt of the daughter of My people slightly, saying, Peace, peace; when there is no peace.« »With lies ye have made the heart of the righteous sad, whom I have not made sad; and strengthened the hands of the wicked, that he should not return from his wicked way, by promising him life.« Jeremiah 8:11; Ezekiel 13:22 »Woe be unto the pastors that destroy and scatter the sheep of My pasture! ... Behold, I will visit upon you the evil of your doings.« »Howl, ye shepherds, and cry; and wallow yourselves in the ashes, ye principal of the flock: for your days for slaughter and of your dispersions are accomplished; ... and the shepherds shall have no way to flee, nor the principal of the flock to escape.« Jeremiah 23:1-2; 25:34-35, margin

Ministers and people see that they have not sustained the right relation to God. They see that they have rebelled against the Author of all just and righteous law. The setting aside of the divine precepts gave rise to thousands of springs of evil, discord, hatred, iniquity, until the earth became one vast field of strife, one sink of corruption. This is the view that now appears to those who rejected truth and chose to cherish error. No language can express the longing which the disobedient and disloyal feel for that which they have lost forever – eternal life. Men whom the world has worshiped for their talents and eloquence now see these things in their true light. They realize what they have forfeited by transgression, and they fall at the feet of those whose fidelity they have despised and derided, and confess that God has loved them.

The people see that they have been deluded. They accuse one another of having led them to destruction; but all unite in heaping their bitterest condemnation upon the ministers. Unfaithful pastors have prophesied smooth things; they have led their hearers to make void the law of God and to persecute those who would keep it holy. Now, in their despair, these teachers confess before the world their work of deception. The multitudes are filled with fury. »We are lost!« they cry, »and you are the cause of our ruin;« and they turn upon the false shepherds. The very ones that once admired them most will pronounce the most dreadful curses upon them. The very hands that once crowned them with laurels will be raised for their destruction. The swords which were to slay God's people are now employed to destroy their enemies. Everywhere there is strife and bloodshed.

»A noise shall come even to the ends of the earth; for the Lord hath a controversy with the nations, He will plead with all flesh; He will give them that are wicked to the sword.« Jeremiah 25:31 For six thousand years the great controversy has been in progress; the Son of God and His heavenly messengers have been in conflict with the power of the evil one, to warn, enlighten, and save the children of men. Now all have made their decisions; the wicked have fully united with Satan in his warfare against God. The time has come for God to vindicate the authority of His downtrodden law. Now the controversy is not alone with Satan, but with men. »The Lord hath a controversy with the nations;« »He will give them that are wicked to the sword.«

The mark of deliverance has been set upon those »that sigh and that cry for all the abominations that be done.« Now the angel of death goes forth, represented in Ezekiel's vision by the men with the slaughtering weapons, to whom the command is given: »Slay utterly old and young, both maids, and little children, and women: but come not near any man upon whom is the mark; and begin at My sanctuary.« Says the prophet: »They began at the ancient men which were before the house.« Ezekiel 9:1-6 The work of destruction begins among those who have professed to be the spiritual guardians of the people. The false watchmen are the first to fall. There are none to pity or to spare. Men, women, maidens, and little children perish together.

»The Lord cometh out of His place to punish the inhabitants of the earth for their iniquity: the earth also shall disclose her blood, and shall no more cover her slain.« Isaiah 26:21 »And this shall be the plague wherewith the Lord will smite all the people that have fought against Jerusalem; Their flesh shall consume away while they stand upon their feet, and their eyes shall consume away in their holes, and their tongue shall consume away in their mouth. And it shall come to pass in that day, that a great tumult from the Lord shall be among them; and they shall lay hold everyone on the hand of his neighbor, and his hand shall rise up against the hand of his neighbor.« Zechariah 14:12-13 In the mad strife of their own fierce passions, and by the awful outpouring of God's unmingled wrath, fall the wicked inhabitants of the earth – priests, rulers, and people, rich and poor, high and low. »And the slain of the Lord shall be at that day from one end of the earth even unto the other end of the earth: they shall not be lamented, neither gathered, nor buried.« Jeremiah 25:33

At the coming of Christ the wicked are blotted from the face of the whole earth – consumed with the spirit of His mouth and destroyed by the brightness of His glory. Christ takes His people to the City of God, and the earth is emptied of its inhabitants. »Behold, the Lord maketh the earth empty, and maketh it waste, and turneth it upside down, and scattereth abroad the inhabitants thereof.« »The land shall be utterly emptied, and utterly spoiled: for the Lord hath spoken this word.« »Because they have transgressed the laws, changed the ordinance, broken the everlasting covenant. Therefore hath the curse devoured the earth, and they that dwell therein are desolate: therefore the inhabitants of the earth are burned.« Isaiah 24:1, 3, 5, 6

The whole earth appears like a desolate wilderness. The ruins of cities and villages destroyed by the earthquake, uprooted trees, ragged rocks thrown out by the sea or torn out of the earth itself, are scattered over its surface, while vast caverns mark the spot where the mountains have been rent from their foundations.

Now the event takes place foreshadowed in the last solemn service of the Day of Atonement. When the ministration in the holy of holies had been completed, and the sins of Israel had been removed from the sanctuary by virtue of the blood of the sin offering, then the scapegoat was presented alive before the Lord; and in the presence of the congregation the high priest confessed over him »all the iniquities of the children of Israel, and all their transgressions in all their sins, putting them upon the head of the goat.« Leviticus 16:21 In like manner, when the work of atonement in the heavenly sanctuary has been completed, then in the presence of God and heavenly angels and the hosts of the redeemed the sins of God's people will be placed upon Satan; he will be declared guilty of all the evil which he has caused them to commit. And as the scapegoat was sent away into a land not inhabited, so Satan will be banished to the desolate earth, an uninhabited and dreary wilderness.

The revelator foretells the banishment of Satan and the condition of chaos and desolation to which the earth is to be reduced, and he declares that this condition will exist for a thousand years. After presenting the scenes of the Lord's second coming and the destruction of the wicked, the prophecy continues: »I saw an angel come down from heaven, having the key of the bottomless pit and a great chain in his hand. And he laid hold on the dragon, that old serpent, which is the devil, and Satan, and bound him a thousand years, and cast him into the bottomless pit, and shut him up, and set a seal upon him, that he should deceive the nations no more, till the thousand years should be fulfilled: and after that he must be loosed a little season.« Rev. 20:1-3

That the expression »bottomless pit« represents the earth in a state of confusion and darkness is evident from other scriptures. Concerning the condition of the earth »in the beginning,« the Bible record says that it »was without form, and void; and darkness was upon the face of the deep.« [The Hebrew word here translated »deep« is rendered in the Septuagint (Greek) translation of the Hebrew Old Testament by the same word rendered »bottomless pit« In Revelation 20:1-3] Genesis 1:2 Prophecy teaches that it will be brought back, partially at least, to this condition. Looking forward to the great day of God, the prophet Jeremiah declares: »I beheld the earth, and, lo, it was without form, and void; and the heavens, and they had no light. I beheld the mountains, and, lo, they trembled, and all the hills moved lightly. I beheld, and, lo, there was no man, and all the birds of the heavens were fled. I beheld, and, lo, the fruitful place was a wilderness, and all the cities thereof were broken down.« Jeremiah 4:23-26 Here is to be the home of Satan with his evil angels for a thousand years. Limited to the earth, he will not have access to other worlds to tempt and annoy those who have never fallen. It is in this sense that he is bound: there are none remaining, upon whom he can exercise his power. He is wholly cut off from the work of deception and ruin which for so many centuries has been his sole delight.

The prophet Isaiah, looking forward to the time of Satan's overthrow, exclaims: »How art thou fallen from heaven, O Lucifer, son of the morning! how art thou cut down to the ground, which didst weaken the nations! ... Thou hast said in thine heart, I will ascend into heaven, I will exalt my throne above the stars of God: ... I will be like the Most High. Yet thou shalt be brought down to hell, to the sides of the pit. They that see thee shall narrowly look upon thee, and consider thee, saying, Is this the man that made the earth to tremble, that did shake kingdoms; that made the world as a wilderness, and destroyed the cities thereof; that opened not the house of his prisoners?« Isaiah 14:12-17

For six thousand years, Satan's work of rebellion has »made the earth to tremble.« He had »made the world as a wilderness, and destroyed the cities thereof.« And he »opened not the house of his prisoners.« For six thousand years his prison house has received God's people, and he would have held them captive forever; but Christ had broken his bonds and set the prisoners free.

Even the wicked are now placed beyond the power of Satan, and alone with his evil angels he remains to realize the effect of the curse which sin has brought. »The kings of the nations, even all of them, lie in glory, everyone in his own house [the grave]. But thou art cast out of thy grave like an abominable branch. ... Thou shalt not be joined with them in burial, because thou hast destroyed thy land, and slain thy people.« Isaiah 14:18-20

For a thousand years, Satan will wander to and fro in the desolate earth to behold the results of his rebellion against the law of God. During this time his sufferings are intense. Since his fall his life of unceasing activity has banished reflection; but he is now deprived of his power and left to contemplate the part which he has acted since first he rebelled against the government of heaven, and to look forward with trembling and terror to the dreadful future when he must suffer for all the evil that he has done and be punished for the sins that he has caused to be committed.

To God's people the captivity of Satan will bring gladness and rejoicing. Says the prophet: »It shall come to pass in the day that Jehovah shall give thee rest from thy sorrow, and from thy trouble, and from the hard service wherein thou wast made to serve, that thou shalt take up this parable against the king of Babylon [here representing Satan], and say, How hath the oppressor ceased! ... Jehovah hath broken the staff of the wicked, the scepter of the rulers; that smote the peoples in wrath with a continual stroke, that ruled the nations in anger, with a persecution that none restrained.« Verses 3-6, R.V.

During the thousand years between the first and the second resurrection the judgment of the wicked takes place. The apostle Paul points to this judgment as an event that follows the second advent. »Judge nothing before the time, until the Lord come, who both will bring to light the hidden things of darkness, and will make manifest the counsels of the hearts.« 1 Corinthians 4:5

Daniel declares that when the Ancient of Days came, »judgment was given to the saints of the Most High.« Daniel 7:22 At this time the righteous reign as kings and priests unto God. John in the Revelation says: »I saw thrones, and they sat upon them, and judgment was given unto them.« »They shall be priests of God and of Christ, and shall reign with Him a thousand years.« Revelation 20:4, 6 It is at this time that, as foretold by Paul, »the saints shall judge the world.« 1 Corinthians 6:2 In union with Christ they judge the wicked, comparing their acts with the statute book, the Bible, and deciding every case according to the deeds done in the body. Then the portion which the wicked must suffer is meted out, according to their works; and it is recorded against their names in the book of death.

Satan also and evil angels are judged by Christ and His people. Says Paul: »Know ye not that we shall judge angels?« Verse 3 And Jude declares that »the angels which kept not their first estate, but left their own habitation, He hath reserved in everlasting chains under darkness unto the judgment of the great day.« Jude 6

At the close of the thousand years the second resurrection will take place. Then the wicked will be raised from the dead and appear before God for the execution of »the judgment written.« Thus the revelator, after describing the resurrection of the righteous, says: »The rest of the dead lived not again until the thousand years were finished.« Revelation 20:5 And Isaiah declares, concerning the wicked: »They shall be gathered together, as prisoners are gathered in the pit, and shall be shut up in the prison, and after many days shall they be visited.« Isaiah 24:22

CHAPTER 42

THE CONTROVERSY ENDED

At the close of the thousand years, Christ again returns to the earth. He is accompanied by the host of the redeemed and attended by a retinue of angels. As He descends in terrific majesty He bids the wicked dead arise to receive their doom. They come forth, a mighty host, numberless as the sands of the sea. What a contrast to those who were raised at the first resurrection! The righteous were clothed with immortal youth and beauty. The wicked bear the traces of disease and death.

Every eye in that vast multitude is turned to behold the glory of the Son of God. With one voice the wicked hosts exclaim: »Blessed is He that cometh in the name of the Lord!« It is not love to Jesus that inspires this utterance. The force of truth urges the words from unwilling lips. As the wicked went into their graves, so they come forth with the same enmity to Christ and the same spirit of rebellion. They are to have no new probation in which to remedy the defects of their past lives. Nothing would be gained by this. A lifetime of transgression has not softened their hearts. A second probation, were it given them, would be occupied as was the first in evading the requirements of God and exciting rebellion against Him.

Christ descends upon the Mount of Olives, whence, after His resurrection, He ascended, and where angels repeated the promise of His return. Says the prophet: »The Lord my God shall come, and all the saints with Thee.« »And His feet shall stand in that day upon the Mount of Olives, which is before Jerusalem on the east, and the Mount of Olives shall cleave in the midst thereof, ... and there shall be a very great valley.« »And the Lord shall be king over all the earth: in that day shall there be one Lord, and His name one.« Zechariah 14:5, 4, 9 As the New Jerusalem, in its dazzling splendor, comes down out of heaven, it rests upon the place purified and made ready to receive it, and Christ, with His people and the angels, enters the Holy City.

Now Satan prepares for a last mighty struggle for the supremacy. While deprived of his power and cut off from his work of deception, the prince of evil was miserable and dejected; but as the wicked dead are raised and he sees the vast multitudes upon his side, his hopes revive, and he determines not to yield the great controversy. He will marshal all the armies of the lost under his banner and through them endeavor to execute his plans. The wicked are Satan's captives. In rejecting Christ they have accepted the rule of the rebel leader. They are ready to receive his suggestions and to do his bidding. Yet, true to his early cunning, he does not acknowledge himself to be Satan. He claims to be the prince who is the rightful owner of the world and whose inheritance has been unlawfully wrested from him. He represents himself to his deluded subjects as a redeemer, assuring them that his power has brought them forth from their graves and that he is about to rescue them from the most cruel tyranny. The presence of Christ having been removed, Satan works wonders to support his claims. He makes the weak strong and inspires all with his own spirit and energy. He proposes to lead them against the camp of the saints and to take possession of the City of God. With fiendish exultation he points to the unnumbered millions who have been raised from the dead and declares that as their leader he is well able to overthrow the city and regain his throne and his kingdom.

In that vast throng are multitudes of the long-lived race that existed before the Flood; men of lofty stature and giant intellect, who, yielding to the control of fallen angels, devoted all their skill and knowledge to the exaltation of themselves; men whose wonderful works of art led the world to idolize their genius, but whose cruelty and evil inventions, defiling the earth and defacing the image of God, caused Him to blot them from the face of His creation. There are kings and generals who conquered nations, valiant men who never lost a battle, proud, ambitious warriors whose approach made kingdoms tremble. In death these experienced no change. As they come up from the grave, they resume the current of their thoughts just where it ceased. They are actuated by the same desire to conquer that ruled them when they fell. Satan consults with his angels, and then with these kings and conquerors and mighty men. They look upon the strength and numbers on their side, and declare that the army within the city is small in comparison with theirs, and that it can be overcome. They lay their plans to take possession of the riches and glory of the New Jerusalem. All immediately begin to prepare for battle. Skillful artisans construct implements of war. Military leaders, famed for their success, marshal the throngs of warlike men into companies and divisions.

At last the order to advance is given, and the countless host moves on – an army such as was never summoned by earthly conquerors, such as the combined forces of all ages since war began on earth could never equal. Satan, the mightiest of warriors, leads the van, and his angels unite their forces for this final struggle. Kings and warriors are in his train, and the multitudes follow in vast companies, each under its appointed leader. With military precision the serried ranks advance over the earth's broken and uneven surface to the City of God. By command of Jesus, the gates of the New Jerusalem are closed, and the armies of Satan surround the city and make ready for the onset. Now Christ again appears to the view of His enemies. Far above the city, upon a foundation of burnished gold, is a throne, high and lifted up. Upon this throne sits the Son of God, and around Him are the subjects of His kingdom. The power and majesty of Christ no language can describe, no pen portray. The glory of the Eternal Father is enshrouding His Son. The brightness of His presence fills the City of God, and flows out beyond the gates, flooding the whole earth with its radiance.

Nearest the throne are those who were once zealous in the cause of Satan, but who, plucked as brands from the burning, have followed their Saviour with deep, intense devotion. Next are those who perfected Christian characters in the midst of falsehood and infidelity, those who honored the law of God when the Christian world declared it void, and the millions, of all ages, who were martyred for their faith. And beyond is the »great multitude, which no man could number, of all nations, and kindreds, and people, and tongues, ... before the throne, and before the Lamb, clothed with white robes, and palms in their hands.« Revelation 7:9 Their warfare is ended, their victory won. They have run the race and reached the prize. The palm branch in their hands is a symbol of their triumph, the white robe an emblem of the spotless righteousness of Christ which now is theirs. The redeemed raise a song of praise that echoes and re-echoes through the vaults of heaven: »Salvation to our God which sitteth upon the throne, and unto the Lamb.« Verse 10 And angel and seraph unite their voices in adoration. As the redeemed have beheld the power and malignity of Satan, they have seen, as never before,

 that no power but that of Christ could have made them

conquerors. In all that shining throng there are none to ascribe salvation to themselves, as if they had prevailed by their own power and goodness. Nothing is said of what they have done or suffered; but the burden of every song, the keynote of every anthem, is: Salvation to our God and unto the Lamb.

In the presence of the assembled inhabitants of earth and heaven the final coronation of the Son of God takes place. And now, invested with supreme majesty and power, the King of kings pronounces sentence upon the rebels against His government and executes justice upon those who have transgressed His law and oppressed His people. Says the prophet of God: »I saw a great white throne, and Him that sat on it, from whose face the earth and the heaven fled away; and there was found no place for them. And I saw the dead, small and great, stand before God; and the books were opened: and another book was opened, which is the book of life: and the dead were judged out of those things which were written in the books, according to their works.« Revelation 20:11-12

As soon as the books of record are opened, and the eye of Jesus looks upon the wicked, they are conscious of every sin which they have ever committed. They see just where their feet diverged from the path of purity and holiness, just how far pride and rebellion have carried them in the violation of the law of God. The seductive temptations which they encouraged by indulgence in sin, the blessings perverted, the messengers of God despised, the warnings rejected, the waves of mercy beaten back by the stubborn, unrepentant heart – all appear as if written in letters of fire.

Above the throne is revealed the cross; and like a panoramic view appear the scenes of Adam's temptation and fall, and the successive steps in the great plan of redemption. The Saviour's lowly birth; His early life of simplicity and obedience; His baptism in Jordan; the fast and temptation in the wilderness; His public ministry, unfolding to men heaven's most precious blessings; the days crowded with deeds of love and mercy, the nights of prayer and watching in the solitude of the mountains; the plottings of envy, hate, and malice which repaid His benefits; the awful, mysterious agony in Gethsemane beneath the crushing weight of the sins of the whole world; His betrayal into the hands of the murderous mob; the fearful events of that night of horror – the unresisting prisoner, forsaken by His best-loved disciples, rudely hurried through the streets of Jerusalem;

the Son of God exultingly displayed before Annas, arraigned in the high priest's palace, in the judgment hall of Pilate, before the cowardly and cruel Herod, mocked, insulted, tortured, and condemned to die – all are vividly portrayed.

And now before the swaying multitude are revealed the final scenes – the patient Sufferer treading the path to Calvary; the Prince of heaven hanging upon the cross; the haughty priests and the jeering rabble deriding His expiring agony; the supernatural darkness; the heaving earth, the rent rocks, the open graves, marking the moment when the world's Redeemer yielded up His life.

The awful spectacle appears just as it was. Satan, his angels, and his subjects have no power to turn from the picture of their own work. Each actor recalls the part which he performed. Herod, who slew the innocent children of Bethlehem that he might destroy the King of Israel; the base Herodias, upon whose guilty soul rests the blood of John the Baptist; the weak, timeserving Pilate; the mocking soldiers; the priests and rulers and the maddened throng who cried, »His blood be on us, and on our children!« – all behold the enormity of their guilt. They vainly seek to hide from the divine majesty of His countenance, outshining the glory of the sun, while the redeemed cast their crowns at the Saviour's feet, exclaiming: »He died for me!«

Amid the ransomed throng are the apostles of Christ, the heroic Paul, the ardent Peter, the loved and loving John, and their truehearted brethren, and with them the vast host of martyrs; while outside the walls, with every vile and abominable thing, are those by whom they were persecuted, imprisoned, and slain. There is Nero, that monster of cruelty and vice, beholding the joy and exaltation of those whom he once tortured, and in whose extremest anguish he found satanic delight. His mother is there to witness the result of her own work; to see how the evil stamp of character transmitted to her son, the passions encouraged and developed by her influence and example, have borne fruit in crimes that caused the world to shudder.

There are papist priests and prelates, who claimed to be Christ's ambassadors, yet employed the rack, the dungeon, and the stake to control the consciences of His people. There are the proud pontiffs who exalted themselves above God and presumed to change the law of the Most High. Those pretended fathers of the church have an account to render to God from which they would fain be excused. Too

 late they are made to see that the Omniscient One is

jealous of His law and that He will in no wise clear the guilty. They learn now that Christ identifies His interest with that of His suffering people; and they feel the force of His own words: "Inasmuch as ye have done it unto one of the least of these My brethren, ye have done it unto Me.« Matthew 25:40 The whole wicked world stand arraigned at the bar of God on the charge of high treason against the government of heaven. They have none to plead their cause; they are without excuse; and the sentence of eternal death is pronounced against them.

It is now evident to all that the wages of sin is not noble independence and eternal life, but slavery, ruin, and death. The wicked see what they have forfeited by their life of rebellion. The far more exceeding and eternal weight of glory was despised when offered them; but how desirable it now appears. »All this,« cries the lost soul, »I might have had; but I chose to put these things far from me. Oh, strange infatuation! I have exchanged peace, happiness, and honor for wretchedness, infamy, and despair.« All see that their exclusion from heaven is just. By their lives they have declared: »We will not have this Man [Jesus] to reign over us.«

As if entranced, the wicked have looked upon the coronation of the Son of God. They see in His hands the tables of the divine law, the statutes which they have despised and transgressed. They witness the outburst of wonder, rapture, and adoration from the saved; and as the wave of melody sweeps over the multitudes without the city, all with one voice exclaim, »Great and marvelous are Thy works, Lord God Almighty; just and true are Thy ways, Thou King of saints«; Revelation 15:3 and, falling prostrate, they worship the Prince of life. Satan seems paralyzed as he beholds the glory and majesty of Christ. He who was once a covering cherub remembers whence he has fallen. A shining seraph, "son of the morning;" how changed, how degraded! From the council where once he was honored, he is forever excluded. He sees another now standing near to the Father, veiling His glory. He has seen the crown placed upon the head of Christ by an angel of lofty stature and majestic presence, and he knows that the exalted position of this angel might have been his.

Memory recalls the home of his innocence and purity, the peace and content that were his until he indulged in murmuring against God, and envy of Christ. His accusations, his rebellion, his deceptions to gain the sympathy and support of the angels, his stubborn persistence in making no effort for self-recovery when

God would have granted him forgiveness – all come vividly before him. He reviews his work among men and its results - the enmity of man toward his fellow man, the terrible destruction of life, the rise and fall of kingdoms, the overturning of thrones, the long succession of tumults, conflicts, and revolutions. He recalls his constant efforts to oppose the work of Christ and to sink man lower and lower. He sees that his hellish plots have been powerless to destroy those who have put their trust in Jesus. As Satan looks upon his kingdom, the fruit of his toil, he sees only failure and ruin. He has led the multitudes to believe that the City of God would be an easy prey; but he knows that this is false. Again and again, in the progress of the great controversy, he has been defeated and compelled to yield. He knows too well the power and majesty of the Eternal.

The aim of the great rebel has ever been to justify himself and to prove the divine government responsible for the rebellion. To this end he has bent all the power of his giant intellect. He has worked deliberately and systematically, and with marvelous success, leading vast multitudes to accept his version of the great controversy which has been so long in progress. For thousands of years this chief of conspiracy has palmed off falsehood for truth. But the time has now come when the rebellion is to be finally defeated and the history and character of Satan disclosed. In his last great effort to dethrone Christ, destroy His people, and take possession of the City of God, the archdeceiver has been fully unmasked. Those who have united with him see the total failure of his cause. Christ's followers and the loyal angels behold the full extent of his machinations against the government of God. He is the object of universal abhorrence Satan sees that his voluntary rebellion has unfitted him for heaven. He has trained his powers to war against God; the purity, peace, and harmony of heaven would be to him supreme torture. His accusations against the mercy and justice of God are now silenced. The reproach which he has endeavored to cast upon Jehovah rests wholly upon himself. And now Satan bows down and confesses the justice of his sentence.

»Who shall not fear Thee, O Lord, and glorify Thy name? for Thou only art holy: for all nations shall come and worship before Thee; for Thy judgments are made manifest.« Verse 4 Every question of truth and error in the long-standing controversy has now been made plain. The results of rebellion, the fruits of setting aside the divine statutes, have been laid open to the view of all created intelligences. The working out of Satan's rule in contrast with the government of God has been presented to the whole universe. Satan's own works have condemned him. God's wisdom, His justice, and His goodness stand fully vindicated. It is seen that all His dealings in the great controversy have been conducted with respect to the eternal good of His people and the good of all the worlds that He has created. »All Thy works shall praise Thee, O Lord; and Thy saints shall bless Thee.« Psalm 145:10 The history of sin will stand to all eternity as a witness that with the existence of God's law is bound up the happiness of all the beings He has created. With all the facts of the great controversy in view, the whole universe, both loyal and rebellious, with one accord declare: »Just and true are Thy ways, Thou King of saints.«

Before the universe has been clearly presented the great sacrifice made by the Father and the Son in man's behalf. The hour has come when Christ occupies His rightful position and is glorified above principalities and powers and every name that is named. It was for the joy that was set before Him – that He might bring many sons unto glory – that He endured the cross and despised the shame. And inconceivably great as was the sorrow and the shame, yet greater is the joy and the glory. He looks upon the redeemed, renewed in His own image, every heart bearing the perfect impress of the divine, every face reflecting the likeness of their King. He beholds in them the result of the travail of His soul, and He is satisfied. Then, in a voice that reaches the assembled multitudes of the righteous and the wicked, He declares: »Behold the purchase of My blood! For these I suffered, for these I died, that they might dwell in My presence throughout eternal ages.« And the song of praise ascends from the white-robed ones about the throne: »Worthy is the Lamb that was slain to receive power, and riches, and wisdom, and strength, and honor, and glory, and blessing.« Revelation 5:12

Notwithstanding that Satan has been constrained to acknowledge God's justice and to bow to the supremacy of Christ, his character remains unchanged. The spirit of rebellion, like a mighty torrent, again bursts forth. Filled with frenzy, he determines not to yield the great controversy. The time has come for a last desperate struggle against the King of heaven. He rushes into the midst of his subjects and endeavors to inspire them with his own fury and arouse them to instant battle. But of all the countless millions whom he has allured into rebellion, there are none now to acknowledge his supremacy. His power is at an end. The wicked are filled with the same hatred of God that inspires Satan; but they see that their case is hopeless, that they cannot prevail against Jehovah. Their rage is kindled against Satan and those who have been his agents in deception, and with the fury of demons they turn upon them.

Saith the Lord: »Because thou hast set thine heart as the heart of God; behold, therefore I will bring strangers upon thee, the terrible of the nations: and they shall draw their swords against the beauty of thy wisdom, and they shall defile thy brightness. They shall bring thee down to the pit.« »I will destroy thee, O covering cherub, from the midst of the stones of fire. ... I will cast thee to the ground, I will lay thee before kings, that they may behold thee. ... I will bring thee to ashes upon the earth in the sight of all them that behold thee. ... Thou shalt be a terror, and never shalt thou be any more.« Ezekiel 28:6-8, 16-19

»Every battle of the warrior is with confused noise, and garments rolled in blood; but this shall be with burning and fuel of fire.« »The indignation of the Lord is upon all nations, and His fury upon all their armies: He hath utterly destroyed them, He hath delivered them to the slaughter.« »Upon the wicked He shall rain quick burning coals, fire and brimstone and an horrible tempest: this shall be the portion of their cup.« Isaiah 9:5; 34:2; Psalm 11:6, margin Fire comes down from God out of heaven. The earth is broken up. The weapons concealed in its depths are drawn forth. Devouring flames burst from every yawning chasm. The very rocks are on fire. The day has come that shall burn as an oven. The elements melt with fervent heat, the earth also, and the works that are therein are burned up. Malachi 4:1; 2 Peter 3:10 The earth's surface seems one molten mass – a vast, seething lake of fire. It is the time of the judgment and perdition of ungodly men – »the day of the Lord's vengeance, and the year of recompenses for the controversy of Zion.« Isaiah 34:8

The wicked receive their recompense in the earth. Proverbs 11:31 They »shall be stubble: and the day that cometh shall burn them up, saith the Lord of hosts.« Malachi 4:1 Some are destroyed as in a moment, while others suffer many days. All are punished »according to their deeds.« The sins of the righteous having been transferred to Satan, he is made to suffer not only for his own rebellion, but for all the sins

 which he has caused God's people to commit. His punishment is to be far greater than that of those whom he has deceived. After all have perished who fell by his deceptions, he is still to live and suffer on. In the cleansing flames the wicked are at last destroyed, root and branch – Satan the root, his followers the branches. The full penalty of the law has been visited; the demands of justice have been met; and heaven and earth, beholding, declare the righteousness of Jehovah. Satan's work of ruin is forever ended. For six thousand years he has wrought his will, filling the earth with woe and causing grief throughout the universe. The whole creation has groaned and travailed together in pain. Now God's creatures are forever delivered from his presence and temptations. »The whole earth is at rest, and is quiet: they [the righteous] break forth into singing.« Isaiah 14:7 And a shout of praise and triumph ascends from the whole loyal universe. »The voice of a great multitude,« »as the voice of many waters, and as the voice of mighty thunderings,« is heard, saying: »Alleluia: for the Lord God omnipotent reigneth.« Revelation 19:6

While the earth was wrapped in the fire of destruction, the righteous abode safely in the Holy City. Upon those that had part in the first resurrection, the second death has no power. While God is to the wicked a consuming fire, He is to His people both a sun and a shield. Revelation 20:6; Psalm 84:11

»I saw a new heaven and a new earth: for the first heaven and the first earth were passed away.« Revelation 21:1 The fire that consumes the wicked purifies the earth. Every trace of the curse is swept away. No eternally burning hell will keep before the ransomed the fearful consequences of sin. One reminder alone remains: Our Redeemer will ever bear the marks of His crucifixion. Upon His wounded head, upon His side, His hands and feet, are the only traces of the cruel work that sin has wrought. Says the prophet, beholding Christ in His glory: »He had bright beams coming out of His side: and there was the hiding of His power.« Habakkuk 3:4, margin That pierced side whence flowed the crimson stream that reconciled man to God – there is the Saviour's glory, there »the hiding of His power.« »Mighty to save,« through the sacrifice of redemption, He was therefore strong to execute justice upon them that despised God's mercy. And the tokens of His humiliation are His highest honor; through the eternal ages the wounds of Calvary will show forth His praise and declare His power.

»O Tower of the flock, the stronghold of the daughter of Zion, unto Thee shall it come, even the first dominion.« Micah

4:8 The time has come to which holy men have looked with longing since the flaming sword barred the first pair from Eden, the time for »the redemption of the purchased possession.« Ephesians 1:14 The earth originally given to man as his kingdom, betrayed by him into the hands of Satan, and so long held by the mighty foe, has been brought back by the great plan of redemption. All that was lost by sin has been restored. »Thus saith the Lord ... that formed the earth and made it; He hath established it, He created it not in vain, He formed it to be inhabited.« Isaiah 45:18 God's original purpose in the creation of the earth is fulfilled as it is made the eternal abode of the redeemed. »The righteous shall inherit the land, and dwell therein forever.« Psalm 37:29 A fear of making the future inheritance seem too material has led many to spiritualize away the very truths which lead us to look upon it as our home.

Christ assured His disciples that He went to prepare mansions for them in the Father's house. Those who accept the teachings of God's word will not be wholly ignorant concerning the heavenly abode. And yet, »eye hath not seen, nor ear heard, neither have entered into the heart of man, the things which God hath prepared for them that love Him.« 1 Corinthians 2:9 Human language is inadequate to describe the reward of the righteous. It will be known only to those who behold it. No finite mind can comprehend the glory of the Paradise of God.

In the Bible the inheritance of the saved is called »a country.« Hebrews 11:14-16 There the heavenly Shepherd leads His flock to fountains of living waters. The tree of life yields its fruit every month, and the leaves of the tree are for the service of the nations. There are ever-flowing streams, clear as crystal, and beside them waving trees cast their shadows upon the paths prepared for the ransomed of the Lord. There the wide-spreading plains swell into hills of beauty, and the mountains of God rear their lofty summits. On those peaceful plains, beside those living streams, God's people, so long pilgrims and wanderers, shall find a home.

»My people shall dwell in a peaceable habitation, and in sure dwellings, and in quiet resting places.« »Violence shall no more be heard in thy land, wasting nor destruction within thy borders; but thou shalt call thy walls Salvation, and thy gates Praise.« »They shall build houses, and inhabit them; and they shall plant vineyards, and eat the fruit of them. They shall not build, and another inhabit; they

 shall not plant, and another eat: ... Mine elect shall

long enjoy the work of their hands.« Isaiah 32:18; 60:18; Isaiah 65:21-22 There, »the wilderness and the solitary place shall be glad for them; and the desert shall rejoice, and blossom as the rose.« »Instead of the thorn shall come up the fir tree, and instead of the brier shall come up the myrtle tree.« »The wolf also shall dwell with the lamb, and the leopard shall lie down with the kid; ... and a little child shall lead them.« »They shall not hurt nor destroy in all My holy mountain,« saith the Lord. Isaiah 35:1; 55:13; Isaiah 11:6, 9

Pain cannot exist in the atmosphere of heaven. There will be no more tears, no funeral trains, no badges of mourning. »There shall be no more death, neither sorrow, nor crying: ... for the former things are passed away.« »The inhabitant shall not say, I am sick: the people that dwell therein shall be forgiven their iniquity.« Rev. 21:4; Isaiah 33:24 There is the New Jerusalem, the metropolis of the glorified new earth, »a crown of glory in the hand of the Lord, and a royal diadem in the hand of thy God.« »Her light was like unto a stone most precious, even like a jasper stone, clear as crystal.« »The nations of them which are saved shall walk in the light of it: and the kings of the earth do bring their glory and honor into it.« Saith the Lord: »I will rejoice in Jerusalem, and joy in My people.« »The tabernacle of God is with men, and He will dwell with them, and they shall be His people, and God Himself shall be with them, and be their God.« Isaiah 62:3; Revelation 21:11, 24; Isaiah 65:19; Revelation 21:3

In the City of God »there shall be no night.« None will need or desire repose. There will be no weariness in doing the will of God and offering praise to His name. We shall ever feel the freshness of the morning and shall ever be far from its close. »And they need no candle, neither light of the sun; for the Lord God giveth them light.« Revelation 22:5 The light of the sun will be superseded by a radiance which is not painfully dazzling, yet which immeasurably surpasses the brightness of our noontide. The glory of God and the Lamb floods the Holy City with unfading light. The redeemed walk in the sunless glory of perpetual day.

»I saw no temple therein: for the Lord God Almighty and the Lamb are the temple of it.« Revelation 21:22 The people of God are privileged to hold open communion with the Father and the Son. »Now we see through a glass, darkly.« 1 Corinthians 13:12 We behold the image of God reflected, as in a mirror, in the works of nature and in His dealings with men; but then we shall see Him face to face, without a dimming veil between. We shall stand in His presence and behold the glory of His countenance.

There the redeemed shall know, even as also they are known. The loves and sympathies which God Himself has planted in the soul shall there find truest and sweetest exercise. The pure communion with holy beings, the harmonious social life with the blessed angels and with the faithful ones of all ages who have washed their robes and made them white in the blood of the Lamb, the sacred ties that bind together "the whole family in heaven and earth« Ephesians 3:15 – these help to constitute the happiness of the redeemed.

There, immortal minds will contemplate with never-failing delight the wonders of creative power, the mysteries of redeeming love. There will be no cruel, deceiving foe to tempt to forgetfulness of God. Every faculty will be developed, every capacity increased. The acquirement of knowledge will not weary the mind or exhaust the energies. There the grandest enterprises may be carried forward, the loftiest aspirations reached, the highest ambitions realized; and still there will arise new heights to surmount, new wonders to admire, new truths to comprehend, fresh objects to call forth the powers of mind and soul and body.

All the treasures of the universe will be open to the study of God's redeemed. Unfettered by mortality, they wing their tireless flight to worlds afar – worlds that thrilled with sorrow at the spectacle of human woe and rang with songs of gladness at the tidings of a ransomed soul. With unutterable delight the children of earth enter into the joy and the wisdom of unfallen beings. They share the treasures of knowledge and understanding gained through ages upon ages in contemplation of God's handiwork. With undimmed vision they gaze upon the glory of creation – suns and stars and systems, all in their appointed order circling the throne of Deity. Upon all things, from the least to the greatest, the Creator's name is written, and in all are the riches of His power displayed.

And the years of eternity, as they roll, will bring richer and still more glorious revelations of God and of Christ. As knowledge is progressive, so will love, reverence, and happiness increase. The more men learn of God, the greater will be their admiration of His character. As Jesus opens before them the riches of redemption and the amazing achievements in the great controversy with Satan, the

hearts of the ransomed thrill with more fervent devotion, and with more rapturous joy they sweep the harps of gold; and ten thousand times ten thousand and thousands of thousands of voices unite to swell the mighty chorus of praise. »And every creature which is in heaven, and on the earth, and under the earth, and such as are in the sea, and all that are in them, heard I saying, Blessing, and honor, and glory, and power, be unto Him that sitteth upon the throne, and unto the Lamb for ever and ever.« Revelation 5:13

The great controversy is ended. Sin and sinners are no more. The entire universe is clean. One pulse of harmony and gladness beats through the vast creation. From Him who created all, flow life and light and gladness, throughout the realms of illimitable space. From the minutest atom to the greatest world, all things, animate and inanimate, in their unshadowed beauty and perfect joy, declare that God is love.

Appendix

General Notes

Revisions adopted by the E. G. White Trustees November 19, 1956, and December 6, 1979.

Look up on the English page numbers!

Page 50. Titles.

In a passage which is included in the Roman Catholic Canon Law, or Corpus Juris Canonici, Pope Innocent III declares that the Roman pontiff is "the vicegerent upon earth, not of a mere man, but of very God;" and in a gloss on the passage it is explained that this is because he is the vicegerent of Christ, who is "very God and very man." See Decretales Domini Gregorii Papae IX *(Decretals of the Lord Pope Gregory IX), liber 1, De Translatione Episcoporum, (On the Transference of Bishops), title 7, ch. 3;* Corpus Juris Canonici *(2d Leipzig Ed., 1881), col. 99; (Paris, 1612), tom. 2, Decretales, col. 205.* The documents which formed the decretals were gathered by Gratian, who was teaching at the University of Bologna about the year 1140. His work was added to and re-edited by Pope Gregory IX in an edition issued in 1234. Other documents appeared in succeeding years from time to time including the Extravagantes, added toward the close of the fifteenth century, all of these, with Gratian's Decretum, were published as the Corpus Juris Canonici in 1582. Pope Pius X authorized the codification in canon law in 1904, and the resulting code became effective in 1918.

For the title "Lord God the Pope" see a gloss on the Extravagantes of Pope John XXII, title 14, ch. 4, Declaramus. In an Antwerp edition of the Extravagantes, dated 1584, the words "Dominum Deum Nostrum Papam" ("Our Lord God the Pope") occur in column 153. In a Paris edition, dated 1612, they occur in column 140. In several editions published since 1612 the word "Deum" ("God") has been omitted.

Page 50. Infallibility.

On the doctrine of infallibility as set forth at the Vatican Council of 1870-71, see Philip Schaff, The Creeds of Christendom, *Vol. 2, Dogmatic Decrees of the Vatican Council, pp. 234-271,* where both the Latin and the English texts are given. For discussion see, for the Roman Catholic view, The Catholic Encyclopedia, *Vol. 7, art. "Infallibility," by Patrick J. Toner, 790ff.;* James Cardinal Gibbons, The Faith of our Fathers *(Baltimore: John Murphy Company,*

110th ed., 1917), chs. 7, 11. For Roman Catholic opposition to the doctrine of papal infallibility, see Johann Joseph Ignaz von Dollinger *(pseudonym "Janus")* The Pope and the Council *(New York: Charles Scribner's sons, 1869);* and W.J. Sparrow Simpson, Roman Catholic Opposition to Papal Infallibility *(London: John Murray, 1909).* For the non-Roman view, see George Salmon, Infallibility of the Church *(London: John Murray, rev. Education, 1914).*

Page 52. Image Worship.

"The worship of images ... was one of those corruptions of Christianity which crept into the church stealthily and almost without notice or observation. This corruption did not, like other heresies, develop itself at once, for in that case it would have met with decided censure and rebuke: but, making its commencement under a fair disguise, so gradually was one practice after another introduced in connection with it, that the church had become deeply steeped in practical idolatry, not only without any efficient opposition, but almost without any decided remonstrance; and when at length an endeavor was made to root it out, the evil was found too deeply fixed to admit of removal. ... It must be traced to the idolatrous tendency of the human heart, and its propensity to serve the creature more than the creator. ...

"Images and pictures were first introduced into churches, not to be worshiped, but either in the place of books to give instruction to those who could not read, or to excite devotion in the minds of others. How far they ever answered such a purpose is doubtful; but, even granting that this was the case for a time, it soon ceased to be so, and it was found that pictures and images brought into churches darkened rather than enlightened the minds of the ignorant - degraded rather than exalted the devotion of the worshiper. So that, however they might have been intended to direct men's minds to God, they ended in turning them from him to the worship of created things." – *J. Mendham, The Seventh General Council, the Second of Nicaea, Introduction, pages III-VI.*

For a record of the proceedings and decisions of the Second Council of Nicaea, A.D. 787, called to establish the worship of images, see Baronius, Ecclesiastical Annals, *Vol. 9, pp. 391-407 (Antwerp, 1612)*; J. Mendham, The Seventh General Council, the Second of Nicaea; Ed. Stillingfleet, Defense of the Discourse Concerning the Idolatry Practiced in the Church of Rome *(London, 1686)*; A Select Library of Nicene and Post-Nicene Fathers, *2d series, vol. 14, pp. 521-587 (New York, 1900)*; Charles J. Hefele, A History of the Councils of the Church, from the Original Documents, *B. 18, ch. 1, secs. 332, 333; ch. 2, secs. 345-352 (T. and T. Clark Education, 1896), vol. 5, pp. 260-304, 342-372.*

Page 53. The Sunday Law of Constantine.

The law issued by the Emperor Constantine on the seventh of March, A.D. 321, regarding a day of rest from labor, reads thus: "All judges and city people and the craftsmen shall rest upon the venerable day of the sun. Country people, however, may freely attend to the cultivation of the fields, because it frequently happens that no other days are better adapted for planting the grain in the furrows or the vines in trenches. So that the advantage given by heavenly providence may not for the occasion of a short time perish." – *Joseph Cullen Ayer, A Source Book for Ancient Church History (New York: Charles Scribner's sons, 1913), div. 2, per. 1, ch. 1, sec. 59, g, pp. 284, 285.*

The latin original is in the Codex Justiniani *(Codex of Justinian), [681] Lib. 3, Title 12, Lex 3.* The law is given in Latin and in English translation in Philip Schaff's History of the Christian Church, *Vol. 3, 3d period, ch. 7, sec. 75, p. 380, footnote 1*; and in James A. Hessey's Bampton Lectures, Sunday, *Lecture 3, par. 1, 3d ed., Murray's printing of 1866, p. 58.* See discussion in Schaff, as above referred to; in Albert Henry Newman, A Manual of Church History *(Philadelphia: the American Baptist Publication Society, printing of 1933), rev. Education, 305-307*; and in Leroy E. Froom, The Prophetic Faith of Our Fathers *(Washington, D.C.: Review and Herald Publishing Assn., 1950), vol. 1, pp 376-381.*

Page 54. Prophetic Dates.

An important principle in prophetic interpretation in connection with time prophecies is the year-day principle, under which a day of prophetic time is counted as a calendar year of historic time. Before the Israelites entered the land of Canaan they sent twelve spies ahead to investigate. The spies were gone forty days, and upon their return the Hebrews, frightened at their report, refused to go up and occupy the promised land. The result was a sentence the Lord passed upon them: "After the number of the days in which ye searched the land, even forty days, each day for a year, shall ye bear your iniquities, even forty years." Numbers 14:34. A similar method of computing future time is indicated through the prophet Ezekiel. Forty years of punishment for iniquities awaited the kingdom of Judah. The Lord said through the prophet: "Lie again on thy right side, and thou shalt bear the iniquity of the house of Judah forty days: I have appointed thee each day for a year." Ezekiel 4:6. This year-day principle has an important application in interpreting the time of the prophecy of the "two thousand and three hundred evenings and mornings" *(Daniel 8:14, R.V.)* and the 1260-day period, variously indicated as "a time and times and the dividing of time" *(Daniel 7:25)*, the "forty and two months" *(Revelation 11:2; 13:5)*, and the "thousand two hundred and threescore days" *(Revelation 11:3; 12:6)*.

Page 56. Forged Writings.

Among the documents that at the present time are generally admitted to be forgeries, the Donation of Constantine and the Pseudo-Isidorian Decretals are of primary importance. "The 'Donation of Constantine' is the name traditionally applied, since the later Middle Ages, to a document purporting to have been addressed by Constantine the Great to Pope Sylvester I, which is found first in a Parisian manuscript *(Codex lat. 2777)* of probably the beginning of the ninth century. Since the eleventh century it has been used as a powerful argument in favor of the papal claims, and consequently since the twelfth it has been the subject of a vigorous controversy.

At the same time, by rendering it possible to regard the papacy as a middle term between the original and the medieval Roman Empire, and thus to form a theoretical basis of continuity for the reception of the Roman law in the Middle Ages, it has had no small influence upon secular history." – *The New Schaff-Herzog Encyclopedia of Religious Knowledge, vol. 3, art. "Donation of Constantine," pp. 484, 485.*

The historical theory developed in the "Donation" is fully discussed in Henry E. Cardinal Manning's The Temporal Power of the Vicar of Jesus Christ, London, 1862. The arguments of the "Donation" were of a scholastic type, and the possibility of a forgery was not mentioned until the rise of historical criticism in the fifteenth century. Nicholas of Cusa was among the first to conclude that Constantine never made any such donation. Lorenza Valla in Italy gave a brilliant demonstration of its spuriousness in 1450. See Christopher B. Coleman's Treatise of Lorenzo Valla on the Donation of Constantine *(New York, 1927)*. For a century longer, however, the belief in the authenticity of the "Donation" and of the False Decretals was kept alive. For example, Martin Luther at first accepted the decretals, but he soon said to Eck: "I impugn these decretals;" and to Spalatin: "He [the pope] does in his decretals corrupt and crucify Christ, that is, the truth."

It is deemed established that (1) the "Donation" is a forgery, (2) it is the work of one man or period, (3) the forger has made use of older documents, (4) the forgery originated around 752 and 778. As for the Catholics, they abandoned the defense of the authenticity of the document with Baronius, Ecclesiastical Annals, in 1592. Consult for the best text, K. Zeumer, in the Festgabe fur Rudolf von Gneist (Berlin, 1888). Translated in Coleman's Treatise, referred to above, and in Ernest F. Henderson, Select Historical Documents of the Middle Ages *(New York, 1892), p. 319*; Briefwechsel *(Weimar ed.), pp. 141, 161.*

See also The New Schaff-Herzog Encyclopedia of Religious Knowledge *(1950), vol. 3, p. 484*; F. Gregorovius, Rome in the Middle Ages, *vol.*

2, p. 329; and Johann Joseph Ignaz von Dollinger, Fables Respecting the Popes of the Middle Ages *(London, 1871).*

The "false writings" referred to in the text include also the Pseudo-Isidorian Decretals, together with other forgeries. The PseudoIsidorian Decretals are certain fictitious letters ascribed to early popes from Clement *(A.D. 100)* to Gregory the Great *(A.D. 600)*, incorporated in a ninth century collection purporting to have been made by "Isidore Mercator." The name "Pseudo-Isidorian Decretals" has been in use since the advent of criticism in the fifteenth century.

Pseudo-Isidore took as the basis of his forgeries a collection of valid canons called the Hispana Gallica Augustodunensis, thus lessening the danger of detection, since collections of canons were commonly made by adding new matter to old. Thus his forgeries were less apparent when incorporated with genuine material. The falsity of the Pseudo-Isidorian fabrications is now incontestably admitted, being proved by internal evidence, investigation of the sources, the methods used, and the fact that this material was unknown before 852. Historians agree that 850 or 851 is the most probable date for the completion of the collection, since the document is first cited in the Admonitio of the capitulary of Quiercy, in 857.

The author of these forgeries is not known. It is probable that they emanated from the aggressive new church party which formed in the ninth century at Rheims, France. It is agreed that Bishop Hincmar of Rheims used these Decretals in his deposition of Rothad of Soissons, who brought the Decretals to Rome in 864 and laid them before Pope Nicholas I. Among those who challenged their authenticity were Nicholas of Cusa (1401-1464), Charles Dumoulin *(1500-1566)*, and George Cassender *(1513-1564)*. The irrefutable proof of their falsity was conveyed by David Blondel, 1628.

An early edition is given in Migne Patrologia Latina, CXXX. For the oldest and best manuscript, see P. Hinschius, Decretales PseudoIsidorianiae at Capitula Angilramni (Leipzig, 1863). Consult The New Schaff-Herzog Encyclopedia of Religious Knowledge *(1950), vol. 9, pp. 343-345.* See also H. H. Milman, Latin Christianity *(Vols.), vol. 3*; Johann Joseph Ignaz von Dollinger, The Pope and the Council *(1869)*; and Kenneth Scott Latourette, A history of the Expansion of Christianity *(1939), vol. 3*; The Catholic Encyclopedia, *Vol. 5, art. "False Decretals,"* and Fournier, "Etudes sure les Fausses Decretals," In Revue D'Historique Ecclesiastique *(Louvain) vol. 7 (1906), and vol. 8 (1907).*

Page 57. The Dictate of Hildebrand (Gregory VII).

For the original Latin version see Baronius, Annales Ecclesiastici, *Ann. 1076, vol. 17, pp. 405, 406 of the Paris printing of 1869*; and the Monumenta Germaniae Historica Selecta, Vol. 3, p. 17. For an English translation see Frederic A. Ogg, Source Book of Medieval History *(New York: American Book Co., 1907), ch. 6, sec. 45, pp. 262-264*; and Oliver J. Thatcher and Edgar H. McNeal, Source Book for Medieval History *(New York: Charles Scribner's sons, 1905), sec. 3, item 65, pp. 136-139.*

For a discussion of the background of the Dictate, see James Bryce, The Holy Roman Empire, Rev. Ed., Ch. 10; and James W. Thompson and Edgar N. Johnson, An Introduction to Medieval Europe, 300-1500, *pp. 377-380.*

Page 59. Purgatory.

Dr. Joseph Faa Di Bruno thus defines purgatory: "Purgatory is a state of suffering after this life, in which those souls are for a time detained, who depart this life after their deadly sins have been remitted as to the stain and guilt, and as to the everlasting pain that was due to them; but who have on account of those sins still some debt of temporal punishment to pay; as also those souls which leave this world guilty only of venial sins." - *Catholic Belief (1884 ed.; Imprimatur Archbishop of New York), p. 196.*

See also K. R. Hagenbach, Compendium of the History of Doctrines *(T. and T. Clark ed.) vol. 1, pp. 234-237, 405, 408; vol. 2, pp. 135-150, 308, 309;* Charles Elliott, Delineation of Roman Catholicism, *B. 2, ch. 12;* The Catholic Encyclopedia, *vol. 12, art. "Purgatory."*

Page 59. Indulgences.

For a detailed history of the doctrine of indulgences see Mandell Creighton, A History of the Papacy From [684] the Great chism to the sack of Rome *(London: Longmans, Green and Co., 1911), vol. 5, pp. 56-64, 71*; W.H. Kent, "Indulgences," The Catholic Encyclopedia, *vol. 7, pp. 783-789;* H. C. Lea, A History of Auricular Confession and Indulgences in the Latin Church *(Philadelphia: Lea Brothers and Co., 1896)*; Thomas M. Lindsay, A History of the Reformation *(New York; Charles Scribner's Sons, 1917), vol. 1, pp. 216-227*; Albert Henry Newman, A Manual of Church History *(Philadelphia: The American Baptist Publication Society, 1953), vol. 2, pp. 53, 54, 62*; Leopold Ranke, History of the Reformation in Germany *(2d London ed., 1845), translated by Sarah Austin, vol. 1, pp. 331, 335-337, 343-346*; Preserved Smith, The Age of the Reformation *(New York: Henry Holt and Company, 1920), pp. 23-25, 66.* On the practical outworkings of the doctrine of indulgences during the period of the Reformation see a paper by Dr. H. C. Lea, entitled, "Indulgences in Spain," published in Papers of the American Society of Church History, *Vol. 1, pp. 129-171.* Of the value of this historical sidelight Dr. Lea says in his opening paragraph: "Unvexed by the controversy which raged between Luther and Dr. Eck and Silvester Prierias, Spain continued tranquilly to follow in the old and beaten path, and furnishes us with the incontestable official documents which enable us to examine the matter in the pure light of history."

Page 59. The Mass.

For the doctrine of the mass as set forth at the council of trent see The Canons and Decrees of the Council of Trent In Philip Schaff, Creeds of Christendom, *Vol. 2, pp. 126-139*, where both Latin and English texts are given. See also H. G. Schroeder, Canons and Decrees of the Council of Trent *(St. Louis, Missouri: B. Herder, 1941).*

For a discussion of the mass see The Catholic Encyclopedia, *vol 5, art. "Eucharist," by Joseph Pohle, page 572ff.*; Nikolaus Gihr, Holy Sacrifice of the Mass, Dogmatically, Liturgically, Ascetically Explained, *12th ed. (St. Louis, Missouri: B. Herder, 1937)*; Josef Andreas Jungmann, The Mass of the Roman Rite, its Origins and Development, translated from the German by Francis A. Brunner *(New York: Benziger Bros., 1951).* For the non-Catholic view, see John Calvin, Institutes of the Christian Religion, *B. 4, chs. 17, 18;* and Edward Bouverie Pusey, The Doctrine of the Real Presence *(Oxford, England: John H. Parker, 1855).*

Page 65. The Sabbath Among the Waldenses.

There are writers who have maintained that the Waldenses made a general practice of observing the seventh-day Sabbath. This concept arose from sources which in the original Latin describe the Waldenses as keeping the Dies Dominicalis, or Lord's day (Sunday), but in which through a practice which dates from the reformation, the word for "Sunday" has been translated "Sabbath."

But there is historical evidence of some observance of the seventhday Sabbath among the Waldenses. A report of an inquisition before whom were brought some Waldenses of Moravia in the middle of the fifteenth century declares that among the Waldenses "not a few indeed celebrate the Sabbath with the Jews." – *Johann Joseph Ignaz von Dollinger, Beitrage zur Sektengeschichte des Mittelalters (Reports on the History of the Sects of the Middle Ages), Munich, 1890, 2d pt., p. 661.* There can be no question that this source indicates the observance of the seventh-day Sabbath.

Page 65. Waldensian Versions of the Bible.

On recent discoveries of Waldensian manuscripts see M. Esposito, "Sur quelques manuscrits de l'ancienne litterature des Vaudois du Piemont," In Revue D' Historique Ecclesiastique *(Louvain, 1951), p. 130ff.*; F. Jostes, "Die Waldenserbibeln," In Historisches Jahrbuch, 1894; D. Lortsch, Histoire de la Bible en France *(Paris, 1910), ch. 10.*

A classic written by one of the Waldensian "barbs" is Jean Leger, Histoire Generale des Eglises Evangeliques des Vallees de Piemont *(Leyden, 1669),* which was written at the time of the great persecutions and contains first-hand information with drawings.

For the literature of Waldensian texts see A. deStefano, Civilta Medio-evale *(1944)*; and Riformatori ed eretici nel medioeve *(Palermo, 1938)*; J. D. Bounous, The Waldensian Patois of Pramol *(Nashville, 1936)*; and A. Dondaine, Archivum Fratrum Praedicatorum *(1946).*

For the history of the Waldenses some of the more recent, reliable works are: E. Comba, History of the Waldenses in Italy *(see later Italian edition published in Torre Pellice, 1934);* E. Gebhart, Mystics and Heretics *(Boston, 1927)*; G. Gonnet, Il Valdismo Medioevale, Prolegomeni *(Torre Pellice, 1935)*; and Jalla, Histoire des Vaudois et leurs colonies *(Torre Pellice, 1935).*

Page 77. Edict Against the Waldenses.

A considerable portion of the text of the papal bull issued by Innocent VIII in 1487 against the Waldenses *(the original of which is in the library of the University of Cambridge)* is given, in an English translation, in John Dowling's History of Romanism *(1871 ed.), B. 6, ch. 5, sec. 62.*

Page 80. Wycliffe.

The historian discovers that the name of Wycliffe, has many different forms of spelling. For a full discussion of these see J. Dahmus, The Prosecution of John Wyclyf *(New Haven: Yale University Press, 1952), p. 7.*

Page 85. Papal Bulls.

For the original text of the papal bulls issued against Wycliffe with English translation see J. Dahmus, The Prosecution of John Wyclyf *(New Haven: Yale University Press, 1952), pp. 35-49;* also John Foxe, Acts and Monuments of the Church *(London: Pratt Townsend, 1870), vol. 3, pp. 4-13.*

For a summary of these bulls sent to the archbishop of Canterbury, to King Edward, and to the chancellor of the University of Oxford, see Merle

D'Aubigne, The History of the Reformation in the Sixteenth Century

(London: Blackie and son, 1885), vol. 4, div. 7, p. 93; August Neander, General History of the Christian Church *(Boston: Crocker and Brester, 1862), vol. 5, pp. 146, 147*; George Sargeant, History of the Christian Church *(Dallas: Frederick Publishing House, 1948), p. 323*; Gotthard V. Lechler, John Wycliffe and his English Precursors *(London: The Religious Tract Society, 1878), pp. 162-164*; Philip Schaff, History of the Christian Church *(New York: Charles Scribner's Sons, 1915), vol. 5, pt. 2, p. 317.*

Page 104. Council of Constance.

A primary source on the Council of Constance is Richendal Ulrich, Das Concilium so zu Constanz gehalten ist worden *(Augsburg, 1483, incun.)*. An interesting, recent study of this text, based on the "Aulendorf Codex," is in the Spencer Collection of the New York Public Library, published by Karl Kup, Ulrich von Richental's Chronicle of the Council of Constance *(New York, 1936)*. See also H. Finke *(ed.)*, Acta Concilii Constanciensis *(1896), vol. 1;* Hefele, Conciliengeschichte *(9 vols.), vols. 6, 7*; L. Mirbt, Quellen zur Geschichte des Papsttums *(1934)*; Milman, Latin Christianity, *vol. 7, pp. 426-524*; Pastor, The History of the Popes *(34 vols.), vol. 1, p. 197ff.*

More recent publications on the council are K. Zahringer, Das Kardinal Kollegium auf dem Konstanzer Konzil *(Munster, 1935)*; th. F. Grogau, The Conciliar Theory as it Manifested itself at the Council of Constance *(Washington, 1949);* Fred A. Kremple, Cultural Aspects of the Council of Constance and Basel *(Ann Arbor, 1955)*; John Patrick McGowan, D'ailly and the Council of Constance *(Washington: Catholic University, 1936).*

For John Huss see John Hus, *Letters, 1904*; E. J. Kitts, Pope John XXIII and Master John Hus *(London, 1910)*; D. S. Schaff, John Hus *(1915)*; Schwarze, John Hus *(1915)*; and Matthew Spinka, John Hus and the Czech Reform *(1941).*

Page 234. Jesuitism.

For a statement concerning the origin, the principles, and the purposes of the "Society of Jesus," as outlined by members of this order, see a work entitled Concerning Jesuits, edited by the Rev. John Gerard, S.J., and published in London, 1902, by the Catholic Truth Society. In this work it is said, "The mainspring of the whole organization of the Society is a spirit of entire obedience: 'Let each one,' writes St. Ignatius, 'persuade himself that those who live under obedience ought to allow themselves to be moved and directed by divine Providence through their superiors, just as though they were a dead body, which allows itself to be carried anywhere and to be treated in any manner whatever, or as an old man's staff, which serves him who holds it in his hand in whatsoever way he will.'

"This absolute submission is ennobled by its motive, and should be, continues the ... founder, 'prompt, joyous and persevering; ... The obedient religious accomplishes joyfully that which his superiors have confided to him for the general good, assured that thereby he corresponds truly with the divine will.'" – *The Comtesse R. de Courson, in Concerning Jesuits, page 6.* See also L. E. Dupin, A Compendious History of the Church, *cent. 16, ch. 33 (London, 1713, vol. 4, pp. 132-135)*; Mosheim, Ecclesiastical History, *cent. 16, sec. 3, pt. 1, ch. 1, par. 10 (including notes)*; The Encyclopedia Britannica *(9th ed.)*, art. "Jesuits;" C. Paroissen, The Principles of the Jesuits, Developed in a Collection of Extracts from their Own Authors *(London, 1860 - an earlier edition appeared in 1839)*; W. C. Cartwright, The Jesuits, Their Constitution and Teaching *(London, 1876)*; E. L. Taunton, The History of the Jesuits in England, 1580-1773 *(London, 1901)*. See also H. Boehmer, The Jesuits *(translation from the German, Philadelphia, castle press 1928)*; E. Goethein, Ignatius von Loyola und die Gegenreformation *(Halle, 1895)*; T. Campbell, The Jesuits, 1534-1921 *(New York, 1922).*

Page 235. The Inquisition.

For the Roman Catholic view see The Catholic Encyclopedia, *Vol. 8, art. "Inquisition" By Joseph Blotzer, p. 26ff.*: And E. Vacandard, The Inquisition: A Critical and Historical Study of the Coercive Power of the Church *(New York: Longmans, Green and Company, 1908).*

For an Anglo-Catholic view see Hoffman Nickerson, The Inquisition: A Political and Military Study of its Establishment. For the non-Catholic view see Philip van Limborch, History of the Inquisition; Henry Charles Lea, A History of the Inquisition of the Middle Ages, *3 vols.*; A History of the Inquisition of Spain, *4 vols.*, and The Inquisition in the Spanish Dependencies; and H. S. Turberville, Medieval Heresy and the Inquisition *(London: C. Lockwood and Son, 1920 – a mediating view).*

Page 265. Causes of the French Revolution.

On the far-reaching consequences of the rejection of the Bible and of Bible religion, by the people of France, see H. von Sybel, History of the French Revolution, *B. 5, ch. 1, pars. 3-7*; Henry Thomas Buckle, History of Civilization in England, *Chs. 8 , 12, 14 (New York, 1895, vol. 1, pp. 364-366, 369-371, 437, 540, 541, 550);* Blackwood's Magazine, *Vol. 34, no. 215 (November, 1833), p. 739*; J. G. Lorimer, An Historical Sketch of the Protestant Church in France, *Ch. 8, pars. 6, 7.*

Page 267. Efforts to Suppress and Destroy the Bible.

The Council of Toulouse, which met about the time of the crusade against the Albigenses, ruled: "We prohibit laymen possessing copies of the Old and New Testament. ... We forbid them most severely to have the above books in the popular vernacular." "The Lords of the districts shall carefully seek out the heretics in dwellings, hovels, and forests, and even their underground retreats shall be entirely wiped out." – *Concil. Tolosanum, Pope Gregory IX, Anno. Chr. 1229. Canons 14 and 2.* This Council sat at the time of the crusade against the Albigenses. "This pest [the Bible] had taken such an extension that some people had appointed priests of their own, and even some evangelists who distorted and destroyed the truth of the gospel and made new gospels for their own purpose ... (They know that) the preaching and explanation of the Bible is absolutely forbidden to the lay members." – *Acts of Inquisition, Philip van Limborch, History of the Inquisition, chapter 8.*

The Council of Tarragona, 1234, ruled that: "No one may possess the books of the Old and New Testaments in the Romance language, and if anyone possesses them he must turn them over to the local bishop within eight days after promulgation of this decree, so that they may be burned lest, be he a cleric or a layman, he be suspected until he is cleared of all suspicion." *- D. Lortsch, Histoire de la Bible en France, 1910, p. 14.*

At the Council of Constance, in 1415, Wycliffe was posthumously condemned by Arundel, the archbishop of Canterbury, as "that pestilent wretch of damnable heresy who invented a new translation of the Scriptures in his mother tongue."

The opposition to the Bible by the Roman Catholic Church has continued through the centuries and was increased particularly at the time of the founding of Bible societies. On December 8, 1866, Pope Pius IX, in his encyclical Quanta cura, issued a syllabus of eighty errors under ten different headings. Under heading IV we find listed: "Socialism, communism, clandestine societies, Bible societies. ... Pests of this sort must be destroyed by all possible means."

Page 276. The Reign of Terror.

For a reliable, brief introduction into the history of the French Revolution see L. Gershoy, The French Revolution *(1932)*; G. Lefebvre, The Coming of the French Revolution *(Princeton, 1947)*; and H. von Sybel, History of the French Revolution *(1869), 4 vols.*

The Moniteur Officiel was the government paper at the time of the Revolution and is a primary source, containing a factual account of actions taken by the assemblies, full texts of the documents, etc. It has been reprinted. See also A. Aulard, Christianity and the French Revolution *(London, 1927)*, in which the account is carried through 1802 - an excellent study; W. H. Jervis, The Gallican Church and the Revolution *(London, 1882)*, a careful work by an Anglican, but shows preference for Catholicism.

On the relation of church and state in France during the French Revolution see Henry H. Walsh, The Concordate of 1801: A Study of Nationalism in Relation to Church and State *(New York, 1933)*; Charles Ledre, L'Eglise de France sous la Revolution *(Paris, 1949)*.

Some contemporary studies on the religious significance of the Revolution are G. Chais de Sourcesol, Le Livre des Manifestes *(Avignon, 1800)*, in which the author endeavored to ascertain the causes of the upheaval, and its religious significance, etc.; James Bicheno, The Signs of the Times *(London, 1794)*; James Winthrop, A Systematic Arrangement of Several Scripture Prophecies Relating to Antichrist; with Their Application to the Course of History *(Boston, 1795)*; and Lathrop, The Prophecy of Daniel Relating to the Time of the End *(Springfield, Massachusetts, 1811)*.

For the church during the Revolution see W. M. Sloan, The French Revolution and Religious Reform *(1901)*; P. F. La Gorce, Histoire Religieuse de la Revolution *(Paris, 1909)*.

On relations with the papacy see G. Bourgin, La France et Rome de 1788-1797 *(Paris, 1808)*, based on secret files in the Vatican; A. Latreille, L' Eglise Catholique et la Revolution *(Paris, 1950)*, especially interesting on Pius VI and the religious crisis, 1775-1799. For Protestants during the Revolution, see Pressense *(ed.)*, The Reign of Terror *(Cincinnati, 1869)*.

Page 280. The Masses and the Privileged Classes.

On social conditions prevailing in France prior to the period of the Revolution, see H. von Holst, Lowell Lectures on the French Revolution, *Lecture 1;* also Taine, Ancien Regime, and A. Young, Travels in France.

Page 283. Retribution.

For further details concerning the retributive character of the French Revolution see Thos. H. Gill, The Papal Drama, *B. 10*; Edmond de Pressense, The Church and the French Revolution, *B. 3, ch. 1.*

Page 284. The Atrocities of the Reign of Terror.

See M. A. Thiers, History of the French Revolution, *Vol. 3, pp. 42-44, 62-74, 106 (New York, 1890, translated by F. Shoberl)*; F. A. Mignet, History of the French Revolution, *ch. 9, par. 1 (Bohn, 1894)*; A. Alison, History of Europe, 1789-1815, *vol. 1, ch. 14 (New York, 1872, vol. 1, pp. 293-312).*

Page 287. The Circulation of the Scriptures.

In 1804, according to Mr. William Canton of the British and Foreign Bible Society, "all the Bibles extant in the world, in manuscript or in print, counting every version in every land, were computed at not many more than four millions. ... The various languages in which those four millions were written, including such bygone speech as the Moeso-Gothic of Ulfilas and the Anglo-Saxon of Bede, are set down as numbering about fifty." – *What is the Bible Society? rev. ed., 1904, 23.*

The American Bible Society reported a distribution from 1816 through 1955 of 481,149,365 Bibles, Testaments, and portions of Testaments. To this may be added over 600,000,000 Bibles or Scripture portions distributed by the British and Foreign Bible Society. During the year 1955 alone the American Bible Society distributed a grand total of 23,819,733 Bibles, Testaments, and portions of Testaments throughout the world. The Scriptures, in whole or in part, have been printed, as of December, 1955, in 1,092 languages; and new languages are constantly being added.

Page 288. Foreign Missions.

The missionary activity of the early Christian church has not been duplicated until modern times. It had virtually died out by the year 1000, and was succeeded by the military campaigns of the Crusades. The Reformation era saw little foreign mission work, except on the part of the early Jesuits. The pietistic revival produced some missionaries. The work of the Moravian Church in the eighteenth century was remarkable, and there were some missionary societies formed by the British for work in colonized North America. But the great resurgence of foreign missionary activity begins around the year 1800, at "the time of the end." Daniel 12:4. In 1792 was formed the Baptist Missionary Society, which sent Carey to India. In 1795 the London Missionary Society was organized, and another society in 1799 which in 1812 became the Church Missionary Society. Shortly afterward the Wesleyan Missionary Society was founded. In the United States the American Board of Commissioners for Foreign Missions was formed in 1812, and Adoniram Judson was sent out that year to Calcutta. He established himself in Burma the next year.

In 1814 the American Baptist Missionary Union was formed. The Presbyterian Board of Foreign Missions was formed in 1837.

"In A.D. 1800, ... the overwhelming majority of Christians were the descendants of those who had been won before A.D. 1500. ... Now, in the nineteenth century, came a further expansion of Christianity. Not so many continents or major countries were entered for the first time as in the preceding three centuries. That would have been impossible, for on all the larger land masses of the earth except Australia and among all the more numerous peoples and in all the areas of high civilization Christianity had been introduced before A.D. 1800. What now occurred was the acquisition of fresh footholds in regions and among peoples already touched, an expansion of unprecedented extent from both the newer bases and the older ones, and the entrance of Christianity into the large majority of such countries, islands, peoples, and tribes as had previously not been touched. ... "The nineteenth century spread of Christianity was due primarily to a new burst of religious life emanating from the Christian impulse. ... Never in any corresponding length of time had the Christian impulse given rise to so many new movements. Never had it had quite so great an effect upon Western European peoples. It was from this abounding vigor that there issued the missionary enterprise which during the nineteenth century so augmented the numerical strength and the influence of Christianity." – *Kenneth Scott Latourette, A History of the Expansion of Christianity, Vol. IV, The Great Century A.D. 1800 A.D. 1914 (New York: Harper & Brothers, 1941), pp. 2-4.*

Pages 327, 329. Prophetic Dates.

According to Jewish reckoning the fifth month (Ab) of the seventh year of Artaxerxes' reign was from July 23 to August 21, 457 B.C. after Ezra's arrival in Jerusalem in the autumn of the year, the decree of the king went into effect. For the certainty of the date 457 B.C. being the seventh year of Artaxerxes, see S. H. Horn and L. H. Wood, The Chronology of Ezra 7 *(Washington, D. C.: Review and Herald Publishing Assn., 1953)*; E. G. Kraeling, The Brooklyn Museum Aramaic Papyri *(New Haven or London, 1953), pp. 191-193;* The S.D.A. Bible Commentary 3:97-110 *(Hagerstown, MD: Review and Herald Publishing Assn., 1954, 1977).*

Page 335. Fall of the Ottoman Empire.

The impact of Moslem Turkey upon Europe after the fall of Constantinople in 1453 was as severe as had been the catastrophic conquests of the Moslem Saracens, during the century and a half after the death of Mohammed, upon the Eastern Roman Empire. Throughout the Reformation era, Turkey was a continual threat at the Eastern gates of European Christendom; the writings of the Reformers are full of condemnation of the Ottoman power. Christian writers since have been concerned with the role of Turkey in future world events, and commentators on prophecy have seen Turkish power and its decline forecast in Scripture. For the latter chapter, under the "hour, day, month, year" prophecy, as part of the sixth trumpet, Josiah Litch worked out an application of the time prophecy, terminating Turkish independence in August, 1840. Litch's view can be found in full in his The Probability of the Second Coming of Christ about A.D. 1843 *(published in June, 1838);* An Address to the Clergy *(published in the spring of 1840; a second edition, with historical data in support of the accuracy of former calculations of the prophetic period extending to the fall of the Ottoman Empire, was published in 1841);* and an article in Signs of the Times and Expositor of Prophecy, August 1, 1840. See also article in The Signs of the Times and Expositor of Prophecy, February 1, 1841; and J. N. Loughborough, The Great Second Advent Movement *(1905 ed.), pp. 129-132.* The book by Uriah Smith, Thoughts on Daniel and the Revelation, *rev. ed. off 1944, discusses the prophetic timing of this prophecy on pp. 506-517.*

For the earlier history of the Ottoman Empire and the decline of the Turkish power, see also William Miller, The Ottoman Empire and Its Successors, 1801-1927 *(Cambridge, England: University Press, 1936)*; George G. S. L. Eversley, The Turkish Empire from 1288 to 1914 *(London : T. Fisher Unwin, Ltd., 2d ed., 1923)*; Joseph von Hammer-Purgstall, Geschichte des Osmanischen Reiches *(Pesth: C. A. Hartleben, 2d ed., 1834-36), 4 vols.*; Herbert A. Gibbons, Foundation of the Ottoman Empire, 1300-1403 *(Oxford: University Press, 1916)*; Arnold J. Toynbee and Kenneth B. Kirkwood, Turkey *(London, 1926).*

Page 340. Withholding the Bible From the People.

The reader will recognize that the text of this volume was written prior to Vatican Council II, with its somewhat altered policies in regard to the reading of the Scriptures. Through the centuries, the attitude of the Roman Catholic Church toward circulation of the Holy Scriptures in vernacular versions among the laity shows up as negative. See for example G. P. Fisher, The Reformation, *Ch. 15, Par. 16 (1873 ed., pp. 530-532)*; J. Cardinal Gibbons, The Faith of Our Fathers, *ch. 8 (49th ed., 1897), pp. 98-117*; John Dowling, History of Romanism, *b. 7, ch. 2, sec. 14; and b. 9, ch. 3, secs. 24-27 (1871 ed., pp. 491-496, 621-625)*; L. F. Bungener, History of the Council of Trent, *pp. 101-110 (2d Edinburgh ed., 1853, translated by D. D. Scott)*; G. H. Putnam, Books and Their Makers During the Middle Ages, *vol. 1, pt. 2, ch. 2, pars. 49, 54-56.* See also Index of Prohibited Books *(Vatican Polyglot Press, 1930), pp. IX, X*; Timothy Hurley, A Commentary on the Present Index Legislation *(New York: Benziger Brothers, 1908), p. 71*; Translation of the Great Encyclical Letters of Leo XIII *(New York: Benziger Brothers, 1903), p. 413.*

But in recent years a dramatic and positive change has occurred in this respect. On the one hand, the church has approved several versions prepared on the basis of the original languages; on the other, it has promoted the study of the Holy Scriptures by means of free distribution and Bible institutes. The church, however, continues to reserve for herself the exclusive right to interpret the Bible in the light of her own tradition, thus justifying those doctrines that do not harmonize with Biblical teachings.

Page 373. Ascension Robes.

The story that the Adventists made robes with which to ascend "to meet the Lord in the air," was invented by those who wished to reproach the Advent preaching. It was circulated so industriously that many believed it, but careful inquiry proved its falsity. For many years a substantial reward was offered for proof that one such instance ever occurred, but no proof has been produced. None who loved the appearing of the Saviour were so ignorant of the teachings of the Scriptures as to suppose that robes which they could make would be necessary for that occasion. The only robe which the saints will need to meet the Lord is the righteousness of Christ. *See Isaiah 61:10; Rev. 19:8.* For a thorough refutation of the legend of ascension robes, see Francis D. Nichol, Midnight Cry *(Washington, D.C.: Review and Herald Publishing Assn., 1944), chs. 25-27,* and Appendices H-J. See also Leroy Edwin Froom, Prophetic Faith of Our Fathers *(Washington, D.C.: Review and Herald Publishing Assn., 1954), vol. 4, pp. 822-826.*

Page 374. The Chronology of Prophecy.

Dr. George Bush, professor of Hebrew and Oriental Literature in the New York City University, in a letter addressed to William Miller and published in the Advent Herald and Signs of the Times Reporter, Boston, March 6 and 13, 1844, made some important admissions relative to his calculation of the prophetic times. Dr. Bush wrote:

"Neither is it to be objected, as I conceive, to yourself or your friends, that you have devoted much time and attention to the study of the chronology of prophecy, and have labored much to determine the commencing and closing dates of its great periods. If these periods are actually given by the Holy Ghost in the prophetic books, it was doubtless with the design that they should be studied, and probably, in the end, fully understood; and no man is to be charged with presumptuous folly who reverently makes the attempt to do this.... In taking a day as the prophetical term for a year , I believe you are sustained by the soundest exegesis, as well as fortified by the high names of [Joseph] Mede, Sir Isaac Newton, Bishop [Thomas] Newton, [William] Kirby, [James] Scott, [Alexander] Keith, and a host of others who have long since come to substantially your conclusions on this head.

They all agree that the leading periods mentioned by Daniel and John, do actually expire about this age of the world, and it would be a strange logic that would convict you of heresy for holding in effect the same views which stand forth so prominent in the notices of these eminent divines." "Your results in this field of inquiry do not strike me so far out of the way as to affect any of the great interests of truth or duty." "Your error, as I apprehend, lies in another direction than your chronology." "You have entirely mistaken the nature of the events which are to occur when those periods have expired. This is the head and front of your expository offending." See also Leroy Edwin Froom, Prophetic Faith of Our Fathers *(Washington, D.C.: Review and Herald Publishing Assn., 1950), vol. 1, chs. 1, 2.*

Page 435. A threefold message.

Revelation 14:6, 7foretells the proclamation of the first angel's message. Then the prophet continues: "There followed another angel, saying, Babylon is fallen, is fallen.... and the third angel followed them." The word here rendered "followed" means "to go along with," "to follow one," "go with him." See Henry George Liddell and Robert Scott, Greek English Lexicon *(Oxford: Clarendon Press, 1940), Vol. 1, p.* 52. It also means "to accompany." see George Abbott-Smith, A Manual Greek Lexicon of the New Testament *(Edinburgh: T. and T. Clark, 1950), page 17.* It is the same word that is used in Mark 5:24, "Jesus went with him; and much people followed Him, and thronged Him." It is also used of the redeemed one hundred and forty-four thousand, Revelation 14:4, where it is said, "these are they which follow the Lamb whithersoever He goeth." In both these places it is evident that the idea intended to be conveyed is that of "going together," "in company with." So in 1 Corinthians 10:4, where we read of the children of Israel that "they drank of that spiritual Rock that followed them," the word "followed" is translated from the same Greek word, and the margin has it, "went with them." From this we learn that the idea in Revelation 14:8, 9is not simply that the second and third angels followed the first in point of time, but that they went with him. The three messages are but one threefold message. They are three only in the order of their rise. But having risen, they go on together and are inseparable.

Page 447. Supremacy of the Bishops of Rome.

For the leading circumstances in the assumption of supremacy by the bishops of Rome, see Robert Francis Cardinal Bellarmine, Power of the Popes in Temporal Affairs *(there is an English Translation in the Library of Congress, Washington, D. C.);* Henry Edward Cardinal Manning, The

Temporal Power of the Vicar of Jesus Christ *(London: Burns and Lambert, 2d ed., 1862)*; and James Cardinal Gibbons, Faith Of Our Fathers *(Baltimore: John Murphy Co., 110th ed., 1917), Chs. 5, 9, 10, 12.*

For Protestant authors see Trevor Gervase Jalland, The Church and the Papacy *(London: Society for Promoting Christian Knowledge, 1944, a Bampton Lecture)*; and Richard Frederick Littledale, Petrine Claims *(London: Society for Promoting Christian Knowledge, 1899)*. For sources of the early centuries of the Petrine theory, see James T. Shotwell and Louise Ropes Loomis, The See of Peter *(New York: Columbia University Press, 1927)*. For the false "Donation of Constantine" see Christopher B. Coleman, The Treatise of Lorenzo Valla on the Donation of Constantine *(New York, 1914)*, which gives the full Latin text and translation, and a complete criticism of the document and its thesis.

Page 565. Quotations from Josiah Strong.

In his first edition of Our Country, Josiah Strong, without access to primary sources, incorrectly referenced the statements attributed to Pope Pius IX. The correct reference for the first citation is Pope Gregory XVI's encyclical letter of August 15, 1832. The relevant paragraph is here quoted in full: "This shameful font of indifferentism gives rise to that absurd and erroneous proposition which claims that liberty of conscience must be maintained for everyone. It spreads ruin in sacred and civil affairs, though some repeat over and over again with the greatest impudence that some advantage accrues to religion from it. 'But the death of the soul is worse than freedom of error,' as Augustine was wont to say. When all restraints are removed by which men are kept on the narrow path of truth, their nature, which is already inclined to evil, propels them to ruin. Then truly 'the bottomless pit' is opened from which John saw smoke ascending which obscured the sun, and out of which locusts flew forth to devastate the earth. Thence comes transformation of minds, corruption of youths, contempt of sacred things and holy laws - in other words, a pestilence more deadly to the state than any other. Experience shows, even from earliest times, that cities renowned for wealth, dominion, and glory perished as a result of this single evil, namely immoderate freedom of opinion, license of free speech, and desire for novelty." – *As printed in Claudia Carlen, Ihm, The Papal Encyclicals, 1740-1878 (Ann Arbor, Michigan: The Pierian Press, 1990) 1:238.*

The second citation should be credited to Pope Pius IX's Syllabus of Errors, which accompanied his encyclical letter of December 8, 1864. Included among the 80 errors anathematized are: "24. The church has not the power of using force, nor has she any temporal power, direct or indirect. – *Apostolic Letter 'Ad Apostolicae,' August 22, 1851.*" "78. Hence it has been wisely decided by law, in some Catholic countries, that persons coming to reside therein shall enjoy the public exercise of their own peculiar worship. – *Allocution 'acerbissimum,' Sept. 27, 1852.* "79. Moreover, it is false that the civil liberty of every form of worship, and the full power, given to all, of overtly and publicly manifesting any opinions whatsoever and thoughts, conduce more easily to corrupt the morals and minds of the people, and to propagate the pest of indifferentism. – *Allocution 'Nunquam Fore,' December 15, 1856. – As printed in Anne Fremantle, ed., The Papal Encyclicals in their Historical Context (New York: G. P. Putnam's Sons, 1956), 146, 152.* It should also be noted that the oath of allegiance to the pope, quoted in the last paragraph of the citation from Strong, was the bishop's oath, not one taken by cardinals.

Page 565. Witholding the Bible from the people.

see note for page 340.

Page 578. The Ethiopian Church and the Sabbath.

Until rather recent years the Coptic Church of Ethiopia observed the seventh-day Sabbath. The Ethiopians also kept Sunday, the first day of the week, throughout their history as a Christian people. These days were marked by special services in the churches. The observance of the seventh-day Sabbath has, however, virtually ceased in modern Ethiopia. For eyewitness accounts of religious days in Ethiopia, see Pero Gomes de Teixeira, The Discovery of Abyssinia by the Portuguese in 1520 *(translated in English in London: British Museum, 1938), p. 79*; Father Francisco Alvarez, Narrative of the Portuguese Embassy to Abyssinia During the Years 1520-1527, in the records of the Hakluyt Society *(London, 1881), vol. 64, pp. 22-49*; Michael Russell, Nubia and Abyssinia *(Quoting Father Lobo, Catholic Missionary in Ethiopia in 1622) (New York: Harper & Brothers, 1837), pp. 226-229*; S. Giacomo Baratti, Late Travels into the Remote Countries of Abyssinia *(London: Benjamin Billingsley, 1670), pp. 134-137*; Job Ludolphus, A New History for Ethiopia *(London: S. Smith, 1682), pp. 234-357;* Samuel Gobat, Journal of Three Years' Residence in Abyssinia *(New York: Ed. of 1850), pp. 55-58, 83-98.* For other works touching upon the question, see Peter Heylyn, History of the Sabbath, *2d ed., 1636, vol. 2, pp. 198-200;* Arthur P. Stanley, Lectures on the History of the Eastern Church *(New York: Charles Scribner's Sons, 1882), lecture 1, par. 1; C. F. Rey, Romance of the Portuguese in Abyssinia (London: F. H. and G. Witherley, 1929), pp. 59, 253-297.*